Three Bad Men (c) 2013

G1701-105

Three Bad Men:
John Ford, John Wayne, Ward Bond

SCOTT ALLEN NOLLEN

Foreword by Michael A. Hoey

McFarland & Company, Inc., Publishers

Jefferson, North Carolina, and London

ALSO BY SCOTT ALLEN NOLLEN AND FROM MCFARLAND

Paul Robeson: Film Pioneer (2010);
Abbott and Costello on the Home Front: A Critical Study of the Wartime Films (2009);
*Warners Wiseguys: All 112 Films That Robinson,
Cagney and Bogart Made for the Studio* (2008);
Louis Armstrong: The Life, Music and Screen Career (2004; paperback 2010);
Jethro Tull: A History of the Band, 1968–2001 (2002);
*Robin Hood: A Cinematic History of the English Outlaw
and His Scottish Counterparts* (1999; paperback 2008);
*Sir Arthur Conan Doyle at the Cinema:
A Critical Study of the Film Adaptations* (1996; paperback 2005);
Robert Louis Stevenson: Life, Literature and the Silver Screen (1994; paperback 2012);
*Boris Karloff: A Critical Account of His Screen, Stage,
Radio, Television and Recording Work* (1991; paperback 2008);
The Boys: The Cinematic World of Laurel and Hardy (1989; paperback 2001)

Frontispiece: Ward Bond, as "John Dodge" in *The Wings of Eagles* (MGM, 1957), delivers an uncanny interpretation of his mentor, tormentor, friend of three decades, and surrogate father, John Ford.

LIBRARY OF CONGRESS CATALOGUING-IN-PUBLICATION DATA

Nollen, Scott Allen.
Three bad men : John Ford, John Wayne, Ward Bond /
Scott Allen Nollen; foreword by Michael A. Hoey.
p.   cm.
Includes bibliographical references and index.

ISBN 978-0-7864-5854-7
softcover : acid free paper ∞

1. Ford, John, 1894–1973. 2. Wayne, John, 1907–1979. 3. Bond, Ward,
1903–1960. 4. Motion picture producers and directors — United States —
Biography. 5. Motion picture actors and actresses — United States —
Biography. I. Hoey, Michael A. II. Title.
PN1998.3.F65N65 2013   791.43'0233'092 — dc23   [B]   2013004062

BRITISH LIBRARY CATALOGUING DATA ARE AVAILABLE

On the cover: Publicity still from the 1957 film *The Wings of Eagles*
showing (left to right) Ward Bond, John Ford and John Wayne

Manufactured in the United States of America

*McFarland & Company, Inc., Publishers
Box 611, Jefferson, North Carolina 28640
www.mcfarlandpub.com*

In memory of the remarkable talent of fifteen fellow Midwesterners, eight Iowans and seven Nebraskans, each inextricably linked to the pleasure and pain wrought by John Ford:

Wardell Edwin ("Ward") Bond
actor: born in Benkelman, Nebraska

Henry Jaynes ("Hank") Fonda —
actor: born in Grand Island, Nebraska

John P. Fulton
special effects pioneer: born in Beatrice, Nebraska

Edmund Richard ("Hoot") Gibson
actor: born in Tekamah, Nebraska

Raymond William Hatton
pioneer actor: born in Red Oak, Iowa

Charles B. ("Good Chuck") Hayward
stunt man and actor: born in Alliance, Nebraska

Dorothy Marie Johnson
author, "The Man Who Shot Liberty Valance":
born in McGregor, Iowa

Hans F. Koenekamp
pioneer cinematographer: born in Denison, Iowa

John Tylor ("Ted") Mapes
stunt man and actor: born in St. Edward, Nebraska

Karen Morley
actor: born Mildred Linton in Ottumwa, Iowa

Nathaniel Greene ("Nat") Pendleton
actor and athlete: born in Davenport, Iowa

Donna Reed
actor: born Donna Belle Mullenger in Denison, Iowa

John ("Duke") Wayne
actor, producer and director:
born Marion Robert Morrison in Winterset, Iowa

Norton Earl ("Hank") Worden
actor: born in Rolfe, Iowa

Darryl Francis Zanuck
writer, producer and mogul:
born in Wahoo, Nebraska
and for my home boy,

David ("What Would Ward Do?") Craft
writer, editor and film aficionado: from Ames, Iowa

Table of Contents

Foreword: Working for Mr. Ford

by Michael A. Hoey

I was 25 years old and had been working in the business for about seven years, and had just come over from Disney Studios where I had assisted on the first couple years of *The Mickey Mouse Club*. I had become aware of John Ford when his first cavalry film, *Fort Apache*, had come out in 1948, and had seen it and the follow-ups, *She Wore a Yellow Ribbon* and *Rio Grande*, dozens of times, so you can imagine how thrilled I was when the head of the Warners editorial department told me that I was to assist Ford's regular editor, Jack Murray, on *Sergeant Rutledge*, another John Ford cavalry film. The only thing missing was my other idol, John Wayne. My father had appeared with Wayne in *Wake of the Red Witch*, also in 1948, and, after I had visited the set and met Wayne, he became my favorite actor for a long time after that. As I grew up and entered the film business, I became aware of John Ford's real masterpieces, like *The Grapes of Wrath*, *How Green Was My Valley*, *My Darling Clementine*, and my all-time favorite war film, *They Were Expendable*.

When I first read the *Sergeant Rutledge* script, originally called "Captain Buffalo" and written by the producer, Willis Goldbeck, I was surprised to see the strong emphasis that was placed on racism and the fact that the protagonist was an African-American soldier in the U.S. Cavalry. I was also excited to learn that Ford was planning to return to his favorite location, Monument Valley, to film the exteriors with the troop of Buffalo Soldiers. The company had returned from the Monument Valley location a few days earlier, when Jack Murray took me down to visit the set and to meet the "Old Man."

I was nervous as hell as we entered the stage and walked toward where the company was filming on the deserted railroad station set. Most of the soundstage was pitch-black, except for a pool of illumination where cameraman Bert Glennon was lighting the railroad station for the next set-up. Off to one side, stage flats had been set up to enclose a long table and a number of folding chairs. Several work lights brightened the area, and Jack explained to me that that was where Mr. Ford rehearsed his cast. There was a bearded man, seated on a stool playing "Red River Valley" on an accordion, who's name was Danny Borzage. Ford liked to have mood music, and Danny, who was director Frank Borzage's younger brother, had been a fixture on every Ford set for years and would remain so until Ford stopped making films in 1966.

Mr. Ford was seated in the corner of the set with a work light beside him, reading the script. He was wearing a baseball cap with naval "scrambled egg" on the brim and had his glasses pushed up on his forehead and the eye-patch that he'd worn since his cataract oper-

1

ation in 1953 flipped up. He held his script just inches from his nose and was chewing on a dirty handkerchief. Jack Murray pushed me forward slightly as he said, "Skipper, this is my assistant, Mike Hoey."

Mr. Ford flipped down the eye-patch and the glasses in one movement and then stared up at me for what felt like an eternity before he spoke. "Hoey," he asked, "is that Irish?"

My father's real name was Hyams, but he had chosen Hoey as a stage name, and I had been christened Hoey. So grateful that he'd picked a name from the Auld Sod, I squeaked out a "Yes, sir, it is."

Ford went back to his script and, without looking at Jack, muttered, "He'll do."

I didn't see Mr. Ford again until we ran the editor's cut for him a week after he finished filming. Ford never went to dailies or visited the cutting room, and he relied on Jack Murray's report each day at 4 P.M. after he had viewed the film. He did send a note down to the cutting room that he wanted some music placed over a montage that he had filmed in Monument Valley, and Jack asked me to go to the music library and pick out something. I found a piece of music that had been written the previous year by a composer named Howard Jackson for a Clint Walker Western called *Yellowstone Kelly*.

On the night that we ran the picture for Mr. Ford, he arrived with his driver, Bill Ramsey, and a large thermos of black coffee that he proceeded to share with us. I took one swallow of my coffee and almost choked — it was 90-percent Irish whiskey. The screening went well, with surprisingly few notes, but then Jack Murray had been Mr. Ford's editor since 1936 and *The Prisoner of Shark Island*, and he knew the "Old Man's" taste better than anyone. Mr. Ford liked the music I selected so much that he hired Howard Jackson to write the final score, with one condition: that he use the same piece of music over the montage. I think Howard changed it slightly, but Mr. Ford never noticed.

I consider myself very lucky to have worked for both Mr. Ford and for Jack Murray, who died the following year. *Sergeant Rutledge* isn't one of John Ford's greatest films, but it has an honesty about it that resonated with me, and Woody Strode gave the best performance of his life in that film. Woody's son, Woody, Jr., was a second assistant director on a television episode that I directed in the '80s, and we talked about his dad and the film. Woody, Jr., told me that his father considered John Ford the greatest director in films and that he remained friends with him right up to Ford's death in 1973.

I first met Scott Nollen several years ago at a Sherlock Holmes film convention in Indianapolis where we had both been invited to speak about books that we had recently written. Scott had created a magnificent analysis of every film adaptation made of Sir Arthur Conan Doyle's famous literary detective. My father had played Inspector Lestrade in the Universal Pictures Sherlock Holmes series of the 1940s, and I had written an account of his and my careers in Hollywood and of our sometimes difficult relationship. We exchanged books and became good friends. Scott visited me in San Clemente last summer on his journey of discovery through John Ford's America and spoke of his passion to write about his three heroes. Now it is finished and Scott's passion has been realized, and now it is our turn to enjoy his rollicking account of *Three Bad Men*.

Preface: What Would Ward Do?

Ford's political views ... have been inadequately understood. Too often he and his films were roughly equated with the reactionary politics of his favorite actors, John Wayne and Ward Bond... — Joseph McBride[1]

John Ford walked through life setting stories in motion regardless of whether he ever captured them on film.... The need to lie was already within him while he slept peacefully in his mother's womb.... John Ford was the world's greatest storyteller because he was the world's most convincing liar. He rarely told the truth and he rarely lived the truth. John Ford was shooting a script, no matter what he was doing. — Maureen O'Hara[2]

The complex relationships John Ford had with John Wayne and Ward Bond encompassed the professional (the mostly good), the political (the usually bad) and the personal (the often ugly). It is an association unparalleled in the history of Hollywood cinema.

The electricity for this book struck 30 years ago, while I was a film student at the University of Iowa, attending a John Ford class taught by a professor visiting from his usual stomping grounds in Austin, Texas. He, like most academics of the era, was concerned with the cultural and sociopolitical aspects of the films, while largely ignoring the talent of the artists who created them.

The auteur theory was still all the rage. The making of motion pictures was, not a collaborative effort, but the work of an *author*. And a film was no longer a film, but a *text*. The professor particularly disliked my "celebratory" comments about John Wayne moving "like a ballet dancer."

If Ford had been there to hear all this "auteur" this and that, he probably would have responded, "I would say that is *horseshit*."

This discussion occurred *before* I read Ford's own admission that Wayne moved "like a dancer!" I also discovered that Raoul Walsh made a similar observation when casting *The Big Trail* in 1930. Watch the opening scene of Howard Hawks' cinematic character study *Rio Bravo* (1959), when Duke, as Sheriff John T. Chance, dressed in a cowboy hat, jacket and boots, and wielding a rifle in one hand, *pirouettes* in the barroom while whipping the weapon across Claude Akins' forehead.

In Ford's *The Man Who Shot Liberty Valance* (1962), Wayne, a bit older and heavier, as Tom Doniphon, effortlessly kicks the outlaw's psychotic sidekick, Floyd (Strother Martin), in the head with his right leg *as* he walks toward Valance (Lee Marvin), who has tripped

Ransom Stoddard (James Stewart), causing Doniphon's huge steak to slide onto the restaurant floor. It's one of the finest moments in the Western genre, achieved by a superb ensemble cast and Ford's spare use of editing. When Doniphon, with cool menace, states, "That's *my* steak, Valance," everyone, on screen and off, feels the innate power, controlled yet coiled for action, of this "good bad man."

These are just two examples of the man, born Marion Robert Morrison in Winterset, Iowa, but transformed, primarily with the help of three great directors, into one of the most charismatic and powerful film actors in history. No one other than Wayne could fuse such instinctive choreography with outright, ferocious violence. However, the catlike way Duke moved was not innate, but deliberately developed, first by Raoul Walsh and then refined by John Ford and character actor Paul Fix. Over time, Wayne was able to work acting wonders with the *back* of his body, particularly in two masterpieces of the Western genre, Hawks' *Red River* (1948) and Ford's *The Searchers* (1956).

A very insightful actor, Rex Reason, in his most mellifluous baritone, once told a film-convention audience that I was "chained to the oar" that all writers must endure. I never dreamed I'd become the literary equivalent of a galley slave.

Very few of us mortals have the genius of a John Ford. But I think I've come to understand Ford enough to create an *impression* of him.

I have pulled that oar through archives, libraries, residences, book and memorabilia shops, and cemeteries. Like Hank Fonda, Duke Wayne, and others in Pappy's films, I've had a meaningful (though a bit one-sided) conversation with a tombstone or two. I've even been referred to (by a fellow film lunatic) as a "Sherlock Holmes of the Movies." I don't think anyone could bestow a higher honor, particularly since there is rarely any satisfaction with the position of the galley after it's dry-docked.

Creating this book required a degree of psychological struggle matching the physical effort Ward Bond expended while pulling a pair of britches over his prominent, John Ford-celebrated rear end. A man who claimed that nature made him "always Left," Ford also joined the Motion Picture Alliance for the Preservation of American Ideals, a conservative bully-boy club that supported the House Committee on Un-American Activities, helping to create the Hollywood blacklist (which Wayne insisted "did not exist").

This un–American outfit was run by President Ward Bond, a prestigious "office" later conferred upon John Wayne. Although neither of these "super-patriots" served his country during World War II (Bond was legitimately classified 4-F; Wayne's lawyers and employers were kept busy obtaining deferments), they both were gung-ho in their

"Playing Pappy" (October 2011). The author, decked out in "Fordian" garb (with a pair of Ward Bond's screen-worn jeans draped over his shoulders), captured between some familiar sandstone buttes in Monument Valley, Navajo Nation, on the border of Utah and Arizona.

criticism of men who were "soft," and they were ready to kick "Commie" ass after the combat turned Cold.

The truth is an elusive concept, especially in a world in which everyone fibs a little, and a lot of us (like John Ford) lie a lot.

An estimable friend has often asked, "What would *Ward* do?"

Well, Bond's admirable Major Seth Adams, in *Wagon Train*, would simply answer, "Now, enough of this! Let's *get goin'!*"

John Ford was one of the most complex, contradictory, and downright confounding men who ever burned daylight. Ford, the *director*, was so busy spinning tall tales that Feeney, the *man*, remained largely unrevealed.

He was married to one woman for 53 years, but Mary McBride Ford rarely saw her husband, who, when not making films, either commercially or while "directing" World War II for the OSS, was cruising on his yacht, engaging in Naval Reserve missions, having extramarital affairs, or, at his nadir, crawling into a sleeping bag with a case of whiskey to drink himself into a lengthy oblivion. The wrap-up of the bender usually required a rehydration trip to the hospital and a burning of the foul bedroll.

Ford did have *friends*; but to attain this distinction, most of these fortunate few had to endure verbal attacks, outright humiliation, and even physical abuse. The more a person revealed his affection for Ford, the more sadism he received in return. Ford often demonstrated his love for others (including John Wayne) by kicking them in the ass.

Ford began his directing career in 1917 with Wayne's boyhood hero, Harry Carey; but the "Bronx Cowboy" initially was Ford's *teacher*, so after the younger man achieved a level of control over their films, the "Bright Star in the Early Western Sky" had to disappear from the scene (with a lone exception, a small, but significant, role in *The Prisoner of Shark Island* [1936]).

Ford's second big star, the Greek-godlike, beefcake phenomenon George O'Brien, whom he discovered on the Fox lot, played the leads in his two great silent Westerns, the sprawling epic *The Iron Horse* (1924) and the arguably superior *3 Bad Men* (1926). O'Brien then went on to further stardom in F. W. Murnau's expressionist masterpiece *Sunrise* (1927) and Michael Curtiz's epic *Noah's Ark* (1929) before landing on Ford's shit list for 16 years, due to his unscheduled "side trip" during one of Pappy's binges during a South Seas cruise in 1931.

Contrary to popular belief, Ford never had a real "falling out" with the equally extraordinary, versatile Victor McLaglen. Between the making of *The Long Voyage Home* (1940), which Vic turned down due to Pappy's offer of only $25,000 (half the big man's usual salary), and *Fort Apache* seven years later, Ford was away at war for several years, and none of the commercial films he made (*How Green Was My Valley*, *They Were Expendable*, *My Darling Clementine* and *The Fugitive*) offered a suitable role for the Oscar-winning actor.

Though nearly a decade would pass between Ford's first films involving Wayne and Bond, and the significant career boosts they received from him in the late 1930s, Ford liked having them around on a personal level, to hang out on the *Araner*, play cards, cruise to Catalina or along the coast of Baja, go fishing, and consume near-lethal amounts of "Who Hit John?"

Ford often said that the charismatic Wayne was his favorite actor, but the more personally flamboyant yet professionally versatile Bond was employed more often and spent more time with the director, especially during the early 1930s, when Wayne was frozen out after "defecting" to star in Walsh's *Big Trail*. And after that innovative, expensive epic bombed at the box office, Wayne, without Ford's support, labored on Poverty Row for the next eight years, until Pappy cast him as the Ringo Kid in *Stagecoach* (1939).

Bond, who also appears in *The Big Trail* (but not in a starring capacity), was closer to Ford than any other male actor in his "Stock Company." As a result, Ward endured the heaviest doses of Ford's sadism; but the big, blustering "gorilla" let it roll right off his strong, gridiron-conditioned back. Though Wayne spread the rumor that Bond was nicknamed "The Judge" because he spent so much time on the USC bench, it was the Duke who got cut from the main football squad, lost his scholarship, and dropped out.

This volume opens with a brief biography covering Bond's early years in Nebraska and Colorado, and continues with an in-depth look at the complex, love-hate relationships that he and Wayne developed with Ford. The events of Ford's life are included, as well as a thorough look at his art and how his rapport with these men informed his unique cinematic legacy. Wayne and Bond's lives and work for others are intertwined in this infinitely tangled skein.

Ford's crucial relationship with his big brother and mentor, Francis, an unjustly forgotten cinematic pioneer, hopefully gets its due. Other important players who had a lasting, perhaps unconscious, influence are genius humorist Will Rogers and the much-maligned comic Lincoln Perry (aka "Stepin Fetchit").

Mentored by his brother and Harry Carey, and absorbing the films of D. W. Griffith, Ford helped develop the language and techniques of the cinema, but he also imbued it with much of its heart and soul. Even his most consciously stylized projects support his maxim that the reason for making a film is to "tell a damn good story," an art that has been eroded in the decades since Ford's death, when style often has overtaken substance, in a cinematic realm of continuous, distracting camera movement and attention-deficit-disorder editing.

Ford's last silent Western, *3 Bad Men* (and his last before returning to the genre with *Stagecoach* 13 years later), features his favorite story about a group of outlaws ("bad" men) who, affected by someone in need, reveal their "good" inner selves and are redeemed (usually requiring martyrdom). *Marked Men* (1919), Ford's final Universal Western with Harry Carey, also was his first adaptation of Peter B. Kyne's story "Three Godfathers," in which outlaws discover a dying woman in the Mojave Desert and are forced by fate to care, even unto death, for her newborn baby.

Based on a different source, the novel *Over the Border* by Herman Whitaker, *3 Bad Men* features a trio of outlaws (Tom Santschi, J. Farrell MacDonald and Frank Campeau) who aid and become guardians of a young woman (Olive Borden) stranded in the desert after her father is killed. Ford's breathtaking Technicolor version of *3 Godfathers* (1948), featuring both Wayne and Bond, with one of the trio played by Harry Carey, Jr. (the film is dedicated to his late father), thereafter became one of director's favorites.

John Ford, John Wayne and Ward Bond were real-life "good bad men": Mr. Ford, a sadistic, dictatorial bully on the set, a poor husband and father, and often an unapproachable, tragic alcoholic, was also the nation's most honored director, a Purple Heart recipient who risked his life to film warfare, and an artistic genius with a sensitive, poetic inner self he publicly denied; Mr. Wayne, a misogynist, periodic drunk, celluloid "war hero" and political pretender, was also one of the cinema's finest actors, a loyal friend, good sailor, and a walking, worldwide legend in his own time; and Bond, a sometimes arrogant, carousing, uncouth palooka and informer, was also an intelligent, reliable and generous man, a genuinely gifted, versatile actor, respectable singer, and would-be pianist who loved jazz.

In 1997, an attempt at debunking Ford's mythology was made in *John Wayne's America:*

The Politics of Celebrity by Gary Wills. Portions of the book include brilliant analyses exposing Pappy's self-aggrandizing tales, but the author's openly anti–Ford bias (with respect to his personality and behavior) resulted in too many factual errors.

Wills' chapters on *The Quiet Man* and *The Searchers* are illuminating, as is his lengthy siege upon *The Alamo*, which exposed Wayne's further mythologizing of a legend based on few, if any, historical facts. But Wills was so intent on painting Ford as a right-wing Cold Warrior in the Wayne and Bond mold, that he omitted coverage of the director's historic, often strategically important, contributions to the Allied victory during World War II.

It *is* difficult to accept at face value many of the tales spun by the wily, irascible Ford. This book is not a "definitive" study of his life or films. Several excellent volumes already have been published. In particular, *Searching for John Ford*, the monumental 2001 volume by Joseph McBride, is the "ardent Fordian's" bible, one unlikely to be surpassed. Scott Eyman's *Print the Legend: The Life and Times of John Ford*, published in 1999, is also a well-researched read.

An excellent, intimate volume was written by someone who *was there*: Harry Carey, Jr., honestly recounts his experiences in *Company of Heroes: My Life as an Actor in the John Ford Stock Company* (1994). Woody Strode's 1990 memoir, *Goal Dust*, is also worthwhile; but the passages recalling what Ford told him are based on the same lies his "Papa" fed to everyone else! The most impressively researched, accurate, myth-busting biography of the Duke is Randy Roberts and James S. Olson's massive *John Wayne: American* (1995).

This volume is merely an *attempt* to "discuss the legend and print something closer to the facts." In *John Wayne's America*, Gary Wills attempts to be Ransom Stoddard (James Stewart), "The Man Who *Didn't* Shoot Liberty Valance," and he often succeeds.

It can be a precarious thing, trying to be Stoddard. I don't think the formidable Tom Doniphon (Wayne) is needed to gun anyone down, but it *would* be reassuring to have the mighty Pompey (Woody Strode) watching my back.

A great deal of research was gleaned from my extensive collection of original Ford, Wayne and Bond memorabilia, including handwritten letters (two of which are reproduced in these pages), compiled over the course of three decades. All 60 illustrations were scanned directly from rare originals, many published here for the first time.

Vivid recollections from members of the Ford Stock Company also help tell the tale. Anna Lee was a fine performer and a lovely, very open person who sincerely admired Ford, both as an artist and godfather to her children. By the time I was privileged to befriend Henry Brandon (during the last two years of his life), he was a feisty old Leftist harvesting an "herb garden" behind his home on Spaulding Drive in North Hollywood. The last time we spoke, during the summer of 1989, the 77-year-old Henry had been arrested for possessing a "controlled substance," a charge he denied, stating that the homegrown produce was "only for his personal use." (He subsequently used the experience as research for a role on *Superior Court*!)

Born Heinrich Kleinbach in Berlin, Brandon left the Fatherland with his German-émigré parents to become an artistic asset to the United States. He portrayed nearly every conceivable ethnic role, had an egalitarian philosophy, and made no bones about his disdain for people with tunnel vision.

He appreciated Ford as a master filmmaker, but didn't mention what he thought of Wayne and Bond as *artists*. Their arch-conservative politics had soured his view of them as professionals. He cared little for Wayne, and even less for Bond. When Chief Cicatriz ("Scar") stands up to Ethan Edwards in *The Searchers*, there's very little acting there.

As for Brandon himself, "He spoke good American — for a *German!*" The Monument Valley Navahos shared a lot of laughs, calling him the "Kraut Comanche."

I also had the good fortune of corresponding with several storied actors who worked for Ford, all of whom are now available only in recorded form: Ralph Bellamy, James Cagney, Myrna Loy, James Stewart and Gene Tierney. Family members of departed "Ford veterans" include Mrs. Ben Johnson, Sara Jane Karloff and Francesca Robinson-Sanchez. I must also acknowledge a thumbs-up from Vera Miles, and the considerable assistance of the American Film Institute and Turner Classic Movies.

My good friend, writer and filmmaker Michael A. Hoey (whose father, Dennis, appears with Bond in *Joan of Arc* and Wayne in *Wake of the Red Witch*), worked for Ford as assistant editor on *Sergeant Rutledge* in 1960, and has recalled that experience for the fine foreword. Acknowledgment is also due the very kind Frankie Avalon, who reminisced about Wayne's *The Alamo.*

The appendices provide a detailed listing of the Ford titles featuring Wayne and/or Bond; a complete Bond filmography (including titles missing from previous published and electronic sources); and a complete record of Bond's television appearances, including all the *Wagon Train* episodes produced during his 1957–1960 span. (Most of these shows also are covered in Chapters 12 and 13.)

This is an honest account of incredible ingenuity, creativity, toil, perseverance, bravery, debauchery, futility, abuse, masochism, mayhem, violence, warfare, open- and closed-mindedness, control and chaos, brilliance and stupidity, rationality and insanity, friendship and a testing of its limits, love and hate, all committed by a "half-genius, half-Irish" cinematic visionary and his two surrogate sons: *Three Bad Men.*

Introduction:
Gluteus Maximus and the
Power of Feeney's Myth

[John Ford was] the old sentimental cruel genius bastard son of a bitch, who knew what he was doing, always and for fifty years, and without whom there would be no American cinema as we know it. — Darcy O'Brien[1]

Two [actors] who have never received anywhere near the credit they deserve are two of my closest friends and men with whom I've made many films, John Wayne and Ward Bond. — John Ford[2]

In many respects, Ward Bond may be considered the ultimate *American* character actor. Though his 28 collaborations with John Ford are his main claim to fame, Bond is also notable as one of the most prolific actors in Hollywood film history, racking up a total of 261 film appearances (excluding television work) in a 30-year career. If not for his career damaging, ultra-rightwing, postwar political activities and his premature death at age 57, this total would be far greater.

Prior to starring in the number-one rated television show in the United States, *Wagon Train*, on which he also served (unbilled) as producer, editor and writer, Bond displayed both a believable, naturalistic performance style (an unadorned character-actor version of the Midwestern sensibility crafted by frequent collaborator and fellow Nebraskan Henry Fonda) and an impressive versatility, creating a vast array of characters from nearly every walk of life: Western good and bad men; hillbillies; railroad workers; football players, boxers and wrestlers; coaches, instructors and promoters; sailors and soldiers; military and police officers; "G" Men, detectives and prison guards; taxi and bus drivers; ship and airline stewards; reporters; film directors; historical figures, medieval knights and ancient gladiators; gamblers, bums, corrupt cops, convicts and death-row inmates; henchmen, gangsters, rapists and crazed killers; doctors, politicians, religious leaders and men of the cloth; and even a gendarme in the village of *Frankenstein*! In 1957, he attained the supreme honor of "becoming" his mentor and surrogate father, slightly "disguised" as John "Dodge," in *The Wings of Eagles*.

Appearing in nearly every conceivable genre, Bond worked for a dreamlike list of Hollywood filmmakers. Along with Ford and Raoul Walsh, the two men who "created" his career, he honed his craft with more than 50 major directors, including Busby Berkeley, Frank Borzage, Frank Capra, Michael Curtiz, Cecil B. DeMille, Allan Dwan, Henry Hathaway, Howard Hawks, John Huston, Fritz Lang, Mervyn LeRoy, George Marshall, Lewis Milestone, Nicholas Ray, Jean Renoir, Norman Taurog, Jacques Tourneur, W. S. Van Dyke, William A. Wellman and William Wyler.

Aside from his pal, John Wayne, Bond supported a stunning "Who's Who" of Golden Age Hollywood. Silent stars who had survived the transition to sound included Richard Barthelmess, Lionel Barrymore, Warner Baxter, Wallace Beery, Charles Bickford, Harry Carey, Ronald Colman, Donald Crisp, Richard Dix, Edmund Lowe and Lewis Stone.

Some actors who had cut their teeth during the silent era became stars and screen favorites during the 1930s (Bond's most prolific decade, during which he acted in 183 feature films): Gary Cooper, Joan Crawford, Alan Hale, Helen Hayes, Jean Hersholt, Jack Holt, Walter Huston, Boris Karloff, Myrna Loy, Bela Lugosi, William Powell and Basil Rathbone.

Bond appeared on screen with scores of major stars, including Ingrid Bergman, Humphrey Bogart, James Cagney, Claudette Colbert, Marlene Dietrich, Errol Flynn, Clark Gable, Susan Hayward, Katherine Hepburn, Carole Lombard, Fred MacMurray, Fredric March, Paul Muni, Gregory Peck, Tyrone Power, Edward G. Robinson, Barbara Stanwyck, James Stewart, Spencer Tracy and Loretta Young. On one occasion, he was punched out by Cary Grant.

His colleagues included versatile actors who could play lead roles, striking leading ladies, juvenile stars, great comics and musical performers, African-American favorites, memorable character actors, and the B-Western heroes who provided some of his first prominent supporting parts. There also were his colleagues in the Ford Stock Company, major stars and character actors alike. Only two other performers appeared in more of Pappy's productions: Ford's brother Francis (32) and bulldog-mugged, former Marine D.I., and bit actor supreme Jack Pennick (42).

In 1998, Bond received unique notoriety for appearing in more of the American Film Institute's "100 Greatest Movies of All Time" than any other actor: *It Happened One Night* (1934), *Bringing Up Baby* (1938), *Gone with the Wind* (1939), *The Grapes of Wrath* (1940), *The Maltese Falcon* (1941), *It's a Wonderful Life* (1946) and *The Searchers* (1956). *The Maltese Falcon* also stands out for giving Bond the last word in one of the great film masterpieces. Following Sam Spade's reference to the Black Bird as "the stuff that dreams are made of," Bond's Detective Tom Polhaus mutters, "*Huh?*" a beautifully ambiguous, prime contender for the briefest closing line in cinema history.

Some degree of interpretive subjectivity is involved when writing a book like this one, making history, not a science, but what aspires to be an art. However, in what Sherlock Holmes' friend, Dr. John H. Watson, might call "The Singular Case of Mr. Wardell E. Bond," the proof of his supremacy as Hollywood's Greatest Character Actor can be *argued* qualitatively and *proved* quantitatively. Using the material provided here, just do the math. The sum will be *Ward Bond*.

Though Bond was a mere eight years younger than Ford, Pappy literally was a father figure to his protégé, whom he often treated with the sort of abuse only a "tough loving" parent can dish out to a child to get the desired results. Ford also unleashed this dictatorial cruelty on other actors, most notably Wayne, but it took on a greater significance with Bond, whose own letters to his parents, written as early as 1930, testify to the close relationship he had with both John and Mary Ford. Over the years, Ford spent far more time with Bond (and others in his troupe, including Wayne) than with his own children, Patrick and Barbara.

If Ford and Bond, celebrities of the 20th century, had held a similar status in an earlier place and time, say Ancient Rome (with Ford as Emperor and Bond as his favorite gladiator),

Ward could easily have been known as *Gluteus Maximus*. Another of Bond's unique contributions to film history was Ford's frequent use of his prominent posterior as a compositional element. The Old Man was fond of calling attention to the decidedly equine contour of his protégé's rear end, and often referred to him (on and off the set) as the "Horse's Ass."

In his 1979 biography *Pappy: The Life of John Ford*, the director's grandson, Dan Ford, suggests that becoming an independent producer gave his grandfather the freedom to begin featuring "Bond's butt" during the filming of *Fort Apache* in 1947. However, a close scrutiny of all the Ford films in which Bond appears proves that the director already was using these ATB ("around the butt") shots, rather than OTS ("over the shoulder") shots, as early as 1931: Appearing in only one scene of *Arrowsmith* as a police officer, Bond is introduced from *behind*, his rear end displayed for all eyes to see.

(In the not too distant past, a critic raised the question, "Can writing about an actor's butt be considered 'film scholarship?'" When the complex, contradictory conundrum of a man, John Ford, is the subject, such an inquiry is superfluous, as the following pages prove beyond a reasonable doubt.)

In the preface to his 1995 book *John Ford: Hollywood's Old Master*, historian Ronald L. Davis provides a succinct summation of John "Bull" Feeney:

> As a craftsman he was without peer, his composition equal to the Renaissance masterpieces. Not content merely to photograph scenes, Ford painted with a camera, capturing nuances that were invisible to the naked eye.... But he also ranks among the twentieth century's most famous mythmakers. Through his individualized reading of westward expansion, and despite prejudices and misconceptions, Ford has exerted more influence on the way the world views America's past than have colleges of historians.[3]

Above, Ford is described as the modern counterpart to a Caesar. However, taking a page from Davis, perhaps he was the American equivalent of Homer, the mythmaker of Ancient Greece. After all, *Stagecoach* and *The Searchers*, to name just two of his Western tours de force, possess *Iliad*- and *Odyssey*-like elements. And this Homeric director's greatest muses: Duke and Judge.

Davis also noted:

> Privately John Ford was an elusive figure, his true identity perhaps a mystery even to himself ... he created ... an image of the tough iconoclast so convincingly that the sensitive individual inside grew bereft, sequestered from family and intimate friends. Ford's life was one of loneliness and inner turmoil, but he turned his pain into cinematic masterworks, finding solace mainly in his craft.[4]

A significant part of "his craft" was the Stock Company, whose members helped realize his myths. Ford's family was comprised of those individuals who were necessary, time and again, to bring his cinematic works, both masterful and otherwise, to life. Duke and Judge were the two most prominent representatives of this exclusive club, and Wayne later would borrow other members for his own productions, therefore fashioning his stock company, in Pappy's indelible image.

The loneliness that plagued Ford, made worse by his debilitating and ultimately destructive alcoholism, was often assuaged by his two best pals, and their complicated relationships were absolutely essential to Pappy's art and life. The mythology of the American Old West, created in the East by New England writers, painters and dime-novel hacks, to preserve the romanticism of the fading (mythical) Frontier, and most famously voiced in Horace Greeley's 1837 admonition "Go West, young man, go forth into the Country," would reach its fullest flower in the films of John Ford, who, along with John Wayne and Ward Bond, all "went West" as far as possible, meeting up in a near-mythical place called Hollywood.

1

The Boy from Benkelman

On a fair-weather day during the early 1880s, homesteaders Mr. and Mrs. W. H. Bond forded the Mississippi, trekking the rugged miles from Illinois to Dundy County in southwestern Nebraska, bordering Kansas and Colorado. Recently, the settlement of Collinsville, at the junction of the north and south forks of the Republican River, had been renamed Benkelman. An event that subsequently would dominate the plots of countless Western stories and films, the new village was the domain of local cattle baron J. G. Benkelman, who had built a major shipping site nearby.

The days of the Open Range were coming to an end, due to a Nebraska embargo on Texas cattle and the influx of farmers spurred by the Homestead Act, signed into law by President Abraham Lincoln 20 years earlier. When the Bonds arrived, fears of an "Indian menace" continued to circulate, and hundreds of cowboys still rode the prairie covered with tall, thick buffalo grass.

In 1882, the Burlington Railroad established a local depot, and Benkelman flourished when its businessmen began transporting several essential commodities, including livestock, grain and cream. Beginning in 1885, a wave of immigrants, primarily of German, English and Irish ancestry, helped spur the incorporation of the Village of Benkelman on February 8, 1887. A courthouse was built, and the Dundy commissioners selected the town as the county seat the following year.

Another homesteader couple, Mr. and Mrs. W. V. Hundley, who recently had moved from Franklin, a small town in central Nebraska near the Kansas border, chose Benkelman as the spot to raise their three sons and two daughters. Mr. Hundley, raised on the East Coast, left behind a career as a master carpenter and builder to become a pioneer in the West.

The Bonds, successful in the hotel, café and livery businesses, were even more prolific at procreation, perhaps affected by the fertile buffalo grass environment while conceiving a brood of 11 children. Both the Bonds and Hundleys were often mentioned in Benkleman's newspaper, the *Dundy County Pioneer*, the first such publication "in all the territory from McCook to Denver."[1]

The Bonds' second child, John W., married the Hundley's younger daughter, Mable, on April 9, 1902, and they settled into a life of farming. Exactly one year later, on April 9, 1903, a baby boy, sporting brown hair and gray eyes, was born, and the happy parents christened him Wardell Edwin Bond. In due course, he was joined by a baby sister, Bernice. Mable later recalled their life in Benkelman:

> [T]hose were the happiest days of our lives. I shall never forget how we would drive many miles to dances held at various homes ... and of how we would dance until sun-up in sod houses without a thought of getting weary. How I so often wish that I could shove the calendar back to those happy, happy days.[2]

J. W. purchased a transfer line, and soon was selling all manner of necessary goods to the community. First making sure that his family was well-supported, he spent his "spare time" sharing his hard-earned good fortune with others (a charitable disposition that would be passed on to his son).

J. W. provided help to neighbors and other families struggling with illness and exhaustion, and his many nights of going without sleep while sitting up with a friend earned him the honor of being named Benkelman's "leading citizen." J. W.'s philanthropy even extended to making funeral arrangements and, if needed, personally digging a grave for a deceased resident.

In 1906, young Ward barely survived a three-week bout with rheumatic fever (a common inflammatory disease eventually constrained by the development of antibiotics). A streptococcus infection which led to his illness could have contributed to his later development of epilepsy and a predisposition to various cardiac problems.

Ward also was rendered unconscious on at least two occasions: after accidentally being hit by a car; and, at age 13, barely surviving electrocution from high-voltage conducted by a lightning rod charged during a Fourth of July electrical storm. (Both of these incidents would eerily be repeated during his adulthood: the latter in a low-budget film, and the former in an all too real accident that nearly killed him, leading to a recurrent disability that hampered his physical abilities on film sets for 15 years. By the time he reached his teen years, Ward had developed health problems that, exacerbated by a devil-may-care attitude, did not bode well for a long life.)

At the Benkelman grade school, Ward proved a prompt and active student. As a teenager, he joined the "Young Bloods," a group of "elite" boys who prowled the small-town streets, on the lookout for suitably attractive girls. But his educational and social life was interrupted in 1918, when J. W. decided to sell his current house-moving operation and move farther westward to Denver, 210 miles away from the home town to which his son had become deeply attached.

Four years later, Ward graduated from Denver's East High School, the city's first such institution, founded in 1875 but referred to as "Old East" after being demolished in 1925. (Other East High School students who went on to Hollywood success include Douglas Fairbanks, Sr. [who was expelled], Harold Lloyd, Paul Whiteman, Hattie McDaniel, Pam Grier and Don Cheadle.)

Ward remained with his parents and sister as they moved at yearly intervals, first to Tacoma, Washington, then to Los Angeles and on to Klamath Falls, Oregon. They ultimately settled in California, purchasing a home in Oakland, which would become the Bond family's new home town. Ward intended to become an architect, and worked steadily for a few years to build up his savings account. His triumphant return to Los Angeles involved enrolling at the University of Southern California to study for an engineering degree.

Though Ward was a cocky attention-seeker, he also was a serious, capable student and an excellent athlete. During the fall semester of 1928, he earned a starting tackle position on Head Coach Howard Jones' USC Trojan football squad. At 6'2" and 195 pounds, he was one of the largest, toughest men on the team, who won nine of their ten games that season. The highly defensive October 28 contest with the California Golden Bears ended in a scoreless tie.

At age 25, Ward was a few years older than his classmates. He thoroughly enjoyed the college scene, especially the prestige of living in a notable fraternity house and the glory attained on the gridiron. Ultimately, his success as an athlete would lead him in a completely different and remarkable direction, and introduce him to the two most significant people in his life.

2

Genesis and John Wayne

I don't give a damn about him.
— Mary ("Molly") Morrison, about her eldest son, Marion[1]

John Ford.
— John Wayne, when asked what made him Western incarnate[2]

John Martin Feeney, son of Irish immigrants John Augustine Feeney and Mary Curran (who bore 11 children, six of which survived), was born in a farmhouse at Cape Elizabeth, Maine, on February 1, 1894. At age 12, while struggling through a year-long recovery from diphtheria, young Feeney's suffering was partially assuaged by his older sister, Mamie's, reading of great novels, including Robert Louis Stevenson's 1881 masterpiece *Treasure Island*, one of the maritime tales that later would inform his own cinematic works (particularly a scene in *How Green Was My Valley* [1941]).

When Ward Bond was seven, attending grade school in Benkelman, Feeney, fully recuperated, was excelling as a running back at Portland High. Dubbed "Bull" by his teammates and "the human battering ram" in the local newspapers, the 6'2", 175-pound bruiser earned three football letters and helped Portland win two state championships. Coaches from several Eastern colleges pitched recruitment, but young Feeney also was influenced by teachers who helped develop his intelligence and artistic talent. Impressed by the storytelling engendered by his imaginative Irish father, John's English instructor encouraged a clear, economical writing style, and the school principal furthered his intense interest in U.S. history.

Plagued by poor eyesight, John nonetheless had demonstrated a talent for drawing, an acute visual sense bolstered by the Portland school system's emphasis on art. His love of the sea and local landscape was boosted during summer days at Winslow Homer's studio, located on the Prouts Neck peninsula in Scarborough, seven miles south of Portland.

In 1908, John became fascinated by the first nickelodeons in Portland. Soon he was working as an usher at the Gem Theatre on Peaks Island, where he instinctively noticed the basic techniques used in making films, including some of the earliest efforts of D. W. Griffith, who had just begun to direct for the American Mutoscope and Biograph Company in Manhattan. He also became enthralled with the stage, landing a fulltime ushering job at the Jefferson Theatre, where he saw nearly every popular play of the period. Just as he had studied the visual technique of the movies, he began to scrutinize the acting styles of top performers whose tours stopped in Portland.

Sometimes he doubled as an errand boy, carrying buckets of beer from his father's saloon to thirsty actors, including comic Maclyn Arbuckle, an elder cousin of Roscoe "Fatty"

Arbuckle. He even played the small role of a telegram messenger in a production featuring Sidney Toler, then star of the resident stock company. Noticing the tension in the neophyte actor, Toler began improvising to make him more uncomfortable (a practice Ford eventually incorporated into his own infamous directorial tactics). In 1914, after failing the Annapolis entrance exam, John considered attending the University of Maine, but soon decided to follow in the footsteps of his older brother, Francis "Frank" Feeney, who had achieved success using the name Francis *Ford* making "flickers" in the Arizona desert before moving to a newly developing suburb of Los Angeles called Hollywood.

A full-blown vagabond and black sheep of the Feeney clan, Francis, more than 12 years John's senior, had continually come and gone from the family nest, been booted out of army basic training for being underage, hit the road after a brief marriage to a local girl whom he'd impregnated, and then disappeared without a trace. One of the Feeney children eventually "located" him, at a movie theater, when a familiar face flashed onto the screen as star of the picture!

Frank had found his first film work in New York City and Fort Lee, New Jersey, playing small roles in short subjects for the Centaur, Edison and Melies companies. In December 1909, he and his second wife, Elsie, followed producer Gaston Melies (brother of French film pioneer George Melies) and his son, Paul, when they moved their operation to a ranch near San Antonio, Texas, a location ideally suited for making Westerns and Civil War films. Melies christened the new venture the Star Film Company, and soon Frank began moving up the ladder from prop man to director and featured actor. His first major effort, *Under the Stars and Bars*, was released in October 1910.

By April 1911, Frank was working for producer Thomas H. Ince's Bison Films in California, directing and starring in two-reel Westerns made by his own outfit, the Broncho Motion Picture Company. Creating elaborate makeups, he played the title character in *Custer's Last Fight* (1912) and Abraham Lincoln in several successful shorts, *On Secret Service* (1912), *When Lincoln Paid* (1913), *The Battle of Bull Run* (1913) and *The Toll of War* (1913). He and his mistress, actress and writer Grace Cunard, then moved on to "Uncle" Carl Laemmle's Universal Film Manufacturing Company, where Frank again portrayed the Great Emancipator in *From Rail Splitter to President* (1913).

Unlike the "original screen cowboy," William S. Hart, whose style was quite melodramatic, Frank Ford was a more naturalistic performer. Director Allan Dwan said, "Francis was a hell of a good actor, one of our top stars. He was an exception because we didn't have good actors in movies then."[3]

By the time Ward Bond moved to Denver, John *Ford* had been lured to Hollywood by his big brother, who insulted him with the presentation of a shovel shortly after his arrival in July 1914. (Later in life, Ford, when asked what "had brought him to Hollywood," was fond of sarcastically replying, "The *train*.") Toiling as a ditch digger for a weekly 12 dollars at the recently christened Universal City was an inauspicious beginning, but he eventually found his calling, first working as a property man (alongside Henry Hathaway) and occasional actor.

The role of Dr. John H. Watson in Frank's two-reel version of Sir Arthur Conan Doyle's seminal Sherlock Holmes story, *A Study in Scarlet*, adapted by Cunard, was credited to actor "Jack Francis," but it is now believed that John Ford (using the pseudonymous union of his and his brother's names) played the character. Released on December 29, 1914, *A Study in Scarlet* was intended to be the first in a series of Sherlock Holmes films, but Laemmle's failure to purchase the rights to the Conan Doyle stories nixed the project.

Soon after appearing as companion to the Great Detective, John played one of the Klansmen in D. W. Griffith's *The Birth of a Nation* (1915), alternately the most technically groundbreaking and polemically racist film ever made in the United States. (Ironically, Ford, idolizer and future screen chronicler of Abraham Lincoln, worked for a man who, in political terms, was quite arguably the "John Wilkes Booth of the Cinema.")

"Jack" primarily toiled as a stunt man for Frank, who often resorted to verbal and physical abuse. While doubling his brother in a Civil War film, he nearly was killed when Frank set off a large gunpowder blast beneath the desk at which he was seated. Suffering from a broken arm and other injuries, he spent the next six weeks in the hospital.

Recovered from his near-death experience, Jack finally graduated to assistant director at Universal, where Frank, now doing triple duty as actor, writer and director, and Grace Cunard cranked out a series of two-reel serials. By 1916, 21-year-old Jack already had developed the stern leadership style for which he later became famous, hardened by the cavalier treatment from his brother, and necessarily having to control rough and rowdy extras, stuntmen and cowboys who had migrated to movies from the Wild West shows. As Ford's grandson, Dan, vividly wrote, "Just barely removed from the real thing, as a group they were mean, stupid, and cruel, respecting only rattlesnakes and live ammunition."[4]

Francis Ford (Universal, 1913). Frank Ford remains a largely forgotten cinematic pioneer, known today for the Shakespearean fool roles he plays in his younger brother's much-heralded films. This original sepia portrait is one of the extant artifacts from Frank's career as an actor, writer and director for Universal, Hollywood's first "film factory," founded by self-made mogul "Uncle" Carl Laemmle on June 8, 1912.

The brotherly belittling of Jack continued, as Frank later lambasted, "As a prop man he stunk; as an assistant director, he was worse, and as an actor — well, such a ham!"[5] Allan Dwan, for whom Jack worked as an assistant, recalled:

> Jack Ford was a leader and he could handle men. He used his own language when he lined the cowboys up.... It was, "Come on, you bastards, get in line and shut up."... He was a natural director.[6]

In April 1917, when President Woodrow Wilson, who had vowed to keep the United States out of the Great War, did exactly the opposite, many film industry personnel were given deferments because of their value as producers of anti–German propaganda. Ford volunteered to become an aerial combat photographer, but was turned down because of his terrible eyesight. Nonetheless, he later generated a myth about his own World War I service as a U.S. Navy "bluejacket."

Continuing his training with Francis (whose mentorship helped refine his already prodigious talent for photographic composition), Jack was teamed with actor Harry Carey, a NYU Law School "premature alumnus" (expellee) called the "Bronx Cowboy," who was old enough to be his father. Carey, disgusted with director Fred Kelsey, gave Jack a tryout after Frank caught wind of his intention to find a new collaborator. *The Soul Herder* (1917), starring Carey as "Cheyenne Harry," was the first of 26 films they made together, the earliest of which were shot in five days or less. Jack, Harry and his wife, Olive, and an assistant

Cheyenne's Pal (Universal, 1917; directed by John Ford). **This rare photograph, featuring both Hoot Gibson and Harry Carey (on bar, left to right), is one of the earliest surviving artifacts from Ford's nascent career as a director. This two-reel "Cheyenne Harry" Western was Ford's fifth directorial effort (and the second of 26 films with Carey), after graduating from his jack of all trades apprenticeship as actor, stuntman and crew member.**

director improvised most of the shooting, and then had a writer jot down a continuity from which a releasable picture could be edited. Ford recalled:

> They weren't shoot-'em-ups, they were character stories. Carey was a great actor, and we didn't dress him up like ... Mix and Hart and Buck Jones ... so we decided to kid ... the leading men — and make Carey sort of a bum, a saddle tramp, instead of a great bold gun-fighting hero.[7]

The term "soul herder" referred to the Western "good bad man" pioneered by William S. Hart. Though his acting could be histrionic, Hart's characterizations influenced Ford and Carey's development of a more realistic, working cowboy character, an outlaw who comes to the aid of a community mired in social hypocrisy, regardless of their puritanical disdain for his incongruous lifestyle.

In July 1917, Carey collaborated with Ford, who had continued to study the cinematic techniques of Griffith, in the bold move of writing a feature-length screenplay, *Straight Shooting*. Laemmle, who didn't want to deviate from the financially successful two-reel series, rejected it out of hand.

Undaunted, they went ahead and shot the picture, acquiring enough film stock after Ford lied about accidentally losing his supply in a stream! When *Straight Shooting*, also featuring Edmund "Hoot" Gibson, was completed, Laemmle, irked by their insubordination, demanded that the 90-minute film be butchered for the two-reel (20-minute) format. Impressed by their writing and Ford's inspired direction, 18-year-old whiz kid Irving Thalberg, then working as Laemmle's executive assistant, persuaded his boss to release the full-length version, which quickly became a box-office success.

In 1966, when asked about his early influences in filmmaking, Ford replied:

> [M]y brother Frank. He was a great cameraman — there's nothing they're doing today ... that he hadn't done; he was ... a hell of a good actor, a good director — Johnny of all trades — and *master* of all; he ... was the only influence *I* ever had, working in pictures.[8]

Ford then added, "D. W. Griffith influenced all of us. If it weren't for Griffith, we'd probably still be in the infantile phase of motion pictures."[9]

Australian-born actor Frank Baker (a member of the Ford Stock Company who appeared in 17 of the director's films over four decades) claimed:

> In everything John Ford did, I could see the reflection of Frank. ... Ford suffered tremendously from a great inferiority complex, and sitting right at the foundation ... was his brother Frank. He realized that he was just walking in his brother's footsteps ... and he took it out on Frank for the rest of his life.[10]

Jack worked 84-hour weeks, never took a day off, and indefatigably honed his prodigious writing, compositional and directing skills while making more than two-dozen Westerns with Carey in just two years. As Dan Ford pointed out, "Working under this kind of pressure taught him the greatest lesson of all: to find beauty in simplicity."[11] Their last film together was also the most elaborate: *Marked Men* (1919), Ford's first adaptation of Peter B. Kyne's short story "Three Godfathers." Ford, referring to Universal's decision to change the release title, later growled, "They would, the bastards.... That's sort of my favorite [of the early films].... I liked the story — that's why I asked to remake it years later."[12]

In December 1919, Laemmle loaned Ford to a competitor, William Fox, to make two features, *Just Pals* and *The Big Punch*, with Buck Jones. After developing his position as one of Hollywood's most capable and prolific cinematic dynamos, Ford had been waiting for an opportunity to direct for a more prominent studio, where his paycheck instantly doubled. However, his drive for success and recognition (coupled with rumors about his sexual orientation spread around the Carey ranch by actor Joe Harris), had damaged his relationship with Harry.

Ford already had begun to spend his off-hours imbibing alarming amounts of alcohol during long binges, after which he needed several days to recover. The Volstead Act had been in effect since October, but Prohibition didn't exactly accomplish what the temperance folks had intended.

On March 17, 1920, Ford, who currently shared digs with Hoot Gibson, accepted an invitation from fellow director Rex Ingram to attend a St. Patrick's Day dance at the Hollywood Hotel, where he met the attractive and witty, 28-year-old divorcee Mary McBride Smith. Arguably, there would be no more appropriate event at which Ford could meet a future wife.

Jack and Mary began to see each other frequently, dining on the Venice Pier and hitting all the speakeasies across Los Angeles. Less than four months after the Irish-American holiday, they were married at the L.A. courthouse on the morning before another major celebration, Independence Day (a rare day when Ford didn't "make pictures"). Next, the happy

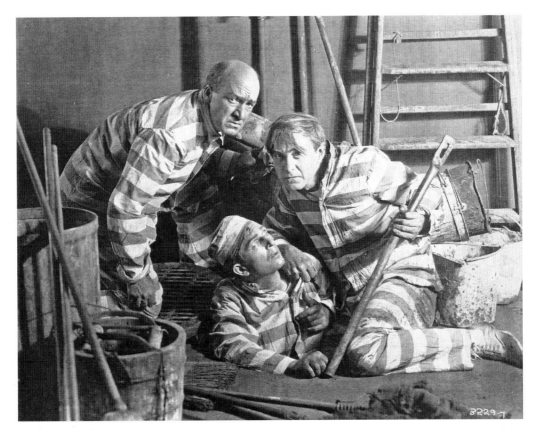

Marked Men (Universal, 1919; directed by John Ford). Ford's first production based on Peter B. Kyne's short story "Three Godfathers," this feature, starring (left to right) J. Farrell MacDonald, Joe Harris and Harry Carey, marked the last of 26 films he made with his first star and cinematic mentor. Ford was not pleased when the studio changed the title from *Three Godfathers* to *Marked Men* at the last minute.

couple immediately set to work producing a new Ford model, Patrick, born in April 1921, nine months after the nuptials.

A direct descendant of Sir Thomas More, Mary was a Scots-Irish Presbyterian whose family had prospered in America since the Colonial era. Her uncles and cousins included Annapolis and West Point graduates and a U.S. Surgeon General. Her father was a stock speculator on Wall Street. As Dan Ford wrote, his grandfather "wouldn't have admitted it, [but] he had married above himself."[13]

The union necessitated moving into a larger home at 6860 Odin Street, near the Hollywood Bowl. Sunday afternoons were spent cooking and imbibing bootleg hooch (which Ford stashed behind a sliding panel in his "secret den") with filmdom's finest, including Gibson, the hard-drinking Tom Mix, and histrionic heartthrob Rudolph Valentino. Weekends also involved one of Jack's favorite diversions: football games.

During Ford's absence from Universal, the Carey series was helmed temporarily by Harlan, Iowa-born Lynn F. Reynolds, another pioneering cinematic jack of all trades. (Reynolds' work for Universal and Fox ended suddenly on February 25, 1927, when he shot himself in front of party guests following a heated argument with his wife, Kathleen O'Connor, who had acted in the Ford-Carey feature *A Gun Fightin' Gentleman* [1919]).

Ford's two collaborations with Buck Jones had been well received, and soon he was back toiling on the Universal lot. William Fox was particularly pleased with *Just Pals*, a "modern," seriocomic Western blending genre trappings with speeding automobiles in "Norwalk, on the border of Nebraska and Wyoming." Jones gives a restrained performance as Bim, the town idler ostracized by the community until his relationship with a homeless boy (George Stone) leads to his heroic exposure of an embezzler (William Buckley) and winning of school teacher Mary Bruce (Helen Ferguson), whose involvement with the villain nearly leads to her downfall. Before he can achieve this victory, however, poor, misunderstood Bim is laughed at, punched out, hog-tied, almost drowned, nearly rail-ridden and just about lynched!

Ford's depiction of social hypocrisy is already prominent in this entertaining 50-minute feature released on October 21, 1920. His ability to create striking compositions in exterior settings using natural light and his strategic use of the close-up to capture the subtle facial expressions of his actors (in an era of mostly *un*subtle acting) are also well to the fore. Most importantly, *Just Pals* marked the first time Ford worked with cinematographer George Schneiderman, who played a major role in the development of his visual style on 20 more Fox films over the next 15 years.

Inspired by his father's backing of the Sinn Fein during the Irish nationalists attempt to end British rule, Ford (concocting a lie that his name was actually "Sean Aloysius O'Fearna") became engrossed with "The Troubles" raging in the homeland of his ancestors. On November 19, 1921, he sailed on the S.S. *Baltic* from New York to Liverpool, and then traveled to Holyhead in Wales, where he boarded the steamer TSS *Cambria*, bound for Dublin.

Ford claimed he was followed and briefly brutalized, but eventually located his cousin, Martin Feeney, an IRA cell leader, hiding out in the Connemara Mountains. Jack contributed some money to the cause and spent a few days in Galway before being escorted to a British boat by the Black and Tans, who ordered him never to return, lest he be tossed into prison. Dan Ford explained, "The trip to Galway was one of the most important experiences in John Ford's life ... [he] had found a facet of himself that he would never forget — his Irishness.[14]

When Ford signed his long-term contract with Fox, he joined a formidable roster of fine directors, including Allan Dwan, Howard Hawks, Raoul Walsh and William Wellman. His first films for the studio were formula pictures, including two melodramas, *Jackie* and *Little Miss Smiles* (both 1921), featuring child star Shirley Mason.

Upon his return from Ireland, he directed *The Village Blacksmith* (1922), based on the poem by Henry Wadsworth Longfellow, and *The Face on the Barroom Floor* (1923), a serious feature version of the poem by Hugh Antoine D'Arcy previously adapted as a comedy short (1914) by Charles Chaplin. *Barroom Floor* featured Henry B. Walthall, longtime colleague of Griffith, who had starred him in *The Birth of a Nation*. By the time these two Ford films were released, Francis had fallen on hard times, drinking even more heavily after being left by Grace Cunard.

Ford always had been credited as "Jack," but the Fox production *Cameo Kirby* (1923), an A picture starring John Gilbert, Alan Hale and Jean Arthur (in her screen debut), put the more distinguished *John* Ford on screen for the first time. Gilbert's starring role as an antebellum gambler also ensured that Ford had an ample budget, some of which was lavished on an exciting riverboat race. Given a chance to demonstrate his talent for "always knowing where to place the camera," he was acclaimed for the powerful visuals used in telling a dramatic story, even if it was based on a hoary, previously filmed play.

Critical success was matched by greater financial security and further family developments. On December 16, 1922, his 20-month-old son was joined by a sister, Barbara, and John decided that Mary should enjoy the assistance of a governess, Maude Stevenson.

On March 16, 1923, Paramount's epic Western *The Covered Wagon*, directed by James Cruze, premiered in New York City. By this time, Ford, now 29, already had directed 50 films, including 36 Westerns. Anxious to capitalize on the commercial success of the Paramount blockbuster, William Fox put up the huge sum of $450,000 to make *The Iron Horse*, an ambitious historical drama about the construction of the transcontinental railroad.

Having nearly exhausted all financial resources, Fox asked Ford, who was hired as director and producer, to cast an "unknown" in the lead role of Davy Brandon. Following a screen test, bodybuilder and former boxer George O'Brien, who had been working as an assistant cameraman under George Schneiderman, proved ideal for the physically demanding, heroic part. In the words of Dan Ford, "With his sleek dark hair, Roman nose, and a physique that rippled with muscles, he looked like an Irish Valentino."[15]

Before Charles Kenyon and John Russell wrote their treatment, Fox gathered research materials from railroad and Western historians, as well as professionals at the Smithsonian, American Museum of Natural History, Library of Congress and the public libraries of New York, Los Angeles, San Francisco, Sacramento and Omaha. Though Kenyon also was credited with writing the scenario, Ford improvised a number of scenes during production.

Ford's older brother Eddie, who had served as his assistant director at Universal, also signed on for the project. Stubbornly independent, Eddie chose to be billed as "Edward O'Fearna," using the family's Gaelic surname. Fox executive Sol Wurtzel hired a train used by the A. G. Barnes Circus to transport and house the cast and crew of 200 at the rugged location near Reno, Nevada, where *The Covered Wagon* had been filmed. Even though the shoot began in early January 1924, the company failed to prepare properly for inclement weather and suffered through a series of brutal snowstorms.

Ford hired local residents, including Piute Indians and immigrant railroad workers from China and Ireland, as extras. The ragtag outfit was a blend of saints and sinners. On one hand, Ford characteristically had befriended an Irish priest, Father Brady, to say Sunday Mass on a makeshift altar in the mess tent at "Camp Ford"; on the other, many of the men spent the Sabbath imbibing bootleg booze and enjoying the services of hookers who "commuted" from Reno. Eventually a local madam set up a special on-site bordello, where a man could have a bath, haircut, laundry services and a wild night, all for the princely sum of $5.00.

Ford attempted to honor his policy of sobriety while filming, but fell off the wagon one day after learning that Rollie Totheroh, Chaplin's cameraman, had brought some Scotch to keep warm during production of *The Gold Rush* near Truckee. Jack got loaded, started tearing up the camp, and was found passed out with some extras. When *The Iron Horse* ran over the four-week shooting schedule, Fox considered shelving it, but after Wurtzel witnessed the courageous efforts of the freezing filmmakers and the striking quality of Ford's footage, the project was expanded.

Ford completed production in mid–March, returned to Hollywood, and worked with editor Harold Schuster to assemble a 150-minute picture from the enormous amount of footage. He chose not to attend the August 28 premiere at the Lyric Theater in Manhattan, where William Fox joined Ford's wife and parents.

"Nana" and "Grampy," as Ford called them, stayed in New York for a week, and especially enjoyed a visit to Fox's Long Island home, where the serving of Jameson's Irish Whisky proved as big a hit as *The Iron Horse*, which became a major commercial and critical success. As part of the massive promotional campaign, Ford imported 25 Shoshone and Arapaho Indians from Wyoming to parade down Hollywood Boulevard for the West Coast premiere, held at the brand-new Grauman's Egyptian Theater on February 21, 1925.

Dan Ford wrote that his grandfather "had found his great theme as a chronicler of the American experience: personal happiness is tied to national progress."[16]

Pappy later remarked:

> [W]e had a hell of a time ... we had to spend more and more money and eventually this simple little story came out as a so-called "epic," the biggest picture Fox had ever made. Of course, if they had known what was going to happen, they never would have let us make it.[17]

George O'Brien may look like an "Irish Valentino" (especially during his climactic, beefcake-laden fight with Fred Kohler), but his acting is far more subtle than that of the Italian matinee idol, whose over-the-top leering and posturing has been generating more laughs than swoons over the decades. Aside from Madge Bellamy (whose wide-eyed portrayals of Victorian innocence *really* suffered after the coming of sound), the performances are quite restrained, in a film that derives its power from Ford's quasi-documentary historical authenticity in the exterior scenes involving thousands of immigrant workers laying over 1,600 miles of tracks against formidable obstacles, both environmental and human.

The early scenes featuring real-life Reno Justice of the Peace Charles Edward Bull as a positive clone of Abraham Lincoln (whose signing of the Railroad Act on July 1, 1862,

John Ford (Fox, 1924). Official Fox portrait of the 30-year-old Ford, used to publicize the Transcontinental Railroad epic *The Iron Horse*.

earned his memory the film's dedication) are matched in their majesty by the closing scenes depicting the driving of the golden spike celebrating the joining of the Union Pacific and Central Pacific railroads at Promontory Point, Utah, on May 10, 1869. In between, the clichéd love-triangle subplot involving Davy, Miriam Marsh (Bellamy) and Peter Jesson (Cyril Chadwick) is admirably balanced by spectacular sequences of bison thundering across the plains, an enormous herd of cattle being driven through a river, and a Cherokee war party attempting to prevent completion of the rail line.

Other historical figures include William "Buffalo Bill" Cody (George Wagner), "Wild" Bill Hickok (John Padjan, who also plays Leland Stanford) and General Grenville Dodge (Walter Rogers). Many of Ford's trademarks, including "Irish" humor (primarily perpetrated by his pal from the Carey days, J. Farrell MacDonald), the barroom that doubles as a courtroom, and location shots prefiguring his passion for Monument Valley, are already in evidence.

On August 1, 1924, Fox had signed Ford to a new 42-month, $1,500-per-week contract, with the guarantee of an eventual raise to $2,250. Over the next year, he was relegated to cranking out six commercial programmers, although reviewers continued to praise his directorial style. The best of the bunch, the boxing drama *The Fighting Heart* (1925), re-teamed him with George O'Brien and Francis, who continued to scrape for work as a character actor.

Another member of the cast was making his debut in a Ford picture: self-confident, Kentish-born and South African-bred Victor Andrew de Bier Everleigh McLaglen, son of an Anglican bishop, former heavyweight champion of the British Army, World War I officer, Deputy Provost Marshal of Baghdad, *and* film actor on both sides of the Atlantic. Just prior to working for Ford, he played Hercules, the strongman, in director Tod Browning's *The Unholy Three* (1925), one of Lon Chaney, Sr.'s finest films, also featuring Mae Busch, Matt Moore and Harry Earles.

McLaglen was the sort of bold and vibrant, yet graceful actor whom Ford preferred in lead or major supporting roles. When he discovered such a performer, he relied on him time and again (especially if the poor soul was capable of withstanding his frequently abusive directorial methods). Eventually this preference led to the evolution of the Ford Stock Company.

One of 10 children, McLaglen (who, like Francis Ford, had been discharged from his nation's army for being underage) had four brothers, Arthur, Clifford, Cyril and Kenneth, who also became film actors in England during the early 1920s. In 1934, Cyril, attempting to grab the coattails of his famous elder brother, arrived in Hollywood, where he also became a member of the Stock Company (playing small roles in five Ford films between 1936 and 1940). After appearing in five films in England and four in Australia, Arthur, too, attempted to capitalize on his big brother's success (after Ford gave him a small part in *The Informer* [1935], he actually *played* Victor in Columbia's *It Happened in Hollywood* [1937] before retiring!). A fifth brother, Leopold, also gave the cinema a try, but appeared in only one film, Stoll Productions' *Bars of Iron* (1920), produced in London.

Though he continued to make formula pictures for Fox, Ford began to demonstrate great versatility and range. The studio planned to make a sequel to *The Iron Horse*, allocating a $650,000 budget to star Western heroes Tom Mix, Buck Jones and George O'Brien as *3 Bad Men*. Ford wanted to direct another major Western, but insisted that novelist Herman Whitaker's "good bad" outlaws be interpreted by more realistic actors.

When location shooting began at Jackson Hole, Wyoming, in March 1926, cowboys "Bull" Stanley, Mike Costigan and "Spade" Allen were played by Tom Santschi, J. Farrell McDonald and Frank Campeau, respectively. McDonald had made a major contribution to *The Iron Horse*, as did George O'Brien, who was cast as romantic lead Dan O'Malley. In the Teton Mountains, Ford's company, again surrounded by ice and snow, endured harsh conditions to make a gritty, historical drama depicting the Dakota land rush of June 25, 1877.

The rush sequence that brings the film to a dramatic conclusion includes the most famous shot in all of Ford's silent films (and the most directly irresponsible act of his career): a baby girl, mistakenly left sitting on a dried-up lake bed, barely escapes death under the wheels of 150 thundering wagons when a man's arm reaches in to whisk her away. Harry Carey had thought of the scene years before, but he and Ford knew that no sane mother would allow her child to be placed in such a precarious position. In those untamed days, events on the screen, for the most part, had to be done for *real*.

Though he could have used process photography, Ford chose cinematic "realism" over the welfare of the child. The day before the scene was scheduled to be shot outside Victorville, California, he approached a stuntman's wife, promising that her baby would appear in the shot, totally safe and riding on a wagon. Soon after the mother arrived the following day, Eddie O'Fearna escorted her off the set, explaining that it was standard policy for parents not to be present during shooting. The baby was set on the lake bed, the wagons rolled like the devil and, with his own life at stake, longtime Ford prop man Lefty Hough saved her in a hair's breadth. He recalled:

> It was set up for a left-handed man. The camera was shooting out of a pit and I was on the running board of an automobile standing off to the side with the motor idling. As soon as I had a grip on her, the car raced off just ahead of those galloping horses. If I'd missed, I would have fallen on the kid.[18]

Ford claimed, "[S]everal of the people in the company had been in the actual rush.... For example, the incident of snatching the baby from under the wheels of a wagon actually happened."[19]

The film *3 Bad Men* was previewed in Los Angeles in August 1926. Poor audience

3 Bad Men (Fox, 1926; directed by John Ford). Ford's silent Western masterpiece, featuring "good bad" outlaws (from left to right) "Bull" Stanley (Tom Santschi), Mike Costigan (J. Farrell MacDonald) and "Spade" Allen (Frank Campeau), is a gritty historical drama depicting the Dakota land rush of June 25, 1877. The film also stars George O'Brien and Olive Borden (pictured in the inset at right).

reception sent Ford back to the cutting room and, the following month, a shortened, tighter version was screened in Modesto to considerable acclaim. Though it subsequently was a critical success, *3 Bad Men*, a bluntly violent film for its time, was not a big hit with the masses. The believable narrative and emotionally engaging characterizations, deftly integrated with the epic events, are arguably superior to those in *The Iron Horse*.

J. Farrell MacDonald and his compatriots (who "weren't exactly thieves, but they had a habit of finding horses that nobody lost") contribute ample doses of comedy; but, unlike the comic scenes in *The Iron Horse*, the humor arises naturally from the events, rather than being used to relieve dramatic tension. When Bull Stanley decides that the fatherless Lee Carlton (Olive Borden, a fine actress and an enormous improvement on Madge Bellamy in *The Iron Horse*) cannot face the land rush alone, he vows to Spade and Mike, "We'll find a marryin' man if we have to shoot him." The attempts at matchmaking are a comic highpoint, and the three thoughtful outlaws eventually pair Lee with the handsome, gallant *and* Irish Dan O'Malley, referred to as a real "*man.*"

The film ends with all three outlaws sacrificing their lives to save the couple from the corrupt Sheriff Layne Hunter (Lou Tellegen, wearing *Nosferatu*-like makeup) and his gang of cutthroats. (This S.O.B. of a "lawman" orders the local church, with the preacher and congregation inside, burned to the ground; the outlaws save them, too). Just as the "3 Bad Men" ride into the film, framed in a classic Ford long shot and silhouetted against the sunset, their ghost riders head back into the setting sun at the end, as the happy couple, cradling their baby son, Stanley Costigan Allen O'Malley, watch from the window of their newly built cabin.

The film *3 Bad Men* is loaded with characters, events and themes that would become further developed throughout Ford's career as a "maker of Westerns," particularly in *Stagecoach*, *3 Godfathers* and *The Searchers*. As pointed out by Joseph McBride, it also features "some of the most complex compositions of any Ford movie," yet "always unfolds with effortless naturalness, and the images never come across as mannered or overly studied."[20]

Ford (without receiving screen credit) next aided Raoul Walsh in directing Fox's World War I epic *What Price Glory* (1926), costarring Victor McLaglen and Edmund Lowe, a successful pairing that would be repeated in several films over the ensuing decade. Ford also oversaw the shooting of World War I sequences for Fox's *Seventh Heaven* (1927), which won Frank Borzage the first Best Director Academy Award.

In February 1927, Ford, accompanied by Mary, boarded the SS *Hamburg* on a voyage to Germany financed by Fox. During their stay, Jack was to film background footage in the Tyrol for the upcoming *Four Sons*, based on I. A. R. Wylie's short story, "Grandma Bernle Learns Her Letters," depicting the relationship between a Bavarian widow and her sons during World War I. While in Berlin, Ford received a private impromptu seminar in expressionist filmmaking from the great F. W. Murnau, who recently had signed a contract with Fox that brought him to Hollywood to make the extraordinary *Sunrise: A Song of Two Humans* (1927).

Ford spent a month in the German capitol, where he screened Murnau's *Nosferatu* (1922) and *The Last Laugh* (1924), Robert Weine's *The Cabinet of Dr. Caligari* (1919), and Fritz Lang's *Destiny* (1921) and *Metropolis* (1927), all of which had a profound influence on the consciously stylized visual and performance techniques he brought to *Four Sons*. Ford imitated Murnau's work, particularly *The Last Laugh*, so closely that the film, shorn of his name in the credits, appears as if it was made entirely in Weimar Germany. Much of *Four Sons*, in fact, was shot on the leftover sets constructed for *Sunrise*.

The joyful residents of the Bavarian village include Frau Bernle (Margaret Mann) and her four sons, one of whom, Joseph (James Hall), migrates to New York, establishing a German-American delicatessen, while the other three remain behind. When the Great War erupts, two of the boys, Franz (Francis X. Bushman, Jr.) and Johann (Charles Morton) are killed in Russia, and the third, Andreas (George Meeker), is conscripted by the reactionary Major Von Stom (Earle Foxe).

Drafted into the U.S. Army, Joseph, during combat, discovers the fatally wounded Andreas, who dies in his brother's arms. The emotionally intense film concludes with Frau Bernle "learning her letters" so she may emigrate to the States, where she confusedly wanders off from Ellis Island but is found by a friendly policeman who takes her to Joseph, his wife and small son.

Though he had created a film blatantly "borrowing" the style of another filmmaker (one who would continue to affect his self-conscious tendency toward expressionism), Ford was showered with accolades for *Four Sons*, including *Photoplay* magazine's Gold Medal Award for the Best Picture of 1928. Ford's friend Jack Pennick, as "The Iceman" who fights alongside Joseph in battle, enjoyed his first major supporting role in the film, which, rather than depicting actual combat, relies on expressionistic acting (stylistically matching Ford's use of costume and set design, lighting and a highly mobile camera) for its dramatic power. One of the most moving sequences involves Frau Bernle sitting alone at her dining table, joined only by the superimposed "ghosts" of her sons slaughtered in the war.

Prior to making *Four Sons*, Ford shot a more conventional film, *Mother Machree* (1928), an Irish-American melodrama featuring Victor McLaglen as "The Giant of Kilkenny." Among the crewmen on the Fox lot during the summer of 1927 was Marion "Duke" Morrison, a 20-year-old laborer who was herding a flock of geese to be used by Ford.

Born Marion Robert Morrison in Winterset, Iowa, on May 26, 1907, he had lived in California since age seven. In 1916, his parents, Clyde, a druggist who had attempted to farm in the Mohave Desert, and Mary (known as "Molly"), had moved Marion and his younger brother, Robert (whose birth in 1912 brought about the change of Marion's middle name to "Mitchell"), to the Los Angeles suburb of Glendale.

At the Sixth Street Elementary School, Marion hated being teased about his "girl's name," which sparked the expected childhood brawls. But, in 1918, he was forever relieved of this unmanly moniker by a group of local firefighters who were joined every weekday by the Morrison family dog, an Airedale terrier named "Duke," who would nap at the fire station until Marion was dismissed from school. The men first attached the nickname "Little Duke" to the boy, and then shortened it to "Duke," which stuck.

From childhood, Duke maintained a safe emotional distance from females. His mother, who preferred his younger brother, often berated him, in between arguing with his father, with whom he enjoyed a close, understanding relationship. Around Glendale, he quickly became fascinated by the Hollywood companies filming on location.

By 1920, two of his pals, twin brothers Robert and William Bradbury, both were acting in a series of short films directed by their father, Robert N. Bradbury, a specialist in Westerns and action programmers. (The younger Robert later would transform himself into B-Western star Bob Steele.)

After graduating from Wilson Intermediate School, Duke attended Glendale Union High from 1921 to 1925, excelling as an honor student, class president, debate team captain, yearbook advertising salesman, and member of the student council, newspaper staff and dramatic society, which he represented at the Southern California Shakespeare Contest during his senior year. He also played top guard position on the football team, helping to win the state championship in 1924.

Like Ford, his hopes of attending the U.S. Naval Academy were dashed, but Duke was offered a football scholarship by the University of Southern California, where he registered for the 1925 fall semester, majoring in pre-law. When the football season ended, he had more time for a social life, including dates with Josephine Saenz, the 16-year-old daughter of a "Hispanic Blueblood" doctor who had built a successful chain of pharmacies throughout the Southwest. Aware that Duke's Protestant parents were not listed in the Los Angeles social register, the Catholic Saenz family disapproved of the courtship.

In 1926, legendary USC head coach Howard Jones cut a deal with Tom Mix, trading box seats at the football stadium for the Western star's promise to arrange summer jobs at Fox for some of his best players. In June, Duke went to work at $35 per week, informed that he would travel to Colorado as a trainer for Mix and possibly play a bit part in the film *The Great K & A Train Robbery*. However, when the company arrived at the location, Duke, laboring as a prop man, was unable to speak to the star. Back in Hollywood at the end of the month, he was put on a swing gang, moving heavy furniture.

The persistent tale is that Duke's introduction to Ford included grappling with him during some gridiron shenanigans. After supposedly decking the director with a kick to the *chest* (expertise in, not football, but martial arts would be needed to perform such a maneuver), Duke heard Pappy order the cast and crew, "Come on, let's get back to work — that's enough of this bullshit!"

Wayne later recalled:

> Jack appreciated the fact that I was more than just another prop man, that I was trying to get an education.... I watched how he handled people, how he got his actors to communicate without the spoken word. I ... began to appreciate what a great artist he really was.
> The other kids who were going to law school all had connections ... I had none ... and the more I thought about the picture business, the more attractive it became. I had no thoughts about becoming an actor — I wanted to be a director like Jack Ford. He was my mentor, my ideal....[21]

One week before workouts for the 1926 football season began at USC, Duke seriously injured his right shoulder while bodysurfing at a popular point between Seal and Huntington Beaches. In excruciating pain, and unable to handle his tackle position, he was dropped to the scrubs by Jones, who was furious. This demotion jeopardized his scholarship and, at the close of the 1927 spring term, his status as a ridiculed dishwasher induced him to leave school and seek a full-time job.

At the suggestion of George O'Brien, Duke headed for San Francisco. While rooming with some of O'Brien's friends, he discussed job possibilities with the actor's father, the city police chief. Weeks passed and, with no hope of employment, Duke stowed away to Honolulu aboard the SS *Malolo*. After four days, the starving stowaway asked to see the captain, who promptly ordered him thrown into the brig. At the end of the round trip, Duke was jailed in San Francisco, but Chief O'Brien, asking the steamship company not to press charges, gave him a ticket for a Los Angeles–bound train.

Duke went back to Fox, working as Lefty Hough's assistant prop man, when Ford offered him an extra part in *Mother Machree*. During August 1927, on a day when Ford was preparing to shoot a dramatic scene for *Four Sons*, Margaret Mann was not doing well during rehearsals, and Duke repeatedly had to blow leaves onto the porch set and then sweep them up. After nearly eight hours of tedium, Duke, his concentration on the wane, didn't realize that Ford finally was shooting an actual take. While sweeping up the leaves, unknowingly entering the frame as the camera was rolling, he heard Pappy shout, "*Cut!*"

Realizing that he had ruined the take Ford was trying to capture all day, Duke frantically ran off the stage, but a crew member was ordered to stop him. Ford then escorted him back to the set, told a Serbian actor to pin a German Iron Cross on him, and commanded, "Assume the position." Duke, kneeling down as the cast and crew looked on, received a swift kick in the ass.

"All right, it was just an accident," Pappy assured the embarrassed prop assistant. Ford later added, "We were all laughing so much we couldn't work the rest of the day. It was so funny — beautiful scene and this big oaf comes in sweeping the leaves up."[22] Duke's absent-mindedness earned him another extra part.

He also landed two extra roles in *Hangman's House* (1928), Ford's first film to touch on The Troubles, starring Victor McLaglen as Citizen Denis Hogan, an exiled Irish patriot serving in the Foreign Legion who returns to the Auld Sod to kill John D'Arcy (Earle Foxe, even more loathsome than in *Four Sons*), the rake responsible for his sister's suicide. Informed that he is terminally ill, Lord Chief Justice James O'Brien (Hobart Bosworth), known to the locals as "Jimmy the Hangman," forces his daughter, Connaught (June Collyer), to marry D'Arcy, much to the chagrin of Dermot McDermot (Larry Kent), the man she really loves.

Hangman's House (Fox, 1928; directed by John Ford). Citizen Denis Hogan (Victor McLaglen, standing at left) prepares to leave India to seek vengeance in his troubled homeland. (John Wayne served as prop man and plays two bit roles in this atmospheric melodrama set primarily in Ireland.)

Threatened by Hogan, D'Arcy informs on him (seven years before McLaglen himself would do the same thing as Gypo Nolan in Ford's *The Informer*), but his fellow rebels break him out of jail. Both Hogan and Dermot plan to kill D'Arcy, but the former first challenges the cad to a dagger fight, then agrees to use pistols, only to be shot in the back while preparing for the duel. D'Arcy tips over a candelabrum, sets fire to Hangman's House, and then plunges to his much deserved death from a balcony. "A great yellow stain has gone from the green of Ireland," says Hogan before he bids farewell to Dermot, Connaught and Ireland to return to his military life "in the desert."

Duke briefly appears in a steeplechase scene (some of which Ford had shot in Ireland following the visit to Germany), in which he tears down a picket fence to lead the spectators racing toward the winning horse. He also appears in silhouette during a flashback sequence, when the dying, guilt-ridden O'Brien stares into the blazing fireplace, imagining haunting visions of past executions. This scene is a highpoint of a visually stunning film which is not an F. W. Murnau imitation, but an expressionist-influenced *John Ford* production. (As noted by Joseph McBride, *Four Sons* marked "the one time he tried to be someone else."[23])

Ford cast his pal J. Farrell MacDonald in the comedy *Riley the Cop* (1928), a silent with ludicrous music and sound effects, before attempting his first "talkie," *Napoleon's Barber* (1928), a 32-minute short, which bluntly introduced him to the perils of early dialogue recording. He had been accustomed to shouting directions to his cast and crew, who now had to join him in being completely quiet when "Action!" was called. The enormous, noisy sound cameras, which had to be housed in padded booths, and the microphone "stranglehold" that plagued even the finest filmmakers who had perfected their silent craft during the mid– to late–1920s, also shackled Ford for a time.

J. Farrell MacDonald and Irish-American writer James Kevin McGuinness joined him for the Victor McLaglen vehicle *Strong Boy* (1929), another silent feature with music and sound effects. McGuinness had been a publicist for the Catholic Church and now enjoyed the one-two combination of drinking and filmmaking with Ford, who called him "Seamus" in exchange for the equally Gaelic "Sean." Fox put up $400,000 for their next collaboration, *The Black Watch* (1929), an adaptation of Talbot Mundy's colonial novel *King of the Khyber Rifles*.

Ford, assisted by Edward O'Fearna and brother-in-law Wingate Smith, a decorated World War I veteran, shot *The Black Watch* as a semi-expressionistic silent with Victor McLaglen and Myrna Loy in the starring roles. After Ford and editor Alex Troffey finished cutting the picture, Sol Wurtzel and producer Winfield Sheehan, impressed by the success of Raoul Walsh's sound Western *In Old Arizona* (1929), announced that all subsequent Fox releases would be talkies.

The completed cut of *The Black Watch* was then given to Lumsden Hare, a British stage director, who inserted several lengthy sound sequences featuring McLaglen and Loy (as with many talkies made in 1929–30, comprised of stilted dialogue and static shots resembling a filmed play). This executive decision ruined the flow of the narrative, but reviewers unknowingly criticized Ford for the asymmetry of the film. Ford explained, "Winfield Sheehan ... got Hare to direct some love scenes.... And they were really horrible — long, talky things, had nothing to do with the story — and completely screwed it up. I wanted to vomit when I saw them."[24]

Ford had a totally different reaction toward Loy, however, and invited her to a party at his Odin Street home, where a group of his young friends, including Duke Morrison, were gathered. Mary Ford had no idea Loy would attend, and Myrna was unaware that she would be the sole female highlight of a stag gathering! She was a tough little cookie who could stand up to any man, on screen or off, and had a grand time that evening. She would remain one of Ford's pals for many years.

Ford, deeply disappointed by the commercial failure of his past three films, was becoming increasingly uncomfortable with the sound format. Also influenced by Raoul Walsh's *In Old Arizona* (the film that cost the action-oriented yet versatile director his right eye when, on location, a jackrabbit smashed into his car's windshield), James Kevin McGuinness realized that shooting an exciting adventure film in a remote area might be the key to attracting audiences. His screenplay, *Salute*, about two competitive brothers who attend West Point and Annapolis, respectively, greatly interested Ford. In early 1929, McGuinness, George O'Brien and cinematographer Joseph August joined him on a trip to the East Coast to scout locations.

One of the high points of *Salute* is a depiction of the annual Army-Navy football game. An apocryphal story, told by John Wayne and documented many times over the years, runs thusly:

> For the casting of players, Ford asked Duke if he could line up 25 members of the USC Trojan squad. Duke met with one of his former Sigma Chi brothers, George von Kleinsmid, son of the USC President, to discuss ... approaching his father on behalf of Ford.
>
> Ford filled most of the parts with the Sigma Chi frat boys, but a few others also managed to get hired. When they all assembled at the Sante Fe Depot ... one mug showed up, toting nothing but a jug of bootleg gin: Ward Bond, a brazen member of the Sigma Tau fraternity, whom Duke tried to avoid.
>
> "Who is that great, big ugly guy?" asked Ford.
>
> "Which one?" inquired Duke.
>
> "The one with the liver lips and the big mouth," Ford replied.
>
> "His name is Bond, *Wardell Bond*," said Duke. "He's just a big loudmouth who thinks he can play football.... We call him 'The Judge' because he spends so much time on the bench."[25]

The available evidence reveals that Marion Morrison (no longer associated with USC, but now a card-carrying member of the Motion Picture Studio Mechanics' Union, Local No. 37) successfully accomplished his assignment by enlisting one player who was on Howard Jones' 1928-1929 football roster: Wardell E. Bond. To show his appreciation, Ford instructed Duke to share a sleeping compartment with Bond on the 2,700-mile, cross-country trip. By the time they reached the East Coast, the two former "antagonists" had become great friends.

Wayne later explained:

> You couldn't help but notice Ward in a crowd. He was always getting himself into trouble by opening his mouth before he knew what he was going to say. But he was really fun, and right away Jack kinda took to him.[26]

At Annapolis, Ford hired a Marine D.I. to instruct the extras how to portray Navy midshipmen. Using George O'Brien as his exemplar, the D.I. ordered the rest of the men to follow suit. For their efforts, each was paid $50 per week, plus expenses.

Duke later recalled some of his on-location exploits with Bond:

> Ward had an unshakeable ego and all the gall in the world.... One night we wanted to go out drinking. Ward said, "Come on, I'll get some money from Jack Ford." He didn't know Jack nearly as well as I did, but he just marched up to Jack's door and banged on it and said, "Hey, it's me, Ward, open the goddamn door and let me in." Jack was sitting in the bathtub shaving.... We went in and on top of the dresser was about fifteen dollars in cash. Ward reached up and said, "Jack, I'm taking fifteen bucks," and before he could say anything, we were out the door![27]

When interviewed by Peter Bogdanovich in 1966, Ford very succinctly recalled the moment when he hired the two men who would become a vital element in his life and work:

> Ward Bond and Wayne were on it — they were both perfectly natural, so when I needed a couple of fellows to speak some lines, I picked them out and they ended up with parts. Wayne used to work for me.... I knew him so well.[28]

During the filming of *Salute*, Duke continued to work in several capacities, contentedly following all orders issued by Ford. The aspiring actor played the small role of a midshipman *and* served as wardrobe man for African American comic Stepin Fetchit, who, in his first of several Ford films, received fourth billing. Ford immediately befriended Fetchit (born Lincoln Theodore Monroe Andrew Perry in Key West on May 30, 1902), and personally arranged for him to stay in the Annapolis commandant's guest house during the shoot. Fetchit later praised Ford as "one of the greatest men who ever lived."[29]

Ford's depictions of blacks and other minority groups continued throughout his career, particularly in his later films, and are generally positive. Ford later recalled growing up as the son of Irish immigrants in Portland, where African Americans "lived with us.... They didn't live in barrios. Our next-door neighbors were black. There was no difference, no racial feeling, no prejudice."[30]

The "Stepin Fetchit" comic character was created as a way to make a living for Perry, who became the first African American performer to earn $1 million in the film industry. When he wasn't playing the slowly walking and talking, often unintelligible, but lovable fool, Perry, who was an extremely literate man, ironically enjoyed a second lengthy career writing for the African American newspaper *The Chicago Defender*. Joseph McBride observed:

> Ford's typically sly and convoluted satire of racial stereotyping shaped the comedian's character.... For nearly a quarter of a century, Ford employed Stepin Fetchit ... to ridicule and subvert the conventions of American racism. For this both men have been maligned by humorless critics who fail to understand what the African American film historian Albert Johnson observed in 1971, that "cooler second sight must admit that Stepin Fetchit was an artist, and that his art consisted precisely in mocking and caricaturing the white man's vision of the black...."[31]

Trailblazing African American athlete and actor Woody Strode, who later appeared in four Ford films and became one of his closest friends, wrote:

> I remember when I was in Las Vegas making *The Professionals* [1966] for Columbia Pictures.... The black actors were criticizing Stepin Fetchit. He was one of our greatest comedians and the first black actor to get star billing. I took a stand for him. I said, "If it hadn't been for Stepin Fetchit, I wouldn't be here. Somebody had to start it." They're going to do his story some day and all this history will come out. John Ford loved the guy; so did Will Rogers.... As a child, the only black movie star I had ever heard of was Stepin Fetchit.... I saw him when I was a kid; he was driving a pink convertible Rolls Royce.[32]

Interestingly, Perry's "Stepin Fetchit" may have been a primary influence on Ford, who was delighted to feature similar slow-witted, mentally challenged or drunken, but Caucasian, characters in his later films, often played by Francis, or Stock Company regulars Hank Worden and Ken Curtis (who was Ford's son-in-law from 1952 to 1964). Ford depicted a totally insane character in *The Lost Patrol* (1934), directing Boris Karloff into a frenzy as the crazed religious fanatic Sanders, arguably the most wildly demented chap that the "King of the Horror Films" played in a career loaded with brilliantly realized nutcases, fiends and monsters. Although *Tobacco Road* (1941) is literally populated with inbred imbeciles, including

Salute (Fox, 1929; directed by John Ford). Marian Wilson (Joyce Compton) dances with Cadet John Randall (George O'Brien) as Midshipman Harold (Ward Bond) looks on in disapproval. (An unbilled John Wayne, who plays Midshipman Bill, also served as Stepin Fetchit's wardrobe man during production.)

Bond's Lov Bensey, James Arness, as Floyd Clegg in *Wagon Master* (1950), may take the prize as the most obtuse, seemingly brain-damaged character in Ford's entire *oeuvre*.

James Kevin McGuinness constructed the *Salute* script in a way that allowed Ford to shoot the action scenes without sound, which later was dubbed in after they returned to Fox, and the talking scenes included only enough dialogue to move the story along. Ford thoroughly enjoyed their time at Annapolis, where he further developed the love of U.S. Navy life that would subsequently inform his life and career.

During the 2,700-mile train trip back to Hollywood, Bond quickly earned the enmity of Eddie O'Fearna (who repeatedly skimmed from the meal funds) when he devoured an enormous breakfast that set the company back a whopping 20 bucks (twice the per diem). Duke explained to Ford that a football player needed all he could get. Just to pour salt into his brother's wound, Jack, accompanied by George O'Brien, followed suit with a 40-dollar feast and then signed Eddie's name to the check. "Eddie got sore as hell and blamed it on me," Wayne later admitted. "I don't think he ever forgave me for that."[33]

Wayne biographers Randy Roberts and James S. Olson noted:

Ward and Duke became a pair in Ford's mind. Although Duke was reserved and kept a respectful distance from Ford, Ward's antics and outrageous boasts drew Duke into constant controversies.

Ford was so delighted with Bond's unconventional behavior that Duke benefited by association. By the end of the trip East, the three had formed a friendship that would last until the end of their lives....[34]

Though Duke and Ward's contributions to *Salute* were in the can, Ford returned to Annapolis to work on the film through the late spring of 1929. On Sunday, May 12, during a break in production, he went home to Portland, where he spent a somewhat uncomfortable Mother's Day with the emotionally distant Abby Feeney, who once said of her brood, "All the children are normal, except the youngest, Johnny."[35]

In June, Ford was back in Hollywood, shooting the interior scenes for *Salute*, when he was asked by Kenneth Hawks, the younger brother of Howard, to play himself in *Big Time* (1929), the young director's first solo effort, featuring Lee Tracy, Mae Clarke (in her film debut) and Stepin Fetchit as vaudevillians who try their luck with talking pictures. Ford was glad to oblige the promising young filmmaker who, tragically, never completed another production. On January 30, 1930, he and nine crewmen were killed when their camera planes collided over Santa Monica Bay while shooting aerial footage for *Such Men Are Dangerous*.

At age 31, Kenneth Hawks left Mary Astor a widow after less than two years of marriage. (Though she landed major roles in several subsequent prestige films, including Ford's *The Hurricane* [1937], and won a Best Supporting Actress Oscar for *The Great Lie* [1941], her personal life was wracked by alcoholism, three divorces, and a botched suicide.)

Duke and Ward soon appeared together in another Fox film, *Words and Music*, directed by James Tinling. (The fact that the film was released on August 18, 1929, two weeks before *Salute* hit theaters, has led to the erroneous belief that it was the first, not the second, picture to include both Morrison and Bond, who also was playing the *second* role of his acting career.) However, Duke Morrison, in the major role of frat boy Pete Donahue, received on-screen billing for the first time; while Bond was cast as a supporting character appropriately named "Ward." Staying true to form, Bond then accepted a small role, as another USC football player, in MGM's *So This Is College* (1930), starring Elliott Nugent and Robert Montgomery.

The actual USC team opened its 1929 schedule with a 76–0 victory over UCLA, and followed up with eight more wins and two losses. The season was capped with the Trojans' 47–14 national-championship trouncing of the Pittsburgh Panthers at the Rose Bowl, played in Pasadena on New Year's Day 1930. USC quarterback Russ Saunders, who threw three touchdown passes and scored a fourth on a 16-yard run, was named Most Valuable Player.

With the big game won, Ward decided to take a semester off, grab as many bit roles as possible and decrease his academic debt. At Fox, he played a townsman in *The Lone Star Ranger* (1930), the latest Western starring George O'Brien, while Duke went back to work for Ford.

James Kevin McGuinness had written another maritime story, set on a submarine disabled on the ocean floor, which Jack then turned over to U.S. Navy veteran and former New York *World* reporter Dudley Nichols, who combined extensive military detail with a talent for crafting economical dialogue. Ford took drafts by both writers and authored a final shooting script titled *Men Without Women*. Blending scenes filmed on the Fox lot with location footage shot on Catalina Island, he and cinematographer Joseph August created a dynamic visual style to offset the fact that the majority of the 77-minute production is set inside the wrecked submarine. This time, Ford gave Duke some dialogue and a close-up, making his brief role as a navy radioman much more noticeable than his previous extra parts. Ford, perhaps once more exaggerating Duke's participation, claimed, "I asked the stuntman to dive overboard and he refused.... So John Wayne ... says, 'I'll double them all.' And he put on different clothes and dove overboard."[36]

After completing *Men Without Women*, Ford claimed that he was asked by Raoul Walsh if he knew of any good-looking, tough, young leading men who could be cast on the cheap. Ford took credit for suggesting Duke, screening his brief performance as the navy man for Walsh, and landing him the lead role in an upcoming epic Western to be shot in the new 70mm "Fox Grandeur" process.

Walsh denied that Ford had anything to do with his choice of Marion Morrison to star in his opus, tentatively titled "The Oregon Trail." He claimed that, after watching the physically striking young prop man effortlessly lugging furniture on the Fox lot, he told his casting director, Eddie Grainger, to shoot a screen test. As soon as Walsh saw it, he wanted Duke for the role of wagon-train scout Breck Coleman, but Winfield Sheehan refused to put the name "Marion Morrison" on the screen. A Revolutionary War buff, Walsh wanted to borrow the moniker of a favorite general, "Mad" Anthony Wayne, but Sheehan thought it sounded "too Italian." Eventually, they settled on "John Wayne," and Duke had no say in the matter.

Ford also claimed that he and Duke, not Walsh, concocted the screen identity. Joseph McBride accurately assessed, "All that's certain in this matter is that for Ford and Walsh, those two master bullshit artists, naming the Duke was a cherished example of 'When the legend becomes fact, print the legend.'"[37]

History is permeated with fairy tales, legends and myths. The many creation myths are the most persistent, from Gilgamesh down to the fabrication of cultural figures like "John Wayne." In this case, a genesis and evolution occurred, until the contrived Wayne persona subsumed much of what existed within Marion Morrison.

Morrison came to believe that he really *was* John Wayne. The public acceptance of the image includes the supposition that, among other falsehoods, this Paul Bunyan–like cinematic character singlehandedly won World War II, when the *real* man, prompted and aided by his Hollywood bosses, remained Stateside.

Much of the world clung to John Wayne, even when he inevitably became an anachronistic caricature of his "original self." Like most legends, as more time passes, the verity of Marion Morrison will be lost, while the lore about John Wayne will continue on its inexorable path.

It doesn't matter who began the mythologizing. Three men (John Ford, Raoul Walsh and Howard Hawks) are primarily responsible for the creation and development of John Wayne, the character who became the fourth architect of his own legend. However, Harry Carey, Jr., writing in 1994, insisted that it was, not his "Uncle Jack," but his father-in-law, character actor Paul Fix, who "was the man who gave Duke his first insight into forming the mold which was to be his persona ... the first man to put the John Wayne image into [his] head."[38]

Though Ford believed that Monument Valley was the most awe-inspiring locale on Earth, the Wayne myth he helped foster eventually grew to match, in power and majesty, that ancient, river-hewn desert wonder. Sometimes an environmental marvel can be explained more easily than a cultural entity.

Former President Bill Clinton provided specific evidence of the efficacy of the Wayne phenomenon:

On [August 11, 1993] I nominated Army General John Shalikashvili to succeed Colin Powell as chairman of the Joint Chiefs of Staff.... Shali, as everyone called him, had entered the army as a draftee and risen through the ranks to his current position as the commander of NATO and U.S. forces in Europe. He was born in Poland, to a family from Georgia in the former Soviet Union.... When Shali was sixteen [1952], his family moved to Peoria, Illinois, where he taught himself English by watching John Wayne movies.[39]

The most enduring myth in the culture of the United States is that of the Frontier, from which sprang the Western, first in lore, then in print (thanks primarily to Easterners), painting, on stage, and in motion pictures. When Ford arrived in California to join his brother, filmmaking was still a "frontier." There was no UCLA film school, where he could learn to create "motion pictures" with computers and without using film. Ford said that "black and white is real photography," and to make movies in Hollywood's pioneer days, a director had to understand, or learn very quickly, the complicated principles of that visual art.

The "rules of cinema" were still being established, and directors like Thomas Ince, Francis and John Ford, Raoul Walsh and Cecil B. DeMille were helping to develop and refine them as they cranked out as many titles as possible. In those days, these trailblazers actually had to *do* things physically; even "faked" events had to be accomplished, exposed on film, developed in a dark room and then manually cut and "cemented." There was no CGI studio waiting for them to fake things digitally and "fix it in post."

Though filmmakers of later generations have been more concerned with "realism," rather than symbolism, metaphors and stylized acting, they have been pursuing an impossible dream. The only way realism can be experienced is in *real* life, not *reel* dreamland, where every minute aspect is manipulated for maximum effect. The only way to achieve "realism" would be *not* to use a script, editing, visual and sound effects — or a camera.

Commercial motion pictures were developed as a visual form of *storytelling*. Many of the films made during the silent and early sound periods are more pleasant to watch because the filmmakers were concerned with photography, rather than jerking a hand-held camera in all directions and cutting every half-second to hold the gaze of audiences who have developed mass attention-deficit disorder.

Many film historians, concerned with facts about the past, have been intent on "exposing John Ford's myths." The truth is that, the first time Ford directed a film, he was making a *Western*, the genre most steeped in legend, in which he primarily worked for the first seven years of his career. While going about his daily "job of work," as he referred to it, he indirectly went to myth-making school. The fact that the great films of his mature period are loaded with mythology is understandable. He reinforced existing myths, created them, replaced old with new, *and* subverted and exposed them.

Raoul Walsh's *The Big Trail*, the first attempt to make a Frontier epic during the sound era, was affected in every aspect by 27 years of Westerns that preceded it. The first narrative motion picture ever made, Edwin S. Porter's *The Great Train Robbery* (1903), was a Western. When Wayne (after enduring a regimen of acting lessons and "cowboy" training) and Bond saddled up with Walsh to head out for Arizona and other rugged locations to make this bold, difficult attempt to outdo what the genre already had produced, the last thing on their minds was mythology.

Busy with his new career in the motion-picture business, Bond hadn't been corresponding properly with his concerned parents in Oakland. On Wednesday, March 5, 1930, two months after helping the USC Trojans win the Rose Bowl, he took pencil in hand to write a long letter, laced with his usual blend of eloquence and levity (including a signature no doubt inspired by his Latin studies), in which he finally dropped the bomb on his folks:

> Surprise! Surprise! I am really writing—no fooling after so long. Yours of very recent date at hand and beg to state that your contemplated action of communicating with either Mr. Clarke or Mr. Templeton concerning my welfare is entirely unnecessary, as I am in good health, better spirits and excellent care.
>
> *There.* I have no broken bones, unless they are in my head, and don't expect to have any, and my heart and hand are still in one piece or rather two pieces, one at the end of my arm and the other somewhere in my midsection.
>
> Am really very sorry to have caused you all so much mental anguish.... I'll try to do better. *Please* don't worry—*ever.*
>
> Well I am not in school *this* semester. Which means that I finished last semester about Feb 15 and have been working in pictures since that time. Did a small part in John Ford's new picture, some football work in "Good News" at M.G.M. and am starting tomorrow at Fox on another college picture which I think will take about a month, maybe less.
>
> The reason I stayed out of school is very apparent especially to anyone who might have had access to the contents of my pocketbook at that time. The resources therein were sadly depleted and hence the time out for recuperation of said contents of said pocketbook.
>
> It is my honest intention to return to school in September and finish my studies at S.C. and of course enjoy another year of football if possible.
>
> I want to work as much as I can until that time and pay off a few debts so that I can finish OK. If work does not continue as good as it should, I may take a trip on a boat—So. America—Europe—China or any place just for the trip. A coupla kids from school want to go, too, but that is only in case the work in movies doesn't hold out....
>
> All my love to you all and all the folks you correspond with. Don't forget to write more often.
> Affectionately Your Son
> Wardus Edwinus Bondus[40]

(Bond's Sigma Tau fraternity brothers, Eugene Clarke played an end position on the USC team, and George Templeton played center.)

Soon after Duke Morrison landed a job on the Fox lot, he wanted to make filmmaking his career. Cut from the USC football team, he lost his scholarship and dropped out of college. Ward Bond used film acting as a way to make money so he could *remain* in college and complete his degree. His sincere attempts to take care of his debts and focus on his studies at USC are documented in the letters written to his parents: hard, primary evidence that Bond, like Victor McLaglen, was not just the fun loving, hell-raising halfwit that film historians have characterized over the years.

The innocent John Wayne of Walsh's *The Big Trail* retained some of his original, "pure" qualities over time, but eventually became the complex, conflicted, ineffable *force* of Ford's annihilating *The Searchers* and mournful *The Man Who Shot Liberty Valance*. Contrary to the long-held critical belief that Wayne was typecast, this was another "cowboy" altogether. What critic Greil Marcus wrote about *The Searchers* settles the whole shebang: "Wayne changes from a man with whom we are comfortable into a walking Judgment Day ready to destroy the world to save it from itself."[41]

The facts about "John Wayne" begin with *The Big Trail*, but Ward Bond was a real person who had appeared briefly in six films prior to joining his old pal, Duke, to work on Walsh's project. For MGM's film adaptation of the Broadway musical smash *Good News* (1930), directed by Nick Grinde, Ward received an extra's pay for suiting up to play football. Unlike the deliberate Morrison-Wayne fusion, who, from the beginning, was groomed to be a *movie star*, the natural Bond began his career as a character actor who eventually would demonstrate a great versatility; but it would require the narrative scope of television to, not only make him a star, but allow him further to develop and display his wide dramatic range.

While the credit for Wayne's success can be attributed to three men, all of whom sensed his inherent gift, it was John Ford who recognized Bond's talent, eventually bringing him to the attention of nearly every important director in Hollywood. During the final three years of Bond's abbreviated life, he would craft the complex character of Major Seth Adams on *Wagon Train*. Like its feature-film predecessor, Ford's *Wagon Master* (1950), this television series was a literal descendant of *The Big Trail* that brought a new, fictionalized chapter of the pioneer saga into American living rooms every week. (Wayne's Breck Coleman would heavily influence the development of Robert Horton's "Flint McCullough," a similar, very capable *Wagon Train* character.)

During the winter and spring of 1930, nearly three decades before Bond became the wagon master on the small screen, Walsh took his large company to arduous locations throughout the West to shoot his seminal widescreen epic. On the evening of Saturday, April 19, 1930, the cast lodged at the Hotel del Ming in Yuma, Arizona, "The Sunshine Capital of the United States," where Bond wrote a letter to his parents in Oakland, expressing uncertainty about his role as Sid Bascom in the film:

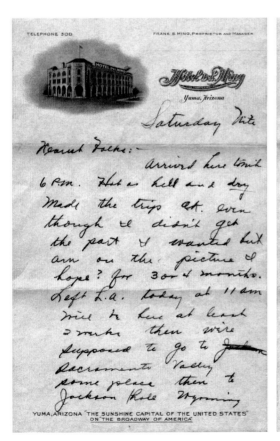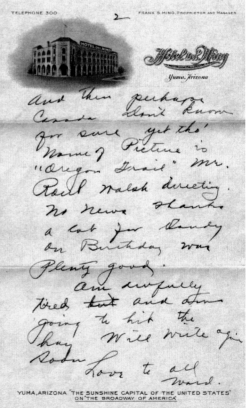

Handwritten Letter from Ward Bond to His Parents (April 20, 1930). Ward, writing from Yuma, Arizona, informs Mr. and Mrs. John N. Bond, in Oakland, California, that he currently is working on Raoul Walsh's epic Western "Oregon Trail," eventually released by Fox as *The Big Trail.*

Dearest Folks:

Arrived here tonight 6 P.M. Hot as hell and dry. Made the trip OK, even though I didn't get the part I wanted but am on the picture I hope? for 3 or 4 months. Left L.A. today at 11 A.M. Will be here at least 2 weeks then we're supposed to go to Sacramento Valley some place, then to Jackson Hole, Wyoming, and then perhaps Canada. Don't know for sure yet. The name of [the] picture is "Oregon Trail." Mr. Raoul Walsh [is] directing.

No news. Thanks a lot for candy on [my] birthday, was plenty good.

Am awfully tired and am going to hit the hay. Will write again soon.

Love to all,
Ward[42]

After sinking $2 million into what became *The Big Trail*, Walsh had a 70mm widescreen epic, stunningly filmed by Arthur Edeson, which only could be shown in *two* theaters (Grauman's Chinese and New York's Roxy) equipped to project this oversize format. The film also was issued in a standard 35mm version, shot by Lucien Andriot, in which much of the film's visual splendor is lost; and, though "John Wayne" is a great looking, energetic lead, his middling performance (due in part to the confining conditions imposed by the early sound recording process), alongside Marguerite Churchill, failed to impress audiences. Comparing Wayne to two of the film's other male actors, Tyrone Power, Sr. (as wagon boss Red Flack) and Ian Keith (as gambler Bill Thorpe), Gary Wills observed:

> Keith stalks Wayne cautiously; Power gropes and lumbers; Wayne glides. The *pictorial* interplay of the three is at the heart of the film. That explains why Walsh was so quick to promote an untried furniture mover to the starring role. Wayne looked right; he moved right; he offered just the visual contrast with the other characters that Walsh desired. Sound had just come to Hollywood ... but Walsh was trained in the silent era, and still thought more in pictures than in words.[43]

Bond appears throughout the film, but his dialogue is confined to a few brief scenes. To look more like a rugged mountain man, he grew an enormous, bushy beard, providing quite a physical contrast to the youthful, clean-shaven Wayne. Ward speaks one line in the opening scene, as Sid Bascom discusses the forthcoming journey with his father (Frederick Burton), just before Breck Coleman rides into the camp. Typical of an inexperienced actor, Bond has trouble knowing what to do with his hands, tending to fiddle with his beard as he listens to the others.

Handed the job of directing *Born Reckless* for Fox, Ford was unimpressed with the disjointed script focusing on smalltime mobsters given the choice of either going to prison or using their finesse with firearms on the battlefields of World War I. Always attempting to infuse some effective humor into his work, Ford said:

> [I]n the middle of the picture, they go off to war; so we put in a comedy baseball game in France. I was interested in *that*. In those days, when the scripts were dull, the best you could do was to try and get some comedy into it.[44]

Born Reckless, a strange conglomeration of the gangster, war and comedy genres, stars Edmund Lowe (Victor McLaglen's frequent screen partner) as Louis Beretti. In his second appearance for Ford, Bond plays an army sergeant who enjoys giving the once-over to his volunteers, including the trio of hoods, led by the wisecracking Beretti.

Although Bond isn't billed in the credits, Ford's appreciation of his "natural" talent is proven out, as the green actor of *The Big Trail* here gives the, albeit brief, performance of a seasoned professional. Jack Pennick and Harry Tenbrook also make their obligatory contributions for Ford, and even Wayne again appears as an extra in one scene. To top off an

FEARLESS SCOUT and fighter, he guarded hundreds of lives amid privations and dangers of pioneer times. But one, most precious of all, he cherished day and night, dreaming of happiness and peace at the end of the trail.

John   Marguerite
WAYNE   CHURCHILL
EL BRENDEL

Tully Marshall Tyrone Power David Rollins
and
20,000 more
Story by
Hal G. Evarts

The BIG TRAIL

SEE Indian hordes attack the wagon train, the dangers, joys and sorrows of brave men and loyal women.
HEAR savage war cries, thunder of stampeding buffalo, roar of floods.
LIVE with the characters in this greatest picture ever produced.

The Big Trail (Fox, 1930; directed by Raoul Walsh). In his first starring role, John Wayne plays frontier scout Breck Coleman, supported by Marguerite Churchill as Ruth Cameron. (Ward Bond appears in the small, unbilled role of Sid Bascom.)

interesting cast, Randolph Scott makes a play for Beretti's sister, Rosa (Marguerite Churchill), only to have the door rudely slammed in his face.

Ford and his stalwart cameraman, George Schneiderman, utilized some inventive techniques in creating the three scenes involving mob murders: one mug is shot through the glass pane in a door; another as the lights go out; and the last, "Big Shot" (Warren Hymer), is dropped by a slug from Beretti as the camera tracks backward through the swinging doors of a speakeasy. These incidents would be used similarly in subsequent gangster films, particularly the Warner Bros. classics starring Edward G. Robinson and James Cagney usually credited with transforming the genre.

Though Bond had mentioned a Fox "college picture" in his letter of March 5, he next appeared in a project set at a different type of "college" altogether. During the early 1930s, film industry executives kept a keen eye on newspaper headlines in an attempt to cash in on hot topics. Following an inmate uprising at Auburn Prison in New York during the spring of 1930, MGM rushed its prison epic *The Big House* into production, spurring Fox to shelve writer Maurine Watkins' script dealing with prison life titled *Up the River*. Working with longtime pal William Collier, Sr., Ford rewrote the screenplay, converting it into a comedy about "Bensonatta, a Penitentiary in the Middle West," a Joint resembling a racially integrated college campus, where inmates want to break *back in* to play championship baseball against a team from another prison!

In New York, Ford saw John Wexley's play *The Last Mile* starring Spencer Tracy and Humphrey Bogart. After attending a second time, he called Winfield Sheehan, enthusiastically recommending Tracy for the top spot in *Up the River*, but the producer said that the actor already had failed a screen test at the studio. Back in L.A., Ford watched the test, which featured Tracy obscured by thick makeup and facial hair. Fox had considered hiring him as a character actor, but Ford knew Tracy had the presence and credibility to carry a film. After a second screen test, the studio signed Tracy for his first feature *and* Bogart for his second. Ford recalled:

> More than anything else, I was tantalized by [Tracy's] movement. I don't think many people were ever conscious of Spence's bodily discipline.... He made every movement sharp and meaningful, and didn't waste a single turn.... He had the power of a consummate actor.[45]

To avoid "plagiarizing" the popular, hard-hitting *Big House*, Ford and Collier (who plays "Pop," the "lifer" baseball manager) had immediately jettisoned the "bunch of junk" written by Watkins, replacing it with satirical, often absurd material. Bond is back, briefly appearing as a baseball-bat toting, 30-year prisoner in three scenes, one of which features him arguing with Bogart's morose Steve Jordan until he's punched out by Tracy's take-charge "Saint Louis."

As Dannemora Dan, another of his lovable, delightfully vacuous characters, Warren Hymer nearly steals the show, allowing Ford to work in a comic bit involving his hero Abraham Lincoln. After temporarily breaking out of the Joint with Saint Louis to aid the recently paroled Steve, Dan, while surveying the mantelpiece in the Jordan family home, mistakes the 16th President for his former cellmate's old man!

Ford had hated the project at first, but reworking the story into a comedy inspired him to make a very entertaining film that had film exhibitors roaring with laughter at the preview. "One guy actually *did* fall out of his chair," claimed Ford. As to working with his two new leading men, he recalled, "We did it in two weeks ... they were great — just went right in, natural."[46]

A bit of "realism" was added to the farcical film with the casting of Joan Marie Lawes, the eight-year-old daughter of Sing Sing warden Lewis E. Lawes (in her only screen appearance), as Jean, the child of Bensonatta's push-over Irish warden (Robert Emmett O'Connor). But the highlight for Ford was Tracy's intuitive understanding of the cinematic medium:

> Spence was as natural as if he didn't know a camera was there, or as if there had *always* been a camera when he acted before. His speech was decisive. He knew a straight line from a laugh line. If he had a chance for a laugh, he played it in a way that would get it.[47]

Bogart, however, was Pappy's low point. His unforgivable mistake of calling Ford "Jack" landed him "in the barrel," where he remained for the entire shoot. In the end, Ford had taken a straightforward look at life behind bars and transformed it, in the words of Joseph McBride, into a "subversive film portraying prison life as preferable to the hypocrisy and emotional isolation of the outside world."[48]

Tracy continued to hang out with Ford, who introduced him to other Irish-American, hard-drinking cronies. Unfortunately, when Spence developed a chronic alcohol problem, he attempted to sublimate his denial by blaming Ford for stealing him away from Broadway and turning him into a drunk, prone to hell-raising that landed him in the real slammer on two occasions.

Men consigned to the "crossbar hotel" also figure in *The Doorway to Hell* (1930), the first Warner Bros. gangster film to feature James Cagney (in a supporting role), while improb-

Up the River (Fox, 1930; directed by John Ford). Ford's charming prison parody features (left to right) Warren Hymer (who, as "Dannemora Dan," nearly steals the show), Humphrey Bogart (in his second film role), William Collier, Sr. (who co-wrote the screenplay), and Spencer Tracy (in his film debut). (Ward Bond appears as a baseball-bat toting, 30-year prisoner in three scenes, one of which features him arguing with Bogart until he's punched out by Tracy!)

ably starring baby-faced Lew Ayres as mob boss Louis Ricarno. Bond briefly appears as a police officer (his first of many) in this Archie Mayo–directed melodrama.

Now 27 years old, Ward returned to USC for the fall 1930 semester, and held his tackle position on the football team for a third year. The season resulted in eight victories and two defeats, with USC outscoring its opponents 382 to 73. The California Golden Bears again suffered outright humiliation, being demolished 74–zip.

Released on November 1, 1930, *The Big Trail* took a nose dive at the box office, due mainly, not to Wayne's unsure performance, but to the technological exhibition problems. This fiasco badly damaged Wayne's potential for stardom (a similar fate suffered by Marguerite Churchill), and Ford, for reasons unexplained (even to the Duke), shut the actor out of his life for the next several years.

The most feasible explanation is that Ford was furious when Duke "turned coat" on his "mentor" by accepting the offer from Walsh, one of Pappy's few directorial peers (though many of Walsh's stories about his past, unlike Ford's, were *true*: such as laboring as a real cowboy, and traveling to Mexico in 1914 to meet with and make a film for Griffith about rebel leader Pancho Villa *during* the Revolution.) This was Wayne's first experience with

Ford's near-megalomaniacal selfishness during what Gary Wills referred to as "their close but tortured relationship."[49]

In mid–October 1930, Ford and George O'Brien, armed with another Dudley Nichols maritime script, were back on Catalina to make the World War I submarine film *Seas Beneath*, costarring Warren Hymer (as his usual lovable lug, this time in a sailor suit) and John Loder (as a German naval officer). Ford enjoyed the combination of camaraderie and discipline while working with naval officers and men, as well as shooting on the S-47 and V-4 submarines, with the latter also serving as his sleeping quarters during production.

Considering the stage-bound nature of most films made during the early sound period, *Seas Beneath*, with its realistic scenes shot on the Pacific, particularly the secret U.S. Navy "Mystery Ship," or Q-boat, commanded by Robert Kingsley (O'Brien), at battle with the German U-boat 172, with Baron Ernst von Steuben (Henry Victor) at the helm, seems like a documentary by comparison. (Some of the staged combat shots, masterfully captured by cinematographer Joseph H. August, anticipate Ford's filming of the real thing while commanding the Field Photo unit during World War II.)

Ironically, London-born John Loder had been with his father, General W. H. M. Lowe, at Irish Republican Brotherhood leader Patrick Pearse's surrender in Dublin following the Easter Rebellion of 1916. While serving in the British Army during World War I, Loder was captured by the Germans, whose language he learned well enough to remain in Berlin, where he eventually landed small roles in several films before trying his luck in London and Hollywood. His believable performance as Franz Schiller matches that of George O'Brien, who effortlessly moved into "talkies" from his starring roles in the silent epics of Ford, Murnau and Curtiz.

In an example of Ford's seamless integration of humor and drama, O'Brien deadpans, "C'mon, Mac. You've lived long enough," to the youthful Lieutenant McGregor (Larry Kent) as their burning vessel begins to sink. The scene then cuts to a striking image of the German officers standing atop their submarine as it descends down to Davy Jones (with August's camera taking the viewer along with them). The film's only real detriment is the performance of Wisconsin-born Marion Lessing as the U-boat commander's sister. Rather than becoming stoically submerged with her Teutonic comrades, she regretfully ascends into a scenery-chewing stratosphere.

Seas Beneath was the final film Ford directed at the Fox lot on Western Avenue. During 1930 and 1931, the effects of the Great Depression hit William Fox hard, and his beloved studio fell into receivership. He sold his remaining stock to General Theaters Equipment Company president Harley L. Clarke and retired from the film business. Ford was still retained, however, under the provisions of his contract, which ran through October 1932.

Fox again tried the Wayne and Churchill pairing, in the B college-campus comedy *Girls Demand Excitement* (1931), which began shooting on November 24, 1930, under the direction of Seymour Felix, a choreographer who seemed to think he was filming a ballet. Duke despised the film, which he said "was just so goddamn ridiculous that I was hanging my head."[50]

Following *The Big Trail*, Bond worked fairly steadily at Fox. On the same day that Duke realized that *Girls Demand Excitement*, David Butler began directing the latest Will Rogers epic, *A Connecticut Yankee* (1931), in which Ward briefly appears as a knight in the court of evil temptress Queen Morgan le Fay (Myrna Loy).

In December, Duke was cast opposite his friend, Loretta Young, in *Three Girls Lost* (1931), a crime drama directed by Sidney Lanfield. Bond also landed a small role, as an airline steward, in what turned out to be Wayne's final Fox film. Although Duke signed a five-year contract, the studio had included a six-month option clause which was not renewed.

Strictly a freelancer, Ward kept working at Fox well into the summer of 1931, playing a police officer in every film until, intending to "branch out," he strayed over to Warner Bros. to portray — a highway patrolman. In January, he again came up against Spencer Tracy, who was playing hood Daniel J. "Bugs" Raymond, in *Quick Millions* (1931), Rowland Brown's directorial debut. Anxious to make his millions as quickly as possible, Raymond becomes a big-time racketeer who has his bodyguard, Jimmy Kirk (George Raft, in his fourth film and first major role), whacked after pulling a job that grabs the local headlines.

Expectations were high when famed art director William Cameron Menzies teamed with Kenneth McKenna to direct some films for Fox. Days before production began on the Edmund Lowe and Bela Lugosi fantasy classic *Chandu the Magician* (1932), which Menzies co-directed with Marcel Varnel, he and McKenna completed a similar Lowe film, "The Midnight Cruise," based on the story "The Man with the Miracle Mind" by Samri Finkelle and released as *The Spider* (1931). Bond, surviving this fantastical experience to repeat his cop act for the James Dunn vehicles *Sob Sister* and *Over the Hill* (both 1931), used the checks to help pay the tuition for his final semester at USC.

On January 16, 1931, Ford, planning to tour the Far East for the next three months, left Mary behind in favor of George O'Brien, who joined his director aboard the *Tai Yang*, a Norwegian tramp steamer ready to disembark from San Pedro. Not surprised by Jack's preference for the more "tolerant" nature of male companionship, Mary left on her own little excursion to Hawaii.

While in the Philippines, O'Brien became impatient when Ford refused to leave his Manila hotel room, into which he'd retreated with a case of hooch several days earlier. At one point, O'Brien stuck his head into the room, imploring him to sober up long enough to attend a dinner, but Ford quickly told him to go to hell, kicking empty booze bottles from under the covers and onto the floor. Unaware that, even in a nearly comatose state, this was Ford's way of testing the loyalty of his most intimate associates, O'Brien became fed up and took a 10-day side trip, hoping that Jack would be in a coherent state upon his return.

When O'Brien arrived back in Manila, Ford indeed was sober and gung-ho about continuing on to China. However, in the words of O'Brien's son, D'Arcy, "He did not work for John Ford again for seventeen years, and never had the lead again in a Ford picture."[51]

Four decades later, George O'Brien admitted that, after spending several months with Ford, he "knew less about him than ever before ... even though I loved him I guess the truth is that I never really understood him."[52]

Based on the 1916 play by Maude Fulton, *The Brat* (1931), starring Sally O'Neil as a poverty-stricken young woman exploited by a caddish writer (Alan Dinehart), was another "of those damn things they handed you," said Ford, "but we had a fight between these two women — and it turned into a real one — they hated each others guts and really went at it.... Pulling hair and slugging one another — there was no faking about it. Very funny."[53] Considered one of Pappy's worst films, *The Brat* at least provided another bit role for Bond.

In June 1931, Ward donned highway patrol garb for Roy Del Ruth, who was directing "Larceny Lane" at Warner Bros. Teamed with Joan Blondell for the second time, James Cagney, in a breezy comic role, is the antithesis of his stone-cold killer in the star-making *The Public Enemy*, which had been generating great interest and box-office since April 23.

Released as *Blonde Crazy*, the new Cagney-Blondell hit marked Bond's second of many parts, from bits to major supporting roles, he would play at Warners over the course of his career.

On July 27, after sweating through a hot Sunday morning at the Sigma Tau Fraternity House at 2719 Ellendale Road, Ward drove over to the home of his recently divorced girl-friend, Doris Sellars Childs. With some time on his hands, he sat at a wobbly card table to pen a very entertaining, six-page letter to his parents, humorously announcing that he had earned his university degree:

> My Dear Mr. and Mrs. Bond:
> It is with the greatest pleasure that I take my pen in hand this hellish hot day to convey to you some of my sentiments concerning many and various things.
> Doubtless you have almost forgotten that you have an offspring of the male sex. At least you would if you depended upon the number of letters he writes....
> Let me tell you that it is so damned hot here that I am dripping a salty solution, commonly called sweat, all over these pages.
> Well, as you know, school is out — and I have graduated, finished, ceased to be a student, or whatever you may call it. And I am *glad* to be out.
> Immediately after graduation I started work for Fox Films and made 2 pictures — not much money or much to do in them but better than anything else I could have found.... This lasted about 5 weeks, since which time I have been doing nothing. However, I start again Tuesday — for how long, I don't know. Am told I am to be a blacksmith. Have a couple other irons in the fire for later on. Don't know yet how they'll turn out....
> Am over to Doris' house today. The damned, dumb nurse is out so we have the kid today. Are going out to some friends' ranch this P.M. to drink beer and go swimming in their pool. They have a beautiful place up the valley about 30 minutes from here. Suppose we'll have big time, what with watching out for the brat, etc. Well — so it goes.
> Things are not too well in L.A. generally. Still lots of people out of work. However I believe conditions are some better than they were....
> Don't know when I'll see you, if at all before this fall. But be good and consider yourselves all kissed. How about it?
> Best love and regards to those you write to and better than that to you, Mother, Dad & Sister....
> Thank you ladies and gentlemen. Cheerio. See you later.
> Doris says, "Hello."
> G'bye again.
> Station W.E.B. signing off for the present.[54]

During the blazing summer, Francis Ford, continuing to play small, unbilled roles, handled *two* in the same film: *Frankenstein* (1931), directed by James Whale at Universal. Starring Colin Clive, Mae Clarke and John Boles, this hugely successful horror thriller brought stardom to Boris Karloff who, as the Monster, brutalizes (off camera) a villager named Hans, Francis' second appearance in the film. His first is a "blink and you'll miss him" performance as one of the students attending the phrenology lecture of Professor Waldman (Edward van Sloan).

In early September 1931, Pappy was loaned out to Samuel Goldwyn to direct playwright Sidney Howard's adaptation of Sinclair Lewis' Pulitzer Prize–winning novel *Arrowsmith*, starring Ronald Colman as an obsessively ambitious Midwestern doctor whose quest for achieving great medical discoveries leads to the deaths of his wife (Helen Hayes) and infant son, as well as unethical experimentation on humans. Before production began on this "prestige picture," Goldwyn asked Ford to sign an oath to remain sober throughout the shoot. Joseph McBride noted, "Ford's unhappiness and distraction while making *Arrowsmith*

Frankenstein (Universal, 1931; directed by James Whale). Toppled from the heights: By 1929, Francis Ford's directing career was behind him. During the early 1930s, his acting roles were no larger than Ward Bond's, but occasionally he appeared in an important film. Here, cradled by Dr. Henry Franken-stein (Colin Clive), Francis appears as Hans, a villager attacked by the Monster, in the film that made future John Ford actor Boris Karloff a star.

was reflected in its extreme stylistic unevenness, its highly episodic nature, and its schizoid variations in mood."[55]

One day, when Ford was planning to shoot a scene with the principal actors in an oth-erwise empty set, assistant director H. Bruce Humberstone had filled the space with a crowd of extras. Insisting that they clear out, Ford was visited by Goldwyn, whose unwanted pres-ence induced the director to walk out, suggesting that the producer either take his place or call him at home if he wanted the picture finished.

By the time Ford reached the Odin Street house, Goldwyn already had phoned five times, but he just ignored them, drove to San Pedro, boarded the *Araner*, and headed to Catalina to get supremely inebriated. After studio representatives found him on October 9, he returned to the set, but was in such an incoherent state that he was unable to work. During post-production, Ford went AWOL twice more, inducing Goldwyn to send him packing back to Fox, where he was fired on October 22.

Though *Arrowsmith* suffers from a patchy, confusing narrative that suddenly jumps years ahead at several points (and wastes an opportunity to give Myrna Loy an actual char-acter), it does not (as some critics have suggested) lack singularly "Fordian" touches. The early, small-town scenes include some trademark comic moments (John Qualen makes the first of his several appearances for Ford as a "Swede"), Arrowsmith continually neglects his wife to pursue his work in the company of men, and Bond appears as a policeman in an early scene (when introducing his pal, Ford's placement of the camera behind him created the first-ever shot highlighting the actor's prominent posterior). The presence of African American actor Clarence Brooks as the educated, highly articulate Dr. Oliver Marchand is the film's one truly trailblazing aspect, although it is he who allows Arrowsmith to use "native people" in the West Indies as human guinea pigs when testing a bubonic plague serum.

Nine days after he was sacked by Fox, on Halloween 1931, Ford, accompanied by Mary, left on another long voyage to Hawaii and the Philippines. After becoming so alcoholically incapacitated at Honolulu's Royal Hawaiian Hotel, Mary checked him into a hospital. Upon his recovery, they fetched Pat and Barbara from their private school and traveled on to Manila, where Ford again abandoned his family, this time to go on an excursion to the East Indies with Fox representative Larry de Prida and artist Malvina Hoffman.

Wayne, also dumped by Fox, was scrambling to accept any available acting offers. He first tried his luck at Columbia, where Jack Holt, Buck Jones and Tim McCoy were still starring in Westerns and other action-oriented films, but he unintentionally pissed off Harry Cohn and, after being demoted to the B Western unit, was given the boot.

Maker of Men (Columbia, 1931; directed by Edward Sedgwick). Abandoned by Ford after *The Big Trail* went bust, John Wayne re-teamed with Ward Bond on the cinematic gridiron. Head Coach Dudley (Jack Holt, center) advises his players, including Dusty Rhodes (Wayne, third from right) and Pat (Bond, not visible).

Bond was cast in the small role of a football player in *Maker of Men* (1931), Wayne's final Columbia film, starring Jack Holt as a tyrannical college coach whose hard-headedness nearly leads to his son's (Richard Cromwell) death on the field. Duke appears in the thankless supporting role of Dusty Rhodes, a shiftless player who sells out the team.

During the last months of 1931, Bond played a taxi driver in Samuel Goldwyn's comedy *The Greeks Had a Word for Them* (1932), starring Joan Blondell, and a major supporting role in Columbia's Buck Jones Western *High Speed* (1932). He returned to the Fox lot in early 1932 to appear in three films, all of which had him back in a police uniform: two Joan Bennett vehicles, *Careless Lady* and *The Trial of Vivienne Ware*; and *Bachelor's Affairs*, starring Adolphe Menjou and Minna Gombell.

Cut loose from Columbia, Duke landed at Mascot, toiling in serials demanding constant physical acrobatics but little opportunity for character development. However, Mascot's mogul, Nat Levine, recalled:

> I was impressed with his honesty, his character.... There was nothing phony about the guy, and that came through on the screen. As an actor, he wasn't the best and he wasn't the worst.... What helped him the most was his naturalness — along the lines of Spencer Tracy.[56]

While making the 12-chapter *The Shadow of the Eagle* (1932), Wayne met the peerless stunt man Enos Edward "Yakima" Canutt, who not only devised and performed the stunts, but also played the small role of a henchman. The multitalented Canutt worked as a rodeo rider, action-sequence director, and an absolutely fearless double. He literally created the modern, carefully planned and safety-conscious art of cinematic stunt work. Under Canutt's tutelage, Wayne continued to develop two of the most essential physical abilities of a cowboy actor: how expertly and gracefully to handle a horse (an animal he always disliked) and all manner of firearms.

After pulling an elaborate practical joke on Duke, the two men became friends, and soon "Yak" would prove to be another of the major "architects" of the John Wayne image. Duke later recalled:

> I spent weeks studying the way Yakima Canutt walked and talked. He was a real cowhand. I noticed that the angrier he got, the lower his voice, the slower his tempo. I try to say my lines low and strong and slow, the way Yak did.[57]

Nat Levine began preparing the next 12-chapter serial, *The Hurricane Express* (1932), while Duke landed another job at one of the major studios, Paramount. In *Lady and Gent* (1932), he plays the role of "Buzz" Kinney, a college student and pugilist who knocks out aging boxer "Slag" Bailey (George Bancroft), an event that sparks a series of disasters.

Back at Mascot, Duke again worked with Yak on *Hurricane Express*, in which he plays Larry Baker, the son of an L & R Railroad engineer (Ford's frequent collaborator, J. Farrell MacDonald) who dies in the first of a series of train "accidents" devised by the mysterious "Wrecker." At the end of the 12th chapter, the dastardly villain is literally unmasked by the intrepid young Baker in time to win the hand of lovely Gloria Stratton (Shirley Grey).

3

Jack of All Genres

Christ, if you learned to act you'd get better parts.
— John Ford, to John Wayne[1]

He's always been dynamite!
—"Cappy" (Frank Darien), commenting on Ward Bond's
character, "Big Red" Kincaid, in Universal's *Prison Break* (1938)

On January 2, 1932, Mary Ford's 35-year-old brother, John Willis Smith, asphyxiated himself in the Odin Street garage, which subsequently went up in flames. When a neighbor ventured forth to investigate, he discovered Smith's burned body, with a suicide note clutched in its hand, slumped in the back seat of the car. Mary and the children returned to Los Angeles, but Jack continued on the Far East trip, finally arriving home on March 8.

Bond spent the spring and summer of 1932 finding work at several studios. At Columbia, he played another supporting role in a Buck Jones Western, *Hello Trouble*, also featuring Russell Simpson, whom he would befriend in the Ford Stock Company. Norman Taurog directed Ward, as yet another football player, in the Wheeler and Woolsey comedy *Hold 'Em Jail* at RKO, before he went back to Columbia, once again to menace Buck Jones, who stars as the Native American Pony Express rider *White Eagle*. Aptly referred to as "Henchman Bart," Bond convincingly does the dirty work for his boss, Gregory (Robert Ellis), a bogus express agent, whose idea of compensation is a bullet after the job is completed.

One of Ward's best roles to date arrived back at Fox, in the lively gangster parody *Rackety Rax* (1932), his first film with Victor McLaglen. As "Brick" Gilligan, a former Sing Sing inmate turned football coach, he is hired by racketeer Frank "Knuckles" McGloin (McLaglen), who has purchased the mortgage on Canarsie College, to whip his gang of mob goons into a winning team. Trained to play rough and dirty, the Canarsie outfit hammers out quite a victory streak, until all hell breaks loose at the "big game" against Lake Shore Tech. The ball is gunned down, a battle royal rages on the field, and McGloin and his competitor-cum-partner, Joe Gilotti (Stanley Fields), are both whacked by a car bomb.

As Frank, an amiable taxi driver, in Columbia's *Virtue* (1932), Bond enjoyed enough screen time to develop an actual character. Frank shares digs with fellow cabbie Jimmy Doyle (Pat O'Brien), advising him not to marry Mae (Carole Lombard), a woman he met on the job. Unknown to Jimmy, Mae is a former streetwalker ordered to leave New York. After she secretly loans Jimmy's nest egg to Gert Hanlon (Shirley Grey), Frank informs the couple that their "friend" has been shaking down everyone she knows. Gert is accidentally killed in a tussle with the two-timing "Toots" O'Neill (Jack LaRue), and Mae is arrested, but the testimony of Jimmy and Lil Blair (Mayo Methot), Toots' vengeful girlfriend, sets her free.

Virtue provided Bond with an early opportunity to display his "effortless" naturalism and comic timing. The faithful friend and bachelor, Frank overlooks the marriage "mistake," ultimately ending Jimmy's three-day bender with news that Mae, charged with murder, is in the slammer. While waiting at the police station, Frank unleashes a "prophetic" line (screenwriter Robert Riskin's work), describing Toots as being "no Clark Gable." (Lombard, then married to William Powell, would become entangled with Gable four years later.) Interestingly, under the direction of Edward Buzzell, Bond, a major beefcake at age 29, is shown wearing only a shirt and boxer shorts. Later, he enters the apartment, bends over in front of Lombard, and orders O'Brien to give him the swift kick. O'Brien obliges.

Faced with no work and, worse, no income, Ford signed with his first filmmaking home, Universal, to direct *Air Mail* (1932), an aviation film written by Lieutenant Commander Frank "Spig" Wead. A former Naval hero, Wead had become paralyzed after breaking his neck in a household accident. Unable to continue the military life, he channeled his considerable experience into writing successful stories, stage dramas and screenplays. The excellent *Air Mail* cast features Ralph Bellamy, Gloria Stuart, Pat O'Brien, Slim Summerville, and Bond, back with Pappy to play the small role of Joe Barnes. O'Brien, who considered Ford a perfectionist and harsh taskmaster, also appreciated his artistry:

> He would incorporate tiny things into a picture that sounded like nothing when he told you. Then when you saw the dailies, something came off the screen that was revelatory, something you weren't cognizant of while you were shooting.[2]

Now freelancing, Ford migrated to MGM to direct the bizarre love-triangle melodrama *Flesh* (1932), starring Karen Morley and Ricardo Cortez as Americans who complicate the life of Polokai (Wallace Beery), a wrestler and beer garden waiter, while stranded in Germany! Where Ford went, Bond surely followed, tackling the colorful role of grappler "Muscles" Manning, a type of two dimensional heavy he often would play throughout the decade. Following this turn in the ring, nearly six years would pass before the Judge and the Coach worked together again.

Wayne, enjoying the nonexclusive clause in his Mascot contract, was now at Warner Bros. to make a series of six B Westerns. To keep budgets low, the studio incorporated Duke's new material with action scenes from silent Ken Maynard Westerns made at First National, which had merged with Warners in 1928. Wayne closely resembled his heroic predecessor in the stunt-oriented long shots, especially when riding "Duke, the Devil Horse," a close match to Maynard's famous mount, "Tarzan."

Beginning in the summer of 1932, Wayne starred in *Ride Him, Cowboy, The Big Stampede, Haunted Gold, The Telegraph Trail, Somewhere in Sonora* and *The Man from Monterey.* He also scored small roles in the Warners A films *Central Airport* (1932), *The Life of Jimmy Dolan* (1933) and *Baby Face* (1933), featuring a steamy pre–Production Code performance by Barbara Stanwyck.

In February 1933, Ford was back at Fox, directing *Pilgrimage*, a visually stunning, heartrending World War I drama adapted from a short story by I. A. R. Wylie and beautifully acted by Henrietta Crosman, Marian Nixon and Norman Foster. Crosman plays the stern, pathologically selfish Hannah Jessop, who arranges to have her son, Jim (Foster), enlist in the Army and sent to his death, rather than see him wed his "trash" sweetheart, Mary Saunders (Nixon). Ford atypically includes a breathtaking scene of the two young Arkansan lovers sneaking out for a late-night rendezvous in a hayloft (the culmination of which is only suggested, but masterfully "painted" by Ford and the great George Schneiderman).

At the instant of Jim Jessop's death during the ghastly Battle of the Argonne, Mary gives birth to a healthy baby boy. When Hannah learns that her son has been killed, Schneiderman pans the camera with her as she slowly walks away, isolating herself from the others (an example of Ford's credo only to use camera movement when necessary, here done both for physical and narrative reasons). Hannah also shuts down psychologically by ignoring the fatherless "Jimmy."

While on a pilgrimage from Three Cedars, Arkansas, to Paris with other "Gold Star Mothers" whose sons died in the war, she meets young lovers (Maurice Murphy and Heather Angel) whose own dilemma with a headstrong mother (Hedda Hopper) initiates her redemption. The scene in which Hannah admits that *she* killed Jim before collapsing on his grave is one of the most powerful moments in Ford's work, made startlingly effective by the film's stringently unsentimental tone.

Unlike many of Ford's films, which depict the erosion of traditional family life by social and environmental factors, *Pilgrimage*, in the words of Joseph McBride, "locates the source of destruction within the family itself ... [it] is unique among surviving Ford films for making a deeply flawed mother its central focus."[3] Ford had a problematic relationship with his own mother, who passed away soon after he wrapped *Pilgrimage*.

Another atypical element is the role played by Francis Ford. Rather than providing comic relief as his stock Shakespearean fool, he appears respectably as Elmer Briggs, the town mayor, who informs Hannah that her son has been suffocated by a collapsed trench in France. (This time, the film's [spare] humor is provided by a pipe-smoking, female hillbilly, Tilly Hatfield [the legendary Lucille LaVerne], who has lost *three* sons in combat.)

Aside from a bit in the William Boyd vehicle *Lucky Devils* (1933) at RKO, Bond appeared in five consecutive films for Columbia, where he was gaining more screen time in B Westerns and crime capers. On Wednesday, January 4, 1933, he had just finished playing a Mormon elder in the Buck Jones saga *Unknown Valley* (1933) and moved on to another substantial role in Columbia's latest Jack Holt drama, costarring the lovely Lilian Bond. During a break, he managed to write a long letter to his parents in Oakland, thanking them for sending Christmas gifts to him and Doris:

> Got your letter yesterday — apparently you expected me to come up, and I intended doing so providing I did not have to work. However the Western I was working on with Buck Jones did not finish until Friday before New Year's, and I had to start work on another picture at Columbia, called "Fever," right away....
>
> Saw the football game New Year's and liked it of course. Naturally we think SC has a great team and really deserve the national championship.

Ward described the good fortune delivered by Santa Claus, and then some major news about two other big names in his life:

> Well, Duke (John Wayne) announced his engagement to the dame he's been going with for so many years. Too bad too — such a good guy. There's only a few of us left (bachelors, I mean) and our ranks are fastly being depleted.
>
> The John Fords returned from Xmas in Maine the other day. Spent New Year's Eve at their house and went to the game with them Monday. I start a picture with him at Fox as soon as we get this one put away. Then he wants me to go to Tahiti with him and I think I'll go for about a month. South Seas wouldn't be so bad, eh? Can't tell yet, though.

Bond closed the letter on a very serious note, indicating that alcoholism may already have been plaguing him:

I took two glasses of sherry wine Xmas, and that was all so am back on the wagon for another year. Doubt very much if I ever drink anything again. Have sort of lost the desire. It's been a year now, you know....

Must go now. They're yelling for me so will say thanks again and "good awfternoon" for the present.

Love,
Ward[4]

Filmed under the working title "Fever," the Jack Holt feature was released by Columbia as *When Strangers Marry* on May 25, 1933. Billed fifth, Bond plays Billy McGuire, the trusted assistant of Holt's railroad engineer, "hardnosed" Steve Rand.

Ward also appeared in some impressive projects at Warner Bros., including two pro–New Deal, "social problem" films directed by William Wellman: *Heroes for Sale* (1933), starring Richard Barthelmess as a down and out World War I veteran; and *Wild Boys of the Road* (1933), a heartbreaking look at the Great Depression starring Frankie Darro, Edwin Phillips and Dorothy Coonan as a trio of teenagers who join the "homeless waifs" riding the rails, looking for jobs, in the wake of their parents' unceasing unemployment.

Bond doesn't appear until the closing minutes of *Heroes for Sale*, playing one of the

Wild Boys of the Road (Warner Bros.–First National, 1933; directed by William A. Wellman). This uncompromising look at teenagers who ride the rails, looking for work during the height of the Great Depression, is one of the most powerful films of the pre–Production Code era. Red, the railroad brakeman (Ward Bond), is beaten by the boys (including Edwin Phillips, far left, and Frankie Darro, far right) after he rapes a girl aboard one of the boxcars.

vagrants moving from town to town, always herded out by local law enforcement. Like Warners' earlier *I am a Fugitive from a Chain Gang* (1932), the film deals with the travails of a wronged veteran, but its constantly shifting, often heavy-handed narrative (symbolized by Robert Barrat's annoying caricature of a fair-weather communist) hastily deals with the Depression in the final scenes, and the simplistic plaudits for FDR arrive as abruptly as Bond's character, as he is shoved into a freight car.

If Warners hadn't managed to complete the superior *Wild Boys of the Road* prior to the institution of the Production Code, it is doubtful if the film could have been made. A forerunner of *The Grapes of Wrath, Wild Boys* features a quasi-documentary depiction of unemployed, weary, ill and abused victims of the Depression. There also are several sexually suggestive scenes, including one in which Bond, as "Red," a railroad "security man," expecting to clear the riffraff from a freight car, finds only a single, attractive female, stripped down to her bra, drying a sweater over a small fire.

The scene cuts to the kids at trackside; but when they fight their way back onto the train, they discover the terrified girl (who obviously has been raped) and Red leering down from a window. He makes the mistake of heeding the challenge of Eddie (Darro), who leads the wildly flailing mob. One of the boys, throwing a right jab, connects with the bruised and bloodied Red's chin (Bond actually was struck hard in the face), and he falls backwards out of the car, to be crushed on the tracks below. Though confined to a single scene, Bond's brutish performance stands out in a film filled with shocks: a boy's leg run over by a locomotive and the resulting rail-yard amputation; railroad men and cops being pummeled with eggs and produce; plus the bizarre sight of a youthful Sterling Holloway soaking one of his legs in a container of milk.

At Columbia during 1933, for every criminal he played, Ward earned two appearances as a cop. In the "domestic melodrama-earthquake spectacular" *The Wrecker*, he supports Jack Holt and George E. Stone. Following a one-shot bit for Frank Capra in the Runyon-esque comedy *Lady for a Day* (stolen by two ladies, May Robson and Glenda Farrell), he tackled another major B role, in *Police Car 17* (1933), as Tim McCoy's radio patrol partner, "Bumps" O'Neill.

Originally titled "Life's Worth Living," *Doctor Bull* (1933), adapted from the James Gould Cozzens novel *The Last Adam*, was the first collaboration between Ford and another of the nation's great artists: prolific cowboy humorist, writer and actor Will Rogers. Rather than being "half genius, half Irish," like Jack, "Bill" (as Ford called him) could be labeled, "three-fourths genius, one-fourth Cherokee."

Born on November 4, 1879, into a Cherokee Nation family on the Dog Iron Ranch in Indian Territory (which became part of Oklahoma in 1907), Rogers aspired to be a cowboy, first traveling to Argentina to seek a job as a gaucho, then working on a ranch in South Africa before entering show business as a trick roper in Texas Jack's Wild West Circus. Prior to becoming a sensation in American vaudeville, the restless vagabond also performed as a rider and roper for the Wirth Brothers Circus in Australia.

After Mark Twain passed away in 1910, Rogers was truly without peer. His down-home, humble, kind and seemingly bashful personality, combined with a razor-sharp wit, brilliant observations about society, and a lightning-quick talent for improvisation, made him irresistible to audiences.

By 1915, Rogers was working for Florenz Ziegfeld on Broadway; and three years later, he made his Hollywood film debut for Samuel Goldwyn in *Laughing Bill Hyde* (1918), which led to a three-year contract, a ranch in Santa Monica, and his own production company.

In 1924, he began making films for comic specialist Hal Roach. Five years later, when the development of talkies allowed him to unleash his extraordinary wit, he already had starred in 48 silent pictures.

In 1929, Fox announced that Ford would direct Rogers in an adaptation of Twain's *A Connecticut Yankee in King Arthur's Court*, but the film was postponed for two years, only to be reassigned to director David Butler, who previously had appeared in four of Ford's films made at the studio. By the time Rogers walked onto Ford's set at Fox, he had headlined 10 sound feature films.

Ford began production on "Life's Worth Living" by turning Rogers loose before George Schneiderman's camera on Monday, June 5, 1933, and wrapped in mid–July. He later recalled:

> [N]o writer could write for Will Rogers.... Some of the lines he'd speak from the script, but most of the time he'd make up his own; he'd stop and let people pick up their cues and then go on ... just get in front of the camera and get the sense of the scene in his own inimitable way.[5]

Ford actually admitted that he worked "*for* Bill." Unlike power-hungry studio bosses, Rogers was a fellow artist who liked to say, "I am not a member of an organized political party. I am a Democrat." Ford added, "*Doctor Bull* was a downbeat story, but Bill managed to get a lot of humor into it — and it became a hell of a good picture. It was one of Bill's favorites."[6] Rogers' Dr. George Bull is a small-town medico who simultaneously battles typhus and the narrow-minded views of the local populace.

The Irish novelist Liam O'Flaherty recently had arrived in Hollywood to try his hand at screenwriting. A hard-drinking, intense man with socialist ideals, O'Flaherty had written one of Ford's favorite books, *The Informer*, the tragic tale of Gypo Nolan, an IRA Communist who sells out his best mate, Frankie McPhillip, for some Judas coin during the 1921–23 civil war. The novel already had been adapted for the screen in England by German director Arthur Robison in 1929.

Intending to direct his own expressionistic version of *The Informer*, Ford optioned the book but warned O'Flaherty that the political content might prove a difficult sell to any of the Hollywood studios. Ford already had voted for FDR (for the Leftist tenets of the New Deal *and* repeal of the cataclysmic Volstead Act), but the more he and O'Flaherty talked politics as they quaffed alarming quantities of Guinness Stout and Jameson's Whisky, his support for both Irish independence and the efforts of the working man grew by leaps and bounds.

At Warner Bros., William Wellman's *College Coach* (1933), costarring Dick Powell, Ann Dvorak and Lyle Talbot, offered Wayne only one line, while Bond, upstaging his pal, played an assistant to Calvert head coach James Gore (Pat O'Brien). A well-made gridiron drama, *College Coach* was one of the first feature films to expose the corruption in university-level football.

In March 1933, Wayne and costars Jack Mulhall, Raymond Hatton and Creighton Chaney (later known as Lon Chaney, Jr.) headed out for Yuma, Arizona, to shoot his third and final 12-chapter Mascot serial, a French Foreign Legion update of *The Three Musketeers*. Duke plays the unimaginatively named "Tom Wayne," a heroic pilot who saves the day during an Arab uprising in North Africa (actually the Mohave Desert, where the blazing heat nearly roasted leading lady Ruth Hall).

Bond was busy with another major B role at Columbia: Krull, a murderous henchman, in *The Fighting Code* (1933), duking it out with Buck Jones, and finally landing in the slammer at the film's end. "Ball and chain" being the order of the day, during the afternoon of June 24, 1933, he attended the wedding of Josephine Alicia Saenz and "Marion Mitchell Morrison," a social affair held in the gardens at the Bel Air estate of Loretta Young's mother and stepfather.

Duke's decision not to convert to Catholicism ruled out a church wedding, but the service was performed by Monsignor Francis J. Conaty. Young was matron of honor, and Duke's best man and eight ushers were all former Sigma Chi fraternity brothers. Grant Withers, Wayne's pal, Young's ex-husband, and one of Ford's favorite actors and drinking buddies, was also there.

On August 30, 1933, Universal "horror star," the genial Boris Karloff, boarded a train bound for Yuma, joining his friend Reginald Denny and fellow Britons Victor McLaglen, Wallace Ford, J. M. Kerrigan, Billy Bevan and Douglas Walton, to shoot Ford's *The Lost Patrol* (1934) for RKO Radio. At 6:30 the following morning, the cast assembled in nearby Buttercup Valley, a location dubbed "Abdullah Alley" by the crew.

Karloff occasionally had enjoyed a single-malt Scotch or two with Ford, but this grueling production in 120-degree desert heat was his first and only professional collaboration with the director he called "wonderful." When asked about the film, Karloff merely replied, "That was directed by Jack Ford, who of course speaks for himself."[7]

Though Richard Dix had been cast, Ford knew that McLaglen had been born to play the part of the World War I British sergeant whose section becomes lost in the brutally hot, sand-swirling Mesopotamian desert after the soldier carrying their orders "in his head" is shot dead by a crafty, "invisible" Arab. Fifteen years before shooting *The Lost Patrol*, McLaglen had served in the British Army as Provost Marshal of Baghdad in Mesopotamia (which became independent Iraq in 1938). In 1919, when Victor returned to the McLaglen home in England, he brought with him an "Arabian servant" named Abdullah. (Interestingly, McLaglen's younger brother, Cyril, had played the same role in *Lost Patrol*, a British silent adaptation of Philip MacDonald's novel directed by Walter Summers in 1929.)

A bugler awakened *The Lost Patrol* company every morning at 4:30, breakfast was served promptly at 5:00, and then they all had time to visit the "six-holer" latrine and six outdoor showers before reporting to Ford and cinematographer Harold Wenstrom at 6:30. Billed second under McLaglen, Karloff created one of his most unusual characterizations (in a career of brilliant, bizarre and spine-chilling performances) as a soldier and religious fanatic who goes mad in the desert.

The company toiled from 6:30 to 11:00 A.M., and then broke until 2:00 P.M. to avoid the worst heat of the day. Shooting as economically as possible, Ford completed the location schedule in a mere two weeks, even though the oven-like atmosphere and constant sandstorms sometimes stressed the actors to the breaking point. During a meal, one of the cooks refused to serve an African American laborer, and Wallace Ford punched him out.

When he was asked by RKO to speed up production by cutting the lunch break from three hours to 30 minutes, Ford refused. "I'm not going to have a lot of sick people on my hands—sunstroke and everything else," he explained. About an hour after defying Cliff Reid's directive, Ford discovered that the producer had been taken to the Yuma hospital to be treated for heat exhaustion.

The temperatures were stifling, but the actors managed some comfort by playing many scenes stripped to the waist. This powerful, dramatic film, ending on a bleak note with only one soldier (McLaglen's sergeant) surviving, became a major popular and critical success.

Ford was continuing to build his reputation by directing successful films in a variety of genres, while Wayne was still laboring on Poverty Row. At Monogram, where B Westerns were cranked out at a breakneck pace, Duke fortunately was able to collaborate with major talent, including cinematographer Archie Stout, director Robert North Bradbury, and, most importantly, stunt coordinator Yakima Canutt.

Canutt's infinite patience with Duke while carefully choreographing their screen brawls and other physical feats added immeasurably to the appeal of the Monogram programmers, but acting was not one of the stunt wizard's strong points. Wayne wisely studied the distinct mannerisms and understated delivery of his hero, Harry Carey, and also benefited from the style of Paul Fix, with whom he'd worked at Fox, Warner Bros., and Monogram, where the laid-back performer, equally at ease in heroic or villainous roles, became his unofficial acting coach.

As much as he had observed Yak, several of Wayne's colleagues (including Harry Carey, Jr.) claimed that it was Fix who helped him develop his unique, trademark gait; not John Ford, nor Raoul Walsh. Mary St. John, Wayne's personal secretary and close friend for three decades, admitted, "Paul taught Duke to walk. Duke's mannerisms were more studied than most people realize."[8]

Much to the chagrin of directors, the Canutt-trained Wayne insisted on doing many of his own stunts and all of his screen fights, developing a convincing "fake" punch into which he threw his entire body, resulting in a powerful, sledgehammer blow that looked as if it truly decked his opponents. This unique wallop became a Wayne trademark that other actors tried in vain to emulate. He continued these practices throughout his career, passing on Yak's techniques to many other stuntmen over the years.

During the autumn of 1933, Bond worked steadily at Columbia, appearing with Tim McCoy, a very young Betty Grable, and even Clark Gable and Claudette Colbert, playing a bus driver in *It Happened One Night* (1934), his second small role for Frank Capra, who would continue to cast him over the next two decades. He also did a bit with Joe E. Brown in Warner Bros.' *Son of a Sailor* (1933), and played gunfighter Ben Murchison in *Frontier Marshal* (1934), Fox's first of three fictionalized films dealing with the Wyatt Earp story (Bond appears in all of them, the third being Ford's *My Darling Clementine* [1946]). This first adaptation of Stuart N. Lake's book about Earp stars George O'Brien as Michael Wyatt, Alan Edwards as "Doc" Warren, and George E. Stone as David Ruskin, a Jewish shopkeeper (a variation on his Sol Levy character in *Cimarron* [1931]), whose stagecoach is held up on its way to Tombstone.

Bond completed his last job of the year in late November, as another cop, in Universal's Edward Everett Horton comedy *The Poor Rich* (1934), also featuring Thelma Todd and future Ford fixture Andy Devine. During 1934, Ward appeared in 22 films, maintaining his steady pace at Columbia, augmented by small parts for Universal, Warner Bros., Paramount, MGM and Darryl F. Zanuck's 20th Century Productions.

Plenty of criminal, convict, cop and coach characters came Bond's way, as well as a prize fighter and detective. He continued to play B-film sidekicks to Tim McCoy and get his rear end kicked by Buck Jones. In A pictures, he appeared with Gable, Ralph Bellamy, Fredric March, Jean Arthur and Joan Crawford.

In *The Circus Clown* (1934), another Warner Bros. Joe E. Brown comedy, Ward adds a deft touch as an audience member continually complaining about the poor quality of the so-called spectacle. As a stadium guard in MGM's bizarre baseball murder mystery *Death on the Diamond* (1934), he briefly aids Robert Young in his efforts to nab the serial sniper who guns down players on the St. Louis Cardinals team. Frank Capra used him again, as

Douglas Dumbrille's henchman, in the Warner Baxter–Myrna Loy horseracing opus *Broadway Bill* (1934), adapted from Mark Hellinger's story by Robert Riskin.

Over the next two years, Duke played a variation on the same character, a wandering cowpoke who, while nearly getting lynched, aids the good people of a dusty little town, one of whom is always a pretty filly, in 16 dirt-cheap "Lone Star" Westerns running just under 60 minutes. The first of the series, *Riders of Destiny* (1933), is the most outlandish, with producer Paul Malvern introducing Duke as "Singin' Sandy" Saunders, a gunslinger who vocalizes and strums a guitar, even when heading straight into a quick-draw shootout. This was not the Harry Carey–Paul Fix type of believable Western hero Wayne had in mind, and his singing was so bad that the numbers had to be overdubbed by R. N. Bradbury's son Bill, who had a strong baritone voice.

"Singin' Sandy" was ditched after *Destiny*, and Malvern was suitably impressed with Wayne's screen presence and work ethic (shooting an entire film in three to six days) that he was sure his new cowboy actor who rode into town, eventually saving the citizens from corrupt bankers and businessmen, would prove a hit with bread-and-butter audiences across Depression America. Indeed, with a new vehicle hitting 5,000 small-town screens about once each month, Duke finally experienced some success; and occasionally the formula would be altered enough to keep the series interesting.

Released in June 1934, *Randy Rides Alone* benefits from a macabre opening, with Wayne's express agent riding down from the hills to discover an isolated saloon full of stiffs, as the player piano still pounds away. (The long shot features an obvious miniature of a large, multi-room complex, while the full-size "Half Way House" consists of one room and a "secret passage.") The outlaw responsible for the murders, Marvin Black, disguised as the *hunchback* storekeeper "Matt the Mute" Mathews, played by a clean-shaven, pre–"Gabby" George Hayes, is a highlight. But the pinnacle of this bizarre effort is the contrast between Wayne's spare performance and the awful acting of Yakima Canutt, who, as "Spike," Matt's top henchman, is saddled with pages of dialogue. (Screenwriters on Duke's early Westerns discovered that, by keeping his lines to a minimum, he was more comfortable in front of the camera, providing the latitude for him to develop the deliberate tempo and use of dramatic pauses that became his trademark.)

During the same month that moviegoers watched Duke discover a dive decorated with dead men, Ford laid out $30,000 for the *Faith*, a 110-foot, diesel powered ketch, built in Essex, Massachusetts, and previously owned by a Pasadena banker. He rechristened her the *Araner*, and ordered a refit at the Fellows and Steward Yard in San Pedro. By the time the work was completed, Ford had his own private maritime retreat, with a beautiful teakwood deckhouse, comfortable cabins, two fireplaces and two bathrooms. He hired George Goldrainer, a licensed master, and spent the latter part of the summer in the Isthmus Harbor off Catalina. Bond was among the frequent visitors, joining Preston Foster, Dudley Nichols and Grant Withers in the fishing, card playing, heavy drinking and general hell raising.

Wayne hadn't spoken to Ford since 1930, but finally was welcomed back into the fold after being spotted getting lubricated with Bond at Christian's Hut, a popular Catalina watering hole. Ford's young daughter, Barbara, had come into the bar to tell Duke that "Daddy" wanted him to come out to the yacht, where a group of people were enjoying the usual blarney. Thinking that she had been sent to summon Bond, Wayne suggested that she leave the bar; but, when Mary Ford appeared, repeating Jack's "request," he hightailed it to the *Araner*.

After holding court and "dismissing" the guests, Ford asked Duke to stay for dinner.

Nothing was said about the four-year cold shoulder following *The Big Trail*. Wayne later recalled:

> I found myself spending a lot of time on the *Araner*.... We'd go over to Catalina for two or three weeks at a time. Jack would bring in a cord of books, and I'd read one while he read three.... We had a nice comfortable relationship.... On most of these trips Jack never drank. The *Araner* was one place where he felt completely relaxed without belting the brew.[9]

Ford's next Fox assignment, *The World Moves On* (1934), starring Franchot Tone, Madeleine Carroll and Reginald Denny, is an ambitious, multi-generational epic following the ups and downs of a family of cotton barons from 1825 through World War I and into the early days of the Great Depression. More vast in scope than *Pilgrimage*, and far more ponderous, the film excels only in the combat sequences, occasionally featuring a documentary quality anticipating Ford's later work with the Field Photo unit. The hard-hitting violence of these scenes is balanced by Ford's inclusion of several asides featuring Stepin Fetchit, whose character, "Dixie," is on an equal footing with his comrades, who show genuine respect and concern for him.

Of *The World Moves On*, Ford said, "I'd like to forget that. I fought like hell against doing it ... but I was under contract and finally I had to do it, and I did the best I could, but I hated the damn thing."[10]

Stepin Fetchit plays Jeff Poindexter in Fox's *Judge Priest* (1934), sidekick to the title character (Will Rogers, again injecting comic magic into a Ford project), who brings to light the ethnic intolerance rampant in his community, an "old Kentucky town in 1890." Rogers and Fetchit had been close friends for years. While shooting *Judge Priest*, Ford allowed Rogers to demonstrate his improvisational talent by performing an uncanny impression of Fetchit in one scene.

Ford's admiration for Fetchit was matched by his casting of Hattie McDaniel, giving this prodigious singer, songwriter, comedian and actress her first major screen role (her previous appearances in 14 feature films had been small, unbilled parts). She also became fast friends with Rogers and, soon after appearing in the film, joined the Screen Actors Guild.

McDaniel's role in *Judge Priest* is the familiar "black servant" stereotype of the period, but she imbues "Aunt Dilcy" with a bit of the fire she later would ignite in *Gone with the Wind* (1939). Ford subversively toyed with depictions of blacks during this period, and here he attempted to include a scene in which Priest saves Jeff from a lynching and then publicly condemns such hate crimes. However, when white censors in the South complained about the sequence, Fox consigned it to the cutting-room floor. Ford admitted that Rogers had improvised "one of the most scorching things you ever heard."[11] Scott Eyman wrote:

> As for Stepin Fetchit, there's no question he's a stereotype. So are the white people. Ford often used stereotypes as convenient hooks, then went deep into character and made the stereotypes come alive, confirming Stepin Fetchit's own estimation of the film: "When people saw me and Will Rogers like brothers, that said something to them."[12]

(One of the people to whom the film spoke was Rogers' friend, President Roosevelt, who expressed his admiration in a letter, dated October 8, 1934.[13])

Ford's comic "forte" is evident in the broad shenanigans perpetrated by his brother. Billed as "Juror No. 19," just above "McDaniels" (the spelling used in the credits) and Fetchit, Francis continually chews tobacco, effortlessly spitting it into a ubiquitous cuspidor, especially during the courtroom scenes, when the bailiff, in an effort to quell the crowd's riotous laughter, moves it farther away each time.

Judge Priest (Fox, 1934; directed by John Ford). A rare candid of five cinematic pioneers enjoying a break on the set: (left to right) star Will Rogers; director Ford; writer and actor Irvin S. Cobb; alpha film actor Henry B. Walthall, star of Griffith's *Birth of a Nation*; and Lincoln Theodore Monroe Andrew Perry, aka "Stepin Fetchit."

Nearly five years had passed since Bond had worked for Raoul Walsh in *The Big Trail*. During September 1934, the director was shooting "East River," the latest Fox Edmund Lowe and Victor McLaglen adventure, about "sand hogs" who dig New York's subway tunnels. Rather than being Quirt and Flagg, this time Ed is "Shocker" Dugan and Vic is "Jumbo" Smith. Buff as ever, Ward played the small role of a prize fighter in the notable he-man cast featuring Charles Bickford as rival sand-hog boss "Nipper" Moran. Loaded with all the drinking, gambling, skirt-chasing and brawling expected from a Lowe and McLaglen opus, the film was released as *Under Pressure*, a reference to the compressed air in which the sand hogs labor.

On September 12, 1934, Ford was appointed lieutenant commander in the U.S. Naval Reserve by Captain Herbert Jones during a ceremony in San Diego. Dan Ford wrote:

> As a product of Hollywood, John had a romantic, idealized notion of what the navy was all about.... But it also meant respectability, for in those years before the technocrats took over the military, a commission, and particularly a naval one, gave a man status as a gentleman.[14]

Two weeks later, James Cagney and Pat O'Brien were on the Coronado Peninsula, costarring in a sequel to their successful Warner Bros. military comedy *Here Comes the Navy*

(1934). For three weeks, director Lloyd Bacon filmed "Flying Marines" on location at Naval Air Station San Diego on North Island. One of Cagney's weakest 1930s vehicles, the film, re-titled *Devil Dogs of the Air*, suffers from a script in search of a plot, poorly developed characters and tedious incidents showing USMC flight training. Cagney and O'Brien repeatedly go over the top (as they do in several films together), but the reliable Bond remains down to earth as Jimmy, the senior flight instructor.

Ward then played a small role at Warner Bros. in "Black Hell," the latest Paul Muni "social problem" vehicle, directed by Michael Curtiz. Ward plays Mac, a police officer hired by McGee (Barton MacLane), a company thug who brutalizes striking coal miners. Released as *Black Fury*, the film also features once-and-future Ford performers Karen Morley, John Qualen, J. Carrol Naish and Mae Marsh. In one scene, Bond helps rough up Muni, whose melodramatic portrayal of immigrant miner Joe Radek earned him a "write-in" Best Actor Oscar nomination.

While shooting the comedy *The Whole Town's Talking* (1935) at Columbia during the autumn of 1934, it's doubtful if Ford had to use his bullying tactics to inspire a great performance from his star, who personally had requested him as director. In a career filled with diverse portrayals, Edward G. Robinson, in a dual role, as ruthless gangster "Killer" Mannion and his look-alike, meek office clerk Ferdinand Q. Jones, created *two* of his finest characterizations under Ford's guidance. The scene in which the teetotaler Jones gets loaded on booze and cigars in his boss' office features Robinson giving a brilliant, very subtle, comic drunk performance.

Jean Arthur, who'd made her feature-film debut in Ford's *Cameo Kirby* 12 years earlier, was perfectly cast as Jones' wisecracking coworker and secret love interest. She recalled:

> Ford always had a handkerchief or a pipe hangin' out of his mouth. He chewed on it and you never knew what he said. And Robinson had a pipe that *he'd* chew.... I'd say, "How do I know what I'm gonna do if you don't talk?" And they said, "Well, we talk with our brains. We don't need to verbalize things."[15]

Ford set Mexican towns talking during the winter of 1934-35, when he took the *Araner* on a two-month cruise along the Baja coast, destined for La Paz and Mazatlan. Wayne, Bond, Dudley Nichols and Henry Fonda (who just had moved to Los Angeles from New York) were all on board, fishing during daylight hours and consuming prodigious quantities of beer and tequila in the evenings. One day, Ford, still loaded, swore he saw a green sea serpent surface near the boat.

The madness increased when the crew reached Mazatlan, hitting every bar, partying into the wee hours, pounding down tequila and paying local mariachis to bring their lively traditional tunes aboard the boat as the carousing climaxed with everyone lapsing into a quasi-coma. As always, Bond effortlessly stole the show, calling his buddies "assholes" and "sons of bitches," bragging that he knew everything under the sun, growing more loud and obnoxious with every shot of booze, and being firmly told by Hank Fonda, "Oh, go fuck yourself!" On another occasion, Ford tossed a bottle, barely missing Bond's head.

As if reality wasn't insane enough for Ford, he had to exaggerate to another level by planting a bogus log in George Goldrainer's cabin. Pappy's own handwriting notes that, on New Year's Eve, the yacht master had gone ashore *twice* to bail Himself, Wayne, Bond and Fonda out of the local calaboose. Then, at 9:30 that evening, Mexican officials ordered them all to leave town.

The log goes on to claim that, on the following day, New Year's 1935, Ford attended Mass and then returned to the *Araner* with the priest in tow. Witnessed by the padre, Ford signed a pledge to remain sober and then celebrated by pouring champagne and brandy. The coup de grace was delivered when "Goldrainer" observed "the cook" (Wayne) urinating into Ward's personal jug of gin.

Somehow surviving his two-month vacation, Bond worked in eight pictures for five different studios during the first two months of 1935. In MGM's *Times Square Lady*, starring Robert Taylor and Virginia Bruce, he briefly appears as Dugan, a tough Glendale hockey player. At Warner Bros., he played small, unbilled roles in three films: a patron at Al Jolson's Broadway nightclub in *Go Into Your Dance*, directed by Archie Mayo; and thugs in the William Keighley projects *Mary Jane's Pa*, with Aline MacMahon, and the prestige picture *"G" Men*, starring James Cagney as Jim "Brick" Davis. An attorney-cum-federal copper, Davis was based on FBI agent Melvin Purvis, who had pursued and "eliminated" John Dillinger just minutes after the renegade gangster watched his favorite actress, Myrna Loy, in MGM's *Manhattan Melodrama* at the Biograph Theater in Chicago the previous July.

Bond appears briefly as one of the hit men (also including Warners "wiseguys" Russell Hopton and Noel Madison) in a recreation of the infamous "Kansas City Massacre," a June 17, 1933, Tommy-gun ambush organized by a quartet of mobsters assisted by Charles "Pretty

"G" Men (Warner Bros., 1935; directed by William Keighley). "Public Enemy Number One" Danny Leggett's hit men (left to right: Russell Hopton, Noel Madison, Ward Bond, Mike Lally, unidentified actor) in a recreation of the infamous "Kansas City Massacre," a June 17, 1933, Tommy-gun ambush of law-enforcement agents organized by a quartet of mobsters assisted by Charles "Pretty Boy" Floyd.

Boy" Floyd. When the smoke cleared, a federal (BOI) agent, an Oklahoma police chief, two KCPD detectives, and mobster Frank "Jelly" Nash were slumped dead in a Chevrolet and on the street outside Union Station.

Floyd intended to free Nash, "the most successful bank robber in U.S. history," who was being escorted from Hot Springs, Arkansas, back to Leavenworth Penitentiary. But "Pretty Boy" and two other freelance gangsters, Vernon C. Miller and Adam C. Richetti, badly botched the hit and subsequently were gunned down by agents, whacked by a rival mob, and executed in Missouri's gas chamber, respectively. Later evidence suggests that Nash, one of the detectives, and BOI agent Raymond J. Caffrey (the model for Robert Armstrong's "G" Man, Jeff McCord, in the film) were killed, not by the gangsters, but accidentally by BOI agent Frank Lackey, who had borrowed a shotgun from the police chief.

The film's "Public Enemy Number One," Danny Leggett (Edward Pawley), was based on Vernon Miller. If the viewer blinks during the "Machine Gunners Butcher Officers" scene, Bond's mug may be missed amid the mayhem, but this potential disappointment will be alleviated by the magnificent Ann Dvorak, as Jean Morgan, the moll with a heart of gold, who comes to a tragic, violent end, gunned down by her own husband, mob boss Brad Collins (Barton MacLane).

During early 1935, Monogram and Mascot Pictures, both in debt to Consolidated Film Industries, a group of processing labs, were merged, along with the even smaller Chesterfield, Liberty, and Majestic Pictures, into a single company by C.F.I. President Herbert J. Yates, who christened the new outfit Republic Pictures. While Yates assumed the position of Chairman of the Board, Monogram founder Ray W. Johnston was named President, and Monogram's Trem Carr and Mascot's Nat Levine were put in charge of production. Aside from slightly larger budgets, little changed about Duke's Westerns, but he soon signed another eight-picture contract.

Bond continued his studio hopping throughout the spring, playing a naval homicide victim in *Murder in the Fleet* and a police detective in *Calm Yourself* at MGM, and featured roles alongside Tim McCoy at Columbia. In *Justice of the Range*, he is Bob Brennan, a rancher working both sides of the fence during a range war, who nearly winds up dead before aiding detective Tim Condon (McCoy) in identifying cattle rustler Hadley Graves (Guy Usher), ending a feud between the Brennans and the neighboring McLeans.

The Informer, turned down by Columbia, Fox, MGM and Warner Bros., finally began shooting at RKO Radio on February 11, 1935. David O. Selznick, who now was in charge of the small, ramshackle studio, didn't mind the political content, and Ford was pleased to meet adventurer, World War I pilot, and "jungle documentary" filmmaker Merian C. Cooper, Selznick's right-hand man. Ford's intention to make *The Informer* a stylized, expressionistic drama filmed entirely in the studio would hold down budget costs, a fact that appealed to Cooper, who would prove an important, longtime production partner over the decades.

Though *The Informer* screenplay is credited to Dudley Nichols, it was dictated to him during many long, brutal sessions in the living room of Ford's home on Odin Street. Ford didn't care for the writer's tendency toward verbosity, and mercilessly minimized the dialogue. As Dan Ford pointed out, "In an era of wordy talkies, there was so little dialogue in *The Informer* that the picture could have been shot as a silent film."[16]

Ford again called on Wallace Ford to play a major supporting role, that of the doomed Frankie McPhillip, and cast his drinking buddy Preston Foster as rebel leader Dan Gallagher. For the title role of Gypo Nolan, there was only one choice: big, powerful Victor McLaglen, although Ford assumed he would have to browbeat the fun-loving actor into giving a successful, emotionally complex performance (an extreme tactic, considering the excellent work McLaglen had just contributed to *The Lost Patrol*). Throughout production, Ford changed the schedule behind McLaglen's back, filmed what he called "rehearsals," and verbally abused the gentle giant to wring out a characterization that would win a Best Actor Academy Award. McLaglen earned it, developing severe stress, insomnia and weight loss during the month-long shoot.

Like the other legends either instigated or supported by Ford, *The Informer* has long carried this one:

> On the evening before filming the powerhouse scene of Gypo confessing his betrayal to the rebel court of inquiry (including Francis Ford, who plays "Judge" Flynn), Pappy told Victor to stay home the next day, and then arranged for friends to take him to a party. The stressed-out actor lustily proceeded to hammer himself stupefied, stumbled around and passed out on top of a piano. A few hours later, he was called to the studio and, wracked by a brutal hangover, gave a brilliant, improvised performance. At one point during this cycle of Fordian abuse, McLaglen vowed to quit the acting profession, right after murdering the director.

McLaglen's son, Andrew, said, "My father was the furthest thing from the blowhard that story makes him out to be. He was a quiet, soft-spoken man, not an alcoholic. He didn't drink when he was working."[17]

Thinking *The Informer* wouldn't amount to much, Selznick and Cooper left Ford alone to do whatever he wanted, and were surprised by the unusual, stunning quality of the film during its initial screening. After it was premiered for a dumbfounded Los Angeles audience in April 1935, Ford actually exited the theater and vomited in the street.

A second preview for a more literarily astute crowd was a smash; and, on May 9, *The Informer* opened at Radio City Music Hall in New York. A critical success, the film failed to attract filmgoers until it went into wide release, when Ford's innovative direction and McLaglen's multifaceted acting drew large crowds. This "unimportant picture" shot in a "storage shed" at RKO was deemed a masterpiece and crowned Best Film of the Year by the New York Film Critics. Oscars were awarded to McLaglen, Ford, Dudley Nichols and composer Max Steiner.

Although he won the much-heralded Best Actor Academy Award (and later would be nominated for his supporting performance in *The Quiet Man*), McLaglen remains a seriously underrated actor, often described as having a "limited range." The truth is that he had a remarkable scope, when he wanted to give it some exercise. Like Wayne and Bond, he was a natural whose range covered a vast spectrum from subtle, comforting whispers to broad, commanding declarations that threatened to blow his fellow actors right off the screen. He often needed no words, but only the slightest of gestures, to convey deep emotion and meaning. His characters could be humorous, joyous, rambunctious, likeable, lovable (sentimental or otherwise), defiant, macho, pitiable, pathetic, irritating and sometimes downright obnoxious. Referring to *The Informer*, Joseph McBride summed up McLaglen's triumph:

> His Gypo is a moving portrait of a man of limited intelligence groping for truth and understanding.... A walking embodiment of guilt and original sin, McLaglen's Gypo is like a huge errant child who wanders the streets of Dublin bleeding money as he tries to rid himself of the evidence of his crime.[18]

Due to friction between the craft unions and the Academy, Dudley Nichols, a member of the Screen Writers' Guild, refused his Oscar statuette. So did Ford, initially. When he finally relented and took it home, there were more than a few grumbling remarks tossed around the Screen Directors' Guild.

The Headline Woman, a tedious, no-budget newspaper film, began shooting at Mascot on April 12, 1935, and was ready for release just one month later. Russell Hopton and Bond, killers in *"G" Men*, are two of the scoop-crazed reporters in this programmer involving gambling, gangland murders and imbecility, provided in large part by Ford Sterling as Hugo Meyer, an obtuse German police officer, played for a patsy by newsmen led by Bob Grayson (Roger Pryor). Bond, an embodiment of the lethargic pacing of director William Nigh, provides sarcastic comic relief as Johnson, a slacker who, with eyes closed tight, phones in his stories while lying on a sofa or bed. "You're fired!" shouted by *Express* editor Harry Chase (Robert Gleckler) signals his sudden, merciful exit from the film.

In May, the filmmakers responsible for *King Kong* (1933), Merian Cooper, director Ernest B. Schoedsack, and writers James Ashmore Creel-

John Ford (RKO, 1935). Official RKO portrait of Ford taken during production of *The Informer*.

man and Ruth Rose, re-teamed for the RKO Radio "historical epic" *The Last Days of Pompeii*, starring Preston Foster as Marcus, a blacksmith-cum-gladiator who rises to great wealth just as his benefactor, Pontius Pilate, "washes his hands" of the fate of Jesus, after the "teacher" miraculously cures Marcus' injured son (David Holt). Bond barnstorms his way through the brief but memorable role of Murmex of Carthage, the blustery gladiator responsible for ending the undefeated reign of Marcus. Although Foster receives top billing, the real stars of the film are the splendid Basil Rathbone as a wonderfully regretful Pilate and the impressive, realistic special effects of Willis O'Brien, who had masterfully created Kong and the other gigantic creatures for the earlier RKO spectacle.

During 1935, Darryl F. Zanuck and his partner, Joseph Schenck, merged their successful 20th Century Productions with the financially strapped Fox, thus forming the new 20th Century–Fox, where the Nebraska-born, hard-nosed Zanuck, who had been a formidable writer and producer at Warner Bros., quickly began replacing most of the staff. But administrative measures were only the beginning: Zanuck also intended to maintain creative control over the company's product. He informed all Fox filmmakers of his intention to supervise the writing of every A-picture screenplay, which then would be turned over to a producer, who would summon the director only after all pre-production details had been completed.

This system would allow 20th Century–Fox's top directors to shoot several pictures in a single year, all of which would be a "Darryl F. Zanuck Production." The new mogul insured this by drafting memos ordering his hired hands to forget about any individual "directorial touches" (stylistic, dramatic or comic) that might slow production. When the shooting was completed, the footage was to be turned over to the boss, who ultimately oversaw the editing, giving him "final cut" and insuring his total control of each film prior to its release. Zanuck, the only studio head who was not a Jewish immigrant, had made himself King over his own feudal empire.

Ford's first professional contact with Zanuck had occurred before the merger, in April 1935, when he attempted to pitch a treatment called "Glory Hunter," a decidedly atypical, unsympathetic account of the tragic follies of General George Armstrong Custer. (He would successfully revive the idea at RKO 12 years later with *Fort Apache*, starring Henry Fonda as the Custer-like Colonel Owen Thursday.)

Following the Zanuck takeover, Ford had just completed his third feature with Will Rogers, *Steamboat Round the Bend* (1935), which was quickly seized by the mogul to be re-edited. Having enjoyed relative independence under Sol Wurtzel and Winnie Sheehan (Wurtzel remained, while Sheehan had been paid off and sent packing by Zanuck), Ford was not pleased to see many of his signature comic touches (again featuring Stepin Fetchit) hit the cutting-room floor. Nonetheless, the film is arguably the funniest of all the "Jack and Bill" collaborations, especially since most of the best laughs occur in a frenetic steamboat race during which Dr. John Pearly's (Rogers) crew (including Fetchit at his apex; Francis, playing his drunken fool characterization to perfection; and Berton Churchill, contributing a scene-stealing turn as "The New Moses") burn nearly everything on board (including the deck!) to prevent the hanging of the doc's innocent nephew, Duke (John McGuire), in Baton Rouge.

The scene in which Rogers performs some of his formidable roping skills, at one point lassoing the New Moses and dragging him through the river toward the steamboat, is a comic highpoint. The performances are uniformly excellent, especially the believably touching Anne Shirley's Fleety Belle, a "swamp girl" in love with Duke.

The "Southern" atmosphere of the two earlier Ford-Rogers films is interestingly tempered this time around, with Pearly calling everyone "Brother" regardless of color, and the white and black characters working equally, side by side, while practically torching the boat (eventually using jugs of hooch as fuel) to save Duke and insure a happy ending. Ford (whose comic "forte" is aptly represented, regardless of Zanuck's meddling) was exercising equal opportunity imbecility in *Steamboat Round the Bend*.

Ford wrapped *Steamboat* in early July 1935, asking Rogers to join him aboard the *Araner* for a cruise to Hawaii. Rogers declined, informing Ford that he planned to indulge his love of aviation during an exploratory excursion from Alaska to Russia with Wiley Post, the first pilot to make a solo flight around the globe.

On August 15, when Post's plane, a nose-heavy hybrid of two Lockheed models that he had cobbled together against the advice of the aviation company, crashed into a lagoon near Point Barrow, Alaska, killing them both instantly, Ford was devastated. In Honolulu, he organized a memorial service for Rogers attended by several other Fox employees, including Sol Wurtzel, Henry King, Janet Gaynor and Shirley Temple. Across the nation on August 22, the U.S. flag was flown at half-mast, and movie theaters shut down their projectors for a two-minute period of remembrance. During Rogers' funeral at Forest Lawn, film production was put on hold at all the Hollywood studios.

Bond was busy during the summer of 1935, working for five different studios in a dozen films. Columbia continued to provide him with colorful B supporting characters, including "the notorious bandit" LaCrosse in *Western Courage*, starring Ken Maynard. The small roles kept coming at Universal and Warner Bros., where he appeared as a stage actor in Roman garb in *I Found Stella Parrish*, directed by Mervyn LeRoy and starring Kay Francis, and a two-bit Broadway bodyguard for mobster Jack LaRue in the charming Sybil Jason vehicle *Little Big Shot*, directed by Michael Curtiz and featuring Glenda Farrell and Robert Armstrong.

Two-bit *everything* describes *Waterfront Lady*, a Mascot casino-ship potboiler, in which Bond (as Jess, bodyguard of gambling czar Jim McFee [Charles C. Wilson]) is joined by Ford regulars Frank Albertson, J. Farrell MacDonald (as a drunken skipper), Grant Withers, Mary Gordon and Jack Pennick. Ann Rutherford's feature-film debut, though shot in part at San Pedro harbor, suffers from cramped interiors, forced double-entendre dialogue, stilted acting and tacky miniatures.

During the autumn, Republic began operations at its new studio in the San Fernando Valley. Duke's first picture, *Westward Ho*, already had been released in mid–August; and, aside from having more money ($34,000) to spend, Trem Carr's production crew changed little from the Monogram days: Paul Malvern, R. N. Bradbury, Archie Stout and Yakima Canutt. Although production values were better, and the shooting schedule longer, the screenplay, by Robert Emmett and Lindsley Parsons, was the same old Monogram formula; and, to make matters worse, it reverted Duke to a singing cowboy! Luckily, he was able to blend his own uncertain vocals with those of a backing group called the "Singing Riders" (Chuck Baldra, Jack Kirk, Charles Sargent and, of all people, Glenn Strange).

Coupled with the continuing "lone hero of the range triumphs over greedy town capitalists" message, the higher production values (which eventually led to full music scoring, beginning with *The Lawless Nineties*, in February 1936) scored bookings in urban theaters, increasing revenues and attracting critical attention from major newspapers. Following personnel changes, including replacing Bradbury with Joseph Kane as director of Duke's films, Yates and Levine bought out Johnston and Carr, who became a producer at Universal. Soon, Yates, who knew nothing about films but a lot about money, would buy Levine's stock and run Republic his way.

Bond had been signed to play "Nick, the Lineman" in Warner Bros.' adaptation of the hit Broadway gangster melodrama *The Petrified Forest*, starring Leslie Howard, Bette Davis and Humphrey Bogart, directed by Archie Mayo from October 14 to November 3, 1935. At some point, he was replaced by character actor Eddie Acuff and cast in another Warners film, *Boulder Dam*, directed by B specialist Frank McDonald.

Originally titled "Backfire," *Boulder Dam* stars Ross Alexander as "Rusty" Noonan, a Detroit auto mechanic who unintentionally kills his shop foreman (William Pawley) during a fistfight. On the lam, he reaches the Nevada desert, where he meets Ann Vangarick (a role intended for Ann Dvorak, but played by Patricia Ellis), whose kind immigrant family welcomes down-and-out men, helping them to find work at the nearby dam.

As one of Pa Vangarick's (Egon Brecher) beer-drinking pals, Bond appears in one brief scene, while Eddie Acuff, his replacement in the more important *Petrified Forest*, outdoes him again by playing the much larger role of Ed Harper, who plunges to his death from a dangling scaffold. Warners then tossed Ward another bit part as a cop, in the lavish Dick Powell–Ruby Keeler musical *Colleen*, which Alfred E. Green began shooting on November 5.

During the last three months of 1935, Bond alternated his work for Warner Bros. with three bit roles at RKO. After playing a bank robber in *We're Only Human*, starring one of the Ford gang, Preston Foster, he transformed from criminal to cop for *Two in the Dark*, featuring two more Ford veterans, Alan Hale and Wallace Ford, and then shifted back to gangster mode for *Muss 'Em Up*, another Preston Foster vehicle.

Bond enjoyed working with old pals, even if he was only called in for a single day's shooting. Before the end of the year, he also landed two projects at Republic: *Hitch Hike*

Lady, playing a motorcycle cop who threatens the perambulations of Judy Martin (Mae Clarke) and her accidental companion, Amelia Blake (Alison Skipworth); and *The Leathernecks Have Landed*, an imperialist adventure set in Shanghai, starring Lew Ayres and featuring Ward in the supporting role of Tex, a U.S. Marine captured briefly by Chinese warlord Chang (Victor Wong).

All told, Bond was very busy during 1935, having acted in a staggering total of 30 films. The man really got around, working at all of the major studios except Paramount, for several minors, and one Poverty Row outfit.

On December 23, 1935, a Screen Directors Guild meeting was held at the home of King Vidor. Nearly three years of industry-wide pay cuts called for by the studios and instituted by AMPAS necessitated organization by Hollywood's filmmakers. Ford was joined by Frank Borzage, Lloyd Corrigan, William K. Howard, Gregory La Cava, Rowland V. Lee, Lewis Milestone, A. Edward Sutherland, Frank Tuttle, Richard Wallace and William Wellman. The SDG, having attracted 75 members, was incorporated the following month and, in no time, rumors abounded that the organization was "Communist inspired." Ford, who was elected the union's first treasurer, had referred to the film industry as a "racket ... controlled from Wall Street," and stressed that the SDG must stand in solidarity with all the workers, from the ground up:

> Let's try to get back to the old days — when the people on the set looked to the director for leadership.... I grant you that the producers haven't recognized us, but for Christ's sake, and I say that with reverence, let's not get into a position where the workers of the industry don't recognize us.[19]

Since November 12, Ford had been shooting his first new project for Zanuck, *The Prisoner of Shark Island*. Nunnally Johnson's screenplay based on Dr. Samuel A. Mudd (Warner Baxter), who was imprisoned for treating the fleeing John Wilkes Booth, seemed tailor-made for him, but "Bull" Feeney, as if he was back on the Portland High gridiron, quickly began butting heads with the equally combative producer.

Ford's policy of shooting as few takes as possible (often only *one*), then delegating the examination of the printed rushes to his assistant director and editor, enraged Zanuck, who ended up with very little footage (especially the lack of expected "coverage") he could recreate in his own image. The producer didn't give a damn that a man under studio contract had been making films, most of them *his* way, for two decades, and recently won a Best Director Academy Award.

Shark really began to bite Ford when he refused to discuss Warner Baxter's use of a Southern accent, something Zanuck had *ordered* him to eliminate. Though Baxter was a thorough professional, with decades of screen performances on his resume, he wasn't particularly effective with dialects, a fact painfully obvious to everyone working on the set. "If you don't like the way I'm directing this goddamn picture," Ford told Zanuck, "then take me off of it."

"Don't you ever threaten me again," raged the producer. "If I didn't want you on this picture, you wouldn't be on it. Let's get one thing straight right now. I'm in charge of this studio and when I say do something, you sure as hell better do it."[20]

In an unexpected move, Ford told Baxter to ditch the accent and re-shot the footage, which Zanuck edited to his personal satisfaction. The film, one of Ford's first to provide a well-balanced fusion of dramatic realism with his stunning, expressionist-influenced visual style, fared well with audiences and reviewers, but his experience with "Darryl F. Panic," the name he used in private, "had left him with a bitter taste in his mouth."[21]

Nunnally Johnson, whose script was improved by Ford's direction, recalled, "It was on the set that John made all of his contributions to the picture. These were in the staging of the scenes, the shaping of the characters, and his wonderful use of the camera."[22]

Without the heavy accent, Warner Baxter is excellent as Dr. Mudd, although the version put on film by Johnson, Zanuck and Ford is somewhat fictionalized. The Lincoln assassination is portrayed fairly accurately (though, for dramatic effect, the President dies in his theater seat, rather than across the street at Peterson's boarding house the following morning), but Mudd's actual sociopolitical views and participation in the affair are bowdlerized.

Dr. Mudd did help fight a yellow fever epidemic at the prison where he was incarcerated on the Dry Tortugas, and eventually was pardoned by President Andrew Johnson, but he was not the wholly innocent, heroic figure championed by the film. Baxter's loving family man who develops a touching friendship with Buckingham "Buck" Milford (Ernest Whitman), one of his former slaves, is often a fine testament to Ford's egalitarian values, but a far cry from the historical Mudd, who had met John Wilkes Booth prior to the assassination and believed that slavery was "divinely ordained."

Ford's positive depiction of blacks (one of his improvements on Johnson's script) reached a high point in *Shark Island*, with the expected contemporary stereotypes well-balanced by the major role African Americans play in the narrative. In a film featuring many fine actors (Gloria Stuart, John Carradine, O. P. Heggie and Harry Carey, making his only appearance in a Ford talkie), Ernest Whitman (in his second screen role) gives a standout performance, both dramatic and comic, making several playful references to the fertility of his wife, Rosabelle (Etta McDaniel, Hattie's older sister), while eschewing the shtick of Stepin Fetchit.

Buck, not Mudd, steals the film's ending as he is reunited with Rosabelle and their 12 children. Having been consigned to the back of the carriage by Dr. Mudd, the true hero of the film thanks his former "massa" for being allowed to save the white man's life, and then happily runs toward his family and into the concluding fadeout. Ford didn't even bother to shoot the reunion of the doctor and his family. Joseph McBride observed, "In one of the sweetest 'grace notes' in all of his work, Ford shows where his deepest emotional allegiance lies in this grim chapter of American history."[23]

Frank McGlynn, Sr., who had played the Great Emancipator in John Drinkwater's play *Abraham Lincoln* (1918), several short silent films, and Fox's Shirley Temple vehicle *The Littlest Rebel* (1935), was an inspired choice. After *Shark Island*, he would portray Honest Abe in seven more films, including Republic's *Hearts in Bondage* (1936), the only feature directed by Lew Ayres, and Paramount's *The Plainsman* (1936), directed by Cecil B. DeMille.

From February 25 through April 23, 1936, Ford was at RKO, shooting an adaptation of the Maxwell Anderson play *Mary of Scotland* for David O. Selznick. But on this set, Ford's head-butting occurred, not with the studio boss, but with the star of the picture — and a *woman* to boot! The blue-blooded, brilliant, snobbish, and often histrionic Katherine Hepburn disagreed with Jack on just about everything, going so far as to complain about his direction of a particular scene. After Ford told her to direct it herself and walked out, Hepburn *then* followed his orders. The two polar-opposite personalities clashed so much that, by the end of the shoot, they had fallen in love. (Ford had first met Hepburn in 1932, when he was assigned by Fox to direct her screen test for *The Warrior's Husband*, a film eventually made with Elissa Landi as "Antiope.")

When they weren't meeting at Hepburn's home in Laurel Canyon, "Sean" and "Kate" were having the time of their lives aboard the *Araner* on the weekends. With *Mary of Scotland* wrapped, they spent a month at the Hepburn family estate at Saybrook Point, Connecticut, sailing on Long Island Sound and playing that most Scottish of games, golf, at the local country club.

But Ford knew that the relationship would never work. Dan Ford explained:

> Both were volatile, creative, strong, and self-centered. Both were opinionated, pigheaded, and difficult to live with.... John was better off married to someone who had a stabilizing effect on him, a woman who could tolerate his energies and absences and could make him a home. Deep down, he knew he was better off with Mary and he let the relationship end.[24]

Mary of Scotland is a lavish, highly fictionalized historical epic, blending a complex web of 16th-century Stuart vs. Tudor politics with a love affair involving Mary and the Earl of Bothwell (Fredric March, using a Lowland Scots accent). The actual Earl of Bothwell, James Hepburn, the queen's third husband, was an ancestor of the actress, thus his surname is not emphasized in the film.

John Carradine steals the (mostly over-reverent) show as the Italian courtier David Rizzio, Mary's singing, lute-strumming private secretary, who was brutally stabbed to death by conspirators in league with Henry Stuart, Lord Darnley. Mary's second husband, Darnley was jealous of their relationship, claiming they were having an adulterous affair. The murder, featuring Douglas Walton as Darnley, is one of the most historically accurate, powerful scenes in the film.

Bothwell's imprisonment in Denmark's Dragsholm Castle, where he went insane and died, is also depicted truthfully, but a scene involving Elizabeth (Florence Eldridge) visiting Mary on the eve of her execution is pure fiction, though one of the dramatic highlights and a fitting climax to Hepburn's underrated performance. (Though she gave many affected, stagey performances, Hepburn's histrionics are somewhat tempered by Ford's direction.)

Mary's ascension up a long flight of stairs toward the (off-camera) scaffold, amidst a brewing storm that bathes the scene in expressionistic shadows, is a romanticized version of the actual execution, which required the doomed queen to walk up five steps to a small platform, where she was decapitated with a gory axe previously used on animals. (Two blows and sawing were required to remove the queen's head, but Ford created a tasteful, stylized portrayal of martyrdom as Mary focuses on her faith and, as she imagines hearing the bagpipes, undying love for Bothwell, who awaits her in paradise.)

In early 1936, Bond played "Gunner" Brady under the command of Charles Bickford's tough Sergeant Steve Riley, who "never missed a fight — or a girl!" in Columbia's *Pride of the Marines*. Trumpeted by the studio as "a tender human interest yarn flavored with gay romance, pathos and hilarious comedy," this period flag-waver loaded with "stirring scenes of military pageantry" was filmed on location at the San Diego USMC base, where 2,600 "fighting leathernecks" of the 6th Regiment worked with the cast and crew. From January 10 to February 3, they roomed at the U.S. Grant Hotel in the city and reported to work at 7:30 each morning.

The year had begun like a déjà vu experience for Bond, again overloaded with too much work; but the fact that official studio publicity campaigns were mentioning his contributions was encouraging. For *Pride of the Marines*, Columbia claimed:

> For-ward ... march! ... rang out the stentorian command and the troops of the Sixth Regiment of U.S. Marines ... moved forward in a wave.
> In the ranks of marching men were Charles Bickford, Joseph Sawyer, George McKay and Ward Bond who play leading roles in the stirring screen drama.
> For Bickford, McKay, Sawyer and Bond the day's activities meant only one thing — work! With

the regular Marines they charged over the top, laid in swampy ground and fired the howitzer and light field guns at the "enemy" and packed eighty-seven pounds of equipment on their back during maneuvers.[25]

An argumentative brawler who had been acquitted of attempted murder at the age of nine, Bickford served in the U.S. Navy prior to joining a burlesque troupe, Boston's John Craig Stock Company, and honing his craft while touring with a road outfit for a decade. He eventually landed on Broadway during the mid–1920s, when he befriended neophyte actor James Cagney. A no-nonsense, down to earth performer who had no time to suffer fools, he provided quite an example for Bond during the three weeks they worked together. The previous year, while filming Fox's *East of Java*, he had nearly died after being mauled by a lion. The extensive scarring ended his starring status at the studio, and he shifted to playing gritty character roles.

Bickford's espousal of Cagney's dictum that an actor "planted his feet, looked the other person in the eye, and *told the truth*" went a long way with Ward. Between more bits in A films at 20th Century–Fox and Paramount, he played the villain in another Columbia Ken Maynard Western, *Avenging Waters* (1936). This time around, Bond isn't "Lacrosse," "Lanky," "Heavy" or simply "So-and-So's Henchman," but sports the more believable moniker "Marve Slater," as the neighboring rancher who works the old "damn up the water and dry out the competition" racket. Less than an hour passes before Slater's scanty property is destroyed in the flood of his own design.

Unfortunately, Ward's character name cannot save a film marred by bad direction, writing, acting, editing, costumes, props, stunt fights, miniature and back-screen projection sequences, and off-key musical numbers. Columbia's production values may be a slim notch above those of Monogram, but even Bond is hamstrung by the indescribably awful dialogue of that legendary cinematic scribe, Nate Gatzert. *Avenging Waters* may be worth one viewing, however, for the reliable performance of Maynard's horse, Tarzan, and the sight of women attired in mid–1930s fashions fearing "road agents" and "Indian massacres!"

The uninspired location shoot at Kernville, California, posed no physical threat to Ward (although *viewing* the film may have required hospitalization). On April 28, 1936, he was in fine form to wed his longtime girlfriend, Doris Sellers Childs, aboard the *Araner*. Earlier that month, he had signed a contract with Hal Roach to portray "Mr. Fitch" in the comedy *Mister Cinderella* for $350-per week, but director Edward Sedgwick eventually made the film with Sid Saylor in the role.

Less than three weeks after *Avenging Waters* burst onto kiddie matinee screens across the nation, Bond again squared off with Ken Maynard, as *The Cattle Thief*. Another Columbia collaboration between "screenwriter" Nate Gatzert and director Spencer Gordon Bennet, this cinematic cow chip, though set on a "ranch," is less Western and more a hybrid of the B-gangster genre and Mack Sennett's Keystone Kops.

Maynard is a man on a mission, sent by the local cattlemen's association to stop the organized rustling operation of Ranse Willard (Bond). Known only as "the mystery rider," Ken wears a mask by night, and masquerades as a mentally challenged peddler during the day. In the end, he lassoes and hogties Ranse, leaving Ward on the ground, looking like a trussed-up Texas steer.

The basic elements of cinema are so often absent that *The Cattle Thief* doesn't really qualify as a motion picture. The writing and direction are so bad that even a good actor (Bond is all by his lonesome here) cannot bring it one hoof's-breadth from the chasm. Insipid in the extreme, the only "thievery" in this bovine miscarriage is its taking away 57 precious minutes of the viewer's life. In the words of Ward's Ranse Willard, "It looks like we've been double-crossed."

During May and June 1936, Bond played bits in three A productions: the Barbara Stanwyck comedy *The Bride Walks Out* for Edward Small and RKO; and two 20th Century–Fox films, *High Tension*, directed by Allan Dwan, and an adaptation of Jack London's *White Fang*, directed by David Butler. He also portrayed a California Highway Patrol drill master in Universal's Jack Holt programmer *Crash Donovan*, in which Ford's tough as nails old pal (with one of the best toupees in the business) is the title character, a motorcycle stunt driver who joins the law enforcement agency.

Bond alternated between RKO and Columbia throughout the summer of 1936, playing small but diverse roles: politician, policeman, gambler and airline pilot. In Columbia's *The Man Who Lived Twice*, he plays ex-boxer John "Gloves" Baker, sidekick to the notorious Johnny "Slick" Rawley (Ralph Bellamy), a killer who undergoes experimental brain surgery in exchange for plastic surgery to help him evade the law. Though hampered by a contrived script and Slick's bad makeup, the film is saved by the performances of Bellamy and Bond, whose "Glovesy," attempting to go straight, admits to Dr. Clifford Schuyler (Thurston Hall), "Look, Doc, I love that guy. I'd do anything for him—*anything*."

And he *means* it. In a unique plot twist, Gloves commits suicide by crashing his car, also taking out Peggy Russell (Isabel Jewell), the only other subpoenaed witness against Rawley, aka Dr. James Blake, after the now-eminent physician's pre-treatment identity is discovered.

Columbia's *Legion of Terror*, starring Bruce Cabot and Marguerite Churchill, features Ward as Don Foster, a Stanfield, Connecticut, working man murdered for trying to expose the "Hooded Legion," a pseudo–KKK "patriotic" organization that proves to be a front for local racketeers. Based on the actual "Black Legion" in Detroit, where Charles Poole, a WPA worker, was killed in May 1935, the film, shot as "Legion of Horror," was made concurrently with Warner Bros.' *Black Legion*, starring Humphrey Bogart and featuring Dick Foran in the "Poole" role. Though the Warners film went into production nearly three weeks earlier, the shooting of additional scenes necessitated withholding its release until January 1937, when the Columbia version had finished its box-office run. The delay paid off for Warners: *Black Legion* won the National Board of Review's award for Best Picture of 1937, and Bogart was chosen as Best Actor. Columbia's film soon was forgotten.

In July 1936, Ford, still at RKO, began shooting another Irish "dream project," an adaptation of Sean O'Casey's play *The Plough and the Stars*, set during the disastrous 1916 Easter Rebellion. Unfortunately, the studio was unwilling to hire Dublin's Abbey Players to fill the roles, instead saddling Ford with Barbara Stanwyck, who never could make her Brooklyn accent sound Irish. Though Preston Foster hailed from Ireland, was one of Ford's drinking buddies, and had been adequate in *The Informer*, he proved decidedly lackluster as Stanwyck's husband (Ford had offered the part to Spencer Tracy, but MGM withdrew its loan-out). However, Ford did cast a handful of Abbey Players, including Barry Fitzgerald and his younger brother, Arthur Shields, and Denis O'Dea, the street singer in *The Informer*.

New RKO production head Sam Briskin, believing that filmgoers were uninterested in watching a married couple, ordered Ford to shoot additional scenes of Stanwyck and Foster occurring *prior* to their wedding. Rather than cave in to such a ridiculous demand, Ford went on a blinding bender, eventually holing up at the Odin Street house while Mary was away. Finally, Cliff Reid approached Katherine Hepburn, to see if she could persuade him to sober up. The wily Kate managed to drag "Sean" into her car, drive back to the RKO lot, and administer a "lethal dose of whiskey and castor oil." Hepburn later recalled:

> I thought he was going to die. And he thought he was going to die. Then he fell asleep and I thought he was dead.... I took him to the Hollywood Athletic Club and they pulled him together.... I'll never forget it. I really nearly killed him.[26]

At that point, Ford many not have cared. RKO's compromised adaptation of *The Plough and the Stars* (including scenes directed by George Nicholls, Jr.) was such a seriocomic mess, he asked that his name be removed from the credits. Briskin and Reid didn't oblige him on that count, either.

Now that former Monogram producer Trem Carr was at Universal, he offered Wayne, whose Republic contract was coming up for renewal, a six-picture, $36,000 deal. Carr was planning lower-budget ($70,000) versions of the successful, non–Western adventure films being made at the major studios, particularly Warner Bros., where Errol Flynn's career had taken off in such blockbusters as *Captain Blood* (1935) and *Charge of the Light Brigade* (1936).

Duke's first Universal film, *Sea Spoilers*, a Coast Guard crime drama directed by Frank Strayer, began production in early July 1936 and was released by the end of September. Director David Howard began shooting the follow-up, under the working title "The Showdown," while *Spoilers* was still in post-production. This drama dealing with racketeering in the boxing ring, released as *Conflict* (1936), is notable mainly for cinematically bringing Wayne and Bond back together for the first time since they'd bumped into each other while making Warners' *College Coach* three years earlier.

Duke and Ward had the pleasure of being billed first and third, respectively, with gorgeous Universal contract player Jean Rogers sandwiched in between. Duke plays Pat Glendon, a young lumberjack turned boxer, who becomes involved in bogus fights with Gus "Knockout" Carrigan (Bond), the "champion" of a syndicate run by Sam Stubener (Frank Sheridan). Things run smoothly until Pat, in love and troubled by his conscience, refuses to cheat more honest people out of their hard-earned cash. After all hell breaks loose, Pat defeats Carrigan in a bona fide bout.

Wayne remained at Universal to make four more films, while his buddy continued to freelance between the studios and independent producers. As usual, Columbia provided some of Bond's most visible roles, including "Sidecar" Wilson in the naval submarine adventure "The Depths Below," which director Erle C. Kenton began shooting on September 8, 1936. Costarring Richard Dix, Dolores del Rio and Chester Morris, this remake of the popular Jack Holt films *Submarine* (1928), directed by Frank Capra, and *Fifty Fathoms Deep* (1931), directed by Roy William Neill, was released as *The Devil's Playground* in January 1937.

During the summer of 1936, comic Joe E. Brown, in a major career move, chose not to renew his Warner Bros. contract. Seeking more creative control, he signed with independent producer David L. Loew, who had made a distribution deal with RKO. Bond had appeared in two of Brown's Warners films, and the newly liberated artist cast him as a police detective in the first Loew picture, *When's Your Birthday?* At midpoint, Ward arrests Brown's Dustin Willoughby, a busboy-boxer studying for a D.A. ("Doctor of Astrology"), for "telling fortunes without a license."

One subpar film away from Warner Bros., where he had taken for granted the top talent and high production values, taught Brown that he had made a tragic mistake, and the remainder of his film career lasted just a wee bit longer than Bond's brief performance in

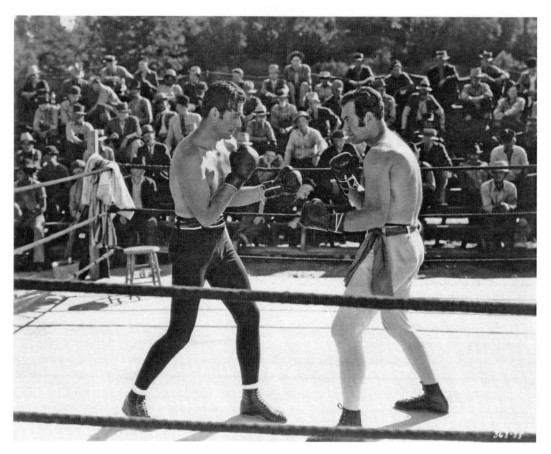

Conflict (Universal, 1936; directed by David Howard). Under contract to Universal, John Wayne (left) meets freelancer Ward Bond in the boxing ring.

Birthday. Apropos of Ford, the funniest line arrives when Willoughby, ordered locked up until he can fight a Friday night bout, responds, "But Jerry (Marian Marsh) and I were going to see *Mary of Scotland* tonight!"

During the closing months of 1936, Bond worked for the formidable Fritz Lang in the Sylvia Sidney–Henry Fonda crime thriller *You Only Live Once*, the Austrian director's second Hollywood film, and with former Ford favorite George O'Brien in the independently made quickie *Park Avenue Logger* (1937). The ludicrous nature of the latter film, based on the 1935 short story by Bruce Hutchison, only begins with its title.

Incorporating footage of logging camps in the Great Northwest, this serial-like feature pits New Yorker Grant Curran (O'Brien), son of Timberlake lumber magnate Michael Curran (Lloyd Ingraham), who calls his college-educated heir an intellectual "sissy," against Paul Sangar (Bond), roughneck field boss of the rival O'Shea logging camp in Oregon. Completely clueless, Old Man Curran has no idea that his beefcake son wrestles as "The Masked Marvel," nor that his camp manager, Ben Morton (Willard Robertson), is conspiring with Sangar to derail the entire O'Shea operation. Aided by Nick (Bert Hanlon), an immigrant who agitates for a workers' pension while running the Timberlake mess hall, Grant, the intellectual *he-man*, rights all wrongs and steals the fetching Peggy O'Shea (Beatrice Roberts) from Sangar, who is last seen being dragged off to the slammer by two cops.

"What can you do with a guy like that?" Grant's father asks a psychiatrist. "He doesn't drink, doesn't smoke, doesn't even *cuss*!" Nearly as wide as he was tall (5'10¾"), George O'Brien first shared the screen with Bond (who was four inches taller) in Ford's *Salute* eight years earlier. In this inauspicious "reunion," George, aiming upward, convincingly pretends to knock out Ward with just one right jab to the jaw. After all, as Nick, referring to Bond's Sangar, so astutely observes, "Nobody loves him, except his *mother*!"

When Ford returned to 20th Century–Fox in late January 1937, Darryl Zanuck ordered him to direct *Wee Willie Winkie*, a Kipling-based Shirley Temple vehicle set in colonial India. Was this assignment punishment for his "insubordination" while shooting *The Prisoner of Shark Island*?

Ford's initial impression disappeared upon learning that the male lead was his old colleague, Victor McLaglen, a good friend of the top-billed child star. However, he wasn't thrilled that Vic's character, Sergeant Donald MacDuff, would die from battle wounds two-thirds through the film. Determined to direct a solid Temple and McLaglen picture, Ford successfully collaborated with Zanuck this time around, taking advantage of the Scotsman's premature demise to create a dramatic highpoint.

First, Ford directed a subtly touching scene during which Temple's "Private Winkie" hands MacDuff a small bouquet of flowers and sings Robert Burns' "Auld Lang Syne" as her friend peacefully passes away. Ford set up a shot that limited McLaglen to play his death scene using only his hand, which the actor allowed slowly to fall limp as Temple sang the classic Scottish song of camaraderie. Ford then followed it with an inspired, beautiful sequence, as he later recalled:

> [I]t had been raining — but the clouds were so nice, and they had that occasional streak of light.... I had a great cameraman, Artie Miller, and I said, "We've got to do something ... with these clouds." I said, "We've got everybody here — let's bury Victor!" ... So we put in the funeral.[27]

This superbly acted film, culminating with two warring factions in an imperialist nation negotiating peacefully through the intercession of an innocent child, may be a bit fantastical, but Ford's inspired direction (which blends his comic "forte" with drama and action, and admirably resists over-sentimentalizing the MacDuff-Winkie relationship) handed Zanuck a minor masterpiece that remains seriously underrated. Temple, who playfully called the director "Ford V-8" throughout production, gave the performance of her life, and her uncharacteristically restrained Winkie is matched by another brilliant turn by McLaglen, who proved that his feat as *The Informer* was no fluke.

After shooting his final scene, the veteran actor, emerging from the sergeant's eternal sleep, told the little trouper, "If I wasn't already dead, I'd be crying, too."

Walking over to the deathbed, Ford put his arm around Temple, assuring her that her grief had been played with "perfect restraint." Of her 30-plus feature films as a child star, *Wee Willie Winkie* always remained Temple's favorite. Cesar Romero, who plays Khoda Khan, said:

> Shirley ... wasn't a spoiled brat.... She was also very smart, always knew her lines and yours, too. If you blew a line, she'd tell you what it was! Her mother did a really great job with this child, because she was not the little precocious child star at all.[28]

In February 1937, Bond was back at Universal, tangling with *Lost Patrol* veteran Boris Karloff (and Jean Rogers as his daughter) while playing "Fingers," a mob goon who aids his boss, "The Kid" (Alan Baxter), in shaking down the inventor of a new, supposedly foolproof, burglar alarm system. In an attempt to rework Karloff's screen image but still capitalize on his prodigious villainy, J. Cheever Cowdin and Robert Cochrane, the "New" Universal's owner and president, respectively (who cared much about Wall Street but little about Hollywood Boulevard), booted out the Carl Laemmle regime (including 70 employees) and rushed its stars into hastily prepared B pictures.

In *Night Key*, a potboiler blending tenets of the horror and gangster genres, Karloff plays Dave Mallory, the kindly inventor who runs afoul of racketeers. Betrayed by unscrupulous industrialist Steve Ranger (Samuel S. Hinds), who convinces him to sign a cutthroat contract, Mallory is strong-armed into aiding the Kid, Fingers and Carl (Frank Reicher) during several burglaries.

Although the film features Karloff in a rare "heroic" characterization, it suffers from the pedestrian direction of Lloyd Corrigan, who was forced to work with a tiny $175,000 budget. One of the highlights involves Mallory "electrocuting" Fingers (Bond does his best in an absurd situation) with what looks like a device left over from the set of *The Bride of Frankenstein* (1935)!

Wayne's final four Universal vehicles, *California Straight Ahead*, *I Cover the War*, *Idol of the Crowds* and *Adventure's End* (all 1937), allowed him to work with Arthur Lubin, one of the studio's most competent "house" directors; but these attempts to make Duke a non–Western star failed to generate popular interest. Once again having bombed at a studio outside of Poverty Row, he accepted a one-film offer to costar with Johnny Mack Brown in Paramount's B-Western *Born to the West* (1937), which promised the excitement of a cattle drive, gambling, shootouts and even a few fillies. But under the direction of Charles Barton (who later presided over Abbott and Costello at Universal), this Paramount picture looks like it was made at Monogram or Republic.

Bond continued on his inexorable path throughout 1937, playing bits for the majors and support for the minors. In the Spencer Tracy vehicle *They Gave Him a Gun*, MGM's contribution to the "World War I veteran turned gangster" subgenre, Ward briefly asserts his authority as an M.P. In Hal Roach's comedy classic *Topper*, he plays a cab driver who gets punched out by Cary Grant. And he's unforgettable as a doorman in Samuel Goldwyn's *Dead End*, the film that introduced the "Kids" of the same name, plus offered Humphrey Bogart his first "prestige" gangster role following *The Petrified Forest*. Originally cast but dropped from the Warner Bros. mob melodrama, Bond now made the first of his several film appearances with Bogie.

In May 1937, Ford lobbied to be rehired by Samuel Goldwyn, to direct an adaptation of the Charles Nordhoff and Norman Hall novel *Hurricane*. Goldwyn, willing to put the *Arrowsmith* debacle behind them, originally had chosen Howard Hawks, but a recent falling out had sent him packing. Having bristled under the gun of Darryl Zanuck, Ford was lured by a sweet deal: $100,000, plus 12 percent of the profits (increasing to 15 percent after a net of $1 million), a contract to lease the *Araner* to appear in the film, and (most importantly) script approval and final cut. Dan Ford observed, "John ... thrived under the studio system.... With his powerful personality and reputation for irascibility, he was able to browbeat even the strongest producers and more often than not make the system work for him."[29]

The cast of *The Hurricane* is headed by a striking screen couple: handsome beefcake star Jon Hall (nephew of the novel's co-author) and the exotic, gorgeous Dorothy Lamour. Raymond Massey leads the solid supporting cast, including Thomas Mitchell, John Carradine and C. Aubrey Smith, all of whom worked frequently for Ford.

The fairly uncomplicated story is set on "Manukura" in the South Seas, where a native sailor, Terangi (Hall), shortly after his honeymoon with Marama (Lamour), daughter of

Chief Mehevi (Al Kikume), is sentenced to prison by the Governor of Tahiti for injuring a white racist (in self defense) during a barroom brawl. Incapable of tolerating confinement, Terangi repeatedly escapes, only to be captured and, without the support of the law-and-order Governor of Manakura, Eugene DeLaage (Massey), handed a longer sentence each time. After racking up a 16-year stretch, he tries to hang himself and then breaks out after accidentally killing a guard.

Following a grueling, 600-mile canoe trip back to Manakura, Terangi, aided by Father Paul (Smith), is reunited with Marama and meets his daughter, Tita (Kuulei De Clercq), at Motu Tonga. While DeLaage commandeers a schooner to search for the escaped convict, storm winds brew into a full-blown hurricane. Many of the Manakurans seek shelter in Father Paul's church, which is destroyed by savage squalls that also uproot the tree to which Terangi has tied himself and his family. DeLaage, having weathered the storm while at sea, returns to the ravaged island but, encouraged by his wife, Germaine (Mary Astor), allows Terangi, Marama and Tita to flee in a canoe.

Ford worked on *The Hurricane* from May 3 through the end of September 1937, initially shooting on location with the *Araner* at Catalina, where the crew bunked in tents set up on the shore of Isthmus Harbor. The interiors were then completed at the Goldwyn Studio in Hollywood. Goldwyn's contractual agreement to leave the production in Ford's hands didn't quite pan out, however. After insulting Merritt Hulburd, an associate producer sent to Catalina to keep an eye on him, Ford clashed briefly with the mogul when asked to shoot additional close-ups of Lamour. As he had done with Zanuck on *The Prisoner of Shark Island*, Ford first went ballistic but then relented, realizing that the suggestion would improve the picture, which was released on November 9, 1937, to terrific box office but lukewarm reviews. Ford later recalled a quieter, gentler version of the incident:

> Sam Goldwyn never interfered with anybody.... But when they ran *The Hurricane* for him, he said, "It isn't personalized enough." ... Our time and budget had run out ... and I had just done what was in the script. So ... I went back and ... put in some closer shots.[30]

Ford not only filmed additional material for *The Hurricane*, but also pitched in to complete some scenes for Goldwyn's ridiculous *The Adventures of Marco Polo* (1938), in which Bond is among the many Anglo actors (Basil Rathbone, Alan Hale, H. B. Warner, even Stanley Fields!) who appears as a Mongol.

Jon Hall gives a powerful physical performance throughout *The Hurricane*, brawling, swimming, fighting his way through wind and waves, and wrestling with a shark, which he then guts with a knife. John Carradine reprises his sadistic prison officer from *Shark Island*, and Thomas Mitchell makes the first of several appearances for Ford as a liberal, philosophical alcoholic (a character not unlike the director), a doctor who delivers a baby in a canoe during the hurricane. C. Aubrey Smith is perfectly cast as Father Paul, who informs the rigid imperialist governor, "There are stronger things in this world than *governments*, DeLaage," shortly before perishing, along with several of the natives, when his church is obliterated by the storm. The hurricane sequences feature the impressive work of special effects artist James Basevi, who worked closely with Ford and assistant director Stuart Heisler.

While still making his way through *The Hurricane*, Ford bought the film rights to "Stage to Lordsburg," a story by Ernest Haycox published in *Colliers* magazine a few months earlier. (Ford rightly claimed that Haycox had based it on Guy de Maupassant's famous short story "Boule de Suif," which is set during the Franco-Prussian War of 1870–71.) Ford hadn't made a Western in over a decade, and was itching to direct an A film that would bring respectability back to a genre that had long been relegated to B status.

Conferring with Dudley Nichols, he began to develop a screenplay that added depth to the diverse group of characters who are thrown together in a stagecoach traveling through the New Mexico Territory rife with Apaches. They transformed the central character, the gunslinger "Malpais Bill," into a more laudable, environmentally scarred outlaw known as "The Ringo Kid." Believing that their economical, exciting script had solid box-office potential, Ford was abruptly given the bum's rush by five studio bosses, including Zanuck, who wouldn't even read it.

During that summer, Ford also joined the Motion Picture Artists Committee, which supported the Loyalist cause in the Spanish Civil War. In July, he had met Ernest Hemingway at the home of Fredric March, where the author screened the film *The Spanish Earth*. Dan Ford explained, "During these years there was an élan, a very special glory, about the Loyalist cause that both the bully-boy Irishman and the liberal man of letters in John were drawn to."[31] Ford also signed on with Melvyn Douglas and writer Philip Dunne as a vice-chairman of the Motion Picture Democratic Committee, a "liberal, internationalist, pro–Roosevelt organization that believed fascism to be a more serious threat to world peace than communism."[32]

Francis Ford's son, Bob, fought with Spain's International Brigade, and was pleased that his uncle was supporting the cause. He wrote a letter to John, explaining that the prevailing belief in the United States that the Loyalists were "Red" was "out and out Fascist propaganda." Ford wrote back:

> I am glad you got some of the good part of the Feeney blood — some of it is God damn awful — we are liars, weaklings and selfish drunkards. But there has always been a stout rebel quality in the family and a peculiar passion for justice....
> Politically — I am a definite Socialistic Democrat — always left. I have watched the Russian experiment with great interest. Like the French Commune, I am afraid it might lead to another Bonaparte.[33]

On the home front, John and Mary, who lived quite modestly by Hollywood standards, had worked past the Hepburn affair. According to Dan Ford, "John had several minor affairs, but they didn't really amount to much ... his real vice was alcohol, not women."[34]

Ford was very strict with his children, and delegated most of the domestic duties to Maude "Mama Steve" Stevenson. He loved the kids, but the most important people in his life were his fellow filmmakers, particularly the Stock Company members who were becoming a professional *and* personal surrogate family. John's brother, Eddie O'Fearna, who had assisted him since 1920, left the ranks in 1937 to work for William "Wild Bill" Wellman, and the top assistant position was filled by his brother-in-law, Wingate Smith, formerly of the U.S. Army and now known as the rough and tough "First Sergeant" of the Stock Company. He became Ford's liaison with the 20th Century–Fox front office, removing some of the pressure created by the daily tribulations of directing.

Ford detested pretense, ostentatious attire, conspicuous consumption, and most material possessions, so he often appeared as the polar opposite of the public's image of the "Hollywood film director." In 1938, when Louis B. Mayer invited him to discuss making a film for MGM, he showed up at the studio gate, unshaven and wearing clothes he'd put on three days earlier. Assuming he was dealing with a skid row drunk, the guard refused to let him enter.

The second half of 1937 brought Bond a variety of roles, including small parts in MGM's Civil War drama *Of Human Hearts* (1938), starring James Stewart, and RKO's screwball comedy gem *Bringing Up Baby* (1938), directed by Howard Hawks and pairing

Katherine Hepburn with Cary Grant. Even the quality of the B films improved, and he charted higher in the billing as the scope of his performances began to increase. He still was handed cop and criminal roles, but these occasionally allowed him to inject deft comic touches.

At Columbia, he worked on the taut prison thriller *Penitentiary* (1938) with director John Brahm (who, two decades later, would become one of his chief collaborators on *Wagon Train*). At Warner Bros., he played Eddie Edwards, an overly ambitious racketeer, in *Over the Wall* (1938), featuring several character actors who were frequent colleagues: Dick Foran, John Litel, George E. Stone and Raymond Hatton.

The multitalented Foran plays Jerry Davis, a two-bit boxer double-crossed by Edwards, whom he later punches out, giving mob boss "Ace" Scanlon (Dick Purcell) the perfect opportunity to eliminate his upstart lieutenant and frame the washed-up fighter for the crime. *Over the Wall* is one of the most bizarre entries in the Warner Bros. urban crime genre, a gangster film doubling as a "prison musical," featuring Foran singing several numbers, including a reverent rendition of Franz Schubert's "Ave Maria" under the guidance of the prison chaplain, Father Neil Connor (Litel).

Arguably the best vocalist ever to work as a B-Western singing cowboy, Foran is a "singing convict" this time around, giving this low-budget forerunner to *Angels with Dirty Faces* (1938) a unique twist on the well-worn "innocent man railroaded to the Joint" plot. Eddie Edwards allows Bond to shine in a conspicuous and colorful supporting role, a slick wiseguy whacked by his boss. (An early scene, set on the beach, allows the well-chiseled Ward to display his superiority over Dick in the beefcake department.) George E. Stone also enjoys a prime scene, as his "Gyp" Hatton, the boss' diminutive sidekick, reveals the truth about the whack just before he takes the Big Sleep.

Like Wayne, Bond was given his most absurd roles by Republic. Produced under the working title "Fools in Paradise," *Escape by Night* (1937) is so ridiculous that it rarely stops being entertaining. Ward plays Peter "Spudsy" Baker, a member of a gang operated by James "Capper" Regan (Dean Jagger), who implicates all his associates by shooting a police officer during their attempt to flee into the country.

Regan remains in the city, but his "mugs" (Bond and Murray Alper) and Nick Allen (William Hall), a bystander who prevented Capper's girlfriend, Josephine (Steffi Duna), from being kidnapped, scram into the sticks. Soon their evil city ways are left behind, as they spend the summer making improvements to a rundown but peaceful farm owned by "Pop" Adams (Charles Waldron), a very accommodating blind man, and Linda (Anne Nagel), his beautiful daughter.

Ward really shines in this potboiler. Not only does Spudsy teach Linda how to cook (while wearing a chef's hat and apron), raise chickens and team up with a German shepherd to plant potatoes (while wearing a straw hat and bib overalls), he also unleashes the legendary Bond "horse whinny" at one point. Working with a ludicrous screenplay, the entire cast delivers believable performances. Even the dog (Bill) deserves his billing in the opening credits. (Proof of Bond's upward mobility during 1937 is provided by his billing *above* a dog in this film. This was not necessarily the case in 1936.)

Bond finished out the year in Republic's *Born to Be Wild*, reportedly the "first non–Western" directed by the studio's resident ace, Joseph Kane. But is this film *not* a Western?

On first viewing, *Born to Be Wild* may *seem* to be the first-ever "trucker musical," but it's actually the same old Republic singing cowboy Western dressed up as possibly the most bizarre film in which Bond appears. Audiences in early 1938 may have thought that the studio had discovered, in Ralph Byrd and Ward Bond, the Poverty Row counterparts of Warner Bros.' Dick Powell and James Cagney. The film could have been released as "Taillight Parade."

Steve Hackett (Ralph Byrd) and Bill Purvis (Bond) are freight haulers whose work records are less than stellar. Offered a $1,000 bonus to drive a load of lettuce to Indian Head, California, they discover the cargo is actually dynamite. After numerous mishaps and sabotage incidents, including the double dealing of lovely young female Mary Stevens (Doris Weston), they boldly reach their destination.

The explosives are sought by the local citizens to blast open dam locks shut down by J. Carroll Malloy (Harrison Greene), a greedy land owner threatening to flood the town. Somehow the resourceful, singing and dancing truckers blow up the rig, save the town, and lose *their* lettuce. They are last seen, harmonizing in fine voice, heading out on another potential suicide mission: Steve and Bill, accompanied by the new *Mrs.* Hackett and her dog, Butch.

Bond scored third billing in this genre-bending, quasi-surrealist hybrid. Billed just below him is the *dog*, a cairn terrier named "Stooge." Unlike "Bill," the multitalented German shepherd, in *Escape by Night*, this canine does — absolutely nothing.

Ward is the multitalented treat of this fantastical mishmash. Though all he really wants to do is sleep, Bill Purvis, aside from his usual trucker duties, is forced to lie in the middle of a highway, dodge bullets, be tied up, beaten and tossed over an embankment, play the piano, sing, impersonate a Latino, and dance the rhumba with the sensual cantina *bailarín* "Manuela" (Sterlita Peluffo), while wearing a huge sombrero and suggestively rubbing a Mexican shawl across his wiggling, equine rear end.

Like Cagney and Powell, Bond and the crooning Byrd never costarred in another film. If Ford ever saw one of the projects his protégé made for another director, it should have been *Born to Be Wild*. Pappy's torture would have been terminal, but Ward would have taken it like the wild man he was born to be.

On Monday, January 10, 1938, during Ford's hiatus from Fox, Bond returned to the studio's Western Avenue lot to work for director James Tinling. He again was appearing as a boxer in a low-budget film, but this time the role was flashy; and he plays "Biff Moran, Heavyweight Champion of the World" to perfection.

To Bond, it was just another bread and butter part. By the time the film was released three months later, his performance, commanding considerable screen time in a major-studio production, was no longer part of "Charlie Chan at the Ringside." One of the most challenging and convoluted projects ever to emerge from a Hollywood B unit, it began with Bond supporting Warner Oland as Chan; but his Biff Moran ended up in a release starring Peter Lorre as a different character!

Tinling's shoot was intended to be the 17th entry in Fox's hugely popular Oland detective series, which had begun with *Charlie Chan Carries On* (1931) and continued to be a major moneymaker. By noon on the first day, the cast and crew were dismissed early after Oland, wracked by alcoholism and an impending divorce, suffered a "sudden indisposition." In reality, the star had just walked off the set.

To make matters worse, Oland failed to arrive for work the next morning. When the suits failed to track him down, his agent claimed that he refused to work on soundstage number "6" because of draughty, "pneumonia inducing" conditions. While Fox negotiated with Oland and the Screen Actors Guild to solve the problem, Bond and his fellow actors were sitting around on the stage, waiting for *something* to happen.

On Thursday, January 13, Oland returned to the Fox lot, pleased to pass through a stage door bearing the numeral "7." What the actor didn't realize was that a worker had painted "7" over the original "6," and the great Charlie Chan was unknowingly delivering his familiar aphorisms on the same "unhealthy" stage.

Two days later, against Tinling's protests, Oland again bolted; and, after returning on Monday morning, claiming that he needed "a glass of water," inexplicably disappeared once more. With only three days of shooting completed, the cast and crew of "Charlie Chan at the Ringside" had seen the beloved star for the last time. Sol Wurtzel paid them their salaries (which drained $100,000 from the budget), suspended Oland, and shut down production.

Wurtzel met with Zanuck to discuss possible ways to salvage the project, combining the completed footage with a reworked script featuring another actor as Chan, or perhaps Keye Luke as "Number One Son," Lee Chan. Concluding that either of these strategies might bomb with audiences who practically believed that Oland *was* Chan, they had to devise a more commercially sound alternative. In the meantime, the studio issued publicity claiming that Oland had suffered a "nervous breakdown" and was recuperating at his home.

With another "Oriental" detective on their roster, Wurtzel and Zanuck retained the plot of "Ringside," replaced the Chinese investigator with their "little Japanese dick," added a subplot involving Lee Chan as a student of the "international" policeman, and changed the title to *Mr. Moto's Gamble*. Minimal changes were made to the dialogue, making it more suitable for the mysterious, often unscrupulous and physically violent Moto; but much remained unaltered, resulting in the character responding with Chan-like, "fortune cookie" wisdom.

By the time Tinling began shooting the reworked material on January 24, Bond had moved on to his next project, the Jack Holt vehicle *Flight into Nowhere*, for director Lewis D. Collins at Columbia. Fortunately the great Biff Moran hadn't appeared in many shots with Chan, so Tinling and editor Nick DeMaggio were able smoothly to incorporate Bond's extant performance with new footage involving Moto, resulting in a characterization that stands out in a cast including Lynn Bari, George E. Stone, Cliff Clark and a young Lon Chaney, Jr. "Slapsie" Maxie Rosenbloom's kleptomaniacal, punch-drunk pugilist, Horace "Knockout" Wellington, lends credibility to Bond's professional boxer, although Moran ultimately loses his title to challenger Bill Steele (Dick Baldwin).

Zanuck negotiated a new contract with Oland, who had been making progress in his recovery, for three more Chan pictures. Intending to begin production on the first of these films, Fox executives again were foiled when Oland suddenly left to visit his mother in Sweden, where he contracted bronchial pneumonia and died at age 57.

The New Year brought Bond reunions with George O'Brien at RKO and Jack Holt at Columbia. In *Gun Law* (1938), Ward and Francis MacDonald (John Wilkes Booth in Ford's *Shark Island*) are the dreaded outlaws "Pecos" and "Nevada," both of whom are easily bested by O'Brien's U.S. Marshal Tom O'Malley. After dispatching Holt on the *Flight to Nowhere* (1938), Ward joined him in the *Reformatory* (1938), also housing "Dead End Kid" Bobby Jordan and "Wild Boy of the Road" Frankie Darro.

Having landed in Columbia's *Penitentiary* and *Reformatory* within a six-month stretch, Bond simply *had* to take Universal's *Prison Break*, which provided one of his most memorable B-film roles of the decade. Directed by Arthur Lubin, the film had three working titles ("State Prison," "Prison Walls" and "Walls of San Quentin") prior to its release on July 15, 1938. Initially planned as the first of four Universal projects to costar Barton MacLane and Glenda Farrell, *Prison Break* was the only film actually produced; and by time it hit theaters, the pair already had appeared in four of the successful "Torchy Blane" installments (*Smart Blonde* [1937], *Flyaway Baby* [1937], *The Adventurous Blonde* [1937] and *Blondes at Work* [1938]) at Warner Bros.

Unlike his small roles in the Columbia incarceration pictures, "Big Red" Kincaid, awarded Bond by Duke's Universal producer, Trem Carr, provides the only real physical presence in *Prison Break*. Inexpensively shot on cramped sets, with stock footage providing its only spatial sense, the film benefits little from Lubin and cinematographer Harry Neumann's use of shadows, but much from Ward's athletic build and menacing, though understated, performance. Like Wayne, Bond had to do very little to convey power, and here he is a stone killer who looms as a legend in the minds of all the yard birds, except for Joaquin Shannon (MacLane), a Portuguese-Irish tuna fisherman, sent to the Big House after being framed for manslaughter by the bigoted father (Victor Kilian) of his fiancée, Jean Fenderson (Farrell).

Barton MacLane was no physical slouch, but his fight scenes are so badly staged that no viewer could believe Shannon actually contributes to someone's death (he takes the rap for his brother-in-law, who didn't do it, either!) or knocks out Big Red in the climactic scene. He and Farrell proved their collective acting prowess by giving good performances while saddled with the clumsy dialogue of screenwriter Dorothy Reid, who adapted Norton S. Parker's story "Walls of San Quentin." However, in the best tradition of Warners' *I Am a Fugitive from a Chain Gang*, she was able (without becoming preachy) to work in a few swipes at antiquated criminal laws.

Somehow the other performers also fare rather well. "Big Red Kincaid — he's always been dynamite," announces "Cappy" (Frank Darien), Shannon's cellmate, when the criminal colossus arrives in the prison yard.

"Welcome home!" shout the other convicts, all of whom recognize him instantly. Effervescent characters like "Soapy" (Paul Hurst, billed above Bond), the slammer's baseball manager, are ubiquitous in the B prison subgenre.

Bond does a bang-up job with his delivery, too. He uses the term "Stir-dude" often, but convincingly each time. After Shannon stands up to Big Red, this murderer of yard captains replies, "Why, you dirty, lyin' Portuge-Mick!" like he really means it (just before engaging in another lame "fist fight").

From late January through March 1938, Ford was back at Fox, directing *Four Men and a Prayer*, a Zanuck-assigned project with a fine cast: Loretta Young, Richard Greene, George Sanders, David Niven, Alan Hale and John Carradine. A film about four English brothers who scour the globe to find members of a munitions racket responsible for having their father, Colonel Loring Leigh (C. Aubrey Smith), dishonorably discharged from the British Army and murdered for "knowing too much," did not excite Ford. He later recalled succinctly, "I just didn't like the story, or anything else about it, so it was a job of work."[35]

David Niven became Ford's whipping boy this time around, and Zanuck even took part in a ruse resulting in the urbane, 28-year-old actor arriving on the set late one morning, stewed to the gills. By the time the befuddled Niven realized that he had been set up, he was forced to handle a snake and a box full of turtles!

In late February 1938, Bond returned to Warner Bros. to play "Tug," a mug in the mob of *The Amazing Doctor Clitterhouse*, a clever, PCA-induced variation on the studio's earlier gangster films. The third teaming of star Edward G. Robinson (in the title role) and Humphrey Bogart (as gangster "Rocks" Valentine), the film also features studio regulars Claire Trevor, Donald Crisp, Gale Page, Henry O'Neill, John Litel, and the greatest gangster's sidekick ever to grace the screen: Allen Jenkins, who backs up *both* Eddie and Bogie.

Okay (Jenkins), Butch (Maxie Rosenbloom) and Tug, originally in Valentine's mob, develop an admiration for the doc's criminality studies.

In order to prove his theory that criminal behavior results, not from sociological problems, but a physiological one, Clitterhouse joins the gang on their "jobs" and then performs a blood test on each mug in their hideout, using "The Hudson River String Quartet" as a front. "Every time I see that needle, I get woozy," Tug admits before grabbing his violin. Bond's comic timing is on display, and the sight of him masquerading as a chamber musician is one of the film's most amusing moments.

Frank Capra used Ward in another small part, Mike, the Detective, in Columbia's *You Can't Take It With You* (1938), a well-acted and genuinely funny all-star cast adaptation of the hit Broadway play by George S. Kaufman and Moss Hart. This successful exercise in "Capra-corn," Bond's fourth film for Frank, also was the populist filmmaker's second to win both the Best Director and Best Picture Academy Awards.

Ford's respite from work was usually provided by the *Araner*, but his temper often flared during the frequent card games (hearts, pitch, poker and his favorite, bridge) played on board with his closest pals. On one occasion when Duke was challenging the Coach, Barbara interrupted to inquire what game they were playing.

Wayne answered, "Honeymoon Bridge."

"Why do you call it that?" she asked.

"Because we're trying to screw each other," Duke explained.

Ford was often so abusive that he, Wayne and Bond had difficulty rounding up a fourth for a game. Duke recalled a particular day when the *Araner* was docked at San Pedro, where he and Ward were relaxing:

> Jack sent George Goldrainer ashore and had him scour through the waterfront bars to find a fourth. He came back with some guy who had been drunk for about five days. He was so drunk he couldn't even sit up at the table. But that's not the half of it. The worst part of it was that Jack made me take this guy for a partner.[36]

Other than the *Araner*, Ford's favorite hangout was the Hollywood Athletic Club on Wilcox Street, where he, Wayne and Bond would rub shoulders with many of filmdom's elite. Of course, the club included all the fitness amenities: weight room, steam bath, swimming pool, massage room and barbershop. But it was the upstairs *bar* set up exclusively for Ford and his pals, including Merian Cooper, Preston Foster, Frank Morgan, Dudley Nichols, Liam O'Flaherty, 20th Century–Fox producer Gene Markey, Wingate Smith and even Tarzan himself, Johnny Weissmuller, that provided the most "fitness" for the group.

To scoff at the local country clubs that excluded show-business types, Pappy and his cohorts jokingly (and *very* inaccurately) named their own club "The Young Men's Purity Total Abstinence and Snooker Pool Association." Membership requirements were a prodigious consumption of booze and frequent trips to the steam room, which was attended by John "Buck" Buchanan, a gracious black man whom they dubbed "The Distinguished Afro-American."

"Jews but no dues" (another direct hit at the L.A. country clubs) was their official slogan, and their charter explained that the club's purpose was to "promulgate the cause of alcoholism." Dudley Nichols, the most left-wing member of the group, was consistently denied membership because of the "socially reprehensible" nature of his political beliefs. This became a running gag at the club, and, according to Dan Ford, "Although Nichols liked to claim that he was a big drinker, and loudly boasted of his alcoholic exploits, he really drank very little, at least when compared with the likes of Messrs. Wayne, Bond and Ford."[37]

Eventually the athletic club grew too claustrophobic for the members, many of whom shared a love of the sea, so the outfit was rechristened "The Young Men's Purity Total Abstinence and Yachting Association." Ford elected to keep the (considerably embellished) minutes of the club's meetings and, not only repeatedly reproached the "temperance" of Dudley Nichols, but also noted the *overindulgence* of another member, Brother Wardell Edwin Bond:

> At the last meeting ... Mr. Ward Bond was summarily dropped from our rolls for conduct and behavior which is unpleasant to put in print. Mr. Dudley Nichols, the well-known Irish-American screenwriter, was elected in his place.

Ford then claimed that "Brother Commodore John A. Buchanan (colored)," while working at the Hollywood Athletic Club, reported:

> On Saturday night, February 27th ... I was amazed by seeing Brother Bond taking a bath.... Later I saw him in the barbershop having a manicure. When I reported this unusual procedure to Brother President Ford, he at once doubted my veracity.... Upon my insistence ... Ford ... proceeded to the barbershop. There we found Brother Bond in a state of total intoxication, drinking Irish whiskey with gin chasers, attempting to kiss the manicurist on the back of the neck with a lighted cigar in his mouth.[38]

By the summer of 1938, the organization had been transformed into the fictitious "Emerald Bay Yacht Club," to honor one of Ford's favorite spots near Catalina's Isthmus Harbor, where *The Hurricane* had been filmed. The slogan and requirements remained the same, and the meetings continued to be held at the Athletic Club. However, to promulgate the sham of establishing a real yacht club, all the members, including James Cagney, Ronald Colman, Henry Fonda, Howard Hawks, James Stewart and William Wellman, began to dress in ostentatious maritime regalia.

After a span of nearly six years, Ford welcomed Bond back to his set in late June 1938, to play the supporting role of Seaman Olaf Swanson in the 20th Century–Fox adaptation of *The Splinter Fleet of the Otranto Barrage* by Ray Milholland. This maritime project set during World War I weathered 10 screenwriters (including William Faulkner) and several titles (one being "Wooden Anchors"), but ultimately was released on November 25, 1938, as *Submarine Patrol*.

Zanuck had given Ford a two-month shooting schedule, with Richard Greene again cast as the male lead, opposite Nancy Kelly in the top female spot. Bond was in good company, because Pappy went all out, loading the supporting cast with drinking buddies and members of his Stock Company: Preston Foster, George Bancroft, J. Farrell MacDonald (as Quincannon, an Irish surname ubiquitous in Ford's films), Jack Pennick and John Carradine. George E. Stone also was cast in a noticeable role; and, for a few brief moments, the studio again tossed a bone to Lon Chaney, Jr., who appears as a Marine sentry.

One heavy drinker, the New York–born, Runyonesque Warren Hymer, who had appeared in *Men Without Women*, *Born Reckless*, *Up the River* and *Seas Beneath*, played his lovable lug for Ford one last time. As the son of playwright John B. Hymer and stage actress Eleanor Kent, he had a fine thespian pedigree, had graduated from Yale's School of the Fine Arts (where he performed with Herbert J. Biberman), and acted on Broadway before moving to Hollywood in 1928.

Warren's penchant for booze got the best of him during the months following his work in *Submarine Patrol*. While freelancing at Columbia, where he appeared in *The Lady and the Mob* and *Coast Guard* (both 1939), Hymer arrived on the set one morning acting as if he'd spent a few days in Ford's sleeping bag. When word of his inebriation reached studio

Submarine Patrol (20th Century–Fox, 1938; directed by John Ford). Ford regulars Jack Pennick (left, holding beer mug), Warren Hymer (kneeling) and Ward Bond (fourth from right) are joined on the crew by ace character actor George E. Stone (far right, grasping handle).

boss Harry Cohn, Warren was ordered thrown off the lot. Reportedly, the "throwing" wasn't sufficient, however, and Hymer somehow made his way into Cohn's office, where he unceremoniously relieved himself of excess metabolized alcohol on the mogul's desk.

This act of drunken defiance *did* get Hymer tossed out; and, though many of his fellow working actors applauded his "courageous" stand, his name was "Piss" with the Columbia suits. For the remainder of his career, Hymer primarily remained in the doghouse at the major studios, given an occasional bone while repeating his familiar shtick at Universal and finally on Poverty Row, where he was re-teamed with Bond in the indescribably awful *Hitler: Dead or Alive* (1942). He continued on his inexorable path of self-destruction along Hollywood's skids until, unable to land a part in over two years, he died of a "stomach ailment" in 1948 at age 42. One of his earliest films had been Raoul Walsh's *The Cockeyed World* (1929), the first "Flagg and Quirt" sequel to *What Price Glory* starring Victor McLaglen and Edmund Lowe.

Ford, lying that he served in the U.S. Navy during the conflict depicted in *Submarine Patrol*, said:

> Having been a Blue Jacket — though I wasn't in the submarine fleet — I had a lot of sympathy for them.... The head of the fleet was an old pal of mine and he helped me on it ... all the comedy wasn't in the script; we put it in as we went along.[39]

The film opened to good reviews, and Zanuck and his wife, Virginia, planned a celebration to honor Ford at their Santa Monica home. Prior to the soiree, the 20th Century–Fox publicity department issued a statement asking journalists not to base their judgments of Nancy Kelly on her acting in *Submarine Patrol*, but hold off until seeing her as Tyrone Power's love interest in the blockbuster *Jesse James*, directed by Henry King. Ford detested this sort of studio backstabbing, and did not attend the party, lying to Zanuck that he had been stranded aboard the *Araner* with a broken-down engine. In a letter to the Fox executives, he wrote:

> [T]his coming out in print is an adverse criticism from my own studio of my direction. I presume I am no longer wanted at 20th Century–Fox to direct pictures, especially pictures with women. I am terribly sorry that the studio should have to take this means of protecting their stars....[40]

4

Boating, Booze and "Boule de Suif"

Ford was a tender loving man, and he was a delicate, artistic man....
Yet he was intrigued with machoism. He wanted to be a two-fisted,
brawling, heavy-drinking Irishman. He wanted to do what John Wayne
did on the screen and clean up a barroom all by himself.... There was a
part of him that Wayne exemplified physically, something he always
wanted to be. So he created that on the screen. — Harry Carey, Jr.[1]

Goddamn, nobody ever enjoyed a picture more than these people
enjoyed Stagecoach. — John Wayne, on the February 2, 1939, preview[2]

From late summer into the autumn of 1938, Bond did his usual work at several studios, playing cops, crooks and heavyweight boxers. He also appeared as Jim Hatton in Selznick International's *Made for Each Other* (1939), a Carole Lombard and James Stewart tearjerker; and was saddled with the moniker Mulligan P. Martinez in RKO's *The Law West of Tombstone* (1939), in which he encounters Harry Carey (as William "Bonanza Bill" Barker, a mining prospector) and Tim Holt (as the outlaw "Tonto Kid").

Amidst all the mayhem generated by his bogus "maritime organization," Ford had managed to generate some interest in his "Stage to Lordsburg" screenplay. Merian C. Cooper, who had signed Ford to a two-picture contract prior to merging his production company, Pioneer, with Selznick International, where he now was vice president, discussed the situation with his boss, who definitely wanted the director to honor the existing agreement.

But Selznick waffled on "Stage to Lordsburg," first agreeing to make it, and then nixing it the following day. Ultimately he decided that only Gary Cooper would have enough star power to make the picture a commercial success. Instead he wanted Ford to direct a Benedict Arnold biopic and, of all things, the pro–Confederate soap opera *Gone with the Wind*, with scenes, particularly those whitewashing slavery, that Pappy would have ripped right from the script.

Finally, Ford managed to find a buyer: independent producer Walter Wanger, an outspoken liberal fond of "message" films, who owed a picture to United Artists. The distributor, however, didn't match the producer's enthusiasm, allocating only $392,000 to a lowly Western retitled *Stagecoach*. Ford knew that all the location shooting he'd written into the script would burn much of the budget, so he settled for a flat fee of $50,000, less than half of what he'd earned for *The Hurricane* and considerably below his 20th Century–Fox salary of $75,000. Dudley Nichols was paid $20,000 for his screenplay.

With only $65,000 allotted to the entire cast, Ford also realized he'd have to talk some of his favorite actors into accepting less than they expected. An essential aspect of his film-making brilliance was casting, and he managed to snag some prodigious talent: Claire Trevor as the female lead, Dallas, a shunned prostitute; Thomas Mitchell as "Doc" Boone, a variation on his alcoholic physician in *The Hurricane*; John Carradine as Hatfield, a gambler who attempts to impersonate a gentleman; Louise Platt as Lucy Mallory, a "respectable" (and pregnant) married lady; old, reliable George Bancroft as Marshal Curley Wilcox; Berton Churchill as Gatewood, a slimy, embezzling banker; and the terminally laryngitic Andy Devine as Buck, the constantly complaining stage driver.

After production began, Ford chastised Devine, "You big tub of lard. I don't know why I'm using you in this picture!"

"Because Ward Bond can't drive six horses," replied Andy.[3]

Ford also cast Donald Meek, Tom Tyler, old buddies Jack Pennick and Harry Tenbrook, Tim Holt, and Francis, who was handed a typically thankless (and unbilled) bit role as Billy Pickett. Regardless of producers' daydreams about bankable stars like Gary Cooper, Ford knew who would play the Ringo Kid from the time he began working on the script, a young man who had learned the basics in cinematic "boot camp" for nearly a decade at Poverty Row dumps like Mascot, Monogram and Republic: one of his two surrogate sons, John Wayne.

Although he levied doses of his trademark abuse upon the Duke, Ford had loved him from the start, and Wayne always viewed the Coach as a mentor, counselor and father figure. But Wayne wasn't just a fun (and funny) guy to have hanging around. Ford had seen flashes of brilliance in his unadorned, naturalistic acting style, and thought he glided his 6'4" body "like a dancer."[4]

Following his parents' bitter divorce in 1929, Duke had remained close to his father, but Clyde, weakened by a heart condition, had passed away during an afternoon nap on March 4, 1937, making his son's time with Pappy on the *Araner* even more personally significant. Tired of the grind and limitations of his B-Western career, Duke nevertheless had signed a new, eight-film contract with Republic on May 7, 1938, to appear, not as the star of his own vehicles, but to replace Robert Livingston as Stony Brooke, one of the "Three Mesquiteers," in a series of modern-day B Westerns (with the same hoary, cowboy versus corrupt authority plots) costarring Ray "Crash" Corrigan (as Tucson Smith) and Max Terhune (as Lullaby Joslin), a frequently annoying ventriloquist, whose dummy, Elmer, was a hit with the kiddies. If Stony happened to fall in love with the female lead (*Overland Stage Raiders* [1938] features Louise Brooks), this situation caused no end of trouble for the cowboy trio, who always ride off together at the film's end. Wayne later referred to these ridiculous hodgepodge pictures as "horrible monstrosities."[5]

Duke recently had been on several fishing excursions with Ford, Bond and Dudley Nichols; but this time, he and Pappy were the only passengers aboard the *Araner* as she left San Pedro harbor for a weekend cruise to Catalina. Duke was expecting the usual card playing, fishing and drinking, so he was surprised when Ford handed him a script titled *Stagecoach*.

During a wee-hours card game, Ford rattled off the names of the fine actors he'd already cast, and then asked Wayne if he knew of anyone who could play the Ringo Kid. Knowing that the Coach was up to something, Duke facetiously suggested Lloyd Nolan, a reply that Ford ignored before bursting into a profane tirade about not being able to find a capable young horseman who could act.

Wayne endured this rant for the remainder of the weekend and, just as they returned to San Pedro on Sunday night, Ford calmly admitted, "Duke, I want you to play the Ringo Kid."

Wayne later recalled that this revelation was like being "hit in the belly with a baseball bat."[6] As Ford's grandson so eloquently observed, "The hand of the giver always did have a vicious backhand."[7]

Ford also had to be rather fierce when standing up to Walter Wanger, insisting that Wayne was his *only* choice for the lead role. Joseph McBride explained that the actor "struck the kind of effortlessly impressive male figure that the former 'Bull' Feeney wished he could have been. Ford found his physical ideal in the Duke, his cinematic equivalent of Michaelangelo's David."[8]

Ford's "David," however, received the paltry sum of $3,000 for his work on *Stagecoach*, at a time when the director's previous favorite, Victor McLaglen, was pulling down $50,000 for a costarring role in the independently produced, Hal Roach–directed adventure film *Captain Fury* (1939).[9] Top-billed Claire Trevor earned the largest salary for *Stagecoach*, $15,000, while Mitchell and Devine, earned $12,000 and $10,624, respectively.

Ford had chosen to spend the location funds in one of the most rugged spots in the Southwest: Monument Valley, a desert region distinguished by breathtaking sandstone monoliths providing endless visual possibilities for the man "who painted with a camera." Some sources claim that the area was first described to him by Harry Carey, who had discovered it a decade earlier, but the location was directly pitched to Ford by Harry Goulding, operator of the local trading post and lodge, who had arrived unannounced at Wanger's office with a collection of stunning photographs. Goulding initially had been tipped off by Mr. and Mrs. John Wetherill, who ran a similar operation 25 miles south of the valley at Kayenta, and had first attracted filmmakers, including George O'Brien, to the area.

Located on the Navajo reservation in southern Utah and northern Arizona, Monument Valley was accessible only by driving from Flagstaff, over 200 miles of rutted dirt roads that required passing *through* numerous dried-up streambeds. The area not only lacked bridges, but all forms of modern communication. Ford was blazing a new trail into an environment even more brutal than the one into which he had driven the sun-baked members of *The Lost Patrol* five years earlier.

The miserable poverty and living conditions Ford witnessed upon arriving at the reservation induced him to hire hundreds of Navajos (at $3 per day) to work with the crew, play bit parts and appear as extras in the action scenes. He befriended many of the local people, including the Brady Brothers, translators and his liaison with the Navajo tribal council. He enlisted the medicine man, Old Fat, to provide weather predictions, cast Fred Big Tree and Chief White Horse in small parts, and promised each man full scale pay. To play Geronimo, who appears only briefly at the beginning of the now-legendary chase sequence, Ford discovered Many Mules, an Apache, who lived in a far-off canyon that required traveling on horseback. By the time he left Monument Valley, the Navajos had performed a ceremony making him an honorary member of the tribe, bestowed with the name *Natani Nez* ("Tall Leader").

Harry Goulding provided his station wagon for Ford, who was welcomed to the set each morning by the melodies of treasured American and Irish folk songs such as "Red River Valley" and "Wild Colonial Boy" emanating from the ubiquitous accordion of Danny Borzage. When the hot and dusty day's work was done, the entire company would return to the lodge for a hearty cowboy meal of beefsteak or barbecued ribs, and a few "lucky" fellows would end up in Ford's room for a rousing game of pitch.

The fallout from Ford's fight to cast Duke landed squarely on the actor's shoulders, which, like those of Victor McLaglen, were broad and resilient enough to take it. Surrounded by longtime veterans of A productions, especially Bancroft, Mitchell and Trevor, whose talent and toughness equaled her beauty, Wayne, the "B actor," already was nervous before shooting began, a fact that played right into Pappy's abusive tactics. Though Ford admitted that Duke moved like a dancer, here he accused him of being "a big oaf" and "skipping like a goddamn fairy." Dan Ford wrote:

> Beyond the sadistic pleasure John took in humiliating Wayne, there was an important political reason for it. The Ringo Kid was the key character.... John had given the part to an upstart actor whom everybody knew was his personal friend and drinking buddy.... By humiliating and harassing him, John got the rest of the company to pull for the kid....[10]

Gary Wills claimed, "One reason actors put up with Ford's abuse was their generally subservient position at the time. Ford's autocratic air on the set was a rebellion against producers' power that the actors appreciated."[11] However, Dan Ford offered a much simpler explanation:

> You've got to be that way. You're under a tremendous amount of pressure. There's a huge amount of money involved. You've got all these people around you. *Somebody's* got to be in charge.... So he built himself up into this *caricature*, this tough, hard-nosed director.[12]

Arguably, Ford's alcoholism played a significant role in his abusive attitude toward others. Vowing to stay sober during the shooting of his films (which he did accomplish more often than not), his withdrawal from booze caused him to be volatile and cranky, and was a reason for his constant mastication of handkerchiefs, rather than more conventional substitutes for drinking, such as smoking, eating candy or chewing gum.

Ford spent only seven days in Monument Valley, shooting action sequences involving a cavalry troop, Native Americans and doubles for the principal actors in the stagecoach. He then took his cast and crew back to California to shoot the thrilling chase scene during which the Apaches, like a force of nature, ride down and attack the fleeing stagecoach. While the sequence appears as if it, too, was filmed in Monument Valley, Ford used a dry lakebed at Victorville, northeast of Los Angeles on the southwestern border of the Mohave Desert, the same location he had utilized so effectively for the land-rush scene in *3 Bad Men* nearly 13 years earlier.

To aid Ford in the filming of several dangerous maneuvers during this crucial scene, Wayne suggested utilizing the remarkable skills of Yakima Canutt. Aside from his acting role, this proposition to the Coach allowed Duke to make another invaluable contribution to *Stagecoach*. Though an erroneous belief exists that Canutt never again worked on a Ford film, he did perform a stunt for *Young Mr. Lincoln* three months after working on *Stagecoach*. Fourteen years later, at MGM, he also directed some gorilla footage for *Mogambo*, Ford's Technicolor remake of *Red Dust* (1932). (In both cases, Canutt was hired by the studio, but Ford didn't refuse his input.) In between, Yak was a very busy man, capably serving in a myriad of capacities on scores of both A and B pictures (including several with Wayne).

Three weeks into the *Stagecoach* shoot, Wayne was giving the kind of performance Pappy knew had always been inside that 6' 4" dancer. The Ringo Kid isn't just a typical Western gunslinger seeking vengeance; he's a fully realized character, descended from the Hart and Carey "good bad man," and brought to life by Wayne's unique blend of sincere respect, bashfulness, straight-shooting honesty, and that indefinable quality called charisma.

Stagecoach provided a glimpse of the Wayne character that later would emerge with a

Stagecoach (Walter Wanger–United Artists, 1939; directed by John Ford). John Wayne as the Ringo Kid.

vengeance: the solitary individual who believes in the "justice" of civilization, but ultimately can't subject himself to it. Like the Ringo Kid, the later Wayne characters accept justice, as long as it is defined by their own codes of conduct. Though Ringo does become "domesticated" by riding off with a woman at the end of *Stagecoach*, she is another individual who has followed an unconventional lifestyle.

Harry Carey, Jr., later revealed that Wayne, who was "paralyzed with fear" by the prospect of carrying off such an important role, had, while shooting the studio scenes in Hollywood (and behind Ford's back), worked on his characterization every evening at the home of Paul Fix. Carey claimed:

> Because Duke was kind of heavy-footed and used to trudge more than walk, Paul told Duke to point his toes when he walked, and the "John Wayne walk" was born.... When Duke first did it, it was ballsy as hell. As the Wayne legend began to form, the walk became more pronounced.[13]

Eventually, Ford not only eased off on Wayne, but took him beyond earshot of the others and whispered, "Duke, you're doing just great."[14] One acting technique, the wrinkling of his forehead (as a sign of puzzlement, confusion, or subtle jest), was suggested by Ford during production (and would become a Wayne trademark for the next four decades).

In Hollywood, Ford realized that the compelling Ringo Kid needed a more spectacular introduction, so he wrote a brief sequence in which Duke fires his Winchester to halt the stagecoach, then twirls the rifle like a handgun as cinematographer Bert Glennon's camera dollies in for a close-up. Ford's last-minute decision added the perfect touch of star-making excitement to the first glimpse of Ringo (and created one of the most unforgettable entrances for an actor in cinema history). Completely ignoring the facts about the genesis of this last-minute addition, Gary Wills took an unsubstantiated shot at Ford:

> Renowned as this shot has become, it is deeply flawed. It is a process shot done in the studio. It would have been more impressive if Wayne were standing in real space, with Monument Valley around him. Furthermore, this seems to be a one-shot — or at least the editor had nothing better to use than this one, where the camera loses focus and fumbles back into it as it tracks forward. And Wayne's "take" is crude, easily improved if Ford had had the patience to reshoot. It looks as if Ford did not realize how important this shot was — not what one would expect if Ford had planned the movie for launching Wayne as a star.[15]

This is balderdash (Ford would have used a stronger word). The shot *is* flawed, but there are similar temporary "losses of focus" in many tracking shots in Golden Age Hollywood films. Very little of *Stagecoach* was actually filmed in Monument Valley, and this shot of Wayne was *not* in the script, but created by Ford *after* the cast and crew had returned to Hollywood. Therefore, it would have been impossible to shoot this setup while in the valley; and after Ford decided to add the shot, it is very unlikely that Walter Wanger would have increased the budget just to send the company back to the location to capture one setup.

Furthermore, Wills' accusation that Ford was "impatient" reveals an ignorance of the director's shooting methods, including his distaste for "coverage." Ford often said that film is expensive, and he didn't like to waste it, but anyone familiar with his work knows that he deliberately shunned alternate shots that could be used by producers or editors to alter his personal vision. If he liked the first take, he printed it; and he *liked this one*. Suggesting that the director "did not realize how important this shot was" is ludicrous, tantamount to concluding that Ford was, not a cinematic genius, but actually the idiot savant "Ol' Mose" Harper (Hank Worden) in *The Searchers*.

Ford personally supervised editors Dorothy Spencer and Walter Reynolds in preparing a cut to be shown to a few select colleagues, including Merian Cooper, Gene Markey and Jim McGuinness, all of whom were mightily impressed, particularly by the visual power of the location work and the incredible rhythm of the chase sequence. Ford then told Walter Wanger that there would be no worrying about the box-office performance of the film.

Some scholars have considered *Stagecoach* just a higher-budgeted B Western with better writing and acting, with Ford copying setups he had used in his early silents with Harry Carey. As Randy Roberts and James S. Olson pointed out:

> Similar to Ford's *The Informer*, *Stagecoach* demonstrates the director's artistic debt to German expressionism.... Ford's use of interior ceilings, deep focus, high and low camera shots, and low-key lighting has more in common with the later films of Orson Welles and William Wyler, with *Citizen Kane* and *film noir*, than with Westerns or any other films of the 1930s.[16]

In fact, Orson Welles, who named Ford as his favorite director, claimed that he studied *Stagecoach* "over forty times" before directing *Citizen Kane*.[17]

While Ford and Wayne were making *Stagecoach*, Bond appeared in several films, including three major Warner Bros. productions. Directed by Busby Berkeley, *They Made Me a Criminal* (1939) was the studio's second adaptation of the play *Sucker*, by Bertram Millhauser and Beulah Marie Dix, filmed with Douglas Fairbanks, Jr., as *The Life of Jimmy Dolan* in 1933. In his first starring film role, John Garfield plays the framed, presumably dead, boxer Johnnie Bradfield; Claude Rains is Phelan, the disgraced cop seeking redemption by hunting him down; and the Dead End Kids are the boys being "rehabilitated" on the Arizona ranch where "Jack" finds his salvation.

Bond had known Billy Halop, Leo Gorcey, Huntz Hall and the East Side crew since making the original *Dead End* the previous year, and he enjoyed seeing them while playing Lenihan, promoter of the Gaspar "Bull" Rutcheck (Frank Riggi) fight, during which Jack raises $2,000 for the boys to open a service station. Executive producer Hal Wallis, impressed with a rough cut, ordered additional scenes that beefed up the production to A status.

During the summer of 1938, Warner Bros. embraced the Western as a medium for casting major adventure and gangster stars in different, less stereotypical roles. The results were often quite unpredictable. The first of these high-budget projects, *The Oklahoma Kid* (1939), is one of the most strangely cast cowboy films ever made.

As ridiculously duded-up cowboy Jim Kincaid, James Cagney adds just the right

The Oklahoma Kid (Warner Bros., 1939, directed by Lloyd Bacon). In the first film to cast both James Cagney and Humphrey Bogart as rootin', tootin' cowboys, Bond plays minor bad man Wes Handley (center), here caught up in a poker game with Bogie's "Whip" McCord (left).

amount of tongue in cheek humor to make his performance believable. Though associated with urban "tough guy" roles, Cagney was actually an accomplished horseman and farmer. However, his costar, Humphrey Bogart, as villain in black "Whip" McCord, is merely a mob boss in a Stetson, a racketeer on the range.

As Wes Handley, a henchman in McCord's gang, Bond enjoys some quality screen time. In one scene, during which Kincaid orders the pianist to play "I Don't Want to Play in Your Yard" and then begins to sing along, Handley attempts to shut him down. Instead, Kincaid knocks the much larger man to the floor with a right to the jaw, and then resumes the song. (Cagney always insisted that, if he was to throw a punch in a film, his rival had to be physically larger, and Bond certainly qualified.)

While shooting a scene in which McCord and Handley thunder by as Kincaid stands on a rock above, Cagney, who had never used a lariat, asked the wrangler if he could perform the lassoing of Bond's horse himself. He wanted to add some realism to the sequence, so he grabbed the rope, tossed the loop directly over the horse's head, and stopped Bond cold. Cagney held on for a second, and then let go, prompting Lloyd Bacon to yell, "Cut! Why didn't you hang on?"

"What did you want me to do?" asked Jim. "Kill Ward?"

"Why not?" replied Bacon.[18]

Bond also worked on Warners' first lavish Technicolor Western, *Dodge City* (1939), directed by Michael Curtiz and starring Errol Flynn, who fits into the boots of Wade Hatton as effortlessly as he does the buckskin of Sir Robin of Locksley in *The Adventures of Robin Hood* (1938). Also on hand are Flynn's eternal sidekick, Alan Hale; his favorite leading lady, Olivia de Havilland; Flynn and Wayne's wily pal, Bruce Cabot; and Ford favorite Russell Simpson.

Bond plays Bud Taylor, a "stupid" henchman who acts like a tough hombre until Hatton applies the third degree, grilling him in the glow of two overhead lights and a table lamp until, wringing with sweat, he informs on Yancey (Victor Jory), the cold-blooded killer of newspaper editor Joe Clemens (Frank McHugh). Nearly every memorable element of the classic Western genre flows through *Dodge City*, one of the most sweeping Curtiz films, and a stunning example of Technicolor used, not to overwhelm, but to enhance content. Among all the lauded films released in 1939, many of which have dated badly, it is timeless.

Warner Bros. held a gala premiere in Dodge City, Kansas, on April 1, 1939. Several cast members and other studio players were transported to the location on the Santa Fe Special, and a parade led by Errol Flynn preceded the screening. Anticipating great box-office success, Warners had made certain to include, in the film's closing scene, a virtual introduction for a sequel, *Virginia City*, which also would be written by Robert Buckner and directed by Curtiz.

Bond returned to Universal during November 1938, to play the tiny part of a gendarme in the horror extravaganza *Son of Frankenstein*, director Rowland V. Lee's expressionistic follow-up to James Whale's masterpieces, *Frankenstein* and *The Bride of Frankenstein*. Though Lee was one of the studio's top filmmakers, his continual changes to a script that was never finished, as well as scheduling and budget overruns, caused endless problems.

Intending to wrap on Christmas Eve 1938, Lee didn't complete the shoot until January 5, 1939, just *two days* prior to the scheduled preview. Much to Universal's relief, shortly after its official premiere at Los Angeles' Pantages Theatre on January 13 and the New York release two weeks later, *Son of Frankenstein* became a box-office smash, inaugurating a second successful "cycle" of Hollywood horror films.

Though he was part of this historic reinvigoration of the genre, Bond, having contributed just one day's work, had long moved on to other projects. His entire performance consists of his police guard blocking the entrance to Castle Frankenstein and yelling at the shepherd's horn-playing Ygor (Bela Lugosi), bosom companion of the Monster. "Ygor! Shut up!" he commands. "You've been playing that thing *all night!*" Unlike his experience working on *Night Key*, he didn't even cross paths with Boris Karloff this time around.

Ward finished out 1938 with several more bit parts at the major studios. At 20th Century–Fox, he played "Sailor Sam," a wrestler, in the opening scene of *Mr. Moto in Danger Island*, his second contribution to the Peter Lorre B series, which reunited him with the infamous Warren Hymer, who excels as the detective's dimwitted but congenial sidekick.

At Paramount, he was one of the tracklayers building the *Union Pacific*, Cecil B. DeMille's railroad epic starring Barbara Stanwyck (giving her second bad performance while attempting an "Irish accent"). DeMille probably hadn't bothered to watch Ford's *The Plough and the Stars*, but his legendary tendency not to see the actors for the all-important sensational sets and effects is on full display here.

At Warner Bros. Ward appeared as blacksmith Ladislaus "Tiger" Klewicki in one scene of "Broadway Cavalier," directed by Lewis Seiler and starring Pat O'Brien and Joan Blondell. A candidate for the most bizarre name of his career, Klewicki is the only Bond character introduced into a film while *unconscious*. Released as *The Kid from Kokomo*, the film is an unabashed rip-off of the studio's superior fight-racketeering opus *Kid Galahad* (1937), directed by Michael Curtiz and starring Robinson, Bogart, Bette Davis and Harry Carey. Wayne Morris plays the same wooden title character in both pictures. In *Kokomo*, he knocks out Klewicki for saying that "Mother's Day is a racket dreamed up by the greeting card people." Jerry Wald and Richard Macauley's screenplay was based on a story by Dalton Trumbo.

During the winter months, Ford again cruised the *Araner* down the West Coast into Mexican waters, where he, Wayne, Bond, Preston Foster, Dudley Nichols and Wingate Smith enjoyed the sites, deep sea fishing and, habitually, the local libations. On one of the fishing expeditions, Ford landed three marlins; Foster, Nichols and Smith caught several each; Duke reeled in seven; but the frustrated Ward was left high and dry.

Bond's love of booze may have had something to do with his inability to haul in the mighty marlin. Wayne later recalled one of Ford and Bond's trips together:

> One day Ward and Jack got a couple cases of beer, took one of the *Araner*'s launches, and went out fishing. When they got out to sea, Jack told Ward to hand him a beer. Bond reached into the cooler and got the beer, then realized he had committed the unpardonable sin: he had forgotten the opener. Ward rummaged through the tackle box looking for something to use, and all the while Jack was ... calling him a "liver-lipped baboon" and telling him, "I've met eggplants with higher IQs." Finally Ward said, "Dammit, Jack, I'll open it." He raised the beer up to his mouth and opened it with his teeth. That day Jack made Ward open a whole case of beer with his teeth ... the beer wasn't in bottles, it was in cans.[19]

In Mazatlan, the gang lodged at the Belmar Hotel, which housed Ford's favorite bar, situated on the beach, where imbibers could watch the beautiful sunsets over the rippling water. On one particular evening, when Bond (whom Ford had dubbed "The Class Clown") passed out early from his customary acts of overindulgence, Ford (in a reprise of his joke on David Niven while shooting *Four Men and a Prayer*) borrowed a pet boa constrictor from the owner of the bar and gently dropped it on his whipping boy's lap. Eventually, when Ward blearily awakened, he saw the snake, sprang up, and tossed the reptile back at

Jack. Now that he was at least semiconscious, he joined the others in rowing out to the *Araner*, with a mariachi band aboard, to play Mexican songs for them as they topped off the night with high-octane tequila.

Ford's drinking became more pronounced on each subsequent excursion to Mexico, and he often would spend entire weeks consuming nothing but alcohol until he reached complete oblivion. He always became sentimental and depressed, sometimes absolutely morbid. Wayne admitted:

> Drinking was the one way Jack could really relax and shut off his mind.... He always ... saved those real benders for times when he was around people ... who he felt he could trust.... Maybe once a year he would really pin one on, but I'll tell you, they were long ones when he did it."[20]

Stagecoach was previewed in Westwood on February 2, 1939. Wayne, who had been told by Ford, "You may get some real parts from this one ... you're actually going to have to go out and buy some clothes," was in attendance at the Village Theater, where the audience gave *Stagecoach* a standing ovation.[21] United Artists released the film on March 3, and Ford's boast to Wanger was quickly transformed into truth. The public turned out in droves, and the critical reception included such superlatives as "the best Western in years" and "rare screen masterpiece."

The day before the *Stagecoach* preview, Warner Bros. and director Anatole Litvak made a bold political move by beginning production on the powerful anti-fascist drama *Confessions of a Nazi Spy*, starring Edward G. Robinson as an FBI agent (ironically, J. Edgar Hoover recently had established a file on EGR to document all of his anti-fascist activities). As soon as the cameras rolled, death threats were received via telephone by Robinson and Jack Warner, who stood his ground, refusing to give in to German protests at the U.S. State Department and especially the Third Reich's gangster-like intimidation tactics.

The plot was based on an actual case involving the German-American Bund, a fascist organization popular in Wisconsin and on Long Island. At one point, screenwriter John Wexley saw notorious witch-hunter Martin Dies leaving Warner's office, having just warned the mogul not to malign a "friendly country" like Germany. Apparently, Dies also had requested that the script place some dreaded "Commies" alongside the Nazis, but Wexley and cowriter Milton Krims refused.

In a casting move that subsequently seems both appropriate (for the time) and ironic (in retrospect), Litvak chose Bond as the actor to voice the film's message in a few brief lines of dialogue. During a public speech to the German-American Bund in New York, Dr. Karl F. Kassel (Paul Lukas) calls for the total destruction of "democracy ... a fanatical faith," as represented by the Constitution and the Bill of Rights. In a brief, sincerely believable performance, Bond, playing an American Legionnaire, rises from his seat, vowing to fight for these sacred American foundations. "We don't want any 'isms' in this country except Americanism!" he shouts. As a fight breaks out, he adds, "I have a right to speak in an open meeting! This is a free country!" This scene provides another prime example of Bond's ability to generate credibility in even the smallest role.

Understandably excited about being a major part of an A feature's success, Wayne was bitterly disappointed upon his return to Republic, where Herb Yates behaved as if nothing had changed. Prior to the general release of *Stagecoach*, Duke already had finished his scenes for the "Robin Hood" Western *The Night Riders*, the first in another series of four "Three Mesquiteers" kiddie-matinee programmers with Corrigan and Terhune. By the time the last title, *New Horizon*, was ground out, Terhune had been replaced by Raymond Hatton, and Wayne's Stony Brooke completely dominated the storylines. Still under contract to

Republic, he also could be loaned out to other studios, with Yates doing nothing but sitting back and collecting the fees.

In mid–February 1939, director David Howard began shooting the B Western *Trouble in Sundown* at RKO. Again cast opposite George O'Brien, Bond played "Dusty," another henchman who, despite his best efforts to aid a crooked land grabber (Cyrus Kendall), winds up in the calaboose. He also scored small parts in two Latin tales: an accused cattle rustler in 20th Century–Fox's *The Return of the Cisco Kid* (1939), starring Warner Baxter; and a wrestler branded "Mexican Pete" in RKO's *The Girl from Mexico* (1939), featuring Lupe Velez.

The Warner Bros. B unit began providing Bond with more noticeable roles, including Mart Handler, a drunken longshoreman who falls to his death in the wake of union politics, brawling (with star Dennis Morgan) and murder, in *Waterfront* (1939), shot on location at San Pedro. The higher-budget crime drama *Dust Be My Destiny* (1939), starring Warners' "new Cagney," John Garfield, typically offered Ward the brief part of a hot-headed robber who tangles with the smaller but tougher, misunderstood antihero.

The raves about Ford's "resurrection" of the A Western inspired him to create three more major cinematic achievements, all for 20th Century–Fox, before the year ended. From the time he began shooting *Stagecoach*, in late October 1938, until wrapping his final film of 1939 in mid–November, Ford (in the words of his grandson) "made four films ... that together stand as the greatest collective achievement in the history of the cinema. With them, John established himself as the premier director of American motion pictures."[22]

The first project, a historical drama about his political hero, *Young Mr. Lincoln*, with Henry Fonda in the lead role, began shooting in early March 1939. Three months earlier, Ford, aware that two similar plays about Lincoln recently had been produced on Broadway, told Zanuck he thought filming Lamar Trotti's screenplay about the 16th President's early years was a bad idea. However, after Zanuck badgered him relentlessly to read the script, which the mogul had supervised personally, Ford, realizing that Trotti had written a masterpiece, capitulated.

Fonda, too, originally passed on the project. His response, like Ford's initial refusal, only brought on a barrage from Zanuck *and* Trotti, so the actor agreed to do a screen test just to get them off his back. After seeing the results, however, he was even more adamant. "I am *not* going to play Abraham Lincoln," he informed them.

Ford then called Fonda into his office. "What's all this bullshit about you not wanting to play Abraham Lincoln?" he growled at the actor. "You're not playing the Great Emancipator. You're playing a jack-legged lawyer from Springfield, Illinois, a gawky kid still wet behind the ears who rides a mule because he can't afford a horse."[23]

When production began, Ford and Fonda hit it off very quickly. Born in Grand Island, Nebraska, "Hank" had learned the art of acting the hard way (by just going out and treading the boards), with the help of Marlon Brando's mother, Dodie, at the Omaha Community Playhouse. In 1928, he migrated to the East Coast, where he played a role at the Cape Playhouse in Dennis, Massachusetts, before joining the University Players, an intercollegiate stock company whose members included Joshua Logan, Kent Smith, his future best buddy, James Stewart, and future wife, Margaret Sullivan. In New York, while seeking roles on Broadway, his brief 1931 marriage to Sullivan ended in divorce, and he moved in with Stewart. In 1934, when Stewart headed for Hollywood, Fonda soon followed, to play the lead role in 20th Century–Fox's *The Farmer Takes a Wife*, and they again roomed together, right next door to Greta Garbo.

Ford appreciated Fonda's fusion of formal training with a naturalistic style, his easygoing approach to working, and the personal, Midwestern honesty that effortlessly imbued his performance with the kind of integrity expected from Abraham Lincoln. Of Ford, Fonda later admitted:

> I had never met anyone remotely like him. Pappy was full of bullshit, but it was a delightful sort of bullshit.... He had great instincts ... did everything intuitively.... John focused on the common, everyday aspects of Lincoln's life, demythologizing the legend to find the real flesh-and-blood man underneath.... Predictably, John and Zanuck disagreed over the pacing.... [John] printed only one take and destroyed the negatives of any others. He "camera cut" by surrounding his scenes with built-in dissolves.... There was little that Zanuck could do.[24]

Fonda's graceful performance is augmented by an excellent supporting cast, including Alice Brady as Abigail Clay, the grief-stricken mother of two sons (Richard Cromwell, Eddie Quillan) accused of murder; Marjorie Weaver as Mary Todd; Pauline Moore, in a brief appearance as the tragic Ann Rutledge; and Bond (in an excellent turn, wearing the same pair of tell-tale tartan trousers throughout the film) as John Palmer Cass, the man whom Lincoln eventually unmasks as the actual murderer of Scrub White (Fred Kohler, Jr.). Ford includes one of his "veiled" references to Bond's rear end, in a courtroom scene during which Lincoln playfully questions Cass about why he calls himself "J. Palmer Cass" while some folks know him as "Jack."

Honest Abe's utterance of "*Jack Cass*" sets the courtroom howling; even the judge (Spencer Charters) eventually joins in the laughter. Ford's comic interjections also include Francis (in drunken Shakespearean fool mode) as Sam Boone, one of the jurors selected by Lincoln during the murder trial.

A beautiful film (supporting Ford's argument for the supremacy of black and white over color), *Young Mr. Lincoln* is one of the strongest examples of his intuitive talent for creating stunning *mise en scène*. He not only knew exactly where to place the camera, but he also knew precisely where to place his actors within the frame. Each shot featuring Fonda is calculated to make the actor physically resemble Lincoln. Costume designer Lewis Royer Hastings brilliantly augmented Fonda's lean 6'1" frame by creating boots adding three inches to his height, and then shortened his trousers and shirt sleeves to make him look even lankier.

Ford's uncanny placement of the character (particularly the actor's extremities) within his compositions, combined with Fonda's ballet-like movements (John Wayne wasn't the only Ford actor who moved like a dancer), creates some of his most stunning imagery, making it seem as if the real Abraham Lincoln is on the screen. Although Lamar Trotti's screenplay is a fictionalized version of an actual 1858 criminal case in which Lincoln served as attorney for the defense (the film is set in Illinois during the late 1830s), Fonda, wearing "Royer's" (Oscar nominated) costumes while being directed by Ford, created an outstanding, authentic portrait of the young jackleg lawyer who would become the 16th President of the United States.

Deliberately paced, reverent, and quite moving, *Young Mr. Lincoln* simultaneously offers 100 minutes of John Ford's finest visual poetry and a look at the development of an extraordinarily uncommon "common man" from the heartland of America. Ronald L. Davis wrote an excellent summation of Ford's approach to presenting history in cinematic form:

> Ford tended to agree with Hegel, who argued that the purpose of a hero is "to bring a new world into existence." The filmmaker felt that Abraham Lincoln had done that; he had abandoned his law practice to alter the course of American history. Lincoln emerged the great democrat, respon-

Young Mr. Lincoln (20th Century–Fox, 1939; directed by John Ford). John Palmer Cass (Ward Bond) sits in the witness chair (second from right foreground), as the "jackleg lawyer" (Henry Fonda, center) from Springfield, Illinois, defends accused murderers Adam and Matt Clay (seated at table: Eddie Quillan, left, and Richard Cromwell), as their mother (Alice Brady, behind Quillan) and sister (Arleen Whelan, behind Cromwell, with baby) observe the proceedings.

sible for the modern American state.... [Ford's] reading of history mingled truth with dreams. He invented an American past that restored faith and taught lessons, and he laced history with poetry and myth to glorify the American character and illustrate a superior existence. He viewed ritual and formalized behavior as anchors that stabilized society in the face of sweeping change. Without intellectualizing his work, Ford created images on multiple levels, many of which supported the ideals he believed were being lost.[25]

While getting *Young Mr. Lincoln* underway, Ford, to honor the fact that so many Irish-Americans were in its ranks, the Emerald Bay Yacht Club planned an elaborate St. Patrick's Day dinner at the Ambassador Hotel's Coconut Grove, where all the alcoholic revelry was capped off by a furious food fight. When the hotel management requested that the club never return to the premises, Ford answered in a letter, "I neither understand nor condone your allegations regarding our behavior at a recent *fete galante*, but unfortunately, I am not in a position to remember it."[26]

Thereafter, the Irish fest was celebrated at Hollywood's House of Murphy restaurant, where the shenanigans of the uniformed drunks were tolerated. Of course, Wayne and Bond were there to jumpstart the inebriation, followed in due course by the likes of Frank Borzage, John Buchanan, Philip Dunne, Preston Foster, Tay Garnett, Frank Morgan, Liam O'Flaherty,

Wingate Smith, Johnny Weissmuller, and even that "temperance man," Dudley Nichols. As Vice Commodore, Ford held court at the head of the table, where he could salute his cohort, Gene Markey, who was perched at the opposite end.

Completing *Young Mr. Lincoln* at the end of April 1939, Ford took a brief Hawaiian vacation aboard the *Araner* before moving on to his next 20th Century–Fox historical drama, *Drums Along the Mohawk*, which began shooting on June 28. Again working from a screenplay by Lamar Trotti, who had adapted the novel by Walter Edmonds, Ford was pleased to have Henry Fonda back as the male lead, but instantly was beset with problems created by female costar Claudette Colbert, a fine actress but also a perfectionist whose demands affected every aspect of her participation. To voice his disdain for such behavior, Ford referred to the Paris-born Colbert as "Froggy."

Filming the experiences of a newlywed couple against the backdrop of the American Revolution was a challenge for Ford, who was ordered to shoot in Technicolor for the first time in his career. He said:

> It's much easier than black and white for the cameraman ... black and white is pretty tough — you've got to ... be very careful to lay your shadows properly and get the perspective right.... For a good dramatic story ... I much prefer to work in black and white; you'll probably say I'm old fashioned, but black and white is real photography.[27]

The terrific pace that Zanuck continually demanded in his memos to Ford made the arduous location shooting in the Wasatch Mountains near Cedar City, Utah, even more difficult. Though he again enjoyed working with Fonda, whose relationship with the director was given an added boost by the excellent reviews pouring in for *Young Mr. Lincoln*, Ford was becoming exhausted. He hadn't bothered to take a real break from physically and mentally taxing work for nearly a year.

Ford decided to scrap the three weeks scheduled to shoot the brutal August 6, 1777, Battle of Oriskany, in which General Nicholas Herkimer, commanding a troop of militiamen and Oneida Iroquois, was mortally wounded by an enemy force of Patriots loyal to the British crown. Instead, he filmed Fonda giving a harrowing eyewitness account after Gil Martin dazedly returns home. Pappy let the camera roll while he asked questions, and Hank improvised his responses, which then were edited with cutaway shots involving the amputation of the general's (Roger Imhof) leg. (In the film, the general dies that evening, but the historical Herkimer lived for 10 days before a botched operation led to his death from profuse blood loss.) The gory details of Gil's description are temporarily interrupted by Bond's helpful Adam Hartman (his bum, providing "relief," fills the shot).

Based on Revolutionary War hero Adam F. Helmer, who, on September 16, 1778, warned the inhabitants of German Flatts, New York, of the impending arrival of a combined force of Tories and Native Americans, Gil is the film's champion, who makes the incredible, death defying run from the fort to the settlement. However, Adam Hartman becomes Ford's focus in many of the scenes, including three that include prolonged ATB shots (in which the Bond bum, at center, nearly fills the screen). Ford had wanted both Gil and Adam to make the run, but he was overruled by Zanuck, rightly giving Fonda the glory.

Ford had given Bond a good role in *Young Mr. Lincoln*, but his cowardly murderer, Jack Cass, has nothing in common with his charming, hard-working Adam, who is Gil's most loyal friend. The humor in *Drums Along the Mohawk* is more subdued than in many of Ford's films, and Bond's comic contributions are the most naturalistic. The role was his first for Ford to place him so often in the spotlight.

When Gil and his wife, Lana (Colbert), first arrive at the fort in the Mohawk Valley,

Drums Along the Mohawk (20th Century–Fox, 1939; directed by John Ford). Surrounded by their Mohawk Valley neighbors, (left to right) Adam Hartman (Ward Bond), Joe Boleo (Francis Ford, background), Gilbert Martin (Henry Fonda) and Lana Martin (Claudette Colbert) observe the destruction wrought by an Iroquois attack. (Man at right not identified.)

they are greeted by Adam and Joe Boleo (Francis Ford, who is *not* a drunken imbecile this time around). The fearless Ford wiseacre (a role later commanded by Victor McLaglen) is a woman, the widow Mrs. McKlennar (Edna Mae Oliver), who continually mentions Barney, her deceased husband, and becomes the object of Adam's affectionate shenanigans.

Adam begins "courting" Mrs. McKlenner after she presents her unused cradle to Gil, who is waiting for Lana to give birth. "What good is it to me?" the childless woman asks.

"You can never tell," Adam laughs, "good-lookin' widow like you."

"Aw, shut up!" she replies. "You make me sick. Great, big, good for nothing loud-mouth — even if you *are* good lookin'!"

When the baby arrives, Adam runs outside, hugs Joe and guzzles from a moonshine jug. (The image of Ward embracing Francis is priceless.) This scene is paralleled soon after, during the wedding reception of John Weaver (Robert Lowery) and Mary Reall (Dorris Bowdon), as Adam dances a jig with Mrs. McKlennar, and then hugs and gives her one of the longest screen kisses of the Production Code era. (The comic intent accounts for its incredible intensity and eight-second duration.)

Confident that she had never received a better smooch, Adam is informed, "Barney McKlenner was a *real* man. When he kissed you, you *stayed* kissed!"

"Let's see if he taught you to hold your liquor!" he responds. (The ferocity of Adam's kiss makes one wonder about the proclivities of Barney.)

Later, when the widow refuses to leave her home set ablaze by the Iroquois, Adam demands, "Come on, Sara!" and, draping her over his shoulder, rushes from harm's way.

During the climactic battle, Joe volunteers to run for reinforcements, but is captured and bound in a hay cart. Just as the Iroquois release flaming arrows, the Reverend Rosen-krantz (Arthur Shields) reluctantly fires a flintlock rifle, putting the old man out of his misery. (Perhaps Ford's sacrificial torching and shooting of his brother was cinematic payback for the real-life explosive experience engineered by Francis two decades earlier.) Pappy injects more comic relief by cutting to a bum shot of Bond that lingers for six seconds, and then knocks Adam out of the running by giving him a flaming arrow in the chest. (Ward actually was shot and briefly set on fire.)

Mrs. McKlenner also takes an arrow, but her wound proves fatal. Adam cradles her as she says, "Goodbye, good lookin'" before calling out for her husband.

When the Tory scoundrel Caldwell (John Carradine) is killed by Gil's pal, Blue Back (Chief John Big Tree), the proud Iroquois emerges donning the dead man's signature eye patch (a very overt Fordian touch).

Judiciously leavened with humorous touches, *Drums Along the Mohawk*, graced with superb art direction (Richard Day and Mark-Lee Kirk), set decoration (Thomas Little) and costume design (Gwen Wakeling), is one of Ford's more historically accurate films. It concludes at the end of the Revolutionary War with the raising of the first American flag in the Mohawk Valley.

As most directors would do, did Ford choose his male star to perform this patriotic act?

No. Characteristically, the actor who does fervently climb up to hand the red, white and blue to the flag-raiser is not Hank Fonda, but his fellow Nebraskan, 12th-billed Ward Bond. Joseph McBride noted that this ending

> offers one of the director's most joyously optimistic, if somewhat naïve, affirmations of American national unity.... All are symbolically gathered in multiracial harmony to celebrate the birth of the nation. For Ford, the fact that the new nation was "conceived in liberty" is enough for the African American and the Native American to celebrate, even though their personal liberty has yet to be won.[28]

Seeking a little more liberty of his own, Wayne had gone to Herb Yates, insisting that, although he had several years left on his contract, his new status won by *Stagecoach* entitled him to step up from B-film fodder. He especially looked forward to being loaned out for other studio's A films, the success of which could only increase the box-office take for Republic's own Wayne films.

At 20th Century–Fox, Bond appeared in the studio's second adaptation of Stuart N. Lake's *Frontier Marshal* (1939), this time as the indolent Tombstone town marshal who is replaced by Wyatt Earp (Randolph Scott). Fox's *Heaven with a Barbed Wire Fence* (1939), the film debut of both Glenn Ford and Richard Conte (then using his actual first name, Nicholas), required Ward to resurrect his debauched *Wild Boys of the Road* sex fiend. Appropriately called "Hunk," he attacks Anita Santos (Jean Rogers), tangles with Joe Riley (Ford), and is decked by "The Professor" (Raymond Walburn), an educated hobo who "abhors violence" but wields a wicked walking stick. Adapted from a Dalton Trumbo story, *Barbed Wire Fence* is among a handful of films directed by Ricardo Cortez (an Austrian transformed into a Spaniard by Paramount), after his acting career had descended into the B unit at Warner Bros.

Ford held on to Henry Fonda for his final Fox assignment of the year, Nunnally Johnson's adaptation of John Steinbeck's Oklahoma Dust Bowl novel, *The Grapes of Wrath*, scheduled to begin shooting on October 4, 1939, and including location work in California, New Mexico, Arizona and Oklahoma. Zanuck had pitched it while both director and star were still on location shooting *Drums Along the Mohawk*. Fonda accepted immediately, but Ford, emphasizing that he was exhausted from working 18-hour days without a break, said he would make the film *only* if given a month to recover before the start of production. Zanuck, knowing that Ford's political values, particularly his support of the working man, made him the perfect director for the picture, agreed.

As soon as he completed *Mohawk* in late August 1939, Ford, accompanied by his wife and surrogate son, Ward Bond, headed for Catalina aboard the *Araner*. Many of "the usual suspects," including Preston Foster and Gene Markey, already were there, partying the nights away on Isthmus Harbor.

On September 2, Pappy was beginning to shake off the stress brought on by months of intense artistic concentration and physical labor. While playing cards with Mary, Ward and Preston, he heard a radio report describing Hitler's invasion of Poland, and the subsequent declaration of war against Nazi Germany by Great Britain and France. When he next saw Gene Markey, a fellow officer in the Naval Reserve, they discussed getting back to 20th Century–Fox to make their scheduled films before Uncle Sam came calling.

Wayne's first Republic loan-out, to RKO Radio, resulted in *Allegheny Uprising* (1939), a black and white, pre–Revolutionary War muddle released just one week after *Drums Along the Mohawk*. The assumption that reuniting Wayne with Claire Trevor would guarantee a box-office bonanza was compromised by a bad script by P. J. Wolfson, a historical hodge-podge with an unflattering portrayal of the British, as represented by the pompous Captain Swanson (George Sanders, who arguably could portray snobbery better than any other actor in film history), flashing across U.S. screens just as Great Britain had begun fighting Nazi Germany.

Meanwhile, Bond had landed a "prestigious" supporting role, Yankee Captain Tom, in the film that Ford refused to direct, David O. Selznick's epic adaptation of author Margaret Mitchell's historically impertinent *Gone with the Wind*, which was in production during half of 1939. Interestingly, as the Great Depression raged on, and Steinbeck was publishing *Of Mice and Men* (1937) and *The Grapes of Wrath* (1939), progressive, New Deal-inspired masterpieces honoring the common man (and a fascist nation built on anti–Semitism was on a destructive march through Europe), Selznick, the son of a Jewish family from Pittsburgh, was producing a romanticized film bemoaning the end of a secessionist society that enslaved its fellow human beings.

The film is worth seeing for the stunning production design of William Cameron Menzies and many fine performances, particularly those of Clark Gable (who was born to play Rhett Butler), Leslie Howard, Olivia de Havilland, and Hattie McDaniel. Bond is among several veterans of Ford films, including McDaniel, Thomas Mitchell, J. M. Kerrigan, Yakima Canutt, Tom Tyler, Ernest Whitman and George Meeker.

Ward first appears after the intermission, 155 minutes into this 233-minute epic. Captain Tom, representing the villainous Yankees threatening the sanctity of Southern womanhood, raps on the door of the Wilkes household, which is quickly surrounded.

Bond's screen time runs a mere 3:17. Following his "interrogation," Tom is sent packing by the wily Rhett Butler, who concocts a lie about the supposedly drunk Ashley Wilkes (Howard) having been, not at a political meeting, but with him at a whorehouse.

Gone with the Wind (Selznick International–MGM, 1939; directed by Victor Fleming). **In what remains the most popular film ever produced in Hollywood, Ward Bond plays Yankee Captain Tom (center left), with Olivia de Havilland as Melanie Hamilton, "King" Clark Gable as Rhett Butler (center right), and Leslie Howard as Ashley Wilkes.**

If Ward had to play an invading Yankee, at least Tom is a considerate one. He says, "I'm sorry" three times and, casting a sideways glance at Rhett, begs the "forgiveness" of Mrs. Wilkes (de Havilland) while backing toward the door.

The film concludes with Rhett Butler's famous line, "Frankly, my dear, I don't give a damn." In a badly contrived response, the pathologically self-absorbed Scarlett O'Hara (Vivien Leigh), gives herself a pep talk, recalling memories that "*land* is the only thing that matters," and finally declares, "*Tara* ... I'll go home ... after all —*tomorrow is another day!*"

The conservative backlash that occurred after the publication of *The Grapes of Wrath* was paralleled publicly (albeit unconsciously) by the $20-million box-office take of *Gone with the Wind*. (In May 1936, when the unpublished manuscript of Mitchell's novel arrived at Selznick's office, he claimed he was too busy to read it. After hastily skimming through a 57-page condensation of the story, he gave the manuscript to his then-story editor, Val Lewton, who, after plowing his way through the entire opus, told the producer not to bother with such "ponderous trash."[29])

Arguably, *Gone with the Wind* is its generation's *The Birth of a Nation*, although the ahistorical content and racist stereotypes are better hidden beneath all the Technicolor gloss. During the film's first MGM release, African American playwright Carlton Moss, published

"An Open Letter to Mr. Selznick" in the January 9, 1940, issue of *The Daily Worker*, claiming, "Whereas *The Birth of a Nation* was a frontal attack on American history and the Negro people, *Gone with the Wind* ... is a rear attack ... sugar-smeared and blurred by a boresome [*sic*] Hollywood love story.[30]

As if institutional bondage in the United States never existed, the opening credits bill the black characters as, not slaves, but "house servants." To the tune of "Dixie," the Old South is called "a pretty world of cavaliers and cotton fields," and described in these nostalgic, fairytale terms:

> Here was the last ever to be seen of Knights and
> their Ladies Fair, of Master and Slave.
> Look for it only in books, for it is no more than
> a dream remembered.
> A civilization gone with the wind....

More than a few viewers have considered this description, in its correlation of "Slave" and "civilization," a might peculiar. Though the film was nominated for 13 Academy Awards (and won eight), it was completely shut out by the National Board of Review.

For Bond, his "big scene" with Clark Gable in such a monumental production plays remarkably well amidst the spectacle; but, in acting terms, required little that differed from any of his other small roles of the period. Afterwards, it was business as usual. In September 1939, he appeared in two more Latin-flavored projects: one a billed part in Fox's *The Cisco Kid and the Lady*, starring Cesar Romero; and yet another bit as a cop, in RKO's *Mexican Spitfire*, with the tragic Lupe Velez in the title role.

Henry King's production of *Little Old New York* (1940), a fictionalized look at Robert Fulton's development of the steamboat, was a major undertaking for 20th Century–Fox. To create an "authentic" early 1800s atmosphere, three ships and two dozen smaller boats were built, and actual New York locations were filmed to be used in extensive process shots.

Bond was cast in the standout role of Regan, a browbeating shipyard owner, who attempts to halt Fulton (Richard Greene), but winds up with a good shellacking. Darryl Zanuck intended *Little Old New York* to showcase the acting abilities of top-billed Alice Faye; but, following a preview, fan complaints induced him to add a production number, transforming the film into another lavish romantic musical. The mogul had wanted Henry Fonda to portray Fulton's shipbuilding colleague, Charles Browne (who also becomes involved in the predictable Hollywood love triangle), but the part ultimately went to Fred MacMurray.

Zanuck, eager to make *The Grapes of Wrath*, Steinbeck's story of the Joad family and their fellow displaced "Okies," was dealing with pressure from both ends of the political spectrum. From the Right, he was warned by the studio's board of directors that the novel was "radical ... subversive ... [and] not suitable to put on the screen"; from the Left, critics who championed Steinbeck's socialistic denunciation of the American system expected a faithful cinematic representation.[31]

Attempting to strike a delicate balance, Zanuck advised Nunnally Johnson, who was a Southern conservative, to focus on the personal struggles of the Joad family, rather than making any broader generalizations of an overtly political nature. In the end, Johnson adapted only portions of the novel, integrated several nods to FDR's New Deal, and ended the screenplay with a scene in which Tom Joad, before leaving his family's roost in a government camp to work as a labor organizer, bids farewell to his mother with an earnest declaration that he'll "be there" for the little man, regardless of the circumstances. (This beautifully written sequence, performed with great sensitivity and conviction by Fonda, became one of the most memorable and powerful in all of Ford's films.) Ford later revealed what attracted him to the project:

> The whole thing appealed to me — being about simple people — and the story was similar to the famine in Ireland, when they threw the people off the land and left them wandering on the road to starve.... It was a timely story.[32]

The supporting roles were filled by 20th Century–Fox contract players, many of whom were, or became, members of the Ford Stock Company: Jane Darwell as Ma Joad; John Carradine as Casey, the "tetched" former preacher; Charley Grapewin as Grandpa Joad; Dorris Bowdon as Rosasharn; Russell Simpson as Pa Joad; O. Z. Whitehead as Al; John Qualen as the tragic little Muley; Eddie Quillan as Connie; Zeffie Tilbury as Grandma Joad; and Frank Sully as Noah. Ford also managed to create small parts for Bond, who appears in one scene as a policeman (a role he could have played in his sleep), and Francis, who briefly contributes his familiar portrayal of an affable old geezer.

Ford couldn't stand Carradine's titanic ego, but had cast him in major supporting roles in eight films over the past four years. In a career that truly ranged from the sublime to the ridiculous, the actor enjoyed some of his best roles under Ford, and was impervious to extraordinary amounts of abuse. Pappy would direct him to play an imbecile, but Carradine often would enact his own interpretation when the camera rolled. He recalled:

> No matter what Ford hired me for, he'd always want me to slobber, drool or squint. I used to fight him, not verbally, because you didn't do that with Ford, but just go ahead and do it my way.... [I]n the scene where Casey's talking about another preacher ... to illustrate a point, I wanted him to jump over a fence. Ford comes over, just like I knew he would. "What was that?"
> "Oh, nothing, just an actor's pipe dream."
> "What was it?"
> So I told him while he was chewing on his handkerchief. And he said, "Oh, all right, go on, do it. But I had to make *him* ask *me*.[33]

Art director Richard Day worked with Ford to develop the visual style, providing sketches to cinematographer Gregg Toland, whose exceptional services Zanuck had secured on a loan-out from Sam Goldwyn for a mere $50,000. Ford and the equally meticulous Toland then agreed on emphasizing stark contrasts to create a quasi-documentary style not unlike the work of the Great Depression's finest still photographers (Margaret Bourke-White, Dorothea Lange) and filmmakers such as Pare Lorentz, whose highly influential, New Deal–sponsored film about the Oklahoma Dust Bowl, *The Plow That Broke the Plains*, had been released three years earlier.

Ford wrapped *The Grapes of Wrath* on November 8, 1939, and his work on the project ended there. However, to give Zanuck as few editing choices as possible, he had shot the film as quickly as possible over the 43-day schedule. The entire cast had followed his lead in focusing with absolute precision, and the result allowed Ford to use only half the film stock that most directors would expose during a typical A-picture shoot.

Fonda stayed in character for much of the principal photography, and was able to adapt to any situation and improvise without losing motivation. His combination of Midwestern naturalism and aloof personality made him the ideal Tom Joad, a good man whose time in prison has given him the courage and ability to fight back, if necessary. Tom's farewell speech to Ma (which Fonda and Darwell did in a single take) is one of cinema's transcendent moments:

I'll be all around in the dark. I'll be everywhere. Wherever you can look — wherever there's a fight, so hungry people can eat, I'll be there. Whenever there's a cop beating up a guy — I'll be there. I'll be there in the way guys yell when they're mad. I'll be there in the way kids laugh when they're hungry, and they know supper's ready, and when people are eatin' the stuff they raised, and livin' in the houses they built — I'll be there, too."

Ford wanted to end the film as it begins, with Tom walking over the hill, but Zanuck had the last word, making sure to include Johnson's scripted epilogue featuring Ma making a positive statement about "the people" not being licked. Ford later said, "[W]e wanted to see what the hell was happening to the mother and father and the girl; and the mother had a little soliloquy which was all right."[34]

Soon after Zanuck completed the editing, Ford wrote a letter containing his "review." After butting heads with the mogul several times, he committed to Hollywood Athletic Club stationery his praise for the producer's work (however, his degree of sincerity, and perhaps the effect of any possible alcohol consumption that day, can never be known):

Dear Darryl:
    Several nights ago I had the pleasure of seeing "Grapes of Wrath" and so I set *my* pen to write my first fan letter. The editing. The daring musical score. The whole treatment was revolutionary. It was sheer genius. No one person in our industry would have the courage to do what you achieved. The sound effects — the croaking of the frogs, the railroad whistles in the background were inspired.
                    My heartfelt thanks,
                    Jack

John Ford
Odin St. Hollywood[35]

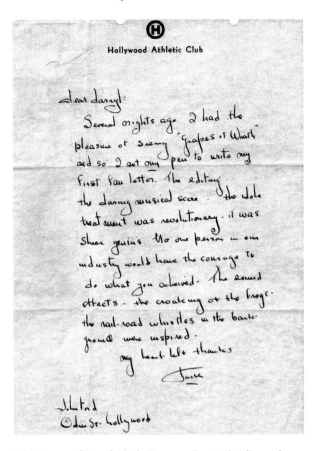

The Grapes of Wrath (20th Century–Fox, 1940; directed by John Ford). Soon after Darryl F. Zanuck finished editing *The Grapes of Wrath*, Ford wrote this unusual letter containing his "review." After butting heads with the mogul several times, he committed to Hollywood Athletic Club stationery his praise for the producer's work. This letter is proof of the collaborative nature of filmmaking under the Hollywood Studio System (and should inform those who cling to the auteur theory). Ford said, "It is wrong to liken a director to an author. He is more like an architect."

This unusual letter, especially from Ford, is positive proof of the collaborative nature of filmmaking under the Hollywood Studio System (and should prove informative to those who cling to the auteur theory). Ford said, "It is wrong to liken a director to an author. He is more like an architect."[36]

To answer liberal journalists who were accusing Zanuck of watering down the sociopolitical content of the novel, 20th Century–Fox waged a publicity campaign emphasizing the faithfulness of Johnson's screenplay, which had been given the "unqualified approval" of Steinbeck.[37] On January 24, 1940, the premiere at New York's Rivoli was attended by 12,917 people who literally squeezed themselves into the theater. For weeks afterward, lines formed around the block and disrupted traffic so often that the NYPD ordered the management to leave the turnstiles open.

Bond's policeman who briefly chats with the Joads in *The Grapes of Wrath* is a major role compared to his bit in *Virginia City*, Michael Curtiz's follow-up to *Dodge City*, which began shooting with Errol Flynn and Randolph Scott at Warner Bros. in late October 1939. Jack Warner still didn't know what to do with Humphrey Bogart, going so far as to cast him as a zombie (a role intended for Boris Karloff) in the horror film *The Return of Dr. X* (1939), but there was no doubt that the temperamental actor was tired of playing gangsters. Following Bogie's portrayal of a cowboy in *The Oklahoma Kid*, Warner decided to give him the bigger challenge of playing a *Mexican* bandit. Needless to say, *Virginia City* would be Bogart's final Western.

Following a Civil War battle at Morgantown, Kentucky, the film's opening line is spoken by Bond, as a Confederate sergeant checking the passes of travelers. The stagecoach, carrying Miriam Hopkins to Richmond, Virginia, hits the road, and Ward is never seen again.

Bond immediately went from Warner Bros. to Paramount, where director Mark Sandrich had cast him and Morris Ankrum in crucial supporting roles, outlaws who cause trouble for Jack Benny and sidekick Eddie "Rochester" Anderson, in the Western spoof *Buck Benny Rides Again* (1940). In his inimitable, absurdist style, Benny, believing a bank robbery a ruse, becomes a hero when he and his pet bear, Carmichael, apprehend the armed and dangerous Bond and Ankrum. Having proved that he truly is a "Man of the West," Benny wins the leading lady (Ellen Drew). Ford favorite Andy Devine plays "himself," and Ernest Whitman ("Buck" in *The Prisoner of Shark Island*) also makes a brief appearance.

From November 29 to December 23, 1939, Wayne starred in Republic's Western *Dark Command*, and additional shooting was scheduled for the first two weeks of February 1940. The most expensive film the studio had made to date, this "historical drama," loosely based on the Missouri-Kansas border raids of teacher turned Confederate guerrilla William C. Quantrill during the early years of the Civil War, spends more time on the rivalry, both personal and professional, between Will Cantrell (Walter Pidgeon) and Bob Seton (Wayne).

For the third time, Claire Trevor was cast opposite Duke, but her character, Mary McCloud, eventually marries Cantrell. Seton, a Texas cowboy who becomes marshal of Lawrence, Kansas, is eventually forced to gun down Cantrell, here depicted as a teacher who degenerates into a hell-raising mercenary, raiding Yankees and Confederates alike for his own selfish ends. For good measure, Republic also cast B-Western star Roy Rogers (as Mary's brother, Fletch) and George "Gabby" Hayes (in sidekick mode, as "Doc" Grunch). Directed by Raoul Walsh for the first time in a decade, Duke fared much better in Bleeding Kansas than he did on *The Big Trail*.

The national release of *The Grapes of Wrath* on March 15, 1940, met with considerable box-office success. Critics, as well as John Steinbeck, were equally enthusiastic.

Ford didn't wait around to see how the film fared. He rounded up Wayne and Bond, along with Preston Foster, Wingate Smith and George Schneiderman; and, with Mary, George Goldrainer and a crew of six on board, pointed the bow of the *Araner* toward Mexican waters.

On this occasion, Pappy had an ulterior motive for the voyage: Ellis Zacharias, Chief

Intelligence Officer for the 11th Naval District, had asked him to carry out a "semi-official" reconnaissance mission to determine if any Japanese activity was afoot in the Gulf of California. He again was thoroughly overworked, but was excited about performing a duty that might benefit his country, advance his position in the Naval Reserve, and provide a little extra adventure.

Ford said nothing about the "mission" to his companions. To make it seem like the trip was "business" as usual, Goldrainer dropped anchor at the same watering holes along the way: Magdalena Bay, Cabo San Lucas and Mazatlan. When they entered Guaymas harbor at the north end of the Gulf, Ford spotted a Japanese fleet of 14 trawlers and two mother ships which he believed were being used as spy vessels.

Now the reason for Schneiderman's presence came into play: Pappy relied on his expertise to capture numerous telephoto shots of the alleged fishing boats. The Japanese crews went on liberty on December 30, and Ford followed, making a detailed, seven-page report to turn over to Zacharias. He studied the men closely, noting their "military carriage" and "aristocratic" features.[38] "I would call them Samurai or Military Caste.... It is my belief that the crews and officers of this shrimp fleet belong to the Imperial Navy or Reserve," he wrote.[39] After completing the account, he and his comrades headed back toward Mazatlan, returning to San Pedro in January 1940.

For *Stagecoach*, Ford received the best director award from the New York Film Critics, and Thomas Mitchell and composer Richard Hageman won Academy Awards at the February 29 Coconut Grove ceremony. (This was a fine showing, considering the spate of popular 1939 films, particularly *Gone with the Wind*. The Best Supporting Actress Oscar went to trailblazer Hattie McDaniel, and no one was more pleased than her friend, Clark Gable, who was topped by Robert Donat in the Best Actor category.)

Ford's mind was taking him far away from Hollywood and filmmaking. In March 1940, Merian Cooper abandoned his vice-president position at RKO Radio to aid fellow aviator Claire Chennault in establishing a unit of pilots for Chiang Kai-shek called the Flying Tigers. Ford knew that he, too, must join his fellow progressive artists in the fight against the fascism that was spreading like a political cancer across the planet. The following month, he began recruiting Hollywood's finest filmmakers for a revolutionary Naval Reserve Unit that would document the global crisis that he knew would eventually involve the United States.

Acting independently, with no authorization from the U.S. Navy or any other governmental institution, Ford signed up writers Garson Kanin and Budd Schulberg, editor Robert Parrish, sound engineer Sol Halperin, special effects artist Ray Kellogg, and two of his favorite cinematographers, Joseph H. August and Gregg Toland. He called his outfit the Naval Field Photographic Reserve (which, in time, was referred to as "Field Photo"). As far as finding a "D.I." to whip his men into military readiness, Ford grabbed up Jack Pennick, a bulldog-faced veteran of many of his pictures but, more importantly, a former U.S. Marine who had fought in World War I. At Faxon Dean's military supply house, Pappy convinced a clerk, Mark Armistead, to lend the outfit equipment in exchange for a commission, following official sanction by the U.S. Navy.

To supply his ragtag band with "military regalia," Ford lifted uniforms from the Western Costume Company, and rifles and swords from the property department at 20th Century–Fox, where they carried out their drills on one of the huge soundstages. Ford oversaw the training exercises until October 1940, when he met the man who could make the unit legitimate: Jack Bolton, a liaison between the U.S. Navy and the Hollywood studios who had solid connections in Washington. Already having developed a lightweight 35mm camera designed by photographic engineer Harry Cunningham and mounted on a rifle stock, Field Photo attracted scores of volunteers following its official recognition.

Political causes, like the social events so important to his wife, were of little concern to Duke, who was doggedly focused on his film career. Later in life, he claimed being a "socialist" during his university days, having a "liberal" outlook in order to consider all sides of an issue before forming his own opinions.[40] During the 1930s, he had spent time with noted Hollywood liberals, including Ford, Dudley Nichols, and Melvyn Douglas; but he also had a number of conservative friends, the most outspoken of which was his buddy Ward. By 1940, his views had moved further to the right; but as his star continued to rise in Tinsel Town, Wayne, as Henry Fonda noted, "never talked politics."[41]

Ford was eager to make a film for Darryl Zanuck reflecting the current wartime situation in Europe. He proposed an "updated" remake of his own *Four Sons*, but the project was dropped when they discovered that MGM, on February 8, 1940, had begun shooting *The Mortal Storm*, a powerful drama set in Nazi Germany starring James Stewart and Margaret Sullivan. Interestingly, Bond had been cast by director Frank Borzage in a standout supporting role as a vicious, brown-shirted, fascist thug.

At this point, the reliable Dudley Nicholas rose to the fore, suggesting that he and Ford adapt four Eugene O'Neill one-act plays set aboard an English tramp steamer during World War I (*The Moon of the Caribees*, *In the Zone*, *Bound East for Cardiff* and *The Long Voyage Home*) into a screenplay, updating them and focusing on the anti-war theme. Choosing the title *The Long Voyage Home* for the project, they visited O'Neill in Danville, California, several times while preparing the script. Due to the ditching of the *Four Sons* remake, Ford had no intention of offering this new work to Zanuck, but instead had his agent pitch it to Walter Wanger, who was thrilled about the prospects of a film based on the works of America's greatest playwright.

At Republic in late March 1940, Wayne began working on *Three Faces West*, written by Samuel Ornitz, F. Hugh Herbert and Joseph Moncure March, a semi–Western mixing elements of *The Grapes of Wrath* with the current Popular Front anti–Nazi pictures. Duke plays John Phillips, head of a farmer's association in Asheville Forks, North Dakota, who becomes involved with Dr. Karl Braun (Charles Coburn) and his daughter, Leni (Sigrid Gurie), immigrants who were driven from Vienna by the Nazis. Seeking a community in need of a physician, Dr. Braun was summoned to Asheville Forks after speaking on the *We the People* radio program.

During a brutal dust storm, Leni wants to leave, but her father will not shirk helping the beleaguered farmers. Leni develops feelings for John but, learning that her fiancé, Eric, is still alive, leaves to join him in San Francisco. As the dust storms rage on, John convinces the farmers to resettle in Oregon where they can work the land, and not become impoverished fruit pickers like the Okies. The plot then follows the standard formula of an agitator (Trevor Bardette) attempting to turn the people against their leader, but John reassures them that Oregon, not California, is their promised land. Having bade farewell to John, Leni and her father leave San Francisco for Oregon after discovering that Eric has joined the Nazis.

Duke received favorable notices for his performance, but *Three Faces West* was almost universally panned by the major critics. The screenwriters' muddled attempt to fuse social commentary with a melodramatic love triangle resulted in what a journalist for the *New York Times* described as a "fairy-tale version of *The Grapes of Wrath*."[42]

For *The Long Voyage Home*, Ford created a gritty, claustrophobic, highly dramatic depiction of the endless challenges faced by a group of tormented men at sea, characters he knew could best be portrayed by his usual crew: Wayne and Bond (together in their first Ford film since *Salute*), Thomas Mitchell, Barry Fitzgerald, John Qualen, Arthur Shields, Joseph Sawyer, J. M. Kerrigan, Jack Pennick, Danny Borzage, Douglas Walton, Billy Bevan and Victor McLaglen's brother, Cyril. (Previous reports that a "falling out" occurred after Victor turned down Ford's offer of $25,000, half the actor's standard salary, to star in the film have been greatly exaggerated.) Pappy also cast stage actress Mildred Natwick (in her film debut) and the versatile South African-born, English actor Ian Hunter.

Ford, again using "master of deep-focus" Gregg Toland as director of photography, began shooting *The Long Voyage Home* on April 17, 1940, one day after Duke completed his work on *Three Faces West*. The expressionistic, closed-in atmosphere that plagues the doomed Gypo Nolan in *The Informer* permeates this project, "one of the most avant-garde films ever made in Hollywood."[43] Ford later explained:

> We purposely kept it in confined spaces — that was what the story called for. Life on a ship is claustrophobic, but you get accustomed to it. You make friends and you make enemies, you kick about the food, you kick about everything. I found that sailors who don't kick about the food are lousy sailors.[44]

Ford added: "When *The Long Voyage Home* was made, I wanted it very, very sharp, as a razor, and it was. I wanted to see everything. I didn't want any tricks. It's a story of character."[45]

Though *Citizen Kane* (1941) is often praised for its "innovations" in deep-focus cinematography, Toland shot Orson Welles' much lauded opus immediately *after* completing *The Long Voyage Home*. The cameraman's inclusion of ceilings in his compositions was nothing new in 1940, and his expressionistic style already had been demonstrated with Ford before he moved on to Welles (who admitted using *Stagecoach* as inspiration for *Kane*). Ford may have told Toland that he "didn't want any tricks," but Welles had him use every trick in the book, plus others they created, for *Kane*.

The Long Voyage Home begins in the West Indies, where the tramp steamer *Glencairn* is ordered to collect U.S. munitions for the British war effort and transport them across the Nazi patrolled Atlantic. Each sailor, plagued by inner demons, faces a dangerous, dark future. The only member of the crew who maintains an upbeat attitude is the likeable, naïve Ole Olsen, a major acting challenge for Wayne.

Although saddled with the difficulties of playing his role with a "Swedish" accent, Duke (who worked on the dialect with Danish actress Osa Massen) struggled valiantly to make Olsen nothing like the stereotypical, comic Swede familiar to American filmgoers (especially since John Qualen, a "stage Swede" specialist, was handling that shtick). Knowing that their mate has the potential for some future in his homeland, the rest of the crew mother him through hell and high water to make sure he gets aboard the proper ship.

In the end, Wayne came through, even working some humor into his part; and, with Massen's help, avoiding the broad comic strokes he heard from Qualen every day. Perhaps inspired by the hard work of his pal, Bond gave one of his finest performances to date. Although his "Yank" Lawson is mortally wounded early in the film, his moving death scene, stunningly composed and lit by Ford and Toland, is unforgettable.

Ford marks the 11-year reunion of his two favorite actors by opening the film with them. "Spanish girls" writhe erotically against palm trees as Bond's simpleminded Yank Lawson, silently blowing smoke rings as he leans on the ship's rail, is the first sailor to appear. Olson slowly walks up from behind to join him in viewing the lovely ladies on the beach.

Invited by Driscoll (Thomas Mitchell), who has sneaked ashore, the women are rowed out to the ship, where the booze- and sex-starved sailors nearly go berserk, dancing to Irish tunes and pounding down contraband rum smuggled in fruit baskets. Yank is the most lusty of all, breaking off the neck of his bottle to pour the rum down his throat, before stealing a basket from one of the women (Carmen Morales) to lure her into the cabin. When she temporarily escapes, he runs back out on deck to fetch her (Ford includes the film's one ATB shot as Bond picks up the flailing female and slowly carries her away).

During a savage storm, as some of the sailors labor to lash canvas over the cargo hold loaded with TNT, Yank hears the anchor break loose and slam against the hull. He runs out of the cabin, is hit by a ferocious squall, and punctures a lung as he is washed down the deck. As he had done in *Drums Along the Mohawk*, Ford allows Bond to shine (this time in stark counterpoint to his joyous character in the previous film), and his death is the emotional highpoint of the *Long Voyage*. His closest friend, Driscoll, holds his hand and attempts to give him water and a puff from a cigarette, as he again blows smoke rings before expressing regret for killing a man "in self-defense" and asking for "something nice" to be purchased for a barmaid in Cardiff.

In a rare move for Ford, he depicts the film's alcoholic, "Smitty" (Ian Hunter), as a

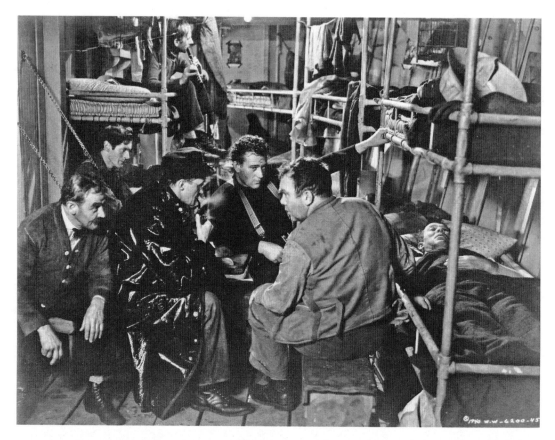

The Long Voyage Home (Walter Wanger–United Artists, 1940; directed by John Ford). Ward Bond's unforgettable demise: Yank (far right) lies dying, as Axel (John Qualen, top left) plays the flute during a vigil held by crewmates (left to right) Cocky (Barry Fitzgerald), Scotty (David Hughes), Donkeyman (Arthur Shields), Olsen (John Wayne) and Driscoll (Thomas Mitchell).

tortured, tragic man, unable to return to his wife and children, who arrive to collect his body in England after he is killed by German machine-gun fire (from an off-screen aircraft). Wayne's dialogue is wisely kept to a minimum, except during an extended sequence set in a pub, where Olson is asked about his background by party girl Freda (Mildred Natwick), who regretfully sets him up to be shanghaied.

Driscoll leads the crew in the rescue of Ole from the "devil ship" *Amindra*, though he is injured and pressganged for his efforts. The following morning, when all the sailors except Olson and Driscoll return for another voyage aboard the *Glencairn*, Donkeyman (Arthur Shields) drops a newspaper, with the headline "*Amindra* Torpedoed!" into the harbor.

The Long Voyage Home features none of the typical romanticism of the sea; only gritty portraits of men who sail upon her, not because they want to, but out of necessity. Like career criminals, they return time and again, victims of a vicious circle, to a ship whose name translates as "Valley of the Graves." The gloomy film (and all the performances, including Wayne's) fared highly with the critics, but failed to recover its costs at the box office. After co-writing the screenplay with Ford, Dudley Nichols, inspired by Eugene O'Neill, left Hollywood, intending to focus on "legitimate" writing back in Connecticut. After viewing *The Long Voyage Home*, he wrote to Ford:

> I know you've got a magnificent picture.... You're a thorny guy, but a grand thorny guy ... nobody who works with you ever wants to work with anyone else. In that sense, you've deprived me of an easy living. I can no longer sit on my ass with a fat contract and turn out crap.[46]

Though Dan Ford assumed the film was "too grim" for audiences, others have suggested that Nichols' "politically ambiguous" screenplay, having no clear-cut heroes and failing to depict "evil German fascists," was the reason it failed financially.[47] (Nichols later returned to writing screenplays, including the powerful film noir *Scarlet Street* [1945], directed by Fritz Lang and starring Edward G. Robinson.)

Bond played one of his most visible roles to date in independent producer Edward Small's *Kit Carson*, which director George B. Seitz began shooting on location at Cayente, Arizona, in May 1940. Jon Hall portrays the title character in this fictionalized adventure based on the exploits of legendary mountain man and "Indian fighter" Christopher Carson (1809–1868), whose fame was assured during the 1840s by his successful scouting expeditions for expansionist military man John C. Fremont (played in the film by Dana Andrews).

The film was shot quickly and with little regard for actual geography. Though the historical events covered territory from the Missouri River, along the Oregon Trail, and into California, the cinematic depiction never leaves the area around Monument Valley, its buttes even being visible from the "Murphy Hacienda" in Monterey! Ironically, the land of the Navajo Nation is seen throughout this whitewashed account of a man who, under orders, played a major part in the lethal "relocation" of these native people during the 1860s. The reality of this "move or die" ultimatum, however, is reflected in the Manifest Destiny-bred attitudes voiced throughout the film. (Ford's depiction of the Apaches in *Stagecoach* seems like a "pro–Indian" account by comparison.)

Hall's romanticized version of Carson is countered briefly by the 5'7" Raymond Hatton's hilarious performance as grizzled, jaded frontiersman Jim Bridger, who leaps up to be cradled like a baby by "Ape" (Bond), Kit's huge right-hand man (who is eight inches taller). As usual, Ward provides a believable anchor to many of the fanciful actions swirling around him. The mucho beefcake scene in which Ape, Carson and Lopez (Harold Huber) all share a bath is a highpoint. However, Ape's martyrdom in a massive gunpowder explosion (saving

California from the army of evil Mexican general Castro [C. Henry Gordon]) may be the result of always wearing a beaver cap in the desert!

Anatole Litvak, who had directed Bond as the adamant, anti-fascist American Legionnaire in *Confessions of a Nazi Spy*, chose him for a small but important role in Warner Bros.' James Cagney epic *City for Conquest*, which began shooting on May 31, 1940. Cagney had serious aspirations for the film, based on Aben Kandel's best-selling novel including subplots set during 1907–1927 in New York's Lower East Side, where the actor had been born (in 1899) and raised. However, when the multiple-plot structure resulted in a two hour-plus film, Jack Warner insisted that several important elements be cut, resulting in a butchered 101-minute version that Cagney proclaimed "a trite melodrama ... I said to hell with it."[48]

In order for the revised edition to make sense, Litvak used Frank Craven as an "Old Timer," a bewhiskered bum whose on-screen philosophizing sets up key segments. However, filmgoers who patronized the version originally released on September 21, 1940, didn't see Bond's contribution, which the cinematically circumscribed Warner had cut.

Later, when two of the excised minutes were restored, viewers were welcomed into the Warner Bros. world *by* Bond, as an amiable policeman listening to the introductory remarks of the "Old Timer." It is possible that Ward had been cast by Raoul Walsh, whom Warner had hired and then replaced with "prestige" director Litvak, whom Cagney considered a "squirrelly son of a bitch" and a "natural-born asshole."[49] As future filmmaking would prove, the powerhouse actor greatly admired Bond's talent. (During his first decade as an actor, Bond played a civilian law-enforcement officer in at least 35 films. By the time he shot his scene for *City for Conquest*, he was, not only naturalistic, but nearly *was* a cop! Ward Bond, a police officer? What magic the cinema weaves.)

Following the success of Universal's comic Western *Destry Rides Again* (1939), the formerly washed-up Marlene Dietrich began a smashing second career in Hollywood. Her new contract included casting approval of her leading men, actors with whom she could have affairs, both on- and off-screen. For Universal's *Seven Sinners*, which began shooting in July 1940, she reportedly saw Wayne in the studio commissary, and ordered director Tay Garnett, "Daddy, buy me *that*."[50] Producer Joseph Pasternack originally had considered Franchot Tone for the role.

An entertaining film graced with a diverse cast including Broderick Crawford, Albert Dekker, Anna Lee (in her American film debut), Mischa Auer, Samuel S. Hinds, Billy Gilbert and Reginald Denny, *Seven Sinners* stars Dietrich as "Bijou" Blanche, a saloon singer "with a reputation" who is exiled from one tropical island after another. Duke plays Lieutenant Dan Brent, who falls for her hard enough to propose marriage, but she returns to her wandering ways rather than risk tarnishing his career in the U.S. Navy. Universal press releases claim that Garnett briefly appears as one of the drunken sailors in the monumental bar fight, which reaches a nearly surreal level as men literally are *thrown* in every direction, with some landing in the wagon-wheel "chandeliers."

Though the mythical "John Wayne" was being established, on screen and in studio publicity, as the trustworthy, all–American, tough yet gentle, man devoted to his family, the reality was something else altogether. His marriage had never been satisfying, and with Josie continuing to honor the high society life, Duke moved further into the Hollywood scene, including a very public affair with Dietrich that would continue for the next three years.

Wayne may have been quite busy with la Dietrich, but Bond merely took a little time off during the early summer before beginning work on the next Warner Bros.–Michael

Curtiz Western epic, "Diary of the Santa Fe," in which he was cast as Townley, one of the followers of fanatical abolitionist and martyr John Brown (Raymond Massey). Much of the shoot, which began in mid–July 1940, was done on location at the Lasky Ranch in the San Fernando Valley, with Errol Flynn (as J.E.B. Stuart) happily costarring with his usual female lead (Olivia de Havilland) and sidekick (Alan Hale), plus Ronald Reagan (as a fairytale version of the young George Armstrong Custer) and Van Heflin (as a traitor and mercenary supporter of Brown).

Bond rated a grand sendoff by Flynn this time around. Ordered by Brown to hang Stuart, Townley begins to fix the noose around his neck. But the wily Southerner pulls Townley's pistol and shoots him, point blank, before escaping through a barn. Ward's role ends, not with Stuart swinging in the wind, but as Townley lies dying on the ground.

Re-titled *Santa Fe Trail*, the film premiered in the capital of New Mexico on December 13, 1940. The general release two weeks later proved a box-office bonanza, regardless of Robert Buckner's freewheeling historical distortions, including a very negative depiction of Brown, who is portrayed by Massey as a megalomaniac intent on destroying the Union. (The following year, Warner Bros. would give Custer an even bigger whitewashing, courtesy of Raoul Walsh, with Flynn playing the role, in the historically heinous yet exciting and well-acted *They Died with Their Boots On*. In 1955, Charles Marquis Warren presented a more evenhanded portrait of Brown, again played by Raymond Massey, in Allied Artists' *Seven Angry Men*, on which Sam Peckinpah served as dialogue director.)

Wayne and Bond again teamed up during the autumn of 1940, giving each other holy hell, not on Ford's boat, but while shooting scenes for Paramount's *The Shepherd of the Hills* (1941), marking the first time either of them had acted for another of Hollywood's pioneer directors, Henry Hathaway. Wayne was particularly anxious to appear in the film, which also introduced him to Harry Carey, whose down to earth, convincing style had been a major influence on his own development as an actor.

The third screen adaptation of Harold Bell Wright's popular moralistic novel set in the moonshine drenched mountains of the Ozarks, Hathaway's *Shepherd of the Hills*, shot partially on location at Big Bear Lake, was the first film to feature Wayne in vibrant Technicolor. This temporary "graduation" from monochrome also presented Duke with the challenge of playing "Young Matt" Masters, a character faced with fulfilling a "blood oath" imposed by his Aunt Mollie Gibbs (Beulah Bondi), who raised him following his father's desertion, an act that led to his mother's premature death.

Ordered to seek out and murder his pappy, Matt gradually falls under the moderating influence of Daniel Howitt (Carey), a friendly stranger who arrives to purchase "Moanin' Meadow," the property on which his mother is buried. Upon learning that Howitt *is* his father, Matt attempts to shoot him with a rifle, but the older man is too quick on the draw. Like the "Cheyenne Harry" character in Ford's silent Westerns, Carey's "Howitt" pulls a pistol from under his belt; but, in this powerful and astonishing scene directed by Hathaway, he plays a man forced to gun down his own son.

Having been accidentally decked by Sammy Lane (Betty Field) following a brawl with his cousin, Wash Gibbs (Bond), earlier in the film, Matt is leveled for real this time, but rallies after hearing Howitt tell the girl that he acted to prevent his son from becoming a murderer faced with life in prison (the place from which he has just returned). Carey took Duke under his wing during the shoot, and their real-life rapport is reflected in their excellent scenes together.

Carey's calm demeanor provided a welcome balm for the harsh orders routinely meted out by Hathaway, another stern taskmaster, who kept prodding Wayne to "act more like Gary Cooper." Originally cast as a hillbilly, Henry Brandon became so irritated by the director's abuse that he "resigned" before production was completed. He recalled:

> *Shepherd of the Hills* had a marvelous cast: not only Wayne and Bond, but Harry Carey, Beulah Bondi, James Barton, Marjorie Main, Betty Field, Marc Lawrence (who was amazing as the halfwit), and another actor from Ford's stock company, John Qualen.
>
> Ward Bond could whinny exactly like a horse, which sometimes amused John Ford, but these shenanigans didn't go over so well with other directors. To Ford, he was always the necessary "Horse's Ass."
>
> During the filming of one of the cabin scenes, Hathaway and the cast and crew were inside the set. Bond, who had a small role, wasn't in the scene. Hathaway had just about completed a take when, somewhere outside the cabin, a *horse* began to whinny.
>
> "Shit! God damn it!" Hathaway yelled, and then he ran out to find the horse. Well — there was no horse. So he went back inside to shoot a second take — and, just as the cast nearly nailed it, the horse began to whinny again, but even louder this time.
>
> Hathaway went berserk, rushed out of the cabin set, yelling, "God damn it! Jesus Christ!" and — again — no horse.
>
> After this happened a third time, Ward Bond was *standing there*, laughing himself sick, when Hathaway came running out. Of course, Wayne thought it was funny, but Hathaway was *not* amused.
>
> For some unknown reason, Bond didn't become the whipping boy on that picture. Hathaway decided to take out all his frustrations on me — and *I* became the whipping boy — so I asked out.[51]

(Though he is not credited in the finished film, Brandon's "Bald Knobber" can be glimpsed in the background of some scenes, and he also appears on one of the original-release lobby cards, as well as the window card, on which he is shown, directly behind Bond, leaning against a large boulder.)

One evening while on location, Wayne was explaining to some of his colleagues how he planned to branch out as an actor, to seek a variety of roles rather than be typecast as the hero in every film. After the actors left the room, Olive Carey, who had overheard this pronouncement, really ripped into the Duke:

> You big, stupid son of a bitch. Would you like to see Harry do all these things you were telling these people? People have accepted you. They've taken you into their homes and their hearts now, and they like you as a certain kind of man.[52]

Ford's next picture for Zanuck, an adaptation of Erskine Caldwell's novel *Tobacco Road* shot in November and December 1940, has been described as an outrageous parody of the proletarian characters in *The Grapes of Wrath*. Jack Kirkland's stage adaptation, which had opened in New York on December 4, 1933, had attracted the attention of several Hollywood studios, but potential censorship issues had prevented anyone from purchasing the screen rights.

Encouraged by the success of *The Grapes of Wrath*, Zanuck, who had received the green light by the Production Code Administration, finally bought the rights for $150,000 against a percentage of the box-office gross. Though Ford hadn't read the novel nor seen the play, he nonetheless accepted the assignment. The role of Jeeter Lester, played on stage by Henry Hull, was intended for Henry Fonda; but after Ford became attached to the project, Charley Grapewin was cast as the shiftless head of the white-trash clan.

Due to possible protests from religious organizations, Zanuck and Ford canceled plans to shoot on location in Augusta, Georgia. Much of the outdoor work was done at Sherwood Forest in California, and the "poor farm" sequences were shot at Encino. Ford recalled, "I enjoyed making the picture.... Poor Charley Grapewin was a fine actor, and a wonderful guy to work with, always cracking jokes and playing practical jokes, and then he'd go and get right into his part again."[53]

Joseph McBride noted:

> *Tobacco Road* looks like something Ford would have made on a drunken bender.... Schizoid in the extreme, it alternates between the crudest, most grating low-comedy scenes ... and some deftly sketched moments of sentiment as moving as any he ever put on the screen.[54]

The PCA had advised that the sexual relationship between Lov Bensey and Ellie May Lester could not be depicted in an "overt" manner; therefore, McBride's comment, "the embarrassing spectacle of Ward Bond and Gene Tierney writhing toward each other in the dirt to convey sexual passion are among the lowest points in Ford's *oeuvre*" is rather misplaced.[55] Pappy wasn't allowed to use a serious approach, so he created an outrageously comical one.

Portions of the film, especially those featuring the over the top performance of William Tracy as Dude Lester, Jeeter's automobile-obsessed son, are downright obnoxious. Aside from the poor-farm section, the most palatable scenes involve Jeeter and Lov, who first appears, five minutes into the film, carrying a Croker sack of turnips to the Lester shack.

Tobacco Road (20th Century–Fox, 1941; directed by John Ford). Lov Bensey (Ward Bond), Jeeter Lester (Charley Grapewin), Dude Lester (William Tracy), Ada Lester (Elizabeth Patterson) and Ellie May Lester (Gene Tierney) in Ford's outrageous adaptation of Erskine Caldwell's controversial play.

Though the 13-year-old Pearl Lester is married to Lov (pronounced "love"), she refuses even to talk to him, and he arrives, whining incessantly about his personal predicament:

> I tried every way I know how. I kicked her, and I poured water on her, and I chucked rocks and sticks at her, and all she does is bawl a lot when she's hurt. You can't call that talkin'!

Jeeter and his wife, Ada (Elizabeth Patterson), advise Lov to "trade-in" Pearl, but he rejects the alternative of marrying Ellie May, whom he considers "too old" at 23. Caked in dry mud, Tierney is quite a sight as Ellie, saying she wants "just one bite" (of a turnip), while slowly sliding her rear end across the dusty ground. When she makes contact with Lov, the rest of the family, including the dog, ambush him and steal the turnips. Lov beats the retreat, and Bond disappears from the film for more than an hour.

When Lov returns, Jeeter runs like hell. Crashing through a fence, Lov explains that he is not angry about the turnips, but again looking for Pearl, who has taken off for Augusta. "I wasn't doin' a thing to that girl, except tyin' her up with some rope!" he admits.

Filmed alongside Grapewin in a lengthy tracking shot, Bond plays his "crying scene" in a single take (running 1:35). This image of the 37-year-old actor as the dimwitted, highly emotional hick is another of the film's truly bizarre elements, but his comparative underplaying makes it watchable. Jeeter finally is able to talk Lov into accepting Ellie May, although she is "awful old for a wife."

As Lov walks down the road toward his home, the crazed Dude nearly runs him down, swerves into a fence, jumps out of the car, and slaps him in the face. In a nice touch, Bond "sweeps" a small portion of the dirt road with one hand before setting down his half-eaten turnip with the other. He then throws a very convincing punch, sending William Tracy tumbling into the ditch. Lov is last seen loping down the middle of the road after overturning Dude's car with his back!

According to Nunnally Johnson, the rampant imbecility in the film was due, not to his screenplay, but added entirely by the director:

> Ford did a lousy job on *Tobacco Road*.... To Ford a low, illiterate cracker and a low, illiterate Irishman were identical. Since he didn't know anything about crackers and he did know about the Irish, he simply changed them all into crazy Irishmen.... When you send the thing in red and it comes out green, that's a disappointment. But I didn't have any control.[56]

Viewers who had read Erskine Caldwell's novel or seen the stage version recognized little in the film. Despite negative reviews, *Tobacco Road* did respectable business, as described by the *Hollywood Reporter*:

> *Tobacco Road* is getting away to a big start in New England as a result of the wide open exploitation possibilities offered by the censorship situation here. All the New England censor boards passed the picture but, by contrast, the stage play was banned throughout this part of the country except in four cities. As a result, the exhibitors are capitalizing plenty on the chance to see the film version of the long-barred play.[57]

On January 3, 1941, Wayne returned to Republic to begin shooting *A Man Betrayed*, an urban crime drama utilizing the same basic plot as his Westerns. Following the murder of an innocent young man at a gambling joint, country lawyer Lynn Hollister arrives in Temple City to encounter widespread scandal and corruption backed up by a gang of thugs; but by the final reel, he has everything cleaned up, nice and tidy, and lands the daughter of the crooked political boss, whom he manages to get released on parole.

Like its predecessor, *Three Faces West*, *A Man Betrayed* was an attempt by Republic to cash in on several popular genres (in this case, mystery, social expose and screwball comedy) resulting in an unbelievable potboiler. Duke deserved better, as did his fine supporting cast: Frances Dee, Edward Ellis, Wallace Ford, Alexander Granach (who plays the Renfield character in Murnau's *Nosferatu*), and Bond as Floyd, the glassy-eyed killer at the casino, who is a few cards shy of a full deck.

While Duke remained to star in more Republic programmers, Bond went back to the major studios to play character roles in top A films of the period. At Warner Bros., he made his first appearance for Howard Hawks, in the topical, $2-million spectacular "The Amazing Life of Sergeant York," starring Gary Cooper as World War I hero Alvin C. York, a formerly drunken and aimless young man from Tennessee's Cumberland Mountains, who, after "finding religion," had to overcome his conscientious objector status before using "turkey shooting" methods to storm singlehandedly two German machine gun nests and capture 132 prisoners during the Battle of the Argonne.

A recipient of the Medal of Honor and the French Croix de Guerre, York had been turning down the making of a biopic by Jesse Lasky since 1919, but now the pioneering producer convinced the modest veteran to consider the current European war and recent passing of the Selective Service Act, and then do his "patriotic duty." York, seeking funds to build an interdenominational Bible school, finally gave his word to make the film; but when the studio considered Pat O'Brien or Ronald Reagan to play him, Lasky had a bogus telegram signed with York's name sent to Gary Cooper, and he arguably saved the film from becoming a miscasting disaster. (Surprisingly, Jack Warner didn't insist on using Bogart.)

Now dated by heavy doses of sentimentality and the bombastic score of Max Steiner (who relied too heavily on manipulative leitmotifs), Gary Cooper's performance still holds up (although, nearly 40 during production, he was far too old for the part). Hawks' use of baby-face, 16-year-old Joan Leslie (whose "accent" is about as Tennessee mountain as a New York minute) to play Coop's fiancée (even by "hillbilly" standards) borders on perverse. York's "biography" prior to April 1917 fills two-thirds of the 134-minute running time, but the emphasis on character development leads up to rousing montage when his extraordinary wartime feat is dramatized. Like the real York's life, a global conflict is required to jump start the reel version's, as well.

Five writers, including Abem Finkel and John Huston, worked on the screenplay, retitled simply *Sergeant York*. Shooting began February 3, 1941, on a revolving "Tennessee Valley" set constructed on the studio's largest soundstage, and location work was done in the Simi Hills, Santa Susana Mountains and at the Warner Bros. Ranch. In a supporting cast led by Walter Brennan (wearing one of the most ludicrous wig and eyebrow combinations ever pasted onto an actor), George Tobias, Stanley Ridges and Margaret Wycherly, Bond received seventh billing as Ike Botkin, one of York's Cumberland hell-raising buddies, who brings some genuine humor to the film's first half. (His third hillbilly role in six months, Ike, when fully loaded, is reminiscent of Lon Chaney, Jr.'s Lennie in *Of Mice and Men* [1939].) Made with strategic timing, *Sergeant York* became an enormous critical and commercial success.

The 13th Academy Awards ceremony, held at the Los Angeles Biltmore Hotel on February 27, 1941, was the first to use the sealed envelope. (The previous year, the *L.A. Times* had utilized leaked information to publish results prior to the event.) Jane Darwell won the Best Supporting Actress Award for *The Grapes of Wrath*, but Henry Fonda's groundbreaking, realistic as the Oklahoma Dust performance as Tom Joad ironically was ousted by his buddy James Stewart's comic turn in *The Philadelphia Story*. Claiming the Best Actor Oscar was a "consolation" for not giving it to Stewart for the previous year's *Mr. Smith Goes to Washington*

(1939), Joseph McBride noted that Fonda's "Joad, coiled with feral rage yet still capable of the most selfless generosity, is the performance of a lifetime."[58]

As he had done the previous year for *Gone with the Wind*, David O. Selznick leaned on the Academy mightily for his *Rebecca*, the first Hollywood film directed by Alfred Hitchcock. This half thriller, half soap opera, glittering adaptation of Daphne du Maurier's 1938 novel won out over *The Grapes of Wrath* for the Best Picture Award (*The Long Voyage Home* also was nominated), but Ford *was* honored with the Oscar for Best Director.

On March 3, 1941, Wayne began working on yet another Republic programmer, *Lady from Louisiana*, a period piece on which the studio spent most of the A-level budget on art direction and costumes, with little left over for anything else. Unlike *A Man Betrayed*, which at least features a host of fine actors (including Bond as the psycho), this New Orleans melodrama supports Duke with a bland cast led by Ona Munson, Ray Middleton, Helen Westley, and Ford perennial Jack Pennick (as a killer). (The film is worth seeing, however, just to catch 18-year-old Dorothy Dandridge in a small supporting role.)

An "unofficial" remake of the 1932 Howard Hawks–Edward G. Robinson love-triangle adventure *Tiger Shark*, "Hard to Get" was assigned by Warner Bros. executive producer Hal B. Wallis to Raoul Walsh, whose finished product would be called *Manpower*, seemingly the perfect title for the work of the one-eyed macho man. In fact, the entire production, which began in late March 1941, involved a fleet of macho men, some of whom actually ended up in the film.

The casting began with the female lead: Duke's lover, Marlene Dietrich. For the role played by Robinson in *Tiger Shark*, Wallis originally considered Victor McLaglen (who had worked with Walsh as much as he had with Ford) and Broderick Crawford. But Jack Warner still was having problems with the irascible Humphrey Bogart, who played the ridiculous roles forced on him, rather than be suspended without pay for weeks or months.

Dropped from the cast of *Out of the Fog* (and replaced by John Garfield), Bogart was tossed "Hard to Get," but the equally obstinate George Raft, who had worked with "Hump" before, claimed that his costar was being miscast again. The simple truth is that George couldn't stand the competition.

Bogart was dumped after his wardrobe test, during which he began arguing with Raft's double, Mack Gray. For a moment, George was relieved, but became even more pissed off when the original Robinson role went to — Edward G. Robinson, the studio's heaviest hitter. Rather than the tuna fisherman of *Tiger Shark*, Eddie would play an electrical lineman in *Manpower*, battling Raft for the fair hand of Dietrich.

The shoot was not a pleasant one for Walsh, who had to direct amidst two feuds: a producers' struggle between Wallis and associate Mark Hellinger; and another, more volatile, continuing scrap between Robinson and Raft on Stage 11. Angry over having to compete with Eddie (in particular) and the downward spiral of his own career (in general; and of his own making), Raft was a constant pain, becoming ferociously jealous over Robinson's attention to Dietrich. Eventually the production ran a week over schedule, with the budget escalating to $920,000.

Fed up, Hellinger quit, allowing writer Jerry Wald to move up in the pecking order. As for Raft, not wanting the audience to perceive him as weak, objected to a scene depicting his character, Johnny Marshall, in the pouring rain, losing his grip on Hank McHenry (Robinson), who then falls to his death. Raft refused to do it, insisting that a faulty rope be responsible for Hank's plummet.

On Wednesday, April 9, 1941, the supporting actor playing McHenry's courageous, pole-climbing colleague, Eddie Adams, celebrated his 38th birthday. For a time, the male bonding so celebrated by Walsh infiltrated the *Manpower* locker room, courtesy of Wardell E. Bond, with a little help from the veteran character star playing fellow lineman "Jumbo" Wells: Rufus Alan MacKahan, aka Alan Hale.

Robinson and Raft stayed away from each other, but each enjoyed separate acts of hijinks. When a photographer visited the set, Bond and Hale provided the axis around which the others revolved: Eddie G. fed Alan biscuits; and stone-cold George actually laughed when Ward poured a libation through a funnel into Alan's trousers. Frank McHugh simply looked on, mesmerized by the collective shenanigans.

Relative peace reigned for nearly two weeks, but the tension peaked again on April 21, during the shooting of a fight scene featuring Bond and Robinson, his sledgehammer right striking Ward so realistically that it can almost be felt by the audience. Robinson and Raft, both diminutive men, were as formidable as Wayne when packing a powerful punch.

Intervening in the brawl, Raft roughed up Robinson, swore when he objected, and then punched him in the side, prompting Bond and Hale to separate them. With Robinson's

Manpower (Warner Bros., 1941; directed by Raoul Walsh). The male bonding so celebrated by Walsh was tested time and again during a volatile two-month shooting schedule. On April 9, Bond celebrated his 38th birthday; and, with a little help from Alan Hale, relative peace reigned on the set for nearly two weeks. Here, stone-cold George Raft (center) actually cracks a smile while Bond pours a libation through a funnel into Hale's trousers; Frank McHugh (far right) and the bit players are simply mesmerized.

permission, Hal Wallis filed Screen Actors Guild charges against Raft; but when the film became a box-office hit, the matter was dropped. (A very amiable man and a bona fide artistic genius, Robinson was quite fearless; but it is possible that Raft's "connections" had something to do with quashing the charges. On the set of Warners' *Each Dawn I Die* during the spring of 1939, Raft saved Cagney from a mob hit ordered by labor racketeer Willie Bioff, whose effort to extort "protection" from Jack Warner had been ignored. In 1955, Bioff was whacked in classic Mafia style: blown up in his car after hiding out it Arizona, posing as a grocer.)

Billed eighth in an impressive cast also including Barton MacLane and Eve Arden, Bond benefited from his previous work with Walsh, who built up his character in several key scenes. During a rain-saturated sequence depicting "Omaha" (McHugh) and Eddie Adams aiding Hank and Johnny in emergency repairs, Johnny is hit by a falling cross arm, and Hank, trying to help, is electrocuted when he steps on a sparking transformer. Both men are taken down to a panel truck, where Adams performs CPR on the unconscious Hank. Johnny recovers and, concerned about his friend, who has been in a state of arrest for 30 minutes, takes over the resuscitation duties.

"Ah, it's no good, Johnny," Adams sighs. "You can't bring him back."

Johnny refuses to stop and, as Hank regains consciousness, his pal asks, "How do you feel, mug?"

Incredibly, old Hank is just fine, suggesting that he also was suffering from hypothermia, brought on by the torrential, chilling rain. (Under normal circumstances, seven minutes of arrest is enough to cause irreversible brain damage.) Ironically, Bond's character helps save the life of Robinson's unconscious Hank, who later punches him out!

The explosiveness of the actors is well-represented by classic Walsh fight scenes, one of which involves Robinson pummeling Bond a second time, prompted by Adams' insensitive remark about Fay Duval (Dietrich). Hank calls Adams a "wiseguy" after smashing him to the locker-room floor (Bond received another real punch). This is *Manpower*'s most tense moment, which is defused when the two men shake hands. (Perhaps the liberal Robinson's actual anger on the set was increased by his distaste for Bond's conservative political views.)

During a savage rainstorm, Adams quits the job, prompting Johnny to tender his resignation, though he agrees to do "one more" project for Hank. But when Fay, who is now married to Hank, admits that she loves Johnny, Hank flies into a jealous, murderous rage, climbs a pole, and takes after Johnny with a huge wrench. Tragically, he fatally falls after his friend attempts to hold onto a strap that slips out of his hand.

A master of montage sequences, Walsh builds the suspense dramatically by having his actors ascend geographically. (He gave Bogart a mountain in *High Sierra* [1941], Robinson a tower in *Manpower*, and his most unforgettable example, the exploding fuel tanks for Cagney, in *White Heat* [1949].)

Manpower gave Bond the opportunity to work with Walsh for the third time; and, as Eddie Adams, developed one of his best (non–Ford) performances to date. His off-camera wisecracking and practical jokes provided desperately needed humor for Raft and, eventually, Eddie Robinson, to lighten up, albeit temporarily.

Screenwriter John Huston renegotiated his Warner Bros. contract in 1941, grabbing a pay raise and the opportunity to direct one film in return for his fine script work. He chose to fill both production roles on a new adaptation of Dashiell Hammett's hardboiled detective novel *The Maltese Falcon*, which he believed had been given short shrift by the studio, who had bought the film rights for $8,500 in 1930.

A semi-serious adaptation by Maude Fulton and Brown Holmes, directed by Roy Del Ruth and starring Ricardo Cortez as Sam Spade, was released the following year, followed by a screwball comedy attempt, *Satan Meets a Lady*, directed by William Dieterle and costarring Warren William and Bette Davis, in 1936. The erudite Huston had the *radical* idea that a film actually could be faithful to its literary source.

On May 22, 1941, Huston met with associate producer Henry Blanke and studio manager Tenny Wright to discuss the new film, which would begin shooting on June 10, with a slim B budget of $381,000. Blanke had cast three supporting actors: Mary Astor (as Brigid O'Shaughnessey), Peter Lorre (as Joel Cairo), and cinematic neophyte Sydney Greenstreet (as Kasper Gutman), a stage actor Huston had seen at Los Angeles' Biltmore Theatre. By June 5, the crew assignments had been made, but the lead role of Sam Spade had yet to be cast.

Humphrey Bogart had done a wardrobe test with Astor the previous day. The part had been promised to George Raft, but when he heard of the low budget and first-time director, he turned it down. (Raft had done the same thing the previous year, refusing to play gangster Roy "Mad Dog" Earle in Raoul Walsh's hard-hitting *High Sierra*. Bogart told Raft it was just another thug role, and then played it himself, to great critical and public acclaim.)

Bogart was on suspension from the studio, but Jack Warner welcomed him back on June 10 to begin working with the director with whom he'd create some of the finest Hollywood films of the next decade. The supporting roles were filled out with the great Gladys George (as Iva Archer, Spade's mistress and widow of his partner), Barton MacLane (as Lieutenant Dundy), Lee Patrick (as Effie, Spade's secretary), Jerome Cowan (as the unfortunate Miles Archer), and Elisha Cook, Jr. (as weasel-like gunsel Wilmer Cook).

For the second time in a very well-cast film, Warner Bros. gave Bond eighth billing, as Detective Tom Polhaus, an old pal whom Spade playfully likes to rib, referring to the Lieutenant as his "boyfriend" and "playmate." These remarks were part of Huston's subtle way of skirting PCA censorship and retaining the novel's gay overtones involving the eccentric Joel Cairo, who is called "queer" by Effie, and a "fairy" by Spade. Huston had to use more innocuous dialogue, but often relied on his visual sensibilities to communicate intent. Cairo's curly hairstyle (which is "smooth" in the novel) and carrying of a phallic cane/umbrella, which he holds close to his face during his initial discussion with Spade, was Huston's way of suggesting Hammett's original "queer" depiction.

Huston, very pleased that he had assembled the "ideal" group of actors, decided to take the unorthodox route of shooting the film in sequence, rather than structuring it later in the cutting room. Prior to production, he sketched storyboards of each shot and then held extensive rehearsals, a laborious process that ultimately paid off as he filmed many scenes in long takes, and (like Ford) wasted little stock on re-takes.

Impressed by Dashiell Hammett's unique prose style, he attempted to create a visual counterpart with lighting, angles and camera movement. Nearly every chapter and section is faithfully scripted, and nearly all the dialogue is represented verbatim or in carefully edited passages. Huston became one of the first filmmakers at a major Hollywood studio to serve as sole screenwriter and director on the same feature film.

In casting Dundy, Huston gave the usually unlikable Barton MacLane a chance to play a more ambiguous character (as in the novel), nearly matching Bond's standout role (a contender for his very best non–Ford performance), no mean feat when sharing the screen with Bogart in his milestone interpretation of Sam Spade, which began the development of his post-gangster, cynical, tough yet "good guy" screen persona. Hammett's dialogue is like music in Bogie's mouth; and, thanks to Huston's innovative shooting schedule, he was able to build his performance dynamically from the first scene to the last.

The final 27 minutes of the film involve the brilliant confrontation (played in real time) between Spade and all the principal Falcon seekers at his apartment. Bogart mesmerizes with supremely controlled pyrotechnics as Spade tells Brigid O'Shaughnessy, "Maybe you love me and maybe I love you.... I'll have some rotten nights after I've sent you over, but maybe that will pass."

Though Bogart is certainly the peak, the entire cast is the exemplary foundation of the acting pyramid. In his film debut, Greenstreet is dazzling, and Lorre (giving perhaps his finest English-language performance) provides the ideal physical counterpoint, as well as a whimpering foil to the Fat Man's calm, sometimes slightly giddy, demeanor.

Having created a masterpiece sequence driven by an ensemble of impeccable actors, Huston ends it (and the film) with a monosyllabic line from Bond, who gets the last word — and the last laugh. Described by Hammett as having "thick" facial features, Tom Polhaus is played substantially as written by Ward, who "effortlessly" parries witty comments with the razor-sharp Bogie. His interpretation provided a new prototype for all the (far more two-dimensionally dimwitted) law-enforcement sidekicks who populate the countless detective series of the 1940s.

Answering Tom's query about the Falcon, Sam Spade explains (with a line written by Bogart) that the "dingus" is "the stuff dreams are made of."

Subtly registering that John Ford-inspired facial expression of slight bewilderment, Polhaus responds, "Huh?" and the characters walk into the fade-out.

Wrapped on July 18, 1941, with some retakes added prior to release, *The Maltese Falcon*, brought in on budget by Huston, did only moderate business (due to an insufficient, B-grade publicity campaign), but was a critical favorite, garnering high praise for the star and director, and Academy Award nominations for Best Picture, Best Screenplay, and Best Supporting Actress for Astor. Unfortunately, at the Oscars, Huston would face some very stiff competition: *wunderkind* Orson Welles and his remarkable first film, *Citizen Kane*; and another masterpiece (just a "job of work") by a guy who dressed like a bum and wanted to be called Sean Aloysius O'Fearna.

Nonetheless, more than seven decades after its release, *The Maltese Falcon*, one of the first and finest of the genre that became *film noir*, remains a timeless classic. (The fact that it was made during the same year as *Sergeant York* stretches the imagination.) Among a formidable cast, most of whom were (or became) notorious scene stealers, Bond more than holds his own.

Darryl Zanuck had bought the film rights to Richard Llewellyn's bestselling novel *How Green Was My Valley* in February 1940. This dramatic story about a proud family living and working in a grimy coal mining community in South Wales was to be adapted by Liam O'Flaherty and directed by William Wyler. Characteristically, O'Flaherty focused on the Leftist political angle at the expense of the human drama, so Zanuck passed the novel on to Ernest Pascal and, finally, Philip Dunne, telling the latter to ignore the existing work. Wyler eventually joined Dunne in polishing off the script, crafting it to the satisfaction of Zanuck, who, planning a Technicolor epic, demanded a faithful representation of Llewellyn's powerful portrait of the Morgan family, whose strong relationships are eroded by the harsh realities of their environment.

Following a lengthy search and audition process, Wyler cast 11-year-old Roddy McDowall, already a veteran of 18 feature films, as Huw Morgan, the character who (as an adult)

The Maltese Falcon (Warner Bros, 1941; directed by John Huston). Writer-director Huston's film noir masterpiece gave Bond one of the finest roles of his career: Detective Tom Polhaus, here seen with his hand up front and center with (left to right) Lieutenant Dundy (Barton MacLane), Brigid O'Shaughnessy (Mary Astor), Sam Spade (Humphrey Bogart) and Joel Cairo (Peter Lorre).

narrates the story (a crucial element added by Zanuck). McDowall already had been directed by the great Fritz Lang in *Man Hunt* (1941), alongside Walter Pidgeon, whom Wyler cast as Mr. Gruffydd, the minister, who has a secret desire for Huw's older sister, Angharad (Maureen O'Hara, whom Ford preferred over Wyler's choice, Katherine Hepburn, which may have proved problematic). The director's other casting choices included Donald Crisp as Gwillym, head of the Morgan household, Sara Allgood as his wife, Beth, and Anna Lee as their daughter-in-law, Bronwyn (Wyler had picked Greer Garson).

Scheduled to begin production during the spring of 1941, *How Green Was My Valley* was postponed by the New York office of 20th Century–Fox, and Wyler went back to his trusted producer, Samuel Goldwyn, to direct his favorite actress, Bette Davis, in *The Little Foxes* (1941), which began shooting on April 28. After one of Hollywood's master filmmakers walked out the door, Zanuck turned over the reins to another cinematic genius he already had under contract: Ford, who wasted no time reshaping the project in his *auteur* image, modeling the Morgan family after the Feeney clan and basing several scenes on challenges he had faced as a child (particularly the year he had spent bedridden with diphtheria).

Prior to production, Ford invited Maureen O'Hara to have dinner with his current Feeney clan at their Odin Street home, an event that proved quite successful, as she later revealed:

I never expected that John Ford and I would become friends before we ever shot a single frame of *How Green Was My Valley*, but we did. It sprouted from our mutual love in all of the world that was Irish. Before I knew it, I was having dinner with his family at their home ... at least once a week during preproduction. In his home, away from the studio and away from the business of making movies, John Ford was very different from the man I had previously met. He was kind, charming, and absolutely wonderful to me.[59]

Ford, after weaving mostly fabricated tales about his family history in Ireland, insisted that O'Hara sing for her supper, always Irish or Irish-American songs, like "Danny Boy" and "I'll Take You Home Again, Kathleen," standing beside her place at the table before she was allowed to sit down. At a dinner in May 1941, she was introduced to Duke, with whom she began to develop a "casual friendship."[60]

Zanuck and Ford wanted to shoot *How Green Was My Valley* on location in Wales, but they knew Great Britain's devastating war with Nazi Germany precluded any such ambitions. Instead, Zanuck spent $110,000 ordering a complete Welsh coal mining village, built to resemble the Cerrig Ceinnen and Clyde-cum Tawe in Wales, on 80 acres of the 20th Century–Fox Ranch in the hills near Malibu.

Zanuck had used all his might in fighting against the New York money men's hesitance to finance such an expensive epic, and his belief in the project fostered a remarkably affable collaboration with Ford, who, working with a budget reduced to $1,250,000, shot the picture in black and white (which he knew suited the realistic material far better than fantastical "*Gone with the Wind* Technicolor"). Production began on June 10, 1941, and, as the mogul watched the dailies, he wrote copious memos to the director, praising him for working to make what would be his "greatest" film, a "masterpiece," and a solid two hours of entertainment to clean up at the box office.

Unlike the underrated British coal mining film *The Proud Valley* (1940), starring the great Paul Robeson and populated with authentic citizens from South Wales, *How Green Was My Valley* features primarily English actors. There are also a few Irish: O'Hara, Sara Allgood, and Ford regulars Barry Fitzgerald and his nearly sound-alike brother, Arthur Shields (all of whom began their careers at the Abbey Theatre). The one true Welshman in the bunch is an actor who was making his film debut as the bare-knuckle fighter Dai Bando: Rhys Williams, born in Merionith, a county constituency in North Wales.

O'Hara explained:

Ford had been making movies for nearly a quarter of a century by the time I started working with him. The dos and don'ts on a John Ford picture were already well etched in stone by this point, and so members of the ... stock company ... advised me on how to stay out of trouble and out of the barrel. You never wanted to find yourself in Mr. Ford's barrel, which meant you were on [the] list to be tortured....[61]

Roddy McDowall always recalled working for Ford as a warm and delightful experience. While he performed in the school sequence in which Huw is forced by the vicious headmaster (Morton Lowry) to sit on the dunce's stool, Ford quipped, "Watch him feel for the chair with his ass. He knows how to act, this kid." Joseph McBride perceptively noted, "Roddy McDowall ... gives perhaps the finest performance by a juvenile actor in movie history."[62]

Huw's choice to follow in his father's footsteps of drudgery, rather than leave the valley to seek an educated profession, is the true tragedy of the film. Tag Gallagher called it Ford's "question of duty and tradition gone astray," while McBride added, "the boy's decision is a highly complex compound of several elements.... Ford does not intend us to endorse Huw's decision to ruin his life, which we judge from within the film's framing device of Huw as a chastened young man in his fifties finally leaving his boyhood home."[63]

Anna Lee, initially worried that Ford would replace her with another actress (perhaps Garson), invented a bogus Irish ancestor, but this blarney didn't fool Pappy, who called her "Limey." She recalled:

John Ford. Now there *was* a director and a lovely man. I thoroughly enjoyed every minute of working for him. He had a sort of "magical" way of directing you when you didn't *realize* he was directing you. It was most unusual. I loved him so much that I went on to make eight pictures with him as a member of the John Ford Stock Company, which was like a family. Pappy also was godfather to my children.[64]

Lee (whose own godfather was Sir Arthur Conan Doyle) actually suffered a miscarriage during the making of the film. Without informing Ford that she was pregnant with twins, she agreed to collapse in a doorway, rather than using a double, and the unexpectedly hard landing caused her to bleed internally (only one of the babies survived). (Though Ford always blamed himself for this accident, Lee considered it a consequence of her job, hence the choice of Pappy as godfather for her subsequent children during 25 years with the Stock Company. Her daughter, Bronwyn, was named after O'Hara's character in *How Green Was My Valley*.)

Ford wrapped *How Green Was My Valley* on August 12, 1941, and, as usual, left the post-production duties to Zanuck. O'Hara recalled, "I can't recall a single retake being shot on the picture.... *How Green Was My Valley* was camera cut, and nearly every inch of film that Mr. Ford shot ended up in the picture."[65]

While Ford made another masterpiece, Wayne took second billing to Ray Milland in Cecil B. DeMille's latest "historical" epic, *Reap the Wild Wind*, which was in production from June 2 to August 31, 1941. Duke initially had turned down the role of Captain Jack Stuart, honest skipper of the *Jubilee*, who falls prey to "salvage profiteers" in the Florida Keys. Earlier in his career, he had attempted to audition for the famous director, only to be rudely snubbed, an event that still stuck in his craw; and, to add insult to injury, DeMille now wanted him to play a character who, in one scene, gets punched out by Ray Milland, who plays Stephen Tolliver, the foppish attorney for the shipping company, who also is his rival for Loxi Claiborne (Paulette Goddard), a "tomboy" who operates a legitimate salvage outfit. The film ends with Stuart sacrificing himself to save Tolliver from a deadly octopus.

After meeting with DeMille several times, Wayne accepted the role and they developed an excellent working relationship, even joining each other for lunch on many occasions. However, Duke had become a good enough actor to realize that DeMille hadn't modified his style since the silent era, remaining an absolute master at helming huge crowd scenes, but alternating them with stilted sequences in which actors had to attempt delivering archaic dialogue with little or no help from the director. In typical DeMille fashion, *Reap the Wild Wind* became a tedious love-triangle romance cloaked in $4-million worth of extravagant period production values and boasting a stellar supporting cast led by Raymond Massey, Robert Preston, Lynne Overman, Susan Hayward and Charles Bickford. A few familiar Ford faces also appear in bit roles: J. Farrell MacDonald, Raymond Hatton, Milburn Stone and Cyril McLaglen.

Fresh from *The Maltese Falcon*, Bond moved on to another prominent supporting role, gangster Barney Millen, in Republic's *Doctors Don't Tell* (1941), directed by Jacques Tourneur. John Beal stars as Ralph Sawyer, a young physician, whose partner, Frank Blake (Edward Norris), becomes connected to a protection racket operated by Millen and Joe Grant (Douglas Fowley). Within a 65-minute running time, Bond takes a bullet, is brought to trial, murders a pharmacist, guns down Blake (after he turns stoolpigeon), and dies in a hail of copper's bullets. Unfortunately, Tourneur, in one of his early feature-film efforts, is hampered by a clichéd love-triangle plot and Republic's standard procedure of including two songs, performed in the nightclub scenes by Diana Wayne (Florence Rice).

Bond made an appearance in, of all things, *Know for Sure* (1941), a government "informational short" about the dangers of venereal disease. Laughable in their own day, these seriously intended projects were made by the United States Public Health Service. This 23-minute dramatization sponsored by the Research Council of Academy of Motion Picture Arts and Sciences and directed by Lewis Milestone, features Bond as a patient, in a diverse cast including Samuel S. Hinds, Tim Holt, Etta McDaniel, J. Carrol Naish and Shepherd Strudwick.

Celebrated French director Jean Renoir had arrived in the United States after the Nazis invaded his homeland. Though he had experienced great international success with the antiwar film *La Grande Illusion* (1937) and a superb adaptation of Emile Zola's *La Bête Humaine* (1938), his satirical *The Rules of the Game* (1939) met with great derision at the time of its release. He found assimilating into the Hollywood studio system quite difficult, but eventually began work on 20th Century–Fox's *Swamp Water* in mid–July 1941.

Walter Brennan stars as Tom Keefer, an escaped convict hiding out in Georgia's Okefenokee Swamp. Revealed to have committed the murder for which Keefer was convicted, brothers Tim (Bond) and Bud Dorson (Guinn "Big Boy" Williams) are driven deep into the swamp. Bud sinks to his death in quicksand, and Tim is last seen fading into the distance. This dark, often frightening film features a fine cast including Walter Huston, Anne Baxter, Dana Andrews, and a contingent from the Ford Stock Company: Bond, John Carradine, Russell Simpson, Joseph Sawyer and Mae Marsh. Henry Fonda again was mentioned as star of a Fox picture, only to be replaced by Andrews. Continually criticized by Darryl Zanuck for working too slowly and moving his camera too much, as well as other stylistic choices, Renoir cancelled his contract with the studio.

Warner Bros. kept Bond busy playing supporting roles in Westerns. *Wild Bill Hickok Rides* (1942), shot during September and October 1941, stars Bruce Cabot (who had proved such a quietly effective villain in *Dodge City*) as the legendary gunfighter, who organizes Wyoming ranchers against scheming land grabber and cattle thief Harry Farrel (Warren William), instigator of the requisite "dam explosion and resulting flood" plan. Constance Bennett is top-billed as gambler Belle Andrews, who relays Farrel's intentions to Hickok, who guns him down. No sniveling henchman this time around, Bond is billed sixth as Sheriff Edmunds.

"Moose Malloy? *That* sounds grotesque," quips Ann Reardon (Lynn Bari) in RKO's *The Falcon Takes Over* (1942), which provided Bond with his final acting role of 1941. Adapted from Raymond Chandler's novel *Farewell, My Lovely* and the "Falcon" stories of Michael Arlen, the film pits Gay Lawrence (George Sanders) against Bond's "Moose," described as being "an ex-wrestler, 6'5", 265 pounds," and he looks it, wearing additional padding over his already substantial frame, inside a neatly pressed, three-piece suit.

Out of the Joint following a five-year stretch, Moose is all inertia, walking and talking very slowly; but, when he receives negative responses to his inquiries about his old flame, Velma, he quickly throttles and *throws* his victims. The doorman and waiter at a nightclub receive this treatment, before he calmly saunters into the office of the manager, who gets the same going over (off-camera) and is left lying dead with a broken neck.

"He's strictly the manglin' kind," reports Jonathan "Goldy" Locke (Allen Jenkins), the Falcon's assistant, who was forced to drive Moose on his getaway from the club. "The guy ain't human — he's a mountain." In a later scene, low-key lighting and Bond's slow, deliberate walk, with hands and fingers outstretched, provides a virtual prototype for Rondo Hatton's later portrayals of "The Creeper" in Universal's *The Pearl of Death* (1944), one of the best Basil Rathbone–Nigel Bruce Sherlock Holmes films, and *House of Horrors* (1946), a thriller with Martin Kosleck.

In the end, Moose finds Velma, aka Diana Kenyon (Helen Gilbert), but she responds with a bullet. Bond is alternately effective and humorous, remaining calmly menacing throughout, regardless of the circumstances. Rather than showing pain when shot, he registers a hint of puzzlement, before stumbling off to die on the ground.

Concurrently, Wayne was playing second fiddle to Joan Blondell in yet another Republic period potboiler, *Lady for a Night*, which began shooting in late September 1941. Duke plays Jack Morgan, co-owner of the 1880s riverboat casino *Memphis Belle*. His partner, entertainer Jenny Blake (Blondell), aspires to Memphis high society, and marries Alan Alderson (Ray Middleton), a drunken gambler with a "proud name," in order to get there. Neither Morgan nor Alderson's family is pleased with this financially necessitated union; and after the riverboat goes up in flames, Jenny is framed for bumping off the worthless inebriate, who keels over after quaffing some poisoned hooch. Fortunately, Jenny is freed when the mentally unstable Aunt Katherine testifies that her sister, Aunt Julia, is actually a homicidal maniac. All of this outlandish folderol is capped off by the sound of wedding bells for Jack and Jenny.

Wrapped on November 14, *Lady for a Night* was in post-production when the Japanese bombed Pearl Harbor three weeks later. In their biography of Wayne, Randy Roberts and James S. Olson noted:

> Few films could have been more out of step. Like so many of the studio's films of the 1930s and early 1940s, it emphasized the class and racial barriers that divided Americans. Its theme was: Stay with your own kind.... It was just a typical Republic quickie, the kind of film that Herbert Yates loved so much because it could be counted on to make money.[66]

On November 25, Bond sent Pappy a telegram, letting him know that even the clouds of war could not darken his creative sense of humor. Addressed to "Seaman First Class John Ford," it read, "Have managed to sell *Araner*. Proceeds do not cover round trip to Avalon. Please wire $4.29 Mexican."[67]

Like *The Grapes of Wrath*, *How Green Was My Valley* was first premiered at a hugely successful gala event, at New York's Rivoli, followed by screenings in Wilkes-Barre and Scranton, Pennsylvania. Just as Zanuck had predicted, its nationwide release on December 26 proved a huge critical and box-office success. By the time the receipts began to roll in, Ford had been gone from the movie capitol for more than three months. Making motion pictures was still going to be his "job of work," but there would be no studios, sets, green valleys — nor John Wayne and Ward Bond — where he was going.

5

Pappy, Wild Bill, Jimmy and Brick

Whatever respect Ford may have had for his old pals John Wayne and Ward Bond faded when neither man showed much interest in serving his country. — Joseph McBride[1]

I better go do some touring — I feel the draft breathing down my neck. — John Wayne, to Marilyn Fix Carey[2]

On September 11, 1941, one month after wrapping *How Green Was My Valley*, Commander John Ford, USNR, received orders to report to the nation's capital. He carefully and quietly prepared for the trip, telling Mary that he would be gone for only a few days. He was dropped off at the train station by Jack Bolton, and began the long trip east aboard the Union Pacific Streamliner. During a stop at the station in Green River, Wyoming, he received a telegram from Zanuck, who had finished editing the film, which had impressed the suits at the front office in New York. No doubt Ford thought to himself, "What in the hell am I doing?" as he left behind fame, fortune and family security for a completely uncertain and dangerous life in the U.S. Navy. Dan Ford provided a succinct analysis of his 46-year-old grandfather's motives:

> He had done everything there was to do in the world of motion pictures.... The very best that was in store for him was more of the same.... He wanted a change for its own sake. He wanted to shake up his life, to move on to new conquests, new adventures.[3]

Ford's Field Photo unit, including Mark Armistead, Ben Grotsky, Ray Kellogg, Carl Marquard, Robert Parrish, Gregg Toland and Jack Pennick, who would serve as Pappy's aide-de-camp, had been ordered to Washington, D.C., not by the U.S. Navy, but by Colonel William Joseph "Wild Bill" Donovan. Already a legend in his own time, this New York lawyer and soldier had hunted for Pancho Villa under General John "Blackjack" Pershing, commanded the "Fighting 69th" during World War I, had been awarded the Congressional Medal of Honor, the Distinguished Service Cross, and two Purple Hearts. Recently he had been appointed by President Roosevelt as an "unofficial" emissary to Great Britain, where he consulted with Prime Minister Winston Churchill and British Intelligence on the wartime situation.

FDR had named Donovan "Coordinator of Information," a position that involved the nearly impossible task of centralizing all the fragmented intelligence services operating within the U.S. government (including the FBI and the State Department), all headed by directors who wanted to maintain their autonomy. Roosevelt's goal was for Donovan to create the Office of Strategic Services (OSS), which would conduct espionage and sabotage operations in the (*very* likely) event that the United States entered the war. (Eventually, Donovan's leadership of the OSS would involve him in head-butting contests with J. Edgar Hoover and General Douglas MacArthur.)

Donovan knew that film was the most effective modern propaganda medium, and who better than Hollywood's greatest filmmaker to direct it? Before anyone at the Department of the Navy could authorize the Field Photo unit, the wily "Wild Bill" grabbed Ford and his colleagues for the COI. Rather than being subjected to a conventional military chain of command, Ford would be the commander of a special naval unit under the personal jurisdiction of Donovan, who was directly accountable to President Roosevelt.

Ford quickly ingratiated himself with Washington's top brass by inviting them to intimate screenings of his recent masterpieces. Robert Parrish admitted, "For Ford, the OSS was no different than 20th Century–Fox.... He had no more respect for bureaucrats and professional military types than he had for producers."[4]

Americans across the nation were about to see *How Green Was My Valley*. Maureen O'Hara recalled that it "opened on October 28 and its success was meteoric. Theaters were packed — huge box-office receipts — and there was overwhelming critical acclaim." As for Roddy McDowall's portrayal of little Huw Morgan, any well-viewed film buff could agree with O'Hara's assessment: "It is arguably the finest performance by a child in movie history, though Roddy, ever modest, always believed that distinction belonged to Jackie Coogan in *The Kid*."[5]

Ford's first orders, received in November 1941, were to produce and delegate to his men the shooting of films showing the readiness of U.S. Army and Navy units. Donovan then screened these films for Roosevelt. On December 7, Ford, accompanied by Mary and Barbara, who had arrived for a visit, and Merian Cooper, who had returned to Washington for a reassignment, were relaxing at the home of Admiral William Pickens in Alexandria, when the maid announced that the "War Department" was on the telephone.

Immediately following the Japanese attack on Pearl Harbor, no one was certain where the next strike might occur, so Donovan ordered Ford to the Panama Canal Zone to shoot footage of the current state of defenses. On December 30, three days after MacArthur ordered his troops to retreat from the Philippines to the Bataan Peninsula, Ford and two cameramen flew to Panama and spent New Year's capturing first-hand evidence to include in a film to show FDR. After viewing the film, which Ford narrated, the President acclaimed the ability of Donovan's organization to produce such an accurate report in record time, without being subjected to the usual red tape that may have made any form of intelligence impossible.

For Ford, the President's praise, coupled with news that he had been named best director of 1941 by the New York Film Critics for *How Green Was My Valley*, provided a great boost following the whirlwind mission to Panama. Regardless of objections from the Navy and Secretary of War Henry Stimson, Donovan next ordered him to produce a "top secret" film in an effort to discover who was "at fault" for the devastating attack on Pearl Harbor. Ford assigned the project to Gregg Toland, who, accompanied by Ray Kellogg, flew to Hawaii, where he edited together actual footage shot by Navy cameramen with restaged scenes created with miniatures. By mid–February, Toland's blatant refusal to keep his controversial work under wraps required a visit from Ford, whose repeated orders to keep the mission covert were ignored.

FDR had ordered the Hollywood moguls to begin tailoring their forthcoming films to benefit the war effort: propaganda had to be integrated with entertainment, or the federal government would impose strict controls on filmmaking, as it had with other "essential" industries such as automobiles, steel, and oil. In February, Selective Service director General Lewis B. Hershey had ordered department officials in California to grant deferments to men whose work was vital to the film industry, which he deemed "essential in certain instances to the national health, safety and interest, and in other instances to war production."

The majority of Hollywood's leading men enlisted, leaving a void at every studio. Traditionally the appeal of the male star was his youth, vigor, strength and virility; but, with the nation now involved in a world war, any such actor remaining on the screen could prompt moviegoers to question why he wasn't in the military. As a result, the "new" leading man was still handsome with an appealing voice, but usually over the upper age limit for the draft (originally 44, but eventually lowered to 38), married, and with at least two dependents at home, or simply classified as 4-F. Good actors who had begun their careers during the silent era were now kept working steadily.

Darryl Zanuck was still at 20th Century–Fox, where Bond was playing a supporting role in *Ten Gentleman from West Point*, which Henry Hathaway had been directing since the day after Christmas. This fictionalized account of the establishment of the U.S. Military Academy, starring former boxer George Montgomery, marked the first time Ward appeared in a film costarring Maureen O'Hara, who walked off the set after receiving a disgusting French kiss from the leading man. Bond, who subsequently would work often with the "fiery Irish lassie," quickly realized that no one messed with Maureen, one of the few women in Hollywood who, like Katherine Hepburn, did not abate any nonsense (even from Errol Flynn: "I would have loved to have knocked him on his ass," she later admitted), one of the reasons Ford became so fond of her.[6]

In March, Ford wrote a letter to Mary, sarcastically growling that the Duke and the Judge were sitting out the war in Hollywood: "Ah, well — such heroism shall not go unrewarded — it will live in the annals of time."[7]

Bond, who turned 39 on April 9, 1942, was unquestionably 4-F due to his epilepsy, a fact he kept hidden for most of his life. When he volunteered to be an air-raid warden, Ford wrote to Wayne, "How does Uncle Ward look with a tin hat and a pair of binoculars?"[8] Wayne was classified 3-A, given a deferment because he was 34 (though four years below the limit), married, and the father of four young children. In his letters to Ford, he mentioned joining the Field Photo unit, but he backpedaled whenever an opportunity was offered, always having another film to complete. The Coach subsequently let the Duke's cavalier attitude infuriate him for many years. Wayne's mother, too, would often remind him that he stayed home to become the nation's greatest movie star, while his younger brother, her beloved Robert, was drafted into the Navy.[9]

As those who remained in Tinsel Town wrestled with their consciences, Ford and several assistants left Pearl Harbor to join Colonel James H. "Jimmy" Doolittle on his "raid" of Japan, which involved launching 16 B-25s from two aircraft carriers, bombing the home island of Honshu, and then flying on to China. Believing that U.S. citizens needed a morale boost, and to plant seeds of doubt in the minds of the Japanese, Doolittle's rationale for the attack was as much psychological as military. On April 14, 1942, four days before the actual raid, Ford, aboard the cruiser U.S.S. *Salt Lake City*, was able to listen to the radio broadcast of the Academy Awards, during which he won the Best Director Oscar for *How Green Was My Valley*, his second consecutive victory and his third in seven years. Darryl Zanuck also picked up the Best Picture Award.

Throughout the perilous mission, which concluded with little material damage to

Japan, but the loss of all aircraft and the death or capture of 11 U.S. servicemen, a makeshift flag, consisting of a gold Oscar on a blue field, flew from the masthead of the *Salt Lake City*. However, the raid had the effect on morale Doolittle had predicted. Soon after, Admiral Isoroku Yamamoto recalled the aircraft carrier fleet of the Imperial Japanese Navy from the Indian Ocean to defend the home islands and, six weeks later, ordered an attack on the small Pacific atoll of Midway, located between Honshu and Hawaii, 1,100 miles northwest of Pearl Harbor. In Honolulu, Ford was exasperated to learn that the U.S. Navy had confiscated the supposedly "top secret" film from Toland, whom the director, at the cinematographer's request, reassigned to Rio de Janiero.

Before returning to Washington, Ford grabbed some stationery from his room at the Moana Hotel and wrote a letter to Zanuck, again giving his boss credit for the success of an exceptional motion picture, but this time adding an unusual request (and a tongue-in-cheek valediction) that perhaps reveals more of his true feelings about the situation:

> Dear Darryl,
>   Congratulations for the award for "How Green Was My Valley." It was a well deserved choice, even you and I will admit that. It was a fitting tribute to your judgment and courage. I know what a scrap you had with the company about its production. Well, you won! Please grant me a favor. Would you have a miniature Oscar made up for me as a memento? You know — quarter size — "best production," etc? Would appreciate it, and it looks like a long time before I compete again. Hoping you are in the best of health and with kindest regards,
>   I am your obedient servant,
>   Jack
>
> Comdr John Ford USNR
> Kaneshe Naval Air Station
> Oahu, T. H.[10]

In Hollywood, Herb Yates had his own "exceptional" kind of picture in mind: a bona fide war film to star Wayne, a combination certain to reap enormous profits at the box office. But this was Republic, and the mini-mogul had no time to waste on innovation. Although credited with writing the "original story," Kenneth Garnet, who shared screenplay credit with Barry Trivers, unabashedly modeled *Flying Tigers* on Howard Hawks' *Only Angels Have Wings* (1939), which focuses on dangerous missions flown by a group of air-mail pilots through the jungles of South America. Firing up his cameras on April 27, 1942, director David Miller nearly made Republic look like a major studio by taking two months to complete this tribute to Colonel Claire Chennault's fearless airmen who had aided China against the Japanese.

Wayne plays Jim Gordon, leader of a group of pilots fighting in China, who is persuaded to join the "Flying Tigers," a squadron commanded by reformed drunk Blackie Bales (Edmund MacDonald). Aided by his top dog, "Hap" Davis (Paul Kelly), Gordon also enlists "Alabama" Smith (Gordon Jones) and "Woody" Jason (John Carroll), a daredevil mercenary whose sole interest is being paid for shooting down "Japs." The excellent female supporting cast includes Anna Lee as the love interest, Red Cross nurse Brooke Elliott; and former leading lady Mae Clarke (*Waterloo Bridge, Frankenstein*) as Blackie's wife, Verna Bales, who talks Gordon into signing on with her husband, who is killed after bailing out of his ship during a ferocious fight. Too busy scoring another kill to aid Blackie, Woody later redeems himself by saving Gordon and sacrificing his own life to blow up a Japanese supply train.

Written specifically for Duke, the Gordon character is the stoic, courageous, quiet hero whose actions speak louder than words, and around whom everyone and everything else revolves: the "John Wayne" who would become, not only the biggest star of World War II, but beloved across the planet for decades to come. Herb Yates thought that *Flying Tigers*, depicting men with various motives coming together as a well-oiled team, would be the ideal film for the feds, but the "reviews" offered by officials at the Office of War Information (OWI) criticized the overemphasis on the individual heroics of U.S. pilots, while downplaying the efforts and abilities of the Chinese characters.

On the contrary, the film puts a very positive spin on Chiang Kai-shek's corrupt, ineffectual administration; and, as for its depiction of the singular feats of various characters, Randy Roberts and James S. Olson's assessment is a direct bull's eye:

> Contentions that filmmakers distort history by focusing on the individual or the small group at the expense of historical reality reveal a deep misunderstanding of the industry — they could be made, no doubt, about every historical movie ever shot.[11]

In fact, these contentions reveal the federal censors' ignorance of basic storytelling, especially when scripted for a fictional feature film based on actual events but made primarily for "folks" seeking to be entertained, not educated nor indoctrinated. Released on October 8, 1942, *Flying Tigers* was the biggest moneymaker Republic had ever made, and the only "Poverty Row" picture to climb into the top 20 box-office grossers of the year.

Reviewers and audiences agreed that the success of the film could be explained in two words, and there was no way Herb Yates was going to let his pot of gold abandon Republic for Uncle Sam, even if Duke desired. The studio's other major star, Gene Autry, already had joined the Army Air Corps, and Wayne's very mention of a possible enlistment reportedly sent Yates into a rage, threatening to sue Duke for everything he already had, plus "every penny" he might hope to make in the future. In short, the war was Herb Yates' personal ticket to the big time, and Duke was the man to ride it for all it was worth. Even at this point, Wayne could have gone to the nearest U.S. Army, Navy or Marines recruiting station and enlisted, but he didn't.

Bond went into battle of a different kind in Warner Bros.' *Gentleman Jim* (1942), giving one of his finest performances as world heavyweight champion John L. Sullivan to Errol Flynn's James J. Corbett, under the direction of Raoul Walsh. Corbett (1866–1933), a San Francisco bank clerk and first boxer to honor the Marquess of Queensberry rules, was nicknamed "Gentleman Jim" because of his handsome features and scientific method of fighting. Born in Boston to Irish immigrants, Sullivan (1858–1918), the last heavyweight to hold the bareknuckle title, also reigned as the first champion of gloved boxing from 1881 to 1892. He was the first athlete in the United States to become a national celebrity.

In New Orleans on September 7, 1892, Corbett defeated the much heavier Sullivan during a grueling, 21-round upset, gaining the championship title. Corbett subsequently appeared in several plays and 16 films, including the features *The Man from the Golden West* (1913) and *The Prince of Avenue A* (1920), and the serial *The Midnight Man* (1919).

For *Gentleman Jim*, producer Robert Buckner hired Ed Cochrane, sports editor of the *Chicago Herald-American* and a Corbett aficionado, as technical adviser. "Mushy" Callahan was one of the trainers who worked with Flynn and Bond, and he also served as a "dancing" double for Flynn in close-ups detailing Corbett's famous footwork. Some location shooting was done at the Baldwin Estate at Santa Anita.

The boxing scenes are extremely well shot (by Sid Hickox) and edited (by Jack Killifer), with Flynn, Bond, Sammy Stein, Wee Willie Davis and others making real contact during the fights. (Doubles were used for Flynn and Bond in some long shots.) The impressive montage sequences, directed by Don Siegel, are an example of economical storytelling at its best.

With all the Irish-American blarney, and veterans of Ford films (Bond, Stein, Alan Hale, John Loder, Minor Watson, Rhys Williams, Arthur Shields, James Flavin, Frank Hagney and Mary Gordon), *Gentleman Jim* is a lot like a John Ford production stripped of its sociopolitical subtext. (During the championship bout, one shot shows Bond's rear end filling the entire frame as he backs into the camera lens.)

As the self-confident Corbett (who boasts that an opponent "can use gloves, no gloves, bare knuckles [or] a baseball bat"), Flynn's fluid combination of graciousness and cockiness provides the ideal counter to Bond's egotistical, blustery Sullivan, supremely convinced that he "can lick any man in the world!" When Jim knocks John L. off his throne, the former champ approaches his conqueror at the post-fight reception, hands over his engraved championship belt and, in quiet, even whispered, tones, discusses Corbett's new style of "gentlemanly" boxing before turning and gallantly walking back through the crowd, triumphant in defeat.

As demonstrated by Corbett afterwards, during his conversation with Victoria Ware (Alexis Smith), his sponsor and object of his affection, *both* proud men have been humbled by the experience. And Walsh doesn't spoil the mood with a typical Hollywood romantic embrace; he shows Jim and the fiery, independent Victoria having yet another argument.

Although the real Sullivan had pawned his belt years before his fight with Corbett, this fictional event provides an impeccable climax for the film. It is the most subtly moving

Gentleman Jim (Warner Bros., 1942; directed by Raoul Walsh). In this boxing classic, Ward Bond (left as John L. Sullivan) gives one of his most understated, heartfelt performances during this poignant scene with star Errol Flynn (as James J. Corbett, who has just defeated him in the ring).

scene in all of Bond's work and, arguably, Walsh's, as well. It is difficult to find a bad film performance by Bond, but Sullivan, his first fully realized period characterization involving the use of an accent (which never falters), provides a rare example of perfect casting. Ward's solid beefcake physical condition (which was superior to Sullivan's) also adds to the authenticity of his acting.

The real Sullivan died at age 59, from the effects of prizefighting *and* a longtime overindulgence in both food and alcohol. In the film, Bond is shown regularly drinking beer as part of Sullivan's training exercises. (His own later life *and* death would eerily parallel Sullivan's.) In today's award-ridden culture, this performance, perhaps his finest in a non–Ford film, could be called "Oscar worthy."

Flynn, six years younger, nearly 50 pounds lighter, and only an inch shorter than Bond, was an equally fine choice. An excellent, if underrated, actor, he clearly was also as handsome as it gets. Similar to Bond's Sullivan-like hairstyle and mustache, Flynn's high, combed back coiffure closely matches that of the real Corbett.

Though every detail in the film may not be historically accurate, these two actors capture the very essence of the real men. In fact, all the roles are well cast, providing a rocksolid element in a great Walsh film. Alan Hale, who dances while singing an Irish song, is at his apex; as is Jack Carson, whose gift for physical comedy is well on display.

There is a lot of Errol Flynn in this version of Corbett. At one point, he tells Victoria, "I can probably drink more than anybody in the world." The morning after Jim's first San Francisco knockout, he and his pal Walter Lowrie (Carson) wake up together in a Salt Lake City hotel bed, having no memory of how they got there!

In the nation's capital, Wild Bill Donovan informed Ford that Ellis Zacharias' Navy cryptographers had broken the Japanese code in time to learn about Yamamoto's plans for the attack on Midway. Admiral Chester W. Nimitz, Commander in Chief of the U.S. Pacific Fleet, was already bolstering the island's defenses, including the deployment of the aircraft carriers *Enterprise, Hornet* (both of which had participated in the Doolittle Raid) and *Yorktown*. Having gained little rest after returning from the Pacific, Ford headed right back in mid–May, initially on a DC-3 to San Francisco, and then aboard a destroyer for the four-day voyage to Pearl Harbor. During a brief layover in the City by the Bay, he had drinks at the Treasure Island Officers' Club with Eugene O'Neill, who praised *The Long Voyage Home* as the greatest film adaptation of any of his plays.

Ford was amazed at how the Pacific base at Pearl Harbor had risen like a phoenix from the ashes and, just one day later, was on a flight to Midway with photographer's mate Jack MacKenzie, the 20-year-old son of Scottish-born cinematographer Jack MacKenzie, Sr., who had shot scores of films for various Hollywood studios. (He had worked on *Mary of Scotland* and filmed Bond in *23½ Hours Leave* [1937], *Fight for Your Lady* [1937], *Hawaii Calls* [1938], *The Girl from Mexico* [1939], and *Mexican Spitfire* [1940].) A third cameraman, U.S. Navy Lieutenant Kenneth M. Pier, shot aerial and sea combat footage with a small 16mm unit while flying on a plane launched from the *Hornet*.

During the early hours of June 3, 1942, the Japanese fleet was spotted by a patrol plane and the troops readied themselves for combat. Ford ordered MacKenzie to shoot his footage atop a generator plant, where he could focus on the faces of the pilots. Contrary to all the "rules" of documentary filmmaking, Ford told him that the shots of planes in combat could always be "faked" later. The director then found his own perch in the airfield's control tower, ready to deliver a running commentary by telephone to the C.O. as he operated his camera with the other hand.

The enemy attacked at dawn the following morning, raining down bombs and strafing the airfield with machine-gun fire that riddled the runway and control tower. Bullets and shrapnel buzzed all around Ford, who, as he kept filming the action in vivid color, suddenly felt a powerful burning sensation and saw the color of deep red on his left forearm. He'd been wounded by a piece of shrapnel but continued to capture the most effective compositions he could, especially the faces of U.S. servicemen engaged in the battle. (One shot of Marines raising a flag amidst all the hellfire was so striking that Ford later had to add narration insuring viewers that the event "actually happened.")

The attack on the atoll was only a prelude to the actual sea battle, during which the U.S. Navy soundly defeated the Japanese, sinking four aircraft carriers and a cruiser (while losing only one carrier and a destroyer) before Yamamoto ordered his remaining forces to retreat. The victory turned the tide of the Pacific War: the Japanese offensive campaign, which had quickly conquered the Philippines, Malaya and the Dutch East Indies (Singapore), was now placed on the defensive.

Back on the island, the wounded Ford and young MacKenzie filmed the military and human costs of the battle, including a memorial service, PT boats carrying flag-draped coffins out to sea, and a shot of FDR's son, Major James "Jimmy" Roosevelt, saluting his fellow Marines who had fallen in combat. Ford then stowed all the footage and hopped on the first available flight to Pearl Harbor, where he climbed aboard a transport ship bound for the mainland. On June 18, the *Hollywood Reporter* boldly reported that he had been wounded while filming the Battle of Midway, but he hastily had his footage printed, wrote his own orders, forged Wild Bill Donovan's signature to them, and left Tinsel Town before any more publicity might hamper his efforts.

As soon as Ford returned to the Field Photo's office in Washington, he broke down the footage and ordered Robert Parrish to catch a flight to Hollywood, where the editor could work without any interference from government publicists or military brass. "Report to your mother," he insisted.

"What about orders?" asked Parrish.

"Fuck 'em," said Ford.[12]

Parrish stayed with his mother, dressed in civilian garb, and slipped onto the lot at 20th Century–Fox to edit *The Battle of Midway*, which was then turned over to Dudley Nichols, who wrote the narration. Back in Los Angeles, Ford found the script too flowery, so he brought in his old pal Jim McGuinness to give the prose a more personal tone, one that would "interest the mothers of America."[13] Ford then brilliantly used the voices of seasoned colleagues Henry Fonda, Jane Darwell, Donald Crisp and Irving Pichel, all of whom were on the lot, acting in William Wellman's powerhouse Western *The Ox-Bow Incident*, based on Walter Van Tilburg Clark's novel about the lynching of three innocent men (one of whom is played movingly by Francis Ford) accused of cattle rustling.

Fonda, Wayne and Bond's frequent companion on hell-raising cruises aboard the *Araner*, was 37, married, and the father of three children; but immediately after shooting his final scene for *The Ox-Bow Incident*, he enlisted at the Los Angeles Naval Headquarters. There was no fanfare, due to Fonda's insistence that his agent keep the event under wraps, so no photographers would be present. Hank had told his wife, "I don't want to be in a fake war in a studio.... I want to be with real sailors, not extras."[14]

Fonda's buddy James Stewart, whose family had a distinguished military record, attempted to enlist in the Army Air Corps, but was rejected for being 10 pounds underweight. At 6'4", he was too skinny to fight. For the next month, he gorged himself on candy and bananas, and washed it all down with beer, a regimen that made him fit for service. In the 10 months following the attack on Pearl Harbor, 2,700 actors, directors, writers, cinematographers and technicians (12-percent of the film industry work force) left Hollywood behind for military service.

Staying one step ahead of the Navy, Ford moved Robert Parrish to a film lab in the San Fernando Valley to work on the sound dubbing for *Midway*. They argued over the sentimental nature of the narration, but eventually completed the film and flew back to Washington, where Donovan set up a screening for FDR. Although a composite print had already been made, Ford, fearing that the President wouldn't pay much attention to the film, ordered Parrish to insert the shot he'd taken of his son, Jimmy, in the middle of the memorial service scene. The unexpected interruption in the soundtrack caught the attention of everyone present: the President and First Lady, New Deal architect and presidential adviser Harry Hopkins, and Admiral William D. Leahy, FDR's senior naval aide.

After the screening, the President, visibly moved, expressed his desire for every American mother to see *The Battle of Midway*. A rousing premiere at New York's Radio City Music Hall was followed by 20th Century–Fox's distribution of 500 Technicolor prints across the nation during September 1942. (Twenty-five years later, when interviewed by Peter Bogdanovich, Ford completely forgot, or perhaps disregarded, the contribution of Jack MacKenzie, Jr., when he claimed, "I did all of it — we only had one camera."[15])

By this time, the studios were under the watchful eye of the Bureau of Motion Pictures (BMP), a branch of the OWI, with one officer, Lowell Mellett, at headquarters in Washington, and another, Nelson Poynter, at an office in Hollywood. Although he knew absolutely nothing about the cinema, in particular how "film grammar" communicated to an audience, Poynter, aided by his staff, cooked up *The Government Informational Manual for the Motion Picture Industry*, which, much like the Production Code of 1934, included a litany of "dos and don'ts," but in this case to guide writers, producers and directors on how to depict the objectives of the U.S. and its unimpeachable allies (to replace a planet plagued by want, fear and persecution with a "new world" of freedom) in the best possible light.

Prior to the establishment of the BMP in June 1942, Wayne made two films, *The Spoilers*, with Marlene Dietrich and Randolph Scott, for Universal, and *In Old California*, with Binnie Barnes and Albert Dekker, for Republic. Although both are Westerns, Duke's characters singlehandedly fight like hell to bring home the wartime message that the *only* way to stop evildoers from stealing the property of others is "might makes right." As noted by Randy Roberts and James S. Olson, "John Wayne became a de facto propaganda machine during the war."[16]

Always nervous from pent-up energy when he wasn't working, Duke was loaned out to MGM, where he took second billing to Joan Crawford in *Reunion in France*, directed by Jules Dassin, who began shooting on June 30. MGM mogul Louis B. Mayer truly believed in the motto he created for his studio's films: *ars gratia artis* (art for art's sake). Every aspect of a production had to reek of glamorous perfection, from the elegantly dressed and coiffed stars, to the finely crafted dialogue, to the lighting, art direction, and musical scores.

Everything was a glossy, fantastical version of human existence, the way "L. B." *wanted* it to be, and very little of what is depicted in MGM's Golden Age films bears resemblance to reality. Occasionally an exception was slipped through a rare crack by a wily (Warner Bros.–style) director, but Jules Dassin certainly didn't achieve such a feat with *Reunion in France*, in which Crawford, in appearance and performance, might as well be tripping the light fantastic opposite Clark Gable in *Dancing Lady* (1933) or any other of her MGM films of the previous decade.

The MGM approach to depicting the war was to hire five writers to make it fit into the gloss and glamour mold, with Crawford playing Michele de la Becque, a French socialite, who is stripped of her property and wealth by the *Boche*, who also whisk away her fiancé, an industrialist turned Nazi collaborator. Joining the Resistance, she aids Pat Talbot (Wayne), an American flying with the RAF Eagle Squadron who has been shot down behind enemy lines. Talbot escapes, Michele is reunited with her fiancé (actually a Resistance fighter who has been "working undercover") and, if there weren't a few swastikas hanging around, the glossy MGM version of France would appear as if no German occupation had occurred.

Officials at the BMP hated the film, and more than a few suggested that women's fashions were its most important element. Journalists agreed that using the war as background for a costume drama was in seriously bad taste; and, this time, Duke also was criticized for being unconvincing in his role. By this time, however, not even an elegant, top-billed MGM star like Crawford could alter the fact that *Reunion in France* was seen as a "John Wayne Movie," and his legion of fans helped make it one of the studio's top 15 grossers of 1943. As noted by Randy Roberts and James S. Olson, "Even a bad Wayne movie made money."[17]

While Dassin was putting the finishing touches on *Reunion in France*, Duke began another loan-out project, *Pittsburgh*, which director Lewis Seiler began shooting at Universal on August 26, 1942. Again forming a triangle with Marlene Dietrich and Randolph Scott, he was cast as Charles "Pittsburgh" Markham, a ruthless big shot in the coal industry who loses everything but rises again to become a selfless home-front patriot working for Uncle Sam's war effort.

Left: World War II Wayne (Republic, 1940s). Though John Wayne did not serve in the U.S. military during World War II, his many popular wartime films created the image of a stand-up, heroic American fighting man embraced by a nation whose sons, husbands and fathers had been hurtled into harm's way. Ironically, he became the very symbol of U.S. military might and right. *Right:* Ward Bond (1942). Though he generally managed to keep his epilepsy a secret, Bond was officially classified 4-F during World War II. His supporting roles in war pictures gained him new fans, to whom he was most generous. While many Hollywood celebrities sent out small, preprinted "signed" photographs, Bond personally autographed this double-weight portrait, either in 8 × 10 or 11 × 14, for his admirers.

On this occasion, the BMP's Nelson Poynter was ecstatic about a Tinsel Town product, a true cinematic sermon saluting the industrial workers turning out essential materials for the U.S. war machine. The stylistic opposite of MGM's fairytale attempt, *Pittsburgh*, however, was viewed by Lowell Mellett and OWI officials in Washington as lacking any real entertainment value for audiences, who would be put off by the blatant propaganda of several lengthy, semi-documentary sequences of actual industrial footage and endless passages of boring, preachy dialogue.

This wordy, visually static film following the dictates of the *Government Informational Manual* proved box-office poison; and, this time, a bad John Wayne movie didn't make money, a phenomenon proving the cinematic ignorance of a Washington agency like the BMP. In the future, the studio moguls would produce films containing wartime propaganda, but they would do it the *Hollywood* way.

Only Tinsel Town could have produced *Hitler—Dead or Alive*, an independent project that began shooting during August 1942. The only time Bond received top billing in a feature, this romp about a trio of convicts (the others being Warren Hymer and Wayne's buddy Paul Fix) who are promised a million bucks if they can parachute into the Fatherland and

Hitler—Dead or Alive (Charles House Productions, 1942; directed by Nick Grinde). Convict turned commando Steve Maschik (Bond), on a million-dollar mission to capture and shave the Führer, hijacks a Kraut beer truck (driver and passenger unidentified), in one of the most ludicrous Hollywood propaganda films made during World War II. The man who sacrifices himself to eliminate Adolf, Maschik proved to be Bond's only top-billed feature film role.

apprehend Adolf, is one of the most ludicrous propaganda products made during World War II.

Drawing on his experience appearing in Robinson, Cagney and Bogart films at Warner Bros., Bond fit right into the role of "underworld czar" Steve Maschik, who impressively shoots down a German plane with a Tommy Gun, highjacks a Kraut beer truck, and ultimately captures Hitler by using a wrestling chokehold.

Aside from "hating clarinets," Adolf has another unique feature by which he can be recognized: his mustache. And the way to distinguish the real Hitler from all his doubles is to locate the scar underneath this facial hair. Reportedly, the poor genocidal megalomaniac was once severely beaten and left for dead by a pack of hostile students wielding beer steins.

"This guy's goin' to get turned into a mess of dog meat!" Maschik promises. While shaving off the captive leader's 'stache, Steve calls him "Baby."

S.S. officers soon catch up with Maschik and the clean-shaven Hitler. Considered one of the doubles, Adolf is whacked by his own men, who then turn their guns on the American and his German underground aides. Initially interested in the mission solely for the pay, Maschik has become appalled by the Nazis' murders of women and children, which he makes quite apparent before he dies. (Once more, Bond somehow doesn't overact, even while shouting absurd dialogue.) A martyr to the cause of world freedom, Steve Maschik is hailed as "a great man — a great American," and the million dollars is donated to purchase new airplanes for the war effort.

Bond worked on the Universal quickie "Sin City" with director Ray Enright during August and September 1942. This pseudo–Western set in the 1910s oil fields features Ward as saloon proprietor Rock Delaney, who is saved from a lynching by Martin "Dude" McNair (Broderick Crawford), only to be bumped off later by "Kentucky" Jones (Ralf Harolde). Constance Bennett, Patric Knowles and Leo Carrillo also appear in what ultimately was retitled *Sin Town*: after all, the small population, depleted by frequent murders, didn't rank the place as a "city."

Leaving *Sin Town* for MGM, Bond, playing Walter Brennan's bodyguard, became *Slightly Dangerous* (1943) for Lana Turner. At 20th Century–Fox, he was confined to two scenes of the Alice Faye–John Payne Technicolor musical *Hello, Frisco, Hello* (1943) as "Sharkey," proprietor of a prominent joint on the Barbary Coast.

Concerned with another coast entirely, Ford left for England to organize Field Photo crews to film "Operation Torch," the Allied invasion of North Africa, to begin on November 8, when British and American troops would land at Oran, Algiers and Casablanca. Ford, Jack Pennick and cameraman Robert Johannes traveled to Algiers, where they joined U.S. Army Captain J. E. Simmerman, who commanded "D" Company, the 13th Armored Regiment of the First Armored Division.

After reaching Tunisia in a British transport ship, Ford ran into his civilian boss, Darryl Zanuck, who was armed to the teeth, driving a Chevrolet Coupe, writing a diary of his adventures, and making a documentary called *At the Front*. Everyone in "D" Company, including Ford, viewed his status as a renegade "glory hunter" with contempt. (The self-proclaimed "combat soldier," who still was collecting his civilian pay, later ran afoul of a Senate Investigating Committee, resulting in his resignation.)

At Soul El Arba, Ford, Pennick and Johannes were forced to take cover in a foxhole when German dive bombers attacked. The situation was grim, until a squadron of British Spitfires arrived, and Ford enthusiastically filmed the ensuing dogfight directly over their heads. When one of the Spitfires shot down a German JU-88, the bombardier emerged from the flaming wreckage that had consumed his comrades. Ford commanded his two men to hop into a nearby jeep, which he drove to the site of the crash.

The German soldier, who understood English, surrendered to Ford, who turned him over to a Free French lieutenant. But when the French officer began brutally interrogating the prisoner, Ford intervened, ignoring the lieutenant's barrage of profanity as he transferred him to the more humane Captain Simmerman.

Mary Ford "did her part" on the home front by accepting the vice presidency of the Hollywood Canteen, which had been opened by John Garfield and Bette Davis in a vacant nightclub at 1415 Cahuenga Boulevard on October 17, 1942. Davis was president, Jules Stein served as business manager, and members of 42 Hollywood unions worked as volunteers.

Two big bands were swingin' for a packed house of 1,600 servicemen each night, and top stars, rounded up by entertainment chairman Bob Hope, performed and helped to serve refreshments to the troops. Kay Kyser lined up the best bands in the land, including those led by Tommy Dorsey, Duke Ellington and Harry James. Since California still outlawed miscegenation, the Canteen was forced to honor "partial segregation," but Willabelle Muse (wife of prolific singer, songwriter and character actor Clarence Muse, who later appeared in *The Sun Shines Bright*, Ford's 1953 remake of *Judge Priest*) worked hard to line up suitable ebony hostesses to dance with African American servicemen.

In December 1942, 20th Century–Fox's "School for Saboteurs" offered Bond third billing, plus a promotion all the way to Chief of the FBI. Carl Steelman (George Sanders), a German-American attorney, is working to infiltrate a Nazi sabotage operation and investigate the enemy's training program for saboteurs. Double agents galore, on the home front and in the Fatherland, certainly complicate matters for the intrepid spy, who executes a series of bold extrications and escapes, eventually leading to the capture and "disposal" of a half dozen saboteurs and the arrest of his father's physician, Dr. Herman Baumer (Sig Ruman), a Nazi sympathizer and informant. Bringing it in line with other recent Hollywood propaganda efforts, the studio released the film with the sensationalistic title *They Came to Blow Up America*.

On March 4, 1943, at Hollywood's Ambassador Hotel, the U.S. Navy received a Best Documentary (Short Subject) Academy Award for Ford's *The Battle of Midway*. It was one of four such Oscars awarded to military films that year: the others being Frank Capra's first U.S. Army-produced "Why We Fight" episode, *Prelude to War*; Artkino Pictures' *Moscow Strikes Back*, narrated by Edward G. Robinson; and the Australia News and Information Bureau's *Kokoda Front Line*.

Living close to the studios, Wayne wasn't as heavily affected by the home-front rationing and shortages that many film industry personnel complained about, especially as U.S. involvement moved well into its second year. On March 31, director William A. Seiter completed RKO's *A Lady Takes a Chance*, a romantic comedy set prior to the war, pairing Wayne (as Western rodeo star Duke Hudkins) with Jean Arthur (as *New Yorker* writer Mollie J. Truesdale). Working with such an intelligent and "effortlessly" funny actress like Arthur sharpened Duke's own comic abilities, both verbal (the keen sense of timing required to parry and thrust with Robert Ardrey's well-crafted dialogue) and nonverbal (the believable, often charming, expressions and gestures that were becoming more familiar with every performance). This "cowboy" variation on *It Happened One Night* (1934) was a major hit with the press and a public growing tired of incessant cinematic flag waving.

Conservative members of Congress, too, were beginning to question the value of the blatantly propagandistic films pushed by Roosevelt's OWI. After the agency's budget was slashed by 75 percent, both Lowell Mellett and Nelson Poynter resigned from the BMP. As a result, Duke spent less time making films and more time raising hell.

Marlene Dietrich had convinced him of the need for a "business manager," so he signed on with Bo Roos, a slick hustler who feigned an "aristocratic" background and loved to "manage" his clients' money into his own pocket while drinking, playing cards, enjoying the outdoor life, and taking expensive junkets to Mexico. Prior to the attack on Pearl Harbor, he had taken Wayne, Bond, Ray Milland and Fred MacMurray along on a trip to explore "investment opportunities" (and other things) in Mexico City. Milland's local connection was a young prostitute named Esperanza Baur Diaz Ceballos, whom he called "his Mexican woman." By the time the Americanos headed back to the States, "Chata" had become *Duke's* Mexican woman, and he and Milland, who had been good buddies, had nothing more to do with each other.

For two years, Wayne, who often stayed away from home for days, usually getting inebriated with Bond and Grant Withers (whose chronic alcoholism stretched back more than a decade, when he was briefly married to Loretta Young), met Chata for trysts in Yuma, Arizona, or Mexico City. Finally, in May 1943, Duke, who had just signed a new, more lucrative contract with Republic, separated from Josephine and left his family (much to the disgust of Catholic friends, particularly Dolores Hope and Mary Ford) to shack up with Chata at the Chateau Marmont and then at the home of Paul Fix. To keep a lid on the sexual shenanigans, Herb Yates had arranged for a U.S. visa and residency documents, capping off the charade by putting Chata under contract for $150 per week, even though she never appeared in a film, nor did anything else, for the studio.

Mary Ford wrote to Jack about Duke's request for a divorce, claiming he had lost his mind and needed some sense beaten into him. Pappy responded by offering some rather ambiguous "advice" in a letter to Wayne, who wrote back, telling his mentor that he'd already made his choice, claiming he didn't even care to see his four children.

With Ford far off, risking his life to make combat films, Wayne and Bond would often show up at the Odin Street house to "comfort" Mary, who, in a June 1, 1943, letter to Jack, admitted, "Bond's drunk three fourths of the time and as Pat says, 'When the cat's away how the mice will play.' Guess without you they're bound for destruction."[18] On one inebriated occasion, Bond passed out on Ford's bed and, when rudely awakened by Wayne to carry on their carousing elsewhere, he told his pal to get lost. Instead, the Duke grabbed a bottle of vodka, soaked the Judge and set his best buddy on fire.

In July, Jack wrote back to Mary, revealing that he was praying the war soon would end, and he could be back home with her, their children and grandchildren, and, of course, the *Araner*. "I'm tough to live with," he admitted, "heaven knows and Hollywood didn't help — Irish and genius don't mix well but you know you're the only woman I've ever loved." In a return missive, she told him that she thanked God every day for their marriage. To celebrate their upcoming 25th anniversary in 1945, she suggested getting roaring drunk on brandy amidst a gang of "equally intoxicated friends" aboard the *Araner*.[19] (Hopefully, the plans didn't include Wayne's dabbling with vodka and a cigarette lighter.)

Duke recently had received word from Washington that the U.S. Army contingent of the Field Photographic Unit still needed men, so he actually began to fill out enlistment papers; but, true to form, Republic intervened, sending him to Perreah, Utah, about 50 miles from Kanab, to make *In Old Oklahoma*, which director Albert Rogell began shooting in late July. On August 1, Wayne wrote to Ford, explaining the latest delay and that he'd give enlistment another try after the new film wrapped in September.

Set in 1906, *In Old Oklahoma* stars Wayne (in another take on the usual Republic plot) as Daniel Somers, Spanish-American War hero and rival of unscrupulous oilman James E. "Hunk" Gardner (Albert Dekker), eventually traveling to Washington to consult President Theodore Roosevelt (Sidney Blackmer). Only after much sabotage by Gardner, who is beaten senseless in the obligatory climactic fistfight, does Somers win Catherine Allen (Martha Scott) and a square deal for all concerned: both he and Gardner, the "little fellers," and the "Indians," under whose land much of the oil resides.

George "Gabby" Hayes appears in his familiar role of a stagecoach driver, "Desprit Dean," supported by Wayne cronies Grant Withers and Paul Fix (painted up as the "Chero-kee Kid," Gardner's "half-breed" henchman, a character the BMP had considered a threat to the nation's veneer of racial and ethnic "unity"). Once again, the heroic Wayne allowed Republic to boast one of the most commercially successful films of the year. Duke and the film both received the praise of critics and, ultimately, the BMP, whose officials were primarily pleased with the finished product.

During August 1943, Ford, Jack Pennick and cameraman Jack Swain flew to New Delhi, India, where Mark Armistead was implementing a process officially called the Intelligence Documentary Photographic Project, but referred to as "Ippy Dippy Intelligence," which used Mitchell 35mm cameras for shooting aerial survey footage. Shortly after their arrival, Ford sought out Fox producer Gene Markey, who currently was working for a Naval Intel-ligence unit attached to the staff of Lord Louis Mountbatten, and knew all the important Allied officers in the country. While hobnobbing with top military men, regaling them with his stories of Hollywood, he was laying the groundwork for Wild Bill Donovan to establish the OSS in India.

While in the Far East, Ford, Pennick, Swain and Guy Bolte flew to Rangoon to aid director Irving Asner in completing *Victory in Burma*, a documentary about mercenary priest Father James Stuart's leadership of a guerrilla band of Kachin tribesmen officially named the 101 Detachment of the OSS. Bolte was assigned the dangerous task of accom-panying the unit into combat to shoot the footage, aided by two cameramen, Bob Rhea and Arthur "Butch" Meehan, another son of a major Hollywood cinematographer. Unfor-tunately, young Meehan was killed while filming the guerrillas behind enemy lines, a tragedy that hit Ford particularly hard.

Though Wayne had completed his forms to join Field Photo, Republic secured another deferment, this time for him to star as "Wedge" Donovan in *The Fighting Seabees*, a tribute to the U.S. Navy Construction Battalions (C.B.s), which had been established at Davisville, Rhode Island, during the summer of 1942. A BMP-friendly film from the outset (only the egotistical female war correspondent, Constance Chesley [Susan Hayward], required an overhaul), this Edward Ludwig-directed propaganda epic is carried by a John Wayne who, not only becomes a hero, but does so by taking the initiative to commit suicide while using his bulldozer like a tank. With Grant Withers and Paul Fix again on hand, *The Fighting Seabees* kept Duke busy from September 20 through early December 1943, at Republic, the Iverson Ranch, and in San Diego, where a few location scenes were filmed.

Executives at 20th Century–Fox had been planning an adaptation of *Phantom Filly*, George Agnew Chamberlain's novel about harness racing, since its publication two years earlier. Winston Miller's screenplay, titled *Home in Indiana*, was written as part of a package deal for Howard Hawks; but the film, which was produced between early September 1943 and mid–January 1944, was directed by Henry Hathaway, who crafted one of his finest films, shot in Technicolor by Edward Cronjager, who received an Academy Award nomination. Today, the film has a timeless quality due in part to its complete lack of references to World War II. (The only hint that it was made during the conflict is the war bond plug included in the end title.)

The opening credits bill Lon McCallister, Jeanne Crain and June Haver as "three young players in their first featured roles," although McCallister already had played a major role in *Stage Door Canteen* (1943), as well as small or bit parts in 27 other films. He was 20 years old when Hathaway began shooting *Home in Indiana*, but the combination of his diminutive size, wardrobe changes and excellent acting make him very convincing as Sparke Thornton, an orphaned teenager slowly transitioning into adulthood. Crain, who was 18, accomplishes a similarly impressive metamorphosis as neighboring "tomboy" Charlotte "Char" Bruce.

Billed third, below Walter Brennan and Charlotte Greenwood, Bond plays Crain's father, horse trainer and driver Jed Bruce, who works for wealthy rancher Godaw Boole (Charles Dingle). During the racing scenes, Ward's large frame provides quite a contrast to McCallister's jockey-like physique. Gruff during his first meeting with Sparke, Jed quickly warms up when realizing he is the nephew of J. T. "Thunder" Bolt (Brennan), a racing legend devastated by Boole's treachery 18 years earlier.

African American actors George H. Reed and Willie Best, as horse handlers "Tuppy" and "Moe Rum," though constricted by period conventions, are a step up from the usual Uncle Tom characters, due to Hathaway's relatively sensitive direction of Miller's script. (Of course, no one would cast Best, a gifted comic, without expecting him to perform some of his trademark shtick.)

Produced simultaneously at Fox, *The Sullivans* (1944) is based on the true story of five brothers from Waterloo, Iowa, who all were serving aboard the U.S. Navy cruiser *Juneau* when it was sunk by the Japanese during the Battle of Guadalcanal on November 13, 1942. The young men, ranging in age from 20 to 27, had obtained special permission to serve together, but their deaths (and a similar incident involving the four Borgston brothers from Thatcher, Utah) prompted the "Special Separation Policies for Survivorship," protecting a family from the draft or combat duty if they already have lost members during military service. In April 1943, the navy launched the destroyer USS *The Sullivans*, which subsequently saw action in the Pacific.

Bond's character, Lieutenant Commander Robinson, was based on the naval officer who had the terrible task of breaking the news to Mr. and Mrs. Thomas Sullivan two months after all their sons had died. Though he appears in only one scene near the end of the film, the commander, required to be calm, diplomatic, and speak in a soothing tone, is one of the character types that Bond played best. Featuring fine performances from Thomas Mitchell, Selena Royle and Anne Baxter, the film did poor business until receiving the more eye-catching title *The Fighting Sullivans*.

More than ever, Wayne's leisure hours were spent with Bond. Like Duke, Ward had grown increasingly distant from his wife, who also aspired to the high-society scene which he loathed with a passion. After eight years of marriage to Doris, Ward could take no more. On October 15, 1943, he admitted that he no longer loved her, moved out, and checked into a room at the Beverly Hills Hotel. Having attempted to talk sense into Wayne, Mary Ford followed suit with Bond, who was carrying on as if he'd never been married. In a November 18 letter to Jack, she claimed that Ward "can't stand Doris and her sloppiness any longer."[20]

Doris' untidiness must have been Olympian, considering that, the further Ward sunk into his own debauched lifestyle, the more Wayne laughed and goaded him on, playing into his buddy's boundless ego. While Doris had found her husband's nightly carousing, attention seeking, and often crude humor less than amusing, Duke intensified the whole shebang, and no amount of baiting and gouging could keep his best buddy seriously angry for too long. Even being set on fire had not affected the Judge's 14-year friendship and working relationship with the Duke.

Eventually Mary realized that neither man had any intention of returning to his wife, and she was pleased when Wayne offered to carve turkeys for the Thanksgiving servicemen's dinner at the Hollywood Canteen. Bond, too, had agreed to serve up some birds, but got so loaded beforehand that he could have posed quite a danger to himself and others with a carving knife in his hand.

Ward was forgiven for his Thanksgiving inebriation when he redeemed himself at Christmas, joining Duke in lavishing gifts on Mary, who had spent the previous evening with their estranged wives. By the time the two "Santa Clauses" had completed their Yuletide visit, the Odin Street house was loaded with perfume, flowers and all manner of appropriate presents. Mary wrote to Jack, who now was in China, that his two boys had definitely been "over-generous."[21]

On December 2, Ford and Pennick had joined Bill Donovan on a flight to Chunking, General Chiang Kai-shek's wartime capitol, where they wanted to set up an OSS base, a move strongly opposed by General Tai-Li, the head of Chinese intelligence. Donovan benefited greatly from Ford's connection to Flying Tiger General Claire Chennault, who allowed them to integrate an undercover OSS unit within his outfit, the 14th U.S. Air Force. Ford spent the next two months instructing the men of the 14th in the methods of the Ippy Dippy process, and personally shooting footage during aerial reconnaissance flights between Chunking and Kunming, the northern terminus of Chaing's supply line, the Burma Road.

After returning to New Delhi on January 14, 1944, Ford and Pennick flew back to Washington. Ordered to meet with Donovan, Ford received a promotion to Captain and assigned the monumental task of organizing and directing the filming of the largest military undertaking in world history: "Operation Overlord," the Allied invasion of Europe, to occur somewhere along the coast of Normandy.

Although Wayne still had failed to enlist, he did join a USO tour of the South Pacific and Australia, using his "entertainment" of the troops as a cover for an assignment from Donovan to become an OSS "informant," specifically to prepare a report on General MacArthur, whose relations with Wild Bill were poor at best. Donovan believed that a "celebrity" might gain access to information off limits to official operatives; but, after Wayne returned in early 1944, he had very little to offer.

The Hollywood publicity machine, however, painted Duke like a returning soldier, with movie magazines publishing photos of him "reunited" with his four children. The fact that he no longer lived with his family and was seeking a divorce from his wife were conveniently ignored in favor of plugging *Tall in the Saddle*, the first of seven features required by his new RKO contract, scheduled to run from 1944 to 1951.

Ford's involvement with the military during the war heavily influenced his politics, which began to move further to the right, eroding his 1937 declaration that he was a "Socialistic Democrat —*always* left." In February 1944, Wayne and Bond were founding members of the ultra-conservative, anti–Communist Motion Picture Alliance for the Preservation of American Ideals. Eventually, Ford joined other Irish Catholics, including his pal Kevin James McGuinness and director Leo McCarey, in denouncing the Marxist anti-religious and generally anti–American ideals he heard being voiced in some circles, and spent some time discussing the matter with Wayne. Other founders included the virulently anti-labor Walt Disney, who infamously ruled his workers with an iron hand, directors Victor Fleming, Norman Taurog and King Vidor, screenwriters Borden Chase (who later co-wrote, with Charles Schnee, the screenplay for Howard Hawks' *Red River*), John Lee Mahin and Morrie Ryskind, and such top actors as Gary Cooper, Donald Crisp, Irene Dunne, Clark Gable, Adolphe Menjou (whose ultra-rightwing beliefs bordered on fascism), Pat O'Brien, Ginger Rogers, Barbara Stanwyck and Robert Taylor.

John T. McManus, a journalist for the left-leaning New York newspaper *PM* identified director Sam Wood as the leader of a Hollywood "handful of noted reactionaries ... [whose] stated purpose [was] running a witch-hunt."[22]

The Fighting Seabees, recommended by the BMP for "special OWI distribution in liberated areas" and released in the U.S. on March 10, 1944, was a smash hit with audiences, even if reviewers were beginning to tire of Republic's recycling of the same formula, whether Western or war film. Randy Roberts and James S. Olson noted:

> With each war film Wayne increasingly came to embody the American fighting man.... According to Republic's schmaltzy formula, his screen image and public persona emerged entirely intertwined with the role of the American hero. His war pictures were really little different from his Westerns; he played only variations of the same hard moral man — ornery and uncompromising, but truthful, loyal, and likable. Now, however, he was the only one to play it, and America desperately needed a hero to celebrate.[23]

(Interestingly, Republic's *Fighting Seabees* quickly spawned an imitator. Filmed at Columbia from January 24 through March 31, and released on August 3, 1944, *Mr. Winkle Goes to War* concludes with a meek U.S. Army mechanic using a bulldozer to prevent Japanese attackers from wiping out his platoon. Although wounded, Winkle recovers to be declared a war hero. Herb Yates did it with John Wayne, so Harry Cohn followed suit his resident tough guy: Edward G. Robinson!)

At Grauman's Chinese Theatre on March 15, *December 7th*, after all the controversy and heavy editing required by the U.S. Navy, followed in the footsteps of *The Battle of Midway* by winning a Best Documentary (Short Subject) Academy Award. This time, the statuette was awarded to the Field Photographic Unit. Another OSS film, *War Department Report*, which covered the military and industrial capabilities of the Axis Powers, also was nominated in the Best Documentary (Feature) category. Reflecting on the content of these films, Joseph McBride noted:

> From *The Battle of Midway* onward, the films shot by Field Photo show a very Fordian preoccupation with mourning the human cost of war.... Sometimes Ford found that he had to mourn the deaths of his own men in Field Photo. Twelve of them died during the war, several in their early manhood.[24]

In March 1944, MGM released *A Guy Named Joe*, a wartime fantasy film that had begun shooting more than a year earlier. Several objections from the War Department and the PCA had delayed production until February 15, 1943, but a near-fatal auto accident on March 31 that put actor Van Johnson out of commission until early July, plus extensive location shooting at Luke Field, Arizona, and Randolph Field, Texas, accounted for most of the delays. Johnson, who had been in critical condition, was nearly replaced, but star Spencer Tracy convinced them that his pal, director Victor Fleming, could "shoot around" the young actor until he was well enough to resume work.

Officials in Washington initially considered the premise about a dead pilot's spirit returning to aid those still fighting of no use to the war effort, and recommended that the project, originally titled "Three Guys Named Joe," be shelved. One of the "guys," Al Yackey, provided Bond with one of the most visible, well-developed characters he ever played in a feature film. As the unflappable, soft-spoken, optimistic bosom buddy of Pete Sandridge (Tracy), he enjoyed ample screen time as Yackey maintained his close friendship with "his best pal's girl," Dorinda Durston (Irene Dunne), while also attaining the rank of Colonel.

A Guy Named Joe benefits from Bond's solid, believable presence, and the undeniable chemistry between Tracy and Dunne, especially during several scenes featuring overlapping dialogue. The screenplay by Dalton Trumbo features great wit and some dialogue exchanges that flew right over the heads of the censors. Though the film suffers from an unconvincing happy ending (the original conclusion, in which Dorinda flies a suicide mission, was nixed by the PCA) and the age gap between Dunne and Johnson (she was old enough to be his mother), the excellent performances and the inclusion of a strong female character are two of many elements that make this one of Bond's best non–Ford films.

In mid–April, Wayne (fresh with another deferment acquired by Republic) and Bond both reported to RKO to shoot *Tall in the Saddle* with director Edwin L. Marin. With sultry film-noir dame Ella Raines added as feisty cowgirl Arleta Harolday, who reluctantly, eventually becomes Duke's love interest, the film pitched Wayne's ranch hand, Rocklin, against Bond's Robert Garvey, actually a bogus "judge" who attempts to swindle Clara Cardell (Audrey Long) out of her rightful inheritance. An action highlight is the climactic fistfight between Rocklin and Garvey in the "judge's office."

The *Tall in the Saddle* screenplay had been adapted especially for Wayne from the Gordon Ray Young novel by Michael Hogan and Paul Fix, who added two specific elements to the film: a major role for Bond; and a further development of Duke's signature walk. Since Wayne was living with Fix at the time, the two men had ample time to collaborate, until the latter's wife caught her husband in an affair with Ella Raines, prompting a quick ejection of Fix, plus Duke and Chata, from the premises.

On April 10, 1944, an official OSS document ordered that "John Ford was placed in charge of all Naval Allied Photographic endeavor on the European invasion." Eight days later, prior to leaving Washington for London to prepare for Operation Overlord, Ford was unexpectedly introduced to PT boat commander Lieutenant John Bulkeley when Mark Armistead came banging on the door of his room at the Carlton Hotel. After being inundated by the incessant pounding for several minutes, Ford, still in bed nursing a massive hangover, shouted, "Well, come on in, goddamn it!"

Armistead approached the extremely disheveled figure of the great film director fidgeting around beneath the covers, but his introduction of Bulkeley resulted in Captain Ford's springing out of his nest to stand at strict attention. "I'm proud to salute the man who rescued General MacArthur!" proclaimed Ford, buck naked.

In London, the OSS reported, "Commander Ford first undertook the gigantic task of analyzing the entire plan of the invasion, with the view in mind of deploying personnel to obtain maximum coverage. A serious shortage of both personnel and equipment existed for a task of this magnitude."

In a report to the OSS, Ford revealed that his job involved coordinating the camera installations of the U.S. Navy, U.S. Coast Guard, Britain, the Netherlands, Poland and France. Seriously short of manpower, he enlisted his friend, fellow director George Stevens, who led a group of 10 U.S. Army cameramen in covering the activities of these various units.[25] For the landing at Omaha Beach, Ford had hundreds of fixed cameras mounted on landing craft and tanks, to supplement the color and black-and-white footage being captured by his combat photographers.

Ford had told the men under his command that he would hit the beach with them on D-Day. Aboard the U.S.S. *Plunket*, he ordered Mark Armistead to be the second Field Photo member to land. Captain Ford would go *first*.

Around 8:00 A.M. on June 6, Ford and his cameramen, none of whom were allowed to carry weapons, left the ship aboard a DUKW landing craft, joining the others making their way through a maze of German mines. Amidst the shelling and wall of machine-gun fire, Ford could hear the troops vomiting as the crafts landed. He hit the beach, ran like hell and ordered his men to take positions behind any cover they could find.

He had told them to lie down while operating their cameras. No filmed event was worth the risk of getting killed or wounded while standing to get the shot. Incredibly, the unit suffered no serious casualties, and only one man, John Flynn, lost his camera, after being blown into the sea by an explosion. "Being a superb swimmer," recalled Ford, he "managed to swim to another destroyer."[26]

Five days after the appalling slaughter of D-Day, which Ford later remembered as "disconnected takes like unassembled shots to be spliced together afterward in a film," a sound motion picture "report" was shown to Winston Churchill in London, and copies were rushed to FDR in Washington and Josef Stalin in Moscow. The film has never been exhibited publicly, due to Ford's belief that the U.S. government was "afraid to show so many American casualties on the screen."[27] (One of the few people who has seen some of the footage is Steven Spielberg, whose incredibly realistic, staged "re-creation" of the event in *Saving Private Ryan* [1998] is the only version the public has seen. Since the actual filmed event has been viewed by so few, Ford and his fellow courageous Field Photo troops, who, totally unarmed, risked their lives to photograph the indescribably brave actions of the men of the U.S. military, many of whom never made it to the beach, did one hell of "a job of work.")

On June 6, 1944, Wayne and Bond, enjoying the pinnacle of their thespian game, were still at RKO making *Tall in the Saddle.* They both got a little banged up during the climactic fistfight (but most of this brawl was performed by stuntmen Fred Graham and Henry Wills). Having co-written the screenplay, Paul Fix also appears in the strong supporting cast with George "Gabby" Hayes, Elisabeth Risdon, Don Douglas, Russell Wade, Raymond Hatton and Ford Stock Company perennial Russell Simpson. The tailor-made role of Robert Garvey allowed Bond, who received third billing, enough screen time to develop the slick yet subtle, smooth-talking villain he again would play opposite Wayne in Republic's *Dakota* (1945).

About a week after D-Day, Ford, at a house on the Cherbourg Peninsula, met up with cinematographer Major William H. Clothier, who was commanding combat cameramen assigned to the Army Air Forces First Motion Picture Unit. One of the men now assigned to Clothier was Junius "Junior" Stout, son of another Hollywood cinematographer, Archie Stout, and a Navy Photographer's Mate First Class who had been one of Ford's lead cameramen during the Normandy landing.

Desperately needing to "unwind," Ford characteristically found a sleeping bag, crawled in, and began pounding down Calvados apple brandy. This continued for several days, until he ran out of booze. Resorting to stealing additional bottles from an officer's locker, he eventually ran into trouble with French guards after he wandered outside, too inebriated to remember his password. Clothier, after witnessing Ford urinating on himself in the sleeping bag, ordered Mark Armistead to escort him from the house.

Soon after, Armistead, aboard Lieutenant Bulkeley's PT boat, heard from Ford, who was on the heavy cruiser USS *Augusta*, asking to join them. When the two crafts converged, an extremely disheveled Ford was cabled across in a boson's chair. Getting reacquainted with Bulkeley, he mentioned MGM's preproduction plans for *They Were Expendable*. The film was to be based on W. L. White's bestseller about the lieutenant's command of the PT boat fleet in the Philippines, shortly after the attack on Pearl Harbor, a mission for which he was awarded the Medal of Honor in August 1942.

Ford came and went during the ensuing weeks, sometimes going ashore to witness more combat firsthand, at other times remaining aboard during running battles with E-boats, the German version of the U.S. PT boat (which the enemy called the *Schnellboot* or *S-boot*). Of these experiences with Ford, Bulkeley later recalled:

> John Ford made up a lot of stuff ... but I never challenged him. I was always very careful about that.... You don't argue with that man. And furthermore, you've got to recognize, as I did, that man is truly a genius.[28]

MGM had bought the rights to White's book in late 1942, and had asked Ford to direct it in April 1943, while he was in Washington. At that time, he didn't want to leave the Field Photo unit, but he did greatly appreciate White's honest account of the PT squadron, whose courageous men had evacuated General Arthur before being defeated and dispersed by Japanese forces. After *December 7th* won the Academy Award, Ford again decided to remain on active duty and not go on leave to make a feature film.

On the home front, Wayne received a shock when the Selective Service, needing extra manpower for major assaults in the Pacific, eliminated the majority of 2-A deferments "in support of national health, safety, or interest." He had been reclassified as 1-A, "available for military service," a status that immediately brought appeals from Republic's attorneys, arguing that the "national interest" was much better served by Duke's film performances than anything he could contribute to the military. Soon his classification was returned to 2-A.

Though he had been exempted from military combat by his epilepsy, the 4-F Bond faced two major personal battles. On July 7, 1944, after more than eight years of marriage, Doris Sellers Childs Bond was granted a divorce by Superior Court Judge George A. Dockweiler on grounds of mental cruelty, specifically that Ward "continually nagged her about the way she ran the house and reared her child from a previous marriage." Though he had been living like a bachelor for nearly nine months, Bond was undoubtedly despondent and, probably having attempted to self-medicate with more than a few libations, was hit by a large automobile while crossing a street in Hollywood.

The injury was critical. His left shin was fractured so severely that doctors were preparing to amputate when an attendant recognized Bond. Phone calls were placed, including one to Republic, where Wayne had just begun starring in a new Western, *Flame of Barbary Coast*, the previous day. The choice was not an easy one for Ward: sacrifice the leg *and* his career; or have it pinned and put in a cast, and hope gangrene didn't develop. Following extensive reconstructive surgery, he rallied; and after being bedridden for a week, proof of an imminent recovery was provided when his infamous, "fun-loving" sense of humor returned with a vengeance. But Bond took his lengthy recovery seriously, to the point where he gave up drinking (a period of sobriety which lasted for nearly three years).[29]

Directed by Joseph Kane, *Flame of Barbary Coast* is yet another Republic Western, this time disguised as a $600,000 "epic," with much of its 91-minute running time devoted to turgid musical numbers. Worse than the pointless songs (and Robert De Grasse's endlessly tracking camera), this thinly plotted rip-off of MGM's *San Francisco* (1936) wastes two excellent actors in formulaic roles that could have been cast with contract players.

The usually believable Ann Dvorak, as the female lead, Ann "Flaxen" Tarry, the star performer at the Eldorado gambling joint, was a fine actress, but not a singer by any means. An actor since childhood, Dvorak had been a star player at Warner Bros. during the previous decade, but her marriage to English actor-director Leslie Fenton and war service as an ambulance driver in London had kept her away from Hollywood for four years.

Though the credits do not reveal who was involved in the voice recording, all but one of Dvorak's numbers were overdubbed during post-production. The difference between her quiet voice and that of the woman whose singing is supposedly emanating from her mouth is painfully obvious. (The sequences often consist of long shots, during which the tracking covers a multitude of sins on the soundtrack, which was nominated for two Oscars.) Worse than the numbers, however, is the emotionless character Dvorak was given to play.

Equally detached, the formidable Joseph Schildkraut is ice-cold, crooked casino owner Tito Morell, who comes up against honest he-man Duke Fergus (Wayne). The chauvinistic cowboy, of course, wins, apparently taking his trophy female to his Montana ranch, but only after all the songs and earthquake (rendered with decent special effects marred by the inclusion of stock footage) are finished.

Wayne, Dvorak and Schildkraut, plus supporting players William Frawley, Virginia Grey (whose scenes also were partially dubbed) and Paul Fix, deserved better from a studio that, sinking most of its money into sets, costumes and outlandish wigs, should have started with a half-decent screenplay. Borden Chase, who later adapted *Red River* from his own short story, really slummed on this ignominy. Butterfly McQueen's brief, sudden appearance as Flaxen's simpleminded African American maid effectively symbolizes the whole hoary affair.

Ford's experiences with John Bulkeley eventually convinced him that *They Were Expendable* had to be made, and his request for inactive status was granted by the Navy on October 20, 1944. When Bulkeley chose not to serve as technical adviser on a project about his own war service, Tony Akers, an officer who had served with him, accepted the job.

MGM had wanted Spencer Tracy to portray Bulkeley, but Ford preferred Robert Montgomery, who, while serving as the lieutenant's executive offer during combat in the South Pacific, had been able to observe him closely. Due to a Navy regulation that disallowed a living service man to be portrayed cinematically under his own name, Bulkeley was altered to "Brickley."

Olive Carey had written to Ford, asking if her son, Harry, Jr., serving as a navy corpsman in the South Pacific, could be reassigned to the Field Photo unit. In his reply to Olive, Ford advised, "Don't let Harry worry about the kid. I know that everything will be all right." Ollie's attempt to thank Ford for pulling the strings that may have saved her son's life was met by a response typical of a man who disdained any recognition of the love he had for others: "Oh, go fuck yourself."[30]

As for young Carey, he had no idea who had initiated the transfer, and was embarrassed and depressed by being forced to leave behind friends he had grown to respect. When he arrived in Washington, he still didn't know whose clout had removed him from the combat zone, nor anything about his new assignment. He recalled, "I was supposed to see Lieutenant English. It was not what you would picture as a typical meeting with a naval officer. In fact, it was about as navy as an Abbott and Costello movie."[31]

Carey finally was informed that he had been reassigned to the Field Photographic

Branch of the OSS, under Captain John Ford. The first and only time Carey actually saw Ford in Washington occurred at the director's office in the Agricultural Building. The recently promoted Petty Officer Second Class could immediately tell that the Captain had been drinking; and, following a brief conversation about his new job (developing classified U.S. and captured German film) and the health of his parents, Carey quickly retreated back to the safety of the darkroom. He wrote of Ford, "God! What a scary man. That was the first time I remembered being alone with him."[32]

Frank "Spig" Wead, sticking closely to the facts, had written a powerful first draft of the script for *They Were Expendable*, though MGM assigned rewrites to other personnel who, to beef up its box-office potential, added fictitious scenes involving domestic relationships that had no relevance to the story. On October 30, Ford, now on inactive status, headed to Hollywood to begin working on the film.

The Navy decommissioned six PT boats to add to the "documentary" style sought by Ford, who assigned the action scenes to second-unit director Captain James C. Havens, USMCR. Ford had also arranged for Robert Montgomery to be placed on inactive status, and this veteran of a PT boat command in the Solomon Islands received top billing above John Wayne as Lieutenant "Rusty" Ryan. For Duke's love interest, Second Lieutenant Sandy Davyss, a navy nurse, he cast another Iowan, the beautiful and naturalistic, 24-year-old actress Donna Reed. Pappy also had the role of a navy chief written for Bond, who, while often "partying" with Mary Ford, had been looking after their children while Pappy was in the service.[33]

After *Flame of Barbary Coast* wrapped in mid–August 1944, Wayne enjoyed a two-month break before returning to RKO on November 6 to begin making *Back to Bataan*, unlike *The Fighting Seabees*, a full-fledged combat film based on MacArthur's historic retaking of the Philippines just 17 days earlier. Knee-deep in the production, which included Duke going head to head with leftist director Edward Dmytryk, he finally was freed from his marriage to Josephine, with whom he hadn't lived since May 1943.

On November 29, 1944, Superior Court Judge Jess E. Stephens granted the divorce on grounds of "extreme cruelty" resulting in both "physical and mental suffering." As time passed, Duke would experience increasing guilt, heightened by the enmity his eldest son, Michael, felt for him. In legal terms, as a bad man, John Wayne had outdone Ward Bond.

Wayne endured plenty of physical suffering of his own while making *Back to Bataan*. His Red-baiting of Dmytryk was happily repaid by the director, who, like Ford, could be abusive to his performers; but, while Ford's sadism usually was expressed verbally, Dmytryk reveled in brute force and the resulting pain. He and fellow leftist Ben Barzman, hired to rewrite portions of the script during production, added several potentially injurious stunts, knowing that Wayne would never allow a double to put a dent in his legendary machismo. In this case, they were right: Duke endured any suffering they could dish out, the worst occurring during the winter weather of early 1945, when he was forced to shoot several takes lying underwater in the frozen-over pond at the RKO Ranch, barely able to breathe through a reed in his mouth.

When Duke began to turn blue, he took a break, drank some whiskey, and advised Barzman, "You better be goddamn sure we don't find out this is something you dreamed up out of your little head as a parting gift."[34]

The making of *Back to Bataan* was supervised by Colonel George S. Clarke, commander of the U.S. Infantry Philippine Scouts. Included in the opening credits is the claim, "This story was not invented. The events you are about to see are based on actual incidents. The characters are based on real people." One of the most effective of all the propaganda films made in Hollywood during World War II, the OWI–appropriate *Back to Bataan* depicts the Asian combatants as absolute polar opposites: the Filipinos are virtuous, freedom seeking peasants; and the "Japs" are innately evil, inhuman monsters.

In *Back to Bataan*, Wayne portrays Colonel Joe Madden, organizer of a band of Filipino guerrillas placed under the command of Captain Andreas Bonifacio (Anthony Quinn) before joining the U.S. forces poised to land General MacArthur at Leyte. Randy Roberts and James S. Olson wrote:

> John Wayne ... brought a believable authenticity to the most cliché-ridden role: the rock-hard American who through dint of personal activity ensures the victory of good over evil.... In his war films he battled for justice and liberty in Europe, Asia and America. True to the form of the classic Hollywood star, he played one variation after another of the same character.... By the end of the war, Americans totally identified John Wayne with that idealized American figure.... His draft status and his divorce were unimportant to his audience.[35]

During pre-production on *They Were Expendable*, Ford learned that Maureen O'Hara was starring in the swashbuckler *The Spanish Main* for Frank Borzage at RKO. O'Hara enjoyed the experience working with Borzage and cinematographer George Barnes, a master who was making her even more fetching in Technicolor. Maureen was resilient, and could handle a knife, sword and gun far better than her costar, Paul Henried, whom she described as "too charming and not tough enough for the role."[36]

O'Hara knew that Pappy had returned to the States to make a film, but she had no idea he would show up, unannounced, at the studio where she was working. As usual, Ford was dressed like a skid row bum, and the young guard at the gate took one look at his old, rumpled attire and promptly gave him the bum's rush. Enraged, Ford drove home and called an RKO executive, chewing him out in every possible direction. After Pappy slammed down the receiver, the suit ran like hell down to the set, describing the imbroglio to O'Hara.

After shooting wrapped for the day, she phoned Ford, explaining that everyone at the studio was feeling sick about the terrible mistake. "If you will please come back tomorrow," she said, "the studio will roll out the red carpet for you." RKO did just that and, when "Mr. Ford" arrived, he indeed, "like a king," drove and walked on a red carpet that led all the way to the set where Maureen was working. Though she had no idea why he was there, she and Borzage soon learned that he wanted her to play the female lead in a film based on a story called "The Quiet Man, to be shot on location in the Emerald Isle.

Ford had dropped hints about making "a picture in Ireland," but O'Hara had considered the remarks wishful thinking. Now she knew the property, and her agreement to star in the film was sealed with a handshake witnessed by Borzage. O'Hara explained:

> From that day forward, John Ford and I had a binding legal agreement that I would play the role of Mary Kate Danaher. Of course, we didn't know it would take another seven years before the cameras would finally roll in the village of Cong.[37]

O'Hara joined John and Mary for a weekend aboard the *Araner*, bound for Catalina, where she and her director would begin to shape the film version of "The Quiet Man," while their families cavorted on the beach. O'Hara revealed:

> Pappy began this artistic process by having me share with him everything about my life growing up in Ireland. I watched as Pappy immersed himself completely in all that was Ireland, and more important, in life experiences and customs that he had never lived himself. In the very beginning, the first role I played in *The Quiet Man* was not Mary Kate Danaher, but that of John Ford's muse.[38]

By the time production began on *They Were Expendable* in Key Biscayne, Florida, on February 23, 1945, Bond's leg had mended to the point where he could stand with the help of a leg brace and crutches. Ford had cleverly rewritten his scenes so that his character, "Boats" Mulcahy, is wounded early in the film, and arranged for him to use the crutches and lean against sturdy portions of the sets for additional support. Pappy then blocked the scenes so that the other actors would move around him as he remained stationary. He actually walks, just two short steps with the crutches, in only one sequence. (This kind of loyalty, especially for a director toward a character actor, is rare in Hollywood, and is the strongest cinematic proof of Ford's devotion to Bond. Perhaps Pappy speculated that a "Commie" was driving that car that ran Ward down.)

Bond was given fifth billing, just below Ford's friend from his earliest days at Universal, Jack Holt, who appears late in the film as General Martin. The role, brief but significant, is perfectly cast, as Holt had a rare ability to imbue "invisibly" even the most resolute character with a nuance of warmth. Martin has the unpleasant task of informing Brickley that there isn't room for the remaining members of his squad on a plane evacuating select men from Bataan, where they are "expendable."

They Were Expendable (Metro-Goldwyn-Mayer, 1945; directed by John Ford). Representing the fighting men who lost a battle to help win the war: (left to right) "Doc" (Jack Pennick), Lieutenant "Rusty" Ryan (John Wayne), Lieutenant John Brickley (Robert Montgomery) and "Boats" Mulcahy (Ward Bond).

Countering the studio's attempt to alter the truth, Ford and Wead constantly re-wrote the screenplay during production. One aspect, in particular, proved a complete about-face from the heroic, loose cannon John Wayne depicted in all the war films made during Ford's active military duty. As Lieutenant Ryan, Duke, although attempting to give up his seat on the plane, follows orders and leaves with Brickley, while many of their men are left behind to die.

Expendability hit Ford for real shortly after production began, when he received news that Navy Photographer's Mate First Class "Junior" Stout, one of his lead cameramen during the Normandy landing, had been killed by German soldiers after his unarmed DC-3 transport plane was forced by inclement weather to land on the enemy-occupied island of Jersey. The Germans had spotted his Cunningham combat camera (mounted on a rifle stock) and, mistaking it for a machine gun, shot him down. Young Stout's unexpected and senseless death capped off more than three years of harrowing war-related experiences, making Ford even more concentrated and tenacious on his movie set.

Ford was especially brutal to Wayne while shooting the picture. At one point, when shards of glass hit him in the face after ball bearings were fired at his boat's windshield (the effects man had forgotten to replace the glass pane with an acrylic one), Duke grabbed a hammer and went after the technician, but Pappy intervened, forbidding him to retaliate. "They're my crew," said Ford.

"Goddamn it, they're my eyes," replied Wayne, nearly causing a fistfight. Duke later admitted, "Jack picked on me all the way through it. He kept calling me a 'clumsy bastard' and a 'big oaf' and kept telling me that I 'moved like an ox.' Now if I couldn't do anything else, at least I *moved* well."[39]

Matters became even worse during the filming of a scene in which both Brickley and Ryan salute Admiral Blackwell (Charles Trowbridge) after he observes their PT boat maneuvers in Manila Bay. After Montgomery and Wayne, with their backs to the camera, performed two flawless takes, Ford called for a third, during which he called, "Cut!" halfway through the performance. In front of a huge crowd of onlookers, he yelled, "Duke — can't you manage a salute that at least looks as though you've been in the service?"

Regardless of the fact that Wayne had not served during the war, Montgomery walked over to Ford, grabbed both arms of his director's chair, and faced him down. "Don't you ever speak like that to anyone again," he ordered the Old Man.

Wayne, for the first and only time in his career, walked off the set, as Montgomery demanded that Ford apologize.

"I'm not going to apologize to that son of a bitch!" replied Ford. Montgomery later recalled that Ford began making excuses, claiming that he "didn't mean to hurt [Wayne's] feelings," and then began to cry.[40]

Production was halted for an entire day before Duke agreed to return. Nearing the end of the shooting schedule, on May 17, 1945, Ford, while directing from a camera scaffold, slipped off and landed on the concrete floor 20 feet below, prompting Wayne to shout vengefully, "Jesus Christ, you clumsy bastard!"[41]

Pappy had fractured his right shinbone, an ironic variation on the injury suffered by Bond, who had been pampered while Wayne experienced endless abuse. Forced to spend two weeks in traction at Cedars of Lebanon Hospital, Ford promoted Robert Montgomery to the rank of temporary director, another act that pissed off Duke. (Montgomery's work began a successful directing career for the former romantic lead, while Wayne's future attempts at direction proved problematic.)

Confined to bed for what seemed like an eternity, with no work or booze, Ford filled the time recalling his war experiences and, according to Dan Ford, "realized that the four years he had spent with the Field Photo had been the most eventful, rewarding, and satisfying period in his life."[42] Joseph McBride observed, "After all the hazards he had faced in actual combat, it was ironic that Ford's only incapacitating injury during the war came on a Hollywood soundstage."[43]

Making the film wasn't complete drudgery for Duke, however. Due to the star status and public persona he had forged during Ford's absence, he was able to make several suggestions regarding his character. His romantic sequence with Donna Reed, a prime example of Ford's emphasis on the purely visual, allowing both actors to communicate primarily with subtle facial expressions (Pappy's maxim of "show the *eyes*"), is arguably the most beautiful "love scene" of Wayne's entire career.

The most fun Duke had, however, centered on tormenting the still hurting but unwavering Bond. He even shared a few laughs with Ford as they devised a practical joke to get the ultra-serious Robert Montgomery, who couldn't stand Ward, to lighten up. Wayne concocted a lie about an "exclusive party" that was being thrown in the Bahamas for visiting British royalty, and convinced the well-connected Montgomery "offhandedly" to mention "his invitation" within earshot of Bond. This charade continued for several days, and eventually Ward, believing that Duke, Bob and Pappy had all been invited to the important soiree, was chomping at the bit.

The "Horse's Ass" was back, in all his glory, making all sorts of creative attempts to be included on the guest list of a mythical shindig. By the time he was involved in the actual shooting, Ward finally got the gag, and Montgomery began to warm up to him.[44]

Long before production began, Ford had decided to place his salary into a trust for an organization he named "Field Photo Homes, Inc.," to build a clubhouse for the veterans of his unit and their families to enjoy after the war. In April 1945, having been paid $300,000 for producing and directing the film, he handed Columbia executive Sam Briskin $225,000 for a 20-acre property in the San Fernando Valley that already included a house, barn, corrals, swimming pool, tennis courts, spacious lawns and plenty of trees.

They Were Expendable was completed in mid–June, when the Allies planned to invade the Japanese home islands, an operation expected to be successful though extremely high in casualties for all concerned, on November 1. But after Japan rejected the July 26 Potsdam Declaration, an ultimatum calling for the government to surrender unconditionally or face "complete destruction" of the military and "utter devastation" of the homeland (the details of which were not revealed), President Truman made the "tragic" decision for the U.S. to detonate atomic (fission) bombs over Hiroshima (August 6) and Nagasaki (August 9).

The second attack was prompted by another Japanese refusal of unconditional surrender, even after the USSR launched its infantry, armor and air forces against Manchukuo, and Truman promised "a rain of ruin from the air, the like of which has never been seen on this earth." Six days after the devastation of Nagasaki, following the intervention of Emperor Hirohito, the Potsdam terms finally were accepted.

At the end of August, Wayne and Bond, pitted against each other as they had been in RKO's *Tall in the Saddle*, completed *Dakota* (1945) with director Joseph Kane at Republic. Expected to lend some credibility to the atrocious "acting" of Czech ice skater Vera Hruba Ralston (Herb Yates' personal "find"), Duke did his best. But, even combined with Bond's admirably understated performance (the best in the film), and the presence of pals Paul Fix and Grant Withers, he could not compensate for Hruba's often unintelligible delivery and,

They Were Expendable (Metro-Goldwyn-Mayer, 1945; directed by John Ford). Following his recent auto accident, Ward Bond, wearing a brace and heavy boot on his left ankle and foot, visits the MGM dressing room of Clark Gable, who currently was starring in *Adventure* (1945), directed by Victor Fleming.

even worse, the rampant scenery chewing of Walter Brennan, whose mean-spirited, racially offensive dialogue, aimed at Nicodemus Stewart (as his shuffling, shiftless riverboat "boy"), sinks this muddy Western travesty, arguably Wayne's worst film of the 1940s.

Lawrence Hazard's mindboggling screenplay, though set in 1870, revels in a reversion to an odious stereotype that Ford, Will Rogers and Stepin Fetchit had turned on its head a decade earlier. Although the OWI had voiced an objection to the "negative racial humor," it was still allowed to remain in the script. (The recipient of three Best Supporting Actor Oscars [twice triumphing over the formidable Basil Rathbone], Brennan, in real life an extreme right-wing bigot who made Wayne and Bond seem like Reds, could have received a "Worst Caricature of a Human Being" statuette for this excruciating portrayal.)

Based on the 1945 novel by Ernest Haycox, Walter Wanger's *Canyon Passage*, featuring a superb screenplay by Ernest Pascal, began shooting on location around Diamond Lake, Oregon, during mid–August 1945, and continued, including interior work at Universal, through mid–December. Shot in Technicolor by Edward Cronjager, this atmospheric, often dark, and morally ambiguous Western set in 1856 Portland bears the stamp of its director, Jacques Tourneur, who recently had honed his skills making three classics of the horror genre, *Cat People* (1942), *I Walked with a Zombie* (1943) and *The Leopard Man* (1943), with producer Val Lewton at RKO.

Wanger initially planned *Canyon Passage* as a project to reunite the cast of *Stagecoach*, namely Wayne, Claire Trevor and Thomas Mitchell, under the direction of another horror-noir specialist, Robert Siodmak. By the time production began, the principal roles were played by Dana Andrews, Brian Donlevy, Susan Hayward and Bond, as "Honey" Bragg, arguably the most repugnant character he ever played. Rounding out this troupe are Hoagy Carmichael (in his favorite role of Hi Linnet, a roving, mandolin strumming shopkeeper who acts as a Greek chorus), Stanley Ridges, Lloyd Bridges, Rose Hobart, Halliwell Hobbes and Onslow Stevens.

British actress Patricia Roc, borrowed from J. Arthur Rank for her American film debut, plays Caroline Marsh, the fiancée of Logan Stewart (Andrews). In the end, Logan winds up in the arms of his true love, Lucy Overmire (Hayward), after her fiancé, gambler, embezzler and murderer George Camrose (Donlevy), is killed. One important member of the *Stagecoach* cast, Andy Devine, does appear in *Canyon Passage*, accompanied by his two sons, Tad and Denny.

Under Tourneur's direction, Bond brings a horror touch to the film, as Bragg, intent on stealing Stewart's gold, and then attempting to beat him senseless, becomes a completely psychotic beast. Blinded by blood during his barroom brawl with Stewart, he mistakenly punches a wooden pillar; and, after being repeatedly pummeled by Logan, retreats, only to return on horseback, in an effort to run him down in the street. Later, in the forest, Bragg tries to bushwhack Logan, as he and Lucy are riding toward San Francisco, but instead guns down their horses and then, spying a young "Indian" woman swimming in the river, rapes and kills her (off screen).

"He *had* to kill something," Logan says at one point, scaring him off with gunfire as the desperate madman runs from the forest toward the town posse. Having burned wagons and homes, and massacred innocent women and children as a result of Bragg's brutal deeds, the "Indians" run him to ground, hacking him to death with tomahawks. Bond gave a physically arduous performance, fleeing through the timber, climbing and hurtling over fallen trees, giving little indication of the pain constantly radiating through his left leg. Earlier in the film, Logan refers to Bragg's leg injury, apparently incurred when the brute crashed through a hotel window after trying to filch his gold-filled saddlebags.

This very adult Western, consistently emphasizing the unsavory aspects of human nature, is often lightened by the charming contributions of Carmichael, who wrote four songs used in the film. "Ole Buttermilk Sky" (co-written with Jack Brooks) was later nominated for an Academy Award (but lost to Harry Warren and Johnny Mercer's "On the Atchison, Topeka and Sante Fe" from MGM's *The Harvey Girls* [1946]).

On September 17, 1945, a little more than three weeks after the Japanese surrender was formalized aboard the U.S.S. *Missouri*, Ford was presented with the Legion of Merit by Bill Donovan who, after pinning the medal on the director's uniform, added an unexpected embrace. Ford, of course, was elated to receive the honor, but this moment of joy was quickly countered the following day, when his beloved Field Photo unit was officially shut down. Only a few cameramen remained in Germany, to photograph the Nuremberg Trials.

The following week, Wayne's financial security skyrocketed when he signed a new seven-picture, nonexclusive contract with Republic guaranteeing a percentage of the gross and his input on each project. Never again would he make an embarrassment like *Dakota* for Herb Yates, who was determined to, not only keep his bread and butter B Westerns, but also produce higher quality films, to the extent of hiring outside, big-name directors for his "Premiere" productions. Together with his long-term RKO contract, the new Republic deal would help make Duke the biggest box-office star in the industry.

On October 15, billed below Claudette Colbert, he began making *Without Reservations* with Mervyn LeRoy at RKO. A meandering but entertaining and well-acted takeoff on *It Happened One Night*, with Duke in the Clark Gable position, the film, released the following May, was a hit with audiences eager to see the bright side of American GIs returning from the war. While the conflict still raged, many of the same filmgoers had seen Colbert in the David O. Selznick–John Cromwell "coming home" tearjerker *Since You Went Away* (1944). And, a few months after the release of *Without Reservations*, they again would be deeply moved, by William Wyler's powerful postwar masterpiece *The Best Years of Our Lives* (1946), made for Samuel Goldwyn and distributed by RKO.

While Duke was abandoning B movies and climbing the financial ladder, Ford was putting the finishing touches on his sincere, poetical narrative about the triumph found in defeat. As noted by Joseph McBride, "With its direction credited to 'Captain John Ford, U.S.N.R.,' *They Were Expendable* signified a new level of aspiration for Ford, a deepened conception of his role as the official cinematic chronicler of American history."[45] The film's credits also include Frank Wead, James C. Havens and Joseph H. August with their military ranks. Montgomery, top-billed, is "Robert Montgomery, Comdr. U.S.N.R.," while Duke, billed below him, is merely "John Wayne."

Dan Ford explained his grandfather's approach to making the film:

John tried to elevate it above the level of a propaganda film.... Reunited with Joe August, his cameraman on *The Informer*, he went after a visual style of great simplicity and strength, with compositions of monumental force, yet never grandiose. He also went after the most delicate touches of human feeling.[46]

World War II was over, a welcome surprise, indeed; but one that consigned *They Were Expendable* to a public status of near-obsolescence. When it was released on December 20, 1945, a little more than four years after the attack on Pearl Harbor, the film itself appeared to be expendable. Randy Roberts and James S. Olson wrote:

Ford believed that it was his duty ... to prepare Americans for the invasion [of Japan] by telling the truth. He wanted no improbable heroics, no scenes of one man taking out a company of Japanese. Nor did he want any race-baiting. No Japanese soldier or sailor ever appears on screen. Ford concentrated his efforts on steeling his fellow countrymen to further sacrifice.[47]

One of the finest and most underrated works ever made about the universal suffering wrought by war, *They Were Expendable* is perhaps the closest Ford ever got to depicting an accurate interpretation of historical events. Here he doesn't "print the legend," although his visual depiction of MacArthur (Robert Barrat) nearly deifies the general (who *was* a bona fide hero at the time).

The only objection to the original script by the OWI had been Ford's attempt (not unlike his earlier *Judge Priest* controversy at Fox) to include an African American soldier, referring to the loss of the Philippines by claiming, "It's gonna be bad back dere in de South — no hemp — what'll dey do for lynchin's?" Following an order from the OWI (which had objected to, but still allowed the abundant "negative racial humor" in *Dakota*), Ford and Wead had to eliminate the dialogue *and* the character. (But this didn't make Pappy give up his quest to visualize his anti-lynching sentiments.)

They Were Expendable was acclaimed by reviewers and received two Oscar nominations (for Best Sound and Best Special Effects), but war-weary Americans showed insufficient interest in a story about, not a propagandistic victory, but a truthful defeat. However, initial box-office receipts were encouraging, and (contrary to previous reports) MGM did reap a worldwide profit of $1.2 million.

Ford's attempt at "documentary" realism wasn't appreciated by some filmgoers who were more comfortable with myths. John Bulkeley, who later was promoted to Admiral, respectfully regarded *They Were Expendable* as "a documentary, yes, but with good actors."[48]

6

The Big Son of a Bitch Learns to Act

John Wayne is pretty goddamn good ... he's a damn good actor. He does everything, and he makes you believe it. He's just a different form of an actor.... I'd say Wayne has to be pretty real.... Ford put Wayne in Stagecoach. *I put him in* Red River. *Wayne did a hell of a job in* Red River, *and Jack Ford said, "I never knew the big son of a bitch could act." So every time I made a picture with Wayne, Ford would come around and watch.* — Howard Hawks[1]

Ford was a dyed in the wool, sentimental, spiritual Catholic, but not a practitioner in the everyday sense. If you'd ever questioned his Catholicism, he'd probably have chopped you down. Had he been in the military on a permanent basis, he would have resisted authority there. He would have ended up in the brig, no question about it. — Charles FitzSimons[2]

Ford had returned to Hollywood, where he and Mary celebrated the 1945 holiday season in grand fashion. Many of his closest friends and colleagues had also "done their part" during the war, and each time one of them was on leave, discharged or retired from the military, a major party raged at the Odin Street home, acclaiming the triumphal homecoming of Lieutenant Colonel Wingate Smith, U.S. Army; Brigadier General Merian C. Cooper, U.S. Army; and Lieutenant (j.g.) Henry Fonda, U.S. Naval Reserve, recipient of a Presidential Citation and the Bronze Star.

Ford also was pleased when the Navy returned the *Araner*, which he put back in trim before resurrecting the Emerald Bay Yacht Club. As secretary of the spurious maritime outfit, Bond lined up all the former "members" of The Young Men's Purity Total Abstinence and Snooker Pool Association for the new, postwar sequel to the original.

On January 3, 1946, the Emerald Bay men assembled for the wedding of Myrna Loy to Commodore Gene Markey, USNR, who had returned to his executive position at 20th Century–Fox. Markey, who had produced *Wee Willie Winkie*, often was accompanied by Wayne and Bond on his fishing expeditions to Catalina.

In the chapel at the Roosevelt Naval Base on Terminal Island, just off San Pedro, Ford was highly honored to give away the bride in the presence of best man Admiral William "Bull" Halsey, Jr., USN, matron of honor Mrs. Collier Young, and Loy's mother, Mrs. Della Williams. The ceremony was performed by naval chaplain Captain Morris M. Leonard, USN.

A decade older than his bride, Markey already had two previous glamorous nuptial conquests under his belt: Joan Bennett, to whom he was hitched from March 1932 to June 1937; and Hedy Lamarr, from March 1939 to October 1941. (His marriage to Loy also would end with a divorce, in August 1950.)

This naval wedding wasn't the only time Ford donned his uniform after the war. As Dan Ford observed, "Having developed a virtual obsession with military glory, John tried to milk his accomplishments in the Navy for all they were worth." Arguably having been Hollywood's worst dresser prior to Pearl Harbor, now he maintained "a closet full of uniforms" fit for any and all social occasions and began wearing navy fatigues and baseball-style cap bearing the captain's eagle.[3]

The war experiences also affected his demeaning attitude toward Francis, whose son, Francis Joseph "Billy" Ford, had served as an infantryman in the South Pacific. Uncle John was so proud of Billy that he was hired as an assistant director. Wayne said:

> It took me a while to realize it, but a big change had come over Jack. Before the war there had always been an edge to him. But after the war, after he had been out there, he was a lot kinder and a lot more sympathetic.[4]

Exactly two weeks after Pappy gave away Myrna Loy, Herb Yates followed suit with Chata Baur at the Unity Presbyterian Church in Long Beach. Wayne's divorce decree had been finalized on Christmas, and he wasted little time getting married again, an act that Bond had attempted to prevent. Ford also tried to convince him that tying the knot was a mistake, but Duke responded that he was truly in love; and, unlike Josie, Chata shared his interests: movies, sports, attending parties with his buddies, and alcohol.

Though Ward, a man who, better than most, certainly was aware of the consequences of a hell-raising lifestyle (in his case, definitely "Do as I say, not as I do"), he dutifully arrived at the church, now walking with the help of a single cane, to serve as Duke's best man. The equally loyal Ollie Carey was Chata's matron of honor, and Wayne's mother momentarily honored her eldest son by hosting a reception for "Mr. and Mrs. Marion Morrison" at the California Country Club.

Following a short Hawaiian honeymoon, the newlyweds who had been living together for more than three years returned to their house in Van Nuys, where Duke's new mother-in-law, Esperanza Baur Ceballos, soon began arriving for lengthy "vacations." In no time at all, Duke realized that three was certainly a crowd.

The official, heavily managed, Hollywood gossip reported that the couple recently had met while working at Republic, where Chata was a "comely Mexican screen actress."[5] Chata had a serious alcohol problem, though Duke, a heavy drinker who was suspicious of men who didn't imbibe, apparently accepted the situation. He loved her, and they continued to enjoy the good times; but Chata eventually began getting inebriated to the point where she physically abused Duke when he attempted to intervene.

During the spring of 1946, Ford spent $75,000, the remainder of his salary for *They Were Expendable*, on improvements at the Field Photo Home and Farm. (Wayne also contributed $10,000.) Per Pappy's wishes, the farm welcomed "everyone, regardless of race, creed or color." A wooden chapel, a multi-denominational place of worship for Catholics, Protestants and Jews, was built on the grounds. An inscription, placed above the altar on which were displayed a crucifix, cross and Star of David, featured the first two lines of a renowned quatrain by English poet A. E. Housman, whose work is permeated with pessimism and the finality of a death unmitigated by religious faith:

> Here dead lie we because we did not choose
> to live and shame the land from which we sprung.

The complete quatrain, ending,

> Life, to be sure, is nothing much to lose;
> But young men think it is, and we were young.

was first published in the collection *More Poems* in 1936, the year of the author's own death.

Dan Ford wrote:
[M]y grandfather recreated the world of his pictures at the Farm.... Everyone that was close to him, whether they were veterans of his unit or actors from his troupe, became involved.... It was a cult, a true community, and one of the most unique institutions ever created in Hollywood.[6]

Intent on developing his own film project under the terms of his new Republic contract, Wayne hired a personal assistant, Mary St. John, who had been supervisor of the studio secretarial pool, and James Edward Grant, a Chicago journalist who had branched out into other areas, namely Hollywood film stories and screenplays (directed by such luminaries as Tod Browning, James Whale, Mervyn LeRoy and Mitchell Leisen) and alcoholism. He was a perfect fit, and eventually would write, whole or in part, a dozen movies for the Duke.

Wayne was impressed with "Angel and the Outlaw," a script about Penelope Worth, a beautiful Quaker woman, whose pacifism eventually tames Quirt Evans, a man who long has lived by the gun. Grant offered it to Duke, with only one proviso: He was so attached to the work that he wanted to try his hand at directing, as well. Planning to work in close collaboration with his friend, Wayne accepted the gambit. Relying heavily on what he had learned from Ford, Duke hired on more pals: Archie Stout as director of photography; Yakima Canutt as stunt coordinator and second-unit director; Bruce Cabot as gunfighter Laredo Stevens; Paul Fix and Hank Worden in supporting roles; and his hero, Harry Carey, to portray Marshal Wistful McClintock.

Retitled *Angel and the Badman*, the film pairs Duke with Gail Russell, a ravishingly beautiful, 21-year-old actress who had begun her film career while still a senior at Santa Monica High School. In 1944, she had played a supporting role in the eerie, atmospheric horror film *The Uninvited* at Paramount; but, unfortunately, she already had begun to self-medicate with alcohol to settle nervousness resulting from inexperience and the victimization of casting-couch lechers. However, Duke now held the reins, not only as an unbilled co-director with Grant, but also as Russell's informal counselor off the set.

Though *Angel and the Badman* has the look of a B Western, there are elements that Wayne cribbed directly from Ford, including an establishing shot of Monument Valley, and a reliance on reaction shots, including (as Pappy had done with the Ringo Kid in *Stagecoach*) close-ups showing the subtle nonverbal responses of other actors to Duke's dialogue. The unconventional story and a neophyte director were bold professional risks for Wayne, but it was the after-hours personal sessions with Russell that got him into trouble.

Influenced by the unfounded suspicions of her mother, Chata believed that her husband was having an affair with the actress. On the day Duke wrapped the shoot, he scheduled a private party, for the cast and crew exclusively, at Eaton's restaurant, located near the studio. By the time the revelry ended at 8:30 P.M., almost everyone, especially Wayne, was well lubricated. When a small group suggested hitting another joint for a nightcap, Duke drove Gail's car, planning to drive her safely home afterwards. Unfortunately, after losing the lead car in traffic, Duke unsuccessfully looked for his pals in a few bars, and then headed for Santa Monica, pulling into Carl's Restaurant to grab a bite to eat.

Some of "Marion's" old high-school buddies recognized him, and after celebrating with a few more cocktails, the midnight hour was fast approaching. Duke drove drunk to Gail's apartment, where she lived with her mother and brother, who phoned for a cab, which arrived about 1:00 A.M. Locked out of his house, and having no key, Duke was forced to ring the doorbell, after which he could hear Chata and her mother quietly chatting.

"Chata!" he shouted. "Open the door. It's Duke."

Still left out in the dark, he smashed a glass panel in the door, stretched in his arm, and unfastened the lock. He could hear the continued whispering, so he collapsed in a stupor onto the couch, only to awaken to find Chata threatening him with a .45 automatic pistol. Mrs. Baur intervened, preventing her daughter from possibly gunning down John Wayne.

When the story broke in the Tinsel Town gossip rags, it was, not Duke's recollection, but Chata's mythical version that was made public. Claiming she had phoned Eaton's and then Duke's production assistant, Al Silverman, who had offered to drive him home, she instead spoke with Silverman's wife, who gave her the phone number of a hotel where Al could be contacted. Failing to discover anything about Duke's whereabouts, she fell asleep, and then was startled at 6:00 A.M. by the sound of shattering glass.

Grabbing one of the two loaded .45s that Wayne kept on his bedside table, Chata was about to shoot the "intruder" when restrained by her mother. Later, Chata claimed that a still-loaded Duke admitted that he spent the night with Gail, alone, in her apartment. Wayne denied the whole sordid tale, and was supported by Mary St. John, who stated emphatically that the "relationship" between her employer and the actress was completely professional and platonic.

In March 1946, Ford, teaming with Merian C. Cooper, also ventured into independent production. Backed by Bill Donovan and three other OSS-connected investors, they filed incorporation papers for the newly organized Argosy Productions. Cooper was named president, but Ford was chairman of the board and would be the creative force behind the company's films, including his adaptation of "The Quiet Man," which he now had owned for more than a decade, having first read it in a 1933 issue of *The Saturday Evening Post*. As Ford began to explore the possibilities of shooting the film on location in Ireland, Cooper negotiated a three-picture deal with RKO Radio which evenly divided the costs and net profits between the producer and the distributor, but granted all creative control to Argosy. The fly in the ointment was that RKO required one financially successful film *before* Ford could make *The Quiet Man*.

Inexplicably, for the first "money-making" film, Ford chose one of the most un-commercial properties imaginable, *The Power and the Glory*, Graham Greene's novel about a Latin American "whiskey priest" who, during his efforts to elude the anticlerical forces on his trail, shacks up with a prostitute in a mountain village. Ford had read the book six years earlier, during one of his cruises to Mexico and, according to Henry Fonda, immediately thought it would make a good film (with Thomas Mitchell in the lead), although the censorship obstacles would be a nightmare: "Jack thought that if he took out the love affair he could make the story acceptable ... and be left with a beautiful Christ allegory."[7]

Since Bill Donovan already had put together a picture deal with a producer in Mexico, Greene's novel seemed a natural fit. Dudley Nichols again teamed with Ford to write the script, a highly sanitized reworking of the story titled *The Fugitive*. Fonda was cast as the priest, whom they transformed from an alcoholic hell-raiser into an irresolute man being hunted by a relentless police lieutenant in a totalitarian country.

Before Ford could begin shooting *The Fugitive* at Mexico City's Churubusco Studios on May 1, 1946, he was contractually obligated to return to 20th Century–Fox to make one more film for Darryl Zanuck. The mogul wanted his top director to sign another long-term contract, guaranteeing a salary of $600,000 per picture, plus a continuation of the freedom to make films for other companies, but Ford remained committed to his new independent venture with Cooper, who was busy with preproduction work for *The Fugitive*. Realizing that this might be his last chance to be Ford's "boss," Zanuck made damn sure that the chosen property had legitimate commercial potential.

While many have assumed that this project was originally designed as a "quintessential John Ford Western," it actually was "suggested" to him by Zanuck, who simply wanted to assure big box office by again adapting Stuart N. Lake's 1931 novel *Wyatt Earp: Frontier Marshal*, a highly fictionalized version of the events culminating with the legendary "Gunfight at the O.K. Corral." (Lake's novel introduced the event to the American public, but the name didn't become ingrained until Paramount released *Gunfight at the O.K. Corral*, directed by John Sturges, in 1957.) Since 1934, Fox already had filmed Lake's book *twice* (as vehicles for George O'Brien and Randolph Scott, respectively, with Bond playing a supporting role in both), but now it had been six long years since Allan Dwan's 1939 effort hit the screen, and Zanuck was ready to stage the phony fight once more.

Ford had screened Dwan's version, telling Zanuck that he thought it could be improved as a bigger-budget Western in Technicolor with Henry Fonda as Earp and popular Fox star Tyrone Power as John "Doc" Holliday. He also noted that the screenplay by Sam Hellman was only "about 40 percent accurate," so Zanuck ordered a fresh script, which was cranked out by Winston Miller and Sam Engel, and this time filmgoers might easily be fooled into thinking they were slapping down 50 cents for an "entirely new" story called *My Darling Clementine*. Ford later told Peter Bogdanovich:

> I knew Wyatt Earp ... and he told me about the fight at the O.K. Corral. So in *My Darling Clementine*, we did it exactly the way it had been. They didn't just walk up the street and start banging away at each other; it was a clever military maneuver.[8]

The truth about the cause of the October 26, 1881, "gun duel" in Tombstone, Arizona Territory, between the Earp brothers, gunslingers who protected the Republican business owners (a Deputy U.S. Marshal, Virgil, not Wyatt, was also town marshal at the time), and the Clanton gang, cowboys (aka "outlaws") in league with local, mostly Democratic, ranchers, still remains hazy. However, a few facts are relatively clear: the fight took place, not at the O.K. Corral, but a block away, in a small vacant lot on Fremont Street, next to a boarding house where Holliday lived; the two parties initiated the conflict while standing only six feet apart; and the entire "duel," during which about 30 shots were fired, lasted about 30 seconds. (To this day, the city of Tombstone draws tourists with a "recreation of the Gunfight at the O.K. Corral" *at* the O.K. Corral.)

"Eruption in the Vacant Lot" does not make for good mythmaking: a process, begun by local, politically biased newspapers and then fueled by decades of tall tales, exaggerations and lies, culminating with Lake's fictional account, published 15 years before Ford and Zanuck approached the subject. The real Tombstone slaughter ended the lives of Billy Clanton and two brothers, Frank and Tom McLaury. Although they were wounded, Virgil and Morgan Earp, along with Holliday, survived. Wyatt Earp emerged unscathed.

Though he had repeatedly made death threats against the Earps, Ike Clanton, unarmed, tried to appeal to Wyatt at the last second, but then, followed by Billy Claiborne, ran like hell after the shooting was initiated, apparently by Wyatt and Billy Clanton. Facing a murder charge filed by Ike Clanton, the Earp brothers and Holliday, following a month-long pre-liminary hearing and grand jury trial, were found not guilty.

Wyatt, Virgil and Morgan, together with two additional brothers, James and Warren, were itinerant veterans of "law and order," while their foes were "cowboys" who apparently had violated a local ordinance against the public wearing of arms. Clanton maintained that, when confronted, Billy and the McLaury brothers, offering no resistance, all had raised their hands before being gunned down in cold blood. During the legal proceedings, witnesses testified that they saw no such act of surrender, and two physicians who examined the locations of the wounds on the dead men corroborated their statements.

Ultimately, *My Darling Clementine*, including location work in Monument Valley, was shot by Joseph August in atmospheric black and white, Ford's preferred and triumphant medium. Henry Fonda was signed as Wyatt, but when his buddy, James Stewart, deferred (to star in Frank Capra's *It's a Wonderful Life*), Victor Mature took on the part of a very morose, tubercular and self-loathing alcoholic "Doc" Holliday, surgeon, gambler and famed gunslinger. (The real Doc was a dentist.)

The supporting roles of Virgil (who, in reality, had been the Earp in charge) and Morgan went to Tim Holt and Bond, respectively, both billed below two females: Linda Darnell, as "Chihuahua," a fiery Latina; and Cathy Downs, as Clementine Carter, the prim and proper WASP woman from the East who catches Wyatt's fancy. (Ford had mentioned Douglas Fairbanks, Jr., and Vincent Price for the Holliday role, and wanted Anne Baxter to play Clementine.) Also in the cast are Ford Stock Company favorites Jane Darwell, Grant Withers, J. Farrell MacDonald, Mae Marsh, Russell Simpson, and brother Francis as "Dad," the town drunk, who this time dons a Union army cap.

Whether or not Ford (or Bond) realized it, casting the Judge in *Clementine* made him the only actor to appear in all three Fox adaptations of *Frontier Marshal* (adding yet another item to his invincible list of unique cinematic achievements). While James Stewart had to choose between Ford's film and Capra's, Bond turned out to be indispensable to both, and their shooting schedules were adjusted accordingly. In a typically facetious letter to Capra, Ford wrote:

> I am writing you regarding using Ward Bond in your picture. As you know, he has already signed a contract to work in my forthcoming production.... I have talked it over with the various members of the cast and they are ... in accord with the idea of Bond working for you.... They are willing to advance you as much as $890.00 if you can get him out of our picture to work solely in yours.[9]

Ford had wanted to cast his buddy Stepin Fetchit as "Buttons," Wyatt's beloved factotum, but pressure from the NAACP led to Zanuck nixing the idea. The comic's prewar shtick was now viewed as an offensive racial stereotype, so the out of work Stepin, victimized by a different kind of blacklisting, was also out of luck. Andrew Sarris wrote:

> Better that Fetchit be permanently unemployed than that he serve as a reminder of a shameful blind spot on both sides of the Mason-Dixon line. But for Ford, Mr. Fetchit was an old friend and a familiar face, and he had to make a living like everyone else.[10]

Superbly played by Fonda, this polite, noble and heroic characterization is a far cry from the real Wyatt, instigator of the March-April 1882 "Earp Vendetta Ride," during which he, now a U.S. Deputy Marshal, and his posse hunted down and murdered four men believed to have been involved in the recent wounding of Virgil Earp (still town marshal) and back-shooting assassination of Morgan Earp (who also had become a U.S. Deputy Marshal).

Ironically, although bitter enemies, both Wyatt Earp (specifically) and "cowboys" (in general) were subsequently romanticized in a positive light by tall tales, pulp fiction, stage dramas and the cinema.

Fonda's Earp, however, does reveal a "dark side" in his racist contempt for Native Americans. "What kind of town is this — selling liquor to Indians?" he asks after subduing a drunken hell-raiser. "Indian — get out of town and *stay out*," he adds before kicking the bewildered man in the ass. This act prompts the first attempt by a Tombstone resident to hire Wyatt as marshal.

While making *Clementine*, Darryl Zanuck didn't expect Ford's cavalier attitude toward the screenplay, which he merely used as a framework for his own transformation, improvised or hastily re-written on the set during production. By the time he finished shooting the picture, several dull, dialogue-laden sequences had been tossed out in favor of his own inventions, resulting in greater character development (realized by some of his favorite actors), charming

My Darling Clementine (20th Century–Fox, 1946; directed by John Ford). Ward Bond as Morgan Earp.

comic touches (including some priceless in-jokes) and unique directorial elements which he called his "grace notes." Even prior to shooting, Ford, realizing that he was veering miles away from any degree of historical truth, suggested giving the characters fictitious names.

Unlike most of Ford's other Westerns, made before and after, very little ambiguity can be found in *Clementine*, an old-style "good vs. evil" morality tale, as Joseph McBride convincingly argued, "deeply influenced" by the director's World War II military experiences:

> *Clementine* emphasizes the devastation caused by frontier warfare, the cost of making the territory fit for "young kids ... to grow up and live safe. Ford's especially poignant treatment early in the film of the death of James Earp (Don Garner) was influenced by the deaths of young men in his wartime command.[11]

Ford's fictionalized version of Old Man Clanton is brilliantly played by a raging Walter Brennan (a forerunner to Lee Marvin in *The Man Who Shot Liberty Valance*). A complete psychopath, he whips one of his own sons for committing a cardinal sin: "When you draw a gun, *kill a man!*" he insists.

Ford's "substitutions" for scripted material included a build-up of Bond's part. Although the real Morgan Earp was murdered, shot in the back while playing billiards, Bond's Morgan is hale and hearty at the end of *Clementine*, having received extra bits of business and camera set-ups drawing attention (however abstractly) to the Ward rear end.

The first ATB shot, with Bond's equestrian form saddled with leather chaps, occurs when the Earp brothers visit the barber shop. The second composition shows Morgan and Virgil standing at the entrance to the jail (with Bond's backside paralleled by one of Monument Valley's largest buttes, and bracketed with a tent and wagon), as Wyatt rides in from visiting James' grave. The scene cuts to a medium three-shot of the men, with Fonda and Holt facing the camera, while Bond stands in half-profile. The "deliver us from all evil" saloon discussion between Wyatt and Doc includes the same Bond profile, as Morgan stands at the bar in the background.

My Darling Clementine (20th Century–Fox, 1946; directed by John Ford). The Earp brothers, Virgil (Tim Holt), Wyatt (Henry Fonda) and Morgan (Ward Bond) observe the drunken Doc Holliday's abusive behavior in the saloon.

A shot Ford added to give Bond his own "grace note" shows Virgil and Morgan leaving to do "a job of work," while Wyatt, leaning back in his chair, with his feet on a wooden pole, does his little Sunday-morning "dance." Linda Darnell appears on the boardwalk, moving away from the camera, as Holt and Bond walk toward her. Just as Holt leaves the frame, Bond pivots toward Darnell and unleashes his uncanny "horse whinny." She responds by emptying her pitcher of milk in his face.

Following Old Man Clanton's murder of Virgil, Wyatt is again seen leaning back in a chair, as the shirtless Morgan washes in a basin behind him. Ford holds the beefcake shot as Bond turns to display his rear before returning to wash, while Wyatt is informed by the Deacon (Russell Simpson) that "the Clantons are at the O.K. Corral." The scene cross-cuts between the Old Man and Ike Clanton (Grant Withers), waiting at the corral, and Doc joining Wyatt and Morgan (as Bond walks to the door, in a medium shot, where he lingers to fill a third of the frame with his backside).

As Wyatt and his men approach the corral, Ford includes a shot of Doc quickly climbing over a fence, while Morgan, back to the camera, slowly walks down the center of the frame. Just after Doc is shot off the fence, Morgan is shown beside him, as Ford juxtaposes Bond's rear with those of a small herd of horses. The scene cuts *to* a horse's rump crossing in front of the camera (right to left), revealing a close-up of Bond (facing the camera) as Morgan fires back at the Clantons.

A shot behind a half-dozen horses cuts to another close-up of a rump crossing the frame (left to right), revealing Bond firing toward the camera. A closer shot of horses cuts to the remainder of the Clanton gang being gunned down, the final bullets fired by Morgan (after Bond climbs onto the fence, triumphantly looming in the center of a low-angle shot). Incredibly, Ford, in orchestrating a major portion of the O.K. Corral gunfight, conveyed the confusion generated during this lethal event while simultaneously constructing the sequence around his favorite actor's bum.

Visually celebrated throughout the film, Bond wasn't Pappy's whipping boy on *Clementine*. When off the set, Ward enjoyed helping Mike Goulding stock the shelves at the trading post. The new man "in the barrel" was Victor Mature, whom Ford rode mercilessly, mocking his half–Italian ancestry with such epithets as "Greaseball" and "Liverlips" (a sobriquet also regularly leveled on Bond). In return, Mature turned in a very controlled, at times dramatically powerful, performance.

Walter Brennan also endured an onslaught of abuse, perhaps Ford's way of verbally punishing the fanatical conservative while cranking him up to become the psychotic, back-shooting killer who undoubtedly would shock many a filmgoer. Following a heated argument between the two men, Brennan swore that this film would mark the first and last time he would work for Ford, a promise he kept (probably to Pappy's relief).

After Zanuck screened Ford's cut of *Clementine*, he insisted it required major changes to address continuity gaps and inconsistencies. Ford vetoed the idea, so Zanuck personally re-cut the film, as he had *The Grapes of Wrath* and *How Green Was My Valley*. The depth Ford had given Chihuahua was eroded by the editing, especially Zanuck's insistence on creating a constant rhythm, leaving little room for the director's leisurely pacing, emphasis on mood, and grace notes. Zanuck called in Lloyd Bacon to film some new shots of Wyatt talking to his dead brother (presumably because James' age was listed incorrectly on the grave marker), and ordered a portion of the ending reshot, replacing Wyatt's farewell shaking of Clementine's hand with a more conventional, albeit believable, kiss on the cheek.

Ford resented these last-minute changes, and the released version of the film received lukewarm reviews. However, *My Darling Clementine* proved very popular with audiences, who paid $4.5 million worldwide to see the picture. By this time, Ford was in Mexico City, working on *The Fugitive*.

In November 1939, Civil War historian Philip Van Doren Stern wrote a short story, "The Greatest Gift," but was unable to find a publisher. Four years later, he privately printed 200 copies to enclose in his Christmas cards. Shortly after the 1943 holiday, the story was read by RKO producer David Hempstead and, in April 1944, the studio, planning to adapt it for Cary Grant, purchased the rights for $10,000. Three different screenplays were written, but RKO was unhappy with them all, and Grant instead chose to star in the Christmas film *The Bishop's Wife* (1947).

"The Greatest Gift" was shelved until RKO boss Charles Koerner passed it on to Frank Capra. Ever since 1933, when he directed *Lady for a Day*, Capra had been making variations on the same theme, honoring the importance of the individual, particularly a man's "inherent qualities of kindness and caring for others."[12] Realizing that Stern's story provided a solid basis for another populist project, Capra bought it for Liberty Films, his new production company. Koerner, pleased to recoup the studio's 10 grand, tossed in all three scripts as a bonus.

Capra wrote his own treatment, borrowed $1.5 million from the Bank of America, and hired Frances Goodrich and Albert Hackett to write the screenplay. Eventually, additional scenes were added by Jo Swerling. The result, *It's a Wonderful Life*, could also be called "Frank Capra's *A Christmas Carol*," as it borrows as much from Dickens as it does from the Stern story.

Many years after the original 1947 release, which proved a box-office disappointment, the copyright for *It's a Wonderful Life* lapsed into the public domain, and soon inferior prints surfaced frequently on television. By the 1980s, the Yuletide airwaves were saturated with what the public now considered one of the most beloved of all Hollywood films. Capra admitted that, not only was *It's a Wonderful Life* his personal favorite, but also the one project for which his other prime films were dress rehearsals.

If Capra had intended *It's a Wonderful Life* to be considered a fantasy film, his simplistic views arguably would not have generated so much critical derision over the decades. As a fantasy, it could have taught an object lesson about the human *capacity* for goodness, rather than optimistically assuming that "good" is always at work, except when threatened by a few, really evil, bad apples (in this case, Mr. Potter, Lionel Barrymore's two-dimensional, undisguised take on Mr. Scrooge). But the fact that the director took the plot seriously makes it the ultimate exercise in "Capra-corn," although an extremely well-acted one. After his experiences during World War II, in the postwar era of disillusionment, represented in the cinema by the expansion of film noir, perhaps Capra believed America needed more corn than ever.

James Stewart and Donna Reed are sensational as George and Mary Bailey, and Capra inspired hitherto unplumbed depths in the dramatic abilities of both performers. Stewart, as a bomber pilot, had participated in the worst hellfire of the war, and his portrayal of Bailey displays the darker edge of his acting genius that would evolve further under the guidance of Alfred Hitchcock and Anthony Mann.

Capra's own genius for casting is apparent in nearly every performance, especially those of the brilliant H. B. Warner, cast against type as Mr. Gower, the alcoholic pharmacist, and Ford veteran Thomas Mitchell as Uncle Billy. The director's casting of "Bert, the Cop" is particularly fascinating: James Stewart, the real-life war hero, plays a man classified as 4-F; but Bond, an actual 4-F, appears as a police officer who becomes a war hero, wounded in North Africa and decorated with the Silver Star.

In his introductory scene, Bert, standing beside the taxi of his pal, Ernie (Frank Faylen), cranes his head over the roof of the cab to check out the sway of beautiful, young Violet Bick (Gloria Grahame), and then comments, "I got to go home and see what the wife's doin.'"

Following the wedding of George and Mary Bailey, in lieu of a honeymoon, the newlyweds are serenaded in a leaky old house by Bert and Ernie, who harmonize outside the window, in a torrential downpour. Bert also provides one of the film's funniest moments when, in an attempt to "calm" the now-paranoid George, he swings his nightstick, only to receive a bite on the arm from Clarence (Henry Travers), the guardian angel. Bert makes his final appearance in the closing scene, accompanying on his accordion dozens of townspeople singing Robert Burns' "Auld Lang Syne."

For the majority of his screen time, Capra shot Bond above the waist or behind a prop, while he remained stationary. However, in the sequences where Bert discovers George peering over the bridge and then attempts to apprehend him, Bond can be seen limping on his left leg, which was continuing to be a painful hindrance to his mobility. *It's a Wonderful Life* was the fifth Capra film in which Ward appeared, and this role would be "the greatest gift" he received from the director. (There is reportedly no direct connection between Bond and Faylen's "Bert and Ernie" and the identically named pair on the PBS television series *Sesame Street*.)

Cecil B. De Mille's Colonial epic *Unconquered*, budgeted at $4 million, had been in the planning stages at Paramount for more than two years when Bond signed on to play the supporting role of John Fraser. Shooting began in early June 1946, and all of the famous director's trademarks, for better or worse, were ready and waiting: the massive sets, the meticulous attention to historical detail (with Iron Eyes Cody and Captain Fred F. Ellis, BMM [ret.] on set as advisors), spectacular action scenes, and an overlong script loaded with stilted dialogue that still smacked of silent-era extravaganzas.

De Mille's longtime collaborator, Henry Wilcoxon, the British, Dominican-born actor who effortlessly fit into "historical" epics, provided a fine thespian balance for the presence of Paulette Goddard, whose beauty could do little to temper the solid slab of North Woods Pine she offered as a performance. Though star Gary Cooper made his usual laconic contribution, the best characterizations were offered by the naturalistic Bond and Boris Karloff, whose East Indian complexion (rendered in stunning Technicolor by Ray Rennahan) fit right into his role as an American Indian, Guyasuta, Chief of the Senecas.

From early September through late December 1946, Wayne worked with Howard Hawks on the epic Western *Red River*, tackling the challenging role of Thomas Dunson, a rancher who gradually degenerates into an obsessive, vengeance-crazed psychotic. After enduring Ford's abuse while playing a homicidal maniac in *My Darling Clementine*, Walter Brennan was pleased to sign on as Wayne's amiable sidekick, Nadine Groot, in a superb cast also including Montgomery Clift, Joanne Dru, John Ireland and *both* Harry Careys, although father and son don't appear in any scenes together.

Harry, Jr., and his mother were the only two people aware of the elder Carey's failing health, as the veteran actor's effortless professionalism covered any trace of his illness on screen. Carey, Jr., wrote:

> Duke wasn't aware that Pop didn't feel well, because Pop still kidded with him and made him laugh. Had Duke known it, I'm sure he would have spoken to Howard Hawks about easing up on him a little. Hawks was wonderful to me when I worked on that same film later.[13]

When production began on *Red River*, Wayne wasn't entirely comfortable with a character he considered an "old man." Hawks recalled:

> I said, "Duke, you're going to be one pretty soon, why don't you get some practice?" He said, "How the hell am I gonna play one?" "Well," I said, "watch me getting up. That's the way to play it." Ford said he didn't know Wayne could act, but I said he could do anything if you've got enough guts to tell him what to do. [Ford] treated him a little like a beginner.... But Wayne adored him.[14]

At the start of production, Ford wrote to Hawks, "Take care of my boy Duke and get a great picture."[15]

Duke's first glimpse of Montgomery Clift made him concerned that the young, neophyte film actor might not be the right choice for the role of his "foster son" who eventually must take away Dunson's herd in order to get the beef to market. "That kid isn't going to stand up to me," he told Hawks. Even after playing a scene with him, Duke said, "There's only one thing that still bothers me, whether he can stand up with me in a fight." Hawks explained:

> I said, "Duke, I don't think I can keep up with you in a fight, but if I got a lucky chance and kicked you in the jaw, I think I'd have a good chance." "OK," he said. And we had Monty kick

him in the jaw. We took four days, and ... I think we made a respectable fight.... In a month [Clift] could really handle a horse, and he really could do anything with a gun. I thought he was a perfect choice....[16]

Building on conventions Wayne had picked up from Ford, Hawks not only added several years to the age of his character, but also re-created him in a more "Hawksian" image. Rather than possessing the historical and ritualized sensibilities of the Ford characters, Dunson is a man merely concerned with the success of his professional ambitions and his "law." Dunson can only tolerate "good" men who operate by his rules of conduct, and when they don't, his neuroses surface. Midway through *Red River*, he has become a psychopath. Hawks scholar Gerald Mast wrote:

Wayne had never played the character ... that he played in *Red River*. Once he had played it ... that persona ... came to represent such a powerful cultural archetype that it served, for many, as a symbol, if not the cause, of the American attitude that produced the Vietnam War ... no star in the history of film other than John Wayne could play this role ... and make it mean what it does and make the story mean what it does.[17]

Following Hawks' initial wrap of *Red River* in late December 1946, Wayne was recalled to shoot additional scenes in late April 1947. In between, he starred in *Tycoon*, his first major A film for RKO, directed in Technicolor by Richard Wallace. After casting Maureen O'Hara to play Duke's resolute leading lady, the studio suits inexplicably replaced her with Laraine Day, whose meager screen presence is overwhelmed by Wayne every time he appears on screen, even with his back to the camera, and regardless of his being saddled with a humdrum character.

A tedious "epic" postwar variation on *Pittsburgh*, *Tycoon* was critically thrashed but still did respectable business. Nonetheless, Duke was disheartened by the whole project, which triggered a mild midlife crisis. At 40, with a few extra pounds and much less hair, he began to wonder aloud if he could still handle he-man leading roles, or wind up in a struggle to learn how to play character parts. He also gave serious thought to concentrating more on producing, or perhaps branching out into directing.

At Estudios Churubusco in Mexico City, Ford, having shed the chains of his Hollywood overlords, was working with a primarily Mexican crew, including the Gregg Toland-trained, master cinematographer Gabriel Figueroa, on his expressionistic, nearly silent art film *The Fugitive*. Early in the shooting, both Dudley Nichols and Henry Fonda became concerned when Pappy, not having to worry about a Zanuck breathing down his neck, tossed entire scenes to the four winds during periods of improvisational frenzy. Dan Ford wrote, "[H]e went after dramatic angles, shadows, backlights, stylized compositions, and ravishing pictorial effects. John's enjoyment took him over the edge of self-indulgence.[18]

Censorship problems had dogged adapting *The Power and the Glory* (published as *The Labyrinthine Ways* in the United States) from the outset. In an effort to satisfy the Production Code Administration, Nichols suggested transforming Greene's decadent "whiskey priest" into the Christ figure in "an allegory of the Passion Play."[19] At that point, Ford decided to co-write the screenplay with Nichols, who was given sole credit in the finished film. The Vatican eventually condemned Greene's novel, and Fonda believed that his character, a cowardly priest, the last of his kind, on the run in a totalitarian country, resulted from inner conflicts engendered by Ford's Catholicism. Joseph McBride explained:

Ford utterly failed to grasp [the] paradox — that God works his will on earth through deeply fallible human beings. Instead, as Greene put it, Ford "gave all the integrity to the priest," which robbed the character of complexity and threw [the] dramatic interest to the fanatically antireligious lieutenant (Pedro Armendariz).[20]

Ford filmed *The Fugitive* at Churubusco and at several locations (Cuernavaca, Taxco, Acapulco, Cholula, Perote, Puebla, Vera Cruz and Tepoztlan) from November 4, 1946, to January 27, 1947. He enjoyed his first collaboration with Armendariz, the great Latin actor known as the "Clark Gable of Mexico." Although born in Texas and educated in the United States, Armendariz was a citizen and resident of Mexico, where his magnetic screen presence had made him a star.

Other Latin American talent contributing to the film included Emilio Fernandez, a director who served as associate producer, but was referred to as a "co-director" by the Mexicans; and the glamorous, groundbreaking Latina star Dolores del Rio (born Dolores Martinez Asunsolo y Lopez Negrete in Durango, Mexico, in 1905), who had been cast with Victor McLaglen in Walsh's *What Price Glory* (1926) and *The Loves of Carmen* (1927) two decades earlier.

Prior to Fonda's casting as the priest, he had suggested to Ford that Puerto Rican actor Jose Ferrer would be better in the role. When Ferrer proved unavailable, due to his commitment to the play *Cyrano de Bergerac*, Ford bargained with Zanuck, promising to direct another film for 20th Century–Fox, *if* the mogul would personally serve as producer on that project and loan Fonda to Argosy for *The Fugitive*. (In 1951, when Ferrer was nominated for a Best Actor Oscar for the film version of *Cyrano*, Bond waged an anti–Communist crusade against him, claiming, "This man is not good for the business."[21])

Referring to Ford's sanitized version of the "whiskey priest," Joseph McBride observed:

> [He] is an ineffectual weakling and anxious teetotaler who seems both spiritually and physically impotent, as Ford may have seen himself in the depths of his alcoholic self-pity. But he seems to identify as strongly with the lieutenant ... and with the "good thief" played by Ward Bond. Known as "El Gringo," Bond's character physically resembles Ford, with his slouch hat, dark glasses, and dirty clothing.[22]

Indeed, Bond looks very much like he would a decade down the road, when Ford cast his surrogate son as "Himself" (though called John Dodge) in *The Wings of Eagles* (1957).

In an effort to inform audiences about the potentially confusing content of the film, and stave off potential negative reactions from Mexican viewers, Ford had Bond narrate the following prologue:

> The following photoplay is timeless. The story is a true story. It is also a very old story that was first told in the Bible. It is timeless and topical, and is still being played in many parts of the world.
> This picture was entirely made in our neighboring republic, Mexico, at the kind invitation of the Mexican government and of the Mexican motion picture industry. Its locale is fictional. It is merely a small state, a thousand miles north or south of the equator — who knows?

Bond first appears as James Calvert, "El Gringo," aboard ship, having robbed a bank in the United States, and heading toward the unnamed country where the "fugitive" is attempting to elude capture and execution. The plot does emulate the Passion Play, with Armendariz's "lieutenant of police" resembling Pilate; "El Gringo," the thief; and the priest, Jesus Christ.

Many contemporary reviewers thought highly of *The Fugitive*, particularly the stunning imagery, Richard Hageman's atmospheric musical score, and Dolores del Rio's elegant performance. The *New York Times* selected it as one of the "Best Films of 1947," but the public reaction in the United States was middling at best.

Although this very "European" film played to excellent business and critical acclaim overseas, it proved a financial disaster for Argosy, forcing RKO to cancel plans to make *The Quiet Man*. Even the subsequent box-office successes of *Fort Apache* (1948) and *She Wore a Yellow Ribbon* (1949) couldn't wipe out the original debt, advances from the studio, subsequent bank loans and accumulated interest.

Two decades after its release, Ford commented on *The Fugitive*:

> It came out the way I wanted it to — that's why it's one of my favorite pictures — to me, it was perfect. It wasn't popular. The critics got at it, and evidently it had no appeal to the public, but I was very proud of my work.... It had a lot of damn good photography — with those black and white shadows.[23]

Countering Ford's assessment, Henry Fonda said, "[T]he perverted son of a bitch, he knew that it wasn't good in the end, but he damn well wouldn't admit it."[24]

Following El Gringo's lengthy cornfield shootout with the fascist police force, he is lured to the priest's "sanctuary" by the film's Judas equivalent, "a police informer" (J. Carrol Naish), with the lieutenant close behind. Bond's death scene, captured in an unedited, two-minute take, is played for all it's worth, as El Gringo pleads, "Beat it, Father," but the priest, knowing he will be captured, remains to pronounce the last rites. Just after the lieutenant's shadow darkens the face of El Gringo, the fugitive's fate is sealed.

The Fugitive (20th Century–Fox, 1947; directed by John Ford). The fugitive priest (Henry Fonda) is warned of his impending doom by the dying James Calvert, "El Gringo" (Ward Bond). As in *The Long Voyage Home*, Ford gave his protégé a memorable death scene.

Bond's gasping performance, a rhythmic counterpoint (ending in death) to del Rio's earlier dancing scene (a brief celebration of life), creates the most dramatically intense event in the film. Ford knew that the physical effort required during the chase through the cornfield (including stumbling through a stone retaining wall) would cause a great deal of pain for Ward, who may have been gasping for real.

The Fugitive may be Ford's most pretentious film, but it's a fascinating *auteur* work nonetheless. During its initial release, Ford was nominated for a Golden Lion at the Venice Film Festival, and several "best film" awards were won internationally.

Aboard the *Araner* during the summer of 1947, Ford and Maureen O'Hara resumed their weekends working on the adaptation of "The Quiet Man." She had been pitching in for more than three years, even after Pappy, angered by a remark she made regarding his completely fictitious "riding with Pancho Villa" (that actually *was* accomplished by Raoul Walsh), viciously punched her out in front of guests, including Frank Borzage.[25]

O'Hara would write down Ford's dictation in shorthand, and then type up the story elements to be used later by the screenwriter. She admitted:

> These were the best times I ever spent with Pappy off the set. We were working together on a story about our beloved Eire, listening to Irish records, speaking with pride of our heritage....
>
> I knew Pappy was fond of me and respected my talent. I didn't know that this fondness would continue to grow over time and change into something far more difficult to explain.[26]

Based on the Pulitzer Prize–winning 1939 play by William Saroyan, *The Time of Your Life* (1948) was the first film made by Cagney Productions to include Bond in a supporting role. Ward's political activities didn't seem to bother (the then-liberal) James Cagney, who had admired his talent and professionalism since they worked together on several projects at Warner Bros. a decade earlier. James and his brother, William Cagney, became independent producers to provide an antidote to the Warners gangster persona, and were making gentler, more contemplative films.

Screenwriter Nathaniel Curtis adapted the highly philosophical stage drama, which immediately met with objections from the Production Code Administration. Forced to alter Saroyan's tragic ending, Curtis wrote a softer version; but after this didn't play well with a preview audience, additional changes had to be made. Cagney's casting of his sister, Jeanne, as a prostitute called Kitty Duval also was forbidden, so she is referred to as a "B girl" in the film.

The Cagney Bros. spared no expense, borrowing large sums from bankers to hire top personnel: director H. C. Potter; cinematographer James Wong Howe; composer Carmen Dragon; and still photographer Madison S. Lacy. The cast features William Bendix, Wayne Morris, Broderick Crawford, James Barton, Gale Page, Robert Benchley and James Lydon.

Regardless of all the talent involved, the film never really clicks, and it's doubtful if film audiences in 1948 understood Saroyan's intellectual musings. (Much of the Broadway carriage trade must have had a similar experience, perhaps taking "The Nap of Their Lives.") Though Bond is inexplicably billed in the opening credits as "McCarthy, 'a blatherskite,'" he appears in only one scene, with minimal dialogue. The real blatherskite is Cagney's forever preaching "Joe ... whose hobby is people." The film fared poorly at the box office, necessitating further deal making by William Cagney, who used future earnings from Warner Bros. to begin paying off the considerable loans.

On June 3, 1947, director George Marshall began shooting Universal's *Tap Roots* (1948), a Technicolor adaptation of James Street's novel about a Mississippi family attempting to keep Levington Valley neutral during the Civil War. Bond plays Hoab Dabney, who becomes head of the family following the sudden death of his father, "Big Sam" (Russell Simpson), and then rallies the locals for support. Hoab's daughter, Morna (Susan Hayward), becomes involved with newspaper publisher Keith Alexander (Van Heflin), who agrees to throw his editorial support behind their courageous effort.

As in *Gone with the Wind*, wartime politics often are overwhelmed by a love-triangle plot, here involving Morna, who becomes paralyzed after a riding accident, her sister, Aven (Julie London), and a Confederate loyalist, Clay McIvor (Whitfield Connor). Boris Karloff again portrays a Native American, Tishomingo, an educated Choctaw, who was Big Sam's close friend and protector. Arthur Shields and Hank Worden appear with fellow Ford comrades Simpson and Bond, who, along with Karloff, again steals the show.

Tishomingo is killed by a Confederate sentry while attempting to stop the recovered Morna from buying time by seducing McIvor, but the valley is attacked, and Alexander and Dabney's men retreat into the nearby swamps. Disgusted by Morna's behavior and his own responsibility for the destruction of the plantation, Hoab goes mad while tramping through the bogs, and then dies in the arms of his wife, Shellie (Sondra Rogers). Alexander guns down McIvor and declares his love for Morna, thus insuring that Big Sam's tap root will continue to grow.

7

Pappy's Inferno

They say I took pleasure killing Indians in the movies. But while today film people shed tears over the fate of the Indians ... more humbly I gave them work.... More than having received Oscars, what counts for me is having been made a blood brother of various Indian nations. Perhaps it's my Irish atavism, my sense of reality, of the beauty of clans, in contrast to the modern world, the masses, the collective irresponsibility. Who better than an Irishman could understand the Indians, while still being stirred by the tales of the U.S. Cavalry. We were on both sides of the epic.— John Ford[1]

"Sergeant—pour me some scripture."—Colonel Owen Thursday (Henry Fonda), to Sergeant Festus Mulcahy (Victor McLaglen), in *Fort Apache*

In March 1947, Ford purchased the James Warner Bellah short story "Massacre," which had appeared in *The Saturday Evening Post* the previous month. His World War II combat experience had instilled his desire to depict the U.S. military tradition as practiced on a frontier cavalry outpost, and a chance to resurrect his longtime idea of making a Western based on the tragic folly of Custer. The extremist political ideology of Bellah's work was problematic, but his hard-hitting, descriptive, economical prose style was ripe for cinematic transformation. Dan Ford provided a splendid summation of Bellah, "The American Kipling":

His works speak of conquest and the white man's burden; his stories are vigorous, energetic, and like Kipling's, given more to vivid expression than to careful logic.... Developing "Massacre" into a screenplay presented some unusual problems.... Although Bellah was a brilliant stylist, he was also a blatant racist, and his nineteenth-century attitude toward the Indians needed to be softened.[2]

In *My Darling Clementine*, Ford had used the names of actual people in a fictional version of events; but for this new Western, the use of fabricated character names actually allowed him to depict history more accurately. Ford explained, "The cavalry weren't all–American boys.... They made a lot of mistakes.... Custer, that was a pretty silly goddamn expedition."[3] On another occasion, he said, "Custer — a great hero. Well, he wasn't."[4]

Needing extensive, correct details to create an authentic historical atmosphere, Ford hired a "research editor," Katherine Cliffton, whose material was then turned over to Frank Nugent, erstwhile *New York Times* critic, and a liberal who would inject the much-needed balancing element of the Native American viewpoint. Cliffton's work was augmented by the input of two technical advisors, U.S. Army Major Philip Kieffer [ret.] and Katherine Spaatz, the daughter of Army General Carl Spaatz.

Working closely with Ford, Nugent wrote detailed biographies of all the characters, adding depth and complexity to the screenplay, titled "War Party," which would benefit from an A budget of $2.5 million, allowing art director James Basevi to design a realistic fort at the Corrigan Ranch in Simi Valley. Nugent and Basevi's work was based on research gathered from the memoirs of Elizabeth Custer, the ill-fated General's widow, histories of cavalry life, and photographs taken by Mathew Brady and his associates. Ford's visual approach was inspired by the paintings of Frederic Remington and Charles M. Russell.

The casting became the ultimate bonanza for the Ford Stock Company, making *Fort Apache* the director's only film to feature top leading men Fonda, Wayne, McLaglen *and* George O'Brien, who, after spending more than 15 years on Pappy's shit list, was back, due to an imploring phone call from his wife. "If you don't give him work and get him out of the house," she explained, "it'll be the ruin of a good Catholic family!"[5] Also on hand were Bond, Anna Lee, Pedro Armendariz, Jack Pennick, Grant Withers and Shirley Temple, whose presence inspired a re-creation of her relationship with McLaglen in *Wee Willie Winkie*.

Ford hired a fleet of stunt performers who would become longtime members of his outfit: coordinator Cliff Lyons, who had developed a safer way to stage horse falls; Frank McGrath, an agile double and memorable comic who played a small role in *They Were Expendable*; Terry Wilson, an athletic stuntman and naturalistic actor who handled horses and men with equal aplomb (McGrath and Wilson later became essential regulars on the *Wagon Train* series); part–Cherokee Oklahoman Ben Johnson, a peerless horseman practically born in the saddle; and Chuck Hayward and Chuck Roberson, respectively dubbed "Good Chuck" and "Bad Chuck" (for reasons obvious to anyone who worked with them).

In late June 1947, Ford gathered up this formidable band of talent and took them to Monument Valley, where many of them lived in tents on the grounds outside Goulding's Lodge, attempting to sleep in 90-plus temperatures that rose to around 115 during the days. And Pappy had a new whipping boy, neophyte John Agar, Shirley Temple's husband, whose inexperience provided endless opportunities for abuse, including being called "Mr. Temple" on the set. After Agar walked out, threatening to quit, Wayne explained Ford's "methods" and convinced him to stick it out.

A few days into the shoot, a plane flew over the location, loudly buzzing the set, interrupting a take and sending Ford into a fury. The culprit: Ward Bond. "Well, you can relax now," Wayne assured Agar, "he's found a new whipping boy."[6] Although his grandfather had been featuring Bond's bum as a prominent compositional element in his films for 16 years, Dan Ford astoundingly pinpointed this production as marking the genesis of this obsession:

> During these years, John liked to make jokes about the size of Ward Bond's rather pronounced posterior. He and Wayne often had their picture taken beside a horse's rear end, and they would send the snapshot to Bond with a note that said, "Thinking of you." On *Fort Apache* John carried this gag one step further. Unbeknownst to Bond, he set up his camera so that it actually featured the actor's butt, and in the finished picture there are several scenes where he actually shoots around Bond's behind rather than over his shoulder.[7]

Ford completed the location work in mid–August, and the company moved to Culver City, where interior scenes were shot at the Selznick studio. Any additional outdoor shooting was done at Corrigan's Ranch.

Although *Fort Apache* is a serious examination of the mythology of the American West, it humorously can be branded Ford's "ass-travaganza." Before Bond's bum even makes its auspicious entrance, Ford, displaying his genius as a visual storyteller by always knowing where to place the camera, introduces, as Bond's son, John Agar, in his film debut, not by including a close-up of his face, but of his rump.

Francis Ford, the first actor to be seen in the film, performs his trademark "tobacco spitting bit," and, just after the chaw hits the spittoon, the scene cuts to a shot behind a shirtless trooper, 2nd Lieutenant Michael Shannon O'Rourke (Agar), bent over while washing his face in a basin. Walking out of the washroom, he is accosted by his "uncles," Sergeants Beaufort (Pedro Armendariz), Quincannon (Dick Foran), Daniel Schattuck (Jack Pennick), and Festus Mulcahy (Victor McLaglen), who takes Ford's gluteal shtick one step further by throwing young O'Rourke across his lap to administer a sound spanking.

During a subsequent sequence, when Sergeant Major Michael O'Rourke (Bond) is reunited with his West Point-graduate son, his rear end remains facing the camera throughout the shot. Later, when Colonel Thursday (Fonda) orders a detail to assess the mayhem wrought by a band of Apaches, Bond's bum fills half the frame as Sergeant O'Rourke stands at the front of his commanding officer's desk.

Ford has often been criticized for including hearty doses of "Irish" slapstick humor in his films. This attitude fails, not only to grasp the general complexity of Ford's work, but also his specific, strategic use of these comic scenes as a subversive device. Joseph McBride wisely equated Ford's "low" comedy with that of Shakespeare, specifically comparing McLaglen's Sergeant Mulcahy to Falstaff:

> Ford uses broad ... comedy to ... puncture the pomposities of the leading characters, giving equal importance to the common man and the king.... Mulcahy mock[s] military rituals while giving Ford's military its true core of humanity.... Low comic interludes do not bother sophisticated modern audiences watching Shakespeare's history plays, perhaps because the archaic language makes everything in them seem equally stylized. But the same kind of humor is widely dismissed as an artistic flaw in Ford....[8]

When Ford watched films, he enjoyed comedy, particularly the work of Laurel and Hardy (often claiming that the pie fight two-reeler *The Battle of the Century* [1927] was his favorite movie) and the Marx Brothers.[9]

The *Fort Apache* scene in which Thursday discovers that mercenary reservation agent Silas Meacham (Grant Withers) has been plying the Apaches with rotgut whiskey hidden in crates marked "Bibles" is one of Ford's finest comic moments. Ordered to pour the Colonel "some scripture" and then "destroy" the toxic hooch, Mulcahy and his comrades, with "a man's work ahead of [them] this day," indeed annihilate the whiskey, which leads to a night in the guardhouse and a morning of "volunteer" detail shoveling horse manure. Wayne's fellow Iowan, Hank Worden, in his first actual role for Ford, stands guard over the hungover sergeants. (Interestingly, Worden's birthplace, Rolfe, is situated in Pocahontas County, which also includes a town called *Fonda*.)

Captain Kirby York (Wayne) speaks with great respect for the Apaches' traditions, including their knowledge of organized warfare and prowess on the battlefield, a viewpoint Colonel Thursday utterly rejects. His narrow-minded, racist view of Cochise (Miguel Inclan) is that no "breech-clouted savage ... murderer and treaty breaker" could be capable of abilities requiring such a high degree of intelligence. The Apaches have left their reservation in Arizona, crossing the border into Mexico, and Thursday wants them punished for their insurrections regardless of the cost.

Fort Apache (Argosy–RKO Radio, 1948; directed by John Ford). **Leading lights of the Ford Stock Company gather to welcome a new man: Lieutenant Colonel Owen Thursday (Henry Fonda), Captain Kirby York (John Wayne), Captain Sam Collingwood (George O'Brien), Second Lieutenant Michael Shannon O'Roarke (John Agar, in his film debut) and Sergeant Major Michael O'Rourke (Ward Bond).**

After York, unarmed and accompanied by Beaufort, who speaks Spanish, rides into Mexico to arrange a peace summit with Cochise, Thursday, refusing to honor a promise made to a "savage," rides out with the fort's full cavalry regiment. When meeting with Cochise, who has returned to Arizona with Geronimo at his side, York fully explains the truth of the situation, but Thursday maliciously calls the great chief a "coward."

Ultimately, Thursday leads his regiment to their doom. As the men ride away from Fort Apache, the women, watching from the rooftops, already know they will never see their loved ones again. "All I can see is the flags," says the wife (Anna Lee) of Captain Sam Collingwood (George O'Brien), the former regimental adjutant whose transfer has, ironically, just come through as he departs.

Among the others who needlessly but dutifully die with their boots on are the rascally Mulcahy and the elder O'Rourke, who soon disappear into the dust storm of the thunderous Apache stampede. Ford shows the massacre, not through the eyes of the reactionary martinet, but through those of the common-sense, tolerant York and young O'Rourke, who, having been ordered to remain with the wagons, watch through binoculars from a hill beyond.

Joseph McBride noted:

The transition from Fonda to Wayne as the essential Fordian hero already was complete by the time of *Fort Apache*.... It is Wayne who plays the humane, outspoken liberal and would-be peace-maker.... Fonda is the arrogant, self-centered bigot and warmonger. And yet York's character is not without troubling ambiguities, as the film's controversial ending sequence demonstrates.[10]

The critical reception of *Fort Apache* was mixed, but the picture eventually made a $2-million profit for Argosy, prompting Ford to plan more projects based on Bellah's cavalry stories. Of Ford's claim that the Irish "were on both sides of the epic," McBride observed, "The ambivalence suggested by that remark ... helps account for the lack of a critical consensus over his Cavalry Trilogy ... films that ... remain some of his most powerful and yet most problematical work."[11]

Does anything close to an *actual* "critical consensus" exist for any work? Was John Ford pro-"Indian" or anti-"Indian?" McBride continued:

The role of the Indians in his cavalry films is endlessly debated by film scholars, with some considering Ford relatively enlightened by the standards of his time and others accusing him of being severely limited by ethnocentrism and a tendency to racial stereotyping.[12]

This "endless debate" between such polar opposites is a waste of time. The only "answer" is that Ford was both, and he was neither. His later claim, in 1968, that his "sympathy is all with the Indians" is another prime example of Fordian folderol, but does indicate a *leaning* toward a pro–Indian perspective. As proved by *Fort Apache*, he understood that, as long as there is more than one point of view about an issue, "answers" must remain expressed ambiguously or from several perspectives. (The use of multiple narrative voices is a treacherously difficult approach attempted by precious few directors.)

The true genius of Ford lies in the contradictory artistry and nature of the man, which is a *realistic* way of viewing the spectrum of human behavior. Anyone expecting to find simple answers in Ford's work will be disappointed and frustrated. Even in his most stylized films, Ford includes a hard dose of reality. He could refer to his being on "both sides" of the "Indian" issue as emanating from his "Irishness," but it really sprang from his genius, which could also be considered plain common sense.

Fort Apache offers both a variation on the spurious legend of Custer and a tribute to the troops who, as described by York, "were all the same — men in dirty-shirt blue and only a cold page in the history books to mark their passing." While Thursday is a racist dictator, his men, ranging from Irish to a Mexican ex–Confederate, represent democracy. Interestingly, Ford allowed Bond, during a fine performance, to deliver the most direct description of Thursday when O'Rourke refers to him as "the madman." An intolerant glory-seeker in life, Thursday is handed heroism ("victory in defeat") only by a brutal death, followed by an ever-escalating trail of lies.

Some writers, including Gary Wills and Charles Ramirez Berg, have suggested that Peter Bogdanovich was wrong in equating the ending of *Fort Apache* (York's lie that Thursday's painted heroics are "correct in every detail") with that of the later *The Man Who Shot Liberty Valance*. Claiming that York "sells out" at the end of *Fort Apache*, these assertions are based on a comment about "printing the legend" made by Ford to Bogdanovich during their 1965 interviews: "We've had a lot of people who were supposed to be great heroes, and you know damn well they weren't. But it's good for the country to have heroes to look up to."[13]

Many historians ignore the fact that Ford was a cunning *liar*. However, Randy Roberts and James S. Olson agreed with Bogdanovich:

He is called upon to follow orders, even when he knows that those orders will lead to disaster, and in the end it is his duty to bury the dead, cover up the mess, and "for the good of the service" tell the world that Owen Thursday died a hero.[14]

The British film scholar Edward Buscombe, in his brilliant 1984 essay "Painting the Legend," concurred:

> Though he knows the truth about Thursday's foolhardy action, York preserves the myth which the painting embodies: when the legend becomes fact, print the legend ... in the [final] scene ... we may assume that the scriptwriters have in mind the many versions of Custer's Last Stand which were painted in the wake of that traumatic event.... Frederic Remington ... did a version ... [which] is rather Fordian, stoicism and dignity in defeat contrasting with the frenzied heroics favored by other artists.[15]

Scott Eyman concluded, "Ford says that the lies are necessary, that the lies are all right, because the most important thing is that the greatest good happens for the greatest number of people."[16]

Ford completed *Fort Apache* on October 2, 1947, and began to prepare the *Araner* for another "fishing excursion" to Mazatlan. His two stars, Hank and Duke, along with perennial fixture Mr. Bond, were aboard and ready for action. This time, after a few days of going ashore to carouse with his pals, Ford got so inebriated that he couldn't leave the boat. Fonda vividly remembered:

> We'd start at the Hotel Central, and then we'd pick up a three-piece mariachi band and go from bar to bar, saloon to saloon, whorehouse to whorehouse. You went to the whorehouses just to sit and drink and listen to the mariachis play. You didn't fuck. You didn't think you should. Those *whoores* looked grungy.[17]

During the autumn of 1947, Bond was cast by his pal Victor Fleming in the plum role of Etienne de Vignolles, "La Hire," French military commander during the Hundred Years War (1337–1453) and comrade of "The Maid of Orleans," in *Joan of Arc*, an epic in the planning stages since 1940. Star Ingrid Bergman joined with Fleming and Walter Wanger to form the production company Sierra Pictures, Inc., and devoted seven months to meticulous research, including material taken directly from the original 1431 trial transcripts. Maxwell Anderson, author of the 1947 play *Joan of Lorraine*, in which Bergman had starred, co-wrote the screenplay with Andrew Solt, and a distribution deal was made with RKO.

Shot in Technicolor at Hal Roach Studios and on location at Balboa and the RKO Ranch, where Joan's burning at the stake scene was staged, the film promised historically accurate events, weaponry and costumes, but the overall Hollywood gloss was decried by many, especially Bergman herself. Nevertheless, though the physical filth of medieval Europe may not be depicted realistically, its absence is duly compensated by the script and acting, which vibrantly display the universal and eternal reality of the corruptive, tragic nature of politics and religion.

Bergman gives an earnest, powerful performance throughout; and, amidst an impressive cast, including Jose Ferrer (in his film debut), Francis L. Sullivan, J. Carrol Naish, Leif Erickson and Hurd Hatfield, Bond (billed fourth) plays the "prickly" La Hire very close to the historical description. Given enough screen time to show his character's gradual transformation from brash warrior to faithful comrade, he also appears in the film's only real dueling scene, during which La Hire drives Sir William Glasdale (Dennis Hoey), the English commander at Orleans, to his demise in a wall of flames. "Death by fire is a horrible thing," Joan prophetically observes.

The original 145-minute cut of *Joan of Arc* premiered in New York on November 11, 1948. Less than two months later, on January 9, 1949, Victor Fleming died of a heart attack in Cottonwood, Arizona. Having directed Bond in three films, he didn't live to see what RKO did to his medieval spectacle, butchering it to 100 minutes, and dubbing in turgid narration to "replace" all the excised scenes. This truncated travesty was released on September 2, 1950 (and was the only version seen by the public until the UCLA Film and Television Archive carefully restored the original cut in 1998).

In early May 1948, two months after the release of *Fort Apache*, Ford began shooting *3 Godfathers*, a stunning Technicolor remake of *Marked Men*, his 1919 collaboration with Harry Carey, based on the Peter B. Kyne short story. (Previous books on Ford erroneously claim that this film was produced before *Fort Apache*.) Carey, a heavy smoker ravaged by a combination of lung cancer and emphysema, had passed away on September 21, 1947, while Ford was wrapping his cavalry epic. This eminent pioneer of American cinema, having made his final film appearance alongside his son's third acting effort, in Hawks' *Red River*, was 69.

Ford had taken a break from completing the *Fort Apache* shoot to help comfort Carey during his final painful hours, reminiscing about the early days when they still made films together. Duke had accompanied Ford, but remained in the next room. When the last flickers of light disappeared from the eyes of his very first star, the stone-cold sober Ford followed Olive out onto the patio of the Carey home, grabbed her and, shaking mightily, wept so hard that he soaked the entire front of her sweater.

Though he had cast his mentor in only one supporting role over nearly three decades, Ford went all out to "produce" an elaborate funeral at the Field Photo Farm. Carey's horse was tied to the chapel's hitching post, a bugler sounded taps, and the large gathering included Wayne, Bond and George O'Brien.

Ford then crafted an awe-inspiring religious allegory as a cinematic homage, including the casting of Harry, Jr. (aka "Dobe"), as William Kearney. Known as the "Abilene Kid," he is a member of a bank-robbing trio led by Robert Marmaduke Hightower (Wayne) and his right-hand man, Pedro "Pete" Roca Fuerte (Pedro Armendariz), who wage an Olympian struggle with death to save a newborn infant while fleeing from Sheriff Perley "Buck" Sweet (Bond) and his posse through the Mohave Desert.

In the 29 years between the release of *Marked Men* and the making of *3 Godfathers*, two other film versions of Kyne's popular story had been made: Universal's *Hell's Heroes* (1930), directed by William Wyler and starring Charles Bickford, Raymond Hatton and Fred Kohler; and MGM's *Three Godfathers* (1936), directed by Richard Boleslawski and featuring Chester Morris, Lewis Stone and Walter Brennan. Since MGM currently owned the story rights, Merian Cooper made a deal with the studio to finance the new adaptation by Frank Nugent and Laurence Stallings. Duke was paid his standard fee of $100,000, while Pappy assured Ward of a $2,500 salary for 10 weeks.

Unlike the overt, expressionistic symbolism that transforms *The Fugitive* into a pedantic visual sermon, *3 Godfathers* achieves a spiritual quality through Ford's organic depiction of three Western "wise men" who battle the formidable elements of nature, not to save their own skins, but to transport the innocent baby, born to a dying mother in a broken-down, abandoned wagon, across the bone-dry desert to New Jerusalem. To achieve the realism he desired, Ford again mercilessly subjected his actors to a brutal regimen, shooting on location for 32 days at Furnace Creek Ranch in Death Valley, where afternoon temperatures soared to 130 degrees.

Harry Carey, Jr. recalled:

There was absolutely no chain of command with John Ford. There was him, and there was us
... and he treated us all the same. If you got your ass chewed out, not to worry — it might be
Duke's turn on the next go-round, or Ward Bond's. But I think Ward liked it. I think he liked
to get Jack riled up, just to see the fireworks. Ward was the biggest glutton for punishment of
any of the Ford actors. To quote Jack on Ward Bond, "Let's face it, Bond is a shit. But he's my
favorite shit!" ... When Duke saw Ward coming, he'd break out laughing ... he'd yell, "Thank
God, fellas, the heat's off. Here comes Ward!" ... Of course, Ward never let us down.

   For openers, right in front of "himself," Ward would greet the day with, "This would be a hel-
luva picture, except Wayne's playing my part!"

   Ford, hearing this, would say, "Well, there goes my day. I thought the son of a bitch had the
day off!" ... Ward was great at his work, and Uncle Jack loved him. In fact, it is hard to guess
which of those two big guys he loved the most.[18]

Before production began on *3 Godfathers*, Wayne told young Carey, "For God's sake,
kid, keep yer mouth shut and yer ears open! And don't make any suggestions, no matter
what the hell he does. An' be careful, 'cause he'll try to suck you into it."[19]

At Furnace Creek, Ford made sure that Dobe would be rooming with Bond, but pre-
tended he didn't know anything about the accommodation. "Oh, God. You poor kid," he
muttered. Carey recalled, "That had been arranged for my benefit, though, because in spite
of all his braggadocio, Ward was a calming influence."[20]

Hank Worden, who roomed with Ben Johnson, plays "Curley," Sheriff Sweet's deputy,
the second of his many idiot savant roles for "Mr. Ford." He recalled, "Ford used to let us
off for a couple of hours at noon when it was really hot, and everybody would hightail it
to the pool, with its natural spring water, for a swim."[21]

To achieve a true, unaffected visual masterpiece, Ford hired Technicolor pioneer Winton
C. Hoch as director of photography. (Plans to use Gabriel Figueroa fell through when the
location schedule was moved from Mexico to Death Valley.) After landing the job by assuring
Ford that he would defer to the director's ability to "always know where to place the camera,"
Hoch nearly lost it during the first day's shooting. Ford, the man who "painted" with a
camera that he rarely needed to move, had chosen a set-up atop a sand dune, but the cinematographer suggested a tracking shot instead. This unintentional mistake unleashed a
typical Fordian tantrum that finally was quelled by a humble, two-word apology from Hoch:
"Sorry, Jack."

Ford called the meticulous Hoch a "very, very pedantic cameraman," but their collaborations, over the course of only eight years, produced the director's most exquisite color
films.[22]

One afternoon, after Ford had finished shooting, the "three godfathers" were in Carey's
cabin when Bond, dressed in a Japanese silk kimono, pulled a station wagon into the gravel
driveway. Beside him in the passenger seat was a diminutive, young blonde, who soon fell
into Ward's mighty clutches. "It was worse than to see Fay Wray with King Kong," recalled
Carey.

"How can she *kiss* that son of a bitch?" Wayne asked; then catching his old pal by surprise, shouted, "What are you doing, Ward?"

Bond bid the young lady a quick adieu, ran into the cabin, and fumed, "What the hell
are you assholes doing here?"

Dobe answered, "I live here, Ward."

"I don't mean you, you red-headed piss-pot. I mean these other two asses!" he bel-
lowed.

Duke responded in kind: "Who the hell are you calling an ass, you ugly asshole? And how can a poor decent girl even kiss such an ugly bastard?"

Carey recalled:

Duke ... was doubled over with laughter and having a marvelous time because he had caught Ward off guard. He'd made Ward look stupid, and that was one of his favorite sports. Ward huffed and puffed some more, called Duke a few more horrible names, but Duke waved him off, and Ward let it go.... You never had to feel sorry for Ward Bond. He was as indestructible as an army tank. Ford's barbs and salvos just bounced right off him — stinging shots that would have withered anyone else....[23]

During the days he worked with Bond, Carey heard him constantly singing "Nature Boy," which was a big hit for Nat "King" Cole at the time. Dobe speculated, "I am sure Ward thought he sang it better than Nat, but he sang it in the style of Louis Armstrong. He actually did a pretty good rendition."[24]

Bond's love of jazz singing often came to the fore during his period of sobriety. Off-camera, while his colleagues drank the nights away, he would make annoying comments about their inebriated behavior. Carey recalled:

Ward ... was always telling me that Wayne should learn to control his drinking. "Look at that big bastard over there, for Christ's sake, making an ass of himself!" he'd say when we were at a party. Ward, cold sober, would sit at the piano and bore Jack and Duke with his imitation of Louis Armstrong. Nat Cole and Louis Armstrong were his favorites, and he really thought he was damned near as good as they were.

I used to think to myself, "My God, what was he like when he was drinking!"[25]

A seasoned veteran like Bond knew what to expect from Pappy, but Dobe Carey was in for quite an initiation. One day, while shooting the scene during which the mortally wounded Abilene Kid takes a walk while singing "The Streets of Laredo" to the newborn baby, Carey could not manage to stay within camera range. "Stop thinkin' so much an' jes do it, goddamn it," Wayne told him. "Let that Old Man do the thinking. You were wanderin' all over the friggin' set!" Carey explained:

Now a word about whether John Wayne was really an "actor" or not. I know he once said, "I'm a re-actor." Well, he was that, too, but Duke was a terrific actor. You only had to play one reasonably well-written scene with him to find that out.[26]

When the day arrived for Carey to play his big death scene, one of the most poignant events in the film, the young actor thought he knew exactly how to nail it on the first take. After he'd finished, however, he received, not a positive response, but the worst abusive onslaught Ford had unleashed on him thus far. His "Uncle Jack" then ordered Wayne, Armendariz, and the crew to retreat, so Dobe could be left alone, without shade or a single drop of water, to roast in the blistering desert sun for the next 30 minutes. When Ford called, "Action" on the second take, Carey's performance was *real*. He remembered:

It was over. Duke lifted me to my feet. He had his arms around me, holding me up. Ford took my face in his hands. He was smiling. "Why didn't you do that the first time? See how easy it was? You done good! That's a wrap!"[27]

Dobe's last scene for *3 Godfathers* was filmed on a soundstage at the RKO Pathé lot, where, during a lull, he drank several cups of coffee and then headed out toward the men's room. As he exited the building, a trailer, transporting his late father's horse, "Sonny," to the lot, caught him by surprise. He walked over, began to pat his old equine friend, and then suddenly was grabbed by the shoulders and turned around. It was Ford, who told him, "Go home, kid. You're not supposed to see this."[28]

As a brief prologue for the film, Ford and Hoch framed an arresting silhouette of Cliff Lyons, doubling for the late Carey, Sr., riding Sonny to the crest of a desert knoll, where he lingers to push the cowboy hat back from his forehead. This Technicolor variation on many memorable Ford-Carey images from the silent days, a striking stimulus for everything that follows in *3 Godfathers*, is accompanied by the dedication, "To the Memory of Harry Carey, Bright Star of the early western sky..."

Though the opening titles include the credit, "Introducing Harry Carey, Jr.," Dobe already had acted in *Red River* and four other Westerns; but now he followed in the prodigious footsteps of Wayne, Bond and McLaglen by impressively surviving, not only the 130-degree temperatures of Death Valley, but the even more ferocious heat of Pappy's Inferno while making *3 Godfathers*. Prior to production, the director had assured the young actor that his enthusiasm and respect would be transformed into "hate" by the end of the ordeal.

A few days after the wrap, Carey, returning to the studio for post-production overdubs, saw Ford sitting outside in his car. Reaching in to shake the Old Man's hand and thank him for the "great education" the film had provided, Dobe triggered a prime example of Ford's refusal to belie his reputation as a son of a bitch by displaying positive emotions. When the only son of his late friend and mentor said, "Uncle Jack, I don't hate you. I love you," Ford "just grunted and drove off."[29]

The making of *3 Godfathers* had provided a kind of reconciliation between Ford and Wayne, who now was a bona fide superstar, a status (regardless of *Red River*) for which Pappy gave himself credit. His rancor over Duke's previous draft dodging behavior began to fade as, on screen, he imbued the Hightower character with affection for the Abilene Kid he could not express to Dobe in real life.

In *3 Godfathers*, Ford shows Bond's bum twice during his initial scene, but this time in glorious Technicolor, including additional emphasis by having Perley swat his wife (Mae Marsh) on the rear end with a small branch torn from a nearby bush. Throughout the film, Pappy similarly showcases Ward's posterior, sometimes juxtaposing it with actual horse's asses. When the outlaws plan their strategy for finding water and escaping across the border into Mexico, Ford (while Bond is off-screen) also works in a verbal reference when Bob Hightower mentions that the Marshal will be "gettin' callouses on his rump."

Ford's depiction of the three "good bad men" is a fully realized expansion of his earlier silent versions; but here, in a sound film, he continuously demonstrates the depth of their relationships visually. The tough, rugged outlaws don't need to verbalize their feelings. The most simple gestures (a hand on the shoulder; refusing the canteen to save precious water for the injured, suffering Kid; never allowing their frustrations with each other escalate to violence) are combined with sensitive actions, such as the reverent behavior toward the pregnant woman by Pedro, the only one of the three who knows anything about childbirth.

Ford's respectful depiction of the Mexican character includes "Pete's" own claim that "Indian" women have a direct connection to the Almighty: "*Nuevo Senior* tells them what to do with babies — how to *born* them — but a *gringa, mama seta.*" Whenever Pete speaks Spanish around the infant, Bob orders him to refrain from using "Mex." Later, as the only living member of the "three wise men," Bob tells the baby, "Adios, *compañero.*"

After Bob buries the woman, who dies soon after giving birth, he removes his hat, Pete prays, and the Kid sings "Shall We Gather at the River?" The understated scene is wrapped up in trademark Ford fashion.

"Is that all, Kid?" asks Bob.

"Them's all the words I know," the Kid replies.

3 Godfathers (Argosy–Metro-Goldwyn-Mayer, 1948; directed by John Ford). *The Pursuers*: Deputy Curley (Hank Worden) and Marshal Perley (Ward Bond) comb the desert for the three fleeing bank robbers.

"Then —*amen*," Bob concludes.

This reverential moment is followed by the sounds of Curley's braying jackass interrupting Perley as he explains to his posse his clever analysis of the escape strategy used by the outlaws. The film concludes with Perley singing "Shall We Gather at the River?" and patting the baby on the rump as Bob rides off to serve his sentence of "one year and one day in prison."

Shortly after completing *3 Godfathers*, Wayne began work on Republic's *Wake of the Red Witch*, an undisguised *Wuthering Heights* meets *Reap the Wild Wind*, directed by Edward Ludwig from mid–July to late October 1948. The convoluted narrative, unfolding in a series of first-person flashbacks, was equally difficult to produce. The original shooting schedule of 70 working days was extended to accommodate innovative underwater footage captured by two independent camera crews.

Duke plays the obsessive Captain Ralls, skipper of the 1860s bullion-laden *Red Witch*, who is attacked by an octopus and later drowns while attempting to retrieve $5 million in scuttled gold. Gail Russell, as Angelique Desaix, plays Cathy to Wayne's hardhearted Heathcliff, and is supported by a superb cast, including Gig Young, Luther Adler, Eduard Franz, Henry Daniell and Dennis Hoey. Wayne's pals Grant Withers and Paul Fix make their obligatory appearances, and Henry Brandon plays the native leader Kurinua, one of his many "ethnic" specialties.

3 Godfathers (Argosy–Metro-Goldwyn-Mayer, 1948; directed by John Ford). *The Pursued*: Bank robbers Robert Marmaduke Hightower (John Wayne), William Kearney, aka "The Abilene Kid" (Harry Carey, Jr.) and Pedro "Pete" Roca Fuerte (Pedro Armendariz) become godfathers of the dying mother's (Mildred Natwick) baby boy (played by a girl, Amelia Yelda).

The typically sprawling Republic storyline and low-budget special effects didn't adversely affect the film's box-office success, or Duke's enthusiasm. As Randy Roberts and James S. Olson noted:

> Everything about the film is larger than life, including John Wayne's role.... He is a Thomas Dunson gone completely over the edge, a swaggering Captain Ahab with an eye for the ladies.

With the film coming so close to *Red River*, Duke knew the type, and he threw himself into the role.[30]

Red River finally was released on September 17, 1948, to sellout audiences across the nation. Eventually raking in $4,150,000 in domestic ticket sales, the film became the second-highest grossing film of the year. Everyone who saw it realized the "big son of a bitch" could act. Roberts and Olson wrote:

> Although he had played the Dunson type before, Duke had never breathed so much life into the character; he had never transformed the type into such a believable person. And it was a character he could play again and again, one that was not constrained by the same biological imperatives as the romantic lead.... Along with John Ford, [Hawks] had revitalized Duke's career ... suddenly he had become the hottest property in the industry.[31]

Against her father's advice, Barbara Ford married actor Robert Walker aboard the *Araner* on July 8, 1948. A somber alcoholic who often flew into violent rages, Walker, still trying to drown the pain of his 1945 divorce from Jennifer Jones, began physically abusing Pappy's daughter just five weeks after the wedding. After she returned home, covered with bruises, Bond threatened to beat the hell out of "that goddamned sissy, son of a bitch," but the Old Man calmed him down.[32] Barbara was granted a divorce on December 16, 1948, and was free to celebrate the holidays with her parents. (Less than three years later, Walker, at age 32, died of an allergic reaction to a sedative, which became toxic when combined with alcohol.)

She Wore a Yellow Ribbon, Ford's second film in his unofficial "Cavalry Trilogy," began production in Monument Valley during late October. Although he had to make the picture on a budget of $1,851,290 ($400,000 less than he had been allotted for *Fort Apache*), Wayne was the only major star he cast, thus leaving ample funds to direct another sumptuous Technicolor Western with Winton Hoch behind the camera. Ford had written to James Warner Bellah:

> Monument Valley ... has never been photographed in color and ... should be breathtaking. At Monument Valley I have my own personal tribe of Navajo Indians who are great riders, swell actors ... have long hair and best of all they believe in me.... They are tall, sinewy and as the poor bastards never get enough to eat unless I make a picture there, they have no excess fat on them....[33]

Having impressed Pappy with his range in *Red River*, the 41-year-old Duke now was given the even greater challenge of playing Captain Nathan Brittles, a cavalry officer in his Sixties on the verge of retirement, who first must deal with a Kiowa uprising before reluctantly turning over his command to the next generation. Wayne rose to the challenge impressively and believably, giving what Joseph McBride aptly described as an "extraordinarily moving performance."[34]

Based on a first-draft screenplay adapted by Bellah from two of his own short stories, "War Party" and "Big Hunt," the final shooting script by Frank Nugent and Laurence Stallings, set in 1876, begins where *Fort Apache* leaves off, fading in on the flag of the U.S. 7th Cavalry and narration that includes the fact that "Custer is dead." Re-joining Wayne from *Fort Apache* are Victor McLaglen, George O'Brien and John Agar. Dobe Carey, fresh from *3 Godfathers*, also is back to continue what became a perennial run as a top member of the Stock Company.

During the train trip from Los Angeles to Flagstaff, "Uncle Jack" tried to pull his usual shenanigans on Dobe *and* Duke. Ford had spotted McLaglen enjoying a wee dram or two in the club car and, claiming that he wouldn't begin shooting *Yellow Ribbon* for another two days, encouraged them to join "Uncle Victor."

"No thanks, Coach," replied Wayne. "I ain't that dumb, an' neither is this red-headed kid here." Knowing young Carey had been well "broken-in" during the making of *3 Godfathers*, Duke looked at him, adding, "Right, ol' Dobe?"[35]

Carey, who had learned to speak Navajo as a child, looked forward to setting foot in Monument Valley, which he previously only had seen in black-and-white while watching *Stagecoach* and *My Darling Clementine*. During the ride from Flagstaff, he shared the back seat of a station wagon with John Agar, while McLaglen, relaxing in the front passenger seat, frequently turned around to discuss the Old Man's "meanness" with the "lads."

When Dobe recalled the grueling *3 Godfathers* experience, McLaglen instantly identified with his younger colleague and admitted that he hadn't even bothered to read the script. "He's a bad one," the veteran whipping boy said of Ford. "A fucking sadist, he is. But ya can't let it bother ya, lad." Carey later wrote:

> Uncle Vic made the trip a joy. He had a wonderful childlike quality and a don't-give-a-damn-what-happens attitude.... With that guilty-little-boy quality inside that huge body and smashed-in kisser, he was a real scene-stealer without trying to be one. Vic never reverted to sly tricks to get a laugh; he just played himself.[36]

Although his Captain York is unable to prevent Colonel Thursday's suicidal charge in *Fort Apache*, Wayne's even more experienced, flexible Captain Brittles, ignoring regulations, briefly takes back his command from young Lieutenant Flint Cohill (Agar) to avoid a repeat of this reactionary disaster when dealing with the Kiowa Chief, Pony That Walks (Chief John Big Tree), who shares his point of view.

"Young men do not listen to me," the Chief tells his longtime friend.

Framed in a tight close-up, Brittles admits, "Old men should stop wars."

Ford later claimed that *She Wore a Yellow Ribbon* was his favorite of the cavalry pictures, specifically referring to the visual approach, inspired by of one of his major influences: "I tried to copy the Remington style there—you can't copy him one hundred percent—but at least I tried to get in his color and movement, and I think I succeeded partly."[37]

Edward Buscombe described the "narrative" content present in Remington's Western paintings:

> [W]hat he chiefly chose to record was the life of hard riding and hard fighting. The focus in his work is on the moment of action frozen at the point of its maximum impact ... even Remington's quieter compositions are founded on tension and suspense, while the most dramatic communicate a sense of action proceeding through time....
>
>   For such paintings the description "cinematic" seems not inappropriate.... Remington's first real success came in 1886 ... [when] the experiments of Eadweard Muybridge in photographically recording the movements of animals were becoming widely known among painters.... The success of the camera in recording what the naked eye could not perceive was capitalized on by Remington to impart a new realism to his work ... there can be little doubt that [this] photographically inspired realism ... helped precipitate the Western as a popular cinema genre.[38]

The most famous shot in *She Wore a Yellow Ribbon*, depicting the cavalrymen on foot, leading their horses through Monument Valley as a blackening sky interrupted by flares of lightning brews overhead, was actually improvised after Ford had called a wrap that day. A myth about Winton Hoch's initial "refusal" to film the additional setup, as freezing rain fell and thunder and lightning raged, circulated for years but finally was laid to rest by Carey, who had heard Ford *ask* the cinematographer if he'd be able to film in such darkness. When Hoch replied that he couldn't "promise anything," Pappy replied, "Winnie, open her up [the lens] and let's go for it. If it doesn't come out, I'll take the rap."

She Wore a Yellow Ribbon (Argosy–RKO Radio, 1949; directed by John Ford). Prior to his official retirement ceremony, Captain Nathan Brittles (John Wayne) checks the breath of Sergeant Quincannon (Victor McLaglen) for any possible trace of alcoholic residue, as witnessed by Sergeant Tyree (Ben Johnson) and Abby Allshard, aka "Old Iron Pants" (Mildred Natwick).

Ford's idea was realized beautifully by Hoch, using film stock that neither of them was certain could be exposed properly by the available light. Carey wrote, "It sure as hell came out! It was a Technicolor breakthrough."[39]

The beautifully written and acted character of Brittles, a fine dramatic match for Ford and Hoch's stunning "Remington color" environment, makes up for the often intrusive, romantic-triangle subplot involving Cohill, Lieutenant Ross Pennell (Carey) and the yellow ribbon-wearing Olivia Dandridge (the ever-fetching Joanne Dru, making her first appearance for Ford, who had been impressed by her performance in *Red River*). Having averted a major Indian War, Brittles ultimately evades the obsolescence of retirement when he is appointed Civilian Chief of Scouts and rides off toward new settlements in California. According to Carey, Wayne worked so hard on the film that he temporarily became a type of Method actor:

> The irony of the whole *Yellow Ribbon* story, where my character was concerned, was that Duke was so into the character of Nathan Brittles that he treated me, Dobe Carey, his old *3 Godfathers* pal, like I really was that horse's ass, even off the set. I must have been giving a fairly convincing performance. We didn't become friends again until the picture was over.[40]

Wayne, who received a cake adorned with one candle, signifying that Ford's discovery "finally had arrived," said, "He never thought of me as an actor, and then he saw *Red River*, and he wanted to top it, and he did. He gave me that part in *Yellow Ribbon* ... and I think it's the best thing I've ever done."[41]

On October 22, 1949, *She Wore a Yellow Ribbon* was released to impressive box-office but only middling reviews, reflecting the film's depiction of the generational division between Brittles and the new command. Dan Ford succinctly described his grandfather's position in the postwar film industry:

> [A]lthough he was making some of the best ... films of his life, his once-exalted reputation with the critics was beginning to fade. Critics of the day liked pictures that broke with the Hollywood tradition to deal with contemporary themes. "Realism" was the order of the day ... [and] they were looking on John as one of Hollywood's grand old men, an honored has-been....[42]

Following his disagreements with the director while shooting *Yellow Ribbon*, Winton Hoch won his first Best Color Cinematography Oscar for his work on a Ford film.

During late 1948, when Monument Valley was hit by a blizzard depositing snow the Navajos described as "two men deep," Ford called some military colleagues. Soon, "Operation Haylift" was underway, with aircraft dropping bundles of food to the stranded and shut-in people.

8

Bond and the Blacklist

There was no blacklist at that time, as some people said. That was a lot of horseshit. Later on, when Congress passed some laws making it possible to take a stand against these people, we were asked about Communists in the industry. So we gave them the facts as we knew them. That's all. The only thing our side did that was anywhere near blacklisting was just running a lot of people out of the business. — John Wayne[1]

Ward Bond was second only to Hedda Hopper in directing the blacklist, literally ending the careers of so many talented people in the industry. I can't say that I enjoyed working with him, but I have to admit that, mainly because of Ford, he was one hell of an actor. — Henry Brandon[2]

The President of the United States was getting tough on Communism, and his "Truman Doctrine" mandated active intervention, economic and otherwise, in the affairs of countries under growing "Red" influence and control. This Cold War mentality also affected the home front, with the federal government requiring its employees to sign "loyalty oaths." Representatives of the House Committee on Un-American Activities (HUAC), including chairman J. Parnell Thomas, had visited Hollywood; and, in September 1947, began issuing subpoenas to those they wished to question at hearings the following month.

In response, John Huston, teaming with fellow director William Wyler, writer Philip Dunne, and former Ford actress Myrna Loy, formed the Committee for the First Amendment (CFA), to protest HUAC's attack on the basic freedoms guaranteed to every American. From the current Ford Stock Company, Henry Fonda was one of the first actors to sign up, soon to be joined by Pappy's erstwhile leading lady and paramour, Katherine Hepburn. By the end of September, the organization had attracted 140 film-industry personnel, including Lauren Bacall, Humphrey Bogart, Ava Gardner, John Garfield, Paulette Goddard, Sterling Hayden, Paul Henreid, Gene Kelly, Alexander Knox, Fredric March, Groucho Marx, Gregory Peck, Edward G. Robinson, Robert Ryan, Frank Sinatra and Billy Wilder.

On October 20, 1947, HUAC officially began its hearings, questioning "friendly witnesses" Louis B. Mayer and Jack Warner, who admitted that he had hired a total of 11 "Communist" writers, including Dalton Trumbo. On the second day, testimony was happily offered by the rabidly right-wing Adolphe Menjou. Though he initially stopped short of "naming names," the actor claimed there were members of his profession who *acted* like Communists, easily working "subversive" gestures into their performances.

Menjou then described a September 1946 Screen Actors Guild strike mediation meeting, praising SAG acting president Ronald Reagan for being on the "right side," while naming four actors on the "wrong side," which had allowed "Communist domination" of labor through its support of the Conference of Studio Unions (CSU): Hume Cronyn, Paul Henreid, Alexander Knox and Edward G. Robinson, whom the borderline paranoid performer wanted to "hang." Returning to a discussion of those on the "right side," he lauded the actions of the Motion Picture Alliance for the Preservation of American Ideals.

Founded in 1944 by ultra-conservative director Sam Wood and the strongly anti-labor Walt Disney, in direct response to Dudley Nichols' support for liberal Vice President Henry Wallace, the MPA was at the forefront of the Hollywood witch-hunters, providing long lists of "Commie" names to HUAC. Several members of Ford's once-and-future troupe ultimately joined the ranks (which Wood estimated to be 1,100 strong): Donald Crisp, Clark Gable, James Kevin McGuinness, Barbara Stanwyck, Frank Wead; and, most prominently, John Wayne and Ward Bond, both of whom eventually served as president of this *un*–American outfit. Gary Wills aptly noted:

> This organization did the one thing guaranteed to make the rest of the movie world hate it. It openly invited the House Committee on Un-American Activities back to California and take up where the [Congressman Martin] Dies Committee had left off five years earlier.[3]

Having referred to himself as a "socialist" just a few years earlier (a period when he was working with Dudley Nichols), Ford, having moved rightward as a result of his wartime experiences, actually joined the MPA, an action (like so many of his contradictory exploits) that has provoked decades of speculation about his "true" political ideology. The simple truth is that Pappy never could allow his "discoveries" (the men he "made") to take *any* kind of leadership role without his personal involvement.

Pappy's relationships, not only with Wayne and Bond, but with "professional Irishman" Jim McGuinness, who spoke with a bogus brogue and flattered Ford by calling him "Sean," pulled him into the MPA. Randy Roberts and James S. Olson wrote:

> John Wayne said that McGuinness was "pleasant company" but a "lousy drunk." ... [W]hen any conversation turned political, he lost his genial Irishman pose and accent and became quite serious. In the early 1930s he had fought a losing battle against Communists in the Screen Writers Guild.... McGuinness remained genuinely concerned about the influence of radicals in Hollywood, and he never slackened his attacks, even though his career suffered as a result.[4]

Less than a year after Louis B. Mayer sacked him from the MGM production roster, McGuinness died. Hailed as a martyr by the Right, he was honored by the MPA with the institution of the James Kevin McGuinness Americanism Award.

Three weeks before the HUAC hearings began, Ford, who had rejoined the Screen Directors Guild in May 1946, was elected chairman of the Special Committee to Investigate Thomas Committee Subpoenas, whose other prominent members included George Sidney, SDG president George Stevens, CFA founders John Huston and William Wyler, and Ford's Argosy partner, Merian Cooper. But, like the CFA, the SDG committee proved highly ineffectual in its attempts to steer a political "middle course." While seeking to defend the civil rights of Hollywood liberals who had been named as "unfriendly," its members literally caved in to HUAC and other blacklisters (in effect, creating their own version of the "loyalty oath") by publicly proclaiming an opposition to Communism.

On October 23, 1947, Gary Cooper, Robert Montgomery (Ford's cinematic Bulkeley), George Murphy and director Ray McCarey appeared at the hearings as friendly witnesses, with Ronald Reagan pledging to aid HUAC in any way possible. The following day, the

CFA ran full-page ads in the Los Angeles papers, including Article I of the Bill of Rights and 100 signatures; and, on October 25, a group of committee performers recorded material for *Hollywood Fights Back*, a radio program that aired nationally the following day. The CFA also sent representatives, including Huston, Bogart and Bacall, to Washington to protest formally at the hearings, but they accomplished little.

On November 24, a group of film industry financiers and producers met at the Waldorf-Astoria in New York, issuing a statement that they would no longer hire any of the artists branded "The Hollywood Ten," a group of writers and directors cited for contempt of Congress, unless they publicly cleared themselves, including admissions that they were not members of the Communist Party. The group also made declarations that basically outlawed anyone who was suspected of "subversive" beliefs or actions, thereby officially greenlighting the blacklist.

Members of the Hollywood guilds arrived at MGM on the morning of November 28 to meet with a committee of West Coast producers selected to enforce the "Waldorf Statement." Ford and Wyler from the SDG, Reagan from the SAG (though he was president of the guild, Ron acted as a "double agent," secretly supporting the blacklist by serving as an FBI informant), and Sheridan Gibney, George Seaton and Harry Tugend from the Screen Writers Guild went up against Louis B. Mayer, Ford's erstwhile producer Walter Wanger, N. Peter Rathvon from RKO, and Edward Cheyfitz of the Motion Picture Association of America.

Fearing heat from Congress, the producers blamed the situation on the MPA and other extremists who had propagandized the degree of "Communist" activity in Tinsel Town; and then "unofficially" admitting that a blacklist did exist, they asked the guild representatives to provide a few patsies who could be used to stave off further bloodletting. Ford boldly informed them that guild bylaws protected their members from being fired for political reasons; and Gibney, supported by Reagan (who already was proving he was a better actor in real life than in the *reel*), referred to the illegality of blacklisting, under California and federal law, including the Taft-Hartley Act and the Wagner Act.

Following further discussions during the first week of December, the guilds, cowed by the producers' bemoaning of box-office losses and protests from anti–Communist and other conservative groups, vented their collective anger but, trying to convince themselves that "the good of the many outweighs the good of the few," went along with sacrificing the Hollywood Ten to the Washington wolves. As to Wayne's involvement, Gary Wills observed:

> [F]rom 1939 to 1947, Wayne's name does not appear on any side of the struggle.... The same careerism that kept him from wearing a uniform kept him from taking a stand. His role, finally, was to emerge after the battle and shoot the wounded. He became "outspoken" only after the Waldorf conference had ended the war and the industry was voicing *only* one side ... by 1948 the Alliance had won, Congress was calling the shots, the studios had capitulated, and actors were making overtones of preemptive cooperation. To step in then was joining a bully, not an underdog.[5]

Duke's views were simple and straightforward:

> [Socialism] isn't going to stop the selfishness of human behavior. It isn't going to stop the greed. If you take twenty dollars and give a dollar to every son of a bitch in a room and come back a year later, one of the bastards will have most of the money. It's just human nature, and you're not going to whip it with a lot of laws.[6]

In early 1948, Ford took another shot at HUAC, using his status as commander of the Motion Picture Chapter of the Military Order of the Purple Heart to deliver a statement of protest, which was provided with additional muscle when read to the committee by CFA member Audie Murphy, recipient of three Purple Hearts and the Congressional Medal of Honor, hailed nationwide as the most decorated U.S. soldier of World War II. However, pressured by fanatical gossip monger Hedda Hopper, Murphy eventually recanted publicly, claiming that the Order of the Purple Heart and other veterans' groups had been duped by Communists.

With Franklin Roosevelt in office, Ford had supported the president's New Deal programs and other progressive causes, both personally (contributing to organizations the FBI considered "Communist fronts") and professionally, by making *The Grapes of Wrath*. And, in 1942, when FDR created the Bureau of Motion Pictures (BMP), which "persuaded" the movie moguls to depict U.S. allies as equal bastions of democracy, pro–Soviet films such as *Mission to Moscow* and *The North Star* (both 1943) were enthusiastically produced. The "Red" content in Hollywood films was created, not by un–American "Bolsheviks" infiltrating the film industry, but by the *United States Government*, which now, through Truman and HUAC, was attempting to ferret out "Commies" from under every rock.

Randy Roberts and James S. Olson pointed out:

> Americans, conservatives and liberals alike, worried about the inroads communism had made throughout the United States, not just in the movies, and the Red Scare was a broad-based political phenomenon that extended well beyond the membership of the American Alliance for the Preservation of American ideals, and the House Committee on Un-American Activities. During that decade, purging Communists was as American as motherhood, baseball, and apple pie.[7]

As for Ford, he was shooting *Fort Apache*, critically depicting a hard-line military martinet in a film with pro–Indian sympathies, ironically represented by a character played by Wayne. Gary Wills added:

> Despite Wayne's image as a nonconformist ... nothing was more conformist in the Hollywood of the 1950s than to berate Communists and to call oneself brave for doing so. Wayne, after all, could not take credit for his one truly nonconformist act in the 1940s—his defiance of all the pressures to join the military. Nor was he known as a rebel or nonconformist in the studios he worked for—no Jimmy Cagney or Bette Davis, who attacked unjust contract conditions. His docility with Ford was almost childlike. Wayne the late-arriving anti–Communist cut no profile in courage.[8]

After Ben Johnson worked as a stuntman and Henry Fonda's riding double in *Fort Apache*, Merian Cooper set out to transform the Oklahoma cowboy into a leading man in *Mighty Joe Young*. Collaborating with fellow *King Kong* veterans (director Ernest B. Schoedsack, writer Ruth Rose, and special effects artist Willis J. O'Brien, who was assisted by a young Ray Harryhausen), Cooper raised the ire of Ford, who didn't appreciate having his name attached to a film aimed at adolescents.

Filmed between mid–December 1947 and early March 1948, *Mighty Joe Young* stars Johnson as a rodeo performer hired by Max O'Hara (Robert Armstrong, in a variation on his Carl Denham character in *Kong*) to capture a marketable creature while on an African safari and transport it back to the States. Argosy vice-president Donald Dewar, admitting that Ford was interested only in producing his own projects, also commented on the chairman's daily lunch ritual:

> Wayne would be there usually, Maureen O'Hara sometimes, Milly Natwick sometimes. But Ward Bond was always there. And he took the most atrocious verbal abuse, horrible beatings. And everybody thought it was funny, except me; I thought it was awful. And Bond's reaction would just be, "Oh, Boss, come on, don't say that...." It was like beating a big puppy. Ford loved to take him apart and he did it repeatedly, over anything at all.[9]

In an attempt to offset his reputation as a "subversive" liberal, Ford now openly participated in MPA activities, following the lead of the ultimate Democratic Cold Warrior, President Truman, who (as later revealed by White House Counsel Clark Clifford) created a propaganda campaign, greatly distorting and magnifying the internal threat of Communism, to help win the 1948 election (just as he had integrated the military in an attempt to capture African American votes).

Harry Carey, Jr., wrote:

> Few people realize that Ford's political beliefs were not aligned with [Wayne and Bond]. His politics fluctuated, depending on who he would like to see as president of his country, and, God, how he loved his country. The "liberals" in [Hollywood] always called him a "right-winger" or a "reactionary," but he was simply a true patriot ... during the shooting of *Yellow Ribbon*, he and I were the only ones in the company to vote for Truman.[10]

While his arch right-wing MPA pals voted for Republican Thomas Dewey, Ford's support for Truman was still a fairly conservative position. Following the HUAC hearings and the Waldorf decision, the MPA turned up the heat in Hollywood, greatly expanding the blacklist by providing, not only names, but entire dossiers to the Congressional committee. Joseph McBride noted:

> Ford's decision to join the MPA's executive committee when Wayne ... [became] president in March 1949 may have been a form of protective coloration to shield himself from political danger from the right. But ... Ford remained prominent in the MPA for much of the blacklist era, lending his considerable prestige to the organization while it was helping to broaden the purge of Hollywood leftists....[11]

Having remained on the home front while so many of their colleagues had forged impressive military careers fighting the Axis during World War II, Wayne and Bond now attempted to bury that bothersome fact by transforming themselves into flag-waving Cold War "super-patriots." Over time, Wayne's political beliefs and activities resulted in an integration of the simplistic patriotic elements of his screen image with his actual personality. Marion Morrison really began to think he *was John Wayne*. Garry Wills explained:

> There is no better demonstration of the power of movies than Wayne's impact on American life. He was not like other actors, who simply hold political views.... Wayne did not just have political opinions. He embodied a politics; or his screen image did. It was a politics of large meanings, not of little policies — a politics of gender (masculine), ideology (patriotism), character (self-reliance), and responsibility. It was a matter of basic orientation. Its dogmas were (usually) implicit. Whatever weight attached to his "real life" was totally derived from the flickering light of his screen appearances.[12]

Wayne's fans hailed his jingoism, even considering him the "Ultimate American." But the critical establishment, disturbed by Wayne's right-wing antics, let political distaste color their views of his artistic work, particularly his recent versatile, full-blooded performances in *Fort Apache, She Wore a Yellow Ribbon* and Hawks' *Red River*.

Bond's growing obsession with tracking down Reds seriously damaged his career, and his once-prodigious cinematic output slowed to a trickle as he was offered fewer roles by Hollywood producers. If Ford, who often was disgusted with his protégé's behavior, and Wayne, who had begun to produce his own films, hadn't continued to hire him, Ward may have reached a point when his voracious eating, drinking, smoking and philandering habits would have become difficult to maintain.

Harry Carey, Jr., explained, "Ford said Ward would do anything that made him feel important, even at the expense of stomping on people, 'cause he was just too thickheaded to really analyze it and see what a phony thing it was." Nunnally Johnson, who had written the screenplays for *The Prisoner of Shark Island*, *The Grapes of Wrath* and *Tobacco Road* (two of which include Bond), added that such self-important, extremist behavior made him "ashamed of the whole industry.... Think of John Huston, having to go out and debase himself to an oaf like Ward Bond and promise he'd never be a bad boy again, and Ward Bond would say, 'All right, then, we clear you, but we've got our eye on you.'"[13]

The social-climbing Bond's ultimate political affront to Ford involved an invitation to a party he was throwing for Senator Joseph McCarthy. His great mentor simply answered, "You can take your party and shove it. I wouldn't meet that guy in a whorehouse. He's a disgrace and a danger to our country."[14]

Though Ford continued to employ him, Bond's status as the director's favorite whipping boy became more apparent each time he stepped on to a new film set. Wayne even began to join the Coach in devising practical jokes intended to make the Judge look like a complete fool in front of his colleagues, but his thick-skinned attitude allowed most of the abuse to run right off his back. Ford recalled, "Duke and I were always spending most of our time playing tricks on Ward. If we spent ... just one quarter of the time reading the script or trying to help the story, we'd have made better pictures."[15]

Anna Lee, who eventually fell victim to the blacklist Bond helped to build, had witnessed the "bizarre" relationship that he and Ford developed over the years. She later said:

It was obvious that Pappy was genuinely fond of Ward. But, one minute, he'd treat him like his best friend — almost like a son — and, the next, would completely turn away or, worse, lambaste him with every terrible name in the book — usually because Ward had done something that Pappy simply couldn't tolerate. I was always aware of Pappy's penchant for calling attention to Ward's substantial rear-end, and I do have one of those photos showing him and Duke, with their backs to the camera, standing on either side of a horse in the same position. Below the horse's behind, Pappy wrote, "Thinking of you," and then sent the picture to Ward. Pappy was always thinking of pranks to play on him, and they became even more rude when Duke joined in.[16]

Bond's next project for Pappy was, not a new film, but his *stage* debut, as the top-billed star in a revival of a popular play with a hearty dose of rebellious attitude. From February 22 through March 11, 1949, he and Pat O'Brien portrayed Captain Flagg and Sergeant Quirt, respectively, in Ford's touring production of *What Price Glory?* Having directed a few scenes for Raoul Walsh's 1926 film version starring McLaglen, Ford was very familiar with the plot about U.S. Marines who bitch about orders but dutifully carry them out (a comic version of Wayne's York in *Fort Apache*), and he was inspired further by a series of variety shows he had produced for World War II veterans.

The "all-star" cast included, not only Bond and Pat O'Brien, but Wayne, Gregory Peck, Maureen O'Hara, George O'Brien, Wallace Ford, Robert Armstrong, Alan Hale, Harry Carey, Jr., Forrest Tucker, Charles Kemper, Henry O'Neill, Ed Begley, Jimmy Lydon, Jim Davis, Luis Alberni and Larry Blake. Ford was thrilled to cast Oliver Hardy, who supported Duke in Republic's *The Fighting Kentuckian* and Bond in Capra's *Riding High* that same year. (After being teamed with Hardy in 1927, Stan Laurel never appeared in a film without his partner. Pappy loved the comic magic they created.)

Ford initially planned to direct the play himself; but, as Pat O'Brien recalled:

[H]e wasn't very good. He finally called in a fine stage director named Ralph Murphy and told him to clean the show up. "I just want you to know that you're not going to get any credit," Jack told him in that crabby way of his.[17]

Murphy actually did receive a "Staged by" credit, but Pappy made sure that his billing topped all: "Entire Production Supervised by John Ford."

Nightly rehearsals were held at the Masquers Club, where Ford was on hand to watch every run-through. Carey recalled, "Ford never once interfered with Murphy ... sat out in the audience and never said a word.... He loved the stage."[18] One evening, when Murphy was unable to attend, Ford filled in, satisfying his sadistic need to berate Bond at every turn. Ward initially had difficulty memorizing the voluminous dialogue, but triumphed by giving an excellent performance as Flagg.

The last dress rehearsal, on February 21, 1949, was held for 450 invited guests, including Secretary of the Navy John Sullivan and former Army Air Corps Captain James Stewart, who served as emcee. The first professional performance graced Long Beach the following evening, and then moved on to San Jose, Oakland, San Francisco, Pasadena (where a reviewer raved that the play was Broadway caliber) and San Gabriel. In Los Angeles, the critic for the *Times* wrote, "Ward Bond, Pat O'Brien and Maureen O'Hara in the leads acquitted themselves admirably. They could star in the play on any stage."[19] The profanity in the

Aboard the *Shamrock Special* (March 17, 1949). En route from Hollywood to Houston to attend the exclusive St. Patrick's Day grand opening of Texas oil tycoon "Wildcat Glenn" McCarthy's lavish Shamrock Hotel, (left to right) Ward Bond, Mrs. Pat O'Brien, Hugh Herbert, and Bond's *Tap Roots* costar, Van Heflin, enjoy lunch aboard a chartered Santa Fe Super Chief temporarily rechristened *The Shamrock Special* for the occasion.

original script was left intact, which created controversy in, of all places, L.A., where columnist Jimmie Fidler actually urged his radio listeners to boycott the show!

Dobe Carey said:

> The audience would just applaud when Ward and O'Brien came on stage. When Wayne made an entrance, they'd just gasp.... With Greg Peck, it was like Frank Sinatra. He was such a heartthrob, the girls would just start squealing when he came on stage.[20]

All proceeds from the play were to be donated to the Military Order of the Purple Heart, but when the accountant took it on the lam with $82,000 in profits, Ford nixed the idea of pursuing him, instead replacing the stolen funds from his own bank account. By that point, Pappy had grown tired of the entire enterprise, but audiences enjoyed his emphasis on the comedy in the original stage version and 1926 film. When James Cagney attended a performance, he particularly reveled in the comic contributions of Hardy: "It was the funniest thing I think I have ever seen. Roland Winters and I had to hang on to each other, we were laughing so much."[21]

Wayne followed these charity performances portraying War of 1812 veteran John Breen in *The Fighting Kentuckian*, yet another rambling Republic frontier "epic," played as much for comedy (provided by Hardy as Breen's rotund sidekick, Willie Paine) as adventure. Though Duke produced the project, Herb Yates still saddled him with Vera Ralston as the female lead, Fleurette DeMarchand. However, he was able to console himself with the dependable presence of Ford-Wayne fixtures Grant Withers, Paul Fix, Mae Marsh, Jack Pennick, Mickey Simpson, Fred Graham, Hank Worden and Cliff Lyons. Set in Alabama, the film was shot primarily at Agoura, California, where Duke and director George Waggner worked closely with French technical adviser Donald Overall-Hatswell to depict accurate cultural and military details.

On St. Patrick's Day 1949, Bond, joined by Mrs. Pat O'Brien, Hugh Herbert, his *Tap Roots* costar Van Heflin, and other Hollywood celebrities, took a chartered Santa Fe Super Chief, temporarily rechristened the *Shamrock Special*, to Houston, where conservative Texas oil tycoon "Wildcat Glenn" McCarthy was throwing "the biggest party" in the history of the city to celebrate the grand opening of his $21 million, 18-storey, 1,100-room Shamrock Hotel. Top stars, comprising a large percentage of the 150 black-tie and evening-gown guests, were flown to Houston Municipal Airport aboard a Boeing 307 Stratoliner that McCarthy recently had acquired from Howard Hughes.

Bond enjoyed partying with several heavy hitters, including Errol Flynn, with whom he'd worked over the years. Outside the complex, 50,000 people clamored to get a glimpse of the famous revelers, and eventually 3,000 of them managed to work their way into the hotel's public areas.

During a nationwide radio broadcast by Dorothy Lamour, the network suddenly cut the feed after a technician unleashed some foul language heard by Americans from coast to coast. Houston mayor Oscar F. Holcombe later claimed, "It was the worst mob scene I have ever witnessed."[22] (Three years later, McCarthy, following an investigation by the SEC, lost the complex to a life insurance company. It subsequently was sold to the Hilton Corporation, whose entertainment director hired the likes of Frank Sinatra and Patty Andrews to headline in the Shamrock's private Cork Club.)

From early June to late August 1949, Wayne gave what Garry Wills aptly called "his most influential performance," for director Allan Dwan at Republic, in the World War II film *Sands of Iwo Jima* (1950), inspired, not by the facts of the original February 23, 1945, flag raising on Mt. Suribachi (photographed by Louis Lowery), but on the myth created by

What Price Glory? (February 22–March 11, 1949; produced by John Ford). In his stage debut, Ward Bond costarred with Pat O'Brien, as Captain Flagg and Sergeant Quirt, respectively (the roles played in Raoul Walsh's 1926 film version by Victor McLaglen and Edmund Lowe). John Wayne (background, left) appeared in the supporting role of Lieutenant Cunningham. This series of live performances marked Bond's only top-billed role (above Wayne!) in a Ford production.

the raising of a *second*, larger flag by a different group of six men (captured in a photo by Joseph Rosenthal and published on the front page of the Sunday *New York Times* two days later).

The far more dramatic Rosenthal version, accompanied by a caption assuring readers that the Battle of Iwo Jima was "still raging" around these valiant Marines, became one of the fabled images of the war, ripe for use as a powerful propaganda tool quickly seized upon by the Marine Corps to boost home-front and military morale. The three men who survived were ordered home to be transformed into overnight celebrities, sent on tour to speak at public events and on radio programs, ostensibly to sell war bonds. Following the Allied victory six months later, the survivors were still on tour, now helping to drum up support for the creation of an awe-inspiring public monument based on the Rosenthal photo.

Commissioned by the Marine Corps, sculptor Felix de Weldon produced a life-size plaster model displayed on Constitution Avenue for the Veterans Day celebration on November 11, 1945. The Marines then sent casts of the sculpture on tour to aid in recruiting efforts, and the original was displayed at the entrance of the Quantico base outside Washington.

Campaigning for a much larger, 100-ton bronze version of de Weldon's work to become a permanent shrine, the Corps agreed to supply Republic with the necessary shooting locations, equipment and attire for *Sands of Iwo Jima* if the second raising would be included as a major scene in the screenplay by Harry Brown and James Edward Grant. As extra impetus, the Marines also contributed the large flag and the surviving men (for minor roles) who had raised it on Suribachi.

Ultimately, the bronze monument would be patterned, not after the poses of the actual Marines in Rosenthal's photograph, but on the Hollywood actors in Allan Dwan's film. (Thus the sculpture, one of the U.S. capitol's leading tourist attractions, depicts, not only a historical myth, but a *fictionalized version* of a myth. In this instance, they definitely "printed the legend.")

The Iwo Jima legend became even more ingrained in the minds of people worldwide after *Sands of Iwo Jima* depicted the men who have been whipped into shape by Wayne's relentless Sergeant Stryker furiously fighting their way up Suribachi to plant the flag. The first flag-raising, and the two patrols which preceded it, were conveniently forgotten. Gary Wills noted:

> Though the movie prospered on the growing legend of Mount Suribachi, its long life in the Wayne legend comes from the character he was given in the script, and from the way he performed. It shows how eager the Corps was to promote the Suribachi myth that it gave in to Hollywood pressures for dramatic license.[23]

(The actual facts of the Battle of Iwo Jima and the Suribachi efforts were dramatized by director Clint Eastwood in *Flags of Our Fathers* [2006], featuring Adam Beach as the ill-fated Native American [Pima], Ira Hayes, who died as a result of alcoholism following his touring as one of the three "celebrity heroes." In an unprecedented effort, Eastwood also directed a companion film from the Japanese perspective, the even more effective *Letters from Iwo Jima* [2006], starring Ken Watanabe.)

Producer Edmund Grainger had estimated that *Sands of Iwo Jima* would cost $2.5 million. With the cooperation of the Marine Corps, authorizing Republic's use of facilities, equipment and troops at Camp Pendleton and from the El Toro air base, the budget was cut down to $1 million. Gone were the exaggerated, suicidal heroics of the films produced during World War II. Grainger said, "[T]his picture ... will show the heroism of the average American as he readjusted from civilian life to the war."[24]

Regardless of James Edward Grant's hoary, cliché-ridden screenplay, Wayne's gung-ho performance earned him a Best Actor Academy Award nomination; and, in the words of Gary Wills, his characterization of "Stryker entered the mythology of right-wing America."[25] This performance also would have an effect on Wayne's subsequent screen persona, not only in war films, but also his work in other genres. Wills concluded:

[*Sands of Iwo Jima*] merged the legend of the Marines and the legend of John Wayne. From now on, the man who evaded World War II service would be the symbolic man who *won* World War II. Its contagious delusions were registered ... in the lives of ... Wayne surrogates who strut about with a need to be tough, to think of life as warfare.[26]

While Wayne was working for Allan Dwan on *Iwo Jima*, Ford was busy at 20th Century–Fox, making a fact-based *comedy* about World War II. *When Willie Comes Marching Home* (1950), stars Dan Dailey as Bill Kluggs, a patriotic G.I. who, aside from one accidental, heroic entanglement with the French Resistance (which he is ordered to keep top secret), winds up stationed back in his hometown of Punxatawney, West Virginia, as a gunnery instructor.

Ford had owed Zanuck a film, due to the mogul's aid in getting *The Fugitive* made, but his attempt to direct an adaptation of Cid Rickett Sumner's novel *Quality*, about a young African American woman (nicknamed "Pinky," who passes for white until she is morally transformed by contact with her ethnic roots) proved disastrous. Chosen because of his friendships with, and previous sympathetic portrayals of, blacks, Ford, who was angry over Zanuck's refusal to let him shoot on location in the South, was replaced with Elia Kazan after he encountered problems directing the highly sensitive Ethel Waters.

Ford's response to Waters' dislike for his direction had been exaggerating an illness, going to bed, and refusing to return to the studio. Philip Dunne later revealed, "I never saw the stuff [Ford] shot, but this is what Zanuck felt: he said the stuff was 'unbelievable.' Ford ... had [Waters] moaning spirituals. He just didn't *understand*."[27]

Kazan also had difficulty directing Waters, whom he said displayed "an odd combination of old-time religiosity and free-flowing hatred."[28] However, Waters recalled the events somewhat differently, claiming that the person responsible for her winning the part of "Granny" was, not Ford himself, but a jazz lover very close to him:

> I'd had a lucky break getting the role.... One of John Ford's closest friends was Ward Bond, the character actor, who had been a fan of mine for years. He was one of the actors who'd always followed my career with interest. He'd caught me every time I'd appeared in Los Angeles and had many of my old records.
> So, being Ward Bond's baby, he suggested I be tested when John Ford started looking for a Granny. And Darryl Zanuck ... remembered my working for him in *On with the Show* and enthusiastically okayed me for the job.

Waters also described her attitude toward Pappy:

> I had always loved John Ford's pictures. And I came to love him, too, but I was frightened to death working for him. He'd never seen me on the stage and he used the shock treatment while directing me. That system has worked with a great many other performers, but it didn't work well with me. I almost had a stroke working for John Ford.... Mr. Kazan, God love him, was able to bring out the very best in me. I was able, through his help, to let myself go and live the part of Granny ... Elia Kazan gave me credit for intelligence.[29]

Kazan's completed version, *Pinky*, released in November 1949, received three Oscar nominations, one for Best Actress (Jeanne Crain) and two for Best Supporting Actress (Ethel Waters and Ethel Barrymore). Though Bond was never nominated for an Academy Award, he ironically had a hand in helping Waters reach that prestigious level.

In 1949, Frank Capra signed a contract with Paramount; but his plans to make *Friendly Persuasion*, *Roman Holiday* and *A Woman of Distinction* all were dashed when studio president Barney Balaban set a strict budget limit at $1.5 million per picture. Negotiating with Harry Cohn, Capra made a deal to trade the rights to *A Woman of Distinction* and for Paramount to loan Ray Milland to Columbia in exchange for the original negative and remake rights to *Broadway Bill*, in which Bond had worked in 1934.

Intending to recall several actors, as well as integrate horseracing scenes from the original, Capra told Balaban that he could make the new version, *Riding High* (1950), for the specified budget. Paramount executives were pleased that Bing Crosby, cast in the role originated by Warner Baxter, would also perform several songs. Unlike most musicals, featuring heavily orchestrated arrangements added to the soundtrack, *Riding High* is a "comedy with songs," performed by Crosby, Clarence Muse and Coleen Gray, with only onscreen instruments as accompaniment. The multitalented Muse reprises his role from the original, and his contributions to the songs written by James Van Heusen and Johnny Burke, something which excited Crosby, who made a point of collaborating with his African American influences (Louis Armstrong, Ella Fitzgerald, Nat Cole), are a highlight of the film.

Bond's racetrack tout, Lee, is an expanded, more benevolent version of his 1934 characterization, and he is joined by other *Broadway Bill* veterans Douglas Dumbrille, Raymond Walburn, Margaret Hamilton, Frankie Darro, Irving Bacon and Charles Lane. This time, Capra's mandatory greedy capitalist, J. L. Higgins, is played by the great Charles Bickford; and cameos are contributed by Oliver Hardy (as a compulsive gambler) and Merwyn "Ish Kabibble" Bogue (complete with his famous "bowl" haircut, as the trumpet player in a polka band). The performances are impressive across the board, led by the always "effortless" Crosby, whose unique triple threat of acting, improvised comedy, and musicianship is at its peak.

Robert Riskin's screenplay is not as heavy-handed as some of his earlier work; and Capra, too, wields a lighter touch. Even though "Broadway Bill" drops dead after winning the big race, the sustained mood of *Riding High*, kept afloat by Crosby, Muse, Gray, and that splendid curmudgeon, William Demarest, results in less "Capra-corn" and forced comedy, and more genuine emotion, an element never reaching the mawkish level of some of the director's earlier films.

An especially merry moment occurs when Capra blatantly "pulls a John Ford." During Bond's first scene, the camera pans from his mug to Crosby's, and then tilts up to a lingering close-up on the horse's ass!

Capra's relationship with Bond extended beyond casting him in supporting film roles. In fact, "socializing" with Ward got out of hand one evening, when he and Duke, deep into their cups, waged a prolonged brawl in the Capra living room. Observing the considerable wreckage, the director's wife, Lucille, insisted that the two miscreants replace the damaged carpeting.[30]

As Sheriff Jim Caradac in the Palomar-Republic Western *Singing Guns* (1950), Bond again worked with Ella Raines and Walter Brennan, as well as Duke's frequent director, R. G. Springsteen, one of the studio's genre specialists. Executive producer Abe Lyman's idea of an "outlaw actor" was singer Vaughn Monroe, who plays the notorious "Rhiannon," ultimately brought to justice by Caradac. By the time this film was made, either Bond was taking a step up, or Ella Raines was taking one down (depending on the perspective): in a role reversal on *Tall in the Saddle*, the striking "film noir actress" was no longer playing Duke's sweetheart, but Ward's.

9

'Cause Wayne Can't Play the Part

*I roomed with Ward many times on location. I always found him a
good man to share a room with. He was a very upbeat, positive person. If
there was something mental that was bothering you, he could usually fix
it by bawling you out. If your problem was physical, he could fix that,
too; he carried a small pharmacy with him. Ward Bond was ... one hell
of an actor. He brought stability to every scene he was in.*—Harry Carey,
Jr.[1]

*Where the hell is Bond? Ward, for Christ's sake, will you pay attention?
We're trying to make a picture here. Why in the hell do I use you? ... Get
your fat ass in here, Ward!*—John Ford, on the set of *Wagon Master*[2]

During the late summer of 1949, Harry Carey, Jr., was enjoying a quiet weekday at
the Field Photo Farm. Preparing to take a relaxing ride, he was grooming his horse outside
the barn when startled by a voice behind him: "Is that ol' Dobe?"

As Carey tried to guess what his "Uncle Jack" was doing there, the Old Man repeated
the question, managing to receive "Yes sir, it is" in return. When Ford didn't recognize the
horse, he asked Dobe what he called the animal.

"Mormon," replied Carey.

"What?" puzzled the Old Man. "That horse's name is *Mormon*?"

As young Carey explained that his father had given the horse a handle appropriate to
its birthplace in Saint George, Utah, Ford said, "Well, I'll be goddamned" and then asked
ol' Dobe if he'd like to ride Mormon in a Western, revealing that he planned to begin shooting one, "in a month or so with you and ol' Ben."

"And Duke?" asked Carey.

"Christ no, not with Duke," Ford answered, emphasizing that he and Ben Johnson
would be the stars of the new film, focusing on a group of Mormons traveling west by
wagon train to Salt Lake City. Pappy had developed the story in his head, and then turned
over the actual writing of the script to his son, Pat, and Frank Nugent, with plans to film
on location in Moab, the actual "promised land" sought by the followers of "Brother Brig-
ham."

After he finished a brief synopsis for Dobe, Ford added that the film could be made
"cheap," for "not ... a lot of dough," and then exclaimed, "Oh, shit! I guess we'll have to
use Ward. Oh, I forgot—you like Ward."[3]

Wagon Master became one of Ford's most smoothly produced, economical efforts, wrapped in 31 days for a negative cost of $848,853. While on location, he was remarkably relaxed, capturing most setups on the first take, creating a documentary-like style for much of the film. Nepotism ran rampant, as he was aided, not only by his film "family," but a passel of real relatives: Pat; Barbara, who worked as assistant editor; and Eddie O'Fearna, Wingate Smith, and Francis Ford, Jr., whose collective finesse as assistant directors, in collaboration with Cliff Lyons' stunt contingent, resulted in very efficient handling of the many horses, wagons, and other animals during the 19 days at Moab.

Since Wayne, nor any other major star, was featured in the picture, Bond enjoyed the comfort of his own room during this location shoot. Though Ben Johnson, Joanne Dru and Harry Carey, Jr., are billed above him in the credits, he was paid the highest fee on the picture ($20,000). Dobe admitted:

> The backbone of *Wagon Master* was Ward Bond.... [He] was superb in the film. He really carried the picture, and of course Jack had his fun with him. The first thing I noticed was Ward's horse. That poor old pony had sure seen better days, and now he had to lug a 230-pound man around for three weeks. Most outsiders didn't know about Ward's physical handicap.[4]

Bond actually had lost considerable weight since appearing in *3 Godfathers* two years earlier. But while filming the scene during which Elder Wiggs and Travis Blue are searching for a river crossing for the wagon train, his horse slipped, as Carey explained:

> Suddenly they hit some sand ... and down went Ward and his old crow-bait horse. The poor old horse groaned as he fell.... Ward struggled up, the camera still rolling, ad-libbed bawling the horse out, and never uttered a swear word.... The accident stayed in the movie, ad-libs and all.
>   That night Ford sent Duke a wire that read: "He fell off his horse." The big story, however, is that the horse fell to the side of Ward's bad leg. Somehow Ward managed to keep it from being crushed.[5]

Bond managed to escape another injury during the scene in which Wiggs breaks up the brawl between Sandy and Sam Jenkins (Don Summers), who are both pursuing Prudence Perkins (Kathleen O'Malley). The altercation was intended to be comical, as neither character was an adept fighter, so Ford decided to create additional mayhem by unleashing two Australian shepherds that had constantly been at each other since filming began. Instructing the dogs' owners to await his cue (the waving of his ever-present, filthy handkerchief), Pappy then scanned the set.

"Where the hell is Bond?" he asked.

Ward, who had wandered a bit far afield, shouted, "Right here, right here, Boss!"

"Ward, for Christ's sake, will you pay attention?" growled the Old Man. "We're *trying* to make a picture here." Then he couldn't resist an opportunity to berate him in front of the cast and crew. "Why in the hell do I use you?" he volleyed.

As usual, Bond had a quick-draw deflection: "Cause Wayne can't play the part," followed by his trademark laugh.

"Get your fat ass in here, Ward!" yelled the Old Man, turning toward the crew to add, "When I cue Ward — by kicking him in the ass — Mister Bond, I hope, comes in and separates the boys. And that is cut. Okay? Everybody got that?"

All was set, Dobe and Don struggled, wrestled, threw wild punches, gouged and bit, and Ford waved his handkerchief for the dogs to join the fray. For the first time, the two animals just stared at each other, before one ran off and the other took after Bond, ripping open his trousers. Again, ever the professional, Bond entered the shot, on cue, and yanked apart Dobe and Don. (At one point, his bum fills the entire frame.)

"Cut and print it!" Ford managed to order while laughing hysterically. "You can't get any better than that!" Then, realizing that his whipping boy may have been injured, he asked, "Ward are you hurt? Did the dog actually bite you?"

"No, no," Bond assured him. "Shit. Goddamn it. I'm all right."

Ford actually appeared to have shown some genuine concern for Bond, but then dispelled the impression with another opportunity for sarcastic abuse. "Oh, that's too bad Ward," he said. "Somebody get the vet out here and give that poor dog a shot, just in case he bit Ward."[6]

Joanne Dru recalled:

> Ward was the most cantankerous man in the world. He was terrible, a real pain in the behind, but I liked him. He and Papa would go at it, and we'd say, "God, here they go."
>
> Papa had a marvelous time on that location. We used to drive out to the set together in the mornings, and he always tipped his hat to the cows as we passed by.[7]

During one scene, Ford depicts his admiration for the Apache tribe, when one of their young women, during a "squaw dance," is sexually assaulted (off-screen) by Reese Clegg (Fred Libby), one of an outlaw family of five, who, pretending to be cowboys, have joined

Wagon Master (Argosy–RKO Radio, 1950; directed by John Ford). Ford depicts his admiration for the Apache tribe when one of their young women (Movita), during a "squaw dance," is sexually assaulted (off-screen) by an outlaw whose family has joined the train. Here, elder Jonathan Wiggs (Ward Bond), respected by the Apaches because of his Mormon beliefs, assures the tribe that justice will be served.

the train. Elder Wiggs, respected by the Apaches because of his Mormon beliefs, orders Reese to be lashed to a wagon wheel and flogged, while his Uncle Shiloh (Charles Kemper), a cold-blooded murderer, watches. Allowing the punishment to be carried out, Shiloh brews a plan for later retaliation with "his boys," including Jesse (Mickey Simpson), Luke (Hank Worden, who is menacingly idiotic this time around), and Floyd (James Arness, who can't even talk).

In the end, the Clegg outfit bites the dust during an explosive gunfight with Sandy and Travis, who both win their women (Johnson finally lands Dru, who lends some subtle eroticism to several scenes) as the wagon train reaches the "promised land" of the San Juan Valley. Although Johnson, Dru and Carey are the stars, and the cast features formidable character actors including Jane Darwell and Alan Mowbray (playing a variation on his Shakespeare-quoting character in *My Darling Clementine*), *Wagon Master* is firmly stolen by Bond in one of his finest characterizations (qualities of which would inspire his "Major Seth Adams" in the subsequent *Wagon Train* series).

Dan Ford wrote, "Once described as an 'intimate epic,' *Wagon Master* is expansive and relaxed and stands as one of the most purely lyrical films John ever made. Though it is a Western, its mood anticipates *The Quiet Man*."[8] Joseph McBride elaborated:

> Ford finds in *Wagon Master* the purity of a vanished era when ... it was still possible for Americans to transcend the divisive forces of social prejudice. *Wagon Master* did not come with the usual trappings of a protest film, but that's what it was. Ford's indirect protest of the darkness, suspicion, and hatred that had enveloped America....[9]

Ford later admitted, "Along with *The Fugitive* and *The Sun Shines Bright*, I think *Wagon Master* came closest to being what I had wanted to achieve."[10]

Wayne, who had just given three of his best performances, in *Red River*, *Fort Apache* and *She Wore a Yellow Ribbon*, thought he now had enough clout to persuade Herb Yates to lure Ford to Republic, where the tightfisted studio boss still expected him to honor his contract. Wayne recalled:

> As long as I was stuck at Republic, I thought I might as well try to get Jack to come out there too. I knew that Yates ... wanted to start making A pictures. I went to him and told him he should get Jack Ford to come to Republic. If he got him, then the other big directors would follow.[11]

On January 4, 1950, hoping to make his longtime pet project, *The Quiet Man*, Ford, joined by Merian Cooper, signed a nonexclusive contract for Argosy to make "at least one and not more than three" pictures for Republic during the next two years. Although Herb Yates agreed to cover the full production costs of the films, he also stipulated that Ford and Cooper would be working with smaller budgets than they had received at RKO, where Argosy also had retained ownership of the pictures as well as stock investment in the studio. After completing *Wagon Master* for RKO in late February, the Argosy office was moved from Culver City to the Republic lot in North Hollywood.

Since December 8, 1949, Wayne had been appearing in *Jet Pilot*, new RKO boss Howard Hughes' attempt to recapture, in Technicolor and widescreen, the success of his earlier *Hell's Angels* (1930) by making an airborne version of *Ninotchka* (1939), with the Greta Garbo role played by Janet Leigh (harnessed in one of the eccentric billionaire's "experimental" brassieres). Hampered by an infantile, anti–Commie Jules Furthman screenplay, *Jet Pilot* was repeatedly withheld from release by Hughes' obsessive attempts to update the aviation technology, and his endless, far-flung searches for perfect cumulus clouds that could be penetrated by his phallic aircraft. *Eight years* after shooting commenced, the film finally was launched to nearly universal critical derision.

While Wayne attempted to work under Hughes' eccentric supervision, Bond made his live television debut on February 20, 1950, in "My Brother's Keeper," an episode of *The Silver Theater*, hosted by Conrad Nagel on CBS. Directed by Frank Telford, the show marked the second time Ward received top billing (something the small screen would frequently provide). Though the romantically oriented series featured some of Hollywood's best character actors (Glenda Farrell had starred the previous week), it ran for only one season.

In 1949, James Cagney, returning to the gangster genre for the first time in a decade, had blasted his way through Raoul Walsh's *White Heat*, right to the top of an oil-refinery tank, where he set off an apocalyptic explosion, disappearing in an enormous mushroom cloud. Still smoldering from the ending, Cagney finally thought he was through with the genre that had made him a star, but his independently produced experimental films hadn't attracted much attention. Although he thought he just had created the most psychopathic killer of his career, Jim was persuaded by his brother to make, for William Cagney Productions, just *one* more gangster film, which they could sell to Warner Bros. for distribution.

Jim didn't want to make *Kiss Tomorrow Goodbye*, but appreciated that the script was based on a novel by hardboiled, Depression-era author Horace McCoy. As producer, Bill Cagney had lined up Yiddish actor Luther Adler, a major force in the Group Theatre, to costar with his brother, who gave in to "an offer he couldn't refuse." Bill also cut a deal whereby Warner Bros. would pay the first $500,000 in receipts to the banks that had financed the poorly received *The Time of Your Life*, in which Bond had played a minor role.

Regardless of Ward's extremist political beliefs, the Cagney brothers liked him and continued to appreciate his straightforward, truthful acting style. In *Kiss Tomorrow Goodbye*, he again was cast as a cop; but this time, teamed up with Barton MacLane, he became one of a pair of corrupt, thuggish detectives on the take.

The plot bears similarities to *White Heat*, but the presentation of the mad criminal differs considerably from the previous film. No matter how sadistic Cody Jarrett may be, he possesses a degree of charm that attracts the viewer. Rather than repeat a similar characterization for *Kiss Tomorrow Goodbye*, Cagney chose to play Ralph Cotter as totally *un*likable. While Jarrett's violent tendencies are the result of hereditary insanity and a bad environment, Cotter is merely a self-interested, cold-blooded killer.

Directed by Gordon Douglas, *Kiss Tomorrow Goodbye* opens at the murder trial of seven "evil" defendants, two of whom are Inspector Charles Weber (Bond) and officer John Reese (MacLane). There should have been eight, but Cotter is already dead, gunned down by his so-called girlfriend, Holiday Carleton (Barbara Payton), who first had explained to him, "You can *kiss tomorrow goodbye*. You shouldn't have killed my brother."

Details about Weber and Reese's racketeering are revealed during the trial testimony. During a scene in which the extortionists are played a secret recording of their last shakedown, Douglas tracks into a tight, chiaroscuro close-up of Bond's face as Weber listens incredulously. The Inspector swats the tone arm from the record, slashing his hand on the needle, and then threatens to whack the lot of them. Keith Mandon (Adler), Cotter's "conscripted" mouthpiece, advises Weber to ease off, revealing that duplicate records will be sent to the D.A. and Chief of Police.

Cotter then bumps off and dumps the bodies of three collectors employed by a local bookie, who orders Weber to find the "missing" men, but he is paid off before any action can be taken. The Inspector's graft operation ends when Cotter is whacked by his sweetheart.

Kiss Tomorrow Goodbye (Warner Bros., 1950; directed by Gordon Douglas). Ward Bond (far left) played one of the most corrupt characters of his career in this hard-hitting gangster film costarring (left to right) Luther Adler, James Cagney, Barton MacLane, Barbara Payton and Steve Brodie.

The entire outfit is found guilty by the jury. Unlike the smooth, cynical villains Bond had played in Duke's Westerns, his Inspector Weber is truly an iniquitous, psychotic bastard who isn't averse to throttling the much smaller Cotter as he slams him against a wall. It is one of his best "tough-guy" characterizations, proving that there is no worse criminal than a cop gone bad.

Released in the wake of the superior *White Heat*, *Kiss Tomorrow Goodbye* fared poorly at the box office and was quickly pulled from release. One of Cagney's seldom-seen films, it is also one of the most underrated. Truly appropriate for his final Warner Bros. gangster role is Cotter's murder at the hands of a woman, cinematic justice for the actor's portrayal of so many broad-bashing mugs over the years.

Referring to Ford's arrival at Republic, Wayne said, "Jack ... made a deal with Yates to make *The Quiet Man* and had moved into an office next to mine."[12] That "deal" required Ford to direct one surefire moneymaker for the studio *before* he would be allowed to make what Yates considered an "art film" destined for low box-office returns. Another clause stated that either Republic or Argosy could cancel the contract after the first picture was released.

This ultimatum resulted in Ford's decision to make another John Wayne Western based on a James Warner Bellah story, "Mission with No Record," which James Kevin McGuinness adapted into the screenplay "Rio Bravo," changed to "Rio Grande Command" during production, and finally released as *Rio Grande* (subsequently branded the last installment in the "Cavalry Trilogy"). More accurately, it could be called Ford's "Cold War Cavalry" picture, with its reactionary attitude toward the Apaches as simplistic savages reflecting, not the more evenhanded approach of the *Fort Apache* and *She Wore a Yellow Ribbon* screenplays by Frank Nugent, but the arch-conservative views of McGuinness, who needed work after being dropped by MGM.

Bellah had based "Mission with No Record" on a May 1873 cavalry raid from Fort Clark across the Rio Grande, commanded by Colonel Ranald Mackenzie under direct orders from General Phil Sheridan. In pursuit of a band of Kickapoo who had fled their reservation for the sanctuary of Mexico, from which they could slip back across the border and attack U.S. installations, Mackenzie claimed that he was following Sheridan's command to wage "annihilation, obliteration, and complete destruction" of the rebellious savages. Mackenzie went so far as to kidnap Kickapoo women and children, carrying them back across the river to hold as hostages. General Sherman was outraged by this violation of an international boundary, stating that he would not tolerate any such illegal actions in the future. The Mexican government also protested the raid as a potential excuse for the U.S. to seize territory south of the border.

Rio Grande (Argosy–RKO Radio, 1950; directed by John Ford). Lieutenant Colonel Kirby Yorke (John Wayne, center right) receives his orders from General Philip Sheridan (J. Carrol Naish, center left), as (at right) Trooper Daniel "Sandy" Boone (Harry Carey, Jr., dark hat) and Trooper Travis Tyree (Ben Johnson) stand at attention. (The sergeant at far left is Ford perennial Jack Pennick; color bearer not identified)

Wayne again portrays Lieutenant Colonel Kirby York, but with a harsher edge (and an "e" at the end of his name) than in *Fort Apache*. In a reversal of the actual 1873 event, Apaches capture white women and children to hold hostage in Mexico, and Yorke must make a covert night crossing of the Rio Grande to rescue them.

Maureen O'Hara, who plays Yorke's Irish wife, Kathleen, was pleased to be working with Wayne. They had been cordial with each other for many years, but their collaboration on *Rio Grande* forged a close friendship that lasted for the rest of Wayne's life. O'Hara revealed:

> Neither John Ford nor Duke really wanted to make this picture. To them it was just a path to *The Quiet Man*. It was understood by all of us that this was the only reason we were doing it. Without that commitment from Yates, *Rio Grande* would never have been made — at least not by John Ford and his company. Duke almost backed out in the beginning. He was having trouble with Yates on a back-salary problem, but Mr. Ford stepped in and settled the matter.[13]

As *Rio Grande* opens, 15 years have passed since Yorke, as ordered by General Sheridan (J. Carrol Naish), torched the plantation owned by the family of his wife, who now arrives at his cavalry outpost, attempting to retrieve their son, Jeff (Claude Jarman, Jr.), who enlisted in the U.S. Army after failing at West Point. Joseph McBride observed, "This emotionally complex family drama is treated by Ford and his cast with great delicacy, intermittently elevating *Rio Grande* above its crudely racist and stridently jingoistic military plot, derived from Bellah's story."[14]

Gary Wills wrote:

> Bellah's tale gave Ford a perfect opportunity for making Wayne repeat his successful role ... as Sergeant Stryker in *Sands of Iwo Jima*. Bellah describes just such a man — one so hard on his subordinates that they have trouble seeing how it could all be for their own good. Ford could never care for such a monster....
>
> In *Rio Grande*, Ford takes Wayne's character as far as possible from the principled thuggishness Bellah admired in "Massacre." ... Wayne goes, not in "hot pursuit" of Indian warriors, but on a mission of mercy.[15]

Ford used two of his favorite ace cinematographers on the film: Archie Stout, who directed the second unit in capturing the spectacular Moab locations; and Bert Glennon, who used stunning chiaroscuro lighting to create an intimate atmosphere in the interior scenes featuring Wayne and O'Hara. The soundtrack, featuring several original songs by Stan Jones performed by Ken Curtis and the Sons of the Pioneers, also adds immeasurably to the mood.

O'Hara, who enjoyed being on location with the Ford Stock Company, nevertheless began to notice, and be victimized by, Pappy's increasingly sadistic behavior, which she only had glimpsed while making *How Green Was My Valley* a decade earlier. She indulged Ford's love of music by performing Irish songs during dinner, when the king held dominion over his court. Pappy's perversion would rise to the fore when he made Wayne follow suit, but his singing had to be off-key so the king could have yet another reason to torment his star fool. O'Hara explained:

> Duke could, in fact, sing — he had a surprisingly nice voice — but he always accommodated Mr. Ford with an awful rendition of the song so that Mr. Ford could laugh and make fun of him.... While we were shooting *Rio Grande*, I clearly saw the darker side of John Ford, the mean and abusive side. It caused me to reevaluate him.[16]

Like *Wagon Master*, *Rio Grande*, aside from requiring Carey, Ben Johnson and Claude Jarman, Jr., to ride "Roman-style," standing up astride two galloping horses, proved to be a pleasant production experience. Carey recalled:

The Old Man told me what to say before each scene — no lines to study on that one. *Rio Grande* was another one of Ford's "vacation" pictures. The filming was extremely easy for him — no strain on him at all. Only a cinematic genius is capable of achieving that day in and day out. He played a lot of his scenes in a master shot.... He used what is called a loose shot ... he left some room on either side of the frame of the lens so there was margin for error....[17]

O'Hara, however, recalled the shoot in far different terms:

[M]ore than anything, it was Mr. Ford's vicious treatment of John Wayne that changed my feelings. He was extremely severe and cruel to Duke on the set. It was horrible treatment, unlike anything I had ever seen. He repeatedly belittled and insulted him in front of the entire cast and crew.... I kept silent, while screaming in my head, "Punch him, Duke. Knock him on his ass. Do something!" But Duke was too much a professional, so he took it — all of it. It made me sick to my stomach....[18]

Though Pappy didn't have a role for Bond in *Rio Grande*, he was welcomed on to the set to visit his pals. After his visit, both Ford and Wayne admitted to "missing" Ward, so they cooked up an infamous "Thinking of you" photograph, showing them bracketing a horse's ass, with its tail raised in the air.

Ford finally realized his dream of securing funds to make *The Quiet Man* after *Rio Grande*, released on November 15, 1950, raked in $2.25 million at the box office. The current Cold War atmosphere, including U.S. involvement in the U.N.–authorized "police action" resulting from North Korean raids across the 38th Parallel into the South, was reflected in the content of the new cavalry picture. As stated by Gary Wills:

Beautifully crafted as *Rio Grande* is ... it also resonated with Cold War concerns, with the duties of empire when the leaders of the free world had a global mission that refused to observe national boundaries. Wayne put a human face on empire — which did not make it any less an empire.[19]

Randy Roberts and James S. Olson noted:

In 1948 ... [Duke] had been one of the more politically inactive stars in Hollywood, remaining distant from the debate that was consuming the industry. By the end of 1950 he was in the middle of the fight, searching for enemies, naming names, and taking stands.[20]

Bond's Western career wouldn't have been complete without an appearance in a film about the James gang. Directed by Gordon Douglas for Paramount, *The Great Missouri Raid* (1951) costars Wendell Corey (as Frank) and MacDonald Carey (as Jesse), with Ward playing the top supporting role of Major Trowbridge, a provost marshal seeking revenge against Frank, who killed his brother (James Millican), a sergeant in the Union Army. The Youngers are represented by Bruce Bennett (as Cole), Bill Williams (as Jim) and Paul Lees (as Bob). Many familiar faces, including those of Tom Tyler, Paul Fix and Ray Teal, populate this relatively accurate version of the James-Younger story, with Bond's corrupt major also biting the dust before the final fadeout.

Bond provided the voiceover narration for Budd Boetticher's *Bullfighter and the Lady* (1951), a fact-based romantic drama Wayne produced for Republic. Boetticher had studied as a novice bullfighter under the matador Armellita, who served as technical advisor during the location shoot centered at Churubusco Studios. Duke had considered playing the lead, American Broadway producer and sportsman Johnny Regan, but he was physically too large for the role, which went to Robert Stack. Gilbert Roland, the son of matador "The Great Paquilo," appears as Regan's mentor, Manolo Estrada.

Herb Yates, who considered the 123-minute director's cut far too long for a Republic release, asked Ford to supervise a drastic re-editing, and the picture eventually was released in an 87-minute version. The development of the Regan-Paquilo relationship, and scenes involving a character played by Paul Fix, were eliminated. Boetticher later claimed, "Ford figured that two men could not love each other unless there was a homosexual situation. That's a lot of baloney, but he didn't like that part and cut it from the picture."[21] (The film was restored 35 years later, with the help of Boetticher and Stack, by the UCLA Film and Television Archive.)

Producer William Cagney again hired Bond for a major role, in an adaptation of Charles Marquis Warren's novel *Only the Valiant*, which Gordon Douglas began shooting in late July 1950. The Cagney brothers originally had planned the film as a follow-up to *The Time of Your Life*, featuring the same cast; but, by time production began two years later, Bond was the only actor who remained. Instead, several cast and crew members from *Kiss Tomorrow Goodbye* were rehired for the Western, including Douglas, Bond, screenwriter Harry Brown, leading lady Barbara Payton, and supporting actors Steve Brodie and Neville Brand. Portions of *Only the Valiant* were filmed on location near Gallup, New Mexico, where the story takes place.

Gregory Peck stars as Captain Richard Lance, a by-the-book cavalry officer whose motives are often misunderstood. Assigned a "suicide mission" to prevent an Apache band led by Tucsos (Michael Ansara) from riding en masse through a narrow canyon passage, Lance loses all but one of his hand-picked motley crew of malcontents, Corporal Timothy Gilchrist (Bond), an alcoholic Irish-American. According to Lance, Gilchrist's drunken misbehavior has resulted "in the destruction of the most Army property" in the history of the U.S. Cavalry!

Many Fordian elements permeate *Only the Valiant*, including *The Lost Patrol*–like plot, the unhappy and misfit officers assigned to a thankless wilderness outpost, and the very presence of Bond in a darker variation of the classic Victor McLaglen cavalry role. Much of this "noir" Western takes place in darkness, an atmosphere reflected in the stern presence of Lance, who, at one point, tells each of his men (who could be called the "Dirty Half-Dozen") just what negative qualities led him to be selected for the risky mission. Gilchrist's McLaglen-like aspects include his claim that he cannot quit whiskey cold turkey because he has consumed "a quart every day," not for his entire life, but just "since the age of three." However, the potentially hazardous consequences of his alcoholic behavior give him a harder edge than the cavalry characters in Ford's "trilogy."

Lon Chaney, Jr., plays Kebussyan, an "Arab" trooper, whose obvious outsider status brings him the expected veiled ethnic slurs of his fellows; but his attempt to kill Lance following two apparent "misjudgments" that led to the death of Lieutenant Bill Holloway (Gig Young) is redeemed by his subsequent heroic stand against the Apaches while the Captain dynamites the pass. Gilchrist also finds a form of redemption by the film's end, depicting Lance reunited with Cathy Eversham (Payton) before the drunken Corporal wanders back toward the fort's canteen, singing his favorite whiskey-soaked ditty.

Bond was reteamed with Wayne for Warner Bros.' *Operation Pacific*, a submarine picture deep-sixed by too much soap opera, which began production on August 29, 1950. *Sands of Iwo Jima* had proved that World War II, the "good war," was the proper vehicle with which to drive home messages pertaining to the Cold conflict, or the warm "police action" in Korea. Written and directed by George Waggner, *Operation Pacific* opens with an "historical" prologue:

> When the Pacific Fleet was destroyed by the Japanese sneak attack on Pearl Harbor, it remained for the submarines to carry the war to the enemy. In the four years that followed our undersea

craft sank six million tons of Japanese shipping including some of the proudest ships of the imperial navy. Fifty-two of our submarines and thirty-five hundred men were lost. It is to these men and the entire *silent service* that this picture is humbly dedicated.

As an officer aboard the submarine *Thunderfish*, skippered by Captain "Pop" Perry (Bond), Wayne brandishes the unimaginative moniker "Duke" Gifford, one of many clichés in this strictly genre offering. The crew's encounters with the Japanese are alternated with a tedious romantic-triangle subplot involving Gifford, his ex-wife, Mary Stuart (Patricia Neal), and navy "fly boy" Bob Perry (Philip Carey), the captain's kid brother. Also in the outfit are Paul Picerni, Martin Milner, Cliff Clark, and the ubiquitous Jack Pennick. The very symbol of the high cost of freedom, Bond was handed a big death scene, as Pop, drowning to protect his crew during a wily "Jap" ruse, becomes a martyr for the cause.

Wayne followed *Operation Pacific* with another World War II picture, RKO's *Flying Leathernecks* (1951), one of the first to incorporate color footage of actual Kamikaze strikes and from the Battle of Guadalcanal. Under the direction of Nicholas Ray, Duke's Major Dan Kirby is pitted strongly against Robert Ryan (a real USMC combat veteran) as his executive officer Captain Carl Griffin, but James Edward Grant's script provides yet another LST-load of genre clichés.

Like *Sands of Iwo Jima* before it, *Flying Leathernecks* was filmed primarily on location at Camp Pendleton and El Toro Air Station. Producer Edmund Grainger also had reviewed footage shot in Korea by USMC Air Wing cameramen, but reports of its inclusion were not confirmed by the studio. Aside from the sparks thrown by Wayne and Ryan, the film was not a critical success; but that mattered little when, after a screening for troops in Korea, General C. B. Gates' pronounced it the "best service picture made to date," and a "command performance" was requested by the U.S. Joint Chiefs of Staff.[22] Perhaps most importantly, both *Operation Pacific* and *Flying Leathernecks* were victorious over audiences, helping land Duke at the summit of *Motion Picture Herald*'s poll of top box-office attractions for 1951.

Arguably, Ford's movement toward the Right was motivated in part by a decision made by the U.S. Army Signal Corps during the summer of 1950. When Secretary of Defense Louis A. Johnson took over the case involving a former naval officer who had worked for the Field Photo unit, but now was considered a "bad security risk," Ford, through guilt by association, also was denied any further access to Signal Corps films. Understandably outraged that his patriotism and World War II service was being dragged through the mud, Ford, attempting to keep the matter under wraps, asked Wingate Smith, a veteran of both world wars, to intercede on his behalf. Announcing his desire to return to active duty as a combat filmmaker during the Korean "conflict," Ford signed a loyalty oath and, serving with the 1st Marine Division, eventually shot enough footage to assemble the propaganda picture *This Is Korea!* released by Republic in August 1951.

While in Korea, Ford, during a discussion with General O. P. Smith, learned that Wayne was about to begin "immediate production" on a picture called "Retreat—Hell!" Concerned that this project would forestall the making of *The Quiet Man*, Ford, on January 19, 1951, wrote a letter to Wayne, asking, "What's this, Junior?" and requesting "the dope" on the deal. Displaying genuine emotion he avoided when in Wayne's presence, Ford continued:

> This is a piss-poor war.... How's our favorite shit-head, Bond? Drop me a line, Duke—will be glad to hear from you. Things are tough here. Had a couple days on a carrier, landing on decks, catapulting off, but got a *bath*—a hot steaming *bath*! Mark "Eager Beaver" Armistead came back from his mission with his plane full of holes. He *likes it*. I was glad to get back on the beach.

We're in good health (knock wood). How about coming out? Douglas MacArthur is a great admirer — runs our stuff at least once a week.

Give my love to Ward and [James Edward] Grant, and Chata ... and take a big slice for yourself, Junior, 'cause I'm very fond of you.

Affection,
Coach

In a postscript, Ford suggested that Wayne abandon the title "Retreat — Hell!" for "the one we use here: 'Operation H.A.O'—'Haul Ass Out.'"[23]

On the morning of January 30, 1951, one day before his mentor turned 57 years old, Wayne sent a telegram to "Capt. John Ford" at the Imperial Hotel in Tokyo. The message read, in part, "Dear Coach.... No Retreat to Hell for me.... Happy Birthday in all languages. Letter Following. Love, Duke."[24]

When MacArthur, removed from command by President Truman in April 1951, saw Ford's positive spin in *This Is Korea!* he reported watching *She Wore a Yellow Ribbon* once every month and that his favorite actors were John Wayne and Ward Bond.[25] This accolade from the World War II hero Ford had depicted in *They Were Expendable,* plus a U.S. Navy Air Medal awarded for "meritorious achievement as Officer-in-Charge of Pacific Fleet Photographic Team ABLE during operations against enemy aggressor forces in Korea," put considerable spit and polish back on his military glory.

The Air Medal made Ford eligible for a promotion to admiral, *if* he made the decision to retire from active service in the Naval Reserve. Rather than putting in another three years, which would have gained him a pension awarded to 20-year men, he characteristically chose the immediate promotion; and, on May 1, 1951, Rear Admiral John Ford, USNR, promoted by President Truman, retired from his beloved service. Dan Ford wrote:

> *This Is Korea* was an important landmark for John. He had freely given his time and talents and was awarded, if indirectly, with his admiral's star. But there is an irony here: he had tried to glorify an unpopular war and had made a bad picture as a result.[26]

On March 29, 1950, Nicholas Ray began shooting "Dark Highway," a thriller combining Gerald Butler's novel *Mad with Much Heart* and an original subplot on which he collaborated with A. I. Bezzerides. A specialist in gritty road stories, Bezzerides had written several screenplays, including adaptations of his own novels for Warner Bros.' *They Drive by Night* (1940), starring George Raft, Ida Lupino and Humphrey Bogart, and 20th Century–Fox's *Thieves' Highway* (1949), starring Richard Conte and Lee J. Cobb.

Ray initially shot "Dark Highway" over a two-month period, partly on location in Colorado, where the atmospheric winter scenes benefited from ample snow and ice, through which his actors had to struggle, both while driving and on foot. Robert Ryan, who initially recommended Butler's novel to RKO, plays Jim Wilson, a Los Angeles patrol cop, whose 11 years on the force have made him an isolated, cynical and bitter man. On the verge of a nervous breakdown, he vents his frustration by beating suspects, resulting in a reassignment to a rural area where a girl has been murdered.

To play Walter Brent, the vengeful father of the victim, Ray considered Lee J. Cobb, Howard Da Silva, Albert Dekker, Rhys Williams and James Bell, but only one actor could provide the intense characterization described as "an agitated, one-man lynch mob": Ward Bond. Exiled from the urban environment in which he "can't trust anyone," Jim Wilson is thrust into an even more reactionary world, where the ineffectual Sheriff Carrey (Ian Wolfe) is easily upstaged by Brent, who bursts into the film wielding a double-barrel shotgun and an oath to empty it into the belly of the killer.

Danny Malden (Sumner Williams), the mentally ill young man who has committed the crime, lives with his sister, Mary (Ida Lupino), who has lost her sight. In an attempt to bring Danny to justice, Wilson must overcome his own psychic upheaval to provide a buffer between highly emotional foes, one who wants the boy sent to an institution, and the other who wants to kill him. Following a harrowing chase through the snow-covered, rocky terrain, Danny falls to his death, after which Brent, realizing that he "was just a *kid*," expresses regret.

After driving back to Los Angeles, Wilson returns to the country, where he is reunited with Mary. An unusual conclusion for a film noir, this redemption scene is made believable by the outstanding performance of Robert Ryan, that rare actor able to transcend the pessimistic, occasionally asinine, conventions of the genre. Bond, too, is superb; and the physical effort he puts into the performance is startling. Temporarily able to stress his left leg, he was required to run convincingly, often through snow and ice, during the shooting of the chase scenes. Lengthy sequences are played without dialogue, with only Bernard Herrmann's signature musical score heard on the soundtrack.

Ray's casting choice for Brent's stern wife, Olive Carey (who was just seven years older than Bond), is an obvious homage to Ford. By the time the heavily re-edited film was released as *On Dangerous Ground* in January 1952, Bond had worked on five more feature films.

On Dangerous Ground (RKO Radio, 1951; directed by Nicholas Ray). Jim Wilson (Robert Ryan) and Walter Brent (Ward Bond) realize that Mary Malden (Ida Lupino) has lost her sight.

Although Ford had signed a loyalty oath to return to combat filmmaking, he refused to do so for any issue not deemed mandatory by the federal government. When the MPA campaigned for a provision requiring everyone in the film industry to sign a non–Communist affidavit, Cecil B. DeMille, who headed his own right-wing "intelligence service," the DeMille Foundation for Americanism, supported the measure at an SDG board meeting on August 18, 1950. Only 14 directors refused to be cowed by such fear tactics, while 547 voted for the oath, which required the guild to send a list of the "traitors" to every producer in Hollywood.

At a subsequent SDG meeting on October 9, this blacklisting measure was adamantly opposed by Joseph L. Mankiewicz and Ford, who reminded his fellow directors that his partner was Merian Cooper, a brigadier general in the U.S. Army, who had vowed not to sign "any goddamn loyalty oath" and be part of a "goddamn blacklist," even if DeMille clapped a pistol to his head.[27] During yet another meeting on October 22, held after DeMille pushed for removing Mankiewicz from his SGD presidency, William Wyler, George Stevens and Rouben Mamoulian fervently spoke out against DeMille's behavior. And then the Old Man rose from his chair, instantly drawing the attention of everyone in attendance, and declared:

> My name is John Ford. I am a director of Westerns. I am one of the founders of this guild. I must rise to protect the board of directors in some of the accusations made here tonight....
>
> We organized this guild to protect ourselves against producers. By producers I don't mean men of the caliber of Zanuck or the late Irving Thalberg.... I mean the little man that creeps in and says that Russians stink. We organized this guild to protect ourselves against those people.
>
> Now somebody wants to throw ourselves into ... an intelligence service and give out to producers what looks to me like a blacklist. I don't think we should ... put ourselves in a position of putting out derogatory information about a director, whether he is a Communist, beats his mother-in-law, or beats dogs....
>
> I think Joe has been vilified, and I think he needs an apology ... [if he] is recalled, your guild is busted up.... Everybody has had their say, and Joe has been vindicated.... I believe there is only one alternative, and that is for the board of directors to resign and elect a new board of directors.... It appears they haven't got the support of the men that elected them.

Mankiewicz retained his presidency, while Ford was named vice president. However, in an inexplicable move, Mankiewicz called for the SDG membership to "voluntarily" sign the loyalty oath, and the motion was ratified on May 27, 1951. Four days later, the turncoat president resigned and moved to New York. (The oath remained in effect for the next 15 years, until the Supreme Court, upholding the ruling of a lower court, declared that the SDG could not base its membership on such a requirement.)

In late 1951, when Frank Capra, a lifelong Republican, was accused of being associated with "Communist" screenwriters, he wrote to Ford, asking for a character reference. Both directors, along with Herbert Biberman and Robert Montgomery, had participated in the 1938 strike at the *Hollywood-Citizen News*, which had been propagandized as being "Communist inspired." Ford went to bat for Capra by writing a letter to the Army-Navy-Air Force Personnel Security Board, claiming that they had been, not participants in, but only "observers" of the strike. Screenwriter Philip Dunne recalled:

> Capra was there formally as president of the [SDG]. Ford has this completely wrong. Jack was not a rational man, he was an emotional man. This is an emotional letter.... Ford had very decent instincts, but he was being pushed around by Ward Bond and John Wayne. He could have been drunk when he wrote it.[28]

Prior to leaving for Korea, Ford had hired *How Green Was My Valley* author Richard Llewellyn to expand Maurice Walsh's "The Quiet Man" to novella length. Combined with the notes he had been compiling for the past 15 years, Ford was sure he'd have plenty of material from which a screenplay could be adapted. However, Walsh already had rewritten the short story as a chapter in his novel *Green Rushes*, wherein the story of Shawn Kelvin deals with aiding his family during "The Troubles" of 1922. Llewellyn used the *Green Rushes* version as his source material; but Ford already had made his IRA film and, as Maureen O'Hara explained, he "knew this would never play to Hollywood studio bosses or American audiences. Most of the work we did on the *Araner* involved removing the politics from the story and focusing it on romance and comedy."[29]

After returning to Hollywood in March 1951, Ford, working with Frank Nugent, began altering Llewellyn's work, including changing the names of the major characters, plus adding three more for good measure. The name of the fictional village became Innisfree (borrowed from William Butler Yeats' poem "The Isle of Innisfree"); Shawn Kelvin was changed to Sean Thornton (Wayne), the forename, of course, after Himself, and the surname after his Irish Thornton cousins; Ellen O'Grady became Mary Kate Danaher (O'Hara), after Mary Ford and Katherine Hepburn; Liam O'Grady became "Red" Will Danaher (Victor McLaglen); and the new supporting characters were Father Peter Lonergan (Bond), the Rev. Cyril Playfair (Arthur Shields) and Michaeleen Og Flynn (Barry Fitzgerald).

Ford and Nugent also added a crucial plot element: Sean's refusal to fight Will due to his guilt for having killed a fellow boxer in the ring, the impetus for abandoning America for the serenity he hopes to find back on the Auld Sod. Incredibly, though Will is Mary Kate's brother, McLaglen, at age 64, was 33 years older than O'Hara when the film was made.

The "art-house" *Quiet Man*, budgeted at $1.75 million, concerned Herb Yates, as one of the most expensive pictures ever made by Republic (in Technicolor, not the inferior Tru-color process), and the first the studio had filmed outside the United States. While Ford and Nugent wrote several script drafts, O'Hara's younger brother, Charlie FitzSimons, was tending to pre-production work in Ireland, gathering an all–British crew to join Yanks Winton Hoch, Wingate Smith, art director Frank Hotaling and prop man Ace Holmes.

When Yates finally beckoned Ford, asking him to reduce the budget, he turned to Wayne, who, out of undying loyalty to the Coach, waved the contractual profit percentage, accepting a flat fee of $100,000, a move that satisfied the Republic mogul. (At one point, Katherine Clifton had suggested Robert Ryan, who had boxed in the Marine Corps, for the lead, but Ford waived her off with his usual "Who's directing this picture?" wisecrack.)

The final draft of the screenplay was completed in April 1951; and Ford, accompanied by Hoch and Argosy production manager Lee Luthaker, flew to Ireland to join "Charlie Fitz" in scouting locations around Galway Bay. In County Mayo, Ford chose the village of Cong as the primary location, and set up shop at nearby Ashford Castle on the shore of Lough Corrib, the second largest lake in Ireland.

The lack of modern conveniences at the 700-year-old citadel may have been incommodious to the company; but, to Pappy, it was a mere trifle. Ashford Castle held a near-sacred place in the heart of Sean Aloysius O'Fearna. The medieval structure had been converted into a hotel by Sir Benjamin Lee Guinness, Lord Mayor of Dublin, Member of Parliament, noted philanthropist and, most significantly, grandson of Arthur Guinness, founder of the St. James's Gate Brewery. Sir Ben had assumed complete control of the brewery in 1839, and his beloved Guinness would be ubiquitous in *The Quiet Man*. (Some of the crew stayed at other local inns and bed-and-breakfast houses.)

Ford had intensified his obsession with the Auld Sod by visiting the family cottage in

Spiddal, where he met with his cousin Martin Feeney for the first time in 30 years. To populate the film with authentic Irish characters, auditions were held at the Abbey Theatre in Dublin. As Ford completed preparations, O'Hara had a chance to observe his extraordinary qualities, particularly his artistic genius:

> John Ford understood the hearts and souls of men better than anyone else I had ever known. He knew our motivations, our desires, and, most of all, our fears. He knew how to elicit reactions of his choosing. His was a unique fascination with the events of life as they unfolded around him — simple or grand moments, it made little difference because all revealed something about the human condition. It was a pure and genuine, God-given fascination.[30]

On the evening of June 6, Ford informed all the major cast members, with the exception of brother Francis, to be fully prepared to begin shooting the following morning. Though he should have known better, Frank took his brother at face value, thinking he could sleep a wee bit late; but when Pappy walked on to the set bright and early on June 7, the *only* character he really needed was Dan Tobin, the old geezer with the long white beard.

Frank was roused rudely from his bed at the castle and dressed quickly while the makeup crew slapped on his bogus beard. Ironically, for *The Quiet Man*, filmed in their beloved Ireland (Francis had directed *The Cry of Erin* in nascent Hollywood 35 years earlier), Ford finally cast his long-suffering sibling in a *positive* light as the primarily sober village elder. Gary Wills rightfully noted, "This is the longest-running, most humane role John Ford ever gave to Frank."[31] The simple truth is that *The Quiet Man*, Ford's most personal, heartfelt project, actually made it possible for him temporarily to forego his pathologically abusive treatment of his brother and, even to some extent, Bond.

Ward had been struggling with his weight ever since the auto accident six years earlier, and it was a battle he usually lost. At age 48, he managed to trim down considerably for the role of Father Lonergan, whose priestly attire has an additional "slimming effect," providing a stark contrast to his hulking Walter Brent in *On Dangerous Ground*, filmed the previous year.

Soon after shooting began, Ford was beset with curious locals gawking out their windows and pedestrians ruining takes by meandering within camera range. Winton Hoch already had completed difficult Technicolor assignments for Ford, but split-second changes in the Irish weather posed a new challenge, necessitating the use of three separate lighting setups, allowing for sunshine, clouds, and rain. The gaffer required an eagle's eye for catching his quick hand signals. Second-unit photography was supervised by Archie Stout.

Herb Yates, perched in his Hollywood office, dissected the daily production reports, making sure that Ford wasn't spending a single penny over budget. He complained about the film's title not being suitable for Wayne and, after viewing some rushes, was exasperated that the footage was "all green." Duke said, "Jack ... was getting a lot of flack from Yates. The 'but-it's-all-green' thing epitomized it."[32]

One morning, Pappy, not feeling up to directing, wanted to stay in bed and get drunk. An entire team (Wayne, Bond, O'Hara, Wingate Smith and Charlie Fitz) did its utmost to make certain this craving was *not* fulfilled. When Smith said that Ford's son, Pat, could direct the film, Bond threatened to quit. Wayne directed the second unit in some footage for the horseracing sequence. Throughout the day, they took shifts to watch over the Old Man, making sure he remained in bed and didn't go out to forage for booze. The following morning, he was up and ready to resume shooting.

Ford's nightly bitching about Yates around the dinner table had begun to erode the expected gouging of Bond, who scored extra points by performing an outrageous and potentially dangerous maneuver on the castle grounds. Climbing to the top of a ruined tower, Ward found a piece of slate that he used to carve a suitably Fordian sentiment into the stone. He then clambered back down to get Wayne, so his pal could witness his thoughtful deed. As Duke reached the summit of the tower, he could clearly see, scraped in huge block letters, "FUCK HERB YATES."

On the weekends, Bond had the time of his life fishing in Lough Corrib. According to an article in the local *Connaught Tribune*, Ward was a far more adept angler than his stream-wading, frustrated Father Lonergan in *The Quiet Man*:

> On Sunday evening Ward Bond brought a 5 lbs. trout off the lake and right proud he was, as it was the best catch of the day. It was also the first brown trout he had ever caught and on that account it was suggested he have it mounted. On hearing that they come up to 17 lbs. on the Corrib, Ward said: "Aw, heck, I'll catch one of the big ones later," and decided to have the 5 pounder for breakfast.[33]

One dinner, near the end of the location shoot, was poignant for Ford. Victor McLaglen's son, Andrew, who worked as second assistant director on the picture, remembered:

> Ford ... got up and made a very soul-searching kind of a speech. He said he was so happy to be here making *this* film, which was his dream film to make, with all the closest friends he had in the business — Duke and Victor and Ward and Maureen. And he said, "This would be the perfect way for me to end my career."[34]

On July 17, 1951, Ford wrapped the location work and returned to Los Angeles, to shoot the interiors and collaborate with longtime editor Jack Murray and composer Victor Young, who based his score on traditional Irish tunes, including "The Kerry Dancers" and "The Rakes of Mallow."

Viewers who allow memories of later Wayne formula pictures to cloud their perceptions of *The Quiet Man* as being "chauvinistic" need only read one of the actor's recollections of how Sean is constantly manipulated by Mary Kate throughout the film:

> Jack and I had only one disagreement on *The Quiet Man*. It was about a scene where Maureen goes and slams the door and locks me out. The way they had written it, I go over, pick up my boxing gloves, and throw them onto the fire. Well, shit! ... I was beginning to wonder if they ever were going to let me show some balls! I brought this up with Pappy and he just gave me a dirty look. But later he ... said, "Duke, I'm going to let you do what you always do when a broad locks you out. I'm going to let you kick the fuckin' door down."[35]

Ford constantly challenged Wayne to confront his established screen persona, to alter certain types of "macho" behavior on which he usually relied. Sean Thornton attempts to live a life of peace, avoiding confrontations that may erupt into violence, but eventually he realizes the only way to resolve his dilemma is to fight Will Danaher. Hoping he will find serenity in Ireland, Sean, manipulated by nearly everyone around him, is confounded by unfamiliar social traditions and "civilization" in general. *The Quiet Man* offers a glimpse at a very different "John Wayne"; and, working with Ford, Marion Morrison proved he had the acting chops to pull it off.

Gary Wills wrote:

> Wayne and Hawks — and Hawks' imitators — were guilty of movie after movie that humiliates women. [*The Quiet Man*] is definitely not one of them.... The comic offering of the stick to beat [Mary Kate] offends some, who forget she offered [Sean] a stick herself, under the priest's censure, and he turned it down. When she happily collaborates with the burning of the 350 pounds, she is proving it was not greed for money ("the purse") that motivated her, but vindication of her claim as an independent person.[36]

While shooting the famous "dragging" scene, O'Hara was hauled through a field adorned with sheep dung (much of it kicked there by Ford and Wayne). She explained:

> Why were Duke and I so electric in our love scenes together? I was the only leading lady big enough and tough enough for John Wayne. Duke's presence was so strong that when audiences finally saw him meet a woman of equal hell and fire, it was exciting and thrilling.... I always gave as good as I got, and it was believable. So during those moments of tenderness ... audiences saw for a half second that he had finally tamed me — but only for that half second.[37]

Andrew McLaglen added, "I'm sure she was a little bit black and blue. That was *very real*."[38]

Another criticism leveled at *The Quiet Man* involves Ford's use of "stage Irish" characters, which is his own twist on a tradition developed by the nation's poets, playwrights and performers, including William Butler Yeats, Sean O' Casey, and the actors of the Abbey Theatre, including Barry Fitzgerald, who best represents the director's endearing characters. Joseph McBride explained:

> Ford's fascination with ethnic characteristics is one of his principal ways of analyzing the structure of a given society; if he treats such traits with humor, it is largely because he finds social hierarchies, other than those based on goodness and achievement, to be ridiculous, offensive, and worthy of mocking.[39]

McBride also pointed out a sly political undertone involving Bond:

> The film ... contains what could be seen as subtle references to blacklisting, such as in Bond's priest threatening Victor McLaglen's ... Danaher by warning, "I'll read your name in the Mass on Sunday," and the squire keeping a book with the names of people who offend him.[40]

Randy Roberts and James S. Olson described Ford's decision to use Bond's character as narrator of this "naturally" developing tale as "a stroke of genius ... from his first line — 'Well, now, I'll begin at the beginning'— the story unfolds as an adult fairy tale." Aye, it is a mystical Ireland recalled from the nostalgic psyche of Father Peter Lonergan:

> Although Ford bragged that he remained true to Irish customs, *The Quiet Man* presents ... a dreamland in the minds and memories of Irish-Americans, where, save for a donnybrook now and again, peace and harmony reign and Catholic parishioners cheer for Protestant bishops.[41]

The film is not only Ford's Irish-American vision, but also a revealing expression of his Catholicism. While *The Fugitive* is a forced, allegorical profession of Ford's faith (one that he described as a "calling"), the Catholic values of *The Quiet Man* develop organically, along with a myriad of other layers, in a very entertaining film. Planning his magnum opus over the course of two decades, Pappy, surrounded by his cinematic family, finally achieved a "seamless" work of art.

Bond is at the center of both Catholic films, but his Father Lonergan in *The Quiet Man*, transformed from the enigmatic, Ford-like El Gringo of *The Fugitive*, *is* Ford, a casting choice suggesting much about Jack's love for "the big, ugly, stupid gorilla." A half-century earlier, Ford's mother had suggested that he enter the priesthood. It took this film, and Ward Bond, to get it done. Though Lonergan's behavior is a wee bit irreverent, Ford's respect for the priesthood resulted in his only prime film with Bond to include no ATB shots.

Victor McLaglen, pushing 65, demonstrated his legendary physical prowess while Ford shot his prolonged battle with the 44-year-old Wayne. Gary Wills noted, "Good as Wayne and O'Hara are, *The Quiet Man* could not work without McLaglen's towering presence athwart their path to happiness."[42] Old Vic, having won the Best Actor Oscar as *The Informer*, would soon earn a Best Supporting Actor nomination for his film-stealing performance as another lumbering, but constitutionally converse, Irish giant.

Wills paid enough attention to this fine actor to describe his vast and quite formidable talents, arguably not in line with a performer whom film scholars have dismissed as having a "limited range":

> McLaglen was a shrewd and successful actor long before *The Informer*.... Some are so little disposed to credit McLaglen's acting ability that they assume the Irish accent ... was his natural speech pattern, like Barry Fitzgerald's brogue.... McLaglen was in fact what Wayne was only in fantasy — a patriot-soldier, military officer, athlete. McLaglen was such a good and enthusiastic horseman that he formed his own uniformed riding club for friends and children.... McLaglen would later have nothing to do with the right-wing activities of Ward Bond or John Wayne.[43]

Wayne's character is the first to appear, but his introduction is prefaced by the voice of Bond. Though Sean Thornton's mother also is heard on the soundtrack, this brief comment is one character's memory, not the "omniscient," guiding tones of Father Lonergan. The priest's first appearance (framed in long shot, behind Bond) is directly foreshadowed by the preceding close-up of a Celtic cross as Sean and Michaeleen drive by in a horse cart.

"Now, then, here comes Myself," the pastor, in voiceover, gently intones with comic sauciness. "That's me, there, walking. That tall, saintly looking man: Peter Lonergan, parish priest." Ford again gives Bond the "*Frankenstein* treatment," first showing him from behind (in an over the shoulder shot), and then cutting to a frontal close-up.

"Ah, yes, I knew your people, Sean. Your grandfather, he died in Australia, in a *penal colony*," Lonergan emphasizes. "And your father, he was a good man, *too*."

As the priest remains by the cart to confer with Michaeleen, Sean walks along the road, lights a cigarette, and experiences a revelation upon spotting Mary Kate. Ford gives the viewer Sean's point of view before cutting to a close-up of the redheaded colleen. Only nine minutes into the film, Ford makes it clear that Bond represents *Himself*, and Duke is the man he would *like to be* (hence the combination of the names of his wife, Mary, and "secret" love, Kate).

Duke's first comment presents Ford's fantasy. "Hey, is that *real*?" Seans asks Michaeleen. "She couldn't be."

"It's only a mirage, brought on by your terrible thirst," the little tippler replies.

The film segues from outside Pat Cohan's pub to inside the chapel, where Sean sits for a few moments and then reverently gets up to leave, followed by Dan Tobin (both Duke and Francis genuflect before heading down the aisle). After Dan makes the sign of the cross with holy water, Sean walks over to the font, where he shares his moistened palm with Mary Kate, who crosses herself and quickly runs off.

"None of that, now. None of that!" scolds Michaeleen. "It's a bold, sinful man you are, Sean Thornton. And who taught you to be playin' patty fingers in the holy water?"

Ford informs his viewers that his expectations of "Ireland" are not wholly realistic. When Sean reveals, "Innisfree has become another word for heaven to me," Mrs. Tillane (Mildred Natwick) replies, "Innisfree is *far* from being heaven, Mr. Thornton." This statement is quickly supported by the sudden arrival of Red Will Danaher, brandishing his very threatening *shillelagh*. After the widow sells Sean his ancestor's estate, White o' Morn, for £1000, the squire growls, "I've got you down *in my book*."

Learning that Sean is the grandson of "Auld Sean Thornton, Himself," he pounds the bar with his stick, announcing that everyone "*will* have a drink!"

Dermot Fahy (Ken Curtis) strikes up "The Wild Colonial Boy" on his accordion, providing a fanfare for Father Lonergan and his associate, Father Paul (James Lilburn), as they enter the pub.

The Quiet Man (Argosy–Republic, 1952; directed by John Ford). Father Peter Lonergan (Ward Bond) observes as Sean Thornton (John Wayne, left) and Squire "Red Will" Danaher (Victor McLaglen) test each other's mettle.

Aspects of Ford's life and personality imbue, not only Father Lonergan, but several other characters: Sean Thornton's name and his desire to return to Ireland; Michaeleen's alcoholism and respect for cultural rites; Francis' very presence as Dan Tobin (the first "respectable" bone tossed by his brother since Mayor Elmer Briggs in *Pilgrimage* 18 years earlier); and even Danaher's attempts to bully desired behavior from others.

Will's refusal to allow Sean to court his sister inspires desperate measures, described by Father Lonergan's narration as having "formed a little conspiracy: the Reverend and Mrs. Playfair, Michaeleen Og, and — saints forgive us — Myself." Spreading a rumor that Will is now pursuing Mrs. Tillane, they expertly bait the squire.

At Sean and Mary Kate's wedding reception, Father Paul plays the spinet while Michaeleen and Owen Glynn (Sean McClory) join him in singing "The Humour Is on Me Now." Father Lonergan slowly walks up behind them, causing a momentary pause, but then sits down to take up the pub-song poke at marriage Himself.

Will, played for a fool, is snubbed by the widow. The "successful conspiracy" of Lonergan and the Playfairs (Arthur Shields and Eileen Crowe) stands by, speechless, as the squire says, "You *all* lied! It's bad enough for *you people*, but *my own priest*!"

Punched to the floor by Danaher, Sean flashes back to the tragic boxing bout in the States (revealing to the viewer, but not the onscreen characters, why he attempts to be the

"Quiet Man"). "Steady, Trooper, steady," advises the Reverend Playfair, the sole citizen of Innisfree to have discovered his identity. Without her dowry, Mary Kate is "no married woman," and Sean spends his nights in a sleeping bag.

Bond plays one of his major scenes as Father Lonergan fly-fishes for the "King of All Salmon," which he has attempted to snare "for 10 years." Mary Kate has just abandoned Sean in the village, due to his unwillingness to grovel for her dowry from the obstinate squire. She and the priest speak "in the Irish" about the marriage situation, to which he responds, "Woman, Ireland may be a poor country, God help us! But, here, a married man sleeps in a bed, not a *bag*— and, for your own good, I'll tell you a thing...." The King strikes, Father's reel unfurls, and he goes berserk, wading into the river after his fishy quarry.

"You've got him, Father!" she cheers. "Well, keep his head up, *you fool*!"

Lonergan loses the salmon. "God help us!" he rages at the sky, lifting his rod from the waters in anger as Mary Kate scampers away. "*Sleeping bag*!" he adds, driving the rod into the river. He retrieves it and makes his way toward the shore, as the scene dissolves to show Sean walking through the rocky countryside.

Cohan's pub is full of depressed men, drinking Guinness and singing "Galway Bay," as Sean strides in to confront Will. Taunted by the squire, he will neither beg nor fight for Mary Kate's "fortune" of £350. Instead, he seeks out the Reverend Playfair; and Wayne plays one of his best scenes as Sean discusses his "murder" of the "good egg" and family man, Tony Gaudello. "I can't fight, or won't fight, unless I'm mad enough to kill," he explains, "and, if that means losing her — I don't know..."

Mary Kate sleeps with Sean, and then she and Michaeleen set him up. Pretending to leave on the Dublin train (in cahoots with the engineer), she is collared and prodded, pulled, pushed and dragged five miles to the Danaher estate. Sean slings her at the squire's feet, calling off the marriage; but when he proceeds to burn the £350, she helps him.

Danaher throws a punch, but Sean ducks, hitting him with a shot to the breadbasket. Casting a sideways glance at the crowd, Mary Kate tells him that "supper will be waiting" and proudly walks back along the path over which she was dragged. Will starts the brawl for real, and Michaeleen begins making book. Ford indulges his love of slapstick (but this time it works), culminating with a shot of Wayne, emerging from a hay pile as he pulls a pitchfork from beneath his bum.

Playfair and the Protestant bishop stop to view the fight through field glasses, just as Danaher, knocked into the river, asks if Sean has "had enough."

"No," he replies. This response occurs at the 120-minute mark, the point at which Ford claimed to have stopped *The Quiet Man* when screening the final cut for Herb Yates and his Republic distributors.

Yates, insisting that audiences would not sit still for a film running longer than two hours, had ordered Ford to excise nine minutes. That he did; but rather than laboriously pruning a few frames here and there, he had the projectionist shut down the film at 120 minutes, knowing full well that, by the time the fight was just ready to rage on, the mogul would be skewered on his own *shillelagh*.

Francis now plays *his* big scene. As Father Paul reads the final rites to Dan Tobin, sounds of the melee can be heard in the distance. The priest runs off to alert Father Lonergan, and Dan, *shillelagh* in one hand as he pulls on his pants with the other, stumbles out of his room and down the road behind the fighters. Lonergan again is forced to abandon his salmon, to "do his duty" and "stop" the fight.

Wayne savors his best comic moment when Sean and Will take a Guinness break at

Cohan's. An argument over who will pay for the pints is ended by the squire, who tosses half his porter in the Yank's face. Duke times his response perfectly. "*Bar towel!*" he orders before asking the publican for the time and then hammering a blow to Danaher's jaw, sending him hurling through the door and into the street.

Best friends through battle, Sean and Will drunkenly sing "The Wild Colonial Boy" while stumbling to White o' Morn. "Woman of the house!" Sean announces. "I have brought the brother home to supper." They sit down and hoist a pitcher of Guinness, followed by the return of the calming tones of Father Lonergan: "Well, then — so peace and quiet came once again to Innisfree..." but the appearance of Mrs. Playfair, hell bent on a bicycle, interrupts. "What's that woman up to now?" the voice asks. "Make way! Make way! She'll be running you down with that *Juge*-gernaut!"

The scene cuts to the live-action version of Lonergan, who, advised of the approach of the bishop, ties a handkerchief around his priest's collar as he informs the crowd, "Now, when the Reverend Mr. Playfair — good man that he is — comes down, I want you all to cheer like Protestants!"

"Hooray! Hooray!" cheers the Catholic crowd as the "prim and proper" Protestant (who lost £15 to Playfair on the fight) passes by. Michaeleen, now acting as chaperone to Will and the widow, pulls up in his horse cart. All the Irish characters, topped by the very-alive Dan Tobin, wave their approval, as do Mary Kate and Sean, who, after hearing her whispered "invitation," chases her across the stream and toward the cottage.

Joseph McBride provided an interesting summation of *The Quiet Man*:

> The ... Technicolor fantasy John Ford made in Ireland at the age of 55 was not the fiercely political *Quiet Man* he would have made at 40.... Like John Wayne's Sean Thornton ... Ford was in flight from violence, material success, and the unexpected consequences of the American Dream. *The Quiet Man* would be his own exorcism of the demon of battle.[44]

One of the most personal, autobiographical commercial films ever made, *The Quiet Man* opened at Radio City Music Hall on February 28, 1952. Long lines formed for each showing, and filmgoers returned for several viewings, a response repeated in cities across the nation. Ford received his best reviews in a decade, and letters of copious praise arrived from many fellow filmmakers, including Frank Capra, Jack Warner and Darryl Zanuck.

The Quiet Man is truly a transcendent film. What began as the sum of one man's ideas was transformed through collective artistry into a *gestalt* experience that any viewer can enjoy.

Herb Yates, the mini-mogul who had protested too much about *The Quiet Man*, now couldn't heap enough superlatives on the first Republic film to garner such business, acclaim, and even Hollywood buzz about Oscar nominations. He waged a monumental publicity campaign, while Ford, fed up with dealing with such a penny-pinching hypocrite, refused to grant interviews or participate in the ballyhoo.

After all, *The Quiet Man* speaks for Himself.

10

One Hell of a Binge

[S]uddenly [Ford] rose up out of the chair and threw a big haymaker
and POW, hit me right in the jaw. It knocked me over backwards, and I
crashed into some furniture.... I was more embarrassed than hurt. I just
walked out of the room. Half an hour later Pappy came up to my room to
apologize.... He just said, "I'm sorry" and turned and walked out. But
from then on, our relationship was never what it once had been.—Henry
Fonda, on the making of *Mister Roberts*[1]

Nobody knew who was in charge of what. Ford was pissed all day.
Ward Bond, for Christ's sake, was directing the picture. At least he kept
the cameras turning when Ford came to and until he passed out again.—
Leland Hayward, producer of *Mister Roberts*[2]

Having produced the stage version of *What Price Glory?*, Ford began directing a new
film adaptation of the Anderson-Stallings play for 20th Century–Fox in mid–December
1951. Incredibly, Darryl Zanuck wanted to remake the 1926 Fox silent, which had costarred
Victor McLaglen, as well as involving Ford as an assistant director to Raoul Walsh, as a
musical.

Ford wasn't enthusiastic about the project from the start: "There wasn't one catchy
tune in the whole score. A quarter of the way through I got disgusted with it."[3]

In reality, Ford, angry at Zanuck for not letting him cast Wayne and Maureen O'Hara,
didn't really give a damn about the whole project, often taking out his frustration on Corinne
Calvet, who had been his "whipping girl" during the making of *When Willie Comes Marching
Home*. That film's star, Dan Dailey, was cast as Quirt opposite James Cagney as Flagg, and
both actors had to deal with a script by Phoebe and Henry Ephron that reduced their characters to mere caricatures of the original McLaglen and Edmund Lowe duo. This fact
induced Cagney to give one of his occasional exercises in relentless scenery chewing.

The Ephrons' addition of an intrusive, sappy romance involving Lewisohn (Robert
Wagner), a soldier who appears only briefly in the play, and Nicole Bouchard (Marisa Pavan),
a local French girl, also got Ford's goat. Having no idea why the director became enraged,
punching him out on the set in front of the cast and crew, the 21-year-old Wagner had to
be lifted from the ground and dusted off by Cagney. Wagner later admitted, "I thought my
career was at an end," calling Ford "a miserable son of a bitch."[4] All of this contempt and
chaos added up to one of the worst films ever to include the credit "Directed by John Ford."

During the inaugural season of the long-running live television series *Schlitz Playhouse of Stars*, Bond received top billing, above Henry Jones and June Lockhart, in "The Apple of His Eye," broadcast on February 29, 1952. The 60-minute program, which ran on CBS from October 5, 1951, through July 31, 1959, featured many top stars and character actors, including Charles Bickford, Walter Brennan, Richard Carlson, Dan Duryea, Kevin McCarthy, Vincent Price and Anthony Quinn. Bond would make two additional appearances during 1956.

Commander Films Corporation, a production company established by producer John C. Champion, completed only one picture, *Hellgate*, filmed from March 25 to mid–April 1952, partially in Los Angeles' Bronson Canyon. This low-budget affair, distributed by Lippert Pictures, was co-written by Champion and Charles Marquis Warren, who also directed.

Based loosely on Ford's *Prisoner of Shark Island*, *Hellgate*, set in 1867 Kansas, stars Sterling Hayden as Gilman Hanley, a veterinarian and ex–Confederate soldier, who treats a stranger proving to be the notorious guerrilla leader Verne Brechene, who has been looting and burning homes, killing innocent women and children in the process. Wrongly convicted of aiding and abetting the gang, Hanley is sentenced to Hellgate Prison, a subterranean series of cells located in the New Mexican desert, run by Lieutenant Vorhees (Bond, at his quietly sly and sarcastic best), whose own wife and child were roasted by guerrillas.

Vorhees is assisted by even more sadistic guards (including the ever-unpleasant Robert Wilkie as a taunting sergeant) and ferocious members of a Pima tribe, who track down escapees in the surrounding desert, earning $25 for a living captive and $50 for a dead one. Deprived of even basic necessities, Hanley endures a tortuous session in the "oven," a metal box sunk into the burning sands, before heroically making his way across the desert to bring a load of water to the typhus-wracked prison. Although a new prisoner who could have cleared Hanley dies before Vorhees can speak with him, the Lieutenant, finally overcoming his hatred, frees him.

This variation on *Shark Island* has other Ford connections, including James Arness and Mickey Simpson in supporting roles, and Andrew V. McLaglen's contributions as assistant director. (Cinematographer Ernest Miller previously had shot dozens of B Westerns and crime films featuring Wayne and/or Bond.)

Republic's *Thunderbirds* (1952) depicts the 1940 maneuvers of a National Guard unit comprised of men from Colorado, Oklahoma, Arizona and New Mexico, and its subsequent service during World War II. Made with the cooperation of the Department of Defense, U.S. Army and Reserve, the film was partially shot on location at Fort Sill, Oklahoma. Bond plays Sergeant Logan, a dedicated soldier who sacrifices himself to save his troops at the brutal battle for Anzio. John Derek and John Barrymore, Jr., are ably supported by Barton MacLane and Mae Clarke.

At Warner Bros. in April 1952, Duke began making *Big Jim McLain*, his own direct anti–Communist propaganda feature, exactly the type of heavy-handed political film he claimed to dislike. Its plot fit squarely into the current Red Scare genre, which included titles seen on double bills that were both ludicrous and bombs at the box office. The Communist characters are invariably crude caricatures: unattractive, humorless and overly sensitive, dressed in underworld attire, and drawing and exhaling cigarette smoke in a very "menacing" way. More often than not, like Mafia hit men, they tend to cheat the FBI by bumping off each other.

Adapted from the story "We Almost Lost Hawaii to the Reds," published in the *Saturday Evening Post*, *Big Jim McLain* relates the exploits of the title character (Wayne) and Mal Baxter (James Arness), two HUAC special agents, who investigate a Communist cell in

Honolulu. Never rising above the level of a formula B picture, it is an embarrassing parade of Cold War stereotypes, slapped together by James Edward Grant, Richard English and Eric Taylor. J. Edgar Hoover became concerned when he learned about the film, but he dropped his inquiry after being assured that it portrayed, not the FBI, but HUAC. The clichéd content of the film mattered little to audiences, who flocked to see the latest Wayne vehicle.

Duke's personal life wasn't faring as well, however. A major battle with Chata erupted on the cruise from California to Hawaii, during which she argued her way into a morass of alcohol. In Honolulu, while attending a party in their honor thrown by George and Anita Vanderbilt, Chata became inebriated and refused to leave at 9:00 P.M., when Duke needed to turn in before his early morning call. Two hours later, he finally left without her, having requested that their hosts phone a taxi. At 4:00 A.M., Anita called Duke, asking him to speak with Chata, but he sent a studio driver to pick her up. Again she refused to leave.

At 5:00 A.M., his phone rang again. "Duke, will you come over and get this Mexican bitch out of my house?" asked Anita. Wayne said it would be best just to let her sleep it off at the Vanderbilt home, and they agreed. But Chata would have none of it, and hitchhiked back to the hotel, looking like something the cat dragged in, at 7:00 A.M., when Duke was preparing to leave for work. Another shindig a few days later brought the same results, but this time Duke forced her to leave, inciting one hell of an argument back at the hotel.

It took two attempts for Chata to book a successful flight to Los Angeles. As for Duke, it was close to the last straw. She had been spending more time in Mexico City, where he purchased a house for her mother. After returning from shooting *The Quiet Man*, they had moved into a larger home in Encino, but soon her mother moved in, and the battles erupted once more. Prodigious alcoholics, mother and daughter constantly enabled one another's destructive habits.

Wayne was informed by his butler that, during his absence in Hawaii, Chata had invited another man, hotel magnate Nicky Hilton, to stay with her. To escape the newspaper coverage, Duke traveled to Peru with his production assistant, Ernie Saftig, planning to scout locations for future films. In Tingo Maria, while observing the shooting of *Green Hell*, he was introduced to a 23-year-old actress, Pilar Pallete Weldy, the estranged wife of their guide, Richard Weldy, an Irishman with a decided weakness for *poteen*.

Chata had threatened to file for a legal separation several times, but Duke always convinced her to give their marriage another chance. This time, when she pulled the act, he filed for divorce, charging her with cruelty. Chata countercharged with claims of Duke's physical and mental abuse, and did everything possible to smear his reputation.

Bond was having more problems of his own. Following the release of *The Quiet Man*, he had appeared in only two films during 1952. Wracked by acute pain in his abdomen, he was diagnosed with appendicitis, and underwent surgery to have the organ removed. Pappy visited him at the same time his brother-in-law and assistant director, Wingate Smith, was having his gallbladder removed. Ford became even more troubled when his colleague Frank Nugent suffered a heart attack.

Following the critical and commercial success of *The Quiet Man*, Herb Yates had no cause to object to Ford's desire to remake *Judge Priest* as *The Sun Shines Bright* (1953), adapted by Laurence Stallings from three Irvin S. Cobb short stories and featuring Charles Winninger, former "Cap'n Andy" of the Broadway and film versions of *Show Boat*. This project had remained in Ford's mind for nearly two decades, since Zanuck had cut Will Rogers' speech against lynching from the original film. Pappy even brought back Stepin

Fetchit to play the same character, Jeff Poindexter, a gesture providing his old friend with some much needed work.

Though a period piece, *The Sun Shines Bright*, filmed from late August to mid–September 1952, strongly reflects the sociopolitical climate at the dawn of the modern Civil Rights era. Joseph McBride wrote:

> Charles Winninger is moving and hilarious as the superannuated judge, displaying a sense of irony and intelligence matching Stepin Fetchit's.... Judge Priest is Ford's 1950s version of Henry Fonda's young Mr. Lincoln, who also stands down a lynch mob (though the men Lincoln saves are not black).[5]

Winninger and Fetchit are joined by several Stock Company stalwarts, including Milburn Stone, Jack Pennick, Russell Simpson, Arleen Whelan, and Francis, back in harness, complete with coonskin cap, as a white-lightning distilling old buzzard appropriately named "Brother Feeney." After honoring his brother with a role of sobriety and dignity in *The Quiet Man*, Ford had him stewed to the gills one final time, as Frank's role in *The Sun Shines Bright* would prove to be his last.

Ford's relationship with Yates reached its nadir during the making of *The Sun Shines Bright*, when he, Merian Cooper and Bill Donovan discovered that Argosy had been ripped off by Republic ever since the contract signing on January 5, 1950. Yates was altering documents, charging fees for personnel and sets used on other Republic films, skimming profits from *The Quiet Man*, and cooking the books, all of which resulted in Argosy being robbed of several million dollars.

While Donovan's law firm began an audit of all financial records pertaining to *Rio Grande*, *The Quiet Man* and *The Sun Shines Bright*, Ford berated Wayne, whom he considered responsible for his involvement with the studio. As the audit continued, Merian Cooper ended his partnership with Pappy to become the production head at Cinerama.

Fed up with Yates' mercenary behavior, Wayne refused to sign another Republic contract. Forming a partnership with producer Robert Fellows, he negotiated a nonexclusive deal with Warner Bros., who possessed the resources to make films in a variety of genres. Randy Roberts and James S. Olson noted:

> As far as Duke was concerned, there was no excuse — ever — for cheating John Ford. Ford's name stood for quality and integrity; he never padded budgets or chiseled employees. Ford had called Republic "a back of the bus operation" and worse, and Duke had to acknowledge that he was right.[6]

Wayne was the most beloved film star in the nation, but he, like Pappy, was not above being shafted by Herb Yates. Against formidable odds, and with Duke's help, Ford finally had realized his dream project; but the same would not happen for Wayne, who had received tacit approval from Yates to make *The Alamo*, only to have it chipped away. Realizing that this mogul of a "cheap poverty-row bullshit" studio would only green light a shoddy, B-Western travesty of his intended magnum opus, Wayne first launched into a shouting match before walking off the lot. Thirty minutes later, he called Mary St. John and told her to pack up and follow. When Yates objected, she immediately let him know the name of her *real* boss. Neither she nor Duke ever returned to Republic.

Without any of his own projects in the works, Ford accepted an offer from MGM's Sam Zimbalist, who was producing *Mogambo*, an updated, Technicolor remake of the studio's earlier jungle potboiler *Red Dust* (1932). Though he had aged a mere two decades, Clark Gable agreed to repeat his starring role, while Ava Gardner and Grace Kelly were signed for the parts originally played by Jean Harlow and Mary Astor. Screenwriter John Lee Mahin retained the basic love-triangle plot, but switched the locale from French Indochina to British East Africa.

MGM announced that *Mogambo* would be the most elaborate picture ever made on location in Africa, where 67 days of shooting had been scheduled in Kenya, Tanganyika and Uganda. In late October 1952, Ford left for Africa, where he remained for more than two months, before flying to London to film the interiors at MGM's Boreham Wood studio. While "on safari," he was responsible for more than 500 cast and crew members who camped in tents and carried firearms.

Meanwhile, Wayne was working on Warner Bros.' *Trouble Along the Way* (1953), playing a divorced coach of an underfunded football program at a Catholic college. Cast opposite Donna Reed, his love interest in *They Were Expendable*, he was concerned that any romantic moves he might make in the film would give Chata further firepower against him. Though portions of the script were altered to make Reed's character the aggressive one, Michael Curtiz shot the scenes as originally written.

Bond also was back at work, making his sophomore live television appearance, in "You Can Look It Up," the October 10, 1952, episode of NBC's *The Gulf Playhouse*. Based on a story by James Thurber, the program was produced by Frank Telford.

On November 7, 1952, Ava Gardner arrived in Nairobi. Unable to cast Maureen O'Hara in her role, Ford either ignored or verbally abused the actress throughout the production. During the first day of filming, Gardner committed the cardinal sin of asking for another take. She later recalled that Ford, "ranting like a madman," said:

> Oh, you're a director now. You know so fucking much about directing. You're a lousy actress, but now you're a director. Well, why don't you direct something? You go sit in my chair, and I'll go and play your scene.[7]

This browbeating occurred even though Gardner's current husband, Frank Sinatra, had accompanied her on location. At a low point in his career, Sinatra, hoping to make a comeback by landing the role of Angelo Maggio in Columbia's *From Here to Eternity*, disliked being referred to as "Mr. Ava Gardner" during the shoot, but was very respectful to Ford, who continually teased him about his size and weight while assigning him the task of preparing Italian dinners for the cast.

When Sinatra received a telegram from the William Morris Agency asking him to report to Columbia for a screen test, Gardner bought a ticket for his 13,500-mile flight back to Tinsel Town. The day after competing with Eli Wallach for the *Eternity* role, Sinatra returned to Nairobi, where he bought Christmas presents for Ford and all the *Mogambo* principals. Grace Kelly recalled:

> [On] Christmas Eve ... Frank even talked John Ford into reciting "The Night Before Christmas" to us, and this wonderful evening ended with 60 Congolese Africans, barefooted, with their blankets around them, singing French Christmas carols. It was a wonderful Christmas, thanks to Frank.[8]

(Sinatra played Maggio for a paltry $8,000 and, as predicted by costar Montgomery Clift, won an Academy Award for his "spontaneous" performance.[9])

Though she recently had starred opposite Gary Cooper in *High Noon* (1952), Kelly had worked primarily on television until Ford persuaded MGM to offer her a contract. During the *Mogambo* shoot, he elicited a performance from her that displayed a smoldering passion beneath her "proper," rather icy, Eastern demeanor. Ford couldn't take all the credit, however, as this sensual quality was no doubt enhanced by her off-camera affair with that legendary lothario, Clark Gable. (Kelly and Gardner both went on to receive Oscar nominations for their work on the film.)

Anxious to thaw his recent freeze-out, Wayne sent five letters and a box of cigars to Ford's room at the New Stanley Hotel in Nairobi. In December, Ford finally wrote back, mentioning Duke's current collaboration with William Wellman on *Island in the Sky* (and, of course, their fellow best buddy) before revealing some undoubtedly embellished, often ribald details about working in the East African bush:

> Do you — like Ward — like to shoot animals in your back yard? This is the place — lions, leopards, rhino, hippo, giraffe, impala, etc., etc., etc. Shootin' 'em ain't crumpet — I mean cricket — so easy. Tonight an askari — native police — came up to us.
>
> "Sir," says he — very Oxford. "I have been forbidden to enter my tent by two lions!" No kidding! We went over and there were two of the biggest lions I've ever seen sitting in front of his tent, chewing their cuds. Twas rutting season, y' know — the birds and the bees — even the flowers! What a performance (yes, I have it in 16mm).
>
> Speaking of rutting season — who doesn't? The English girls are starting to look white to me. I'd better move on. My no. 1 boy promised Gable and I he'd tip us off the minute he heard one of them taking a bath. This was a week ago. This also explains why this letter is hand-written, not dictated....
>
> Frank S[inatra] weighs only 125 lbs. but Gable says 25 lbs. of that is pecker...
>
> I am still true to Meta [Sterne], Mary St. J[ohn, Wayne's assistant], Bea, Grace, Estrellita who sings, Barbara Hagen and Vera Hruba Ralston Yates. (There is a little Irish girl on the second unit from South Africa — but more later.)
>
> Duke, I wish you all the luck in your new film. Give my best to Murph, my favorite pimp — [James Edward] Grant — I wish he were here....

After closing this droll dispatch with the warm valediction, "Much affection," Ford, referring to one of Wayne's missives, added the postscript, "Monument Valley! How lovely that sounds. When?"[10]

In February 1953, Ford was still in London, shooting the interiors for *Mogambo*, when he won his fourth Best Director Academy Award, although *The Quiet Man* was edged out by the grand spectacle of Cecil B. DeMille's *The Greatest Show on Earth* (1952) for Best Picture. Ford's Irish dream had been nominated for seven Oscars, and Winton Hoch and Archie Stout won for their color cinematography, but "Sean" had no interest in being in Hollywood for the ceremony.

Wayne accepted the statuette for his mentor; and, although he hated *High Noon*, also graciously picked up the Best Actor award for the absent Gary Cooper. The fact that Duke wasn't even nominated convinced Bond that the whole thing was a Communist conspiracy. Mary St. John explained, "Duke's politics definitely hurt him that year. *The Quiet Man* was his best performance to date, in a film that was nominated for a half-dozen awards. And they ignored him."

That month, Wayne was making the aviation-survival adventure *Island in the Sky* (1953) with "Wild Bill" Wellman on location near Truckee, California. Screenwriter Eddie Gann also was working on the flight epic *The High and the Mighty*, which Wellman talked Duke into buying. William Clothier was hired to shoot the primarily cockpit-bound film in Cinemascope. Featuring an ensemble cast, the project didn't require big stars, and Wellman chose "competent, fine actors and actresses," including Claire Trevor, Laraine Day, Robert Stack, Jan Sterling, Robert Newton, David Brian and Sidney Blackmer. Spencer Tracy originally was cast as copilot-hero Dan Roman, but his decision to back out left the role for Wayne to handle.[11]

The High and the Mighty was an enormous hit, racking up a tidy profit for Wayne-Fellows. With divorce looming over Duke, Robert Fellows asked if he would buy his interest in the company. As sole owner, Wayne, at the suggestion of his son Michael, named the new production outfit Batjac (after "Batjak," the Dutch shipping company in *Wake of the Red Witch*; the new spelling resulted from a clerical error).

In early February, Bond made a triumphant return to Churubusco Studios in Mexico City, to join Gary Cooper, Barbara Stanwyck, Ruth Roman and Anthony Quinn in Warner Bros.' *Blowing Wild* (1953), an oil-drilling adventure set in 1930s South America. Bond is Dutch Peterson, business partner of Coop's Jeff Dawson. Rendered penniless by bandits, the two men do whatever necessary to rebuild their collective fortune. After Dutch is shot and confined to a hospital, Jeff is hired by old friend Paco Conway (Quinn) as foreman at his petroleum company. Matters are complicated by Paco's wife, Marina (Stanwyck), Jeff's former flame. This complicated affair culminates with the deaths of Paco and Marina, but Dutch, Jeff and his new sweetheart, Sal Donnelly (Roman), make their way home.

On March 15, 1953, Bond costarred with old Hollywood colleague Murray Alper in "Winners Never Lose," an episode of the CBS television series *The General Electric Theater*. Directed by James V. Kern, the program also reunited him with Frankie Darro, one of the kids who beat him bloody in *Wild Boys of the Road* 20 years earlier, and Ford Stock Company favorites Wallace Ford and Pat O'Brien.

Part of the 3-D craze that swept the film industry during 1953, *The Moonlighter*, an unusual Western written by Niven Busch, doesn't include the distracting visual gimmicks associated with the short-lived exploitation format. Shot partly on location at the ranches of Ray Corrigan and Gene Autry, and at Peppermist Falls in the High Sierras, during April and May 1953 by director Roy Rowland, the film stars Fred MacMurray as a "moonlighter," a cattle rustler who works by night, and Barbara Stanwyck as the tough cowgirl who eventually straightens him out. (An arch-conservative, Stanwyck was one of the few stars willing to hire Bond during the early 1950s.)

As he does in his film noir classics, MacMurray, as Wes Anderson, narrates *The Moonlighter*, which takes some startling plot turns, including the wrong man being lynched for his crimes, and his attendance at his "own" funeral, where he robs the mourners to pay the undertaker, Clem Usqubaugh (Charles Halton), whose name is a variation on the Gaelic word for whiskey!

As Anderson begins a rein of vengeance upon lynchers, he is visited by his old friend, the outlaw Cole Gardner (Bond), who persuades him to rob the bank from which his brother, Tom (William Ching) has just been fired. Insisting that he join them, Tom is gunned down during the getaway.

When townsmen are deputized to join the posse, Rela (Stanwyck), Anderson's old flame, who had been seeing his brother, asks to join them. Being told, "We don't deputize *women*" has no effect on her, and off she rides, hell-bent to track down the robbers. Typical partners in crime, Wes and Cole begin to argue immediately after holing up at a mountain cabin hidden behind a waterfall. Bond is a true badass this time around: Cole, following a brutal brawl, during which he and Wes use everything in sight (burning logs, an axe, furniture) as weapons, leaves his "friend" hog-tied and vamooses with all the cash.

Rela spots Cole, who fires at her, but she is too smart for the reckless outlaw. Sneaking around him, she sights her rifle and orders him to drop his; but when he goes for his handgun, she kills him. She then discovers Wes at the cabin, but while taking him at gunpoint toward town, she slips while crossing beneath the waterfall, and he saves her from falling to her death. Back at the hideout, she admits that her previous behavior had driven him to moonlighting, and Wes decides to surrender to the sheriff. Rela promises to wait until he serves his prison sentence, and the couple ride off toward the horizon.

A unique, fast-moving Western (77 minutes), *The Moonlighter* has the distinction of showing the mighty Bond being gunned down by a woman. Stanwyck (in later years, able to ditch the Brooklyn accent that mars some of her earlier films) is impressive as the resourceful Rela, and MacMurray gives one of his delightfully shifty performances.

When Ford returned to California in April, he and Mary lost their home on Odin Street to the City of Los Angeles (by right of eminent domain, it was bulldozed in favor of a parking lot) and moved into William Wyler's former residence on Copa de Oro Road in Bel Air. Compensated $46,000 by the city, they shelled out $95,000 for the new digs. To drown the combined sorrows of losing his beloved home base and nearly losing the *Araner*, damaged during a savage windstorm at Santa Barbara a few months earlier, Ford climbed aboard the boat for a gale-force bender.

While stone-cold sober, Ford's vision had become progressively blurry during the making of *Mogambo*; and, during surgery at Good Samaritan Hospital on June 30, he had cataracts removed from both eyes. Vision was restored in the left eye, but the other would remain sensitive to light indefinitely, a reality that led him to emulate Raoul Walsh by wearing a patch over the right eye for the rest of his days.

The prospect of poor vision adversely affecting his career, which already was being deflated by changing attitudes in Hollywood, seemed a minor issue when Ford learned about the status of his brother's health. Frank, like Jack, loved booze and smoking, but hated doctors, and by the time he underwent exploratory surgery to determine the cause of a painful and debilitating condition, a massive malignancy was discovered. Diagnosed with throat cancer, he was given only a few months to live. Dan Ford wrote:

> I can remember ... going with my grandfather to pick him up at the hospital, and the three of us riding through the streets of Hollywood. When we got to the site of one of the giant studios, we stopped. John and Francis exchanged a look. Then Francis turned to me and said, "I used to own that studio." For a moment he smiled and the old twinkle was there in his eyes. Then it faded away.[12]

At Francis' side when he passed away at 71 on September 5, 1953, Ford claimed that he talked only of Ireland, speaking Gaelic during his final hours. Brother Feeney, "Sean's" mentor, a true cinematic pioneer who had been reduced to playing the inebriated Shakespearean fool for more than two decades, was gone; and most of his work, and the memory of it, would unfortunately disappear with him.

Louis L'Amour's short story "The Gift of Cochise" was published in the July 5, 1952, issue of *Collier's* magazine. Wayne-Fellows Productions purchased the rights, and after James Edward Grant wrote the screenplay, L'Amour expanded his story into a novel, which hit the streets simultaneously with the release of *Hondo* in late 1953.

John Farrow shot *Hondo* on location in Carmago, Chihuahua, Mexico, during the summer of 1953. The 3-D process, accomplished with two cameras borrowed from Warner Bros., not only required extra shooting time, but equipment breakdowns resulted in the actors sitting idle in a small shelter, where they had some protection from the blazing sun. Bond, having shed 15 extra pounds, arrived on the set, proclaiming the benefits of a new artificial sweetener called sucaryl, and nearly driving Duke to distraction. (Some of Ward's lost weight undoubtedly was replaced by the enormous beard he grew to play the aptly named "Buffalo" Baker, who resembles an older, larger version of his Sid Bascom in *The Big Trail*.)

Farrow originally had mentioned casting Katherine Hepburn as the female lead, but Duke wanted to find an actress who looked like an actual pioneer woman. The part went to Broadway star Geraldine Page, a longtime liberal, who listened in "horror" to the political discussions waged by Farrow, Wayne and Bond:

> John Wayne would talk so sensibly, but ... Mr. Farrow was very much a Machiavellian ... and Ward Bond was just an oversimplifying bully.... [Wayne was] a reactionary for all sorts of non-reactionary reasons.... I swear that if John Wayne ever got transplanted out of this circle of people that are around him all the time, that he would be the most anti-reactionary force for ... good.[13]

Duke didn't enjoy shooting his scenes with Page, whose hygiene habits were atrocious. One day, he told Bond, "Jesus Christ, I'm afraid I might puke the next time I have to kiss her. Maybe if I hold my breath it won't be so bad." This comment inspired Ward to play a practical joke on Duke, who, while filming a subsequent romantic scene, was forced to do a second take after his pal "accidentally" bumped the camera.

Without warning, Ford arrived in Carmago one day, advising Farrow that the screen version of John Wayne would not be taken seriously if he was shown falling in love with a woman as unattractive as Page. Subsequently, Farrow had her character, Angie Lowe, look at Hondo Lane and say, "I know I'm a homely woman, but I love you." Mary St. John recalled:

> Do you want to know how bad she smelled [*sic*]? Page did not have the best morals ... and hard-up stuntmen stumbled out of her room every morning. But even Ward Bond wouldn't take advantage of her availability. That's how bad it was.[14]

One evening, St. John pulled a joke on Bond in the dining hall. Just as he began preaching about the wonders of Sucaryl, she announced that *Reader's Digest* had published an article about the sweetener causing impotence in men. In a letter to Ford, Duke wrote that Ward had "dropped the bottle as if it were a rabbi's knife."[15]

Page, however, admired Duke, both as an actor and a man. She easily explained his remarkable screen presence:

> [H]e's terribly bright ... and he learns so quickly. He knows how to do everything....
> He's a terribly honest man.... And that comes across, underlined by the kind of parts he plays. He always plays an honest man, and his own honesty feeds into it, and the simplicity of his acting.

She also recalled an incident involving Farrow's neglect of the Mexican crew, who were left outdoors during a raging storm, that demonstrated Duke's innate decency toward others: "Oh, if you could have seen ... those poor guys out there.... It was a great thing, like out of the movies, because he had gone to bring them a sandwich."[16] Wayne had left his dry, warm motel room to remain out in the cold rain all night, telling stories and singing, while the caterer, whom he had awakened, brought sandwiches, coffee and tequila to the grateful men.

Duke continued to pattern his off-camera hours after Pappy's example, playing cards into the wee hours, throwing in ample doses of whiskey, and exchanging profane stories with Bond and the stuntmen. Page claimed:

> All night long I had such a refresher course in all the foulest language. I'd heard bits of it at different places, at different points through my life, but I never had ... it all gathered together ... an endless stream of it ... it's like rhythm, like music ... on and on and on, it's fantastic.[17]

Lee Aaker, who was nine years old when cast as Angie's son, Johnny Lowe, recalled that Bond, while spending leisure hours by the motel swimming pool, gave him Spanish lessons. Australian actor Michael Pate, who plays the Apache chief Vittorio, remembered:

> Ward was a very tough old bird.... He was a physical person, a rambunctious person. He'd come up and give you a great, big bear hug, and nearly crack your ribs.... But, by god, that character that he stuck up on the screen time after time, is immemorial.[18]

To keep Ford occupied during his visit, Wayne and Farrow sent him out to shoot second-unit action scenes. When Farrow had to return to Hollywood to work on another project, Pappy remained to help Duke finish the picture.

The film depicts Hondo as being "part Indian," offering a more complex and balanced portrait of Native Americans than most Hollywood films of the era. Hondo is foremost an honest man. "I'm not much for lyin,'" he informs Angie; and when Vittorio appears to taunt him, he reveals, "He was testin' me. Indians hate lies."

Later, when asked by Lieutenant McKay (Tom Irish), a young cavalry officer, to ride against Vittorio, Hondo, who has made a promise to the Apache chief, refuses, explaining, "Mister, when I give my word, I keep it."

By contrast, Angie, when learning of Hondo's self-defense killing of her husband, admits, "I married a man who was a liar, a thief and a coward. He was a drunkard, and unfaithful."

Wayne is excellent in this fine film, and the relationship between Hondo and Bond's Buffalo is one of their best. The moral ambiguity, an unusual element in a James Edward Grant script, is admirable for a 1950s Western. When Angie mentions Vittorio's death in battle, Hondo's reply is typically straightforward: "Everybody gets dead. It was his turn."

Informed of the cavalry troops who will follow in the wake of Vittorio's defeat, Buffalo concludes, "That'll be the end of the Apache."

"The end of a way of life," adds Hondo. "Too bad —*good way*."

The initial 3-D release of *Hondo* in late November 1953 was met with the frustration of theater owners and audiences at the mercy of projection problems and the cheap, cardboard glasses needed to view the film. Following its first problematic week, the 3-D version was pulled, and standard color prints, released on January 4, 1954, eventually raised $4.1 million in domestic rentals.

Based on Eric Knight's 1940 novel *Lassie Come Home*, MGM's *Gypsy Colt* was filmed on location in California, Arizona and Colorado during July 1953. Costarring with 10-year-old Donna Corcoran, Frances Dee and the black stallion "Gypsy," Bond made his "family film" debut playing Frank MacWade, a farmer whose crops have been wiped out by an endless drought. Needing cash for seed, to prepare for any possibility of rain, MacWade is forced to sell the horse, but cannot bring himself to tell his daughter. Gypsy twice runs away from his new owner, Wade Gerald (Larry Keating), whose violent trainer (Lee Van Cleef) attempts to convert the animal into a racehorse. Following a 500-mile journey back to the MacWade farm, Gypsy is allowed to stay with his original "family."

Unabashedly sentimental, this beautifully photographed (in Ansco Color) equine version of the Lassie tale features Bond playing a gruff but understanding father, a character he had touched upon in *Home in Indiana* a decade earlier. Excellent performances are contributed by young Corcoran and "Beauty," a truly remarkable horse, whose work was honored with the American Humane Association's PATSY (Picture Animal Top Star of the Year) Award in 1955.

On October 5, 1953, the cast and crew of *The Quiet Man* (with the lamentable exception of Francis) attended an awards tribute to Ford on the Republic lot. Wayne was master of ceremonies, Maureen O'Hara sang Irish songs, and two other Academy honored Ford regulars (Winton Hoch, who won for Best Color Cinematography; and Vic McLaglen, nominated as Best Supporting Actor) were there to help celebrate with Pappy's daughter, Barbara, son-in-law Ken Curtis, brother Eddie O'Fearna, and brother-in-law Wingate Smith. Directors Guild president George Sidney handed Ford the union's gold disc, pronouncing him best director of the year, while the Oscar statuette was rightfully presented to the Coach by none other than the Judge, the honorable Wardell Edwin Bond.

This primarily Ford Stock Company event was far more intimate and meaningful than all the Academy Award ceremonies the director had missed over the past 17 years. As he told the gathering, he was at his ailing daughter's bedside for *The Informer*, "suddenly taken drunk" for *The Grapes of Wrath*, and "somewhere off the shores of Japan" for *How Green Was My Valley*. Visibly moved, he admitted:

> I would be untruthful — at any rate I would be a bad actor — if I pretended modesty tonight. Of course I am proud, enormously so. In fact, I am filled with conceit, if you can imagine such a trait in an Irishman.
> Look here, you'll have to forgive me. This is my first appearance in the role of an award winner.... But here I am now, and I think it's time to state my creed as a director. It is simply this: I ain't no career man. I don't chase after no medals. I simply direct, and if you're good enough, you stars and you cameramen, you supporting players and you set people, if you're good enough, then you make me look like a career man.
> Half of my friends are in those potholes in Forest Lawn because they waited until they had the perfect script, until they signed every big name in the business, until they had three million dollars to throw away, and then the lightning didn't strike 'em. But I simply direct pictures, and if I had my way, every morning of my life, I'd be behind that camera at nine o'clock waiting for the boys to roll 'em, because that's the only thing I really like to do.... You put me here with your talents, your skills, your affection. As for me, if I have a career, you have given it to me.

Joan Crawford purchased the film rights to Roy Chanslor's novel *Johnny Guitar* soon after its publication in 1953. She then sold them to Republic, with the provision that she play the tough heroine in the film adaptation. Philip Yordan wrote the screenplay, and Nicholas Ray, who had directed Bond in *On Dangerous Ground*, began filming, partly on location in the vicinity of Sedona, Arizona, in mid–October. Cinematographer Harry Stradling, benefiting from a Republic "epic" budget, shot the film in the Trucolor process. Victor Young composed an atmospheric score, and Peggy Lee wrote the lyrics for the title song, which she recorded with Young's "Singing Strings."

Recognized as an allegory for the HUAC blacklisting era, *Johnny Guitar* features a vigilante mob led by John McIvers (Bond), whose own reactionary zeal is bested by that of Emma Small (Mercedes McCambridge), whose brother has been killed during a stagecoach holdup. Between them, these two "own the town" and all the surrounding cattle herds. Though no evidence exists, Emma "knows" the crime was committed by the "Dancin' Kid" (Scott Brady), the occasional lover of Vienna (Crawford), who is guilty by association.

Ray knew that Bond was the perfect choice to play the posse leader, an even more narrow-minded version of Walter Brent in *On Dangerous Ground*. Unlike Brent, McIvers is all talk, ready to accuse and condemn, but offers little action, choosing to let others perform the dirty work, including a hanging. Republic's official pressbook, referring to McIvers as a "solid citizen involved in a lynching" and leading "a necktie party," included an article titled, "Ward Bond Scores," playing up his years as a "gridiron athlete" at USC and claiming:

Off screen, Ward Bond is the antithesis of the villainous characters he so frequently portrays. He is quiet, with a good sense of humor. He breeds and raises show dogs, and at one time had six prize-winning white English bull terriers. His main hobby is sailing — anything from a sleek California yacht to a husky apple-bowed fishing barge he discovered in Ireland.[19]

Sterling Hayden plays the title character, John Logan, an erstwhile gunfighter who now is an incognito guitar strummer. Having a "past" with Vienna, he rides to her Arizona casino, where it soon becomes apparent who wears the britches. Crawford knew the role was made for her, and she is excellent as the resilient and courageous Vienna, who stands up to all the men, is nearly lynched (but saved at the last moment by Johnny), and finally shoots it out with Emma, who winds up dead at the bottom of a mountain rise.

This innovative "feminist Western," featuring women who wear six guns, is set up early in the film by Sam (Walter Osterloh), a dealer at Vienna's joint, who tells Johnny, "Never seen a woman that was more man. She thinks like one, acts like one, and sometimes makes me feel like I'm not." Later, Vienna describes to Johnny the societal double standard that holds women up to a rigid moral code that doesn't apply to men.

The fine cast also includes John Carradine (in a rare sympathetic role, as Old Tom, Vienna's soft-spoken kitchen man), Ernest Borgnine (as the outlaw Bart Lonergan), Frank Ferguson (as Marshal Williams, who takes orders from McIvers) and Paul Fix (as Eddie, Vienna's roulette croupier). The climactic gun duel is followed by the embrace of Vienna and Johnny, as the shamed posse stands speechless in the background, and the ethereal voice of Peggy Lee is heard on the soundtrack, singing a few lines from "Johnny Guitar."

Ted Post directed Bond in his debut on NBC's *The Ford Television Theatre*, costarring with Philip Carey in the thriller "Gun Job," aired on December 17, 1953. The 30-minute episode, featuring Ward as Hank Fetterman, paired him with Ellen Drew as his wife, and a supporting cast including old Ford stalwart Kenneth MacDonald.

During this period, Bond decided to end his lengthy dedication to sobriety. Dobe Carey wrote:

> [S]uddenly one night sometime in the early 1950s, I noticed Ward with a Rheingold beer in his hand. Rheingold over ice was his drink. It didn't seem to make too much difference in his behavior, so I wondered why he had gone on the wagon in the first place. Of course beer is not considered drinking by dedicated booze hounds. The Old Man didn't make a fuss over it. He always picked on Ward anyway.[20]

On February 1, 1954, his 60th birthday, Ford was at the U.S. Military Academy, preparing to make "Mister West Point," starring Tyrone Power as Irish immigrant and legendary swimming instructor Martin "Marty" Maher, Jr., whose autobiography *Bringing Up the Brass: My 55 Years at West Point*, inspired the screenplay by Edward Hope. That afternoon, in his room at the Thayer Hotel in West Point, "Mr. John Ford" received the following telegram:

> Dear Coach:
>   This is an important date in my life because I'm more of a man for knowing a fellow who was born on it.
>
>   Happy Birthday,
>   Duke[21]

Leaving Republic and the dreaded Herb Yates behind, Ford had moved his office to Columbia, where he hadn't made a film since being personally requested by Edward G. Robinson for *The Whole Town's Talking* nearly 20 years earlier. Much of "Mister West Point," which would be released as *The Long Gray Line*, was shot on location, with interior scenes later completed at the studio.

Though Columbia mogul Harry Cohn has been perennially painted as a tyrant, he, unlike Yates, respected true cinematic talent. Cast as cadet Dwight Eisenhower in *The Long Gray Line*, Dobe Carey had heard all the tales about Cohn's nearly paranoiac control over the studio:

> You felt his presence all over that little lot.... It's been printed ... many times that Harry had the soundstages and many of the dressing rooms bugged.... All powerful men had spies. They didn't necessarily appoint them. There have always been natural-born stool pigeons who love to tell men of power who is sleeping with whom, who's on dope, who's a closet drinker or a closet gay.... But there were two directors who were absolutely and totally left alone. They called their own shots, and Mr. Cohn did not even walk on their set without being asked — no bugs, no bullshit, and a closed set, at all times. Those two men were Frank Capra and John Ford.... Cohn was a smart man, and he knew he had the best in these two men.[22]

Carey's portrayal, and that of Elbert Steele as the older Ike, had to be approved by the President before shooting could begin on March 15, 1954.

Maureen O'Hara, cast as Maher's wife, Mary, was costarring in her fourth Ford film. Prior to shooting *The Quiet Man*, Pappy had mailed several bizarre "love letters," addressed to "Herself," to the actress, who believed they were part of his creative process in developing the Sean Thornton–Mary Kate Danaher relationship for the film. Since returning from Ireland, he had treated her in a consistently rude manner; but when production on *The Long Gray Line* began, she was, for reasons unknown, "in the barrel":

> Our relationship had changed. There was anger toward me and it was revealing itself in all its ugliness.... Between takes and scenes, Mr. Ford hurried me along by shouting, "Come on! Move that big ass of yours." He was delighted in insulting me in front of everybody.[23]

Ford's references to O'Hara's rear end suggest that some of the heat he'd taken off the "Horse's Ass" during the shooting of *The Quiet Man* was now being transferred to the unfortunate "Herself."

Decades later, O'Hara described an incident in Ford's Columbia office, where she had dropped in to show him some revised sketches of her wardrobe:

> Ford had his arms around another man and was kissing him. I was shocked and speechless.... They were on opposite sides of the room in a flash. The gentleman Ford was with was one of the most famous leading men in the picture business....
>
> Later, that actor approached me and asked, "Why didn't you tell me John Ford was homosexual?" I answered, "How could I tell you about something I knew nothing about?"[24]

"That actor" was the star of *The Long Gray Line*, Tyrone Power. (Although O'Hara did not mention his name, several reliable film industry veterans have confirmed his identity.) Ronald L. Davis wrote:

> In a different age Ford might have turned to homosexuality, but had he done so in the first half of this century, guilt would have overwhelmed him. Without question he preferred the company of men, and male bonding reached inordinate proportions. He may have been physically attracted to men on occasion, but there is no indication that he gratified his appetites homosexually.... His discomfort with behavior that smacked of effeminacy suggests that he was not secure in his masculinity. But his was neither an age nor a society that prized sensitivity in males, and to be labeled an artist made a man suspect in all but the most sophisticated circles. Ford resolved his dilemma by dwelling in a masculine world, enjoying male companionship and post-adolescent horseplay....[25]

In her 2004 account, O'Hara continued:

> I now believe there was a conflict within Ford and that it caused him great pain and turmoil.
>   These kinds of desires were something John Ford could readily accept in others, but never in himself. He saw himself as a man's man. He was a military hero and the compadre of rugged stuntmen. He was also too immersed in the teachings of Catholicism. He would have seen it as a terrible sin.... These conflicts were manifested as anger toward me, his family, his friends, his heroes, and most of all, himself. His fantasies and crushes on women ... were just balm for this wound. He hoped each of us could save him from these conflicted feelings, but was later forced to accept that none of us could. I believe this ultimately led to my punishment and his downward spiral into an increased reliance on alcohol.[26]

One can only speculate on whether or not Ford was a closet "homosexual," but like all the other profound ambiguities that comprised and confounded this enigmatic man, he certainly may have been bisexual. During an age when being "out" was rarely even considered, an artist's honesty (even admitting that he *was* an artist) could be a career killer. When Universal founder Carl Laemmle still reigned at the studio, he and his son appreciated highly the talents of gay artistic genius James Whale; but when the studio fell to Wall Street bankers in 1937, "Jimmy" saw the writing on the wall. One of Hollywood's most innovative directors, Whale made his last feature film, at Columbia, in 1941. His cinematic career lasted only 11 years.

But O'Hara apparently wasn't the only person close to Ford who witnessed or suspected the "conflict" within this "job of work" non-artist. Maureen's youngest brother, Jimmy Fitz-Simons, while visiting the *Long Gray Line* set, was advised by the stuntmen, "Whatever you do, stay away from the Old Man after dark."[27] (This comment brings to mind the "homophobic humor" that helped drive "Jack" Ford away from Harry Carey.)

Ford loved John Wayne and Ward Bond, but his true sexual orientation wasn't something he would have discussed with them, or anyone else. When it came to his own life and psyche, Pappy avoided the truth, exaggerated, lied, or just didn't "have any goddamn idea." The positive emotions he felt for his two favorite actors and whipping boys may have been the underlying cause of his negative, sadistic treatment of them (and himself); but even a lifetime of psychoanalysis may not have "proved" anything.

When Wayne was working with Howard Hawks on the pre-production for *Red River* in 1946, he was visited by Montgomery Clift in his office at Republic. The sensitive, Method schooled, Broadway actor, whom Duke knew nothing about, was Hawks' choice to play cattle baron Thomas Dunson's surrogate son, Matthew Garth, and this was his first meeting with the macho Hollywood star. Randy Roberts and James S. Olson explained:

> Duke ... was not impressed by the frail five-foot-ten-inch actor. Instead of sitting in a chair and talking with him man to man, Clift perched on the back of a sofa, put his feet on its cushions, mumbled inaudible responses to Duke's questions, and avoided making eye contact with anyone in the room. "He's a little queer, don't you think?" Duke asked Mary St. John after Clift left. "Christ, how does Howard expect that kid to stand up to me in a movie? He can't even look me in the eye."[28]

There is no evidence that Wayne or Bond ever said anything about this issue, or even considered that such desires existed in Ford. Regardless of what they may or may not have known, they both loved and respected Pappy, and their loyalty was unbreakable. No matter how abusive or sadistic they were treated, they took it. Wayne was strong and silent. Bond was an attention seeker, the "Horse's Ass." Ford's "gluteal fetish," represented by Ward's equine rear end in so many films, could be understandable in light of these armchair speculations, but Wayne (and Bond, too) also enjoyed the whole sarcastic spectacle. To the Judge, if his center of gravity was the center of attention, so much the better.

When casting *The Long Gray Line*, Bond was the only actor Ford considered for the role of Academy athletics instructor Captain Herman J. Koehler. This picture marked Pappy's first foray into Cinemascope, and he made full use of the frame by showcasing Ward's bum in several scenes. These ATB shots are symbolic of Ford's attitude toward the wide (2.35:1) aspect ratio:

> You've never seen a painter use that kind of composition. Even the great murals weren't this huge tennis court. I like to see the people, and if you shoot them in widescreen, you're left with a lot of real estate on either side.[29]

While making this ponderous and overlong "biopic," Bond was able to steal, not only every scene in which he appears, but the hearts of the actual West Point cadets. Dobe Carey wrote:

> After we'd been there about five days, the cadets invited the cast to dinner in their huge mess hall.... The person they all liked the most was Ward Bond. They loved him, much to Ford's disgust. Bond stole the whole show that night.... You could hear the cadets' laughter from one end of the mess hall to the other.

The Long Gray Line (Columbia, 1955; directed by John Ford). Captain Herman J. Koehler (Ward Bond) sustains a good shot from Martin Maher (Tyrone Power) during their boxing "demonstration."

The Old Man walked over to our table and said to the boys, "That is Mister Bond who is causing the disturbance at that other table. Please do not judge the rest of the cast by his behavior."

"But we love him, sir!" they said in chorus.[30]

Carey again shared a room with Bond, who, when not working, enjoyed his favorite libation, Rheingold beer, at the Thayer Hotel bar, which became his "headquarters for the duration of the shooting." In no time at all, he proved that his behavior off the set hadn't changed since he made his first film (for Ford, at the other military academy, Annapolis) a quarter-century earlier. Like anyone who did time with the Judge, Carey observed:

> Ward Bond thought himself irresistible to women. He thought that all the ladies in the world who had not been bedded by him had been deprived of heaven on earth. West Point had an abundance of attractive women.... Sometimes after hours the bartender would lock the door. God knows at what hour they all went to bed. Ward didn't act like he was a member of the cast; he acted like he was on vacation.[31]

One morning, after "raising hell ... for four or five nights in a row," Bond had been sleeping for about 90 minutes when the phone rang at 5:30 A.M. It was Wingate Smith, relaying the Old Man's orders for him to be in the boxing ring at 8:00 sharp to work "all day."

Muttering to Smith that Pappy was a "mean old bastard," Bond obeyed. Ever the professional on camera, he enduring Ford's sadism for hours, masking the pain and debility caused by his injured leg as he was forced to "vault over the top rope of the ring — many, many times."[32] But after a day's pugilistic workout with Ty Power, he was back in form, doing his best to recover by pounding down Rheingold at the bar.

Bond's activities at the hotel, however, weren't confined to broads and beer. The bar had a television, allowing him to watch the Army-McCarthy Hearings, the first ever live national broadcast of an inquiry held by the U.S. Senate. Convened on March 16, 1954, one day after shooting began on *The Long Gray Line*, the hearings soon attracted heavy press attention, including gavel-to-gavel coverage by ABC and the Dumont network, from April 22 to June 17, one month after Ford wrapped the film.

As chair of the Permanent Subcommittee on Investigations, Joseph McCarthy initiated the conflict by claiming that Communists had "infiltrated" the U.S. Army Signal Corps. After the Army fired back, accusing McCarthy of seeking preferential treatment for his former chief consultant, Private David Shine, a right-wing witch hunter, Harvard graduate and heir to a major hotel chain, who had been drafted the previous November, the tarnished senator was removed from his position on the subcommittee.

The 36 days of broadcasts were viewed by an estimated 80 million people, including Bond and his on-screen wife, Erin O'Brien-Moore, a liberal who countered his admiration for "Tail-Gunner Joe" by cheering for Army Special Counsel Joseph Welch. The probe, which involved, not only allegations of "Communism," but the equally taboo practice of homosexuality, eventually led to McCarthy's downfall. Dobe Carey developed an interesting view of Bond the Red baiter, and how his behavior compared to that of Wayne:

> Ward's political beliefs did not match his personality; you would not think him to be an extreme right-winger. He never brought up the subject, as Duke would. You wouldn't have to know Duke long before he set you straight about his political thinking. I can only speculate that it was Ward's way of getting attention, and a feeling of importance, that made him join ... the Motion Picture Alliance.
>
> Erin O'Brien Moore ... would join Ward ... and watch the hearings and cheer on their heroes.

They liked each other and seemed to treat the whole thing as some sort of sporting match, never getting into any bitter arguing....[33]

The one occasion on which Bond approached Ford about McCarthy, Pappy's "meeting in a whorehouse" response was followed by "He's a disgrace and danger to our country."[34]

Bond also exercised his patriotism by lending his mellifluous narration to "The Red, White and Blue Line," a 10-minute Cinemascope short directed by Ford for the U.S. Treasury Department's current savings bond campaign. Power, O'Hara, Donald Crisp, Betsy Palmer and William Leslie all appeared in a sequence shot on the Maher dining room set, which Pappy augmented with clips from *The Long Gray Line* and an image of two lighting crewmen who made their own sales pitches for Uncle Sam.

Captain Koehler first appears at the cadets' dance early in the film, as Ford repeats the blocking and composition of Bond's introductory shot in *Arrowsmith*, showing him from behind (at screen right). In the boxing ring, Koehler repeatedly decks Marty Maher, who receives the same treatment when he tries to teach a cadet to fight. In Koehler's office, the Captain rises from behind his desk to see Marty out the door, and Ford allows the shot to linger on Bond, who keeps his back to the camera.

Aptly, *The Long Gray Line* has been called "one of Ford's most schizoid films" by Joseph McBride, who argues that it "embod[ies] the director's profoundly contradictory attitudes toward the military and the American dream." Justifiably criticizing the slapstick comedy in the film's early scenes (an unfortunate tendency Ford would repeat in *The Wings of Eagles* three years later), McBride adds:

> Tyrone Power ... gives a buffoonish and corny performance as the mustachioed and heavily brogued Marty Maher, so encrusted with stereotypical Irishness that it's hard to see the character through all the shtick. O'Hara's deftly stylized performance, on the other hand, offers a witty interplay between ethnic role-playing and genuine emotion, conveyed with great economy of gesture.[35]

Produced for $1.75 million, *The Long Gray Line* was not a major critical or commercial success, although it went on to gross $5.6 million at the box office.

From mid–May through early August 1954, Wayne starred as 12th-century Mongol leader Temujin, "Genghis Khan" (a role written for Marlon Brando), in *The Conqueror* (1956), a bloated Howard Hughes Cinemascope epic shot on location in the Escalante Valley near St. George, Utah. The area had been covered with radioactive fallout from several atomic bombs detonated at Yucca Flats, Nevada, the previous year.

Worse than the film was the fate suffered by 91 members of the 220-strong crew, who subsequently contracted cancer (a number three times the norm). To make matters worse, director Dick Powell had 60 tons of the radioactive soil trucked to RKO in Culver City, so the environment of the interior shots would match the location footage. Duke had approached the project as a type of "Eastern Western," and *Time* magazine's review noted that he "portrays the great conqueror as a ... cross between a square-shootin' sheriff and a Mongolian idiot."[36]

Nevertheless, *The Conqueror* stars John Wayne, which insured a box-office bonanza. Further good news came in the form of a divorce decree, which would be finalized on November 1, 1954, when he and Pilar planned to marry in Hawaii.

Robert Bruce "Bob" Mathias (1930–2006) was the first athlete to win gold medals twice in the Olympic decathlon, in 1948 (London) and 1952 (Helsinki), after which he attended USMC boot camp in 1951, and served from the summer of 1954 until 1956. In between Marine Corps duties, Mathias and his wife, Melba, played themselves in *The Bob*

Mathias Story (1954), a film made with grass-roots financing from his home town of Tulare, California. Many residents were cast in small roles, and Bond was chosen to portray Mathias' mentor, Coach Jackson, who induces him to try out for the 1948 Olympics, where he wins decathlon gold. Afterward, Bob attends Stanford, where he excels at football; but Jackson, learning that the Russians will be competing in the 1952 games (an interesting Cold War element right up Bond's alley), helps gear him up for a second decathlon triumph.

While working on the *Mathias Story*, Bond starred in another live television program, the popular mystery series *Suspense*, which was wrapping up its sixth and final season on CBS. Directed by Robert Mulligan, "The Hunted," aired on June 29, 1954, cast Ward as Bill Meeker, a state game warden, who spies "the great hunter," Derek Howard (John Kerr), poaching a doe from the Saddle Mountain Preserve, leaving behind a newborn fawn to fend for itself.

When the repeat offender returns the next day, he obstinately attempts to bribe Meeker. Due to "retire" in a few days (thanks to Howard and his string-pulling father), the wily warden pulls a "Most Dangerous Game" maneuver on him. However, Meeker allows Howard to take his rifle, loaded with three shells, on the run, while pursuing him with a gun and only one bullet. Howard wastes two rounds, falls, injures his leg, and then fires the third, yelling for Meeker to finish the job.

Having taught the cowering young man a lesson, Meeker, carrying an unloaded rifle, helps him off the ground and along the trail, offering to take him home. The two supporting performers, Jane Du Frayne and Steve Parker, appearing in one brief scene, fumbled their lines, while Bond and Kerr were spot-on in this episode that lived up to the series' name.

The formidable James Cagney was impressed when Ford called to offer him the role of the hated Captain of the U.S.S. *Reluctant*, in the screen adaptation of the long-running Broadway hit *Mister Roberts*. Due to the depiction of the Captain as a nasty, over the top tyrant, the U.S. Navy initially resisted approving Frank Nugent's script, so Rear Admiral Ford intervened to smooth the waters, and production was scheduled to begin on location in the South Pacific on September 1, 1954.

Joshua Logan, who had directed Henry Fonda in the stage version 1,157 times over the course of three years, expected to follow the Broadway hit with success on the big screen. However, producer Leland Hayward had other ideas, as explained to Logan by MCA talent agent Lew Wasserman:

> Josh, you *do* want to make money out of *Roberts*, don't you? I know a way of adding a million dollars to the gross. Let John Ford direct it. He's got a reputation for being able to direct men. This is a man's story, and I think he would be the ideal man to do it.[37]

Though he had been invited, Ford did not attend a performance at the Alvin Theatre. The only principal actor from the play to be cast in the film, Fonda became offended by Ford and Nugent's addition of "unnecessary" humor (especially the scenery chewing depiction of the Captain) in what had been a superb script by Logan and Thomas Heggen, author of the novel. Fonda actually had little to complain about, considering that Leland Hayward and Jack Warner, both of whom considered him too old and too long absent from Hollywood, *didn't* want him in the film. Logan actually had opted for Marlon Brando the previous January; but Ford, when consulted, replied, "Bullshit! That's Fonda's part."[38]

Fonda's stage colleagues, David Wayne (Ensign Pulver), Robert Keith (Doc) and William Harrigan (The Captain), had to be satisfied with their theatrical fame. Their cinematic counterparts were handed to Jack Lemmon, William Powell and Cagney, respectively.

Cast as Chief Petty Officer Dowdy, Bond, accompanied by several of the new *Mister Roberts* crewmen, arrived in Hawaii a week before shooting began. Ward had decided to try "the second time around," and, on Monday, August 23, 1954, he married his longtime girl-friend, Mary Lou May, at the home of sportswriter Red McQueen in Kahala. At this happy occasion, everyone was pleased to welcome back their fellow Stock Company stalwart, Hank Fonda, who enthusiastically gave away the bride to the actor whom he'd convicted of murder in *Young Mr. Lincoln*, shared a brotherly bond in *My Darling Clementine*, and led to his death in *Fort Apache*.

Following a decade of bachelorhood, preceded by a divorce and near-disabling accident, Bond considered only one significant person to serve as his best man: the Old Man, Admiral John Ford, USNR, retired. The reception was equally momentous, with native music, hula dancers, and booze that flowed into the wee hours. For Ford, celebrating the nuptials of his "surrogate son" initiated a disastrous binge that would last until his body literally forced him to accept a command he shouted to others on a routine basis: "Cut!"

Dobe Carey, who was curiously cast as the Polish-American Stefanowski in *Mister Roberts*, immediately sensed that "there was never the 'Ford mood' on that set." In fact, he thought that Hayward should have retained Logan and the entire cast of the New York pro-duction for the film, and that Fonda was too entrenched in the role to allow for any "Fordian" touches:

> Ford rehearsed a scene until the pace was right and everyone was comfortable with what they were doing, and then he shot it, nearly always in one take. Henry always wanted a lot more rehearsal, and he felt that Jack was taking too many liberties with the play he loved so much. There was tension building among Ford, Fonda, and Hayward right from the start.[39]

Though the difficulties with the making of the film usually have been blamed squarely on Ford, Carey developed his usual even-handed view of the situation:

> Hayward stayed loose, but in spite of that, *Mister Roberts* was beset with problems. Some of them were Ford's fault.... Marlon Brando accepted, but Ford was adamant about using Fonda. The sad thing is that when the sparks began to fly during the filming, it was Ford upon whom Fonda turned his wrath. It was evident from the first scene that he felt Jack was ruining his beloved play. It is very sad that Henry Fonda ... went to his grave resenting and criticizing Ford as he did in his book [*Fonda: My Life*, 1982].[40]

Fonda said:

> Playing Mr. Roberts on the screen started out as a dream come true for me. After all those years I would be back with Pappy. He was the right man for it for every reason I could think of. He was a navy man, a location man, and a man's director.... He loved me just like he loved Duke and Ward. Still, I was uneasy about the changes he was making.[41]

Carey believed that the film could have been made entirely in the studio, but Ford, who didn't seem to give a damn about the project, at least wanted to use a real U.S. Navy ship on location, in Hawaii *and* on Midway, the site of one of his greatest personal and pro-fessional achievements. While the "top brass" on the film had a contentious experience, there was at least one cast member who, basking in the afterglow of a week-long honeymoon, enjoyed making *Mister Roberts*. According to Carey, "Ward Bond ... was in his glory there on Midway. He appointed himself as the operations officer of the Midway Cocktail Hour."[42] Ford drank only beer while on the atoll, but began adding wine to the mix after returning to Hawaii.

Many actors and technicians who had worked with Ward also noticed the drug habit he had developed. In an attempt to compensate for his overly indulgent lifestyle, he continuously popped "diet pills," a combination of amphetamine and barbiturate called Dexamyl, an "upper" originally prescribed as an antidepressant. Carey admitted:

> During the 1950s it was very common for those who felt they were overweight to take Dexamyl. It was a real pepper-upper and made most people feel terrific, although they didn't necessarily lose any weight. Ward was famous for the "green pills" he always carried with him.[43]

Ford, too, was well aware of his fondness for what came to be known as "Christmas Trees." Ken Curtis celebrated this Yuletide street name by writing lyrics to the tune of the traditional English folk song "Greensleeves" (which famously had been appropriated as the melody for the Christmas carol "What Child Is This?" by William Chatterton Dix in 1865). Ford admired his son-in-law's version so much that it became Bond's "official anthem" during the *Mister Roberts* shoot. Each day he worked on location, he was "piped aboard" by Pappy's order for Ken and Dobe to sing:

> Alas, green pills you've done Ward wrong
> To cast him out discourteously
> When he's relied on you so long
> To bring him comfort from misery.
> Green pills are all his joy
> Green pills are Ward's delight
> Green pills will counteract
> All the Rheingold he guzzled
> The night before.

Carey added, "Of course, Ward thought it was great, and once in a while, he shared some of those green pills with us."[44]

While Bond relied on his uppers, giving a joyful, buoyant performance, Ford, having openly abandoned the "prohibition" he used to demand during production, stayed on his self-destructive downer while making *Mister Roberts*. Following his physical attack on Henry Fonda, while filming on the Navy ship, anchored in Kaneohe Bay off Oahu, he constantly kept an iced case of Heineken beer by his director's chair, pounding it down like there was no tomorrow.

During their ride to the location one morning, Carey and Curtis shared the back seat of a studio car, while Fonda was perched in the front, beside the driver. Carey remembered:

> Henry was looking very grim. He was pissed off! Suddenly a fancy convertible with the top down pulled up even with us, the horn honking. It was the Old Man, and I had never seen him looking happier. He was waving frantically and yelling, "Henry! Henry!" His whole expression was one of joy and goodwill, like, "Isn't this great, Henry? Aren't we having a good time?"
>
> Ford got Henry's attention. Henry turned, leaned way over in front of the driver to make sure Ford could see him, and yelled, "Fuck you, you drunken old son-of-a-bitch!"
>
> Ford looked baffled. What the hell had gotten into Henry? The famous punch hadn't even stayed in his consciousness.[45]

Ford's "apology" obviously hadn't erased the punch from *Fonda's* consciousness; and Carey's description suggests that Pappy, suffering from alcoholic blackouts, had no memory of the incident. Or was he just acting, being Jack Ford, the Ultimate Bullshit Artist?

As that day wore on, however, Ford proved that he was, indeed, in a complete state of stupefaction. Winton Hoch had two cameras set to capture a major action sequence featuring a large group of gorgeous Hawaiian girls, laughing and singing as they paddle their canoes out to the ship and climb on board, much to the delight of the liberty craving sailors. But

Hoch, nor anyone else aboard, knew where to find the director. Their leader, whom the Monument Valley Navajos honored as "Natani Nez," was MIA.

Suddenly, from a flurry of activity on the pier, emerged Jack Pennick and his Hawaiian aide, Sam Kahanamoku, carrying what looked, to Carey, "like an injured football player being helped off the field."[46]

Pouring Ford into a launch, the two men eventually delivered him to the ship, where, beer bottle in hand, he was lifted aboard. Carey wrote:

> I don't think this initial establishing shot ... came off ... it wound up just a mishmash of confusion.... When we see the close shot of Mister Roberts smiling down on us, happy that what he fought so hard for ... was finally a reality, it doesn't really mean very much. Had Uncle Jack been sober, that scene would have brought tears to the eyes of the audience. The bond between an officer and his men was a Ford specialty.[47]

When recalling that day's shooting, Jack Lemmon's account of Ford's drunkenness corroborated Carey's.

During a day off at the Niamalu Hotel at Waikiki Beach, Ford became so inebriated that he removed all his clothes, wrapped himself in a towel, and appeared poolside, where several cast members were lounging in the sun. Climbing up the ladder to the high diving

Mister Roberts (Warner Bros., 1955; directed by John Ford and Mervyn LeRoy). Throughout his career, James Cagney relaxed by practicing the guitar. Here he is joined by (left to right) William Powell, a rather lubricated Henry Fonda, the scene-stealing Ward Bond, and Jack Lemmon, in their tour-de-force serenading for a very attentive German shepherd.

board, he dropped the towel and jumped off, stark naked, into the water. When his head popped out of the waves, his glasses were gone, but a cigar remained clenched between his teeth. Again at the ready, Carey and Curtis dove in and bailed him out.

Continuing to consume alarming quantities of beer after returning to the Warner Bros. lot in Burbank, Ford, slumped in his director's chair, with his feet stretched out onto another seat, pointed toward his abdomen and babbled, "Will you look at this? I can't even button my goddamned pants, for Christ's sake!" As orders were being shouted left and right, Ford told Carey, "I guess they're going to haul my ass off to the hospital and take my gall bladder out."[48] All the alcoholic excess finally had ruptured his *biliary vesicle*, which was removed by his physician, the legendary Dr. Maynard Brandsma.

The last thing Ford said, as he was being carted off the set, was "Anyway, boys, carry on. Good luck."[49] The "boy" who quickly took the directorial reins was Bond, who kept the cameras rolling until Ford was replaced at noon the next day by former Warners house director Mervyn LeRoy (who later claimed that he was responsible for 90 percent of the completed film). However, Jack Lemmon said that Pappy had finished more than half the picture, adding, "I think [LeRoy] did a superb job directing the scenes the way he thought that John Ford would shoot them."[50]

At one point, Logan also was brought in to consult with Fonda and polish certain scenes, including the moving, climactic sequence during which Pulver reads a letter from Mister Roberts. Lemmon and the rest of the cast agreed that the scene needed to be re-shot, but when the young actor visited the recuperating Old Man, he lied about his opinion of the original take, "which [was] a smart thing to do when in a position like that with Pappy Ford." Lemmon later revealed that most of the extra bits of comic business Ford had asked him to perform (while being observed by a disgusted Fonda) did not end up in the finished film.[51]

Logan later said, "I certainly don't look on John Ford as a legend. I think he was a terrible man. He did some wonderful pictures, but he was a mean son of a bitch."[52]

The tension on the set was alleviated when Cagney broke out his guitar for a sing-along jam session with Powell, Lemmon, Bond and (a rather lubricated) Fonda. Critics have faulted Cagney for hamming it to the hilt as Captain Morton, but he was directed to play the character that way, and Jack Warner was delighted with his performance. Cagney, who had worked with Mervyn LeRoy at Warner Bros. during the early 1930s, had never been one of the director's admirers. Ford, who had shot all the exterior scenes, recalled, "A lot of that forced comedy inside the ship wasn't mine."[53]

Mister Roberts opens with a long shot of U.S. Naval vessels at sea, and then cuts to a close-up of Fonda standing on the bridge of the *Reluctant*, peering through binoculars. Several stunning images of ships in the setting sun and a silhouette of Roberts against the sea are telltale Ford compositions. Though three directors (four, if Bond is included) worked on the film, Pappy's distinctive contributions are easy to spot; and even when he wasn't actually directing, his longtime collaborator, Winton Hoch, remained behind the camera.

The Reluctant, or "The Bucket," as known to her men, is a U.S. Navy cargo ship operating in the back areas of the Pacific during the waning days of World War II. LeRoy's claim that he shot "90 percent" of the edited footage proves that he was at least as much, if not more, of a bullshit artist as Ford, who opens the film with a direct reference to Bond's bum, the first of several such verbal or visual homages occurring throughout the film.

As C.P.O. Dowdy announces reveille, one of the sailors snarls, "Okay, Chief. You done your duty. Now get your big, fat can outta here!"

Following the introductions of the Captain's beloved palm tree, Mr. Roberts, Ensign Pulver and Doc, the scene cuts to a medium-long shot as Dowdy enters, screen right: Ford has Bond keep his back to the camera (rear prominent, framing it by placing his hands on his hips) until cutting to a two-shot of Fonda and Bond, who then turns to face the camera before sitting down. This image is the second nod to the beloved bum during the initial 10 minutes. The pajama-clad Captain Morton then emerges from his cabin to water the palm tree. In his final film released by Warner Bros., Cagney, one of the greatest stars *and* actors ever signed by the studio, played second fiddle to Ward Bond's ass.

There are obvious phallic images, as well. When a group of liberty starved sailors (including Dobe) observe and pant over nurses showering on a nearby island, Swede drops a fully extended spyglass to his crotch, holding it like an erection as he complains, "How do you use this thing?"

While requisitioning aspirin on the island, Pulver invites the head nurse to visit the ship that afternoon, when six actually arrive. Here, Ford includes a simultaneously judicious and gratuitous use of the widescreen image: the nurses, backs to the camera, line up at screen left, as Bond enters, screen right, his rear end wiggling its way from foreground to background as he unleashes his infamous "horse whinny." A subsequent shot, moments later, again features the bums of Bond and the nurses.

The film shows, not the sailors' actual liberty, but the appalling aftermath. "Can they walk?" Dowdy asks when the Shore Patrol arrives with two truckloads of inebriated men.

"Walk?" the S.P. replies. "Some of them can't even crawl." At one point, Dolan (Ken Curtis) stumbles up the gangplank with a nanny goat stolen from Rear Admiral Whitworth, intent on turning the Captain's palm tree into "chow."

Is any of this shtick the work of that "90-percenter," Mervyn LeRoy? Every frame of it is as obviously Fordian as anything the director ever put on screen.

Despite Fonda's objections to the screenplay and his brawl with Pappy, he is superb in the film, one of the most entertaining and moving Hollywood productions of the 1950s. *Mister Roberts* had a built-in audience created by the play, performed for record New York crowds from February 18, 1948, to January 6, 1951, before another cast, headed by John Forsythe, took it on the road. Heggen's novel had sold two million copies by the time the film was completed. Ed Sullivan, a big fan of the play, devoted his entire June 19, 1955, *Toast of the Town* program to promote the film, drawing over 50 million viewers to their television sets to watch Fonda, Cagney and Lemmon perform a live reenactment of a major scene.

The ubiquitous palm tree was present, but Bond's equally omnipresent posterior was not. Ford wasn't there, although Leland Hayward did appear; and, when Sullivan asked about the necessity of using two directors, the producer offered a carefully prepared, sanitized explanation, heaping on the manure more than ever:

> Well, we didn't really want to, Ed. Jack got terribly ill in the middle of the picture, and was rushed off to the hospital, late Sunday night for an operation. Mervyn stepped in and started directing the next morning, at nine o'clock. And I think the two of them together made a great team. Next to Jack Ford and Mervyn LeRoy, the best team I know is Josh Logan and Tom Heggen.

The Warners publicity blitz included full-page ads in a dozen national magazines, including *Life*, *Look*, *Photoplay* and *Modern Screen*. One particular newspaper ad must have exasperated Fonda: "Mister Godfrey (Arthur) says *Mister Roberts* is "A terrific picture, infinitely better than the play!" Many years later, Hank's daughter, Jane Fonda, summed it up when she said, "My father never thought the movie was as good as the play, but it was, and still is, an audience favorite."[54]

Fonda was fortunate to be in the movie at all. Brando had been cast, and it was Ford who made certain that Hank, after his lengthy Broadway triumph, would play Mr. Roberts in the film.

More than a decade earlier, the versatile actor who had played the insane Sanders in Ford's *The Lost Patrol*, Boris Karloff, created a sensation on Broadway with a record-setting 1,400 continuous performances in *Arsenic and Old Lace*, a play that had been written expressly for him by Howard Lindsay and Russell Crouse. Karloff, believing that he now was associated entirely with Hollywood films, most famously in the horror genre, didn't think he'd be accepted on the New York stage; but the darkly comic premise of depicting his character, Jonathan Brewster, murdering a man merely for saying that "he looked like Boris Karloff," was an offer he couldn't refuse.

When Warner Bros. hired Frank Capra to direct a film adaptation of the play in 1942, Karloff, in the midst of his tremendously popular run at Broadway's Fulton Theatre, could not jeopardize the producers' profits by temporarily being released from the show to appear in the film. Another actor admitting he killed someone for saying that "he looked like Boris Karloff" doesn't make any sense. Worse, it's not funny.

But Jack Warner didn't give a damn about such things. He and Capra rushed their film version into production, with Raymond Massey (wearing a mediocre makeup by Perc Westmore) cast in the Karloff role, and a hyperactive, scenery chewing Cary Grant as his brother, Mortimer Brewster, a performance often difficult to watch. The film's saving graces are the brilliant Peter Lorre and reliable Jack Carson, whose underplaying provides a partial counter to Grant's cartoonish mania.

But the loser was Karloff, whose legendary characterization was not captured for posterity in the film, produced by money men insisting that the completed cut be released (as "Frank Capra's *Arsenic and Old Lace*") *immediately* after the play closed in 1944. Hank Fonda should have been thankful he didn't get "Karloff-ed" by Leland Hayward and Marlon Brando, and that Ford came to his rescue.

Mister Roberts was not only a box-office smash, but also fared well critically. Jack Lemmon's characterization, particularly popular with audiences, was a career-making performance that won the Best Supporting Actor Academy Award and spawned a sequel, *Ensign Pulver* (1964), directed by Josh Logan for Warner Bros., with Robert Walker, Jr., in the title role. To Ford, what seemed a cinematic hodgepodge, slapped together while he was recuperating from gall bladder surgery, also had been nominated for Best Picture. Though *Mister Roberts* would remain an audience favorite, the director avoided discussing it, joining Dobe Carey in knowing damn well that is wasn't a "John Ford Film."

As for Hank Fonda, he no longer was a member of that elite "inner circle" headed by Duke and Judge. "The love affair was over," he admitted.[55]

Bond returned to the small screen on October 21, 1954, playing Police Lieutenant Ben Annetti in "Segment," an episode of *The Ford Television Theater*, starring William Bendix, with able support from Rosemary DeCamp, Joanne Woodward and Alan Baxter. This excellent Screen Gems–NBC production was codirected by Marc Daniels and Franklin J. Schaffner.

During the *Mister Roberts* imbroglio, Wayne was shooting *The Sea Chase* (1955) in Hawaii. He was joined by Pilar, and they began to make plans for their wedding, but he was troubled by an ear infection that sent him to the hospital on two occasions. Shortly after director John Farrow wrapped production, Duke and Pilar were married at the Kona home of Senator William H. Hill on November 1, 1954. Following their wedding night at Honolulu's Royal Hawaiian Hotel, they left for California the next morning.

Intending to extend their honeymoon to New York, Duke and Pilar were interrupted by a call from William Wellman, who was having problems with leading man Robert Mitchum on the set of *Blood Alley* (1955), an anti–Communist adventure produced by Wayne's Batjac company. Three days into the shooting schedule, the unruly Mitchum, drinking heavily, was openly displaying his contempt for the project. Pressured by Wellman and Jack Warner, who threatened to terminate his distribution deal, Wayne took over the role.

11

Duke Becomes the Devil, Judge Becomes the Coach

Duke ... was always sort of distant and hard to talk to ... unless you were totally alone with him and therefore, had his complete attention, you never felt quite sure he heard a word you were saying.... This trait of his, this sort of, "I don't really know you're here," expression used to drive the people he worked with ... absolutely bonkers.—Harry Carey, Jr.[1]

I think John Ford is the best director who ever lived—no one else is even in his class.... He could speak to your heart, and it meant some-thing—no artifice, nothing between him and you. He had "conservation of line," as the Japanese say. He could do it in two or three strokes, where it would take other good directors seven or eight, and they wouldn't get it as well. He's a storyteller, like Homer. When Homer got through with a story, you had something you could read forever.—John Milius[2]

Bond began 1955 starring on the small screen. In "The Marine Who Was Two Hundred Years Old," the January 4 episode of ABC's *Cavalcade of America*, he played Lou Diamond, supported by ubiquitous character actor James Flavin. On January 27, he again pinned on a familiar sheriff's badge, costarring with Ricardo Montalban in a 60-minute adaptation of Louis L'Amour's "The Mohave Kid," on the popular CBS series *Climax!*

English leading man Ray Milland proved his versatility, not only by playing the title role in Republic's *A Man Alone*, but directing the film as well. Shooting under the working title "The Gunman," production began in early April 1955, with exterior scenes filmed on location at St. George, Utah.

Bond is hardheaded Mesa sheriff Will Corrigan, who is delirious with yellow fever when stranded gunslinger Wes Steele (Milland), after stumbling upon a stagecoach massacre and shooting acting sheriff Jim Anderson (Alan Hale, Jr.) in self-defense, seeks refuge in his cellar. Aided by Corrigan's daughter, Nadine (Mary Murphy), Steele does a good turn by caring for the ailing sheriff, and she comes to understand his plight.

Steele discovers that "his" crimes were actually committed by Stanley (Raymond Burr), the town banker, and a business partner, Luke Joiner (Grandon Rhodes), who receives a bullet in the back after demanding an end to their robberies. Having witnessed the aftermath of their murderous handiwork, Steele is determined to see that justice is served.

Corrigan recovers, and his reactionary behavior is tempered by the reasoning of Dr. Mason (Arthur Space) and Nadine's revelation that she knows about the bribes he has taken

A Man Alone (Republic, 1955; directed by Ray Milland). Ray Milland (seated in director's chair), flanked by his costars, Ward Bond and Mary Murphy, poses with his crew at Republic Studios.

from Stanley, who whips the townspeople into a lynch mob. After helping Steele escape, Corrigan is set to be hanged, but the gunslinger returns to save him and end the corrupt reign of Stanley. Steele remains with Nadine and Corrigan, believing in a better future for Mesa.

Though Bond spends the first half of the film in bed, his subsequent scenes, including Corrigan's near-lynching, more than compensate. Milland's direction is deft and economical, highlighted by a Ford-like, 11-minute opening, in which the story is told visually, sans dialogue. Milland's performance as a complex American gunfighter is also convincing. Shot in the Trucolor process, *A Man Alone* is an innovative and atypical "adult" Republic Western.

Merian Cooper, who had formed a production company with 3M heir Cornelius Vanderbilt "Sonny" Whitney (financier of the Technicolor Corporation), optioned Alan LeMay's novel *The Searchers* in April 1954. "Coop" wanted material suitable for a surefire Ford and Wayne Western, and the story of revenge-crazed Amos Edwards' 10-year, obsessive quest to track down the Comanche who murdered his brother and captured his niece, partially financed by Whitney, attracted all the major Hollywood studios. Warner Bros. ultimately made the best offer, including $125,000 plus 10-percent of the net receipts for Ford, making his payday the best he'd ever received for a single feature.

Ford and Frank Nugent began adapting *The Searchers* during January 1955, changing Amos Edwards' Christian name to Ethan, and creating two additional characters as a seriocomic counter to the very downbeat and violent material suffusing the novel. The Rev.

Samuel Johnson Clayton, who, when not preaching, lawfully wields a shootin' iron as a Texas Ranger, was written especially for Bond; while another Ford favorite, Hank Worden, was presented with the most magnificent idiot-savant of his long career: Ol' Mose Harper, a bald, mentally challenged old buzzard who accomplishes daring deeds while aiding Ethan and conducting a side search of his own, for a rocking chair in which he plans to "retire."

Worden, who'd been playing variations on the fool character for years, recalled overhearing Ford tell Wayne, "If the old son of a bitch will just play himself, he's stupid enough to be what I want." He also revealed that "Duke would put his arm around me and say, 'Hank, you old son of a bitch.' That meant he liked me."[3]

Martin Scorsese commented, "The Mose Harper character, played by Hank Worden, has some of the more eccentric line readings in movie history ... he's got the most poetic and the most fascinating language, and his mind works interestingly."[4]

The Searchers takes place over the course of several years, so it was essential for Ford to depict Ethan carrying on his quest ("as sure as the turnin' of the Earth") without regard to variations in terrain or the changing seasons. He first shot the winter scenes on location in the snows of Gunnison, Colorado, and then sent the second unit to Edmonton, Alberta, where the sequences involving buffalo were directed at Elk Island National Park by Patrick Ford and stunt coordinator Cliff Lyons. Principal photography was scheduled to begin in Monument Valley on June 16, 1955.

Memorial Day was always a revered holiday at the Field Photo Farm, and the services held at the end of May held a special significance for Harry Carey, Jr., whom Ford had just cast in *The Searchers*. Pappy also ordered "Ol' Dobe" to carry out a "grave detail," the placing of wreaths on the final resting places of fallen members of their outfit, at Forest Lawn cemetery.

His duty done, Dobe joined a few of his comrades for drinks that afternoon, an activity that inspired him to journey to an even greater height: the home of the Duke, on Louise Avenue in Encino.

"Get your ass up here!" roared the voice of a delightfully half-loaded Wayne from the loudspeaker at the entry gate.

A few hours later, Duke, Dobe, and another guest, writer James Hennigan, nearly had their eyeballs floating. Grabbing a book from his library, Wayne handed it to Carey, insisting that he perform a dramatic reading of Abraham Lincoln's Gettysburg Address. Inspired by his colleague's patriotic Memorial Day recital while under the influence of a staggering amount of "Who Hit John?" Wayne earnestly brainstormed about a new film he was going to produce on the life of the 16th President, starring none other than red-headed Harry Carey, Jr.

"I'll dye his hair or something!" shouted Duke. "But this asshole is going to play Lincoln!"

In the midst of the alcoholic haze, the hour of 3:00 A.M. rang out. Wayne was arguing, via the house intercom system, with Pilar, as Dobe attempted to make his way out of the house and down to the gate, which he was unable to open. Staggering to his station wagon, he slipped into a temporary coma. Awakened by the rising sun, he ventured back to the gate, discovered the button, and proceeded to drive home. "It probably saved my life, that gate," he later admitted.[5]

Working again with Winton C. Hoch, who shot in Technicolor and VistaVision, the widescreen process with the finest definition and depth of field, Ford explained his visual rationale for *The Searchers*:

When I did *She Wore a Yellow Ribbon*, I tried to have the cameras photograph it as Remington would have sketched and painted it. It came out beautifully and was very successful in this respect, I think. When I did *The Searchers*, I used a Charles Russell motif.[6]

A contemporary of Remington (1861–1909), a New York native overwhelmed by the West during business trips to Montana and Kansas, where he tried his hand at ranching, the Missouri-bred Russell (1864–1926) worked as a cattle hand on a Montana ranch at the dawn of his career in the 1880s. During the last years of his life, he enjoyed many early film Westerns, and befriended Harry Carey, William S. Hart and Will Rogers.

One day, on the front porch at Goulding's Lodge, while Dobe Carey, Ken Curtis and Jeffrey Hunter were harmonizing their best Sons of the Pioneers' rendition of "Tumblin' Tumbleweeds," Ford walked out to have a listen. Suitably impressed, Pappy went back inside the Lodge.

Curtis began regaling his pals with a tale told with what he referred to as a "Colorado dryland accent," and then Hunter fired back with a "country hillbilly" story. This improvising continued as they parried their hick riffs back and forth, much to Carey's delight.

As the dialect-enhanced exchange began to peter out, Ford suddenly reemerged. "Do that again," he commanded Curtis.

Ever the dutiful son-in-law, "Kenny" asked, "What's that, Pop?"

"That routine you and Jeff were just doing," replied the Old Man. "Do it again."

Curtis did his best to talk his way out of the situation, explaining to his Pop that the accent was effective only with specific words, but no one knew better than he that Ford would never consider "No" for an answer. Forced to oblige his father-in-law *and*, more importantly, director, who'd cast him as Charlie McCorry in the film, he launched into a yarn about Italian squash seed, expertly mangling the pronunciation into "*Eye-tal-yan squarsh side.*"

That was all it took for the impulsive, mad genius brain of John Ford to make this immutable decision: "I want you to use that accent in the picture."

Curtis was stunned, as his Pop added, "I want you to play Charlie McCorry that way."

After Ford walked back into the Lodge to play cards, Curtis turned to Carey and Hunter, whispering, "I don't want to do that in the picture. I'll make an ass out of myself."

On location at Mexican Hat, Utah, the following morning, Curtis attempted to perform in his first few shots without the idiotic accent, while desperately trying to devise a plan to convince Ford that it was a bad idea. The entire matter, however, was soon settled by Wayne. Carey explained,

> [T]hat night Duke broke the rules and got plastered. I was rooming with Ward Bond, and Ken was there, shooting the breeze with us.
>
> Suddenly, Duke burst in. His first words were addressed to Ken.
>
> "What in the hell is this crap I hear about you not wanting to do the accent that Pappy asked you to do!"
>
> Kenny went through his routine about it only working with certain words. Duke, subtle as always, said, "Bullshit! Listen, you're a nice lookin' fella, but ya ain't as good lookin' as this Jeff kid, an' on toppa that, yer playing the second lead and there's nothin' more thankless than a second fuckin' lead! Dobe here can attest to that! Play it like the Old Man says, fer Christ's sake, an' you'll be noticed in the goddamned picture!"[7]

Inveterate hell-raiser Frank McGrath also defied the sobriety dictum, and was absent from the stuntman's tent when Ford dropped in, looking for volunteers for his nightly card game. Unable to track down the wiry little scoundrel, Ford promptly "pulled a Warren

Hymer" and urinated all over McGrath's bed. On his way out, Pappy explained, "If the man can drink it, he can lie in it," advising the other "bastards" to keep their mouths shut.[8]

Carey and Bond were rooming beside Dobe's mother, Olive, cast as Mrs. Jorgensen in the picture, and the fetching Vera Miles, who was playing her daughter, Laurie. Though he had spent a lot of private time with Bond, Dobe was flabbergasted by the behavior of his overweight, Christmas Tree-popping pal this time around:

> Ward was insane to molest Vera, and he'd parade around naked in front of the big picture window in the hope that Vera would look in and see him. Vera never looked in that window, so Ward, having failed at everything himself, would try to catch Vera without her clothes on by rushing into her and Mom's room without knocking. He struck out there, too. He reminded me of that silly coyote in the roadrunner cartoons.[9]

After receiving sad news that his father had passed away, Bond left Monument Valley to attend the services and console his mother and sister. When he returned a few days later, he uncharacteristically failed to play a scene the way Pappy ordered, proving that no one on a Ford set was immune from attack. "Get your damned mind off that funeral!" shouted the Coach.

Bond's personal affairs and habits rarely had an adverse affect on his professional obligations, but one incident on *The Seachers* location could have unleashed an earthquake in Monument Valley, *if* Ford had known what actually occurred. Wayne, Hunter and Carey all had prepared themselves for a very difficult scene, during which Ethan tells Brad Jorgensen about finding and burying the violated body of Lucy Edwards (Pippa Scott), his niece and the young man's girlfriend. Ford was shooting the sequence day-for-night, and, as usual, hoping to capture it in a single take.

Carey listened intently as the Old Man explained exactly what was expected of him. As always, Dobe, unsure if his performance would be a rehearsal or the first filmed take, gave it all he had. In fact, the nervous actor overdid it a bit.

The entire ordeal really had been a dry run, so Pappy just said, "Dobe, please don't leap into the shot. Just run in and sit down."

"Action!" was called, Carey performed flawlessly, Wayne gave "the kid" his nonverbal seal of approval, and the camera operator, working under Winton Hoch, was heard whispering something in the background.

"What the hell's all the mumbling about?" asked the Old Man.

During what may have been the cameraman's most frightening moment on Earth, he replied, "The camera stopped, Mr. Ford."

"What?" quizzed Pappy. "The *what*?"

The poor devil struggled for an answer. "It just stopped running." he groaned.

While everyone waited for a Richter-scale explosion, Ford remained reasonably serene. "Well, Christ, fix it, whatever it is," he said. To Duke, Dobe and Jeff, he added, "Sorry, kids. That was fine, but we're going to have to do it again. When we're ready, just do it the same way."

Carey revealed:

> Later on, I found out the reason why the camera quit. Ward Bond had come onto the set with his electric razor. During the high point of the scene, he unplugged the camera, plugged in the razor, and proceeded to shave. John Ford went to his grave never knowing that. He would have dug Ward up![10]

Though Dobe's incredible recollection reads like one of Pappy's own tall tales, it is quite conceivable that Bond, struggling through the aftereffects of the previous night's mournful inebriation, barely made it to the set on time that morning, and he couldn't have been left shaving when the station wagon pulled out! The fact that Ward *was* responsible for the necessity of the second (and *better*, according to Carey) take ultimately was confirmed by the director of photography, as reported by Joseph McBride:

> Winton Hoch told me that several years later, following Bond's death, he ran into Ford at a Hollywood event and told him about the electric razor. Ford's face turned white. He was uncharacteristically speechless, because he didn't have his favorite "horse's ass" to kick around anymore.[11]

Carey revealed that, building on the focused approach he established in *She Wore a Yellow Ribbon*, Wayne created his brilliant characterization through a process that temporarily transformed the ultimate movie star into a Method actor:

> When I looked up at him in rehearsal, it was into the meanest, coldest eyes I had ever seen. I don't know how he molded that character. Perhaps he'd known someone like Ethan Edwards as a kid.... He was even Ethan at dinner time. He didn't kid around on *The Searchers* like he had done on other shows. Ethan was always in his eyes.... Duke was Ethan Edwards ... and no other actor, no matter how great his talent, could have played that part as well.[12]

On the evening of July 2, before reporting the next afternoon to shoot the unforgettable final shot of the film, during which Ethan, rather than following his family, including the rescued Debbie, into their home, stops and then turns to walk alone back into the desert, Wayne fought another ferocious bout with Who Hit John? Of course, this wordless performance, a perfect equilibrium of power and subtlety, given by this American icon, while wracked by a massive hangover, is best, not read, but *seen*.

Ford had created such images nearly 40 years earlier, in his silent films, and his genius still didn't need dialogue to create the apex of cinematic art. But this time, in what is arguably, not just *his* finest film, but one of the very best ever created in the United States, Ford also had a totally absorbed John Wayne, an actor at *his* apex, punishing himself for being such an infinitely complex, utterly fascinating, contradictory bastard called Ethan Edwards. No one else has put into words what Duke does in this shot better than Dobe Carey:

> He was to look and then walk away, but just before he turned, he saw Ollie Carey, the widow of his all-time hero, standing behind the camera. It was as natural as taking a breath. Duke raised his left hand, reached across his chest and grabbed his right arm at the elbow. Harry Carey did that a lot in the movies when Duke was a kid in Glendale, California. He'd spent many a dime just to see that.[13]

This gesture, which Carey frequently employed in his silent Westerns, was also used by other actors in Ford's early films, including Buck Jones in *Just Pals* and Charles Edward Bull as Abraham Lincoln in *The Iron Horse*. Joseph McBride referred to Wayne's spontaneous, profound re-creation in *The Searchers* as "one of the most resonant gestures in the entire body of Ford's work, a gesture movingly encapsulating whole lifetimes of shared tradition."[14]

The Monument Valley Navajos hired by Ford enjoyed calling Henry Brandon "the Kraut Comanche" whenever he came their way. A blue-eyed actor born Heinrich Kleinbach in Berlin may seem an unlikely choice to portray a Comanche chief, but casting Caucasians in every imaginable ethnic role was standard Hollywood practice at the time, and Brandon had been making his living doing it for more than two decades. A busy character player, he would play a Chinese one day, an Arab the next, and his portrayal of "Scar" led to several variations, for Ford and others, well into the 1960s.

Though casting director Jim Ryan advised against hiring Brandon because he was German, Ford was impressed by the ruggedly handsome features and buff, 6'2" frame of the versatile actor, whose status as a World War II veteran was another plus. Brandon, recalling that the Old Man thought his blue eyes "dramatically interesting," addressed his work and the subject of ethnicity:

> There are good and bad people of all races. I have played countless heavies of various nationalities, and never felt that I was maligning any race by doing so. This includes Germans and my adopted nationality — American.
>
> My agent in the Thirties, Abe Sugarman, suggested a name change quite casually one day. I asked him why. With only the slightest hint of a twinkle in his eye, he answered, "Let's say it's too long for a marquee." The dirty words — "too German" — were never mentioned.
>
> I had no objection to changing my name, which was always mispronounced — even as "*Kleenbitch*." "Brandon" is a corruption of my mother's even more Teutonic maiden name — Brandenburg. I have never been ashamed of being German, only ashamed of a very corrupt and evil German government. I even got the guys in my barracks in the Signal Corps at Fort Monmouth, New Jersey, to say, "dirty Nazis" instead of "dirty Germans."[15]

Though Brandon was portraying a Comanche, he wore a Nez Perce hairstyle ("because it looked impressive") and spoke Navajo, which he learned from his technical advisor on location. While discussing the character with him, Ford asked what he thought of an "Indian" bedding down with a white woman. Characteristically, Brandon had no objections whatsoever. They both agreed that "Scar" should not fit the mold of the two-dimensional "red villain" of so many 1950s Westerns, and that the reasons for his motivation should not remain completely ambiguous. Pathological hatred burns in the eyes of Wayne's Ethan, but Brandon revealed, "Ford didn't want me to play Scar that way — to play the hatred."[16]

Rather than use the water-based "Indian" body makeup that needed to be reapplied constantly while working in high temperatures, Brandon ritualistically tanned himself, lying out in the sun, wearing only a tiny bikini swimsuit, every day for three weeks. While the Navajos believed that "the Kraut Comanche" had lost his mind, Ford, evidently incensed by the actor's bold beefcake display, "promoted" him to Official Whipping Boy, an act that again took some of the heat off Bond.

The first "character" to speak in *The Searchers* is "Prince," the Edwards family dog, as Ethan emerges from the desert toward his brother's home. As soon as Martin Pawley jumps, "Indian style," from his horse and enters the house (Ford uses a rare camera movement here, ushering him into his experience with Ethan), Wayne, using just his eyes and body language, immediately projects the "prodigal brother's" racist contempt. He then emphasizes this hate by growling, "Fella could mistake you for a *half-breed*."

The complexity of Ethan's personality is soon suggested when he shows his love for little Debbie (Lana Wood) by giving her his Civil War medal, a proxy gift for the golden locket he previously had presented to Lucy (Pippa Scott). His impending reliance on Mose Harper is then foreshadowed when, during a probing conversation with his brother, Aaron (Walter Coy), he suddenly springs up in anger, leaving a rocking chair moving to and fro in the foreground.

Bond also instantly establishes the demeanor of his character when the Reverend Clayton arrives, expertly interweaving his comments into the overlapping dialogue of all the Edwards family members. (Ford's use of a single, wide VistaVision shot, without resorting to editing, is "pure cinema" at its best.) As the "Reverend Captain" deputizes Aaron and Martin into the Texas Rangers, the camera slowly tracks forward as Ethan moves up behind him. Even before Clayton, drinking his coffee, realizes Ethan is there, he hears, "Captain? The Rev. Samuel Johnson Clayton — *mighty impressive*."

Following their "reunion," during which Ethan emphatically declares his disbelief "in surrenders," Mose is shown in the rocking chair, imparting his wisdom about the recent "Injun" attack. Told to "shut up" by Charlie McCorry (Ken Curtis), he replies, "*Thank* you."

Ethan refuses to let Aaron leave his family, ordering Clayton to "swear him out." Pointing to Mose, the new volunteer admits, "Could be this dodderin' old idiot ain't so far wrong. Could be *Comanch.*"

"*Kind* words, Ethan," replies the rocking Mose, framed in a full shot. "Thank you *kindly.*"

Ethan, claiming "it wouldn't be legal," refuses to be sworn in, raising the suspicions of Clayton, Aaron and Martha about his possible criminal background. Following the introduction of Brad Jorgensen (Harry Carey, Jr.), Lucy's beau, the Reverend, kicking the door closed, turns to see Martha, inside the bedroom, caressing Ethan's coat. Clayton averts his eyes, maintaining his forward gaze as she emerges to hand the garment to Ethan, who embraces and kisses her on the forehead. (Again, a series of actions is depicted in a single wide shot, here done entirely visually, as Ford needs no words to suggest the depth of Ethan and Martha's mutual feelings.)

Within the first 12 minutes, using minimal dialogue and spare editing, Ford brilliantly establishes the web of primary relationships that will become more complicated throughout the film. These associations are given polish by Max Steiner's musical score, which uses the melody of the Civil War ballad "Lorena" as a leitmotif, particularly to suggest Ethan's familial bonds.

Upon discovery of Lars' (John Qualen) slaughtered "prize bulls," Ethan realizes that the Comanche are on a "murder raid," sending the posse, hell-bent, riding the 40 miles to the Jorgensen ranch. Ethan remains behind with Mose, whom he kicks in the ass prior to leaning on the back of his exhausted horse, suspecting that it is already too late to save his own family.

The scene cuts directly to the Edwards home, where dusk begins to fall as the reactions of animals (a flock of birds and the family dog) are an omen of impending doom: the elemental "force of nature" known as "Scar," Cicatriz, and his tribe of Comanche. Here, Ford and Winton Hoch use color brilliantly: outside the house, the Monument Valley sky is blue; viewed from inside, from the family's point of view, it is *red*. A quick camera track into a tight close-up on Lucy, who emits a spine-chilling scream, is all that is needed to signal the imminent horror.

Little Debbie, ordered to hide, is intercepted by the dog, just as she reaches the graves of her ancestors, and Ford introduces Scar by having his shadow loom up and over the child as she stares at him, not in terror, but in wonderment. The scene fades as the Comanche chief, in close-up, blows a signal on his buffalo's horn. The oncoming atrocity *suggested* by Ford is far more effective than any actual depiction of graphic violence.

This economical, poetical strategy again is used when Ethan, accompanied by Mose, and Martin, now on foot, reach the burning ranch house (which is shown twice, from each man's point of view). After Ethan looks into the smoldering ruins, where he discovers Martha's violated body, he punches out Martin to spare him a sight too horrible to share. Mose, concerned about "Marty," effortlessly falls into the nearby rocking chair, which has been spared from the flames, as Prince leads Ethan to little Debbie's doll, lying by the graves.

Ford's favorite traditional gospel song, "Shall We Gather at the River?" (led by Harry Carey, Jr., accompanied by Danny Borzage on accordion) opens Martha's burial scene, but the Reverend's prayers are cut short by a furiously impatient Ethan, who demands that the men begin searching for the two missing girls. After Charlie helps Clayton lift a large stone off the shallow grave of a dead Comanche, Brad pummels the corpse with a rock before Ethan "finishes the job" by shooting out its sightless eyes.

"What good did that do you?" asks the Reverend Sam.

Ethan displays his views on religion when he replies, "By what you preach, *none*; but what that Comanch believes, ain't got no eyes, he can't enter the spirit land — has to wander forever between the winds."

Prior to the shootout at the river, Clayton places his Bible into the hands of the injured Ed Nesby (Bill Steele), who thanks him twice, the second time adding the "already baptized" Mose's tag, "*very kindly*."

The baptism of fire is preceded by Mose's prayer, "That which we are about to receive, we *thank thee*, Oh Lord."

"Hallelujah!" proclaims the preacher after gunning down a Comanche.

Following the enemy's retreat, Ethan demands that he continue alone, but Brad and Marty insist on accompanying him. When Brad wearily expresses his view that the Comanche, "if human at all," must stop to rest, Ethan directly articulates his racist belief: "No, a *human* rides a horse until it dies, then he goes on afoot. *Comanch* comes along, gets that horse up, ride him 20 more miles, then eats him."

Ethan again spares everyone else the sight of human atrocity when he returns from finding Lucy's raped and murdered body. He also doesn't *describe* what he has seen, but later must come clean when Brad believes he has found her. "What you saw was a buck, wearin' Lucy's dress," Ethan tells him, refusing to reveal further details. In a reworking of a scene from *The Lost Patrol*, Brad, impulsively riding off toward the enemy camp, is gunned down as the camera remains on Ethan and Marty.

"About a year" later, having followed the Comanche northward into winter snows, the two searchers temporarily return to the Jorgensen ranch, where Lars' wife (Olive Carey) optimistically states, "*Someday*, this country's going to be a fine, good place to be. Maybe it needs our bones in the ground before that time can come."

The next morning, acting on a tip sent in a letter from trading-post proprietor Jerem Futterman (Peter Mamakos), Ethan rides on. Though Laurie Jorgensen (Vera Miles) attempts to "keep" Marty at the ranch, he soon follows, afraid of what the "crazy" man might do to Debbie in his absence. After paying for information about a *Nawyehkah* Comanche war chief called "Scar," Ethan kills Futterman and two accomplices during an attempted bushwhack on their campsite. A dissolve then indicates the passage of time as the guitar-toting Charlie McCorry rides up to the Jorgensen ranch to deliver a letter addressed to Laurie.

Vera Miles' reading of the missive provides a flashback of the searchers' efforts from Marty's point of view, including, through his trading with a band of Comanche, his accidental acquisition of a "wife," Wild Goose Flying in the Night Sky (Beulah Archuletta), whom they call "Look." This incident, although criticized for containing "misogynistic" elements, shows the positive effects of Marty's relationship with Ethan, especially proof that his "uncle" actually possesses a sense of humor. "Come on, *Mrs. Pawley!*" Ethan calls out to Look as she follows them on horseback. "Come on, Mrs. Pawley! Join our merry group!"

Marty vents his anger by kicking the dutiful "squaw" away from his bedroll. Ethan laughs, informing him, "You know that's grounds for *dee*-vorce in Texas!" Though Ethan outwardly hates the Comanche, he also speaks the language and has a thorough knowledge of their tribal customs. When Look realizes they are searching for Scar, she runs away; but, during the night, she leaves behind a directional arrow made of stones.

Heading back into winter snows, Ethan becomes pathological, attempting to kill as many buffalo as possible, so the meat won't "fill Comanche bellies." Riding away from the sound of a cavalry troop, they reach the burning remains of a Nawyehkah camp, the result of an army massacre. Here, Ford presents a radical departure from the celebratory depictions in his earlier cavalry films: even Ethan speaks with a tone of regret upon discovering the body of Look.

Ford again shifts Ethan 180 degrees, including one of the most memorable and powerful shots in all of his work, a brief tracking shot (a parallel to the earlier track on Lucy's scream) into a tight close-up on Wayne's face, his eyes (bathed in shadow) registering perhaps the coldest expression of hatred in cinema history. Prior to the close-up, observing the behavior of three crazed girls freed from captivity, a cavalry officer says, "It's hard to believe that they're white."

"They *ain't* white — anymore," Ethan replies. "They're *Comanch.*"

Laurie expresses deep disappointment with the conclusion of "Martin Pawley's" account. Ford somewhat lightens the somber mood by having Ken Curtis, drawling his hick accent, sing a few bars of "Skip to My Lou" as Charlie attempts to court her. Max Steiner's score reprises the melody as a dissolve leads to a trademark Ford long shot of the mounted searchers, stunningly silhouetted against the setting sun, riding across the horizon.

The Searchers (C.V. Whitney–Warner Bros., 1956; directed by John Ford). As the two unrelenting searchers, John Wayne and Jeffrey Hunter ride amidst the expanse of Ford's favorite location, Monument Valley.

In New Mexico, they find Mose, looking "mangier than ever," whooping it up in a cantina. "Been helping you, Ethan," he says. "Been lookin,' *all the time*." Ethan mentions the reward, but Mose adds, "Don't want any money ... just a roof over old Mose's head, and a rockin' chair by the fire" before introducing Emilio Figueroa (Antonio Moreno), who has seen Debbie. Saluting with tequila, Ethan reveals that he also understands "Mexican."

"For a price," Figueroa and his men lead Ethan and Marty to Scar's camp. As enemies meet, Ford includes close-ups of Wayne, Hunter and Brandon, all registering the same intense expression. "You speak pretty good American, for a *Comanch*," Ethan informs Scar. "Someone teach ya?"

English, Spanish and Comanche all are spoken in a single wide shot. Figueroa enters the tepee of Scar, who mocks Ethan before allowing him to follow: "You speak good *Comanch*. Someone teach you?"

Inside, both Ethan and Marty are shown a collection of scalps taken in vengeance for the killing of Scar's two sons. The young woman who holds the lance is Debbie. Claiming he will continue the parlay the following day, Ethan leaves to camp for the night. Figueroa, realizing the true nature of Ethan's visit, returns the "blood money" and leaves with his men. Fully utilizing both the width and depth afforded by VistaVision, Ford has Debbie appear on the horizon behind Ethan and Marty, running toward them as they plan their next move.

Marty sees her first. As Debbie explains why she must remain with the Comanche, Marty is ordered to stand aside by Ethan, who draws his pistol. Debbie's "brother" shields her from the approaching executioner, who is struck by the arrow of a Comanche brave, quickly gunned down by Marty. Scar commands a war party to attack, and the searchers are forced to ride for a crevice among the closest rock formations.

Seriously injured, Ethan hands his companion a scrap of paper: a makeshift will, bequeathing all his property to Martin Pawley. Outraged that Ethan claims having "no blood kin," Marty throws the paper back at him, demanding to know, "What kind of a man *are* you, anyway?"

Refusing to accept his racist explanation, Marty moans, "I hope you *die*!"

"*That'll be the day*," Ethan replies.

Ford cuts to the pre-nuptial celebration for Laurie and Charlie McCorry, at which Captain Sam is transformed by his fellow Rangers (one of which is played by Terry Wilson, who later would join Bond on *Wagon Train*) into the Reverend, who (injecting a classic Fordian joke) must complete the ceremony before the bar will be opened. Pappy then foreshadows the fact that this marriage will never happen by having "Shall We Gather at the River?" the same song used for Martha's funeral, performed during the wedding processional.

Just as the ceremony is about to begin, Ethan and Marty arrive in a buckboard. Lars, fearing they will be arrested for the murder of Futterman, attempts to stop them from entering the house. Ethan barges in, opens the bar, and is joined by the rangers, as Charlie leaves to confront Marty.

The obligatory Ford fistfight follows, with the two combatants outside, wrestling around in the red dirt, until the Reverend arrives to establish the formalities (as in *The Quiet Man*'s "use" of the Marquess of Queensberry rules). Bond takes a particular delight in announcing, "Fight fair! No bitin' or gougin'—and no kickin,' either!" After Terry Wilson breaks them up a second time, Ward adds, "No chokin'—no chokin,' no *gougin*'!" The women enjoy every second of the fight, which ends in a draw, mutual apologies, and a cancellation of the wedding.

A little over 100 minutes into the film, Ford includes his first Bond bum scene, (framed in a wide shot, with the camera behind all the principal characters). "Well, Sister Jorgensen," says the preacher, "it was a nice wedding party, considering nobody got married."

Olive Carey, seated behind Bond, responds by slapping his ass with a wooden spoon, a spanking that unleashes Ward's "horse whinny." Having depicted Clayton wearing a long coat or in the saddle throughout all the previous footage, Pappy saved his fetishistic references for the climactic scenes. He more than makes up for it here, with Ethan observing the antics, before the scene cuts to a closer two-shot, when Clayton mentions a required visit to "the state capitol."

"Is this an invite to a *necktie party*, Reverend?" asks Ethan. The scene between Wayne and Bond is their finest mutual moment in the film, with Sam explaining the circumstances of the Futterman killing, and Ethan twirling his handgun with lightning speed before handing it, grip first, to the preacher.

Lieutenant Greenhill (Patrick Wayne) arrives to continue the Ford in-jokes, with Bond enjoying his needling of the (green) actor, who is called "son" by his real father as Ethan crosses between them. The lieutenant's on-screen father, Colonel Greenhill (Cliff Lyons), has ordered a "joint punitive action" by the cavalry and Texas Rangers against a Comanche band led by Scar, the result of information offered by a former captive who "keeps mentioning a rocking chair."

Dragged into the house, old Mose requests his beloved throne before falling unconscious to the floor. In the rocking chair, looking truly deranged, he explains, "Made out like I was crazy.... Ate *dirt*, chewed *grass*. I fooled 'em..." Refusing to reveal the location of Scar's camp to the demanding Ethan, Mose tells Marty, "Seven Fingers," before being ushered away, still calling for his rocking chair. (Hank Worden's performance, arguably his best, is entirely convincing.)

Clayton appoints Ethan and Marty as civilian scouts, to accompany the Texas Rangers the following morning. When Laurie again attempts to stop Marty, this time expressing a view in league with Ethan's, he becomes even more adamant about saving Debbie.

The dawn attack begins with Ethan scouting the valley (Wayne is standing on the formation known as "John Ford's Point") and his revelation to Marty that one of the scalps hanging from Scar's lance had been taken from his own mother. "But that don't change it!" he responds. "But that don't change *nothin'*!" Ethan turns down his request to attempt a rescue of Debbie before they attack, but the Reverend gives him a chance. "It's your funeral," Ethan concludes.

In a parallel to Prince's barks indicating the impending arrivals of Ethan and, more ominously, Scar at the Edwards ranch, a lone dog (off screen) barks outside the war chief's tepee, just after Marty is lowered by Ethan (off John Ford's Point) to the valley floor. Scar emerges, tossing a rock to scare off the animal.

The Rangers' charge is prefaced by another round of Ford shtick, with Wayne again observing the shenanigans (involving young Greenhill's saber) of his teenage son and Bond. The now–Captain tells the young lieutenant, "*I'm* the hard case you're up against out here, not them childish savages."

Marty reaches Debbie but, as they embrace, a Comanche stealthily appears behind him. Alerted by the sound of a rifle cocking and Debbie's scream, he pulls his pistol, quickly firing three times. Hearing the shots, Clayton (clearly intent on Christianizing the heathens) declares to his troops, "*Brethren, we must go amongst them!*"

Riding to the chief's tepee, only to discover that Scar is already dead, Ethan satiates

The Searchers (C.V. Whitney–Warner Bros., 1956; directed by John Ford). "Dodderin' old idiot" Mose Harper (Hank Worden, in rocking chair) explains to Martin Pawley (Jeffrey Hunter, right) where to find the Comanche Chief "Scar," as (left to right) Charlie McCorry (Ken Curtis), Mrs. Jorgensen (Olive Carey), the Rev. Captain Samuel Johnson Clayton (Ward Bond) and Lars Jorgensen (John Qualen) look on.

his bloodlust by scalping the corpse. Knocking Marty into the dust, he rides after Debbie, still appearing intent on killing her. But when he reaches her, at the same alcove where he and Marty had taken cover, his cry of "Debbie!" suggests a change in his attitude. After raising her up to the sky, he cradles her. "Let's go home, Debbie," he says.

These are the final words spoken in the film. Ford follows this poignant climax with the most blatant bum scene in his three decades of films featuring Bond, who actually is shown, bending over, with his pants pulled down around his knees. "Does that hurt, Reverend?" asks one of a trio of Texas Rangers tending to his battered bottom. "Shut up!" he roars before yelling out in pain and then resuming the position.

"Good work, Captain!" congratulates an impressed Colonel Greenhill, whose son is at attention, holding his saber, while watching over the procedure. When Greenhill inquires about the nature of the "wound," Clayton admits that it's neither bullet nor arrow, leaving only one possibility. The incidents of Bond having his ass spanked by Harry Carey's widow and stabbed by John Wayne's son are as carefully structured as everything else in the film, which is all the more effective for seeming to flow so "effortlessly."

In a bookend to the opening scene, the Jorgensen family (now including Mose, with a roof over his head, content in his rocking chair) awaits the delivery of Debbie. His mission accomplished, Ethan looks into the house, but turns and slowly walks back toward the desert as the door is closed behind him (and in front of the viewer). Having scalped a dead man, proving that he is just as bad as those he despises, Ethan knows he cannot join the family inside, and must remain among the "savages." The last gesture made by Wayne is the "Harry Carey pose."

In LeMay's novel, Amos Edwards' fanatical, psychotic search ends in complete disaster. When he finally discovers the young woman he believes is Debbie, she instead proves to be an armed squaw who guns him down. Ford and Nugent's Ethan Edwards lives on to wander the wasteland, and their Debbie, unlike LeMay's character, does not choose to remain with Scar. The literary Martin Pawley (who has no Native American ancestry) kidnaps the girl just before the cavalry raids the Comanche camp, and she undergoes a mental breakdown while being assimilated back into white culture.

LeMay's Amos is a two-dimensional creature of hatred that *must* be obliterated from society. Ethan Edwards is far more complex, carefully developed by Nugent while heeding Ford's command to create a thorough "biography" for each character in the film, including details from the cradle up to his cinematic arrival. Wayne's performance is an ingeniously measured crescendo of (often nonverbal) acting.

Some viewers have commented that Ethan's forgiveness toward Debbie is "sudden" and "unconvincing," but this view ignores the evolving relationship between Ethan and Martin, whose presence gradually has a positive influence on the fearsome hatred within his "uncle." Director John Milius commented:

> In the end, it's all about duty and family—responsibility to your community, no matter how small. Ethan is alone, but he's also part of a family, and his humanity comes through. He may hate Debbie for being defiled, as he himself is defiled, but it doesn't matter. He forgives her. He can forgive her anything.[17]

More simply, *The Searchers*, made during the mid–1950s, when the Production Code was technically still in place, could not have ended any other way. If Ethan was killed (as Amos is in the novel), *no one* in the audience would have accepted such a thing happening to *John Wayne*—and there is no way John Ford would have killed him off in the first place. On the other hand, if Ethan had killed Debbie, the PCA would have demanded his death. *Hanging* the Duke, or merely suggesting such a thing, would have proved even more unacceptable to 1956 audiences!

Many reviewers, still considering Westerns a "juvenile" genre, simply dismissed *The Searchers* with a few terse paragraphs, calling it just another "oater," or dubbing it "lesser" John Ford. The Academy ignored it entirely. The status of the film as arguably the greatest Western ever made, and one of the finest works of the Hollywood cinema, took more than a decade to evolve. Dobe Carey wrote,

> I have it not just at the top, but separated from the rest in a special place with gold letters. I believe it's the finest film John Ford ever directed. The fact I am most proud of in my professional life is that I had the good fortune to be in it—if only for a short time....
> Of all the John Ford pictures I worked on, the set of *The Searchers* was unlike any other. Uncle Jack was much more serious, and that was the tone that pervaded the cast and crew.[18]

During its initial release, *The Searchers* did garner such critical superlatives as "one of the greatest Westerns ever made" and "a Homeric Odyssey," but, as pointed out by Joseph McBride:

> None of the reviewers seemed to understand the film's central themes, since they hardly noticed Ethan's pathological racism. So deeply ingrained were such attitudes in the national culture of

1956 that few even realized something is terribly wrong with this most untraditional Hollywood Western "hero."[19]

So deft is Ford's storytelling, revealed in a cinematic form reaching symphonic proportions, and so powerful is the John Wayne mythos that, more than a half-century later, many viewers of *The Searchers* still don't discern that Ethan Edwards is a racist leviathan. He is arguably the most significant screen character of the era, a cinematic embodiment of the American pioneer who experienced the spectrum of consequences wrought by continental genocide. Laurie Jorgensen, even though she loves the "eighth–Cherokee" Martin Pawley, shares Ethan's racism, going so far as to claim that the deceased Martha would want her brother-in-law to kill her own daughter. McBride added:

> Ford had portrayed racists before ... but the virulent depths of Ethan's racism did represent something of a departure for the director. Wayne's performance is founded, as perhaps most great performances should be, on a deep emotional identification with the character.[20]

During the last years of his life, Wayne often was asked about his affinity for the character, which he adamantly insisted was not a "villain." He admitted, "I loved him and I loved playing him." In fact, Duke loved the character so much that he named his youngest son, born six years after the release of *The Searchers*, John Ethan Wayne.

On one occasion, Duke sternly replied that Ethan was "a man living in his times. The Indians fucked his wife. What would you have done?"[21] This remark, referring to Martha as his "wife," made nearly two decades after the film was made, by the *actor*, John Wayne, suffering from an illness that would kill the *man*, Marion Morrison, five years later, is erroneous, but quite telling. Early in *The Searchers*, Wayne, Bond and Dorothy Jordan brilliantly provide ample, yet subtle, unspoken evidence of Ethan's love for his brother's wife, and this element undoubtedly informed Wayne's multifaceted performance and subsequent, indelible identification with the role.

John Milius said:

> I don't think there is a better acting performance done by any actor in any movie, ever. John Wayne really understood the character of Ethan Edwards. He *got it*. For people to actually sit there and say that John Wayne wasn't a good actor is the stupidest thing in the world. All you have to do is show *The Searchers*.[22]

What did Ford think of Ethan? In 1966, he told Peter Bogdanovich:

> It's the tragedy of a loner. He's the man who came back from the Civil War, probably went over into Mexico, became a bandit, probably fought for Juarez or Maximilian — probably Maximilian, because of the medal. He was just a plain loner — could never be a part of the family.[23]

For *The Searchers*, Ford gave Wayne his greatest character, and personally crafted another for Bond, who often acts like the director Himself. As if he knew he would be doing it for the final time, Pappy, having invented so many variations on the "Horse's Ass" gag over the years, took it to the apex in this, arguably the pinnacle of his work. Henry Brandon said:

> I don't know if Ward Bond realized exactly what role his physique played on-screen, but there were always jokes going back and forth between Wayne and Ford, and Ward would do that whinny that had so exasperated Henry Hathaway.
>
> Even though I had become his whipping boy, Ford rode Bond mercilessly during the whole time we were on location. I think it was that Ward had been his toady for so long, and that made Ford become even more abusive. I didn't put up with it. I stood up to Ford, got mad at *him*, and eventually he eased off me.

At dinner, Ford would berate Bond until he would retreat into the kitchen to hang out with the black help. He'd get away for a while and have the time of his life, joking and singing. It was "tough love," all those years being associated with an evil genius like Ford.[24]

As in *The Quiet Man*, Bond is an on-screen representative of Ford's ingrained, often contradictory, Catholicism. Martin Scorsese observed:

> John Ford's films are very Catholic ... they deal with morality ... they deal with what's right and what's wrong, in a very powerful way. The constant thing is that the language reflects the Old Testament, throughout the whole movie.
> The reverend played by Ward Bond is also a captain. Here you have the double-edged sword, almost like the God of the Old Testament.[25]

Noting the religious aspects of Duke's performance, director Curtis Hanson said:

> Who but John Wayne could say it the way he says it? "As sure as the turning of the Earth." It's *Biblical*.
> It feels, when we watch *The Searchers*, and watch John Wayne's performance ... that we are seeing *the truth*. And because the truth is ugly, and increasingly deranged, and completely contrary to the movie-star image of John Wayne, it seems like an incredibly brave performance.[26]

Completing his work on *The Searchers*, Ford took his usual sabbatical aboard the *Araner*. On November 28, 1955, Wayne, having attended the screening of the finished film, sent an airmail letter to Ala Wai Harbor, Honolulu, expressing his gratitude for being involved in the production:

> Dear Pappy,
> First: I think "The Searchers" is just plain wonderful.... I don't think the music is great, but I think it's all right. At first I had hoped it would be a little nostalgic, but the whole treatment is so different than the usual Western, that I think this music is probably more appropriate. It's just a wonderful picture. You got great performances out of everyone, and it has a raw brutalness [sic] without any pettiness or meanness.
> All I can say is — Thanks again, Coach.
>
> > Your everloving,
> > Duke[27]

On March 31, 1956, less than three weeks after the general release of *The Searchers*, Pilar Wayne gave birth to a baby girl, Aissa. Duke's enthusiasm, like that of a first-time father, was not shared by his four grown children, particularly Toni, whose wedding to law student Don LaCava was scheduled for May 27 at Hollywood's Blessed Sacrament Catholic Church.

One individual instantly inspired by the film was Charles Hardin Holley, known to pop music fans as Buddy Holly, who saw *The Searchers* at the State Theater in Lubbock, Texas, during the summer of 1956. Ethan's oft-repeated phrase of defiance, "That'll be the day," was quickly developed into a song by the prolific tunesmith, who first recorded it with his band, The Crickets, for Nashville producer Owen Bradley in July 1956. In early 1957, Holly and the band, produced by Norman Petty at his studio in Clovis, New Mexico, recorded a new, up-tempo version of "That'll Be the Day" released on May 2. By autumn, the catchy pop number reached the number-one spot on both the U.S. and U.K. charts. ("That'll be the day when I die" unfortunately came far too soon for one of the nation's greatest singer-songwriters.)

On November 20, 1955, the ABC television series *The Christophers* teamed Bond with Joe E. Brown and Ruth Hussey for the 30-minute episode "Washington as a Young Man." During its 10-year run, the program featured a formidable array of talent, including Ann Blyth, James Cagney, Dean Jagger, Pat O'Brien and Barbara Stanwyck.

Ford and Merian Cooper had considered making films for television when the medium was in its broadcasting infancy during the late 1940s. During the autumn of 1955, executive producer Sidney Van Keuren teamed with Hal Roach Studios to create *Screen Directors Playhouse*, a 30-minute anthology series that utilized a major Hollywood director and popular stars in each episode. Joining an impressive roster including Frank Borzage, John Brahm, Stuart Heisler and Leo McCarey, Ford agreed to direct "Rookie of the Year," hiring Frank Nugent to adapt the original story by W. R. Burnett, and casting Wayne and Bond in lead roles.

Duke plays small-town sportswriter Mike Cronin, who, while researching a story on baseball player Lyn Goodhue (Patrick Wayne), discovers that the hot young rookie is the son of disgraced has-been Larry "Buck" Goodhue (Bond). Burnett based Buck on Joseph Jefferson "Shoeless Joe" Jackson, one of the Chicago White Sox (subsequently branded the "Black Sox") who conspired to throw the 1919 World Series.

Bond appears only briefly, but is very effective as a man haunted by his dishonorable past. In the end, Cronin, believing the young rookie's career more important than greater heights for himself, decides not to submit the story. New York editor Ed Shafer (James Gleason) then informs Cronin that every other sportswriter already knows the truth, but no paper will print it. Other members of the Ford Stock Company appearing in the episode include Vera Miles and Willis Bouchey.

Patrick Wayne appears more at ease here than in *The Searchers*. Ford included two interesting elements that touch on his relationships with Duke and Ward: casting Pat as Bond's son; and including a line of dialogue stating that Wayne's character has "a war record a mile wide."

Broadcast by NBC on December 7, 1955, "Rookie of the Year" was preceded one day earlier by another television episode directed by Ford, "The Bamboo Cross," shot in November for the dramatic series *Jane Wyman Presents the Fireside Theater*. Adapted by Laurence Stallings from the book *A Nun in Red China* by Sister Maria del Rey, the episode, starring Wyman, James Hong and Kurt Katch, is a heavy-handed anti–Communist embarrassment intended as Ford's tribute to the Catholic Maryknoll missionaries, whom he ardently supported.

Bond also appeared in two feature films during the autumn and winter of 1955. *Pillars of the Sky* (1956), directed by George Marshall for Universal, features him as Dr. Joseph Holden in an interesting lineup including Jeff Chandler, Dorothy Malone, Lee Marvin and Sydney Chaplin. Based on the novel *To Follow a Flag* by Will Henry, the film was shot on location at LeGrande and around Wallowa Lake in eastern Oregon. The screenplay by Sam Rolfe included early contributions from Patrick Ford and Borden Chase, and presents a relatively balanced view of "both sides of the epic," with members of the Nez Perce, Umatilla and Palouse tribes playing the Native American roles.

The cliché ridden Cold War Western *Dakota Incident* (1956), shot in Trucolor at the Republic stomping grounds, has Bond crawling way out on a limb as the liberal, pacifist, "pious blowhard," Senator Blakeley. The politician's dedication to forging peace between whites and reds (alternated with lusting after red-dressed temptress Amy Clarke [Linda Darnell], who predictably winds up with chauvinistic "good bad man" John Banner [Dale Robertson]) culminates with a Cheyenne arrow through his heart. In an overlong film crawling with stock characters (Regis Toomey, as the mandolin-picking "Minstrel," is a rip-off of Hoagy Carmichael's "Hi Linnet" in *Canyon Passage*), Bond ironically stands out as the dove among the hawks, whose martyrdom inspires a (very unconvincing) rapprochement, suggesting that the only good politician is a dead one.

On May 11, 1956, Bond returned to the *Schlitz Playhouse of Stars*, starring in the grim episode "Plague Ship," supported by Jon Shepodd, who spent a decade playing character parts in various television thrillers, family dramas and Westerns. Ward made his third and final appearance on the series, costarring with Gene Nelson in the opening episode of the sixth season, "Moment of Vengeance," a thriller based on an Elmore Leonard story, broadcast September 28, 1956.

As he had done with *The Quiet Man*, Ford left behind the troubles of Tinsel Town for the ethereality of the Emerald Isle, when he began work on "Three Leaves of a Shamrock," his long wished-for, all–Irish trilogy, shot on location in Galway and Claire from late March through early May 1956. Like *The Quiet Man*, Ford had planned to feature major stars and character actors, including Maureen O'Hara, Alec Guinness, Donald Crisp, Barry Fitzgerald, and even Katherine Hepburn; and, this time, not only in blazing (especially *green*) color, but Cinemascope as well. However, the budget handed down to Pappy by the Irish production company, Four Provinces, and the distributor, Warner Bros., only allowed him the paltry Screen Directors Guild scale of $3,333, and very little to attract marquee-level actors.

Ford shot the film with players from the Abbey Theatre very quickly and economically, wrapping 10 days ahead of schedule and $104,771 under budget. Premiered as *The Rising of the Moon* at the Dublin International Film Festival on May 16, 1957, it played throughout Ireland the following month and the United States during July and August. Even with the addition of Tyrone Power as narrator, the film was a financial and critical disappointment, particularly in Ford's beloved heath. While those in Northern Ireland feared it might encourage revolutionary outbursts, many in the Irish Republic branded it a stereotypical travesty. Ford and Killanin's hopes for establishing an indigenous film industry in Ireland, including the making of their long-discussed, ambitious adaptation of Sir Arthur Conan Doyle's epic historical novel *The White Company*, were dashed.

Instead, Ford returned to Hollywood and familiar cinematic territory, hired by MGM to direct a film about the development of military aviation and the life of Lieutenant Commander Frank "Spig" Wead, which the studio had been planning as a favor for the U.S. Navy since 1953. Pappy was certainly the man for the job, but he approached the project with some trepidation. Wead had been his close friend, a dedicated Navy man who turned to writing for the stage and screen after suffering a broken neck during a fall down a staircase in his home. Ford had directed Wead's screenplays for *Air Mail* (1932) and *They Were Expendable*, two years before his death in 1947.

Ford believed his personal feelings for Wead might jeopardize any objectivity he could bring to the film, but he didn't want any other director to touch the material. And there was only one choice for the actor to play "Spig": the Duke. In his November 28, 1955, letter about *The Searchers*, Duke, while revealing the status of his Wayne-Fellows partnership and other current production possibilities, mentioned the more valuable benefits of taking the lead in his Coach's new film:

> I wanted to tell you ... what I've decided to do. Here goes.
> I built Bob Fellows into such an important character that I can't do anything with him. I find him incompetent, even when he's trying. I've encouraged Bob Morrison [Duke's brother] and Andy McLaglen and moved them up faster than I should have. I'm afraid that if I just fired Fellows and moved someone else in ... I might have just as many headaches with someone else. So I'm going to fold the company up. I can make a hell of a deal at Warners, and an unbelievable one at RKO ... but if I make either one of these deals I couldn't do the Wead story, so to hell with it. It's more important for me to be in a picture with you, career-wise—for my health— and for my mental relief.[28]

In late July 1956, when the Pensacola, Florida, location shooting began on what became *The Wings of Eagles*, Wayne was a 49-year-old man playing a "college kid," a reckless young aviator half his age. But as the story of Wead's naval career, disabling accident, and painful attempts to recover (aided by "Jughead" Carson [Dan Dailey]) unfolded, Wayne (sans toupee in the later scenes) was able to contribute a sensitive and believable performance to a film that, especially during its first half, often veers into the kind of raucous, hell-raising slapstick that Ford enjoyed but could rarely accomplish effectively, especially when such shenanigans were inappropriate and downright distracting.

One of the highlights is the scene in which Wead, now able to walk with crutches, visits the office of John Dodge (Bond's humorous and dead-on impersonation of Ford) to discuss the possibilities of a screenwriting career. Items from Ford's own office and home, including his Oscars, were used to adorn the set; and Bond, attired with sunglasses, pipe and handkerchief, first sprawled out on a sofa, and then offering booze hidden in a walking stick, playfully portrays some of the infamous habits of his beloved mentor and tormentor. Just as Ford chose John Wayne to play his close friend and colleague, he cast the *only* man he would consider to portray Himself, and Bond did not let him down.

Ronald L. Davis wrote, "The picture is interesting for Ward Bond's commendable depiction ... [he] captured Ford's authority, yet avoided self-glorification, proving himself a substantial actor."[29] Gary Wills, suggesting that Ford's "priceless" casting of Bond was a

The Wings of Eagles (Metro-Goldwyn-Mayer, 1957; directed by John Ford). Ward Bond (left) intently listens to Ford's instructions on how to play John "Dodge," as John Wayne enjoys the moment.

further development of an atypical autobiographical element begun with Victor McLaglen in *The Quiet Man*, noted:

> Ford ... put a potent caricature of himself in *The Wings of Eagles*.... He even had ... Ward Bond play the role with authoritarian growls. *The Quiet Man* is a film of self-knowledge. McLaglen's "Danaher," along with Bond's "Dodge," may be as close to such self-knowledge as Ford ever lets us get while we are watching his product.[30]

Dan Ford suggested that Bond's portrayal was only an overt element in a film loaded with covert autobiographical material:

> Spig Wead's story was so much like John's.... A compulsive worker, a man of great obsessions ... like Ethan Edwards — and like John — Wead was incapable of any real home life....
> *The Wings of Eagles* is revealing because it is the story of a belligerent, brave, eccentric visionary, a man of fanatical dedication who, like Ethan Edwards ... is doomed to be alone.
> More than the story of Spig Wead, it is the story of John Ford. The story of a career man.[31]

In Hawaii during the winter of 1956, Ford cast Bond and Ken Curtis in "The Growler Story," a U.S. Navy–produced, 16mm color training film about posthumous Medal of Honor recipient Commander Howard W. Gilmore, a submarine captain who sacrificed his life to save his men during a battle off the Solomon Islands in February 1943. Curtis' portrayal of Gilmore became hampered by Ford's heavy emphasis on Bond's Irish character (characteristically named Quincannon), which he overplayed in every scene (thickly sliced ham the actor rarely served up, unless ordered, during his 30-year film career). At home, the lumbering Irishman commands his eight children to stand at attention and salute him; while aboard the *Growler*, fighting the Japanese, he beats his breast in King Kong–like fashion (perhaps a "gorilla" in-joke demanded by Ford), announces, "God rest their heathen souls," and then registers a wide, wicked smile.

In his official report, Ford claimed he had enjoyed making "The Growler Story," but resented the "advice" offered by a navy admiral, who realized the director was crafting, not an actual training film, but primarily a fictional piece about heroism. Privately, Ford told Wayne that Bond had spent too much leisure time schmoozing and partying with navy officers. (It is possible that, in anticipation of the upcoming holiday season, Ward was popping more Christmas Trees than usual.) The Coach informed Duke that he would be sending the Judge as a yuletide gift:

> From now on, Bond is your exclusive property. You can have him.... In the morning he would be the lazy, kindly old beachcomber, the ex-professor of literature at Harvard, Oxford, Heidelberg, etc. Then in the afternoon he would be a retired gentleman — the younger son of a noble family in England. In the evening he became just a sloppy, goddamned guttersnipe — big, boisterous — could lick anybody — his fly open, a good rich vocabulary of four-letter words, and an all-around pain in the ass. From now on, he's your shit.[32]

On December 11, 1956, Bond costarred with Ben Johnson in the crime drama "Once a Hero," marking his return to ABC's *Cavalcade of America* television series. Produced by Warren Lewis and directed by Lee Sholem, this gripping John Dunkel teleplay also featured Richard and Robert Eyer, brothers who became two of the industry's most prolific child actors. Robert later would appear with Bond in a 1959 episode of *Wagon Train*.

Wayne spent the first three months of 1957 in Libya and Italy with Henry Hathaway, making *The Legend of the Lost*, an interminable "West African Western" in which he plays "Joe January," an American "cowboy" transplanted to Timbuktu, who knows more about the Sahara than anyone on the entire Dark Continent. Not even the visual splendor contributed by his voluptuous female costar, Sophia Loren, shot in Technicolor and "Technirama" widescreen, could sustain this 109-minute celebration of chauvinism and imperialism that arguably rates as one of the most boring films ever made.

As both the star, dragging and carrying the ample Loren through the sand dunes, and co-producer of this collaboration between his Batjac company and Italy's Dear Film Produzione, Wayne more than had his hands full. As foolproof insurance, he had brought Chuck Hayward and Terry Wilson, two permanent members of the Ford Stock Company, along to handle the stunt work.

Back in Hollywood, Ford was editing "The Growler Story," planning an adaptation of Edwin O'Connor's bestselling 1956 political novel *The Last Hurrah*, and attempting to develop a treatment from a mystery story, "The Judge and His Hangman," hopefully to star Duke, Louis Jourdan, Charles Laughton, Basil Rathbone and Erich von Stroheim, in the near future.

Pilar Wayne had been spending time at the Ford home, joining Jack and Mary for dinner and playing cards into the wee hours. On January 25, Ford wrote to Duke, informing him of the itinerary and guest list set for the following evening:

> We — Barbara, Ken, Maizie, Butt Ward, and Mary, are going to your house tomorrow night to see "The Bob Mathias Story." Also "Rio Grande" — my favorite picture. Bob Mathias and his wife, of course, will be there.

Pappy, with his usual degree of levity, also informed Wayne about an auspicious event held the previous evening:

> Had a wonderful press preview of "Wings of Eagles" (Gawd, what a title) aboard the carrier *Lexington* last night. The Navy really put on a great show for us, dinner inspection, the works. The picture went over great. The bluejackets were with it every minute, and during the dramatic moments there was complete silence in that great big hangar deck, which, as you know, is bigger than St. Peter's. Check with Terry Wilson and Chuck Hayward. They know the size, qualifications, height, width and everything about St. Peter's.

In closing his missive, the Coach couldn't resist making a second reference to the Judge's beloved behind:

> Well, give my love to everybody. I hope there are some equestrian statues in Ghadames, or at least a few Arab horses, so we may add to our valuable collection of Bondiana....
> I will now finish, again wishing you all the best and much affection, and proceed to make a pass at Mary St. John.
>
> As ever.
Jack

Pass completed.[33]

12

A Star Steers the *Wagon Train*

Even after Duke became a major star and Bond emerged as an important television personality, John Ford remained Coach and the three continued to be deeply devoted to each other. — Randy Roberts and James S. Olson[1]

[W]hen you get down to the matter of treating various phases of the Old West inaccurately, TV has been a worse offender than the movies ... TV has glamorized and dramatized their heroes inaccurately. And many of the TV Westerns are just plain bad ... I don't sympathize with anyone who sits glued to his set for hours on end watching any of this that comes along. — John Ford[2]

Following nearly three decades of playing diverse character roles, Bond was offered the chance to star in his own weekly television series, *Wagon Train*. While beginning to develop and shoot the first season of episodes, he also accepted a supporting role in *The Halliday Brand* (1957), a low-budget, formula Western about a rancher who "built the town" and still reigns as sheriff. "Big Dan" Halliday is a reactionary bigot disgusted by his family members who become involved with "breeds," a view that incites a lynching, gunfight deaths, and a more "enlightened" son nearly killing his own father.

Most of the story occurs in flashback, recalled by a mortally ill Big Dan, who has tricked his son, "Dan'l" (Joseph Cotten), into coming home. Contradicting his racist views, the Old Man claims he no longer objects to marriage with a "half-breed." The framing story ends with Big Dan, unable to shoot his namesake, dying in bed, as recalcitrant as ever.

Bond was developing his *Wagon Train* character, Major Seth Adams, a considerate peacemaker who resorts to violence only when necessary (usually to tame a reactionary passenger), while playing his "evil twin" in *The Halliday Brand*. Adams is a retired Civil War veteran who works as a rambling wagon master; but Big Dan, possessing a "proud name," is an owner of land he will kill or die to protect.

The stark, black-and-white, often studio-confined film looks as if it was shot by a television crew, though some scenes reportedly were done on location at Newhall, California. In an era when Westerns ruled the small screen, perhaps the claustrophobic feel of this bigscreen release simply went unnoticed by audiences.

One of the highpoints occurs during Daniel's campaign of vengeance, when Big Dan walks into his office to find a noose hanging over the desk, a grim reminder of his collusion in the lynching of Jivaro Burris (Christopher Dark), an innocent man who wished to marry his daughter, Martha (Betsy Blair). Later, Daniel, perched on a rock formation, tells Big Dan that he now "has nobody," just as his horse slowly saunters into the distance.

Surrounded by miscast actors, Bond delivers a believable performance. The film is set in the Southwest, but Big Dan's children, Daniel and Martha, have East Coast accents (Virginia and New Jersey, respectively); while the "breed," Aleta Burris (Viveca Lindfors), somehow has acquired one from Sweden. An exception is reliable Jay C. Flippen, who, as Chad Burris, father of the "breeds," is perfectly matched with Bond's Big Dan. Unfortunately, Dan is forced to gun down old Chad early in the film.

Ward again shifted 180 degrees, donning priestly garb when Frank Borzage cast him as the soft-spoken, erudite, chess-playing Father Cairns in the World War II aviation drama *China Doll*, which began shooting at Samuel Goldwyn Studios on August 15, 1957. The project, coproduced by Batjac and Romina Productions, also involved location work at Saugus, California, and additional footage shot at Kunming airfield in China, which had been used by the Flying Tigers prior to World War II and the Allied Air Forces during the Burma Campaign of 1942–1945.

Bond's *My Darling Clementine* colleague Victor Mature plays Cliff Brandon, a cynical army captain who, while drunk, accidentally "buys" Shu-Jen (Chinese star Li Hua Li, making her English-language debut), whom he, as informed by Father Cairns, must allow to serve him for three months. While delirious with malarial fever, he spends the night with her, and after she becomes pregnant, he (with the help of the priest and "Ellington" [Danny Chang], a local boy) persuades her to marry him.

During a Japanese air-raid, Shu-Jen and Ellington are killed, but the baby is saved when Brandon orders his men to leave the base before sacrificing himself while blasting away with an anti-aircraft gun. An epilogue set in 1957 depicts his 14-year-old daughter, who has been located by Father Cairns, arriving in Los Angeles, where she is met by the veterans of Brandon's outfit (Johnny Desmond, Stuart Whitman and Bond's pal Bob Mathias, who interestingly mentions that the priest had to abandon his Chinese mission when "the Commies took over").

Billed as "Li Li Hua," the celebrated Chinese actress gives a fine performance in her first Hollywood assignment, which includes several incidents quite daring for a Production Code–era film. Unable to show Mature and Hua actually kissing, Borzage nonetheless (very tastefully) worked in a great deal of suggestive material. Li's refreshing presence helps balance the clichéd war-film supporting characters, the stock melting pot of Jew, Italian and Irish (Stuart Whitman's stage accent occasionally disappears completely).

Several Ford and Wayne regulars served on the crew, including cinematographer William Clothier and editor Jack Murray, and the aerial sequences are consistently well-integrated with footage of the actors. Quite different than his priest in *The Quiet Man*, Father Cairns provided Bond with one of his best feature film characters, whose warm, shepherding personality would bloom into full flower during his lengthy tenure as Major Adams on *Wagon Train*.

During the autumn of 1957, Ford again asked his friend Michael Killanin to aid in the making of an off-beat British film, based on J. J. Marric's suspense novel *Gideon's Day*, starring Jack Hawkins as Scotland Yard's chief inspector. Wingate Smith and Duke traveled with Pappy to London, where they lodged at the Savoy Hotel.

Ford thought it would be interesting to try his hand at a mystery, but particularly wanted to make the film to hire the blacklisted Anna Lee. Due to a case of mistaken identity, HUAC had prevented Lee from working for five years, so he insisted on casting his dear friend as the supportive Kate Gideon, who staunchly endures her husband's workaholic lifestyle, heavy smoking, alcoholism, petulance and general neglect.

Wagon Train made its small-screen debut on Wednesday, September 18, 1957. Major Adams quickly became a popular character and role model, giving Bond an opportunity to cultivate a fully realized celluloid personality: outwardly cantankerous and often tough as nails, yet possessing great sensitivity, compassion and *fairness.* Proving his prowess as an actor, Bond invested Adams with qualities that often eluded him in real life.

Wagon Train reflected the versatility Bond had displayed throughout his film career, although here he merged several personalities into a single, complex character. As wagon master, Adams wears many hats (although Ward usually dons the same battered bonnet on screen), including those of former military officer and Civil War hero, leader and authority figure, frontier scout, driver, navigator, quick-draw gunfighter, "Indian" ambassador, moderator, counselor, preacher, detective, attorney, judge, doctor, surrogate brother, uncle, father and grandfather, crusty comedian, sagebrush philosopher and trustworthy friend.

Adams is, in effect, a team of men essential to a grueling, dangerous pioneer trek. Bond plays him naturalistically, often speaking very softly and carrying that big stick of last resort: his powerhouse right cross (very similar to Duke's) that the audience can almost feel when it's unleashed on some bonehead who just can't *get right.*

Wagon Train was developed for Revue Studios (formerly Republic) by veteran producer Howard Christie, who had overseen numerous feature films at Universal, frequently working with the studio's top comedy team, Bud Abbott and Lou Costello, as well as Errol Flynn, Rock Hudson, Joel McCrea, Merle Oberon and Maureen O'Hara. Many of the character actors who had appeared in Christie's films became guests on *Wagon Train.*

Christie's intention was to focus on the lives of both the regular characters and those played by guest actors in each episode. Instead of creating yet another action based Western, he hired writers who could craft character-driven scripts for a series set on a westward wagon train. The inclusion of different stars in a weekly, hour-long anthology series was a groundbreaking concept at the time.

Christie and his directors, including John Brahm, David Butler, Robert Florey, Sidney Lanfield and George Waggner, worked their cast and crew on a six-day shooting schedule eventually reduced to five. Location filming was done at several sites providing the varied terrain necessitated by the continuous movement of the wagon train. Janss Ranch and Thousand Oaks provided hills and wooded areas. Rocky ground with plenty of sagebrush could be found at Iverson's Ranch, while desert scenes were shot at Palmdale. A master shot required up to a dozen authentic Conestoga wagons, each requiring four horses, out-riders on horseback and an actor who could drive it. Oxen, wranglers, stuntmen and 30 to 40 extras also were on hand.

When Bond signed his contract, he was adamant that Frank McGrath and Terry Wilson, frequent coworkers on Ford's films, be hired, not only to handle horses and stage fights, but to play noticeable character roles. Though both were known primarily as stuntmen, they also had played bit parts in many films. Under his guidance, Bond's buddies soon proved that they were fully capable of handling their supporting characters. Harry Carey, Jr., explained:

> Frankie used to be kidded unmercifully on Ford films because he couldn't say a line of dialogue. Ward taught him how to play the role of Wooster, and Frankie didn't have to hit that hard ground anymore. Frankie and Terry went on tour with Ward to rodeos and fairs.[3]

Bond's costar, Robert Horton, cast as lead scout Flint McCullough, recalled:

> When I first met Ward, I had nothing but admiration and respect for him. I had watched him in many films over the years. I thought his performance in *Gentleman Jim* ... was as good as it gets. However, very early on, I became aware that we really didn't have very much in common. We honestly didn't relate at all. At the same time, we enjoyed a great rapport on camera.[4]

Horton described their on-camera relationship and Bond's straightforward acting technique:

> I enjoyed working with Ward. He was always right there. He looked you in the eye and said his lines with honesty and conviction. In all our scenes, whether they were of agreement, disagreement, humor or whatever took place in the moment, Ward and I worked marvelously together. In fact, the relationship between Major Adams and Flint McCullough ... was as good as Gable and Tracy. It was perfect.[5]

The premiere episode, "The Willy Moran Story," directed by Herschel Daugherty, features Ernest Borgnine in the title role, Adams' former Civil War comrade who has descended into a morass of alcohol. Other guest performers include Marjorie Lord, Richard Hale and a 13-year-old Beverly Washburn, who was making the first of three appearances on the show. She remembered,

> Ward Bond was a nice man who would also use some colorful language. Because I was a minor, they had what was called a "welfare worker".... At one point she went to the producer and said if he used one more swear word, she would pull me from the set. So the producer spoke to Ward Bond. Later he came over to me and apologized.... He was really a kind-hearted man, always very nice to me.[6]

"Willy Moran" opens with Bond's narration, followed by the debut of Adams, riding his horse down a dusty main street, as his old comrade is given the bum's rush from the local saloon. Bond immediately establishes the Major's authority, assuring his top aides, Charlie Wooster (McGrath) and Flint McCullough, that *he'll* handle the situation.

Some of Adams' comments that became series trademarks are unleashed during the first few minutes of this initial episode. "Why don't you mind your own business?" he advises Wooster, his (sarcastically and benevolently harassed) whipping boy, before griping, "I wonder where the devil *that McCullough* is?"

Though Adams demonstrates his dead shot with a rifle, he uses violence only as a last resort, after his attempts to reason with reactionary hotheads have failed. The sophomore episode, "The Jean LeBec Story" (September 25, 1957), featuring Ricardo Montalban, Joanna Moore and Ford Stock Company stalwart Grant Withers, includes the Major's admission, "I'm not a man of violence, but I think it's time for a showdown." Between the first two broadcasts, Bond appeared on the September 22 *Steve Allen Show*, a special "NBC Fall Preview" edition on which Rosemary Clooney, Robert Cummings and Eddie Fisher also appeared.

The third *Wagon Train* episode, "The John Cameron Story" (October 2, 1957), established a formula the series would frequently utilize, allowing either Bond or Horton to dominate the narrative, while the other makes brief appearances at the beginning and end, or occasionally sits out the show entirely. Adams brackets this story, while McCullough is featured, with a supporting cast including Michael Rennie, Carolyn Jones and Jack Elam.

"The Ruth Owens Story" (October 9, 1957), directed by Robert Florey, follows suit, with Bond narrating and then appearing during the closing moments, when Adams thunders in to stop a lynching, punch out two men, and remind the people in his charge that *he* is the judge. Russell Simpson is the Ford regular who contributes to this episode.

Florey also directed "The Les Rand Story" (October 16, 1957), featuring a strong performance by Sterling Hayden, whose character's vengeance wrought by the death of his Native American wife is eventually tempered by the intercession of McCullough, the great negotiator, especially in the absence of Adams. Although the Major is conspicuously missing from this episode, it is set in "Ward Bond country," Little Fork, Nebraska.

"Les Rand" deals directly with racism, supporting the pitch that *Star Trek*-creator Gene Roddenberry used when he later described his science-fiction series idea to skeptical television executives as "a *Wagon Train* to the stars." Although the network suits may have thought the great visionary was referring only to the subgenre into which the series fell, Roddenberry undoubtedly admired the social issues the innovative *Wagon Train* tackled on a regular basis.

Bond narrates "The Nels Stack Story" (October 23, 1957), featuring *Red River, She Wore a Yellow Ribbon* and *Wagon Master* leading lady Joanne Dru as Laura Collins, who becomes interested in the title character (Mark Stevens), an ex–Confederate officer whose war experiences have made him a pacifist. Branded a coward by the reactionary Jeff Claymore (Kevin Hagen), Stack causes a stir when he cares for an elderly Native American whose fellow tribesmen have raided their precious livestock. Major Adams' perennial outbursts in this installment include such Midwestern phrases as "Cut it out!" (an example of Bond's frequent improvising).

"The Charles Avery Story" (November 13, 1957), written by Aaron Spelling, provides a glimpse of the social conscience McCullough would reveal as the series progressed. Robert Horton narrates as Adams sends McCullough with a small U.S. Army contingent to escort a Native American chief's daughter (Susan Kohner) carrying a peace treaty from Washington to her tribe. Farley Granger is excellent as Avery, a bigoted lieutenant who has difficulty controlling his even more unpleasant men. As the renegade "Running Horse," Henry Brandon, the "Kraut Comanche," makes his first of several menacing, Scar-like appearances in the series.

"The Mary Halstead Story" (November 20, 1957) features Agnes Moorehead in a superb performance as a dying woman who hopes to find the son she earlier abandoned. Ultimately, she learns from a nearly lynched young man (Tom Pittman) that he killed her boy, who had become the notorious "Abilene Kid" (Tom Laughlin). Moorehead is matched by Bond, whose understated acting convincingly reveals Adams' sensitive side.

In "The Riley Gratton Story" (December 4, 1957), directed by the versatile stylist John Brahm, Bond pays homage to Ford and Wayne (for the first of many times) by uttering Ethan Edwards' mantra, "That'll be the day!" During his introductory narration, he also makes some comments referring, not to his earlier work, but to his birthplace:

> Any time you'd like to know about Nebraska, you just get in touch with me, Seth Adams, Major, U.S. Army, retired, and wagon master. I guess I swallowed enough Nebraska mud and dust to remember the bitter taste of it for the rest of my life....

This Bond in-joke sets up Adams' complaints to Wooster about the multifaceted nature of his job, during which he barks another of his oft-repeated orders, "Why don't you just *shut up?*"

After shooting the first dozen episodes, Bond began having problems with his injured leg; and, without explanation, Major Adams appears, using two crutches, at the close of "The Clara Beauchamp Story" (December 11, 1957), guest starring Nina Foch. The following week's "The Julie Gage Story," another excellent installment written by Aaron Spelling, describes the Major's injury as a strained back incurred while attempting to lift a wagon out of the mud.

Adams makes it very clear that he does *not* want to hear about his need for the crutches; and he again utters "That'll be the day" before McCullough calls him "Grandpa" and rides off. When one of the passengers dies of fever, the Major officiates at the funeral before being asked to "half marry" the deceased man's daughter, Julie Gage (Anne Jeffreys), to unconscious fever victim Tobe Cannon (Robert Sterling), so that she may care for him without being shunned by the "upstanding women" on the train. When Cannon recovers, he doesn't appreciate the "half-married" concept, so Adams performs another ceremony to marry then completely.

Aaron Spelling adapted "The Cliff Grundy Story" from a story by Philip MacDonald for a particularly grueling episode broadcast on Christmas Day 1957. McCullough's old friend, Cliff (Dan Duryea), is seriously mauled during a buffalo stampede; and, when the man must be left behind, Flint remains to care for him, assisted by a passenger, Craig Manson (Russell Johnson), whose mercenary reason is soon discovered when he attempts to wring the location of a gold mine out of the presumably dying man. After Manson disappears into the desert, leaving no water for the others, they prove how two men can help each other survive.

Bond appears briefly in "Cliff Grundy," but is back in the lead for "The Luke O'Malley Story," broadcast on New Year's Day 1958. Guest starring Mary Murphy and Keenan Wynn, who masquerades as an itinerant preacher to escape from a revengeful outlaw, the episode features Bond in fine form. The Major, growing tired of his back malady, threatens to "bend a crutch over [Charlie Wooster's] head!"

Though Adams is down to using only one crutch in "The Jesse Cowan Story," his back problems again are mentioned at the beginning of this episode, guest starring George Montgomery and Lee Van Cleef, aired January 8, 1958, three days after Bond and Horton appeared to promote it on *The Steve Allen Show*.

"As a wagon master, they don't come any better," McCullough says of Adams to the title character (James Whitmore) in "The Gabe Carswell Story" (January 15, 1958), a white man who has long lived with the Arapaho tribe, but wants his "half-breed" son, Jess "Little Elk" Carswell (Scott Marlow), to join the wagon train after all the buffalo have been slaughtered. When McCullough is staked out and left to die in the blazing sun (providing Horton with one of his frequent beefcake scenes), Carswell is forced to kill his own son.

Upgraded to using only a cane, Adams growls another "That'll be the day" to Wooster in "The Honorable Don Charlie Story" (January 22, 1958), about a womanizing gambler (Cesar Romero) posing as a count. Bond appears during two brief scenes of "The Dora Gray Story," in which McCullough encounters two members of the Ford Stock Company, Linda Darnell and John Carradine, as San Francisco–bound "merchants" who sell rifles to the "Indians" after acquiring them by trading whiskey to a U.S. Army sergeant (a pre-*Bonanza* Dan Blocker) and his lieutenant (Mike Connors). To add another Fordian touch to the episode, music supervisor Stanley Wilson used one of the melodies prominently featured in *Stagecoach*.

"The Annie MacGregor Story" (February 5, 1958), guest starring Jeannie Carson and Tudor Owen, is hampered by ethnic stereotypes of "Scotchmen," but features such highlights as Carson singing Robert Burn's ballad "Ye Banks and Braes o' Bonny Doon," the "Indians" being frightened off (like the English before them) by the mighty sound of the Highland bagpipes, and Wooster's wearing of a kilt, held up by suspenders, during the closing scene. Bond again appears nursing his bad back.

During December 1957, while Bond was hobbling about the *Wagon Train* set, Wayne traveled to Japan, where John Huston was preparing to direct "The Barbarian" at Eiga Studios in Kyoto. As Duke soon discovered, working for Ford was a breeze compared to the squall generated by the eccentric, impulsive and self-indulgent Huston.

Huston was impressed by a script called "The Townsend Harris Story" by an old friend, Charles Grayson, who had written screenplays for every conceivable genre, including films featuring Bond and Victor McLaglen. Grayson had adapted his new script from the work of Ellis St. Joseph, who had based his original story on Townsend Harris, who, in July 1856, had been chosen by President Franklin Pierce as the first U.S. General Consul to Japan. Huston believed that Wayne, "a better actor than he knew," was the ideal actor for the role. He wrote:

> [H]is massive frame, bluff innocence and rough edges would be an interesting contrast to the small, highly cultivated Japanese; that the physical comparison would help serve to emphasize their dissimilar viewpoints and cultures.[7]

The role was an enormous challenge for Wayne, but the hefty sum of $700,000 (a record at the time) was enough "persuasion" for him to make the attempt. Pilar Wayne revealed that he (as any actor would expect from a top director) "counted on Huston to help him turn in a creditable performance."[8]

Understandably, Townsend Harris, arriving two years after Commodore Matthew Perry had waged his infamous "gunboat diplomacy" to force the Shogun into accepting President Millard Fillmore's demands for opening trade with the United States, was not heartily welcomed in Japan. Joseph's story and Grayson's screenplay typically took liberties with historical facts, transforming a minor aspect of Townsend's life in Japan into a major piece of sexual sensationalism.

The widely accepted version of events purports that the Japanese government planted a spy, a geisha girl named Okichi, in Harris' household, who then fell in love with him. Following his departure at the order of President Abraham Lincoln in November 1861, Okichi was shunned by Japanese society and eventually committed suicide in 1892.

That's the legend; but here is a more recent revelation (perhaps the fact): Okichi merely served as a housekeeper for Townsend, who dismissed her after only three days for what he perceived as a "skin infection." But to film the legend, Huston needed to find the perfect female to play Okichi; and, true to form, he didn't consider an actress, but merrily made his way through several geisha houses, eventually choosing Eiko Ando, a tall young woman from Hokkaido who appealed to him.

Huston didn't meet Wayne until his arrival in Japan to begin production. Holding a 13-page memo listing all his demands, Duke handed it to the director, who respectfully accepted it; but later, having read none of it, tossed it into the trash. After the first few days of shooting, Wayne, being left to improvise with little direction from Huston, had no idea what was going on. Pilar Wayne recalled:

> Duke wasn't used to working in a totally unstructured atmosphere. He'd learned his craft from directors like Ford and Hathaway, men who wouldn't dream of letting an actor loose in a single scene, let alone throughout the course of an entire production.[9]

Wayne was furious by the time Pilar arrived in Japan to celebrate Christmas. Duke told her:

> I ask him what's on tomorrow's shooting schedule, and he'll tell me to spend more time absorbing the beauty of the scenery and less time worrying about my part. When I tell him I can't memorize the script unless I know what we'll be shooting, the bastard says, "Don't worry, we'll

improvise." ... The son of a bitch can't make a good movie without his father or Bogart to carry him.[10]

Though he declared that he wanted to "kill" Huston, who was openly sleeping with his costar and nearly burned down an entire village while filming one scene, Duke maintained his professionalism on the set.

Huston finished shooting "The Barbarian" in late January 1958, and then followed Darryl Zanuck's edict to head for Africa to make *The Roots of Heaven* with Errol Flynn, Trevor Howard and Orson Welles. During postproduction, 20th Century–Fox changed the title of what Huston thought "was a pretty good picture" to *The Barbarian and the Geisha*, and studio head Buddy Adler, at the insistence of Wayne, had the film edited according to the star's demands, or "Duke ... wouldn't work for Fox again." Huston said,

> It was really a fucked-up proposition. I would have had my name taken off the picture except ... Buddy Adler was a friend of mine and he was dying ... I didn't want him to have further complications.... John Wayne began making demands and Buddy succumbed.... I'd like to forget *The Barbarian and the Geisha.*[11]

After developing a believable, well-rounded character for *Wagon Train*, Bond began to suggest changes to scripts he deemed too violent or containing elements that might prove offensive to a family audience. He eventually became involved in the production and editing of the show. Associate producer Frederick Shore commented:

> We had to submit every script in advance to get approved by both NBC and the censors. I believe we had to have approval of every single person that worked on the show—both cast and crew ... including Ward Bond, who was very right-wing, and I'm sure part of the approval process.[12]

On February 8, 1958, at the annual Directors Guild of America awards ceremony, *Wagon Train* had two episodes in the running for Outstanding Directorial Achievement in Television: "The Clara Beauchamp Story" (Earl Bellamy) and "The Ruth Owens Story" (Robert Florey). Director Don Weis, however, took home the plaque, for the *Schlitz Playhouse* installment "The Lonely Wizard Steinmetz," starring Rod Steiger.

"The Bill Tawnee Story" (February 12, 1958) guest stars MacDonald Carey as a Native American who gallantly served the Union under General Sherman. Of Major Adams, he admits to his wife (Joy Page), "I like him, but I wonder about others." Well-directed by David Butler, the script treads the familiar ground of minority victims of prejudice who become "acceptable" to whites after performing a heroic deed to save their bigoted hides.

Guest star Onslow Stevens is excellent as a headstrong patriarch in "The Mark Hanford Story" (February 26, 1958), in which McCullough must intervene in a family matter between father and son (Tom Tryon) to stop a potential "blood war" with the Cheyenne. Wayne's mentor Paul Fix plays Jake, Old Man Hanford's sensible right-hand man, who ultimately has no choice but to gun down his boss.

One of the best episodes of the first season, "The Bernal Sierra Story" (March 12, 1958), loosely based on historical events, was adapted from an original tale by guest star Gilbert Roland, who plays the title character. Ordered to be executed in 1865 by Maximilian, Sierra is freed by rebels loyal to Benito Juarez. To maintain a cover while searching for a cache of stolen gold meant to buy arms for the revolution, Sierra poses as a deserter, which disgusts Adams, who tells Wooster that he actually saw Juarez, "the Mexican equivalent of Abraham Lincoln." Wooster refers to Juarez as a "little Indian," and angers the Major even further.

Sierra is actually seeking the gold-thieving traitors, Casey Reardon (Louis Jean Heydt), and his Mexican wife, Perdida (Charlita Regis). After one of Reardon's reactionary brothers attempts to kill Sierra, Adams discovers the truth, and Casey confesses his crime after nearly dying from fever. Dr. Morrow (Don Beddoe), who tends to his illness, is a "triple dipper," also being the local pharmacist and undertaker.

"The Marie Dupree Story" (March 19, 1958) benefits from the guest performances of Nick Adams (as an Italian immigrant) and Debra Paget (as a gold digger using him as the pawn in a love triangle). Robert Lowery and the great Sam McDaniel, brother of Hattie, appear in supporting roles.

On March 25, 1958, Ford's *Gideon's Day* was released in England to middling revues. In Hollywood, Columbia ignored it, a sign that the director's name no longer induced instant publicity for a "John Ford Production." The studio failed to market the Technicolor film, instead releasing a black-and-white version, *Gideon of Scotland Yard*, to a limited number of theaters during February 1959.

While *Gideon* languished, Ford returned to developing *The Last Hurrah*, a project that reestablished his liberal leanings. He admitted that he intended to direct a "controversial picture," and Frank Nugent's screenplay depicted the conservative, WASP "Yankee blueblood" opponents of Irish-American, Roman Catholic Mayor Frank Skeffington in a hard-hitting light.

The influence of McCarthy and the results of the HUAC witch hunts had begun to wane. Blacklisted writers were writing Oscar-winning screenplays under pseudonyms openly recognized by many in Hollywood, prompting the Academy to consider ending its ban on allowing "Reds" to receive the award. In an article published in *Daily Variety*, Bond lamented, "They're all working now, all these Fifth Amendment Communists. No point at issue. We've just lost the fight, and it's as simple as that."[13]

Ford and Nugent adapted the screenplay from Edwin O'Connor's novel, based loosely on the unsuccessful 1949 re-election campaign of James M. Curley, a scandal-ridden Democrat who served four separate terms as Mayor of Boston (between 1914 and 1950), twice in the U.S. House of Representatives (1911–1914 and 1943–1947), and once as Governor of Massachusetts (1935–1937). Convicted twice on fraud charges, he also did two stretches in prison, the second being commuted by President Truman in 1947 after supporters of Curley's powerful political machine turned up the heat. In 1950, "Give 'Em Hell, Harry" increased the corruption by issuing a full pardon for both convictions.

Curley, hoping to see a film adaptation of his autobiography *I'd Do It Again*, proposed legal action against the print and screen versions of *The Last Hurrah*, but eventually was persuaded to drop the suit. (He died on November 12, 1958, just 19 days after the film's New York premiere.)

Ford and Nugent's Skeffington has refined blackmail into a fine art, but the character is primarily a conduit for Ford's own disillusionment with 1950s American society. Throughout the film's carefully crafted 122 minutes, he takes pointed shots at trends that have eroded time-honored traditions, represented most visibly by the rapidly increasing influence of mass media.

Ford's production company had secured a bank loan for half the film's budget, but Columbia still had final cut on *The Last Hurrah*, portions of which the studio considered "too daring" and "liable to offend people."[14] Ford, Nugent and editor Jack Murray rallied to replace scenes that had been cut, and Pappy eventually was pleased with the final product.

For the role of Skeffington, Ford first had mentioned Orson Welles to Harry Cohn, information that was distributed to the Los Angeles press. The very next morning, Bond had a "dossier" delivered by messenger to the Columbia mogul *and* AMPAS President B. B.

Cahane, lambasting Welles as a "Commie." Ford, using Wayne's Batjac stationery, revealingly
wrote to Duke:

> Bond did not come to me and protest about Welles' proclivities (alleged). No! He must go to
> Cohn and Cahane.
> You know my very decided views on traitors, Commies, Fellow Travelers and such like. You
> also know my integrity in making films and also my ideas on justice. You are not guilty until
> proven so (and the jury is not necessarily Ward Bond). What ya think of it? I can't get mad.

After signing the letter "Coach," Ford added the postscript, "Fuck Bond...."[15] The
truth is that Bond, who actually had been considered for the lead, wanted to play Skeffington,
and went to extreme lengths to shoot down Orson Welles, who later claimed:

> When the contracts were to be settled, I was away on location, and some lawyer — if you can
> conceive of such a thing — turned it down. He told Ford that the money wasn't right or the billing
> wasn't good enough, something idiotic like that, and when I came back to town the part had
> gone to Tracy.[16]

Wayne and James Cagney also had been contenders for the role, but Ford, at Katherine
Hepburn's request, chose Spencer Tracy. He also cast Jeffrey Hunter as Skeffington's nephew,
Alan Caulfield, a stunning array of character actors who had appeared in his earlier pictures
(Frank Albertson, John Carradine, Ricardo Cortez, Donald Crisp, Ken Curtis, Jane Darwell,
Wallace Ford, James Gleason, Anna Lee, Edmund Lowe, Frank McHugh, Pat O'Brien, Jack
Pennick, O. Z. Whitehead) and, in his first and last performance for Ford, the great Basil
Rathbone.

At Columbia in 1935, Edward G. Robinson had asked Harry Cohn to hire Ford for
The Whole Town's Talking. Now, on April 24, 1958, he was back, again working for the legendary "Poverty Row Tyrant," but Pappy had a very positive view of the mogul: "He was
the kind of a man whose nod and handshake were worth more than a contract drawn up
by a score of Philadelphia lawyers."

Suddenly, three days into the *Last Hurrah*, Cohn died of a heart attack while in Phoenix.
When Ford was informed by a Columbia executive, he was beside himself. He immediately
announced he was shutting down production for the remainder of the day, but was told in
no uncertain terms, "But you can't do that, it's never been done at Columbia!"

"It's being done now," Ford responded.[17]

"I prefer an engaging rogue to a complete fool," states a Catholic clergyman in *The
Last Hurrah*. The complex, sardonic screenplay consistently emphasizes the "lesser of two
evils" nature of American politics. Both Skeffington and his rival's patron, right-wing banker
Norman Cass, Sr. (Rathbone), have congenital idiots for sons; but the WASP moron (Whitehead) is far more mentally challenged than the Irish-American wastrel (Arthur Walsh).

Highpoints are the politically motivated Irish wake for Knocko Minihan, whose widow
(Anna Lee), segregating herself from the pall of cigar smoke and three cases of Old Crow,
receives a $1000 check from Skeffington; and the live television campaign spot attempted
by Republican puppet Kevin McCluskey (Maureen O'Hara's brother, Charles FitzSimons).
Joined by a dog that barks through most of his campaign claptrap, McCluskey's media disaster is a blatant parody of Richard Nixon's September 1952 "Checkers Speech," which had
been televised from Hollywood over 60 NBC affiliates, with additional coverage provided
by CBS and Mutual radio stations.

A fine example of how Ford let subject matter and content drive his visual style, *The
Last Hurrah*, an intimate character piece set in the confined, smoky spaces of old-guard pol-

itics, features far more camera movement and editing than most of his other films. Rather than calling on Winton Hoch or another cinematographer who had worked on his large-scale Westerns, Ford used Columbia's own Charles Lawton, Jr., who had shot *The Long Gray Line*. However, unlike the earlier, Technicolor and Cinemascope (2:55:1) film, *The Last Hurrah* is far less expansive, shot in black and white and a more standard widescreen ratio (1.85:1).

One of Ford's underrated films, *The Last Hurrah* is also one of the most thoroughly *auteur* works ever released by a Hollywood studio. Skeffington, after losing the election, actually uses the term "victorious in defeat"; and when Roger Sugrue (Willis Bouchey), a bitter enemy, arrives at his deathwatch to claim he'd "do it differently" if given another chance, the Mayor emphatically replies, "Like *hell* I would" just before he dies.

Tracy is one of cinema's most celebrated actors, yet his exceptional performance in *The Last Hurrah* is rarely mentioned. Like Tracy, Ward Bond was a "natural" actor, but Frank Skeffington arguably was beyond his scope, and it's difficult to imagine anyone other than Spence playing him. Physically, Bond was completely locked out of the film, but his "presence" is suggested during the television sequence, when Mrs. McCluskey (Helen Westcott) bends over to fill the frame with her (electronically enhanced) rear end. In December 1958, the National Board of Review presented its award for Best Actor to Tracy (for *The Last Hurrah* and *The Old Man and the Sea*) and Best Director to Ford.

Awash in a sea of formidable performers, dimwitted sidekick specialist Edward Brophy, playing Skeffington's faithful factotum, Ditto Boland, stands out as the touching Shakespearean fool of *The Last Hurrah*. In his blissful ignorance, he is perhaps the most fortunate character of all.

One of the most ambitious *Wagon Train* episodes, "A Man Called Horse" (March 26, 1958), was adapted from the short story by Dorothy M. Johnson. Ralph Meeker portrays a Bostonian who travels to the West, is accepted into a Crow tribe, and becomes the surrogate son of an old woman (Cecila Lovsky). The story of Horse is narrated by Bond in flashback, depicting Adams and his colleagues' respect for the tribe, contrasted with the racist beliefs of the public at large. (In 1970, Cinema Center Films produced a feature version of *A Man Called Horse*, starring Richard Harris.)

On April 15, 1958, the 10th Emmy Awards were held at the Coconut Grove in Hollywood. *Wagon Train* was nominated for three awards, Best New Program Series of the Year, Best Dramatic Series with Continuing Characters, and Best Art Direction (Howard E. Johnson), but was topped by *The Seven Lively Arts*, *Gunsmoke*, and *Hallmark Hall of Fame*, respectively.

Aired the following evening, "The Daniel Barrister Story" features brilliant performances by Bond as the level-headed Adams, Charles Bickford as a pious man whose rigid beliefs nearly result in the death of his wife (Peg Hillias), and Roger Smith as a young doctor forced by McCullough to leave a plague-ridden town to save the ailing woman.

Bond expanded his characterization beyond that of a leading ensemble player in "The Major Adams Story," a two-part episode broadcast on April 23 and 30, 1958. Fordian elements imbue the script by Frank W. Marshall, opening with Adams visiting the grave of his lost love, Ranie Webster Douglas (Virginia Grey), to reminisce about their past. The episode is told in a "flashback within a flashback" structure, explaining how Adams, Hawks and Wooster served together in the Civil War. Ranie, believing that Seth had been killed, married another man; and, following his death, she and Adams met again as he led one of his wagon trains westward.

Wagon Train: "The Major Adams Story" (Revue–NBC Television, 1957; directed by Mark Stevens). Two of the Union Army's finest: Corporal Charlie Wooster (Frank McGrath) and Major Seth Adams (Ward Bond), discuss their impending mission.

Bond arguably gives the performance of his small-screen career in this episode, as the Major, seriously wounded in battle, refuses to have his legs amputated (an eerie parallel to his real-life experience in 1945). He then struggles, with the help of Hawks and Wooster, to walk again, and arrives in time to hold Ranie as she lies dying. Her death scene, like the championship belt sequence with Errol Flynn in *Gentleman Jim*, offers an excellent example of the dramatic power Bond achieved with understatement.

"The Dan Hogan Story" (May 14, 1958) also includes a flashback offering details about the past escapades of the Major and Bill Hawks, this time as organizers of an illegal boxing match on Staten Island! Jock Mahoney guest stars as Dan Hogan, an NYPD officer, who knocked out "The Tinsmith" (an overweight Buddy Baer), then married and moved out West, wishing to live a peaceful family life.

After meeting up with Adams in Wyoming where he resides with his wife (Rachel Ames) and young daughter (Dana Dillaway), Hogan is challenged to a duel by Jason Rance (John Larch), the town tyrant, after saving a friend from an unfair business deal. Following an excellent scene in which Adams explains the irrational "Code of the West" to Wooster, Hogan, who has never carried a gun, rather than leaving town and earn the brand of a coward, stands up to Rance, whose pistol is not as fast as Hogan's fist.

John Drew Barrymore is magnetically sinister in "The Ruttledge Munroe Story" (May 21, 1958), spooking the wagon train passengers with his perplexing sense of humor, including his singing of a self-penned ditty about "running away" from the sins of one's past. After saving the Major's life, he attempts to control Ruth Hadley (Mala Powers), a young mother fleeing from her abusive husband, to the point of murdering an innocent young man (Jack Grinnage) standing night watch. Munroe reveals that, during the Civil War, Adams presented evidence at his court-martial resulting in a five-year prison sentence. Revenge crazed, Munroe, lightning fast with a sawed-off shotgun, forces Adams to draw, but is gunned down by Ruth.

"The Rex Montana Story" (May 28, 1958) guest stars Forrest Tucker as a phony Western hero created by the pen of pulp fiction writer Clyde Winslow (James Dunn). After the bogus buckaroo is killed by the father of Loetha (Kristine Miller), the Piute woman he had kidnapped, Adams (in a very Fordian moment) convinces Winslow to leave the legends behind for the kiddies and begin writing the truth about the real trailblazers of the West.

While at Universal, Howard Christie had produced *The Kettles on Old MacDonald's Farm* (1957). For "The Cassie Tanner Story" (June 4, 1958), he hired "Ma Kettle" herself, Marjorie Main, as a cantankerous woman who sets her sights on Major Adams. At first, Bond disliked the script, which placed him in comic scenes he believed clashed with his established characterization. Writer Paul Savage said, "But Bond could play comedy, he went with it, and we captured a lot of the humor."[18]

One of the series' best writers, Richard Maibaum, contributed "The John Wilbot Story," a clever episode based on fantastical rumors that John Wilkes Booth had escaped, and another man had been trapped in the tobacco barn fire and fatally shot through the neck on April 16, 1865. Dane Clark is inspired as Wilbot, an articulate, mysterious man who effortlessly recites passages from Shakespeare plays, carries a clipping about the Booth manhunt in a copy of *Julius Caesar*, and shuffles about with a pronounced limp. Amidst a flurry of accusations from all sides, he admits under duress that he is Booth; but, after being struck down during an "Indian" raid, when asked a second time, he is able only to mutter that his name is "John Wil ..." before he dies.

This serious (albeit contrived) episode opens with a humorous scene depicting Adams' insistence on trading jobs with the injured McCullough.

> MCCULLOUGH: When you get back, you might need a little of Charlie's snake oil there, for the seat of your britches.
>
> ADAMS: Don't you worry about my britches. You just concentrate on fillin' 'em until I get back.
>
> MCCULLOUGH: Well, with plenty of Charlie's cookin' there, and *plenty of time*, I might be able to do just that.
>
> ADAMS: *That'll be the day.*

When Adams returns from scouting at the end of the episode, he forcefully massages his rear end and calls out for "*more snake oil!*"

At the close of its first season, *Wagon Train* had reached number 23 in the Nielsen ratings. Major Adams' successful maiden journey is capped by "The Sacramento Story," narrated by Bond and imbued with the chemistry of Robert Horton and guest star Margaret O'Brien. As Julie Revere, she hints at a possible romance with Flint, who is repeatedly brutalized while investigating a land swindle pulled on her recently deceased father. Dan Duryea, Marjorie Main and Linda Darnell offer comic relief by briefly appearing as their characters from earlier episodes.

On hiatus from *Wagon Train* during the summer of 1958, Bond joined Wayne for *Rio Bravo*, his pal's first re-teaming with Howard Hawks since the trailblazing *Red River* a decade earlier. Although Ward's character, freight hauler Pat Wheeler, is killed early in the film, his death motivates everything that follows.

Hawks built the entire film around the macho Wayne persona for a specific reason. He hated Fred Zinnemann's much lauded *High Noon* (1952) and the Oscar winning character played by Gary Cooper. Hawks explained:

> I didn't think a good sheriff [*sic*] was going to go running around town like a chicken with his head off asking for help, and finally his Quaker wife had to save him. That isn't my idea of a good Western sheriff. I said that a good sheriff would turn around and say, "How good are you? Are you good enough to take the best man they've got?" The fellow would probably say no, and he'd say, "Well, then I'd just have to take care of you." And that scene [is] in *Rio Bravo*.[19]

Another Western cited by Hawks was Columbia's *3:10 to Yuma* (1957), directed by Delmer Daves, which features an even more "chicken hearted" marshal (Ford Rainey), who offers $200 to any man who will escort outlaw Ben Wade (Glenn Ford) to his trial. Interestingly, while Hawks chose to depict Wayne's Sheriff John T. Chance as a lawman who *refuses* all the help offered him in the line of duty, he is practically emasculated sexually. Believing that Duke was getting too old to play romantic roles, Hawks made the female lead, "Feathers" (Angie Dickinson), the aggressor, and the tough sheriff the sexual "prey."

Most of Hawks' films are built on sustained pacing and well-timed dialogue, but *Rio*

Rio Bravo (Warner Bros., 1959; directed by Howard Hawks). Three men who are "good enough": "Colorado" Ryan (Ricky Nelson), Sheriff John T. Chance (John Wayne) and "Dude" (Dean Martin) in Howard Hawks' masterful "anti–*High Noon*" character study.

Bravo moves slowly, relying more on ambience than talk. Even shorn of its "jam session" involving "Dude" (Dean Martin), Chance's alcoholic deputy, "Colorado" (Ricky Nelson), Pat Wheeler's young gun, and "Stumpy" (Walter Brennan), a blustery old galoot who serves as a second "deputy," the film is paced like a musical, with a subtly "choreographed" style lending it a uniquely magnetic quality.

Wayne does move like a ballet dancer in this film, providing strong visual *and* narrative counterpoint when Chance, exceptionally light on his cowboy-booted feet, pirouettes to kick away a spittoon or viciously whip a badass hombre across the mug with his rifle. The sheriff's uneasiness around women is also contrasted with his warm and humorous relationship with Stumpy, who actually receives a playful kiss on the head in one scene.

Wayne and Brennan beautifully play this hilarious example of "Hawksian" male bonding. After Chance smooches the old buzzard's bald noggin, Stumpy spanks his bum with a broom. Though Hawks intended Wayne to portray an "antidote" to Gary Cooper's Will Kane in *High Noon*, he and screenwriters Jules Furthman and Leigh Brackett fashioned a "proper" Western lawman with a complex personality.

On June 8, Wayne, dressed in his *Rio Bravo* wardrobe, joined Ford, Gary Cooper, Walter Brennan, and several other top Western figures for an installment of NBC's *Wide Wide World*, a live, 90-minute, Sunday afternoon television program, hosted by Dave Garroway. Agreeing to a rare "interview," Pappy mentioned *The Iron Horse, She Wore a Yellow Ribbon* and *The Searchers* as his favorite Western achievements, and came as close as he ever would to paying Duke a compliment, warmly grasping his arm at one point.

Featuring brief appearances by an impressive lineup of Western film and television stars, *Alias Jesses James* (1959) stars Bob Hope as Milford Farnsworth, an inept insurance peddler who finally sells a policy, to none other than the notorious Missouri outlaw (Wendell Corey). At the insistence of his irate boss (Will Wright), Farnsworth must track down Jesse, and either buy back the policy or serve as the wanted killer's bodyguard. The finale includes Bond, Gary Cooper, Roy Rogers, James Arness, Gail ("Annie Oakley") Davis, Hugh ("Wyatt Earp") O'Brian, Fess ("Davy Crockett") Parker, and Jay ("Tonto") Silverheels. (Gene Autry also appeared, but his footage was cut from the finished film.)

The second season of *Wagon Train* occasionally suffers from weak scripts, overly contrived plots, and a reliance on antiquated stock footage, but there are also several standout episodes, some of which include further development of the Adams character. The season opener, "Around the Horn" (October 1, 1958), begins in San Francisco, where Adams, Bill Hawks and Charlie Wooster have booked passage on a ship bound for Boston. Rather than continuing to work on the prairie schooners, they plan to settle on the East Coast.

Before their ship sails, they are shanghaied by Captain Matthew Cobb (William Bendix), who forces them to serve as deck hands aboard the *Sea Witch*. Because of his chivalrous efforts to aid Pat (Sandy Descher), Cobb's young daughter, and her teacher, Minnie (Osa Massen, Duke's dialogue coach on *The Long Voyage Home*), Adams is reprimanded, tossed in the brig, and nearly hanged from a yardarm. Meanwhile, Flint McCullough is having the time of his life becoming a blood brother with yet another "Indian" tribe and meeting up with Willy Moran (Ernest Borgnine), who now is a respectable sheriff. Bond is at his best in this episode, which was recycled by NBC for the first-season *Bonanza* installment "San Francisco," broadcast on April 2, 1960.

"The Juan Ortega Story" (October 8, 1958) demonstrates Adams' character flaws when he stubbornly refuses to heed McCullough's warning regarding the presence of the Sioux. "Next time, listen," advises Flint. The Major is very resourceful, but certainly not infallible.

"The Tobias Jones Story" (October 22, 1958) is one of the series' best episodes, arguably featuring Lou Costello's finest performance. His brilliant, touching turn as a drunk accused of murder was part of his dream of becoming a dramatic actor, and an impetus in his decision to end his 20-year collaboration with partner Bud Abbott.

During production, when forgetting his lines during a poignant exchange with Bond, Costello sent everyone rolling with laughter by maintaining a dramatic demeanor while improvising hilarious dialogue. Tobias' touching relationship with a young orphan girl, Midge (Beverly Washburn), reflected Lou's own values; and the scene in which he sits on horseback, unshaven, with a large noose around his neck, is a solemn parallel to the humorous near-lynching that he and Abbott experience in Universal's *The Wistful Widow of Wagon Gap* (1947). Though the role is primarily dramatic, Costello has an opportunity to display his genius for physical comedy, during a drunk scene sans dialogue as Tobias stumbles through the camp.

On the evening of October 28, 1958, Bond appeared in the *Wagon Train* episode "The Liam Fitzmorgan Story," guest starring Cliff Robertson and Audrey Dalton, on NBC. Over at rival network ABC, *The Christophers* installment "Bring Out Their Greatness" featured young actress Gigi Perreau supporting none other than Ward Bond. One of only two other television dramas in which he appeared after the debut of *Wagon Train*, "Greatness" achieved the extremely unlikely feat of airing on the same date as an episode of his own series.

Ford began shooting *The Horse Soldiers* on location during late October 1958. Prior to their departure for southern Louisiana, Duke and Pilar invited Ward and Mary Lou to a party celebrating the remodeling of their home, which recently had been damaged by fire. While Duke and his guests, also including James and Josephine Grant, were waiting in the screening room, Pilar became seriously ill. Wayne, unaware that his wife had been taking medications for depression and anxiety, was furious. Experiencing severe barbiturate withdrawal, she was examined by a family physician, who diagnosed an escalating drug addiction.

The Horse Soldiers shoot also was beset with problems, especially those created by the infuriating Jim Crow laws. While making a Civil War film, Pappy felt as if the actual conflict was still being fought.

After he found an African-American church to use in a scene involving the Confederates' unintentional shooting of Hannah Hunter's (Constance Towers) beloved servant, Lukey (Althea Gibson, the first black woman to win a Grand Slam tennis title), Ford was approached by a local segregationist enforcer. Screenwriter John Lee Mahin recalled:

> Jack ... hired the whole congregation as extras. Then the redneck supervisor of the local board of labor appeared and said, "Now, Mr. Ford, you can't pay these people more than two dollars a day." Jack said, "Oh, I think we can do a little better than that." "Oh, no, Mr. Ford. Two dollars a day. It's the law."[20]

Just as he had done for the Navajos of Monument Valley, Ford treated the blacks of Southern Louisiana with the same professional courtesy. Following further bigoted folderol from the supervisor, Pappy received permission to address the church congregation. He cordially explained:

> I'm paying you people regular Hollywood scale, and I'm serving lunch at twelve noon. It isn't the best food in the world, but it's the best we can do. We would consider it a great honor if you would join us.
>
> I don't want any of you to feel that because you're portraying slaves we are putting you down

The Horse Soldiers (United Artists, 1959; directed by John Ford). Neither John Wayne (left) nor William Holden (right) appears too enthusiastic about Ford's direction.

in any way. Everything in this picture actually happened, and you are playing your grandfathers and grandmothers. You are a part of history, and you should be very proud of it. We are glad to have you as part of our picture.[21]

Soon after their arrival in Alexandria, Louisiana, Duke hired two nurses and had Pilar flown to an Encino hospital. Deprived of Seconal, prescribed to alleviate anxiety and insomnia, she began hallucinating and attempted suicide by slashing her wrists.

On November 25, 1958, Ford wrapped the Louisiana location work, moving the company to Jefferson Military College in Natchez, Mississippi, where Jack Pennick had been drilling cadets in period marching techniques. The sequence featuring the brave young cadets, shot during the late afternoon of November 28, was performed beautifully, following Ford's "necessary" abusing of Anna Lee, who needed to become highly emotional while playing a mother who doesn't want her boy to fight the Yankees. No matter what methods Ford resorted to when directing Lee, she always referred to him as "such a lovely man."[22]

Wayne's character, Colonel John Marlowe, was based on Union Colonel Benjamin Grierson, who led a diversionary cavalry raid through Mississippi to Baton Rouge during the Vicksburg Campaign of April and May 1863. Duke, preoccupied with planning *The Alamo*, joined William Holden in drinking heavily throughout production. Ford became physically exhausted almost daily, but was pleased that his old pal Hoot Gibson, whom he hadn't directed since the early 1920s, had joined the cast. He also enjoyed spending time with Hank Worden, the reliable, modest character actor who had appeared in six of his previous films.

The ultimate crisis was a tragedy so traumatic that Ford "didn't care about the picture anymore."[23] Fred Kennedy, a veteran stuntman cast in a bit part, literally begged to double Holden during a horse fall, so he could buy Christmas presents for his family. Pappy finally relented, and when the out of shape Kennedy (who said nothing about a previous neck fracture) performed the fall, his head snapped back as he hit the ground. As directed, Constance Towers rushed over to embrace Kennedy but, realizing he was mortally injured, recoiled in horror. He was declared DOA at a hospital in Natchitoches.

Ford blamed himself for ending the life of his longtime colleague, moved the production back to Goldwyn Studios in Hollywood, and went through the motions until he was able to wrap *The Horse Soldiers*. Although producer Martin Rackin (who had wanted to cast Clark Gable as Colonel Marlowe) had assumed that the names of Ford, Wayne and Holden would insure a box-office success, he was disappointed when the net profits barely recovered the production cost.

The November 5, 1958, episode of *Wagon Train*, "The Doctor Willoughby Story," guest stars Jane Wyman as an independent woman whose practice of medicine is considered scandalous by everyone, including (initially) Major Adams. During a private discussion, he admits to her, "I don't really know much about women." When the Major forges a truce with a Native American tribe, based on saving the life of a chief shot by white trappers, their ancient code forbids females to act as medicine men. With Carol Willoughby's guidance, Adams successfully performs the operation, adding "surgeon" to his long list of occupational titles. Both Bond and Wyman are excellent, and another flaw in Adams' character is emphasized when she tells him, "You are as stubborn as you are strong."

On November 23, Bond guest starred on a special Thanksgiving episode of *The General Electric Theater* titled "A Turkey for the President." Interestingly, his costars on the show were Ronald Reagan and Nancy Davis.

The great Sessue Hayakawa guest stars in the *Wagon Train* episode "The Sakae Ito Story" (December 3, 1958). Following the death of a Japanese ambassador, his Samurai (Hayakawa) and servant (Robert Kino), having been attacked by a band of Comanche, are discovered on the Kansas prairie. At age 69, Hayakawa had been a screen actor for 44 years, recently earning an Oscar nomination in David Lean's *The Bridge on the River Kwai* (1957). His energetic performance as Sakae Ito is remarkable, and his honorable suicide via harakiri is troubling to Major Adams, but understandable to Chief Sharp Knife (Steven Ritch), who explains, "Samurai more like Comanche." One of the series' most interesting cultural explorations, "Sakae Ito," written by Gene L. Coon, offers another look at the growing complexity of Bond's characterization.

"The Tent City Story" (December 10, 1958) is too heavy-handed in its depiction of Adams' "negative" qualities. Throughout the episode, he flies off the handle with little provocation, yells loudly at McCullough (whom he "fires"), Hawks and Wooster, and engages in forced behavior just to advance a contrived story by Norman Jolley.

The "real" Major Adams returns in the 1958 Christmas episode, "The Mary Ellen Thomas Story," about a young troublemaker (Patty McCormack, star of *The Bad Seed* [1956]) who befriends Sally Mayhew (Jenny Hecht), a terminally ill girl. Realizing that Sally won't survive much longer, Adams arranges for an early holiday celebration, complete with a decorated tree, a visit from Chief Red Cloud (Mario Gallo), and Flint's leading the passengers in a performance of "Silent Night" (a rare opportunity for Robert Horton to sing on the show).

Written and directed by Allen H. Miner, "The Ella Lindstrom Story" (February 4, 1959), is one of the series' finest episodes. Bond and guest star Bette Davis share several poignant scenes in this tale that could have become maudlin with less-talented performers. Davis plays the determined, remarkably democratic mother of seven children who, believing she is going to have an eighth, learns that she has a terminal mass in her abdomen. When she and Charlie Wooster leave Dodge City before the doctor (Alex Gerry) can break the news, Major Adams becomes the reluctant messenger, and then helps the family find a new home for her youngest child, Bo (Bobby Buntrock), who cannot hear nor speak.

"The Last Man" (February 11, 1959) opens with McCullough, while seeking a pass through the mountains, being attacked by a hirsute maniac (Dan Duryea). "Well, I'll be," the Major responds when viewing the ruins of a camp inhabited by a wagon train party that had "disappeared" in severe winter weather. A diary, written by William Capeheart, is discovered; and when some of Adams' passengers read the contents, they assume the survivor, who cannot recall his identity, is the selfish "George Danton" described in the account.

Quite a counter to his John McIvers in *Johnny Guitar*, Bond's Major Adams is the voice of reason who stands up to the lynch mob always brewing under the travelers' veneer of Christian civility. "Vengeance is mine, sayeth the Lord," he quotes when the "eye for an eye" mentality nearly ends the life of the survivor, *William Capeheart*.

Closing the episode, McCullough hints at the depth of understanding he has developed with Adams. "You know, Major, when I first met you — to put it very frank, I didn't think you were any too bright," he claims. "But it's amazing what a couple of years with me has done for you."

"Well, boy, I just want you to know that I am *really* grateful to you," Adams replies with a grin. "*Wagons, Ho!*"

Unable to generate financial backing for his ambitious adaptation of *The White Company*, Ford and Michael Killanin attempted to resurrect "The Judge and His Hangman," which they proposed to shoot in Germany with Wayne and Spencer Tracy; but when Dudley Nichols tragically passed away from cancer a few months later, any chance of a screenplay died with him. (To date, no filmmaker has been able to bring *The White Company* to the screen. In 1995, Conan Doyle aficionado Nicholas Meyer proposed to direct his own adaptation of the massive novel, but was derailed by a death in his family. During a 2011 discussion involving the script that Ford had prepared, Meyer, whose narratively economical approach could have produced an exciting cinematic variant of Conan Doyle's complex prose, frankly said, "My script is better than Ford's."[24])

Ford also was devastated by the loss of his OSS patron and friend, Bill Donovan. The general had suffered from a lengthy series of strokes, and he mercifully passed away at Walter Reed Hospital in Washington, D.C., on February 8, 1959.

On March 27, longtime Stock Company member and Wayne buddy Grant Withers was found dead in North Hollywood. Decades of alcoholism, compounded by weight gain and back problems, had reduced his career to sporadic television roles. Following a guest spot on the series *The Texan*, he committed suicide with an overdose of barbiturates, leaving behind a note, apologizing to everyone he may have slighted during his 33 years in Hollywood.

In 1950, following a brief career as a character actor, Joseph Pevney began directing feature films in a variety of genres. He eventually moved into television production, and directed 24 *Wagon Train* episodes between 1959 and 1965. Prior to shooting his freshman effort, "The Vivian Carter Story" (March 11, 1959), he had become accustomed to ample budgets and adequate shooting schedules but, like several other feature directors who became involved with the series, he was advised by his location crew to forget about "extravagances" such as retakes.

Phyllis Thaxter, a pre–*Bonanza* Lorne Greene, and two Ford veterans, Jane Darwell and Patric Knowles, appear in "Vivian Carter." Unfortunately, the contrived, love-quartet teleplay by Lou and Peggy Shaw, and Kathleen Hite (a prolific writer of female-dominant scripts, including many for the *Gunsmoke* series), torpedoed this group of fine actors.

Directed by Jack Arnold, "The Matthew Lowry Story" (April 1, 1959), guest stars Richard Anderson as a maimed Union Civil War veteran currently following the pacifist tenets of the Quaker faith. English actress Cathleen Nesbitt, then 70, contributes a fine character turn as old and wise Rebecca Pruitt, grandmother of Marian (Dorothy Provine), a lovely young temptress. Lowry is constantly baited by "mad dog" Jed Otis (John Pickard), who accuses him of hiding behind "holier than thou hogwash." Weighed down by his previous "failure" as a medical corpsman, Lowry finds redemption after struggling to stem a breakout of cholera. A *Big Trail*-like scene depicting the passengers hoisting their wagons up a steep cliff consists primarily of stock footage.

In a paraphrase of Soviet Premier Nikita Khrushchev's infamous anti-colonialist rant in Moscow on November 18, 1956, Major Adams, after gunning down "murderous maniac" Jed Otis, shouts at his corpse, "I told you I'd *bury* you!" The irony of this statement, which Adams uses more than once, suggests that Bond may have written or improvised the line.

The "Kraut Comanche," Henry Brandon, returns in "The Swift Cloud Story" (April 8, 1959), which opens with a white-renegade incited (stock footage) attack on the wagon train. With this episode, Brandon was able to add the Chiricahua Apache tribe to the list of ethnic groups he had represented on the screen.

"Your tongue is reckless, White Man!" Fire Cloud sneers at Major Adams, as Bond slowly drawls rudimentary English at Brandon. "You speak with two tongues, White Man!" adds the Kraut Chiricahua.

The chief's disabled son, Swift Cloud (Rafael Campos), fails in his attempt to attack the train. Adams returns to the Chiricahua camp, offering to provide the boy with medical care, in exchange for allowing the train to continue unmolested. "*Ko-to-ma!*" orders Fire Cloud as his son limps toward the encircled wagons.

Fresh from *Rio Bravo*, Angie Dickinson guest stars in "The Clara Duncan Story" (April 22, 1959). Clyrio Soriano (Eduardo Ciannelli) and his future daughter-in-law, Clara, are searching for his son, Claude (Robert Clarke), an artist whose painting "Portrait of a Lynching" has unintentionally attracted newspaper coverage. Drawling halfwit specialist Robert Easton appears as Slim, and comic Roscoe Ates, who began his Western career in *Billy the Kid* (1930) and *Cimarron* (1931), plays the bartender. Unfortunately, Richard Collins and Warren Wilson's heavily contrived plot does the earnest Dickinson an injustice.

On May 6, 1959, Hollywood's Moulin Nightclub held the 11th Emmy Awards, hosted by Raymond Burr. Nominated for Best Western Series, *Wagon Train*, along with *Gunsmoke*, *Have Gun, Will Travel*, and *The Rifleman*, was bested by *Maverick*, starring James Garner.

That evening's episode, "The Kate Parker Story," brought Virginia Grey back to *Wagon Train*, this time as a woman who remains behind to look after Evie Finley (Ruta Lee), an injured passenger, and her husband, Chris (Robert Fuller), who is wanted for a crime he didn't commit. Bond becomes a bit Bogart-like when the Major tells him, "If you were wrong, and I still did nothing about it, I'd be an accessory after the fact, and I'm not sticking my chin out that far for anybody."

Chris tells his wife, "He likes us. We make him laugh. He's sentimental behind that gruff front."

"Chuck Wooster, Wagonmaster" (May 20, 1959), one of the most bizarre episodes, borders on fantasy. During a blizzard, important members of the train begin seemingly to vanish into thin air. The disappearance of Adams leaves Wooster in charge, until he also goes missing. What appears to be supernatural is anything but, when the Major and company (including Harry Carey, Jr., as Wilkins) are discovered held hostage by a white-slavery outfit who supply Canada's *Courteney* ring. The contrivances of this script are somewhat balanced by the absurdist humor. When the "little, bearded turncoat" arrives at the camp overseen by John Loring (Douglas Kennedy), who hires him as cook, Adams, his hands and feet bound, rages, "Nobody's told us anything. They just feed us once a day and keep us tied up in this *stinkin' shack*, that's all!"

The season concludes with several superb episodes, most notably "The Andrew Hale Story" (June 3, 1959). Bond delivers one of his best series efforts, but ironically is eclipsed by the actor who would succeed him as wagon master the following year. Playing a man who has lost his faith, John McIntire carefully builds his performance like a musician, creating a thespian crescendo to match his character's dramatic arc. In the climactic scene, McIntire is spellbinding, and a contender for *Wagon Train*'s finest contribution by a guest star.

Bond, however, regains his briefly stolen thunder in the final episode of the season, "The Jenny Tannen Story" (June 24, 1959). Directed by Christian Nyby (who was nominated for a DGA Award) from a script by the prolific Kathleen Hite, this entry co-stars Ann Blyth, who not only brilliantly plays *two* characters (mother and daughter), but also exercises her sublime singing voice in several poignant scenes.

When Phoebe, the abandoned daughter of former operatic diva Jenny Tannen, is seriously injured and temporarily blinded, Major Adams tenderly cares for the young woman as if she were *his* own child. Bond's ability to shift from the gentle, whispering cadences of a caring father figure to the gruff, growling taunts of the wagon master giving his subordinates holy hell is a fine example of his dramatic range.

After two successful seasons, Bond heard rumors that his pals, Frank McGrath and Terry Wilson, had received a raise in their salaries. Soon he was demanding more money from Howard Christie, who told him, "Ward, this is none of your business. I'm the producer and I'll determine who gets a raise and who doesn't."

Bond wouldn't relent, so Christie visited the wardrobe department, was outfitted in a costume resembling the star's, and walked up to him, threatening, "All right, if you want to be the producer, I'll be the wagon master."

Christie's son, John, recalled, "Bond broke up; and from then on, my father never had a problem being the producer or with Ward Bond being the wagon master."[25]

On September 30, 1959, the third season of *Wagon Train* opened with "The Stagecoach Story," in which McCullough aids a friend, Caleb Jamison (Clu Gulagar), whose stage line is in dire straits. Driving the coach carrying Adams, Wooster and Hawks from San Francisco to St. Louis, Flint and Caleb are horse-jacked by Mexican revolutionists led by Angela DeVarga (Debra Paget), who had fallen in love with McCullough while incognito.

"That'll be the day!" replies the Major after being told the group will aid in the Mexican people's support for Porfirio Diaz. Apparently, enough guns and ammunition are stashed aboard the stagecoach to establish the Porfiriato! Stealing across the border with the weaponry is a breeze, but the Apaches back in the States are another matter. McCullough, however, drives, hell bent for St. Louis, through a wall of fire, and only "Indians" get hurt.

This Jean Holloway–penned episode could have sunk into complete absurdity. Amazingly, the whole thing is held together by the believable performance of Debra Paget as the determined Latina leader, who loves Mexico more than McCullough. At one point, she delivers a politically charged speech, laced with Cold War rhetoric: "When tyranny threatens, or triumphs, anywhere, then freedom is threatened everywhere." Using the institution of the 35-year Diaz dictatorship as a platform for anti–Communism was certainly a peculiar idea, and may have helped put the smile on Bond's face in the closing scene.

"The Greenhorn Story" (October 7, 1959), featuring a masterful comic performance by guest star Mickey Rooney, is one of the most entertaining episodes of the series. Hailing from Pennsylvania, Rooney's Samuel T. Evans represents the Easterner who has "written about the West for years," but has "never been there." The details of preparing for the long journey are compellingly revealed, as Adams' rules on what to take (and, more importantly, what *not* to take) are either heeded or ignored. One of the funniest moments occurs during an early fight scene, in which Bond wages an unconvincing tussle with two bullies, but Rooney, equally convincing and amusing, decks a third man twice his size!

"You're a *radical*!" accuses Major Adams to the title character of "The C. L. Harding Story" (October 14, 1959). "You're so conservative, you're *obsolete*!" Ms. Harding (Claire Trevor) fires back, as if the two actors are playing themselves in this episode, written by Jean Holloway, whose scripts occasionally veer into near-fantastical territory. The fact that Adams keeps the wagon train idle long enough for the "woman newspaper man" to incite a suffragette movement and strike among all the women (and Wooster, who also joins) is difficult to believe.

The most entertaining moment may be the brief appearance of Johnny Cash as Frank Hoag, a newlywed, who tells the Major, "I'm willing to come out for women's rights." The sight of *Stagecoach*'s female lead, 20 years afterward, emotionally selling out C. L. Harding's convictions for Major Adams, whom she calls "a man so tall, so brave, he seemed to fill the universe," could have made Ford cringe.

Pappy, who had been tuning in to *Wagon Train* on Wednesday evenings, told Bond of his dissatisfaction with the teleplays, although several fine writers (Holloway, Gene L. Coon, Milton Krims, Allen H. Miner) were continuing to turn in high caliber material. Though Ford "was delighted with his friend's success," he was relentless with his criticism.[26]

Joseph McBride suggested that Ford, unable to get *The White Company* produced, regarded both *Wagon Train* and Wayne's forthcoming *Alamo* epic "with ill-conceived jealousy and resentment." Bond's rise to stardom in a production independent of the mighty Pappy was judged a "rebellious act" against his father figure: "[W]hen Ford's favorite whipping boy became a household name ... in *Wagon Train* ... modeled (without credit) on Ford's own *Wagon Master*— that was too much for the Old Man to handle gracefully."[27]

Following more badgering and name calling, Bond, the "dumb Irishman" and "big, ugly, stupid gorilla," finally challenged his abusive mentor: "Jack, if you know so much, why don't *you* write one?"[28]

The Old Man said he'd do just that; and, with this professional matter settled, he raised a far more troubling, personal concern. Observing Bond pushing himself to the limit by overseeing every aspect of his series, from story development, to cast and crew choices, to editing, Pappy inquired about his health: the epilepsy, high blood pressure, heavy drinking, chain smoking, and his prolonged drug use, described by Dan Ford as "taking amphetamines as if they were candy."

"I've never felt better in life," was always Ward's way of conciliating the Coach.[29]

Meanwhile, the third *Wagon Train* season rolled on. One of the best episodes, "The Elizabeth McQueeny Story" (October 28, 1959), written and directed by Allen H. Miner, brought Bette Davis back in a guest role, a "theatrical impresario" whose dancing girls cause an uproar among the train's "moral, married women" who quickly form a vigilante group ready to apply tar and feathers. Playing off the perfectly cast Davis, Bond ranges from comic pratfalls to serious discussions of societal values. Adams becomes one of the victims of spotted fever, and his three-day delirium posed a major acting challenge.

When the "plague" is staved off by McQueeny's girls, they give a celebratory dance for the men, with "Liz" shooting the moon at the Major. Adams, referring to the "citizen committee's" remaining prejudice against the young ladies, concludes, "I guess you can't expect people to change their thinking overnight."

Ed Wynn plays the title character in "The Cappy Darrin Story" (November 11, 1959), a lighthearted tale about an eccentric old man who, using nautical methods to navigate on the trail, wanders off and sinks his wagon while attempting to float across a river. As Cappy tells a sea story to his grandson, Tuck (Tommy Nolan), the episode incorporates an expressionistic fantasy sequence featuring Bond, McGrath and Wilson as pirates.

Another Jean Holloway quasi-fantasy, "The Jess Macabee Story" (November 25, 1959), presents Andy Devine and Glenda Farrell as a wacky married couple who haven't welcomed visitors to their isolated, verdant farm during their entire 20-year residence. Having appeared in several feature films with Farrell, Bond unfortunately wasn't able to be reunited with her in this Robert Horton installment.

Directed by Herschel Daugherty, "The Danny Benedict Story" (December 2, 1959) guest stars Brandon De Wilde as the troubled son of Colonel Daniel Morgan Benedict II (Onslow Stevens), the "finest officer" Adams served under during the Civil War. Ashamed of having punished the boy in front of his entire garrison, the Colonel has sunk into an alcoholic haze, but their relationship is redeemed by Adams' intercession. Danny had been flogged for desecrating the flag, but is inspired by the Major's wisdom to follow in his father's footsteps.

Of the 24 *Wagon Train* episodes written by the versatile Jean Holloway, "The St. Nicholas Story" (December 23, 1959) is one of her finest; and, in its remarkable balancing of a diversity of life experiences, a truly transcendent jewel from television's golden age. The juxtaposition of the passengers' cheerful singing of holiday carols with a thunderous attack by a Ute war party (superbly directed by Bretaigne Windust, including none of the familiar stock footage) resulting in the deaths of two beloved men, Papa Kling (Robert Emhardt) and John Reid (Ford favorite J. M. Kerrigan), is one powerful example of Holloway's use of dramatic, moving counterpoint throughout the episode.

Adams must maintain his position of leadership while adapting to each new crisis, serving as military strategist, counselor, surgeon, diplomat and, ultimately, Santa Claus. The climactic scene of the Major, dressed in his Saint Nick suit, first vividly telling the children about the multicultural celebration of Christmas, and then establishing peace with the Utes by clasping hands with the chief (Henry Brandon), is a masterpiece of its kind, featuring one of Bond's most beguiling performances.

The tension generated by real-life adversaries Bond and Brandon in an earlier confrontation scene, during which Adams and the chief negotiate with the lives of two innocent children, one white (Johnny Bangert) and one red (Edward Vargas), is palpable. Every element, including the necessary comic relief of Frank McGrath, is well integrated into the whole, with cinematographer Benjamin Kline and composer Lyn Murray (at one point including an "Indian" variation on "God Rest Ye Merry Gentlemen") providing just the right atmosphere.

As John Reid lies dying in the bed of his wagon, J. M. Kerrigan, in his near-melodic Irish tones, delivers the series' most sound summation of the moral fiber of Adams:

> You're a good man, Seth. I particularly wanted to tell you that. Maybe a little irascible, hard at times, but in times of adversity, a tower of strength. And another thing I always noted about you: Even when you were busy doing the big things, you've never lost sight of the little things — the little things that so often make the big things bearable.

Jean Holloway also wrote "The Lita Folidaire Story" (January 6, 1960), guest starring Diane Brewster as a beautiful young woman whom Bill Hawks discovers, dying after a brutal attack. When she passes away, Adams, who served with her husband, Jess Folidaire (Kent Smith), during the Civil War, vows to track down her killer. Aided by Hawks, the Major questions six individuals, whose recollections are depicted in a series of flashbacks, until proving that Jess, jealous of Lita's relationship with his brother, Clay (Richard Crane), flew into a murderous rage. The familiar love-hate triangle involving two brothers presents nothing new, but the multiple first-person narratives, good performances from Bond and Terry Wilson, and interesting supporting cast (Tom Drake, Evelyn Brent, Paul Birch and Jay Novello), make it an essential episode.

"The Benjamin Burns Story" (February 17, 1960) adds a macabre ambience to the series. Character actor supreme J. Carrol Naish plays an aging former scout who claims he can find the legendary "Shining Water" and save the people of the wagon train, who have hit two dry springs in a row. During the search, Burns is seriously injured after a fall. While most of the party returns to the train, McCullough and John Colter (James Franciscus) remain with the dying man in the blazing heat. Flint becomes delirious from a rattlesnake bite, and Colter, growing paranoid, smothers the old man. In a scene worthy of Val Lewton, as the two men discover Shining Water, the "dead" man, his hands emerging from beneath his cairn, "rises from the grave."

Naish's harrowing performance as Burns struggles back to the train is the high point of this superior episode, written by Gene L. Coon and director Virgil Vogel. When Flint is blamed for the murder, Colter confesses, but Burns denies having any knowledge of the incident. "When we kill a man, he stays killed," the old man tells McCullough. "You know, that's the trouble with this here younger generation. They can't do anything right."

Jean Holloway adapted Charles Dickens' *Great Expectations* for "The Tom Tuckett Story" (March 2, 1960), guest starring Robert Middleton as Nat Burikett, secret benefactor to the orphaned boy who aided him during his escape from Leavenworth in 1854. Disappointed that a "common criminal" is responsible for making him a gentleman, Tuckett (Ben Cooper) is confronted by Major Adams, who refers to Burikett as "a martyr."

Burikett tells Tuck that he was convicted of treason for warning the inhabitants of a Native American village about an impending massacre led by Major Anderson (Don Keefer), a martinet anxious to make a show of force. When the cavalry officers on Burikett's trail are waylaid by war parties from the Cheyenne, Comanche, Sioux, Kiowa and Ottawa tribes, he saves the army after parlaying with the chiefs.

Blackhawk (Frank DeKova), chief of the Ottawa, demands "the life of Burikett, a man of peace ... that we may know there is kindness in the white man, that we may know there is justice, too." An innovative take on Dickens, Holloway's script benefits from the outstanding performances of Middleton and DeKova, a New York–born, Shakespearean actor who often portrayed Native American and Latino characters in films and on television.

Unfortunately, Bond doesn't appear in two episodes featuring his *Maltese Falcon* costars. In "The Tracy Sadler Story" (March 9, 1960), the always entertaining, devilish Elisha Cook, Jr., arguably wears the filthiest hat in television history; while "The Alexander Portlass Story" (March 16, 1960) guest stars Peter Lorre (who was very ill during production) as a dying Aztec treasure hunter called "The Professor" by the "imbeciles" who work for him.

James Dunn contributes an unbilled cameo to "The Christine Elliot Story" (March 23, 1960), starring Phyllis Thaxter as a woman who seeks to fulfill her late father's dream of establishing a school for orphaned boys. The ever-icy Henry Daniell plays Mr. Morton W. Snipple, head of the St. Louis Institute for the Destitute and Homeless, who "tries to snare up eleven helpless little boys." Christine "kidnaps" the lads, and Major Adams (Bond at his most cranky) proves nearly as difficult, refusing to allow a dozen rascals to join his train. Snipple and Deputy Marshal Clancy (Harry Harvey) are finally foiled when Christine marries Philip Ayers (Donald Woods), a teacher traveling to his new position in California.

Virgil Vogel directed another script by Gene L. Coon, "The Joshua Gilliam Story" (March 30, 1960), bringing the great Dan Duryea back for his fourth appearance in the series. Gilliam, a teacher, found badly beaten at the bottom of a ditch, is aided and hired by Major Adams to instruct the children on the train. Possessing a mesmeric ability, Gilliam convinces his young students that Freda Halstadt (Irene Tedrow), the mother of Greta (Bethel Leslie), his intended meal ticket, is a witch. Ending in a ghost town, with Gilliam drowning in an underground cistern, this episode could have been part of Boris Karloff's *Thriller* series, which began airing on NBC in September 1960.

Two episodes, broadcast on April 27 and May 4, 1960, are devoted to Jean Holloway's ambitious "Trial for Murder," guest starring Henry Hull and Henry Daniell as opposing attorneys, while Bond added to the Major's expanding job description by becoming "The Judge" who must determine the fate of a man charged with homicide. The musical score, featuring a dirge-like arrangement of the *Wagon Train* theme played on a mournful cello, immediately sets the mood during the pre-credits sequence, as Charlie Wooster runs into the camp to inform Bill Hawks, "There's been a murder."

Adams initially serves as detective, "arresting" the drunken Brad Mason (Marshall Thompson) and locking him in the prison wagon, charged with the murder of Charles Ivers (Del Moore). Except for one 16-year-old girl, Eileen (Melinda Plowman), the passengers on the train quickly incite a lynch mob mentality. After the Major becomes foster father to Ivers' orphaned son, Davey (Dennis Rush), he tells Hawks, "Brad Mason's going to get a fair trial *by a jury*. Anybody that tries to lynch him is going to have to step over my dead body."

Bond is at his best as he explains the legal authority and responsibilities of the wagon master to Sir Alexander Drew (Daniell). As Professor Mark Applewhite, Hull uses his measured declamatory style to stand up to the formidable Daniell, while Bond provides an anchor of believability. Under the direction of Virgil Vogel, three diverse actors work well together, providing the dramatic core of one of the series' most powerful episodes.

In the shadow of a makeshift gallows, the travelers dress in their finest clothes and prepare food for a lavish party to celebrate the "hanging." Ironically, in an episode featuring Bond as an impartial, unprejudiced man of reason, young Eileen, observing the behavior of her fellow females, declares, "You're on a *witch hunt!*"

Adams and six others, including the attorneys, stand firm as the lynch mob approaches the prison wagon. (Seeing a relatively warm Henry Daniell playing a man on the side of law and order is a rare pleasure.) Forced to pistol whip Miller (Murvyn Vye), the Major commands the vigilantes, all of whom signed the wagon master's articles, to obey the law or "get out of here, and get out now!" Referring to the "dangerous troublemakers," Adams tells the Professor, "We'll be very lucky if we can control them through the trial."

"Tonight, sir," replies Applewhite, "has proven to me that *you can.*"

During the trial, the Professor exposes the unreliability and ineptitude of the witnesses called by Drew. Daniell is particularly effective during Drew's questioning of little Davey, calmly using the soothing tones of his mellifluous voice to comfort the silently grieving child. When Davey identifies Mason, he confesses to the murder, but Applewhite still believes in his innocence.

Drawing part one to a close, Adams (in a tight close-up) tells Drew, "This is a country of law, and the law must be honored, just as the rights of each man must be honored — and *defended* — if we're going to have any justice out here."

Part two opens as Applewhite, addressing the court, asks that, in light of new evidence, the trial be continued and Mason's confession, made under duress, be stricken from the record. Leslie Ivers (Dianne Foster), the victim's widow, has arrived to testify for the defense.

The Professor opens up a new line of testimony, implicating other passengers on the train who were involved with her husband in legal and political issues. Finally, Leslie reveals that she and Brad Mason had entered into a marriage that was annulled by her father, who then forced her to wed Charles Ivers, who actually was Mason's brother.

The second installment suffers from glaring plot contrivances, including the revelation that the real killer is Miller, kingpin of the lynch mob, but is saved by the fiery, incisive performance of Daniell. Bond gets the final speech, however, as the Major informs his passengers,

> Folks, the trial of Bradley Mason is over, but there was more on trial here than just a man. Justice itself was on trial — justice and the rights of free men. I'm proud that, wherever this wagon train is, there is no wilderness. Civilization has arrived.

The brief television career of Floyd Burton consisted of his writing four episodes for *Wagon Train*, two of which, broadcast on May 18 and 25, 1960, are among the finest of the third season. Tommy Nolan plays a disabled boy held back by an overprotective mother (Vivi Janiss) in "The Dick Jarvis Story," in which Joey Henshaw (Bobby Diamond), an abused orphan, flees from his wicked guardian, Sam Hulsey (Richard Reeves), to hide out in one of the Major's wagons.

Ordered to end his friendship with Adams, Dick becomes jealous of the Major's relationship with Joey, and sets in motion a series of near-tragic events culminating with his ability to walk again. Burton wrote some superb scenes for Bond, allowing him to develop further the compassion beneath Adams' gruff exterior. When Hulsey attempts to take Joey, whom he "bought and paid for" with $135, the Major replies,

> Nobody's bought and paid for in this country, *not any more.* That boy doesn't belong to you or anybody else, unless he wants to go with you.... We're not talking about my rights, we're talking about *his*.... Don't push your luck, Mister. You better get on that horse while you still can.

Burton next contributed "Dr. Swift Cloud," a sequel to the second season's "The Swift Cloud Story," guest starring Raphael Campos as the son of the Chiricahua chief Fire Cloud (Henry Brandon), who lies dying just as the young man returns from finishing medical school in San Francisco. After the wagon train is attacked by his people, Swift Cloud attempts to care for the wounded, but the prejudice of the mob prevents him from entering the camp. Following a recollection of his previous experiences with the boy, Adams tells him, "There's an awful lot of ignorance in this world ... and it's not all among your people."

Burton also wrote "The Charlene Brenton Story" (June 8, 1960), a farcical episode tailor made for inveterate scene stealer Frank McGrath. In the midst of some very Fordian "Irish" humor involving large quantities of whiskey and a prolonged bar fight (in which Pappy's pal Sean McClory plays a part), Wooster "steals" an orphaned baby he believes is going to be killed by the citizens of Apache Flatts, who mistakenly think her mother died from bubonic plague. By the time the "bewhiskered old nanny goat" and "old reprobate" manages to improvise a diaper from a flour sack and adapt a whiskey bottle and leather glove to deliver milk to the little girl, her grandfather (Raymond Bailey) arrives with a sheriff (Harry Harvey) in tow.

Bond deadpans the funniest line when the Major, stopping Charlie's wandering supply vehicle, asks the covertly diaper changing old coot how he can "drive from the *back* of a wagon." Ultimately, Wooster becomes so attached to the baby that he rides off, intending to raise her on his own. He even takes two shots at Adams before he is persuaded to turn her over to the grandfather. To honor Wooster's altruistic act, Jim Brenton names the child "Charlene."

Following a run of superior episodes, the third season ends disappointingly with "The Sam Livingston Story" (June 15, 1960), an unconvincing redemption tale, though featuring another good performance by Onslow Stevens; and "The Shadrack Bennington Story" (June 22, 1960), offering too little Bond and too much David Wayne, whose portrayal of an annoying medicine showman is reminiscent of W. C. Fields.

Following several visits to the *Wagon Train* set, where he discussed ideas with Bond, McGrath and Wilson, Ford pitched an original tale of his own involving General Ulysses S. Grant titled "The Colter Craven Story," which he directed (for a paltry $3,500), from a script co-written with Tony Paulson, during May 1960. Ford's episode was scheduled to air during the fourth season, which would begin on September 28, with "Wagons Ho!" an installment scripted by Jean Holloway, directed by Herschel Daugherty, and guest starring Mickey Rooney in a reprise of his comical Samuel T. Evans role from "The Greenhorn Story."

Wagon Train: "Wagons Ho!" (Revue–NBC Television, 1960; directed by Herschel Daugherty). **During production of this episode guest starring Mickey Rooney (second from left), Ward Bond was visited by Arkansas democrat Senator John Little McClellan (second from right), who inscribed and signed this 11 × 14 portrait for his "esteemed friend." Original still owned by Ward Bond.**

During production of "Wagons Ho!" Bond was visited by Arkansas Democrat John Little McClellan, who had served in the United States Senate since 1943 and as chairman of the Permanent Subcommittee on Investigations since 1955. He had participated in the Army-McCarthy hearings, during which he led a Democratic walkout to protest the extremist behavior of Joseph McCarthy.

In light of his Republican support for Richard Nixon, Bond's friendship with McClellan is interesting; but, during the Cold War, no politician in the United States could afford to be branded "soft on Communism." The senator's committee investigations of subversive activities undoubtedly attracted Ward. It is likely that McClellan, who made several television appearances, was in Hollywood shooting the two-part *Armstrong Circle* episode "Sound of Violence" when he met with Bond and Rooney on the *Wagon Train* set.

The senator's investigations eventually resulted in the famous McClellan Hearings, during which he led probes into organized crime, including the illegal Teamsters dealings of Jimmy Hoffa and the mob activities of Sam "Momo" Giancana. During this period, McClellan hired Robert F. Kennedy as chief counsel, vaulting him into the national spotlight.

13

El Shakespeare de San Antone:
"*Buenas Noches, Culo del Caballo*"

Wayne ... felt that the greatest service he could do his country was to make the story of the Alamo, a story that had mysteriously become his touchstone of all the essential American values.... The closest Wayne came to having a real religion, one for which he would sacrifice himself, was his devotion to the Alamo. — Gary Wills[1]

I remembered that the last time I'd seen Ward on the Wagon Train *set, he'd been drinking heavily and seemed very tired.* — Harry Carey, Jr.[2]

Ford was pleased to leave the depression of *The Horse Soldiers* behind when he flew to Honolulu in February 1959, intent on resting aboard the *Araner* and taking rejuvenating morning swims in the Ali Wai Yacht Harbor. An "abandonment" of filmmaking, however, could last only so long.

A few weeks later, he was visited by James Warner Bellah and Willis Goldbeck, who were writing a new script, "Captain Buffalo," hoping to produce it as, not only a new John Ford Western, but another cavalry picture and, this time, with a groundbreaking angle. The Ninth U.S. Cavalry, a regiment of "Buffalo Soldiers" who had fought some of the fiercest battles of the Indian Wars, was comprised entirely of African Americans, and the screenplay used their story as background for a stirring military courtroom drama about Braxton Rutledge, a liberated slave who had risen to the rank of first sergeant, only to be accused of brutally raping and murdering a white girl. The idea for the script had been inspired by a Frederic Remington painting of a troupe of black cavalrymen.

However, the ever-reactionary Bellah's approach to the material was typically pro–Empire and indelibly racist, so Ford diplomatically pointed out a number of "deformities" that could be removed by a course of "deft surgery."[3] Following a 10-day rewrite, Ford was temporarily placed on active USNR duty to make two "orientation films," *Taiwan — Island of Freedom* and *Korea — Battleground for Liberty*, for the "People to People" project, developed by the Department of Defense to provide a counter to current Communist propaganda decrying U.S. imperialism.

Bellah and Goldbeck's reworked "Captain Buffalo" script impressed Ford on two levels: the social, dealing with a positive depiction of blacks; and the commercial, a period film that also would solidly reflect the current climate in Tinsel Town. Pappy's thoughts were outwardly echoed by the suits at every studio, and he accepted the top offer, $100,000 for the screenplay and $300,000 for his direction, from Warner Bros. Goldbeck and Patrick Ford were signed to produce the picture for John Ford Productions.

Joseph McBride wrote:

> By this late stage in his career, Ford had achieved an elegant simplicity of style that some have mistaken for a perfunctory attitude toward his craft. If Ford now seemed less interested in beauty for its own sake, this was ... a result of his pruning away the inessentials to focus attention on the themes ... that most urgently concerned him. More and more obsessively, these revolved around conflicts over race, the most seemingly intractable problem festering within the American psyche.[4]

In 1866, the Ninth and Tenth U.S. Cavalry Regiments were created by recruiting freed slaves and black troops who had fought for the Union during the Civil War. The cavalrymen of the Tenth enthusiastically accepted the term "Buffalo Soldiers," a name apparently bestowed by Native Americans who likened the hair of blacks to that of their most sacred and vital animal. The men of the Ninth followed the lead of their brothers in the Tenth Regiment, led by Colonel Benjamin Grierson, whom Wayne had portrayed in *The Horse Soldiers*. McBride points out the paradoxical reality in Ford's depiction of these black soldiers:

> To Ford, the overriding issue is that, like the Irish in his cavalry films, African Americans are able to strive toward integration ... through loyal military service, a consideration outweighing the tragic irony that they prove their fitness for citizenship by killing Indians.[5]

For the title role of "Captain Buffalo," Ford cast the mighty Woodrow Wilson Woolwine Strode, a 44-year-old former UCLA decathlete, collegiate and professional football star, and professional wrestler. Standing 6'4", Strode had developed a powerful muscular physique that dwarfed all of Ford's previous beefcakes: Victor McLaglen, John Wayne and Ward Bond (in their early days), and even superman George O'Brien. Strode recalled:

> John Ford had a big fight with Warner Bros. because they wanted an established actor like Sidney Poitier or Harry Belafonte to play the title role. Ford said, "They aren't tough enough!" He didn't care that I didn't have a lot of acting experience. He wanted somebody who could portray the image of a fighting man. He didn't want an actor who needed a double. John Ford had power; he won his fight with the studio, and I got the part.[6]

No one else in the Los Angeles area (or anywhere else) looked quite like "Woody," the son of half–African American and half–Native American parents, his father of the Creek and Blackfoot tribes, and his mother of the Cherokee. His shaved head, high cheekbones and expressive, piercing eyes had brought a unique presence to the screen, ever since he began playing small roles two decades earlier. His life was made even more exotic when, in 1940, he wed Princess Luukialuana Kalaeloa, a descendant of Hawaii's last monarch, Queen Liliuokalani (1838–1917), who used "Luana Strode" as her married name. (Though the couple encountered no prejudice in Hawaii, they endured the typical racist abuse in Woody's homeland.)

Though Strode's film debut is often listed as a "tribal policeman" in Henry Hathaway's *Sundown* (1941), he actually appears as a sombrero-clad man (a black vaquero, one of the first cinematic bows to the actual African American cowboys of the Old West) in the saloon near the end of *Stagecoach*. Prior to Pappy's decision to cast him in his first prominent role, Woody had appeared in jungle potboilers (*African Treasure* [1952]), science-fiction adventures (*City Beneath the Sea* [1953], with Robert Ryan), Biblical epics (DeMille's *The Ten Commandments* [1956]), and war dramas (Lewis Milestone's *Pork Chop Hill* [1959] and Stanley Kubrick's *Spartacus* [1960]).

Sergeant Rutledge (Warner Bros., 1960; directed by John Ford). The defendant: First Sergeant Braxton Rutledge (Woody Strode, who succeeded Ward Bond as Ford's "best friend"); the witness: Mary Beecher (Constance Towers); and the attorney for the defense, Lieutenant Tom Cantrell (Jeffrey Hunter).

Ford moved into his offices at Warner Bros. during May 1959 and filmed "Captain Buffalo" (80 percent on the studio lot; 20 percent on location in Monument Valley) from mid–July to early September. At one point, the title was changed to "The Trial of Sergeant Rutledge," but finally shortened to *Sergeant Rutledge* for general release on May 28, 1960.

Ford had great respect for Strode, but treated him no differently when abuse was "required" to achieve the desired performance. Strode explained:

When we really got into shooting the picture, John Ford played every scene for me. He would stand in front of the camera and play my part; then I would step out there and try to do it exactly like he showed me. Sometimes I would be listening to him, but I wouldn't be looking at him.... He'd scream at me.... He'd stomp on my feet, slug me, throw rocks at me. One time he said, "Bend over, you son of a bitch!" and swatted me with the butt end of my rifle.[7]

Like he had done with Wayne and other "green" actors, Ford believed that he had to use extreme measures with Woody to spark the best results. When Ford unleashed the verbal torture, the gloves were off, and it could elicit far greater anger than a kick in the ass, as Strode admitted:

In one scene he really upset me. I was supposed to be spying on the Indians. I was sneaking through the bushes, he hollered, "Woody, you son of a bitch, quit niggering up my Goddamned scene!"

I had been tiptoeing, like I was scared. He wanted me to move with intelligence and cunning. Sergeant Rutledge wasn't a tiptoer; he was proud and dignified. And John Ford knew how to pull that out of me and put it up on the screen.[8]

On another occasion, just as he *claimed* he had done with Victor McLaglen a quarter-century earlier, the Old Man told Woody that, since he was not scheduled to work the next day, he should "enjoy himself," specifically at Pat Ford's, home, where he was handed a large old-fashioned glass full of booze. Strode claimed that "it was more like a beer mug." By the time darkness fell, he "ended up on Sunset Boulevard, whooping and hollering, up and down the street," before Pat tracked him down.

Strode described the next thing he could remember, following his alcoholic blackout:

The next morning I woke up in Mr. Ford's green room. That was like his sitting room, adjacent to his bedroom. As a matter of fact, I fell asleep on his bedspread. And ... in my courtroom close-up, you'll see the imprint of his bedspread on my face.

I woke up wondering, "Where the hell am I?" Then I realized, "Oh, God! What the hell am I doing in this house?" I was terribly hung over, still a little drunk.[9]

Pat drove Woody to Warner Bros., where Pappy arrived, immediately bawling him out for daring to drink the night before.

"I'm sorry. I've never done this before," Strode replied, as Ford sat, with his fists clenched, glaring and growling him into playing his most significant scene:

I took the stand. I felt like an exposed nerve and the Old Man was twisting the knife. He had me all pissed off, emotional, teetering right on the edge. I sat real stoic as the prosecuting attorney started to parade in front of me ... he said, "This Negro raped this little girl and killed her father"....[10]

Attorney Carleton Young's loud exclamations, asking Rutledge why he had returned, made Woody break out in goose bumps as he replied, "Because the Ninth Cavalry is my home and my self respect. If I deserted them, I wouldn't be nothin' but a swamp runnin' nigger. And I ain't that, I'm a *man*."

With tears running down his cheeks, Strode stood up and smashed the chair, prompting Ford to call for a break so he could help calm down his *actor*. Woody admitted:

And that was the truest moment I ever had on the screen.... That old man not only directed me, he split my personality. I almost had a nervous breakdown doing *Sergeant Rutledge*, but it helped me become an actor.

When we finished the picture, they had a special screening at Warner Bros. Mr. Ford invited me to go with him. Ward Bond, Spencer Tracy, John Wayne, Lewis Milestone, all his drinking buddies were there. Mr. Ford said to me, "Come on down front, Woody. I'm going to hold your hand."[11]

Warner Bros. also held screenings for several civil rights activists who expressed very positive views of the film, which didn't fare as well with critics or the general public. However, *Variety* singled out Strode for dominating the film, giving "an unusually versatile performance ... with many shadings of character." Thirty years later, Woody wrote:

> I stole the review, and of all the pictures I've made, I think I'm closest to *Sergeant Rutledge*, because of John Ford. He put me in the saddle.... We became the closest friends because I was honest, strong, and crude. I reminded him of an earlier time in history, a time he was in love with. I became one of the few men that could call John Ford Papa.[12]

While the film was still in production, "Hammerin' Hank" Aaron visited Ford on the set. Pappy, who had been spending more leisure time using his Dodgers season tickets and watching baseball games on television, was visibly moved to meet one of the finest athletes of all time. (At a later meeting of the two "living legends," Aaron told Ford that he had seen *Sergeant Rutledge* six times.)

In 1966, when Ford was interviewed for the French Communist newspaper *L'Humanite*, he forcefully responded to an accusation that his films contained negative racist elements:

> The people who say such things are crazy. I am a Northerner. I hate segregation.... Me, a racist? My best friends are black. Woody Strode, and a caretaker [Ford's majordomo, William Ramsey] who has worked for me for thirty years.

When the Hollywood suits originally mulled over the problems a pro-"nigger" film would cause in the South, Ford explained:

> I got angry and told them they could at least have the decency to say "Negro" or "colored man," because most of those "niggers" were worth better than they. When I landed at Omaha Beach there were scores of black bodies lying in the sand. Then I realized that it was impossible not to consider them full-fledged American citizens.[13]

Scholar Charles Ramirez Berg, in his 2001 essay on Ford's portrayals of ethnicity in his Westerns, wrote:

> Remembering that he was the son of Irish immigrants ... one begins to appreciate the fact that his films emanate from the position of that oppressed ethnic minority and that his stories typically focused on marginalized outcasts. This made his cinema far more different from most Hollywood films, which centered on the WASP Mainstream as a matter of course and looked uncritically at assimilation. Thus, counterbalancing Ford's stereotyping is a richly textured multicultural vision that is nuanced in comparison with the broad strokes that characterized much of classical Hollywood's ethnic representation.[14]

Yes, Ford, who said he was "half genius, half Irish," was actually half a man of his times, and half a man *ahead* of his time. However, those who *still* think his later films dealing with African Americans and Native Americans were made to *redress* elements in his earlier films, don't realize that John Ford, "who never apologized for anything in his life," throughout his entire career, got away with whatever he *could* along the way. In an era when Paul Robeson had to move to Britain to star, above the title, in films *about* black characters, all Hollywood was allowed were those black performers who *had* to play a stereotype so they could survive. Stepin Fetchit, with the help of Ford and Will Rogers, craftily began to subvert it; so, at times, did Hattie McDaniel.

Olympic decathlete Rafer Johnson, who plays Corporal Crump in *Sergeant Rutledge*, often visited Ford at home, chatting for hours about sports, films, and other subjects. He recalled:

We never spoke specifically about race, but in terms of how he handled that film, and us, John Ford might have been a little ahead of his time in terms of looking at the issue, and the problems that existed between society and people of color. That film, and the Rutledge character, showed what Ford really was — a man who respected our people and was concerned about what was going on in our country.[15]

In 1948, shortly after Ford and Merian Cooper had resurrected Argosy, Wayne pitched his idea of a patriotic film about the Alamo, and Pappy soon had his son Pat working on a script. While in Texas to scout possible locations for *3 Godfathers*, Duke and his Coach visited the remains of the mission in San Antonio, where they formally announced their intentions to make the film; but Wayne's increasingly extravagant ideas to produce a monumental epic did not sit well with Ford or Cooper.

Armed with $7.5 million, the largest budget ever lavished on a Hollywood film, and a distribution deal with United Artists, Wayne finally began work on *The Alamo* during the summer of 1959. No expense was spared to create the sets for Duke's dream project, an all–American blockbuster that would inform the younger generation on the nature of true heroism, specifically that of an arch-conservative, anti–Communist hero. At the Brackettville, Texas, ranch of J. T. "Happy" Shahan, Wayne hired 400 workers to construct an exact replica of the San Antonio mission, using only actual adobe and Spanish tiles.

On September 9, 1959, Wayne, playing Davy Crockett, began shooting with Richard

The Alamo (United Artists, 1960; directed by John Wayne). Jim Bowie (Richard Widmark), Davy Crockett (John Wayne) and William Travis (Laurence Harvey) in Duke's "dream project."

Widmark as Jim Bowie, Laurence Harvey as Colonel Travis, "special guest star" Richard Boone as Sam Houston, and a cast including Frankie Avalon, Patrick Wayne, Linda Cristal, Joan O' Brien, Chill Wills, Joseph Calleia, Ford Stock Company perennials Ken Curtis, Hank Worden, Olive Carey and Chuck Roberson, and thousands of extras. The casting of Avalon resulted from financial pressures to attract teenage filmgoers who otherwise had no interest in Duke's American Dream.

Ford had serious doubts that Wayne could pull off producing, directing and acting in such a sprawling project. Although hoping Duke would succeed, he did resent his former whipping boy having the power to create such an ambitious picture without him.

On September 19, just 10 days after Wayne began shooting, Ford could no longer keep his distance. His claim of "taking a vacation" to Brackettville was a pathetic attempt to camouflage his spy mission, much as he had "secretly" observed Bond working on *Wagon Train*. Duke's temper already had begun to boil when Pappy made his first appearance. In no time, the Old Man was lifting his eye patch to look over Wayne's shoulder, slumping down into the director's chair, and even making comments to the crew that Duke was only professing to know how to make a picture.

Sitting next to his veteran collaborator, cinematographer William Clothier, Ford "suggested" camera setups. At one point, he glared at Wayne and Richard Widmark, who both were satisfied with a good take, and barked, "Do it again!"

"*Why*, Coach?" asked Duke.

"Because it was *no damn good*!" Pappy informed him.

Although this was understandably annoying to Wayne, he was largely responsible for the presence of Ford, whose Stock Company (cast, stunt performers and crew) had been substantially raided by its most famous member. Conspicuously absent was Bond, who was too inundated with *Wagon Train*, combined with his frequent schmoozing and carousing on the weekends. To make even a cameo appearance in *The Alamo* would have required a considerable increase in his borderline suicidal intake of Christmas Trees.

When he could stand it no longer, Wayne asked Denver Pyle, "What am I gonna do with the Old Man? I gotta get rid of him."

Gary Wills observed:

> Wayne should have told Ford, the minute he showed up, that he could not have him anywhere around. That is what Ford would have done to any intruder on his set. But Wayne was not ruthless. The screen disciplinarian ... was, off-screen, too nice a guy to be the boss in a situation calling for tough treatment of others. Wayne had always taken Ford's orders submissively, off the set as well as on.[16]

But Duke, considering his mentor's current depressive state, had no intention of making matters worse. Following some brainstorming, Wayne and Clothier, who had brought six state of the art Todd-AO cameras to Texas, decided to create a second unit, responsible for shooting battle and other action sequences directed by Ford. Pappy eventually spent 47 days on location during four trips to Brackettville, and the "second unit" cost producer Michael Wayne much sleep (and his father $250,000). Myths persist that none of Ford's footage is included in the finished film, but the full-length director's cut includes many "second-unit" scenes, including several featuring the principal actors.

Frankie Avalon recalled that Ford was responsible for about "ten to fifteen percent" of the direction. "He was there a lot of the time," especially when Wayne had difficulty directing scenes in which he also played Crockett. Avalon, who "enjoyed making the film," praised Wayne for taking the time to confer with his actors about what he expected from their characterizations: "Ford didn't talk to us much at all. Wayne would discuss the scenes, and he always knew what he wanted. He was very sensitive."[17]

By the time Duke was nearing the end of the *Alamo* shoot, the budget had ballooned to over $12 million. Even after the Yale Foundation contributed $1.5 million to the $8 million previously invested by United Artists and a group of Texas businessmen, he had to sell his land in Mexico, mortgage his homes, borrow money against his yacht and cars, and forego his own salary.

Wayne finally called a wrap on December 15, 1959. Additional retakes were shot at Samuel Goldwyn Studios during August 1960. This massive, expensive project had stretched Duke to the breaking point, but his superstar status eventually attracted enough filmgoers to recover the cost. But his longtime patriotic dream ultimately became both a personal and professional albatross. He not only had to sell his percentage of the film to Universal to recoup his large personal investment, but his future prospects as a director in Hollywood were slim to none.

Of Pappy's view of *The Alamo*, Dan Ford wrote:

John was becoming more liberal ... actively following the presidential aspirations of ... John F. Kennedy.... Wayne, on the other hand, seemed to be growing more and more conservative.... Wayne couldn't talk about anything ... without politics coming into it. While John thought that *The Alamo* was a good story ... he thought Wayne's approach too self-consciously political.[18]

The detractors of *The Alamo* have persistently pointed to the Duke's frequent "preaching" as being intolerable. Setting aside the heavyweight issues involving politics, truth and myth, just consider the *performance* of John Wayne in these sermonizing scenes. His acting (which is quite convincing) sprang from such a font of sincerity that Wayne couldn't help but wax in a manner that reaches near–Shakespearean proportions. (After all, he had performed, however greenly, some of the Bard's material while in the drama club at Glendale Union High!)

Within the "world of the film," to his legendary interpretation of the character of Crockett, there is no line between truth and myth, because Wayne really believed what he was saying. (When Ford later cited *The Alamo* as one of his favorite films, he was, not kicking, but *kissing* Duke's behind.)

As Joseph McBride explained about critics who hail the comedy in Shakespeare but dismiss Ford's Falstaffian interludes as "low Irish," a similar argument can be made about drama. Many learned individuals live with the mistaken impression that all of Shakespeare (whoever he actually was) is "great art." On the contrary, as revealed by noted Shakespearean scholar John McCabe, the Bard was, first and foremost, "a box-office man."[19] He wrote for his audience, who needed comic moments to provide respite from those headman's-axe soliloquies. And "Old Will" didn't *create* "comic relief," both to undermine the pretense and just *to be funny*; it can be traced at least as far back as Ancient Greece.

Most of Shakespeare's "history" is at least as spurious as that of Ford, Wayne and anyone else who has made movies. His demonizing characterization of Richard III, for example, has led to centuries of Bard-inspired balderdash about that particular English monarch, for the simple reason that the plays involving Plantagenet rulers were based on histories written by Tudor historians, propagandists of the conquering Powers that Were.

So why did the Duke act like he was the Tennessee-Texas-Western-patriotic-conservative-hero version of Laurence Olivier? Because both played in grand costume epics based primarily on myths, and their scripts featured soliloquies, ergo "preaching." Arguably, the sincere effort put forth by Wayne as the storybook Crockett in *The Alamo* is just as convincing as Olivier's monstrous turn as the hunchbacked villain in his 1955 adaptation of Shakespeare's very unsubtle *Richard III* (c.1591).

Perhaps the film would work better if it had been titled, "John Wayne's *The Alamo*"; but, then, Wayne thought that "his" *Alamo* and the real event were one and the same. Such is the self-reinforcing, hard-dying power of myth, and Duke had been schooled by the master: his Coach, to whom he would defer to the point of *not* kicking the old, beloved bastard off the set of his own lumbering, self-proclaimed "masterpiece."

The Alamo isn't a masterpiece, but it's not quite the 1960 Western equivalent of Shakespeare's demonized hunchback opus, either. Unfortunately, the ridiculous, politically oriented publicity campaign waged by Russell Birdwell prior to the film's release, made even worse by Chill Wills' self-aggrandizing, embarrassing crusade to win the Best Supporting Actor Academy Award, led to controversy that unduly tainted the film (which has rarely been released in the vastly superior, original director's cut). Wayne actually believed that the film's failure to win six of its seven Oscar nominations (only Gordon Sawyer and Fred Hynes won, for Best Sound) was due to the overriding influence of Hollywood Reds.

Gary Wills speculated on Duke's attempt to "become" a new version of Pappy:

> Happy Shahan was, like Monument Valley's Harry Goulding, a self-promoting promoter of his area. Perhaps Wayne, trying to establish his own identity as a director, saw the possibility of becoming the John Ford of this godforsaken corner of Texas, returning to make films with a stamp of place created by the director's vision. If so, the dream faded fast. The difficulties of building the Alamo in Brackettville jinxed the place in Wayne's mind. Others would make Westerns there, using some of the facilities created by Wayne. But Wayne never went back.[20]

One of those "others" who made a Western at Brackettville was none other than Pappy, who returned shortly after Wayne wrapped *The Alamo*.

In May 1960, while Duke was still editing *The Alamo*, he began a two-hour commute to Point Mugu, California, to star as gold prospector Sam McCord in 20th Century–Fox's adventure farce *North to Alaska*, directed by Henry Hathaway from an unfinished script by John Lee Mahin and Martin Rackin (plus a host of lesser writers), and featuring Stewart Granger, Capucine, and teen idol Fabian (as "Billy Pratt," the actual boyhood name of Boris Karloff!). Hathaway shot the film through mid–August, improvising most of the scenes. The thinly plotted tale of claim jumpers during the 1900 Alaska gold rush is filled out with slapstick comedy, including fistfights, a cataclysmic barroom brawl, a lumberjack pole-climbing contest, plentiful ass kicking, and a monumental wrestling match in the middle of a muddy street (during which Wayne's balding head, sans toupee, can be glimpsed when his hat is knocked off). All the testosterone-fueled mayhem (McCord says, "Women — I've never met one yet that was half as reliable as a horse") resulted in a major box-office hit for Fox (and a prototype for many future mayhem-ridden Wayne films).

Duke immediately moved on to *The Comancheros* (1961), which Michael Curtiz began shooting at Moab in June 1960. Regardless that the film takes place in the forests and swamps between Galveston and New Orleans, Texas Ranger Jake Cutter (Wayne) and gambler Paul Regret (Stuart Whitman) cross "400 miles" of scrub and sandstone desert while heading toward southern Louisiana. Bill Clothier was behind the camera, Cliff Lyons served as second-unit director, and Duke's family (Patrick and Aissa) and friends (Bruce Cabot, Bob Steele and John Dierkes) are in the cast. However, Curtiz's poor health made it necessary for Wayne to direct much of the film, without allowing the once-formidable, now frail and forgetful filmmaker, to realize it. (Curtiz passed away five months after the film's November 1, 1961, premiere.)

In June 1960, producer Sam Shpetner asked Ford if he would direct an adaptation of the Will Cook novel *Comanche Captives*, a violent Western retreading some of the same ground as *The Searchers*, a project he intended to decline. However, the promise of James Stewart and Richard Widmark portraying the two antagonistic men who recapture a group of white children from a Native American band (again led by the "Kraut Comanche," Henry Brandon, playing real-life chief Quanah Parker), plus $225,000 and 25-percent of the net, quickly led him to reconsider.

A satisfying paycheck does not ensure a well-directed film, however; and Ford, who began shooting in mid–October, gave a lesser damn for *Two Rode Together* than he had for *The Horse Soldiers*. But professional dissatisfaction was not the only reason Ford made another mediocre Western. As the location shoot dragged on, a devastating personal tragedy wiped out what little enthusiasm may have remained.

"Wagons Ho!" had opened the new season of *Wagon Train* on September 28. Prior to Ford's "Colter Craven Story," scheduled to air on November 23, the fourth year of Bond's starring enterprise began to feature episodes differing in structure and, to its detriment, believability. Other than "The Allison Justis Story," an October 19 installment featuring Robert Horton, guest starring Gloria DeHaven, and including Edward G. Robinson, Jr., in a supporting role, weeks one through eight were marred by absurd concepts, embarrassing stereotypes, and even a few bad performances. (Lee Marvin's "Mexican" bandit in "The Jose Morales Story" vies with Ken Curtis' "half–Seminole" chief in "The Horace Best Story" as the worst.)

Broadcast on November 2, "Princess of a Lost Tribe," in which Flint McCullough discovers an Aztec civilization, founded by survivors of Cortez and concealed in the American West for four centuries, is the most ludicrous episode made during Bond's years on the series. As "Montezuma IX," Raymond Massey, attired in a costume resembling a reject from Cecil B. DeMille's *The Ten Commandments* (1956), is only one of many preposterous elements in this Jean Holloway–scripted fantasy prefiguring *The Wild Wild West* series (1965–1969). But the love-smitten McCullough's dismantling of an autocratic society ruled by ancient myths is a direct forerunner of Captain Kirk's (William Shatner) identical behavior (violating Star Fleet's "Prime Directive") in a plethora of episodes (about civilizations ruled by computers, legends or misinterpreted mumbo jumbo) that would populate the *Star Trek* series (1966–1969). (In this respect, Gene Roddenberry's show truly did become a "*Wagon Train* to the stars.")

Woody Strode, with "a Sitting Bull–type wig" pulled onto his bald head, "looked just like a squaw."

"Wait a minute, let's try a Mohawk," said Ford, screen testing him for the role of the warrior "Stone Calf" in *Two Rode Together*. Just as he had grown a half-inch of hair for *Sergeant Rutledge* so he would look more African American, Woody needed an aboriginal style for the new film to appear more Native American. Strode explained:

> Ford got into a whole new argument with [the studio] over using a black actor as the Indian.... But, in costume, I looked so much like an Indian that the studio bosses couldn't argue.... Ford had to build my respect with the Indians.... When the Navajos arrived at the fort, [he] told me, "Woody, the Indians are here and I don't want you drinking with them...." He gave me a big lecture.[21]

Around 11 P.M., Woody was relaxing on a small twin bed, studying his scenes in the script, when he heard a knock at the door. Two Navajos, decked out in plaid Western shirts, denim jeans, black cowboy hats adorned with eagle feathers, and moccasins, were standing outside. "The Chief wants to see you," one of them announced.

"Many Mules was lying in bed with a quart of whiskey in his hand," recalled Strode. As he entered the gray-haired, leather-faced, 80-year-old Navajo leader's quarters, an interpreter genially commanded, "Have a drink, Woody." As Strode later admitted, it was an offer he couldn't refuse:

> I knew John Ford would kick my ass for drinking with Many Mules, but here was the Chief of the Navajo Nation, like the President of the United States, saying, "Have a drink!" So I drank. Pretty soon I was wound-up and my curiosity got the better of me. I said, "You know, I've never seen a war dance. Could you show me how that's done?"

Out on the parade grounds, inside a four-foot adobe wall encircling a well, the half Creek-Blackfoot-Cherokee gathered with a group of Navajos, including Many Mules and his drummer. A dilapidated old buckboard used as a tourist attraction was soon lighting the midnight sky with flames, as Woody, boots off and pants rolled up, joined his new friends in the dance, following their steps, gestures and whoops, totally inspired by "booze and the spirit of the ancestors." He later described the result of this alcohol enhanced "traditional ritual":

> The spell was broken when John Ford came running out in his pajamas. "What the hell is going on!" The prop guys showed up with extinguishers and put the fire out. The Indians fell out of their trance. Many Mules gave the order, and the party broke up. John Ford was so mad he just stared at me, didn't say a word. Just stared for about 30 seconds and then just left me standing there.[22]

A few hours later, Strode attempted to eat breakfast with Stewart, Widmark and Ford, who responded by segregating him to another table.

"Papa, what could I do?" asked the disgraced Woody. "When the Chief tells you to drink, you drink." Strode surmised:

> I think Ford secretly enjoyed the dance. And I think it was that part of me that appealed to John Ford. But he couldn't have me upstage him in front of the entire crew. As much as he liked to be one of the guys, he ruled his set with an iron fist.... And he didn't achieve that level of success by letting other people call the shots.[23]

Harry Carey, Jr., working on his first Ford film in five years, roomed with Ken Curtis during the *Two Rode Together* shoot. One evening, just as the two old pals began to pour a drink, Pappy paid an unexpected visit. Carey recalled:

> I was thinking, "Jesus, the Old Man's right across the goddamned hall! He's going to be barging in here every 10 minutes!" ... He was really a very lonely man. He wanted very much to be "one of the boys," but to do that, he would have to give up that mystique and authority he possessed. Ford, the great motivator, the film genius, the man who enabled you to do things you never thought yourself capable of doing ... was there in our room, trying his best to be a "regular guy."[24]

On another occasion, Carey was summoned by Ford, who requested that Richard Widmark be brought to his room. When Dobe roused the no-nonsense actor, Widmark responded to the speechless messenger with a straight shot:

> I know exactly what the old bastard wants! Wayne has called him, and he wants me to go to that goddamned premiere of *The Alamo* in San Antonio! Well, screw it! I'm not going to that goddamned terrible movie. It was enough grief working on it![25]

An hour later, Widmark had undergone a remarkable change of heart. He'd go to the premiere, he told Ford, *if* Carey and Curtis went with him. Dobe remembered the event as "boring as hell, and we returned to Brackettville as soon as we could."[26]

The Old Man also went to see *Sergeant Rutledge* while it was playing at a local theater, and he asked Woody along. At the end of the film, some Texas cowboys walked over to them and said, "Boy, we didn't resent one minute of that. It was beautiful, beautiful!"[27]

Ford had been shooting *Two Rode Together* at Brackettville for three weeks, and expected to wrap the location work after a few additional days. Dobe Carey, whose problems with alcohol had reached a highly depressive stage, was looking forward to returning to Los Angeles. During the afternoon of November 5, 1960, he was sipping coffee in the dining hall, just gazing out the window, when he spotted Wingate Smith chatting with Ken Curtis, who had begun to cry.

Carey abandoned his coffee and ran outside to see what was troubling his friend. Curtis looked up and said, "Dobe, Ward's gone."

The Dallas Cowboys were playing another home game, and Bond was in the midst of another weekend of brown-nosing and hell-raising, courtesy of his oil tycoon buddy, Clint Murchison. He and Mary Lou had checked into the Town House Motor Hotel on Harry Hines Boulevard, and Ward was preparing to take a shower before heading out to the football stadium. While on the toilet, he suffered a massive heart attack, fell headlong against the door, and Mary Lou, unable to open it, ran for help. By the time maintenance and emergency personnel arrived, and the door had been removed, Bond was pronounced dead.

"Does the Old Man know?" Carey asked Curtis, who managed to reply, "No, we have to go tell him now."

Ford was at the location, taking a break, sitting alone away from the action, among the sagebrush and tumbleweeds, when the three men arrived. Curtis had decided that he should break the terrible news to his father-in-law.

Pappy appeared to sense that something was amiss, even before Ken said a word. "What's happened now?" he asked.

Approaching Ford was rarely an easy or enjoyable prospect; but, this time, all Curtis needed to do was choke out two words: "Ward's dead."

The Old Man sat, silent and motionless, as his three family members stood by. "Son of a bitch!" he shouted before falling quiet again.

Others at the location had caught wind of the trouble and began to wander over toward them. Following another pregnant pause, Ford exclaimed, "The doctor told him! The doctor told him over and over again! For months and months, he's been warned." As usual, no one could see his eyes hidden behind the dark glasses. Raising his head toward Curtis, he asked rhetorically, "Heart attack, wasn't it?"

"Yes, sir, it was, Pappy," replied Ken. "I guess it was a big one, too."

Henry Brandon and Andy Devine were two of the first cast members to approach Ford. Looking up at Devine, he announced, "You're gonna have to be my horse's ass now. Ward just died."[28]

Carey, who recalled that the Old Man had referred to Devine as his new "favorite shit," wrote:

> Of course, that was meant to be a compliment to Andy. He knew full well how much Jack loved Ward. He was his most reliable actor. He never let him down. Ward could drive Jack mad with his flamboyant mannerisms and ego, but he knew he would miss Ward terribly as a friend.[29]

The best behavioral portrait of Bond was, not surprisingly, provided by the remarkable insight and tolerance of Dobe Carey, the one veteran eyewitness who survived all the anarchy and mayhem of John Ford's world to tell the tale:

After the McCarthy fiasco, it was said that Ward had trouble getting work. Then he got ... *Wagon Train* ... Ward loved every minute of it. He loved the public's adulation of him as Major Adams.... Ward drank everything that was offered him, chain smoked, and got very little sleep on [his] junkets. Then he would return home, physically worn out, to start a new episode of the show. He fell in with a crowd in Dallas that just loved him to death, literally ... they ... would rest up, but Ward would go back to Hollywood to shoot his series.... No human body can take that kind of punishment, not even a well one. So the Grim Reaper called Ward Bond's name, and Uncle Jack lost his dear friend and favorite actor.[30]

Robert Horton was with Ward the evening before he left on the final jaunt to Dallas:

I dropped by his dressing room. I had issues with a script that I wanted to share with him. After we talked, I said, "Ward, I know we've had our differences, but we both agree this is a terrible script." He placed his hand on my shoulder and said, "Bobby" (he had never called me Bobby before), "we don't have any differences." I smiled, said good night, walked out, and that was the last time I saw him.[31]

Dobe Carey also offered his insider's analysis of the extreme political attitudes for which Bond had become publicly infamous:

Ward liked the power of fame. He loved people, no matter what their beliefs, even though he hurt some with his McCarthyism. He didn't know better. I think Duke did, but not Ward. If looking for commies made him important, then he embraced the cause.... Many of the ones listed as so-called "commies" were friends of mine, and I knew that they were, as I was, good, caring Americans who wanted only the best for their country.[32]

Following Ford's orders, Wingate Smith booked a charter flight to Dallas for the Old Man, Ken and Dobe, and rounded up $1,000 cash for their expenses. Ford's plans were to comfort Ward's widow, make all the necessary arrangements to transport his body back to Los Angeles, where his son-in-law and "honorary nephew," also considered family by "Maisie," would help organize the funeral, to take place at the Field Photo Home. Carey acknowledged:

We flew in a great little plane.... Uncle Jack sat up front with the pilot.... He was anything but solemn.... He talked cheerfully for most of the trip. It was as though he was saying, "Ward! You big dumb bastard. You had to go and do it, didn't you? You're in heaven now, with Harry and all the rest. Damned if I'm going to cry, Ward, but I'll miss you like hell."[33]

At the Dallas airport, the trio were picked up by Gordon MacLendon, a radio station mogul and occasional movie producer, who whisked them off to a private club for dinner and a river of cocktails before dropping them at the home of Bob Thompson, a wealthy pal of Clint Murchison, where "Maisie" was awaiting their arrival. Carey admitted, "I am very ashamed to say that I stayed smashed from that day until we brought Ward's body back to L.A."[34]

In the chapel at the Field Photo Farm, where the flags were lowered to half-mast, Bond's body lie in state in a flag-draped casket as mourners filed past a uniformed honor guard. Having paid his respects to his irreplaceable companion, Ford returned to Brackettville to finish shooting *Two Rode Together*.

On November 7, Mary Ford represented her absent husband at the funeral, during which the casket was carried onto the parade ground by pallbearers Ken Curtis, Frank McGrath, Terry Wilson, and Wayne, who also delivered the heartfelt eulogy. Curtis sang the Bob Nolan song "And He Was There," Carey performed "The Mormon Hymn" ("Come, Come Ye Saints"), and the Sons of the Pioneers harmonized "The Song of the Wagon Master."

Albert J. MacDonald, executive director of the Motion Picture Alliance, couldn't resist marking Bond's passing with a propaganda statement issued to all members of the organization:

> Ward was a giant among Americans, a magnificent patriot who died fighting for his country. The United States is the worse for his going. It was no coincidence that Ward Bond was the third President of MPA to die in office, of a heart attack.... The front rank of the anti–Communist struggle is no place for those unwilling to give everything to it.[35]

Ward had expected to enjoy one last Dallas weekend combining raging parties among rich oil men, real-estate magnates and football stars with his hard-fought Republican campaign for Richard Milhous Nixon. On Tuesday, November 8, 1960, ironically just one day after Bond's funeral, Democratic candidate John Fitzgerald Kennedy was elected, by a microscopic margin, President of the United States.

Prior to the election, Ford had been asked to join Celebrities for Nixon. He replied, "I am a lifelong and fervent Democrat — so frankly I prefer not to be on your committee."[36] On November 9, Wayne sent the following telegram to JFK's brother-in-law, Peter Lawford, in Hyannis Port:

> Please congratulate the President-Elect for me. Now that the battle of the parties is over here is an American who will do anything he can to be helpful. For the next two months I will be in Tanganyika, Africa. Good luck.
>
> John Wayne[37]

Duke was on board the boat from which Bond's ashes were scattered into the channel between San Pedro and Catalina, the location of so many of the good times they had shared with Pappy. A joker to the last, Ward had included a provision in his will ordering a burial at sea, stating, "I loved lobster all my life, and I want to return the favor."

After wrapping *Two Rode Together* at the Columbia ranch, a profoundly depressed Ford flew to Honolulu, where he spent three weeks aboard the *Araner*, self-medicating the wounds wrought by the sudden death of his beloved whipping boy and the irritating experience of consigning two fine actors to an inferior Western. He shut himself up in the yacht, saw no one, and rejected food in favor of a continuous flow of booze. Appearing in a frightful state, he finally was admitted to Queen's Hospital in Honolulu after being diagnosed with severe alcoholic dehydration.

Shirley Jones, miscast as the young female lead in *Two Rode Together*, said, "I thought it was pretty bad.... Jimmy Stewart went at it like he was doing a masterpiece. Without him and Widmark, it ... *would* have been an all time turkey."[38]

Aired on November 23, 1960, "The Colver Craven Story" had been shot in a record six days; but, more impressive than this singular feat was Ford's creation of 72 minutes of usable footage. A two-part episode was considered, but Howard Christie made the decision to edit it down into a well-paced, visually striking 48-minute show that is Fordian in every respect.

To support the regular cast, Pappy gathered a passel of Stock Company regulars, including Willis Bouchey, John Carradine, Ken Curtis, Chuck Hayward, Anna Lee, Cliff Lyons, Mae Marsh, Jack Pennick, Chuck Roberson, Hank Worden, Carleton Young, and even John Wayne, who (billed as "Michael Morris") makes a brief, shadowy appearance as General William Tecumseh Sherman. Assistant director James H. Brown recalled, "Unless you knew it was John Wayne, you couldn't recognize him. But even in silhouette and slumped in his saddle, he was an imposing figure with a tremendous presence. It was something to see."[39]

The centerpiece of the episode is an 11-minute flashback, set in 1854, when Grant (Paul Birch) returns to his hometown of Galena, Illinois, after being dismissed from the U.S. Army for being intoxicated on duty. This set piece is a recollection by Adams for Dr. Colter Craven (Carleton Young), a former Civil War surgeon reduced to alcoholism after experiencing the horrors of the Battle of Shiloh.

The quality of every aspect of Pappy's long-planned "biographical film" about Grant shows that he seriously lavished as much care and attention on this television show as he did on his feature films. Adams' story reveals that Grant, scorned by his father (Willis Bouchey), also instantly fell victim to the reactionary town grapevine. Joseph McBride wrote:

> Throughout this elliptical passage, Ford conveys emotion with the utmost economy, and nowhere more beautifully than in a long shot of Grant's wife and children waiting on a shadowy street corner as he alights from a steamboat.... Ford gets in a jibe at Bond's McCarthy-era rumor mongering. Tired of hearing what "folks say" about Grant, Adams disgustedly tells a pair of busybodies, "You can't always believe what 'folks say.'"[40]

Grant eventually joins the Union Army at the outbreak of the Civil War, and meets up with Adams following the ghastly carnage of Shiloh on April 7, 1862, designated by the Major as "one of the worst days in American history." Adams uses Grant's steadfast refusal to give up fighting in the face of potential annihilation as an inspirational message for Craven, who is making another attempt to triumph over John Barleycorn.

Wayne appears, enigmatically under-lit, in long shot, during the Shiloh scene, the filming of which sparked an argument between Ford and Bond, who wanted to include a close-up of Duke, clearly to emphasize that his buddy was a guest star. Pappy refused, and created the stunning image aptly described by the assistant director.

Wayne and his wife watched the episode in their living room on the evening of November 23. Following the broadcast, Duke turned to Pilar and said, "There will never be another Ward Bond. I remember telling him, a hell of a long time ago, that he was too damn ugly to be a movie star. But I was wrong, Pilar. He was beautiful where it counted — inside."[41] Very unlike the screen's John Wayne, Marion Morrison began to weep uncontrollably.

Following Ward's death, Mary St. John observed a prolonged melancholia in the Duke: "I had never seen him so preoccupied, so subdued, so quiet, so depressed. He lost fifteen pounds over the next two weeks because he didn't want to eat. It was as if someone had cut out his heart."[42]

St. John also revealed that Wayne had planned to include a cameo in Howard Hawks' *Hatari!* (1962), depicting Bond's capture of a rhinoceros. Just to please his pal, Ward was preparing to take a week off from *Wagon Train* to fly to Tanganyika. Duke already had discussed the shooting of the scene with cinematographer Russell Harlan, who was supposed to shoot enough footage to compose a shot juxtaposing the bums of Bond and the rhino. Alas, this touching "tribute" to Ward (and Pappy) was not to be.

Howard Christie made the decision not to write Major Adams out of the *Wagon Train* series. After completing "Colter Craven," Bond had acted in enough footage to be included in five more episodes, which were interspersed with 10 others prior to the introduction of a new wagon master. Veteran character actor John McIntire, who had given a spellbinding guest performance in "The Andrew Hale Story" and was working with Ford on *Two Rode Together* when Bond died, was cast as Christopher Hale.

Christie's initial pitch was to "promote" Flint McCullough into the top spot, but Robert Horton explained that the job would not appeal to his character:

I thought it should be played by an older man ... part of Flint McCullough's appeal was that he accepted responsibility when he chose to. He had never gotten into a situation where he was tied down. He was independent and very much a loner.[43]

Horton did agree to star in four episodes that had been written for Bond, but hearing Major Adams' dialogue spoken by McCullough created many awkward and unconvincing moments. In particular, Flint's behavior in "The Prairie Story" (featuring Beulah Bondi in a fine guest performance) was completely out of character, as Horton explained:

The story involved a woman being dragged off by the Indians. By the time it was cut and edited, it looked as if I stood by and made no effort to prevent it. Now with an older man in that situation, his physical limitations would prevent him from doing anything. Or with Ward in the role, with his knowledge and maturity, he'd say, "There's nothing to be done" and you'd believe it. But when Flint stood by in the prime of his life and did nothing, it invalidated his image.[44]

Horton turned down a substantial new contract after the 1961-62 season, citing the absence of Bond as one of several reasons he decided to leave television for musical theater:

Ward's character was so well-established and the relationship of Major Adams and Flint McCullough so worthwhile that we could make just about anything work, even when there wasn't much of a story to tell.... I liked television and was grateful for the success it afforded me. At the same time, I felt tired, restless and unchallenged.[45]

Terry Wilson experienced similar characterization problems when he was given the reins in "The Sam Elder Story," another episode written for Bond, resulting in Bill Hawks' brief transformation into Major Adams, standing up to the obligatory hot-headed reactionary (Walter Coy) each time he harasses a fellow passenger (Everett Sloane). (Cinematographer Walter Strenge earned an Emmy nomination for his work on this installment.)

Wilson also pulled off quite a character turn in Bond's penultimate episode, "Weight of Command," in which Hawks is forced to challenge a dangerous decision made by the Major, who actually hits him in the face during an argument. Interestingly, Bond's complex, genuinely moving performance, filmed so close to his death, is one of the most powerful he ever gave.

"Weight of Command" also introduced former UCLA athlete and MGM contract player Denny Miller as Duke Shannon, a young scout hired by Adams to assist McCullough. After playing the title role in *Tarzan the Ape Man* (1959), Miller had appeared in several television Westerns, including *Have Gun, Will Travel*, *Laramie*, *The Rifleman* and *The Deputy* (Hank Fonda's first stab at a series, which ran from 1959 to 1961). Bond was so impressed with Miller's naturalistic, affable characterization that he asked Howard Christie to write Shannon into future episodes. Following Ward's death, Miller became a *Wagon Train* regular from 1961 through 1964. (Regardless of his superiority in the beefcake department, Revue insisted that he use a more "manly" moniker: "Denny Scott Miller" eventually was shortened to "Scott Miller.")

Bond's final episode, "The Beth Pearson Story," was broadcast on February 22, 1961. Virginia Grey plays a look-alike of Adams' lost love, Ranie Webster, in this fantastical tale, in which the Major *almost* leaves his job to get married. In the closing scene, a close-up of Ward shouting, "Wagons Ho!" is the last time Adams appears in the series, and his subsequent absence (like that of McCullough, following Horton's departure) is never explained.

Director Virgil Vogel and the editing department adequately cobbled together unused scenes of Bond, generic sequences of the wagon train, and reworked shots from earlier shows, but the use of another actor to perform some of Adams' narration and dialogue is readily apparent (the voice is flat and gravelly, possessing none of Bond's dynamic range nor enunciation). In a myriad of ways, for good, bad and otherwise, there was only one "Judge." Another fine actor might succeed him, but the slender John McIntire would never fill Ward Bond's britches.

When Ward's rather depressing swansong aired, Wayne was in Africa with Howard Hawks, shooting *Hatari!* On February 4, Duke, in a move that would have irritated his late friend, had sent a telegram directly to JFK at the White House:

> Congratulations Mr. President. It was thrilling reading your inaugural speech here in Tanganyika. It made us even prouder we are Americans. Regards.
> John Wayne[46]

Following the travails of *The Horse Soldiers* and *Two Rode Together* (the glories of *Sergeant Rutledge* notwithstanding), it was time for Ford to take another serious stab at a great Western. Always believing that "a good story" is the genesis for a potentially successful motion picture, he paid $7,500 for the rights to the short story "The Man Who Shot Liberty Valance" by Western historian and novelist Dorothy M. Johnson, which had been published in a 1949 issue of *Cosmopolitan* magazine. Three of Johnson's stories already had been filmed: "A Man Called Horse" and "The Bije Wilcox Story" for *Wagon Train* in 1958; and the novel *The Hanging Tree*, starring Gary Cooper and directed by Delmer Daves in 1959.

In March 1961, Ford summoned Bellah and Goldbeck to write the screenplay, which he then shopped to Paramount, where Duke had just signed a major star contract. Though he presented an impressive package including Wayne and James Stewart (pointing out that the film would team the two box-office giants for the first time), Paramount waffled for six months before giving Ford an affirmative answer.

In the meantime, Pappy raised more than $1.5 million (half the proposed budget) through John Ford Productions, while simultaneously directing (for $50,000) the Civil War segment (basically a more brutal version of his Shiloh sequence in "Colver Craven") for *How the West Was Won* (1963), again featuring Duke as General Sherman, with support from Henry Morgan as General Grant. Ford shared the directing credit for this sprawling epic shot in Cinerama (which he hated) with Henry Hathaway and George Marshall.

The official deal for *Liberty Valance* guaranteed Ford $150,000 plus 25-percent of the net profits; Wayne $750,000 plus 7.5-percent of the gross receipts; and Stewart $300,000 plus 7.5-percent of the gross and half ownership of the film after 12 years (Paramount and Ford would split the other half). A coin was flipped to determine the star billing: Wayne lost, so a compromise was struck, whereby Stewart's name appeared first on all the publicity materials, while Duke was given the top spot in the film. (Later Paramount determined that *not* printing Wayne's name first on the posters and other advertising cost them substantially at the box office.)

Ford had negotiated a plum deal on his $7,500 payment to Johnson, now a University of Montana professor of journalism, who had crafted a fascinating tale. Ransom Stoddard, a "greenhorn" Easterner, forges a political career founded on a myth that he saved the Western town of Shinbone by gunning down the iniquitous outlaw Liberty Valance, when the actual killing had been done by a local rancher, Bert Barricune.

Liberty Valance was to be made in color, but Ford changed his mind two weeks prior to production. Working again with cinematographer William Clothier, he chose to shoot in black and white, primarily on studio soundstages, a "back to basics" approach (with expressionistic elements harking back to *Pilgrimage* and *The Informer*) that would focus on well-written characters. He believed that a majestic locale like Monument Valley, filmed in blazing Technicolor, would prove a distraction (particularly during the crucial shootout sequence).

While his choice of shooting in monochrome on the Paramount stages and back lot led critics to believe he was "lazy" and working "on the cheap," Ford instead was making solid artistic and aesthetic statements. The majority of the film is a flashback recollection by Ransom Stoddard including "a dream within a dream" told by the now-deceased Tom Doniphon (Wayne) that reveals the truth about the Liberty Valance killing. Arguably, Ford's choice of shooting in black and white may be the most brilliant use of the format since color became the prominent medium in film production.

As early as 1971, the astute Robin Wood noted the obvious difference in tone between the flashback and the framing story, particularly with regard to the performances:

> The main body of the film has something of the nature of the morality play, the characters conceived more in terms of their functions rather than in terms of naturalistic characterization.... Before one accuses Edmond O'Brien, Lee Marvin or Andy Devine of overplaying or crudity ... [this] element ... is above all what distinguishes the main body of the film from the framework, where this quality is totally absent.[47]

As Ford so wisely reminded Peter Bogdanovich and many others, "Black and white is *real photography*." He proved it with *Liberty Valance*. Bill Clothier said:

> He really was a genius. He'd listen, but if you were smart you'd spend a lot of time listening to him. He knew more about photography than any man who ever worked in the movies. He'd force me into situations where I'd have to sit up and take notice.[48]

From the first frame to the last, *Liberty Valance* benefits from the claustrophobic atmosphere. This film was the first new project Ford had developed since the death of Ward Bond, who hadn't lived long enough to see the last work he and his mentor had made together. Unable to force himself to attend Bond's funeral, Pappy had returned to Brackettville to slop his way through the final shots for the inferior *Two Rode Together*. Now he was carefully making a serious Western that opens with a funeral, that of the long-forgotten Tom Doniphon.

Even before the film begins, John Wayne *is dead* and there are only three people who care enough to pay their respects to Doniphon: the woman who once loved him; her husband, the now-blowhard politician who rose to prominence on a lie that destroyed the dead man's life; and an equally forgotten, old black man mourning beside the pine-box coffin.

Excluding *Sergeant Rutledge* (which is a mixture of genres), *Liberty Valance* would become the first great Ford Western without Ward Bond in more than a decade. And, though he couldn't have known it at the time, it also was his last Western with John Wayne. The Judge was actually dead, so the Coach thought fit to depict the death of the Duke, in a film that, while exposing the mythology of the Frontier, also signaled the death of the traditional Western itself.

Building on Johnson's story, Ford created two additional characters adding greater social and political resonance: Dutton Peabody (Edmond O'Brien), the drunken, Shakespeare-quoting newspaper editor who risks his life for the First Amendment; and Pompey (Woody Strode), Doniphon's African American protector and friend, whose performance in the schoolroom scene involving the Constitution and Ford's hero Abraham Lincoln is one of the most genuinely significant and moving moments in all the director's work.

Shooting began on September 5, 1961, with a supporting cast including more Ford

The Man Who Shot Liberty Valance (Paramount, 1962; directed by John Ford). "I'm not in the habit of eatin' my steak off the floor": Reese (Lee Van Cleef, left) observes as Liberty Valance (Lee Marvin), after tripping "the new waitress," Ransom Stoddard (James Stewart), squares off against Tom Doniphon (John Wayne).

favorites (Andy Devine, Vera Miles, Jeanette Nolan, John Qualen and Carleton Young), plus a new "discovery," Lee Marvin, whom Ford had seen with Wayne in *The Comancheros*, whose Liberty Valance is one of the most evil bastards ever to menace the screen. Marvin enjoyed playing the role so much that it became his personal favorite for the rest of his life.[49]

The blatantly Freudian scene in which Liberty Valance furiously whips Peabody with his silver, phallic cat o' nine tails, while his equally psychotic, but far less violent, henchman, Floyd (Strother Martin), observes with near-orgasmic glee, is one of Ford's most daring elements in this very "adult" Western.

Another change Ford made to Johnson's story was crucial: Stoddard's startling confession that Doniphon, *not* he, is actually "The Man Who Shot Liberty Valance." It is at this point that Maxwell Scott (Carleton Young), the current editor of the *Shinbone Star*, takes his notes documenting the Senator's revelation, rips them in half, tosses them into a wood-burning stove, and utters one of the most unforgettable and profound lines of dialogue in the Ford canon: "The is the West, sir. When the legend becomes fact, print the legend."

When Wayne first read the script, he didn't understand the character of Tom Doniphon. He complained that Pappy had "Jimmy Stewart for the shit-kicker hero. He had Edmond O'Brien for the quick-witted humor. Add Lee Marvin for a flamboyant heavy, and shit,

I've got to walk through the goddamn picture."[50] When he was informed that Doniphon possessed great ambiguity, Duke raged, "Screw ambiguity. Perversion and corruption masquerade as ambiguity. I don't like ambiguity. I don't trust ambiguity."[51]

Ford went to great lengths to persuade Duke to play the role; but, after the cameras began to roll, he became extra-brutal to his friend, commenting on several occasions, in front of the entire company, how inferior the failed football player and military slacker was to Woody Strode, who not only was a trailblazing gridiron star, but had served with great distinction during World War II. Strode, who had no part of the needling, was just happy to be there:

> [H]e kept me working. I made three pictures in a row for John Ford without working for anybody else in between. By the time I got to *The Man Who Shot Liberty Valance*, I was up to $1,500 a week.... I didn't have much dialogue, but since I was John Wayne's right-hand man I was in almost every scene with him. That's the only time I ever worked with John. We were never very close. He was a great guy and I needed John, but as far as John Ford was concerned, I didn't need anyone but him. Papa was very jealous of his relationship, so he put a wedge between us.[52]

The filming of the scene in which Pompey helps the drunken Doniphon stagger to a buckboard, from which the half-crazed inebriate furiously whips the horses as his caretaker climbs into the back, set off a scuffle that could have jeopardized the production. Wayne was unable to control the frightened animals; and when Woody, kneeling behind him, reached up to help with the reins, Duke threw a punch that missed its mark, only to shove the startled Strode aside. Finally, the horses came to a halt and Duke fell out of the wagon. Woody recalled, "I jumped down, and was ready to kick his ass. Ford raced over, 'Woody, don't hurt him! We need him!'"

Pappy shut down production for two hours to let Strode "cool off." The next setups involved Pompey's rescue of "Mister Tom" after Doniphon, intending to roast himself alive, torches his half-built ranch house. Wayne, bitching about having to run into a burning set, asked for his double; but Ford, reminding him that Strode, an "old man" (actually, at 47, Duke's junior by more than seven years), was ready and set to go. That's all it took to send Wayne (and his ego) racing into the flames.[53]

At one point, Ford told Duke that he was considering editing out the crucial scene in which Doniphon admits to Stoddard the truth about the killing of Valance. Of course, to Pappy, this threat was only a cruel joke, while Wayne took it quite seriously. "Jack, that's my main scene. How can you cut that out?" he asked.[54]

On another occasion, Duke, having witnessed Ford treating Stewart with unparalleled consideration throughout the shoot, prompted a situation that finally put his amiable costar "in the barrel." In 1969, Stewart, in his uniquely rambling manner, described his initiation by Ford (which also involved Strode):

> Duke Wayne has been at the bottom of the list, "in the barrel," more than anybody else, which is sort of remarkable, because they love each other. They're like father and son.
>
> In *Liberty Valance* ... the picture was more than halfway finished, and Duke came up to me and said, "How come, that you've gone through this whole thing, and you've never been at the bottom of the list? What is it? Have you been red-applin' the Old Man? What's the idea?"
>
> I said, "I don't know," and I didn't know ... and it went around the company, "Well, Stewart, he's always right up there."
>
> Well, the day before the picture finished, we had a funeral scene, Duke's funeral. And Woody Strode, who played the part of the wonderful Negro friend of Duke's, who was at the funeral ... was dressed in blue overalls, and blue work shirt, and boots. And, for some reason, he does this quite often, but I think this is part of the tension, the part of Ford.... He came up to me before the scene and he said to me, "What do you think of Woody's costume?"

Now ... what possessed me to say what I did, I'll never know. It just came out, and I said, "Well, it looks a little 'Uncle Remus-y,' doesn't it?" And he froze, then walked away. Then he said, "Blow a whistle ... everybody, would you please gather around?" And he said to me, "Would you come over here?"

And, with the whole company around, he said, "Ladies and gentlemen, we have an actor ... here who objects to the costume on Woody Strode. He says that it's 'too Uncle Remus-y.' Now I don't know if this is a prejudice on Mr. Stewart's part. I don't know if he's anti–Negro. I don't know what it is, but I just wanted to point this out to the whole company."

I wanted to shoot myself. I wanted to crawl into a mouse hole ... and I looked at Duke Wayne, and he was beaming like a cat that had just eaten the mouse.

Well, Ford said, "That's all, and everybody's dismissed." And Duke came over and said, "Well, welcome to the club. I'm glad you made it. I *really am*."[55]

Of Stewart and Wayne's characters, Peter Bogdanovich observed:

The movie basically says that the intellectual, the man of law, cannot succeed unless backed by force. And Ford had seen that ... Ford was a Navy man who was in the midst of World War II. He saw the horrors of that war at very close range, and you couldn't argue with Hitler and Mussolini, and win by law. You had to kill them.

So the pacifist, or law-minded intellectual approach, that Jimmy Stewart represents, doesn't work. And when he succeeds, and the wilderness is tamed, there's a yearning for the wilderness that's gone — so the ironies of that movie are staggering.[56]

Joseph McBride's aim was never more dead-on than in his assessment of *Liberty Valance*:

[I]f Ford was behind his time in most superficial ways, he was ahead of the public consciousness in more important respects. With its profoundly skeptical reexamination of American history and mythology, a prophetic quality in anticipating the public's loss of faith in government, and an acknowledgment of the growing brutality in American life and the Western genre, *The Man Who Shot Liberty Valance* now clearly stands out as the most important American film of the 1960s....

For Ford ... *Liberty Valance* represents the true closing of the frontier and that of the film genre he helped create.... Caught up in the tragic rush of history, his characters ... make choices that seem wrong in retrospect but at the time seem almost inevitable.... The wilderness may have become a garden, but it has become poisoned at its heart.[57]

Scott Eyman noted:

In ... *Liberty Valance*, the only true agent of power is time itself, and it does terrible things — the gap between the firmly idealistic Stoddard and the bloviating windbag he becomes is heartbreaking.... *Liberty Valance* deftly, shrewdly, shows the ragged process by which stories become legends, and legends become history.[58]

James Stewart commented that the film "has a tragic sadness about it that always appeals to me ... the human frailty idea. Not to lay it on, but to let it shine through as this sort of inevitable thing."[59]

For the past half-century, many viewers, critics and historians have been utterly confused by "When the legend becomes fact, print the legend," assuming that Ford's own belief matched that of the on-screen newspaper editor, Maxwell Scott. McBride explained, "Unlike Scott, who presumes that the public is better served by being fooled, Ford ruthlessly exposes the myth-making apparatus that underlies much of history and much of the director's own work in the Western genre."[60]

Bogdanovich said of *Fort Apache* and *Liberty Valance*:

Ford has just told you the truth, in two films, vividly showing that Henry Fonda was desperately wrong, and that Jimmy Stewart didn't kill Liberty Valance. So he's printed the truth, *not* the legend. And that's the point of the films: irony, that history is not always necessarily correct.[61]

After Ford wrapped the film, he received a letter from Edmond O'Brien, whose career, both on stage, including major Shakespearean roles, and in major films, having made a brilliant debut in William Dieterle's *The Hunchback of Notre Dame* (1939), was remarkable. He told Pappy, "In all the years, I have never enjoyed an acting experience so much."[62]

Considering all the greatness of *The Man Who Shot Liberty Valance*, including fine performances by the entire cast, there is a missing element that arguably could have made this masterpiece even better. As Andrew Sarris wrote, "[Andy] Devine, Ford's broad-beamed Falstaff, must stand extra duty for the late Ward Bond and Victor McLaglen. Ford, the strategist of retreats and last stands, has outlived the regulars of his grand army."[63]

During the summer of 1961, Duke loaned the battered cowboy hat he had worn in *Rio Bravo* to one of his biggest fans, Sammy Davis, Jr., who was appearing with his "Rat Pack" colleagues, Frank Sinatra, Dean Martin, Peter Lawford and Joey Bishop, in *Sergeants 3* (1962), a comedy remake of the classic adventure film *Gunga Din* (1939), in which Victor McLaglen had costarred with Cary Grant and Douglas Fairbanks, Jr. Directed by John Sturges, *Sergeants 3* was photographed by Ford's frequent collaborator, Winton Hoch, who shot much of the film on location near Kanab, Utah.

While performing at the Prince of Wales Theatre in London on August 29, 1961, Davis sent the hat back to Wayne, accompanied by a letter of gratitude:

Dear Duke,
"Sergeants Three" is now finished and I must, very reluctantly, return your hat. It is a little hard to express with words my appreciation for your kindness but I think you know a little of how I feel. Any success I may have in the picture will be mainly due to your generosity....
If I can ever do anything for you, a benefit for your favorite charity, a walk-on in one of your films, lend you my tuxedo, etc., you know you can count on me.... When I return from England, I hope we can get together so that I may be able to thank you personally.
In the meantime, give our regards to your wife and family.
Most sincerely,
Sammy Davis, Jr.[64]

On December 20, 1961, Paul Newman sent Duke a lengthy, serious letter regarding the arms race and the possibility of nuclear annihilation. After recommending that Wayne read the book *On Thermonuclear Warfare* by Herman Kahn, a military strategist and advisor to the U.S. Strategic Air Command whom he recently had visited, Newman closed his missive with a tongue-in-cheek paragraph:

I am not quite sure when Joanne and I will be coming back to the Coast but I would like to get in touch. Maybe we can "have at it" over a bottle of Jack Daniels. With our combined brain power, there is no reason why we can't set up a benevolent monarchy and then just arbitrarily bomb out the entire area of Russia, except of course that area which is responsible for caviar.
Most sincerely,
Paul[65]

Ford followed *Liberty Valance* with another television production, "Flashing Spikes," to open the second season of the hour-long *Alcoa Premiere* series on October 4, 1962. Like his earlier "Rookie of the Year" episode for *Screen Director's Playhouse*, "Spikes" also deals with a disgraced baseball player (James Stewart), but this time one who has been victimized by a lying witness "namin' names" about suspected bribe takers. Ford again worked in a cameo appearance for Duke (here billed as Michael Morrison), who appears briefly as a Marine sergeant umpiring a game in Korea. Other Stock Company regulars include Patrick Wayne, Tige Andrews, Carleton Young and Willis Bouchey.

Joseph McBride noted:

> Ford's reworking of the ostracization theme of "Rookie of the Year" makes it clear that while both these programs are ostensibly about baseball, their subject is the Hollywood blacklist.... But by approaching the subject obliquely and being several years too late with his public display of moral indignation, Ford made little impact with "Flashing Spikes."[66]

Dobe Carey also plays a supporting role in "Flashing Spikes." Just prior to getting the assignment, he received a call from Ford, who had been giving some thought to the decades of hell-raising that increasingly had spun out of control in recent years, most obviously indicated by the passing of Bond, who literally had overworked and partied himself to death. Carey explained:

> I would always be a kid in the mind of John Ford ... over the phone, he had gone into an elaborate discourse on the past and present drinking habits of the Ford and Carey families, claiming in a most warm and charming way that the whole bunch were alcoholics. And that, last but not least, so was Himself and yours truly. Then, after I said I was in total agreement, he threw in Duke for good measure.[67]

How the West Was Won premiered in Great Britain on November 1, 1962, and went into general release in the U.S. on February 20, 1963. For an overlong epic presented in an unfamiliar format, the film did well at the box-office. More importantly, it began a partnership between Ford and Bernard Smith, a former editor-in-chief at Alfred A. Knopf Publishers and story editor for Samuel Goldwyn who had moved into independent production with *Elmer Gantry* in 1960. Their teaming would culminate with the final two feature films of Ford's career.

14

Do You Miss Ward?

I miss old Ward Bond very much. He played Wagon Master *for me ... and it's possible his very successful TV* Wagon Train *role was modeled after this. He was a great human being and a wonderful actor who was taken for granted because he played Westerns.* — John Ford[1]

Those were great days. You're not supposed to look back, but it's pretty hard not to when there were guys like Ward and Jack. You don't meet them every day. — John Wayne[2]

In his 1971 autobiography, Frank Capra mentioned a conversation with James Edward Grant, who had been involved in writing the screenplays for many Wayne films, including *The Alamo.* One of Grant's forthcoming scripts, for *McLintock!* (1963), directed by Andrew McLaglen, would certainly fulfill the crude writer's comment, "All you gotta have in a John Wayne picture is a hoity-toity dame with big tits that Duke can throw over his knee and spank, and a collection of jerks he can smash in the face every five minutes."[3]

Following the downbeat, black and white *Liberty Valance*, Paramount wanted Ford to direct another John Wayne opus, but this time a comedy *in color.* The script "Climate of Love," based on James Michener's "The South Sea Story," had been bouncing around between eight different writers for several years, and the studio still wasn't satisfied with any of the drafts. In February 1962, Duke had talked Pappy into hiring Grant to rewrite the screenplay; but, after he submitted his draft on April 5, Frank Nugent was brought in to add a greater degree of "refinement" to the "spank and smash" formula.

On July 23, Ford began shooting what became *Donovan's Reef* in Hawaii, spending a little over $3.5 million to reunite Duke and Lee Marvin in a cast including Cesar Romero and Dorothy Lamour, who had survived Pappy's *Hurricane* only to end up stranded in this meandering mess of macho, childish hell-raising set in and around, not a real *reef*, but a *bar* (after which the film was cleverly titled) on the island of Haleakoloha.

After a raft of writers had worked on the script, and Grant had added his sure-fire recipe (which did prove a commercial success), not even the erudite Nugent could salvage a film that Pappy primarily improvised. Paramount, already paying him a $250,000 salary, then shelled out another $5,000 for a lease, so he could also "cast" the *Araner*, now little more than a maritime money pit. When the studio eventually pulled the financial plug, Ford produced the picture with his own money. For the dysfunctional alcoholic Lee Marvin, his on-screen mugging was an extension of the tremendous hangovers he suffered every morning.

Donovan's Reef is the mulligan's stew of Ford films, with Wayne's Michael "Guns" Donovan a hybrid of himself and Himself, a two-year college man who broke his ankle playing football, and then joined the Navy, becoming a World War II hero, along with fellow sailors Aloysius "Boats" Gilhooley (Marvin) and "Doc" Dedham (Jack Warden). Donovan now owns not only the bar, but also the *Araner*. Every year, on December 7, the nativity of both Guns and Boats, the two veterans are reunited, primarily to beat the hell out of each other.

Dedham's "Boston" daughter, Amelia (Elizabeth Allen), sails to Haleakoloha, ostensibly to prevent her Pop from inheriting the family shipping fortune. Amidst the mayhem, Ford again deals with racist issues, specifically Dedham's "half-caste" children whom Donovan, fearing Amelia's disapproval, claims as his own. The usual ethnic insults incite the slapstick bar fight, introduced by an Australian naval officer (Dick Foran, in the Victor McLaglen role) who sings "Waltzing Matilda" while playing the piano, which winds up *on top* of him, and Donovan on top of *it*.

Amelia, whom Guns thinks he has "tamed," proves to have been a tolerant and accepting person all along, and (in typical Hollywood form) marries him, after he presents the bar, renamed "Gilhooley's Reef," as a wedding gift to Boats and longtime girlfriend, Fleur (Lamour). This potboiler of booze, brawling, naval lore, ethnic shtick, and endless in-jokes concludes with Mr. and Mrs. Donovan planning to name their first child William, to "be called *Bill*." *Donovan's Reef* ultimately is Admiral Ford's wild tribute to his hero "Wild Bill" Donovan.

In *McLintock!* Jimmy Grant's "hoity-toity dame" is Maureen O'Hara, who joined Duke and Andrew McLaglen to shoot this "tailor-made blockbuster" on location at Tucson, Nogales and Tombstone, Arizona, in early November 1962. The hoary plot involving the efforts of George Washington McLintock (Wayne) to win back his estranged wife, Katherine (O'Hara), builds to a state of complete anarchy, with 42 people sliding down a bank and fighting in an enormous pool of mud (*North to Alaska* to the 10th power), and ends with Duke spanking Maureen with a small shovel. This is how McLintock "tames" his woman, and wins her back. O'Hara recalled, "I'm always asked, 'Did it hurt?' It sure as hell did. My behind was black and blue for days."[4]

Ford's backside wasn't doing too well, either. During a vacation to Paris with Mary, he had taken a tumble down some stairs, and his muscles now were seizing up on a regular basis. When Woody Strode heard about "Papa's" delicate condition, he and his family visited Bel Air, where Luana could chat with Mary and enjoy the pool along with their children, Kalai and June.

"Ford looked ten years older than the last time I saw him," Strode recalled. "He couldn't lift himself up to shake my hand."

The Old Man asked, "Woody, do you know anything about muscles? I've got all these goddamned knots in my back."

Strode examined his back, discovered several muscle spasms, and replied, "Papa, after thirty years of athletics I ought to know something."

Knowing he had a powerful bird in the hand, Ford asked Woody if his wife would consent to his staying for "a few days" to give him therapeutic massages. There were no objections, so Woody found a quilt and pillow, slept at the foot of Papa's bed, and rose to the occasion whenever he awakened in pain.

Strode remained with Ford for four months, reading a stack of books and discussing U.S. history and sports into the wee hours. Strode's companionship alleviated Ford's loneliness and boosted his ego when he needed it most. They initially shared a bottle of wine in the evenings, but as the quantity steadily escalated, Woody realized, "I had to think of a way to keep him from drinking himself into the grave."

One morning, Ford began asking for hair of the dog beers to ease a hangover. After he chugged one can, Strode began cutting the beer with soda water. None the wiser, Papa was sober by the time darkness fell.

Woody continued to dilute Ford's beer, but the eye patch was raised when he respectfully refused to fetch a "glass full of gin." Threatened that he'd never again act in a John Ford picture, Strode replied, "If you don't like it, why don't you just get out of that bed and try to kick my ass?"[5]

Naturally Strode's living with Ford generated homophobic gossip in the Hollywood community. One day, while attending a funeral, Pat Ford suggested that Woody and his two sons sit with him, but Papa insisted that the big man be at his side.

Following the service, Pat informed Woody that "everyone" was talking about "what the old man is doing with you," so he made the painful decision to move out of Ford's house. Much like Pompey's mourning for Tom Doniphon at the beginning of *Liberty Valance*, Strode became "very emotional" about being separated from his cranky companion:

> John Ford and I had created a father-son relationship but I began to feel uncomfortable because of pressure from the outside. I was becoming closer than friends he'd known forty, fifty years. I realized I had gotten too close.... I learned so much from John Ford.... I sat up there and got an education from that old man.[6]

Joseph McBride concluded:

> There clearly was a homoerotic element in their relationship, at least on Ford's part.... It's no exaggeration to say that Woody Strode was the last great love of John Ford's life. The loss of that intimate relationship served to deepen Ford's sense of isolation.[7]

After directing what he had called a "spoof picture," Ford turned to another of his dream projects, *Cheyenne Autumn*, which he had wanted to make for the past six years. In 1957, soon after the publication of Mari Sandoz's account of the 1878 trek of the Northern Cheyenne from the Indian Territory (now Oklahoma) back to their ancestral home in the Dakotas, he and Dudley Nichols had written a cinematic treatment, but were unable to attract financing for such a "pro–Indian" project. Ford explained:

> [P]eople in Europe always want to know about the Indians. There are two sides to every story, but I wanted to show their point of view for a change. Let's face it, we've treated them very badly — it's a blot on our shield; we've cheated and robbed, killed, murdered, massacred and everything else, but they kill one white man and, God, out come the troops.[8]

To sell the screenplay by James Webb, Bernard Smith made a successful pitch to Warner Bros., who liked the idea of a John Ford Western reflecting the more liberal climate fostered in part by the current Democratic presidential administration. Jack Warner considered such a commercially oriented, $4.2-million project "insurance" against the enormous $10-million budget the studio had just sunk into a far more risky property: the screen adaptation of the hit Broadway musical *My Fair Lady*.

Ford also wanted to incorporate Howard Fast's 1941 novel *The Last Frontier* into the screenplay, but politics and the fact that Columbia owned the film rights officially nixed that idea. Fast, whose other works of pro-civil liberties, historical fiction include *Citizen Tom Paine* (1943), *Freedom Road* (1944) and *Spartacus* (1951), had been blacklisted by HUAC and served a three-month prison sentence for contempt of Congress in 1950. His conviction resulted from his refusal to inform on others who had contributed to a home for orphans of Americans who had fought in the Spanish Civil War. If he had submitted a list of names, the most famous would have been that of former First Lady Eleanor Roosevelt.

Oscar-winning Columbia producer and screenwriter Sidney Buchman had wanted to film an adaptation of *The Last Frontier*, but he also had been blacklisted; and, after refusing to reappear before HUAC in 1952, was sentenced to one year in prison for contempt. The sentence was suspended, but he had to work incognito for the next decade. In his 1990 autobiography *Being Red*, Fast revealed:

> John Ford ... had been pleading with me to talk Buchman into allowing him ... to direct *The Last Frontier*. He said, to quote him, "I'll direct it right out of your book, your dialogue and nothing else. No fuckin' screenwriter — no, sir. Right from the book." And he would have too, and it would have been a splendid film.
>
> But then Columbia ... was told by J. Edgar Hoover that no film was to be made from my book. whereupon Columbia shelved it. John Ford, furious, frustrated by a blacklist he only had contempt for, went to Warner Bros., told them that the story was in the public domain, and then slipped my book to a screenwriter and told him to go ahead and do the screenplay.[9]

Patrick Ford wrote a 90-page treatment for what his father envisioned as a stark, black and white, Native American *Grapes of Wrath*, in which the Cheyenne would not speak English, as "Indians" do ridiculously in the entire history of the Hollywood Western. (The fact that Native Americans were unable to communicate with their English-speaking invaders played a major role in their decimation.) Richard Widmark claimed that, before he was cast in the film, he had given Ford his own historical research on the subject, and this was among the material pored over by James Webb while writing the screenplay.

When the suits at Columbia discovered that Webb had incorporated material from *The Last Frontier*, their attorneys, obtaining a legal hold on the film, threatened Warner Bros. with a plagiarism suit, which was averted by an out-of-court settlement including cash and a profit percentage. Ultimately, Warners released, not a *Liberty Valance*–style, monochrome elegy, but a Hollywood Technicolor epic shot primarily in Monument Valley by William Clothier, using the mega-widescreen, 70-millimeter, Super Panavision process. With a price tag exceeding $4-million, *Cheyenne Autumn* was one hell of a gamble from the outset.

Jack Warner, complaining that the film wouldn't feature "enough stars," had temporarily shut down the project. If only Ford could have shoehorned Wayne into the picture, Warner could have escalated the financial risk by adding yet another million to the budget. Ultimately, the muddled screenplay, cobbled together by Webb from several sources, resulted in an uneven film and some very disappointed contributors. Howard Fast couldn't be acknowledged on screen, but the absence of Pat Ford's name in the credits drove a permanent wedge between a father and son whose relationship had always been problematic. With Duke riding the crest of superstardom, and Ward Bond dead, Woody Strode now became Pappy's surrogate son.

Seeking some degree of realism, Ford's intention to cast Navajos in lead Cheyenne roles was overridden by Jack Warner, who had casting approval and final cut on the picture. The mogul was not going to gamble on unknown Native American performers in significant parts. The same reasoning that led Warner to cast Humphrey Bogart as a Mexican in *Virginia City* now resulted in Mexican actors (Ricardo Montalban, Gilbert Roland and Dolores del Rio) cast as Cheyenne characters.

Though most of the "Indian" parts would have been played by Navajos, Ford wanted Strode to portray the Cheyenne leader Little Wolf. Strode explained:

I look just like him.... But again I was walking uphill because Warner Bros. wanted an established name with marquee value.... About a month away from shooting, John Ford delivered the bad news, "They're going to give the part to Ricardo Montalban...."[10]

Jack Warner knew that Strode was part–Cheyenne, but the African American "half" cost him the part. Montalban, like the other Latino and Anglo actors in Cheyenne roles, speaks English throughout most of the film. The bit and extra roles, however, are played by the Monument Valley Navajos. Ford said:

> The Navajo [are] the best damn fighters in the world. They were tough to beat in the Old West and they've been tough to beat in modern war, in which many of them fought with us and performed heroically. But even today, although the Indian has a better civilized understanding of us, we do not have a much better understanding of him. There is still a lot of prejudice.[11]

Ford was shooting in Monument Valley on November 22, 1963, the day John F. Kennedy was assassinated in Dallas. The next morning, to observe the national day of mourning for the fallen President, the entire cast and crew gathered at Goulding's Lodge, where the flag was lowered to half-staff, a bugler played "Taps," and Ford quietly told his colleagues that, although the nation had "lost a great leader," they could be assured "that the republic was sound." After he read "The Lord's Prayer" to the assemblage, Dobe Carey sang "The Battle Hymn of the Republic." Pappy, wearing a fatigue jacket adorned with his two rear-admiral stars, then "dismissed the company." As reported by Dan Ford, "There was no filming in Monument Valley that day."[12]

Three years later, Ford admitted, "I loved Kennedy. He was a fantastic man, humorous, intelligent, generous. His assassination was a terrible blow to America."[13]

During the evenings, after dinner at Goulding's, Pappy would preside over a game of "20 Questions," challenging his cast and crew to deduce what object he had on his mind. Victor Jory, who plays "Tall Tree" in the film, was among the gathering unable to determine the "animal and vegetable" item in question. Finally, Ford revealed that he was describing "probably one of the most famous props in literature," charging, "It seems that none of you, including Jory, have read Sherlock Holmes."

Pappy enjoyed Conan Doyle's historical novels, particularly *The White Company*, and famous detective stories, especially "The Adventure of the Musgrave Ritual," in which Watson mentions Holmes keeping his tobacco tucked inside the toe end of a Persian slipper. Following the company's inability to identify this article of Sherlockian footwear, the Old Man retired "to call Mother."[14]

On December 20, while shooting winter scenes at Gunnison, Colorado, Ford made the single most inauspicious "entrance" onto the set of his entire 50-year career as a film director. Carey and Ben Johnson knew something was amiss when they arrived to find Richard Widmark (following in the footsteps of Ward Bond) in the director's chair.

Ford apparently injured an ankle trudging through the snow, and had been prescribed codeine painkillers. After observing Widmark helm a scene for about 30 minutes, Carey saw Pappy's station wagon pull up onto an icy flow. Dobe's eyewitness account is unforgettable:

> Uncle Jack was stewed to the gills.... He looked like a circus clown. It was a horrible sight. He was all white around his lips. His tongue was coated white too, and was darting in and out of his mouth....
> I thought, "He's going to fall flat on his face."
> And that's exactly what he did as he stepped out of the car. He had on galoshes at least four

sizes too big. He took a step, but the galoshes didn't move. Then we saw that his pants were on backwards.... The unzipped fly was at his ass, and his shirttail was sticking out of it like a rooster that had just had the shit kicked out of it.[15]

Pleased to see that Widmark had the situation well in hand, Pappy gave up his attempt to maneuver across the ice and snow, clambered back into the station wagon, and was driven back into town.

Ford didn't drink during the shoot, but had become somewhat dependent on drugs (including steroids) to energize him in the morning and sleeping pills to relax at night. The benzodiazepine in the sleeping pills eventually made it difficult to function during the day. On some mornings, Bill Clothier was unable to wake him. In order to generate enough energy to work, Ford began to use Bond's method of relying on uppers.

One morning, when Clothier couldn't rouse Pappy, he walked into the bathroom and flushed all of the pills down the toilet. When Ford couldn't find his amphetamines, he flew into a rage and went searching for the "son of a bitch" responsible for ditching all the drugs. Clothier admitted that he had flushed the dope, and Pappy responded by asking the cinematographer how he would like to have all his lenses sent swirling down the porcelain throne.

Clothier's attempt to diminish the drug abuse had little effect, as Ford had the foresight to hide an emergency stash inside hollowed-out books. One day, when he became totally incapacitated, Wingate Smith called a local sawbones, and George O'Brien sat at his bedside, reminiscing about the earlier films they had made together.

With the film falling behind schedule, second-unit director Ray Kellogg worked with Clothier to shoot whatever footage they could while Pappy recuperated. Although Ford repeatedly claimed that making films was "just no fun anymore," he was adamant about completing the *Cheyenne Autumn* shoot.

The film opens on the Cheyenne Reservation in the Southwest Indian Territory on September 7, 1878. More than a year has passed since the White Man forcibly relocated the tribe here from its "green and fertile country, 1,500 miles to the north." Captain Thomas Archer (Widmark) is not pleased with the U.S. Congressional Committee, "the gentlemen from the East" who don't care that "the Cheyenne have been forgotten ... to most people ... a footnote in history." Promised medicine and food, they have received nothing. Of the 1,000 men, women and children driven to the parched desert location, only 286 remain alive.

The Quaker schoolteacher Deborah Wright (Carroll Baker) naively believes the abandoned tribe will still attend her class, but the soldier explains the difference between "the pitiful reservation Indians" and the innate warrior nature of the true Cheyenne, whom he respects. Fed up with empty promises, the survivors begin to march back to "Yellowstone country."

Ford's Stock Company is well represented by Carey, Ben Johnson, George O'Brien and Patrick Wayne in supporting cavalry roles. Ken Curtis merely does an insidious variation on his Festus Haggin character from the *Gunsmoke* series, as Joe, a racist saddle tramp, who shoots a Cheyenne he meets in the desert, begging for food. "I always wanted to kill me an Injun," he says repeatedly.

Ford follows a tragic scene of White Buffalo slaughter with a comic relief sequence (intended as a near-intermission) set in Dodge City involving Wyatt Earp (James Stewart), Doc Holliday (Arthur Kennedy) and Jeff Blair (John Carradine). Joe and his three cronies enter the saloon, spouting an exaggerated story about "Indian fighting," but Earp ignores the paranoia in favor of his poker game. When the phony cowpokes confront the Marshal, he shoots Joe in the foot, and then cuts out the bullet.

The Fordian shtick goes on far too long during the preposterous "Battle of Dodge City," during which Earp and Holliday accompany a mob onto the prairie to fight the oncoming hordes (only a lone "Indian" is seen). Ford would have been better served by eliminating this superfluous sequence from his serious, though ponderous, attempt to depict the plight of the Cheyenne. (For years, it was cut from release prints, but later included in a restored, full-length version.) Ford claimed:

> It actually happened that way. They were a load of Easterners — not many cowboys there — and they went out thinking they were going to pick up a scalp or something. Someone fired a shot, and they all ran like hell.[16]

Dobe Carey recalled:

> [P]eople wondered why [Ford] stuck a "mini-movie," with Jimmy Stewart ... Arthur Kennedy and John Carradine, in the middle of the picture. That's easy — he wanted to direct these guys once more before saying, "Adios." ... It was all very grim. I never knew what was going on ... I was to discover, however, that no one else did either. They did what the Old Man told them.[17]

In the snows of northern Nebraska, the Cheyenne nation splits, half moving on, the others seeking the protection of Fort Robinson, where the Quaker hopes to save the children. Archer arrives to find that those who have surrendered have been ordered to march back to the reservation through the freezing winter. Captain Wessels (Karl Malden), the by-the-book Prussian commander, insists on obeying the order, but Dull Knife (Gilbert Roland) and "Spanish Woman" (Dolores del Rio) vow to die where they stand.

Incensed, Archer takes leave to visit the "Great White Father," Secretary of the Interior Carl Schurz (Edward G. Robinson), in Washington, where he reveals the truth about conditions at the fort, referring to the imprisonment of the Cheyenne in a freezing warehouse as "murder." After Archer leaves, Schurz walks toward some portraits hanging on his office wall, and Ford cuts to a stunning shot showing Robinson's reflection in a framed daguerreotype of Abraham Lincoln. Schurz asks Ford's hero, "Old friend, what would *you* do?"

At Fort Robinson, the inebriated Wessels is relieved of duty just before unarmed Cheyenne women and children break out of the warehouse, only to be gunned down, their bodies spattering the snow with blood. Utterly shocked, Wessels staggers through the aftermath of the massacre, as the survivors march farther north, into the hills of Dakota. The cavalry lines up for an assault, but is interrupted by Archer, who has brought Schurz with him. The Secretary, informing the commander that the land is Department of the Interior property, "parlays with the Indians."

Spencer Tracy was originally cast as Schurz, but one perusal of the script had him beating the retreat. Ford replaced him with Robinson, whose scenes were shot entirely in the studio. To complete the climactic scene of the Secretary cordially meeting with the Cheyenne, back-screen projection of washed-out images filmed at the actual location was used, an inauspicious cinematic reunion of Ford with one of Hollywood's finest actors, with whom he hadn't worked since making *The Whole Town's Talking* three decades earlier.

Though Ford considered himself a minority who often depicted the downtrodden underdog, his concession to a major studio, depicting a specific, sensitive historical subject within the conventions of commercial epic cinema, invited criticism from "liberal" U.S. journalists who still considered the Western an "inferior, juvenile" genre. *Cheyenne Autumn* only received sensible reviews in Europe, where Ford was considered a major artist. Joseph McBride wrote:

Ford's ambitious attempt to rectify what he perceived as an imbalance in his own work is a testimony to his concern with his artistic legacy and his deep-seated sense of justice.... *Cheyenne Autumn* offers a somber lesson about a tragic period of American history along with a vision of racial reconciliation and healing.[18]

During a rare interview, to promote the film in *Cosmopolitan* magazine, Ford said:

The Indian is very close to my heart.... There's some merit to the charge that the Indian hasn't been portrayed accurately or fairly in the Western, but ... this charge has been a broad generalization.... The fight against the Indian was fundamental to the story of the West. If he has been treated unfairly by the whites in films, that, unfortunately, was often the case in real life. There was much racial prejudice in the West. Some of it was directed against the Negro, too, by the way, something I touched on in *Sergeant Rutledge*.[19]

On a personal level, Dobe Carey admitted, "It was the last time I would work for the man I loved and, at times, tried very hard to hate."[20]

In April 1964, Ford made the first of two preproduction trips to Ireland, intent on directing *Young Cassidy*, a biopic written by John Whiting about the early life of socialist playwright Sean O'Casey. Sean Connery had been cast in the lead role, but his commitment to *Goldfinger* (1964), the third entry in the James Bond series, made it impossible for him to play Cassidy. Australian actor Rod Taylor, a protégé of Peter Finch, took over, working with Irish actor Jack MacGowran to develop a convincing accent. The film was scheduled to begin shooting on July 14, with interiors to be completed at Elstree Studios in London.

Kicking off the second trip in May, Ford got so inebriated that he had to be helped off the Aer Lingus jet in a wheelchair. Before shooting began, he attended a press conference at the Shelbourne Hotel in Dublin on July 9, when he arrived soused on Black Velvet, a cheap blended Canadian whisky, and sarcastically "answered" a few questions, but primarily veered off into expressing his views on the IRA. He remained drunk while shooting the film, having stashed two grocery bags bulging with bottles of Scotch among his luggage.

Barbara Ford's divorce from Ken Curtis on July 23 contributed to Pappy's depressive state. Habitually abusing alcohol until she landed in a sanitarium, attempting to "dry out," Barbara, enabled by her mother, who ran damage control, continued in the sodden cycle until Curtis could stand it no longer.

Hung over during the days, Ford hit the Dublin pubs in the evenings, consuming prodigious quantities of Guinness and Jameson's Irish Whisky. On one occasion, he passed out, turning an alarming shade of gray, before Rod Taylor could carry him back to his room. "I thought he was dead," recalled the actor, "and I was crying my eyes out."[21]

Pappy became so ill that Maynard Brandsma had to be flown in from Los Angeles, while the patient was ordered to rest at Lord Killanin's Dublin estate. Having lost 30 pounds, Ford was diagnosed as "badly debilitated." Forced to abandon *Young Cassidy* after three weeks' work, he left for home on August 4, intending to spend two months recuperating aboard the *Araner*. Renowned British cinematographer and director Jack Cardiff was hired to complete the film.

In Europe to costar with Rita Hayworth in Henry Hathaway's *Circus World* (1964), Wayne nearly lost his life during the shooting of a big-top fire sequence. As circus owner Matt Masters, Duke, performing his own stunts, didn't see the rest of the crew evacuating the blazing tent as he hacked away with an ax. When his toupee began burning, he realized he was trapped, alone in the out of control conflagration. He managed to escape but, suffering from smoke inhalation, began coughing up blood.

During his Honolulu sabbatical, Pappy was frequently visited by Wayne, who now was in Hawaii, starring in Otto Preminger's *In Harm's Way* (1965), a Pearl Harbor aftermath epic. On one occasion, amidst their usual cheating at cards, the Old Man became concerned about Duke's pallid appearance and repeated bouts of coughing. Wayne told him not to worry about some sort of "flu bug" currently afoot.

Pilar Wayne immediately echoed Ford's concern when Duke returned to Los Angeles, insisting that he undergo a complete physical at the Scripps Clinic in La Jolla. As soon as Ford was informed that Wayne had lung cancer, he caught a flight back to the mainland to be at the bedside of his close friend and colleague of nearly 40 years. At one point, he looked at Pilar, admitting, "I love that damn Republican. He's like a son to me." Dan Ford wrote, "With Ward Bond gone, Wayne was the last of the old crowd, and the thought of losing him was too much to even think about."[22]

At Good Samaritan Hospital in Los Angeles on September 14, 1964, Dr. John C. Jones successfully excised a malignant mass from Wayne's left lung, part of which also had to be removed. A complete recovery was expected, and Duke's swift and positive recuperation, followed by an enthusiastic return to filmmaking, inspired others throughout the nation and across the globe.

On December 22, Wayne sent a telegram to another celebrity suffering from lung cancer, the peerless jazz pianist and vocalist, Nat "King Cole, who was being treated at St. John's Hospital:

> Sorry to hear you've joined the club but it can be whipped. I had one snatched with the top half of my left lung three months ago. Don't let it get you down. Was just listening to the radio and heard a record of Christmas songs. Thank you for the joy you've brought me and my family. Keep punching.
>
> John Wayne[23]

Sadly, Nathaniel Adams Coles died, less than two months later, on February 15, 1965. Like Duke a chain smoker for most of his life, he was only 45 years old.

Duke wasn't really part of "the old crowd" to whom Ford had dedicated the Field Photo Home, which also, following a "physical," was in dire need of rescue. The Farm certainly had fulfilled its purpose since World War II; and now, with all the original members either having returned to civilian life or passed away, Ford (who already had downsized the property in 1961) sold the residual land to a developer, whose entire $300,000 payment was donated to the Motion Picture Relief Fund. Though the buildings and grounds had become somewhat run down, Pappy was adamant about keeping the chapel, which was moved onto the grounds of the Woodland Hills Country Home.

Wayne, intent on proving he had "licked the Big C," began the New Year by going back to work, in the rugged, high altitude terrain of Durango, Mexico. Before Henry Hathaway rolled the cameras on *The Sons of Katie Elder* on January 3, 1965, Warner Bros. insured the stubborn star, who insisted on performing many of his own stunts, for $1 million. Duke knew making the film was too much, too soon, but he worked through the shortness of breath, pain and fatigue through sheer force of will. Typically, Hathaway had urged him to do it, both to avoid "babying himself" during his recovery and for the good of his career.[24] Dean Martin, costarring with Duke for the second time, said, "Someone else would have laid around feeling sorry for himself for a year.... He's recuperating the hard way."[25]

Hathaway wrapped *Katie Elder* in March, and Wayne, wanting to drop a few pounds, returned home to focus on maintaining an exercise program including scuba diving and weight lifting. Following a premiere in Chicago, the film was released nationwide on July 1. Though Dean Martin delivers his usual naturalistic, laid-back performance, he cannot overcome Hathaway's miscasting of him as Duke's brother, Tom Elder. As Matt Elder, Earl Holliman is the only actor in the quartet who could pass as a Wayne sibling, but truly incredible is the choice for little brother Bud: British-born Michael Anderson, Jr., who was 36 years younger than Duke! But Wayne was back, slapping leather in a solid, action-packed Western, and audiences responded enthusiastically to the "man's man" who appeared to be able to conquer anything.

As a favor for his colleague, writer-producer Melville Shavelson, Duke moved on to an atypical project, *Cast a Giant Shadow*, a film depicting the role of FDR military adviser and World War II hero David "Mickey" Marcus in the establishment of an independent Israel. Shavelson needed a powerful Hollywood gentile to help balance what was being tagged a "Jewish movie," so Wayne agreed to play a supporting part and provide financing through Batjac. He brought Kirk Douglas and Yul Brynner on board to play Marcus and Israeli commander Asher Gonen, respectively; and the strongly pro–Israel Frank Sinatra, who had supported the independence movement, also was cast in a supporting role.

As U.S. General Mike Randolph, Duke appears in a flashback, liberating one of the Nazi death camps in 1945. The scene presented one of the greatest acting challenges of his life, as Shavelson, deciding not to show actual Nazi atrocities, asked Duke to suggest the horror discovered by Randolph entirely with his facial expressions. Reminiscent of his famous close-up in *The Searchers*, the result is a masterpiece of subtle yet powerful nonverbal acting. Shavelson said, "It depended for effect on what John Wayne could convey to an audience with his eyes."[26]

Completing his work on *Cast a Giant Shadow*, Duke moved into a new home that Pilar had purchased and renovated in Newport Beach. He then went right back to work, reteaming with Howard Hawks to make *El Dorado*, shot partly on location in Arizona, with costars Robert Mitchum and James Caan, and then back to Durango to make *The War Wagon* for Batjac. Costarring Kirk Douglas and featuring Bruce Cabot and young Robert Walker, Jr., this heist-adventure Western, directed by Burt Kennedy, falls squarely into the successful John Wayne formula, with his wrongfully imprisoned Taw Jackson taking the law into his own hands to regain stolen land and a fortune in gold.

Young Cassidy, pairing Rod Taylor with the sublime Julie Christie, premiered in London during February 1965, followed by its New York opening on March 25. Many reviewers credited Ford for the highpoints of the film, most of which had been directed by a very incensed Jack Cardiff. Ford paid little attention to what, for him, was an aborted project, and began brewing new ideas for another modern "minority" film.

Ford had moved into an office at MGM in early November 1964. After reading British novelist Norah Loft's 1935 short story "Chinese Finale," he announced to Bernard Smith, "I want to do a story about women." Although he later said that this deviation in subject matter was "just a job of work," Joseph McBride referred to *7 Women* as Ford's attempt to "confound the shortsighted critics who had failed to treat him with the understanding and deference he deserved."[27]

Ford chose Patricia Neal for the lead role of Dr. Cartwright, an atheist who gives her own life to save a newborn baby and the women of the Unified Christian Missions Educational Society, a culturally imperialist Boston organization seeking to convert the local Chinese. As top-notch female support, he cast Sue Lyon, Margaret Leighton, Flora Robson, Mildred Dunnock, Betty Field, and the beloved Anna Lee. The male roles were filled by Eddie Albert and, as Chinese warriors, Mike Mazurki and Woody Strode (who had just finished playing the deaf-mute Sengal in *Genghis Khan* for director Henry Levin).

Three days into the shoot, Neal, who was pregnant, suffered a series of strokes that nearly proved fatal. A three-week coma and the resulting paralysis left her unable to walk or talk, but, aided by her husband, Roald Dahl, she eventually made a remarkable recovery and gave birth to her fifth child, Lucy, on August 4, 1965. Anne Bancroft took over the Cartwright role, and several scenes were reshot, though Ford was thoroughly disappointed by her performance.

Pappy wrapped the *7 Women* shoot and caught his usual post-production flight to Honolulu, where his maritime sanctuary, the *Araner*, awaited the rear admiral's return. Following the box-office and critical failure of *Cheyenne Autumn*, he already knew that his similar attempt to make a pro-"feminist" film would flop. In fact, he openly stated that it would end his career, a belief that sent him spiraling into one of his most self-destructive alcoholic binges. He said, "We don't make pictures anymore in Hollywood. Madison Avenue and Wall Street make the films."[28]

On January 5, 1966, *7 Women* was released to critics who couldn't wait to lambaste this "aberration" that would prove to be Ford's final feature film. Viewing the film in retrospect, Joseph McBride praised this "mordant drama of religious fanaticism, sexual repression, and social breakdown as one of Ford's masterpieces."[29]

Concerned about his grandfather's deepening depression, Dan Ford, noting that Pappy was drinking "as though he were trying to find real oblivion," came aboard the *Araner* for an extended visit. This time, when "Gramps" was asked about the state of his health, he uncharacteristically offered a direct, honest answer: an admission that he was "not all right." Descending into the deckhouse, he tumbled into the table, sending broken shards of glass in all directions as he hit the cabin floor. Valiantly attempting to make his Gramps as comfortable as possible, Dan quietly praised the "poor old bastard," turned out the light and, while walking back onto the deck, heard him mumble, "I heard that." Dan wrote:

> I stood there for a minute thinking about him: about his fantastic life and his magnificent work. Then I went down below, opened up his liquor cabinet, and got a bottle. Following what I thought was an excellent example, I sat down in the saloon and got drunk myself.[30]

In early 1968, Rear Admiral Ford was commissioned by the United States Information Agency as executive producer of a propaganda film justifying U.S. involvement in the Vietnam War. Director Sherman Beck was hired to direct the location footage shot during the winter of 1968, when Ford also arrived in the war-ravaged country. By this time, the war already was considered a disastrous loss for the United States, but Ford forged ahead, producing a historically dubious film that the USIA actually found embarrassing. Completed in December 1968, *Vietnam! Vietnam!*, a 58-minute exercise in outright jingoism finally went into a limited release in September 1971.

While in Vietnam, Ford had written to Alnah Johnston, a high school classmate, "What's this war all about? Damned if I know. I haven't the slightest idea what we're doing here."[31]

Scott Eyman wrote:

> The vision of Vietnam presented in the film is reminiscent of a Western — overall, the point of view is not dissimilar to John Wayne's *The Green Berets*, which is more or less a World War II movie that had the misfortune to be about Vietnam.[32]

Wayne had read the short-story collection *The Green Berets* by Robin Moore shortly after it was published in 1965. Thinking the book would make a great movie to help counter the antiwar protests, he hinted that it could be an updated version of *The Alamo* when pitching the idea to President Lyndon Johnson, who would have to give his blessing for Batjac Productions to receive support and weaponry from the Department of Defense.

Though the book had been a bestseller, spurring interest among Americans who also helped Sergeant Barry Sadler's song "The Ballad of the Green Berets" become a chart-topper in 1966, U.S. Army and Pentagon brass were not enthusiastic about a film based on the work of a freelance writer (who supposedly served as a member of the Special Forces) which is extremely sadistic, racist, sexually deviant and revealing of a mission carried out prior to Presidential authorization. Garry Wills wrote:

> Moore suggests ... it is all an adventure. The Green Berets in the book are mainly soldiers of fortune from many different nations, men who enjoy their work, exulting in their skills and in the perks of the job (mainly sexual). The author cannot keep himself from joining in the fun. It is an adolescent's dream version of Gunga Din. No wonder the Pentagon hated it.[33]

The screenplay by James Lee Barrett had to be rewritten before the Pentagon would authorize the film and give Wayne access to Fort Benning, as most of the location shooting was planned for Georgia and Alabama. By the time the propaganda fest called *The Green Berets* was released, three years had passed, and conditions on all fronts had worsened. George Beckworth (David Janssen) the bleeding-heart liberal journalist in the film (and the exact opposite of the gung-ho writer in the book), is a symbol for all those on the home front who didn't approve of the war.

When Colonel Mike Kirby (Wayne) insists that Beckworth's criticisms will be refuted by events occurring on the ground, he contradicts the findings of actual U.S. journalists who had issued reports that the Vietnam War was neither winnable nor worth the lives of so many American troops. In order to make the film "entertaining," Wayne had Barrett construct the screenplay along the lines of the World War II movies in which he had so famously fought on Hollywood soundstages while his colleagues were risking their lives in Europe and the Pacific.

This folderol didn't fool the critics, who universally derided the film's naïve, comic-book approach, but the Wayne fans and the "my country, right or wrong" crowd nonetheless made it a commercial success. As Gary Wills noted:

> People who did not want to know about the actual Vietnam War could feel that the national unity and resolve of World War II might turn around this strange new conflict in the far-off jungles of the East. Wayne was fighting World War II again, the only way he ever did, in make-believe ... a memory of American greatness that many still wanted to live by.[34]

Ford, who mercilessly "reminded" Duke that he had proved a coward while his Coach was being wounded on Midway and dodging Nazi machine-gun fire on D-Day, had actually spent real time in Vietnam (not the "VIP tour" that Wayne had undertaken to "cheer up the troops"), wondering why U.S. troops were fighting and dying there.

After directing John Wayne in five films, Howard Hawks said:

> [I]f you don't get a damn good actor with Wayne, he's going to blow him right off the screen, not just by the fact he's good, but by his power, his strength.... Most of the leading men today, the younger men especially, are a little bit effeminate. There's no toughness. McQueen and Eastwood don't compare with Wayne. He *is* tough. The only people who could handle him were Ford and myself.[35]

Wayne's last two films for Hawks, *El Dorado* (1967) and *Rio Lobo* (1970), are virtually remakes of the superior *Rio Bravo*. When queried about this fact by Joseph McBride during the mid–1970s, an aging Hawks, insisting that "they weren't remakes," became quite defensive:

If we make a picture that's a top-biller, that the people like, we're inclined to do a different version of the same picture. And if a director has a story that he likes and he tells it, very often he looks at the picture and says, "I could do that better if I did it again," so I'd do it again. I'll keep on doing them, in a different way. I'm not a damn bit interested in whether somebody thinks this is a copy of it, because the copy made more money than the original, and I was very pleased with it. We found that they liked *Rio Bravo*, and oddly enough, I think they liked *El Dorado* better. Although I think that *Rio Bravo* was a better picture.[36]

A conundrum of contradictions, Hawks' reply insists that *El Dorado* (a huge box-office hit) and *Rio Lobo* are, not "remakes" of *Rio Bravo*, but *copies*. Hawks also believed he could do a "better ... version of the same picture," but knew damn well that *Rio Bravo* "was ... better." The truth is that money talked, John Wayne walked, and the herd maintained its thunderous stampede. Like Ford, Hawks was a notorious bullshit artist, but he couldn't shovel it nearly as well as the master.

"I didn't think [*Rio Lobo*] was any good," Hawks admitted.[37] Perhaps the quality of this film is best summed up when Wayne's Captain Cord McNally, observing that the villainous Ketcham (Victor French) has been set ablaze by a wood-burning stove, flippantly orders, "*Let him burn!*"

Following *The Man Who Shot Liberty Valance*, which provides brilliant insight into the cinematic persona of John Wayne, this legendary character, conceived by Raoul Walsh, molded by John Ford, and hardened by Howard Hawks, had become trapped within his own image. *Liberty Valance* proves the obsolescence of the self-reliant Man of the West representing the Frontier Myth. When the picture begins, the Duke is dead, stripped of his boots by a devious undertaker, and shut up in a cheap pine box.

As aptly demonstrated by *Donovan's Reef*, Ford artistically had done all he could do with Duke, who was consciously playing a burlesque caricature of his image, raising hell in forced comic situations. Hawks' "copies" of *Rio Bravo* depict an obviously aging Wayne stumbling around with a crutch and having difficulty mounting his horse.

Three years prior to *Donovan's Reef*, Duke already had outrageously overdone this deliberate lampoon in Henry Hathaway's *North to Alaska* (1960), in which his extensive interplay with *Fabian* reaches its comic zenith when he squarely kicks the bent-over teen idol (resembling John Agar in *Fort Apache*) in the ass.

Perhaps, finally, Marion Morrison unconsciously was able to achieve a cinematic catharsis for the real-life kicks he'd received (and accepted) from John Ford. Wardell Bond, the "Horse's Ass" himself, already had done the same thing with various young actors in several episodes of *Wagon Train*.

The bottom line is that all that "ass-kicking" of Ford's, both literal and figurative, had made fine actors out of both Wayne and Bond, whom Pappy had considered "naturals" from the beginning. The majority of Wayne's great films were made with Ford who, paying Howard Hawks a compliment by saying he "didn't know the big son of a bitch could act," brought out the very best in the actor. As Gary Wills wrote of Wayne:

Contrary to the general impression, he was not typecast in the Ford movies. Even in the tales most similar by reason of plot and setting, the cavalry stories, he was very different — down to the carriage of his body.... Of course the secret of great movies does not lie in just one artist. Wayne had the advantage, in his critical work with Ford, of the very sensitive writer, Frank Nugent, who saw how to bring nuance to the one-dimensional heroes ... in James Warner Bellah's stories.... But ... the greatest credit for Wayne's fine movies of the 1940s and 1950s must go to Ford....[38]

Without Ford, Wayne made a handful of great films, the best arguably being *Red River*, *Rio Bravo* and *The Shootist*, two of them directed by Hawks. *True Grit* (1969) is a well-made, entertaining film, but awarding Duke the Oscar for his flamboyant portrayal of Rooster Cogburn was the Academy's typical way of recognizing a great actor who should have received the Best Actor statuette far earlier, for *Red River*, *She Wore a Yellow Ribbon* or *The Searchers* (serious Westerns that weren't necessarily taken seriously).

Ironically, Wayne won his Academy Award in a role that Charles Portis, author of *True Grit*, didn't want him to play. Ordered by Henry Hathaway to "settle" the issue with Portis, Hal Wallis, who bought the film rights for Paramount, insisted on casting Duke (who had attempted to purchase the property for Batjac).

Consider another great Ford star, Henry Fonda: arguably one of the finest actors of the 20th century, who could have carried home the Oscar for several of Pappy's films, especially *The Grapes of Wrath*. But Hank was frozen out until they *had* to give the dying man the award for the treacle called *On Golden Pond* (1980), his final film. Although the majority of Bond's roles were supporting and small character parts, he gave excellent performances in, not only a score of Ford's pictures, but some of the finest made by many other top directors, and in three and one-half seasons of *Wagon Train*.

While shooting *The Undefeated* on location in Durango in February 1969, Wayne received another letter, accompanied by a script, from his pal Sammy Davis, Jr., who still was hoping to costar with him in a major feature film:

> Dear Duke,
>   It has been a long search but I believe I have finally found the screenplay for the two of us that we began looking for six years ago. I am so very excited about the enclosed that I am sending it along to you personally and asking you to read it at your first opportunity. I think the two of us in this film would be nothing short of dynamite.... Burt Kennedy ... has read the script and would be available to direct, if you approve of course.... I know you are shooting now and hope there might be a possibility that we could do "THE TRACKERS" upon completion of your current picture. I think you will agree after reading the screenplay that it *must* have DUKE WAYNE and Sammy Davis, Jr.[39]

Davis and Burt Kennedy suggested meeting in Durango to discuss the project, but Wayne unfortunately never found time to make a film with the extraordinary entertainer, whose own schedule was continuously booked. (*The Trackers* eventually was made for television by Aaron Spelling Productions. Directed by Earl Bellamy and pairing Ernest Borgnine with Davis, who also produced the film, it was broadcast by ABC on December 14, 1971.)

On February 2, 1970, Wayne presented the Cecil B. DeMille Award, an honorary Golden Globe acknowledging "outstanding contributions to the world of entertainment," to Joan Crawford during a ceremony at the Hollywood Coconut Grove in the Ambassador Hotel. Bestowed with the award in 1966, Wayne received a letter from Crawford the day after the banquet:

> Duke darling,
>   Thank you so much for presenting me with the Cecil B. DeMille Award last night. I am so deeply, deeply grateful to you. I must say you had the sweetest smile on your face when you presented it; and every time I looked at you, I was so touched by that deliciously small-boy smile....
>   Always,
>   Joan[40]

At the 42nd Annual Academy Awards held at the Dorothy Chandler Pavilion in Los Angeles on April 7, 1970, Barbra Streisand presented Duke with the Best Actor Oscar for his performance in *True Grit*. The next morning, he received the customary telegram of recognition from the President of the United States:

Congratulations. The Oscar recognizes your excellent contribution to the American screen. Mrs. Johnson and I long have recognized your contributions to our beloved country. We join your many thousand other admirers in saluting your success and hope that when your schedule permits you will visit us at the ranch.

Lyndon B. Johnson[41]

Just as the death of Bond had hit Ford hard, the passing of his longtime friend and major domo, Bill Ramsey, in September 1970 was almost too much for him to handle. Evidence of the love he felt for his African American companion was communicated in a letter to Kate Hepburn, in which Pappy admitted that Bill "passed away in my arms."[42]

Wayne continued making his by-the-numbers Westerns in Durango, including *Chisum* (1970) and a project with director George Sherman originally titled "The Million Dollar Kidnapping." By the time the latter production wrapped in December 1970, the verbose title had been changed to the simple, much more Wayne-like *Big Jake*, after his character, Jacob McCandles, another crusty gunslinger with an estranged wife (Maureen O'Hara, in her final film with Duke) he wants to reclaim. With a screenplay by Harry Julian Fink and R. M. Fink (Jimmy Grant was safely six feet under), this entertaining film, set in 1909, concludes, not with a spanking, but with indomitable Big Jake bringing his kidnapped grandson, Little Jake (Ethan Wayne), back home.

As the sadistic outlaw gang boss and mass murderer John Fain, Richard Boone steals the picture from a rather odd, melting pot cast, including Patrick Wayne (as another of Jake's sons); Robert Mitchum's son, Christopher; Duke's drinking buddy, Bruce Cabot, in his penultimate role, as an "Apache" tracker called Sam Sharpnose; singer Bobby Vinton, in his first of two films with Wayne (or anyone else); Welsh comic actor Bernard Fox as a Scottish sheep man; and plenty of faces from the Ford Stock Company: John Agar, Dobe Carey, Hank Worden and Chuck Roberson. Chuck Hayward was also on hand to perform stunts, and Cliff Lyons served as second assistant director and stunt coordinator.

On October 15, 1970, Ford suffered a pelvic fracture after he tripped over a laundry bundle. For the next month, he mended while in traction at St. John's Hospital, and then had to use a wheelchair and walker well into the New Year. But neither the accident, nor the death of his Man Friday, stopped him from planning a film project, one that would carry on his "pro-minority series" that had begun with *Sergeant Rutledge*.

In fact, the new project, which had two working titles, "Appointment with Precedence" and "The Josh Clayton Story," would be a companion piece to *Rutledge*, featuring Woody Strode as a sergeant who chafes under the command of the first black West Point graduate to command an African American cavalry unit. The original story had been written by Robert "Bobby" Johnson, a veteran actor who played Trooper Newcomb in *Rutledge* and directed a powerful African-American film, *Living Between Two Worlds* (on which Ivan Dixon worked as assistant director), in 1963.

Following his longtime tradition of featuring football players in his films, Ford intended to cast NFL great turned "blaxploitation" star Fred Williamson as Josh Clayton. Johnson was joined by James Bellah to write the screenplay, which would include cameo roles for Wayne, Fonda and Stewart. Due to the success of Sergio Leone's "Ford homage," *Once Upon a Time in the West* (1968), and other "Spaghetti Westerns," producers in Italy were interested in financing Ford's project if he could keep the budget under $2 million.

On November 29, NBC broadcast *Swing Out, Sweet Land*, a 73-minute television movie produced by Batjac featuring Wayne, Glen Campbell, Johnny Cash, Bob Hope and George Burns as themselves, with an all-star cast including Roscoe Lee Browne (as Frederick

Douglas), Bing Crosby (Mark Twain), Lorne Greene (George Washington), Dean Martin (Eli Whitney), Hugh O'Brian (Thomas Jefferson) and William Shatner (John Adams). The day after the broadcast, Wayne received a letter of praise from James Cagney, writing from his farm in Stanfordville, New York:

Dear Duke,
    The show was great and all the Cagneys are sending along congratulations. I called Bill [his brother] afterward and he agreed wholeheartedly that it was as fine an offering, as moving an offering, as we had ever seen.
    You were everything that was required, and the boys and girls who helped made it a helluva show with all of it being in the best possible taste....
                                                                    Sincerely,
                                                                    Jim Cagney[43]

Woody Strode had been living in Rome since 1969, appearing in the Italian Westerns *Boot Hill* (1969) and *The Unholy Four* (1970), and currently working on *The Deserter* (1971), co-directed by Niksa Fulgosi and Burt Kennedy, and featuring an all-star international cast including Richard Crenna, Chuck Connors, Ricardo Montalban, Ian Bannen, Slim Pickens and Patrick Wayne. When the "Josh Clayton" project fell through, Ford pitched another script, a religiously oriented Western featuring a white character he wanted rewritten for a black actor (Strode). The rights to the screenplay had a price tag of $20,000, but when the writer heard of Ford's interest in making the film, the fee was increased to $50,000, and this proposed enterprise also was abandoned.

In March 1971, Ford teamed with Frank Capra to make a Revolutionary War film, "Valley Forge," with profits to be donated to the Motion Picture Country House Relief Fund. After gaining the support of Brigadier General Frank McCarthy, whom Capra had worked with during World War II; George C. Scott, who was interested in playing George Washington; and Martin Rackin, whom Ford had forgiven for *The Horse Soldiers* fiasco and the atrocious remake of *Stagecoach* (1966), Columbia refused to sell the film rights.

Ford's other proposed Revolutionary project, an adaptation of Howard Fast's novel *April Morning*, focusing on the 1775 Battle of Lexington, and with Wayne in the lead, also generated no interest. Referring to the Hollywood studio heads who cared little or nothing about their nation's history, Ford said, "These are an ignorant lot of bastards."[44]

Ford attempted, one last time, in March 1972, to get a "Black Western" made. *Variety* reported that "The Grave Diggers," a screenplay by James Bellah and his son, James, Jr., was set to be directed by Ford. The story focused on Benjamin Davis (to be played either by Strode or Williamson), the first black West Point graduate to retire as a major general. Alas, this was the last version of Pappy's African American "dream project" ever announced to the press.

Dobe Carey recalled another Uncle Jack brainstorm:

I think he was always interested in making *The Last Outlaw* [a 1919 Ford Western] again, even then. He wanted to make it with Duke. Oh, I wish it had happened. It would have been marvelous—Duke as an older guy, getting out of prison in the Thirties. Duke always wanted to do it.[45]

During 1972, Wayne remained busy in Durango, shooting *The Train Robbers* and *Cahill, United States Marshal*. During a break from shooting *Cahill* with Andrew McLaglen, Carey, in the café at the Mexico Courts, spied Duke entering "with all his entourage." Thinking about his recent trips to see Ford in Palm Desert, Carey approached Wayne, requesting a private conversation. Duke appeared irritated, but motioned Dobe toward a table at the opposite end of the room.

Carey mentioned his visits with the Old Man, whom he believed was suffering from cancer.

Wayne would have none of it. "Bullshit!" he yelled, claiming that Ford was just slacking off in his "goddamned bed ... feeling sorry for himself because no one will hire him."

Carey was serious enough to make "the big man stop and think," but then Duke just brushed him aside.

The next day, Wayne flew to Palm Desert to see the Coach, and was back in Durango the following morning, quite melancholy as he approached Carey. "You were right, Dobe," he admitted. "He's down there in that goddamned Palm Desert, dying.... And we need him. We need him real bad!"[46]

During exploratory surgery, Dr. Maynard Brandsma had discovered a massive malignancy in Pappy's abdomen. Like his brother Francis before him, John Feeney stoically accepted his fate. Further surgery would not improve his condition. The colorectal cancer was terminal, and he also was suffering from arteriosclerosis.

Jack and Mary each lived in a separate wing of the Palm Desert home. Ford spent increasingly more time in bed, reading and watching television. Though he complained about the historical inaccuracies rampant in serious World War II films, his favorite TV series was *Hogan's Heroes*.

The community he joined was a "Who's Who" of pioneer Hollywood directors: Clarence Brown, Frank Capra, Henry Hathaway, Howard Hawks, George Stevens, William Wyler. Other pals dropped in: Duke, Dobe, Hank Fonda, Lee Marvin, Elizabeth Allen, Robert Parrish, Anna Lee, even Katharine Hepburn, whose tender reunion with Jack was secretly captured on audio tape (and subsequently heard in an extended cut of *Directed by John Ford*, the documentary masterminded by Pappy's biographer and pal, Peter Bogdanovich).

For their final resting place, Jack and Mary purchased a multiple grave plot at Holy Cross, the Catholic cemetery in Culver City. A peaceful, immaculately tended, and green enough for an Irishman (perhaps too green for Herb Yates) burial spot, the headstone merely reads, "Admiral John Ford" and "Mary Ford," with the only "reference" to the film industry being the location of his death noted, not as Palm Springs, but Hollywood. Just a few plots to the right rests his brother Francis, whose headstone notes only his military service in the Spanish-American War.

On March 31, 1973, Ford received the American Film Institute's first prestigious Lifetime Achievement Award. At the ceremony held in the Beverly Hilton Hotel, during which he was referred to as "the most important director since the late D. W. Griffith," President Richard M. Nixon presented Rear Admiral John Ford with the Medal of Freedom, the nation's highest civilian honor.

Ironically, Pappy shared the dais, not only with the scandal-ridden Republican president for whom Bond was campaigning when felled by a fatal heart attack, but also with California Governor Ronald W. Reagan, a former FDR Democrat who had turned right-wing FBI informant during the Red Scare.

Duke, Jimmy Stewart and Maureen O'Hara were there, too; but the Ghost of Ward Bond undoubtedly was smiling down (or *up*, perhaps) on the political implications of this gala affair.

John Ford often exaggerated that, during breaks on location, he and Maureen O'Hara often communicated "in the Irish." He also claimed that, during Francis' final days, Brother Feeney consoled himself by speaking only in Gaelic. When Anna Lee came to visit, she said, "I love you, Sean Aloysius," and he responded, "And I love you, Boniface."[47]

Over the past 35 years, Pappy already had been to heaven many times. Of Monument Valley, he had said, "I feel at peace there. I have been all over the world, but I consider this the most complete, beautiful and peaceful place on earth."[48]

Until the final two weeks of his 79 years and seven months of mortality, John Martin Feeney refused to take the morphine routinely used to ease excruciating pain from the horrific disease that killed Frank and now was murdering him. Along with his Catholic rosary, he still had another comrade for comfort.

Sean Aloysius O'Fearna, as he would like to be called, was an Irishman to the End. This Son of Erin born "across the pond" had what is called, in Gaelic, a *cara*; in English, a friend: Guinness Stout, of St. James Gate, Dublin.

Is fearr de thú Guinness, "Guinness Is Good for You," as the pub signs first proudly proclaimed during the 1920s; and Stout critically consoled the "half genius, half Irish," coach, skipper, socialist conservative, sadist, alcoholic, mean old bastard, evil son of a bitch, rear admiral, "director" of World War II, best goddamn filmmaker of all time, *Natani Nez*, the tall soldier of the Navajos, the man who gave cinema John Wayne and Ward Bond, into the *codlata síoraí*, the eternal sleep, at 6:35 P.M. on August 31, 1973.

Woody Strode had returned from a film shoot in Italy just a few hours before his Papa's passing. Ford may have recalled Alan Mowbray's memorable "Good night, sweet prince" in *My Darling Clementine* as the beloved Woody, his enormous hand gently engulfing that of his surrogate father, bade him farewell as the final moments of consciousness slipped away.

"He was so tough I didn't believe he could die," Strode admitted.[49]

On the day before his death, Ford had no more time for bullshit. While visiting with John Wayne for the last time, he looked up and, with great sincerity in his faltering voice, asked, "Do you miss Ward?"

"I sure do, Jack," replied Duke.[50]

Appendix A

The Films of John Ford Featuring
John Wayne and/or Ward Bond

Also included are the U.S. government shorts, two television programs, and stage play featuring Wayne and/or Bond that were directed and/or produced by Ford. An asterisk [*] indicates that Wayne or Bond is not billed in the on-screen credits.

Four Sons (February 13, 1928)

CREDITS: Director and Producer: John Ford; Screenplay: Philip Klein, Herman Bing, Katherine Hilliker, H. H. Caldwell; Based on the story "Grandma Bernle Learns Her Letters" by I. A. R. Wylie; Directors of Photography: George Schneiderman, Charles G. Clarke; Editor: Margaret V. Clancey; Musical Score: Carli Elinor; Assistant Directors: Edward O'Fearna, R. L. Hough; Costume Design: Kathleen Kay; Wardrobe: Sam Benson; Production Editors: H. H. Caldwell, Katherine Hilliker; Musical Arranger: S. L. Rothafel; Orchestrator: Maurice Baron; Props: **John Wayne**; Fox Film Corporation.

CAST: Margaret Mann (Mother Bernle), James Hall (Joseph "Dutch" Bernle), Charles Morton (Johann Bernle), Ralph Bushman, aka Francis X. Bushman, Jr. (Franz Bernle), George Meeker (Andreas Bernle), June Collyer (Annabelle), Earle Foxe (Major von Stomm), Albert Gran (The Postman), Frank Reicher (The Schoolmaster), Archduke Leopold of Austria (A Captain), Ferdinand Schumann-Heink (A Staff Sergeant), Jack Pennick (The Iceman), Joseph W. Girard (Ellis Island Examiner), Bob Kortman (German Barber), Hughie Mack (Innkeeper), Michael Mark (Von Stomm's Orderly), Tom McGuire (Police Sergeant), Ruth Mix (Johann's Girl), L. J. O'Connor (Aubergiste), Robert Parrish (Joseph's Son), August Tollaire (The Burgomeister), Frank Baker (Soldier), George Blagoi, Stanley Blystone, Carl Boheme, Constant Franke, Hans Feurberg, Hans Joby, Harry Tenbrook, Tibor von Janny, **John Wayne*** (Officers), Carmencita Johnson (Baby), Harry Cording (Bit).

Mother Machree (March 5, 1928)

CREDITS: Director and Producer: John Ford; Screenplay: Gertrude Orr, Katherine Hilliker, H. H. Caldwell; Based on the novel *The Story of Mother Machree* by Rida Johnson Young; Director of Photog-

raphy: Chester A. Lyons; Editors: H. H. Caldwell, Katherine Hilliker; Musical Score: Erno Rapee; Assistant Director: Edward O'Fearna; Props: **John Wayne**; Premiere: January 22, 1928; Fox Film Corporation; 75 minutes.

CAST: Belle Bennett (Mother Machree), Neil Hamilton (Brian McHugh/Brian van Studdiford), Victor McLaglen (Terence O'Dowd, The Giant of Kilkenny), Constance Howard (Edith Cutting), Philippe De Lacy (Brian McHugh as a Child), Ted McNamara (The Harper of Wexford), Billy Platt (Pips, The Dwarf of Munster), Eulalie Jensen (Rachel van Studdiford), Pat Somerset (Bobby de Puyster), Rodney Hildebrand (Brian McHugh, Sr.), Wallace MacDonald (Michael McHugh), John MacSweeney (Father McShane), Aggie Herring (Side Show Woman), Robert Parrish (Child), Joyce Wirard (Edith Cutting as a Child), Ethel Clayton, Jack Rollens (Bits), **John Wayne** (Extra*).

Hangman's House (May 13, 1928)

CREDITS: Director and Producer: John Ford; Screenplay: Philip Klein, Marion Orth, Malcolm Stuart Boylan, Willard Mack; Based on the novel by Brian Oswald Donn-Byrne; Director of Photography: George Schneiderman; Editor: Margaret V. Clancey; Musical Score: Tim Curran; Assistant Director: Philip Ford; Stunts: Audrey Scott; Fox Film Corporation; 80 minutes.

CAST: Victor McLaglen (Citizen Denis Hogan), June Collyer (Connaught "Conn" O'Brien), Earle Foxe (John D'Arcy), Larry Kent (Dermot McDermot), Hobart Bosworth (Lord Chief Justice James O'Brien), Joseph Burke (Neddy Joe, Dermot's Servant), Mary Gordon (Woman at Hogan's Hideout), Brian Desmond Hurst (Horserace Spectator), Eric Mayne (Colonel of Legionnaires), Jack Pennick (Man Bringing Dermot to Hogan), Belle Stoddard (Anne McDermot), **John**

Wayne (Horse Race Spectator/Condemned Man in Flashback*).

The Black Watch (May 22, 1929)

CREDITS: Director: John Ford; Producer: Winfield R. Sheehan; Screenplay: John Stone, James Kevin McGuinness; Based on the novel *King of the Khyber Rifles* by Talbot Mundy; Director of Photography: Joseph H. August; Editor: Alex Troffey; Musical Arrangements: William Kernell; Art Director: William S. Darling; Assistant Director: Edward O'Fearna; Dialogue Director: Lumsden Hare; Sound: W. W. Lindsay, Jr., Willard W. Starr; Props: **John Wayne**; Premiere: May 8, 1929; Fox Film Corporation; 93 minutes.

CAST: Victor McLaglen (Captain Donald Gordon King), Myrna Loy (Yasmani), David Rollins (Lieutenant Malcolm King), Lumsden Hare (Colonel of the Black Watch), Roy D'Arcy (Rewa Ghunga), Mitchell Lewis (Mohammed Khan), Cyril Chadwick (Major Twynes), Claude King (General in India), Francis Ford (Major MacGregor), Walter Long (Harrim Bey), David Torrence (Field Marshal), Frederick Sullivan (General's Aide), Richard Travis (Adjutant), Pat Somerset (O'Connor, Black Watch Officer), David Percy (Soloist, Black Watch Officer), Joseph Diskay (Muezzin), Joyzelle Joyner (Dancer), Harry Allen (Sandy), Mary Gordon (Sandy's Wife), Frank Baker, Arthur Clayton, Tom London, Arthur Metcalfe (42nd Highlanders), Phillips Smalley (Doctor), Gregory Gaye, Bob Kortman, Jack Pennick, Randolph Scott, Lupita Tover (Bits), **John Wayne** (Extra*).

Salute (September 1, 1929)

CREDITS: Directors: John Ford, David Butler; Producer: John Ford; Screenplay: John Stone, Kevin James McGuinness, Wilbur Morse, Jr.; Based on a story by Tristram Tupper; Director of Photography: Joseph H. August; Editor: Alex Troffey; Art Director: William S. Darling; Costume Designer: Sophie Wachner; Assistant Directors: Richard Hough, Edward O'Fearna; Sound: W. W. Lindsay, Jr.; Technical Advisor: Schuyler E. Grey; Costumer for Stepin Fetchit: **John Wayne**; Locations: U.S. Naval Academy, Annapolis, Maryland; Fox Film Corporation; 84 minutes.

CAST: George O'Brien (Cadet John Randall), Helen Chandler (Nancy Wayne), William Janney (Midshipman Paul Randall), Stepin Fetchit (Smoke Screen), Frank Albertson (Midshipman Albert Edward Price), Joyce Compton (Marian Wilson), David Butler (Navy Coach), Lumsden Hare (Rear Admiral John Randall), Clifford Dempsey (Major General Somers), **Ward Bond** (Midshipman Harold), **John Wayne** (Midshipman Bill*), Rex Bell (Cadet), John Breeden (Midshipman), Jack Pennick (Football Player), Harry Tenbrook (Assistant Navy Coach), Lee Tracy (Radio Announcer).

Men Without Women (February 8, 1930)

CREDITS: Director and Producer: John Ford; Associate Producer: James Kevin McGuinness; Screenplay: Dudley Nichols, John Ford, Otis C. Freeman; Based on the story "Submarine" by James Kevin McGuinness; Director of Photography: Joseph H. August; Editors: Walter Thompson, Paul Weatherwax; Musical Score: Peter Brunelli, Glen Knight, R. H. Bassett; Set Decorator: William S. Darling; Assistant Director: Edward O'Fearna; Sound: W. D. Flick, W. W. Lindsay, Jr.; Wardrobe: Sam Benson; Editorial Supervisor: John Stone; Stage Director: Andrew Bennison; Technical Advisor: Schuyler E. Grey; Props: **John Wayne**; Fox Film Corporation; 77 minutes.

CAST: Kenneth MacKenna (Chief Torpedoman Burke), Frank Albertson (Ensign Edward Albert Price), J. Farrell MacDonald (Costello), Warren Hymer (Kaufman), Paul Page (Handsome), Walter McGrail (Joe Cobb), Stuart Erwin (Radioman Jenkins), George LeGuere (Curly Pollock), Charles K. Gerrard (Commander Weymouth), Ben Hendricks, Jr. (Murphy), Harry Tenbrook (Dutch Winkler), Warner Richmond (Lieutenant Commander Briddwell), Ivan Lebedeff (Man with Top Hat), Frank Richardson (Singing Sailor in Shanghai), Pat Somerset (Lieutenant Digby), Roy Stewart (Captain Carson), **John Wayne** (Radioman on Surface*), Frank Baker, Robert Parrish (Bits).

Born Reckless (June 6, 1930)

CREDITS: Directors: Andrew Bennison, John Ford; Associate Producer: James Kevin McGuinness; Screenplay: Dudley Nichols; Based on the novel *Louis Beretti* by Donald Henderson Clarke; Director of Photography: George Schneiderman; Editor: Frank E. Hull; Musical Score: Peter Brunelli, George Lipschultz, Albert Hay Malotte, Jean Talbot; Art Director: John DuCasse Schulze; Costume Designer: Sophie Wachner; Assistant Director: Edward O'Fearna; Sound: W. W. Lindsay, Jr.; Fox Film Corporation; 82 minutes.

CAST: Edmund Lowe (Louis Beretti), Catherine Dale Owen (Joan Sheldon), Frank Albertson (Frank Sheldon), Marguerite Churchill (Rosa Beretti), William Harrigan (Good News Brophy), Lee Tracy (Bill O'Brien), Warren Hymer (Big Shot), Ilka Chase (High Society Customer), Fereke Boros (Ma Beretti), Paul Porcasi (Pa Beretti), Joe Brown (Needle Beer Grogan, Bartender), Ben Bard (Joe Bergman), Pat Somerset (Duke), Eddie Gribbon (Bugs), Mike Donlin (Fingy Moscovitz), Paul Page (Ritzy Reilly), Roy Stewart (District Attorney Cardigan), Jack Pennick (Sergeant), **Ward Bond** (Sergeant), Yola d'Avril (French Girl), Stanley Blystone, Tom McGuire (Newspaper Workers), Edwards Davis (Uncle Jim), Robert Homans (Policeman), John Kelly (Irish Recruit), James A. Marcus (General Sheldon), Randolph Scott (Dick, Joan's Rejected Suitor), Harry Strang (Sergeant), Harry Tenbrook (Beretti Henchman), Bill Elliott (Dance Extra), **John Wayne** (Extra*).

Up the River (October 12, 1930)

CREDITS: Director: John Ford; Producer: William Fox; Screenplay: William Collier, Sr., John Ford; Based on a story by Maurine Dallas Watkins; Director of Photography: Joseph H. August; Editor: Frank E. Hull; Musical Score and Lyrics: James F. Hanley, Joseph McCarthy; Art Director: Duncan Cramer; Costume Designer: Sophie Wachner; Wardrobe: Sam

Benson; Assistant Directors: Edward O'Fearna, Wingate Smith; Sound: W. W. Lindsay, Jr.; Fox Film Corporation; 85 minutes.

CAST: Spencer Tracy (Saint Louis), Claire Luce (Judy), Warren Hymer (Dannemora Dan), Humphrey Bogart (Steve Jordan), William Collier, Sr. (Pop), Joan Marie Lawes (Jean), **Ward Bond** (Inmate*), Joe Brown (Deputy Warden), Bob Burns (Slim), Eddy Chandler, Claude Payton (Guards), Edythe Chapman (Mrs. Jordan), Harvey Clark (Nash), Dick Curtis (New Inmate), Noel Francis (Sophie), Althea Henley (Cynthia Jordan), Elizabeth Keating (May), Richard Keene (Dick), Sharon Lynn (Edith La Verne), George MacFarlane (John Jessup), Louise Mackintosh (Mrs. Massey), Wilbur Mack (Whiteley), Goodee Montgomery (Kit), Robert Emmett O'Connor (Warden), Robert Parrish (Boy), Steve Pendleton (Morris), Pat Somerset (Beauchamp), John Swor (Clem), Mildred Vincent (Annie), Johnnie Walker (Happy), Morgan Wallace (Frosby), Adele Windsor (Minnie), Carol Wines (Daisy Elmore).

Arrowsmith (December 26, 1931)

CREDITS: Director: John Ford; Producers: John Ford, Samuel Goldwyn; Executive Producer: Arthur Hornblow, Jr.; Screenplay: Sidney Howard; Based on the novel by Sinclair Lewis; Director of Photography: Ray June; Editor: Hugh Bennett; Musical Score: Alfred Newman; Art Director: Richard Day; Casting: Robert McIntyre; Assistant Director: Herbert Sutch; Sound: Jack Noyes; Production began early September 1931; Samuel Goldwyn Company–United Artists; 99 minutes.

CAST: Ronald Colman (Dr. Martin Arrowsmith), Helen Hayes (Leora Arrowsmith), Richard Bennett (Gustav Sondelius), A. E. Anson (Professor Max Gottlieb), Clarence Brooks (Oliver Marchand), Alec B. Francis (Twyford), Claude King (Dr. Tubbs), Bert Roach (Bert Tozer), Myrna Loy (Mrs. Joyce Lanyon), Russell Hopton (Terry Wickett), David Landau (State Veterinarian), Lumsden Hare (Sir Robert Fairland, Governor), Erville Alderson (Pioneer), Charlotte Henry (The Pioneer Girl), **Ward Bond** (Cop*), John Qualen (Henry Novak), Adele Watson (Mrs. Novak), DeWitt Jennings (Mr. B. W. Tozer), Beulah Bondi (Mrs. Tozer), Florence Britton (Miss Twyford), Nora Cecil (Nurse), Sidney De Gray (Dr. Hesselink), Walter Downing (City Clerk), Sherry Hall, Mike Lally (Reporters), Theresa Harris (Native Mother), Raymond Hatton (Drunk), George Humbert (Italian Uncle), Carl M. Leviness, Edmund Mortimer (Ship's Passengers), Pat Somerset, Eric Wilton (Ship's Officers), James A. Marcus (Old Doctor), Eric Mayne, Edward Reinach (Dignitaries), Mike Donlin, Bobby Watson (Bits).

Air Mail (November 3, 1932)

CREDITS: Director: John Ford; Producer: Carl Laemmle, Jr.; Screenplay: Frank "Spig" Wead; Based on a story by Frank Wead and Dale Van Every; Director of Photography: Karl Freund; Editor: Harry W. Lieb; Musical Arrangements: David Broekman; Special Effects: John P. Fulton; Aerial Photography: Elmer Dyer; Stunts: Paul Mantz; Locations: Bishop, California; Universal Pictures; 84 minutes.

CAST: Ralph Bellamy (Mike Miller), Gloria Stuart (Ruth Barnes), Pat O'Brien (Duke Talbot), Slim Summerville ("Slim" McCune), Lilian Bond (Irene Wilkins), Russell Hopton ("Dizzy" Wilkins), David Landau ("Pop"), Leslie Fenton (Tony Dressel), Frank Albertson (Tommy Bogan), Hans Fuerberg ("Heinie" Kramer), Thomas Carrigan ("Sleepy" Collins), William Daly ("Tex" Lane), Frank Beal (Passenger to Kansas City), **Ward Bond** (Joe Barnes*), Wade Boteler (Medical Examiner), Edmund Burns (Radio Announcer), Pat Davis, Charles De La Motte (Passenger Plane Pilots), James Donlan (Passenger Passing Out Cigars), James Flavin (Man with Radio Report), Francis Ford (Passenger Who'll Die on a Train), George Irving (John Montgomery), Lew Kelly (Drunken Passenger), Louise Mackintosh (Passenger Writing Postcard), Beth Milton (Flight Attendant), Jack Pennick (Airport Postal Worker), Harry Tenbrook (Airport Worker Yelling "Crash Wagon"), Katherine Perry (Passenger), Jim Thorpe (Indian), Alene Carroll, Enrico Caruso, Jr., Billy Thorpe (Bits).

Flesh (December 8, 1932)

CREDITS: Director: John Ford; Producers: John Ford, John W. Considine, Jr.; Screenplay: Leonard Praskins, Edgar Allan Woolf, Moss Hart, William Faulkner; Based on a story by Edmund Goulding; Director of Photography: Arthur Edeson; Editor: William S. Gray; Musical Score: Alfred Newman; Art Director: Cedric Gibbons; Assistant Director: Dave Taggart; Sound: Douglas Shearer, James Brock; Production Dates: September 26 to late October 1932; Metro-Goldwyn-Mayer; 96 minutes.

CAST: Wallace Beery (Polakai), Ricardo Cortez (Nicky), Karen Morley (Laura), Jean Hersholt (Mr. Herman), John Miljan (Willard), Herman Bing (Pepi, Headwaiter), Vince Barnett (Karl, a Waiter), Greta Meyer (Mrs. Herman), Edward Brophy (Dolan, a Referee), **Ward Bond** (Muscles Manning*), Joe Caits (Referee in Germany), Mike Donlin (Mike, Man in Gym), Charles Sullivan, Jack Herrick (Boxers at Gym), Hans Joby (Hans, Waiter in Germany), Wilbur Mack (One of Willard's Aides), Jerry Mandy (Gym Manager), Larry McGrath (Championship Referee in U.S.A.), Nat Pendleton (Wrestler), Frank Reicher (Warden in Germany), Monte Vandergrift (Radio Sports Reporter), Charles Williams (Sports Reporter), Wladek Zbyszko (Zbyszko, Polakai's Championship Opponent in U.S.A.).

Submarine Patrol (November 25, 1938)

CREDITS: Director: John Ford; Producer: Darryl F. Zanuck; Associate Producers: Gene Markey, Ralph Dietrich; Screenplay: William Faulkner, Kathryn Scola, Rian James, Darrell Ware, Jack Yellen, Don Ettlinger, Sheridan Gibney, Gene Markey, Lieutenant Commander George O. Noville, Karl Tunberg; Based on the novel *The Splinter Fleet of the Otranto Barrage* by Ray Milholland; Director of Photography: Arthur C. Miller; Editor: Robert L. Simpson; Musical Score:

Arthur Lange, Charles Maxwell; Art Directors: William S. Darling, Hans Peters; Costume Design: Gwen Wakeling; Wardrobe Supervisors: Hilda Anderson, David Preston; Makeup Supervisor: Sam Kaufman; Hair Stylist: Jean Adko; Assistant Directors: Edward O'Fearna, Wingate Smith; Sound: Eugene Grossman, Roger Heman, Sr., Jack Lescoulie, Harold A. Root, E. Clayton Ward; Production Manager: V. L. McFadden; Unit Manager: Bernard McEveety; Property Master: Joe Behm; Assistant Property Master: Andy Kisch; Location Managers: Lefty Hough, Ray C. Moore; Technical Advisor: Captain Valentine Wood; Still Photographer: Cliff Maupin; Production Dates: late June to late August 1938; 20th Century–Fox Film Corporation; 95 minutes.

CAST: Richard Greene (Perry Townsend III), Nancy Kelly (Susan Leeds), Preston Foster (Lieutenant [j.g.] John C. Drake), George Bancroft (Captain Leeds), Slim Summerville (Ellsworth "Spuds" Fickett, Cook), J. Farrell MacDonald (CWO "Sails" Quincannon), Warren Hymer (Seaman Rocky Haggerty), Douglas Fowley (Seaman Pinky Brett), Dick Hogan (Seaman Johnny Miller), Elisha Cook, Jr. (Seaman Rutherford Davis Pratt, aka "The Professor"), George E. Stone (Seaman Irving Goldfarb), Jack Pennick (Bos'un "Guns" McPeek), John Carradine (McAllison), Henry Armetta (Luigi), Joan Valerie (Anne), "Slapsie" Maxie Rosenbloom (Marine Sentry Sergeant Joe Duffy), Charles Trowbridge (Rear Admiral Joseph Maitland), Moroni Olson (Fleet Captain), **Ward Bond** (Seaman Olaf Swanson), Robert Lowery (Sparks, Radioman), Harry Strang (Seaman Grainger), Victor Varconi (Italian Naval Chaplain Vanzano), Ernie Alexander, Ray Cooke, Duke Green (Warship Sailors), Murray Alper (Orderly in Maitland's Office), Lon Chaney, Jr. (Marine Sentry), Dorothy Christy (McPeek's Girl), Alan Davis (Maitland's Secretary-Lieutenant), Fred Malatesta, Manuel Paris (Italian Gendarmes at the "Maria Ann"), Frank Moran (Waiter at Dive), Ferdinand Schumann-Heink (German Officer), Dick Wessel (Dock Shore Patrolman), Russ Clark, E. E. Clive, Charles Tannen (Bits).

Stagecoach (March 2, 1939)

CREDITS: Director and Producer: John Ford; Screenplay: Dudley Nichols, Ben Hecht; Based on the story "Stage to Lordsburg" by Ernest Haycox; Director of Photography: Bert Glennon; Editors: Otho Lovering, Dorothy Spencer, Walter Reynolds; Musical Score: Gerard Carbonara; Art Director: Alexander Toluboff; Associate Art Director: Wiard B. Ihnen; Costume Design: Walter Plunkett; Assistant Directors: Wingate Smith, Lowell J. Farrell; Second Unit Director and Stunt Coordinator: Yakima Canutt; Special Photographic Effects: Ray Binger; Sound: Frank Maher; Stunt Rigger: Billy Yellow; Stunts: Iron Eyes Cody, Ken Cooper, Johnny Eckert, W. Frank Long, Jack Mohr, David Sharpe, Henry Wills; Assistant Camera Operators: James V. King, Cliff Shirpser; Still Photographer: Ned Scott; Extras Casting: Lee Bradley, Harry Goulding; Musical Director: Boris Morros; Musical Adaptations: Louis Gruenberg, Richard Hageman, W. Franke Harling, John Leipold, Leo Shuken;

Accordionist: Danny Borzage; Location Manager: Danny Keith; Horse Handler and Wrangler: W. Frank Long; Locations: California, Arizona, Utah; Production Dates: early November 1938 to January 7, 1939; Walter Wanger Productions, Inc.–United Artists; 96 minutes.

CAST: Claire Trevor (Dallas), **John Wayne** (Ringo Kid), Andy Devine (Buck), John Carradine (Hatfield), Thomas Mitchell (Doc Boone), Louise Platt (Lucy Mallory), George Bancroft (Curley), Donald Meek (Peacock), Berton Churchill (Gatewood), Tim Holt (Lieutenant), Tom Tyler (Luke Plummer), Dorothy Appleby, Helen Gibson (Girls in Saloon), Chief John Big Tree (Indian Scout), Ed Brady (Lordsburg Saloon Owner), Yakima Canutt (Cavalry Scout), Nora Cecil (Boone's Landlady), Bill Cody, Buddy Roosevelt (Ranchers), Jack Curtis, Si Jenks (Bartenders), Marga Ann Deighton (Mrs. Pickett), Franklyn Farnum (Deputy Frank), Francis Ford (Billy Pickett), Brenda Fowler (Mrs. Gatewood), Robert Homans (Editor), William Hopper (Sergeant), Cornelius Keefe (Captain Whitney), Florence Lake (Nancy Whitney), Duke R. Lee (Lordsburg Sheriff), Theodore Lorch (Lordsburg Express Agent), Chris Pin-Martin (Chris), Jim Mason (Jim, Tonto Express Agent), Louis Mason (Tonto Sheriff), Merrill McCormick (Ogler), Walter McGrail (Captain Sickel), Paul McVey (Pony Express Agent), Kent Odell (Billy Pickett, Jr.), Artie Ortego (Lordsburg Bar Patron), Vester Pegg (Hank Plummer), Jack Pennick (Bartender in Tonto), Joe Rickson (Ike Plummer), Elvira Rios (Yakima), Woody Strode (Man in Saloon), Harry Tenbrook (Telegraph Operator), Mary Kathleen Walker (Lucy's Infant), Bryant Washburn (Captain Simmons), Whitehorse (Indian Chief), Hank Worden (Cavalryman Extra), Frank Baker, Ted Billings, Wiggie Blowne, Danny Borzage, Fritzi Brunette, Steve Clemente, Patricia Doyle, Tex Driscoll, J. P. McGowan, Mickey Simpson, Chuck Stubbs (Bits).

Young Mr. Lincoln (June 9, 1939)

CREDITS: Director: John Ford; Producer: Darryl F. Zanuck; Associate Producer: Kenneth Macgowan; Screenplay: Lamar Trotti; Directors of Photography: Bert Glennon, Arthur C. Miller; Editors: Walter Thompson, Robert Parrish; Musical Score: Alfred Newman, David Buttolph; Musical Direction: Louis Silvers, Paul Van Loan; Art Directors: Richard Day, Mark-Lee Kirk; Costume Design: Royer; Set Decorator: Thomas Little; Assistant Director: Wingate Smith; Sound: Eugene Grossman, Roger Heman, Sr.; Sound Effects Editor: Robert Parrish; Wardrobe: Sam Benson; Stunts: Yakima Canutt; Locations: Sacramento, California; Production Dates: early March to mid–April 1939; Cosmopolitan Productions–20th Century–Fox Film Corporation; 100 minutes.

CAST: Henry Fonda (Abraham Lincoln), Alice Brady (Abigail Clay), Marjorie Weaver (Mary Todd), Arleen Whelan (Sarah Clay), Eddie Collins (Efe Turner), Pauline Moore (Ann Rutledge), Richard Cromwell (Matt Clay), Donald Meek (Prosecutor John Felder), Judith Dickens (Carrie Sue), Eddie Quillan (Adam Clay), Spencer Charters (Judge Herbert A. Bell), **Ward Bond** (John Palmer Cass), Ernie Adams (Man with

Lynch Mob), Arthur Aylesworth (New Salem Towns-man), Cliff Clark (Sheriff Gil Billings), Francis Ford (Sam Boone), Harold Goodwin (Jeremiah Carter), Charles Halton (Hawthorne), Herbert Heywood (Official at Tug o' War Contest), Robert Homans (Mr. Clay), Dickie Jones (Adam Clay as a Boy), Jack Kelly (Matt Clay as a Boy), Fred Kohler, Jr. (Scrub White), Kay Linaker (Mrs. Edwards), Robert Lowery (Juror Bill Killian), Milburn Stone (Stephen A. Douglas), Charles Tannen (Ninian Edwards), Jim Mason, Ivor McFadden, Steve Randall (Jurors), Louis Mason (Court Clerk), Edwin Maxwell (John T. Stuart), Sylvia McClure (Baby Clay), Tom McGuire (Bailiff), Paul E. Burns, George Chandler, Dave Morris, Frank Orth (Loafers), Jack Pennick (Big Buck Troop), Russell Simpson (Woolridge), Harry Tyler (Barber), Virginia Brissac (Peach Pie Baker), Dorothy Vaughan (Apple Pie Baker), Billy Watson, Delmar Watson (Boys), Sam Ash (Extra), Frank Dae (Bit), Elizabeth "Tiny" Jones, Eddie Waller, Clarence Wilson (scenes deleted).

Drums Along the Mohawk (November 10, 1939)

CREDITS: Director: John Ford; Producer: Darryl F. Zanuck; Associate Producer: Raymond Griffith; Screenplay: Lamarr Trotti, Sonya Levien; Treatment Contributors: William Faulkner, Bess Meredyth; Based on the novel by Walter D. Edmonds; Directors of Photography: Bert Glennon, Ray Rennahan; Editor: Robert L. Simpson; Musical Score: Alfred Newman, David Buttolph, Edward B. Powell, Conrad Salinger, Frank Tresselt; Musical Direction: Louis Silvers; Art Directors: Richard Day, Mark-Lee Kirk; Set Decorator: Thomas Little; Costume Design: Gwen Wakeling; Makeup: Robert Cowan, Steve Drumm, Newton House, Norbert Miles; Hair Stylists: Ann Barr, Irene Beshon, Marie Braselle, Myrtle Ford; Assistant Directors: F. E. Johnson, Edward O'Fearna, Wingate Smith; Production Manager: Ralph Dietrich; Unit Production Managers: W. F. Fitzgerald, Duke Goux, Bernard McEveety; Sound: Roger Heman, Sr., E. Clayton Ward; Sound Effects Editor: Robert Parrish; Assistant Editor: Mary Crumley; Camera Operator: Irving Rosenberg; Wardrobe: Sam Benson; Stunt Double: Jackie Hamblin; Still Photographer: Frank Powolny; Technicolor Director: Natalie Kalmus; Associate Technicolor Director: Henri Jaffa; Techincal Advisors: Thornton Edwards, Harold Lloyd Morris; Locations: Utah; Production Dates: June 28 to late August 1939; 20th Century–Fox Film Corporation; 104 minutes.

CAST: Claudette Colbert (Lana), Henry Fonda (Gilbert Martin), Edna Mae Oliver (Mrs. MacKlennar), Eddie Collins (Christian Reall), John Carradine (Caldwell), Dorris Bowdon (Mary Reall), Jessie Ralph (Mrs. Weaver), Arthur Shields (The Reverend Rosenkrantz), Robert Lowery (John Weaver), Roger Imhof (General Nicholas Herkimer), Francis Ford (Joe Boleo), **Ward Bond** (Adam Hartman), Kay Linaker (Mrs. Demooth), Russell Simpson (Dr. Petry), Spencer Charters (Innkeeper), Si Jenks (Jacob Small), Jack Pennick (Amos Hartman), Arthur Aylesworth (George

Weaver), Chief John Big Tree (Blue Back), Charles Tannen (Dr. Robert Johnson), Paul McVey (Captain Mark Demooth), Elizabeth "Tiny" Jones (Mrs. Reall), Beulah Hall Jones (Daisy), Edwin Maxwell (The Rev. Daniel Gros), Robert Greig (Mr. Borst), Clara Blandick (Mrs. Borst), Frank Baker (Commander of Colonial Troops), Noble Johnson (Native American), Payne B. Johnson (Boy in Wedding), Mae Marsh (Pioneer Woman), Lionel Pape (General), Tom Tyler (Captain Morgan), Clarence Wilson (Paymaster).

The Grapes of Wrath (March 15, 1940)

CREDITS: Director: John Ford; Producer: Darryl F. Zanuck; Associate Producer and Screenplay: Nunnally Johnson; Based on the novel by John Steinbeck; Director of Photography: Gregg Toland; Editor: Robert L. Simpson; Musical Direction: Alfred Newman; Art Directors: Richard Day, Mark-Lee Kirk; Set Decorator: Thomas Little; Costume Design: Gwen Wakeling; Makeup: Gustav Norin; Hair Stylist: Myrtle Ford; Assistant Directors: Edward O'Fearna, Wingate Smith; Second Unit Director: Otto Brower; Production Manager: Ralph Dietrich; Unit Manager: Bernard McEveety; Sound: Roger Heman, Sr., George Leverett, Edmund H. Hansen, Harry Kornfield; Sound Effects Editor: Robert Parrish; Props: Eddie Jones; Assistant Property Masters: Andy Kisch, William Sittel; Wardrobe Supervisor: Sam Benson; Wardrobe: Harry Kernell, Josephine Perrin; Second Unit Director of Photography: Charles G. Clarke; Camera Operators: Lou Kunkel, Bert Shipman; Assistant Camera Operators: Paul Garnett, Eddie Garvin, Cliff Shirpser; Still Photographer: Emmett Schoenbaum; Assistant Editors: Mary Crumley, Jack Wells; Script Supervisor: Meta Stern; Accordionist: Danny Borzage; Locations: California, Arizona, New Mexico, Oklahoma; Production Dates: October 4 to November 16, 1939; 20th Century–Fox Film Corporation; 128 minutes.

CAST: Henry Fonda (Tom Joad), Jane Darwell (Ma Joad), John Carradine (Casey), Charley Grapewin (Grandpa), Dorris Bowdon (Rose of Sharon), Russell Simpson (Pa Joad), O. Z. Whitehead (Al), John Qualen (Muley), Eddie Quillan (Connie), Zeffie Tilbury (Grandma), Frank Sully (Noah), Frank Darien (Uncle John), Darryl Hickman (Winfield), Shirley Mills (Ruth Joad), Roger Imhof (Thomas), Grant Mitchell (Caretaker), Charles D. Brown (Wilkie), John Arledge (Davis), **Ward Bond** (Policeman), Harry Tyler (Bert), William Pawley (Bill), Charles Tannen (Joe), Selmer Jackson (Inspection Officer), Charles Middleton (Leader), Eddie Waller (Proprietor), Paul Guilfoyle (Floyd), David Hughes (Frank), Cliff Clark (City Man), Joseph Sawyer (Bookkeeper), Frank Faylen (Tim), Adrian Morris (Agent), Hollis Jewel (Muley's Son), Robert Homans (Spencer), Irving Bacon (Driver), Kitty McHugh (Mae), Leon Brace, Henry Brahe, Scotty Brown, Cal Cohen, Cecil Cook, Helen Dean, Billy Elmer, Sidney Hayes, E. J. Kaspar, L. F. O'Connor, Walton Pindon, Josephine Allen, Frank Atkinson, John Binns, Joe Bordeaux, Buster Brodie, Hal Budlong, Nora Bush, Delmar Costello, Jane Crowley, W. H. Davis, Lillian Drew, Emily Gerdes, Tyler Gibson, Barney Gilmore, Dean Hall, Edna Hall,

Cliff Herbert, Charles Herzinger, Harry Holden, David Kirkland, Lillian Lawrence, Hazel Lollier, Harry Matthews, Scotty Mattraw, Jules Michelson, Frank Newburg, Walter Perry, Rose Plumer, Chauncey Pyle, Gladys Rehfeld, Waclaw Rekwart, C. B. Steele, Al Stewart, Charles Thurston, D. H. Turner, Pearl Varvalle, Eleanore Vogel, Harry Wallace, John Wallace, Jack Walters, Frank Watson, Jim Welch, Charles West, Bill Worth (Migrants), Wally Albright, George P. Breakston (Boys), Erville Anderson (Arkansas Storekeeper), Arthur Aylesworth (Father), Trevor Bardette (Jule, Bouncer at Dance), Russ Clark, James Flavin, Philip Morris, Max Wagner (Guards), Shirley Coates (Girl in Migrant Camp), Harry Cording, Ralph Dunn, Pat Flaherty, Frank O'Connor, Bob Reeves, Lee Shumway, Paul Sutton, Harry Tenbrook (Deputies), Jim Corey (Buck Jackson), Gino Corrado (Chef), John Dilson (Bookseller), Thornton Edwards (Motorcycle Cop), William Haade (Deputy with Shotgun), Tom Tyler (Deputy Handcuffing Casey), Ben Hall (Bakersfield Gas Station Attendant), Herbert Heywood (Gas Station Attendant), Rex Lease (Cop), Mae Marsh (Muley's Wife), Louis Mason (Man in Camp), Inez Palange (Woman in Camp), Walter McGrail (Gang Leader), Walter Miller (New Mexico Border Guard), George O'Hara (Clerk), Ted Oliver (State Policeman), Steve Pendleton, Robert Shaw (Needles Gas Station Attendants), Jack Pennick (Camp Helper), Dick Rich (Keene Ranch Guard), Gloria Roy (Waitress), Peggy Ryan (Hungry Girl), Georgia Simmons (Woman), Harry Strang (Fred, Trucker at Diner), Glen Walters (Woman Who Gets Shot), Dan White (Poor Man in Transient Camp), Norman Willis (Joe), Bill Wolfe (Square-Dance Caller), Francis Ford (Bit).

The Long Voyage Home (November 11, 1940)

CREDITS: Director: John Ford; Producers: John Ford, Walter Wanger; Screenplay: Dudley Nichols; Based on the one-act plays *The Moon of the Caribees, In the Zone, Bound East for Cardiff* and *The Long Voyage Home* by Eugene O'Neill; Director of Photography: Gregg Toland; Editor: Sherman Todd; Musical Score: Richard Hageman; Art Director: James Basevi; Set Decorator: Julia Heron; Assistant Director: Wingate Smith; Sound: Jack Noyes; Sound Editor: Robert Parrish; Production Manager: James Dent; Special Effects: Ray Binger, R. T. Layton; Musical Conductor: Edward Paul; Still Photographer: Ned Scott; Production Assistants: Lowell J. Farrell, Bernard McEveety, Wingate Smith; Unit Publicist: Bob Burkhardt; Locations: Wilmington and San Pedro, California; Production began April 17, 1940; Argosy Pictures–Walter Wanger Productions–United Artists; 105 minutes.

CAST: **John Wayne** (Olsen), Thomas Mitchell (Driscoll), Ian Hunter (Smitty), Barry Fitzgerald (Cocky), Wilfrid Lawson (Captain), John Qualen (Axel), Mildred Natwick (Freda), **Ward Bond** (Yank), Arthur Shields (Donkeyman), Joseph Sawyer (Davis), J. M. Kerrigan (Crimp), Rafaela Ottiano (Bella), Carmen Morales (Principal Spanish Girl), Jack Pennick (Johnny), Bob E. Perry (Paddy), Constant Franke (Nor-

way), David Hughes (Scotty), Constantine Romanoff (Big Frank), Danny Borzage (Tim), Harry Tenbrook (Max), Cyril McLaglen (First Mate), Douglas Walton (Second Mate), Billy Bevan (Joe, Limehouse Barman), Mary Carewe (Elizabeth, Smitty's Wife), Bing Conley, Ky Robinson (Limehouse Roustabouts), Lita Cortez, Carmen D'Antonio, Soledad Gonzales, Judith Linden, Elena Martinez, Tina Menard (Bumboat Girls), Jane Crowley (Kate), Lowell Drew (Blind Man), James Flavin, Lee Shumway (Dock Policemen), Guy Kingsford, Leslie Sketchley (London Policemen), Art Miles (Captain of the *Amindra*), Lionel Pape (Mr. Clifton), Luanne Robb (Smitty's Daughter), Roger Steele (Smitty's Son), Maureen Roden-Ryan (Meg), Wyndham Standing (British Naval Officer), Sammy Stein (Seaman), Blue Washington (*Glencairn* Cook), Harry Woods (*Amindra* First Mate).

Tobacco Road (March 7, 1941)

CREDITS: Director: John Ford; Producer: Darryl F. Zanuck; Screenplay: Nunnally Johnson; Based on the novel by Erskine Caldwell and the play by Jack Kirkland; Director of Photography: Arthur C. Miller; Editor: Barbara McLean; Musical Score: David Buttolph; Art Directors: James Basevi, Richard Day; Set Decorator: Thomas Little; Makeup: Carrie O'Neal; Hair Stylist: Gene Tierney; Assistant Directors: Edward O'Fearna, Gene Bryant; Production Manager: Ed Ebele; Sound: Roger Heman, Sr., Eugene Grossman; Sound Effects Editor: Robert Parrish; Special Effects: Fred Etcheverry; Wardrobe: Harry Kernell; Camera Operator: Joseph LaShelle; Stunt Driver: Harvey Perry; Location Manager: Ray C. Moore; Publicity Director: Harry Brand; Locations: Encino and Sherwood Forest, California; Production Dates: late November to late December 1940; 20th Century–Fox Film Corporation; 84 minutes.

CAST: Charley Grapewin (Jeeter Lester), Marjorie Rambeau (Sister Bessie Rice), Gene Tierney (Ellie May Lester), William Tracy (Dude Lester), Elizabeth Patterson (Ada Lester), Dana Andrews (Captain Tim Harmon), Slim Summerville (Henry Peabody), **Ward Bond** (Lov Bensey), Grant Mitchell (George Payne), Zeffie Tilbury (Grandma Lester), Russell Simpson (Chief of Police), Spencer Charters (County Clerk), Irving Bacon (Bank Teller), Harry Tyler (Auto Dealer), Charles Halton (Mayor), George Chandler (Hotel Clerk), Robert Shaw (Hillbilly), Erville Anderson (Driver), Francis Ford (Vagabond), David Hughes (Coroner), Mae Marsh (County Clerk's Assistant), John "Skins" Miller (Mechanic), Jack Pennick (Deputy Sheriff), Luke Cosgrave (Bit), Charles Trowbridge, Charles Waldron, Dorothy Adams (Scenes Deleted).

They Were Expendable (December 20, 1945)

CREDITS: Director and Producer: John Ford, Captain U.S.N.R.; Associate Producer: Cliff Reid; Screenplay: Frank Wead, Commander U.S.N., Retired; Based on the book by William L. White; Director of Photography: Joseph H. August, Lieutenant Commander U.S.N.R.; Editors: Douglass Biggs, Frank E.

Hull; Musical Score: Herbert Stothart; Art Directors: Cedric Gibbons, Malcolm Brown; Set Decorator: Edwin B. Willis; Costume Design: Yvonne Wood; Makeup: Jack Dawn; Assistant Director: Edward O'Fearna; Second Unit Director: James C. Havens, Captain, U.S.M.C.R.; Associate Set Decorator: Ralph S. Hurst; Sound: Douglas Shearer; Sound Effects: Michael Steinore; Special Effects: A. Arnold Gillespie, Donald Jahraus, R. A. MacDonald; Stunts: Jack Stoney; Additional Music: Alberto Colombo, Eric Zeisl; Orchestrations: Harold Byrns, Murray Cutter, Wally Heglin; Director, Rear Projection Plates: Robert Montgomery; Locations: Rhode Island, Florida; Production Dates: February 23 to mid–June 1945; Metro-Goldwyn-Mayer; 135 minutes.

CAST: Robert Montgomery, Commander U.S.N.R. (Lieutenant John Brickley), **John Wayne** (Lieutenant [j.g.] "Rusty" Ryan), Donna Reed (Lieutenant Sandy Daiss), Jack Holt (General Martin), **Ward Bond** ("Boats" Mulcahy C.B.M.), Marshall Thompson (Ensign "Snake" Gardner), Paul Langton (Ensign "Andy" Andrews), Leon Ames (Major James Morton), Arthur Walsh (Seaman Jones), Donald Curtis (Lieutenant [j.g.] "Shorty" Long), Cameron Mitchell (Ensign George Cross), Jeff York (Ensign Tony Aiken), Murray Alper ("Slug" Mahan T.M. 1c), Harry Tenbrook ("Squarehead" Larsen S.C. 2c), Jack Pennick ("Doc"), Alex Havier ("Benny" Lecoco S.T. 3c), Charles Trowbridge (Admiral Blackwell), Robert Barrat (The General), Bruce Kellogg (Elder Tompkins M.M. 2c), Tim Murdock (Ensign Brant), Louis Jean Heydt ("Ohio"), Russell Simpson ("Dad" Knowland), Vernon Steele (Army Doctor), Philip Ahn (Army Orderly), Steve Barclay, Franklin Parker, Ernest Seftig (Naval Officers), Bill Barnum, Danny Borzage, Larry Dods, Blake Edwards, Art Foster, Del Hill, Michael Kirby, Stubby Kruger, Ted Lundigan, Bill Neff, Frank Pershing, Robert Shelby Randall, Joey Ray, William Mc-Keever Riley, Phil Schumacher, Sammy Stein, Jack Stoney (Boat Crew Members), Betty Blythe, Jane Crowley, Almeda Fowler, Leota Lorraine, Eleanore Vogel (Officers' Wives), Al Bridge (Lieutenant Colonel), George Bruggeman, Charles Calhoun, James Carlisle, Bruce Carruthers, Tony Carson, Gary Delmar, Frank Donahue, Leonard Fisher, Dick Karl, Michael Kostrick, Paul Kruger, Jack Lee, Jack Lorenz, James Magill, George Magrill, Leonard Mellin, Karl Miller, Wedgwood Nowell, Dan Quigg, Clifford Rathjen, John Roy, Harold Schlickenmayer, Jack Semple, Sam Simone, Reginald Simpson, Leonard Stanford, Larry Steers, Bob Thom, Roy Thomas, Richard Thorne, Brad Towne (Men in Admiral's Office), John Carlyle (Lieutenant James), Tom Tyler (Captain at Airport), Jack Carrington, Fred Coby, Roger Cole, William "Red" Donahue, Frank Eldredge, John Epper, Charles Ferguson, Donald S. Lewis, Bill Nind, Jack Ross, Brent Shugar, Robert Strong, Jack Trent, Hansel Warner (Officers at Airport), Merrill McCormick (Wounded Officer at Airport), Jack Cheatham (Commander), Henry H. Daniels, Jr. (Sailor), William B. Davidson (Hotel Manager), Marjorie Davies, Eve March (Nurses), Patrick Davis (Pilot), Ernest Dominguez, Henry Mirelez (Filipino Boys), George Economides, Michael Economides, Nino Pipitone, Jr., Roque Ybarra, Jr. (Bartender's Children), Lee Tung Foo (Asian Bartender), Mary Jane French (Lost Nurse), Jon Gilbreath (Submarine Commander), Duke Green (PT-41 Boat Starboard Torpedoman), Sherry Hall (Marine Major), Robert Homans (Manila Hotel Bartender), Vincent Isla (Filipino Schoolteacher), Trina Lowe (Gardner's Girlfriend), Jack Luden (Naval Air Captain), Kermit Maynard (Airport Officer), Frank McGrath (Slim Bearded C.P.O.), Margaret Morton (Bartender's Wife), Jack Mower (Officer), Forbes Murray (Navy Captain), Charles Murray, Jr. (Jeep Driver), Robert Emmett O'Connor (Silver Dollar Bartender), Max Ong (Mayor of Cebu), Leslie Sketchley (Marine Orderly), Ralph Soncuya (Filipino Orderly), Pacita Tod-Tod (Nightclub Singer), Emmett Vogan (Naval Doctor), Billy Wilkerson (Sergeant Smith), Jim Farley, Wallace Ford (Bits), Pedro de Cordoba (Scenes Deleted).

My Darling Clementine (December 3, 1946)

CREDITS: Director: John Ford; Producer: Samuel G. Engel; Screenplay: Samuel G. Engel, Winston Miller; Story: Sam Hellman; Based on the book *Wyatt Earp, Frontier Marshal* by Stuart N. Lake; Director of Photography: Joseph MacDonald; Editor: Dorothy Spencer; Musical Direction: Alfred Newman; Art Directors: James Basevi, Lyle R. Wheeler; Set Decorator: Thomas Little; Associate Set Decorator: Fred J. Rode; Costumes: Rene Hubert; Wardrobe: Sam Benson; Makeup: Ben Nye; Assistant Directors: William Eckhardt, Jack Sonntag; Sound: Roger Heman, Sr., Eugene Grossman; Special Photographic Effects: Fred Sersen; Orchestrations: Edward B. Powell; Stunts: Jack Montgomery, Gil Perkins; Double for Russell Simpson: Barlow Simpson; Locations: Arizona, Utah, Wyoming; Production Dates: April 1 to mid–June 1946; 20th Century–Fox Film Corporation; 97 minutes.

CAST: Henry Fonda (Wyatt Earp), Linda Darnell (Chihuahua), Victor Mature (Dr. John "Doc" Holliday), Cathy Downs (Clementine Carter), Walter Brennan (Old Man Clanton), Tim Holt (Virgil Earp), **Ward Bond** (Morgan Earp), Alan Mowbray (Granville Thorndyke), John Ireland (Billy Clanton), Roy Roberts (Mayor), Jane Darwell (Kate Nelson), Grant Withers (Ike Clanton), J. Farrell MacDonald (Mac, the Barman), Russell Simpson (John Simpson), Robert Adler, Jack Pennick (Stagecoach Drivers), C. E. Anderson, Tex Cooper, Duke R. Lee, Kermit Maynard (Townsmen), Don Barclay (Opera House Owner), Hank Bell (Opera House Patron), Danny Borzage (Accordionist), Frank Conlan (Pianist), Aleth Hansen (Guitarist), Jack Curtis (Bartender), Francis Ford (Dad, Old Soldier), Earle Foxe (Gambler), Don Garner (James Earp), Ben Hall (Barber), Fred Libby (Phin Clanton), Mae Marsh (Simpson's Sister), Margaret Martin, Frances Ray (Women), Louis Mercier (Francois, the Chef), Mickey Simpson (Sam Clanton), Charles Stevens (Indian Joe), Arthur Walsh (Hotel Clerk), Harry Woods (Luke).

The Fugitive (November 3, 1947)

CREDITS: Director: John Ford; Producers: John

Ford, Merian C. Cooper; Associate Producer: Emilio Fernandez; Screenplay: Dudley Nichols; Based on the novel *The Power and the Glory* by Graham Greene; Director of Photography: Gabriel Figueroa; Editor: Jack Murray; Musical Score and Direction: Richard Hageman; Art Director: Alfred Ybarra; Assistant Directors: Jesse Hibbs, Zacarias Gomez Urquiza; Sound: Jose B. Carles, Galdino R. Samperio; Orchestrations: Lucien Cailliet; Executive Assistant: Jack Pennick; Production Dates: early December 1946 to late January 1947; Locations: Estudios Churubusco, Mexico City; Argosy Pictures Corporation–RKO Radio Pictures; 104 minutes.

CAST: Henry Fonda (A Fugitive), Dolores del Rio (An Indian Woman), Pedro Armendariz (A Lieutenant of Police), J. Carrol Naish (A Police Informer), Leo Carrillo (Chief of Police), **Ward Bond** (James Calvert, "El Gringo"), Robert Armstrong (Police Sergeant), John Qualen (A Refugee Doctor), Fortunio Bonanova (The Governor's Cousin), Chris-Pin Martin (An Organ Grinder), Miguel Inclan (A Hostage), Fernando Fernandez (A Singer), Rodolfo Acosta, Jack Pennick (Men), Mel Ferrer (Father Serra), Jose Torvay (Mexican).

Fort Apache (March 9, 1948)

CREDITS: Director: John Ford; Executive Producers: John Ford, Merian C. Cooper; Screenplay: Frank S. Nugent; Based on the story "Massacre" by James Warner Bellah; Directors of Photography: Archie Stout, William H. Clothier; Editor: Jack Murray; Musical Score: Richard Hageman; Art Director: James Basevi; Makeup: Emile LaVigne; Assistant Directors: Lowell J. Farrell, Frank Parmenter, Jack Pennick; Second Unit Director: Cliff Lyons; Production Manager: Bernard McEveety; Set Dresser: Joseph Kish; Properties: Jack Colconda; Costume Researcher: D. R. O. Hatswell; Wardrobe: Michael Meyers, Ann Peck; Sound: Joseph I. Kane, Frank Webster; Special Effects: Dave Koehler; Musical Arranger and Conductor: Lucien Cailliet; Lyrics: George Cooper; Stunts: Frank Baker, Fred Carson, John Epper, Richard Farnsworth, Fred Graham, John Hudkins, Ben Johnson, Walt LaRue, Cliff Lyons, Frank McGrath, Gil Perkins, Bob Rose, Danny Sands, Barlow Simpson, Jack Williams, Henry Wills; Stand-in for John Wayne: Sid Davis; Playback Singer: Morton Downey; Technical Advisors: Philip Kieffer, Katharine Spaatz; Dance Sequences: Kenny Williams; Locations: California, Utah; Production Dates: July 24 to late September 1947; Argosy Pictures Corporation–RKO Radio Pictures; 125 minutes.

CAST: **John Wayne** (Captain Kirby York), Henry Fonda (Lieutenant Colonel Owen Thursday), Shirley Temple (Philadelphia Thursday), Pedro Armendariz (Sergeant Beaufort), **Ward Bond** (Sergeant Major Michael O'Rourke), George O'Brien (Captain Sam Collingwood), Victor McLaglen (Sergeant Festus Mulcahy), Anna Lee (Mrs. Emily Collingwood), Irene Rich (Mrs. Mary O'Rourke), Dick Foran (Sergeant Quincannon), Guy Kibbee (Captain Doctor Wilkens), Grant Withers (Silas Meacham), Jack Pennick (Sergeant Daniel Shattuck), Ray Hyke (Lieutenant Gates,

Adjutant), Movita (Guadalupe), Miguel Inclan (Cochise), Mary Gordon (Ma, Barmaid), Philip Kieffer (Cavalryman), Mae Marsh (Mrs. Gates), Hank Worden (Southern Recruit), John Agar (Second Lieutenant Michael Shannon O'Rourke), Cliff Clark (Stage Driver), Frank Ferguson (Newspaperman), Francis Ford (Fen, Stage Guard), William Forrest, Archie Twitchell (Reporters), Fred Graham (Cavalryman), Frank McGrath (Corporal Darice, Bugler), Mickey Simpson (NCO at Dance), Harry Tenbrook (Tom O'Feeney).

3 Godfathers (December 1, 1948)

CREDITS: Director: John Ford; Producers: John Ford, Merian C. Cooper; Screenplay: Laurence Stallings, Frank S. Nugent; Based on the story by Peter B. Kyne; Director of Photography: Winton C. Hoch; Editor: Jack Murray; Musical Score: Richard Hageman; Art Director: James Basevi; Set Decorator: Joseph Kish; Properties: Jack Colconda; Costume Researcher: D. R. O. Hatswell; Wardrobe: Michael Meyers, Ann Peck; Makeup: Don L. Cash; Hair Stylist: Anna Malin; Assistant Directors: Edward O'Fearna, Wingate Smith; Production Manager: Lowell J. Farrell; Sound: Joseph I. Kane, Frank Moran; Sound Effects: Patrick Kelley; Special Effects: Jack Caffee; Musical Arranger and Conductor: Lucien Cailliet; Camera Operator: Harvey Gould; Second Unit Director of Photography: Charles P. Boyle; Second Unit Camera Operator: Edward Fitzgerald; Grip: Tommy Griffin; Still Photographer: Alexander Kahle; Stunts: Michael Dugan, Bryan "Slim" Hightower, Ben Johnson, Cliff Lyons, Jack Montgomery, Jack Williams; Stunt Double for Pedro Armendariz: Frank McGrath; Stand-in for John Wayne: Sid Davis; Technical Advisor: Stan Jones; Script Supervisors: Pat Kelly, Meta Stern; Technicolor Director: Natalie Kalmus; Locations: California; Production Dates: early May to early June 1948; Argosy Pictures Corporation–Metro-Goldwyn-Mayer; 106 minutes.

CAST: **John Wayne** (Robert Marmaduke Hightower), Pedro Armendariz (Pedro "Pete" Roca Fuerte), Harry Carey, Jr. (William Kearney, "The Abilene Kid"), **Ward Bond** (Marshal Perley "Buck" Sweet), Mae Marsh (Mrs. Perley Sweet), Mildred Natwick (The Mother), Jane Darwell (Miss Florie), Guy Kibbee (Judge), Dorothy Ford (Ruby Latham), Ben Johnson (Posse Man), Charles Halton (Oliver Latham), Hank Worden (Deputy Curley), Jack Pennick (Luke), Fred Libby (Deputy), Michael Dugan, Don Summers (Posse Men), Gertrude Astor, Eva Novak (Townswomen), Ruth Clifford (Woman in Bar), Jack Curtis, Harry Tenbrook (Bartenders), Francis Ford (Drunken Old-timer at Bar), Richard Hageman (Saloon Pianist), Cliff Lyons (Guard at Mohave Tanks), Amelia Yelda (Robert William Pedro Hightower [The Baby]).

What Price Glory? (February 22– March 11, 1949) stage play

CREDITS: Director: Ralph Murphy; Supervising Producer: John Ford; Producer: Harry Joe Brown; Production Assistant to John Ford: George O'Brien;

Writers: Maxwell Anderson, Laurence Stallings; Venues: Grauman's Chinese Theater, Hollywood; Long Beach, San Jose, Oakland, San Francisco, Pasadena, San Gabriel.

CAST: **Ward Bond** (Captain Flagg), Pat O'Brien (Sergeant Quirt), **John Wayne** (Lieutenant Cunningham), Maureen O'Hara (Charmaine), Robert Armstrong, Ed Begley, Harry Carey, Jr., Wallace Ford, Oliver Hardy, Charles Kemper, William Lundigan, George O'Brien, Gregory Peck, Forrest Tucker, Larry Blake, Jimmy Lydon, Jim Davis, Luis Alberni.

She Wore a Yellow Ribbon (October 22, 1949)

CREDITS: Director: John Ford; Executive Producers: John Ford, Merian C. Cooper; Associate Producer: Lowell J. Farrell; Screenplay: Frank S. Nugent, Laurence Stallings; Based on the story by James Warner Bellah; Director of Photography: Winton C. Hoch; Editor: Jack Murray; Musical Score: Richard Hageman; Art Director: James Basevi; Set Decorator: Joseph Kish; Makeup: Don L. Cash; Hairdresser: Anna Malin; Costume Researcher: D. R. O. Hatswell; Wardrobe: Michael Meyers, Ann Peck; Assistant Directors: Edward O'Fearna, Wingate Smith; Second Unit Director: Cliff Lyons; Production Manager: Lowell J. Farrell; Properties: Jack Colconda; Sound: Clem Portman, Frank Webster; Sound Effects: Patrick Kelley; Special Effects: Jack Caffee, Jack Cosgrove; Camera Operator: Harvey Gould; Second Unit Camera: Archie Stout, Charles P. Boyle; Gaffer: Robert Campbell; Grip: Tom Clement; Still Photographer: Alexander Kahle; Colorist: Stephen Bearman; Assistant Editor: Barbara Ford; Musical Conductor: C. Bakaleinikoff; Musical Arranger and Orchestrator: Lucien Calliett; Choral Director: Jester Hairston; Stunts: Roydon Clark, Everett Creach, Michael Dugan, John Epper, Fred Graham, Chuck Hayward, Bryan "Slim" Hightower, John Hudkins, Billy Jones, Fred Kennedy, Cliff Lyons, Frank McGrath, Don Nagel, Post Park, Gil Perkins, Bob Rose, Norm Taylor, Jack N. Young; Stand-in for John Wayne: Sid Davis; Technicolor Directors: Natalie Kalmus, Morgan Padelford; Technical Advisors: Cliff Lyons, Major Philip Keiffer, U.S.A. Retired; Script Supervisor: Meta Stern; Gun Wrangler: Barlow Simpson; Locations: Kanab, Mexican Hat, Moab and Monument Valley, Utah; Production Dates: late October to late November 1948; Argosy Pictures Corporation–RKO Radio Pictures; 103 minutes.

CAST: **John Wayne** (Captain Nathan Cutting Brittles), Joanne Dru (Olivia Dandridge), John Agar (Lieutenant Flint Cohill), Ben Johnson (Sergeant Tyree), Harry Carey, Jr. (Second Lieutenant Ross Pennell), Victor McLaglen (Top Sergeant Quincannon), Mildred Natwick (Abby Allshard, aka "Old Iron Pants"), George O'Brien (Major Mac Allshard, Commanding Officer Fort Starke), Arthur Shields (Dr. O'Laughlin), Michael Dugan (Sergeant Hochbauer), Chief John Big Tree (Chief Pony That Walks), Fred Graham (Sergeant Hench), Chief Sky Eagle (Chief Sky Eagle), Tom Tyler (Corporal Mike Quayne,

Leader of Paradise River Patrol), Noble Johnson (Chief Red Shirt), Rudy Bowman (Private John Smith, aka Rome Clay), Lee Bradley (Interpreter), Paul Fix, Peter Ortiz (Gun Runners), Francis Ford (Connelly, Fort Starke Suttlers Barman), Ray Hyke (Trooper McCarthy), Billy Jones (Courier), Fred Kennedy (Badger), Fred Libby (Corporal Krumrein), Cliff Lyons (Trooper Cliff), Frank McGrath (Bugler/Indian), Post Park, William Steele (Officers), Jack Pennick (Sergeant Major), Mickey Simpson (Corporal Wagner, Blacksmith), Don Summers (Jenkins), Dan White (Trooper), Harry Woods (Licensed Suttler Karl Rynders), Irving Pichel (Narrator).

Wagon Master (April 19, 1950)

CREDITS: Director: John Ford; Executive Producers: John Ford, Merian C. Cooper; Associate Producer: Lowell J. Farrell; Screenplay: Frank S. Nugent, Patrick Ford; Based on a story by John Ford; Director of Photography: Bert Glennon; Editors: Jack Murray, Barbara Ford; Musical Score: Richard Hageman; Art Director: James Basevi; Set Decorator: Joseph Kish; Makeup: Don L. Cash; Hair Stylist: Anna Malin; Assistant Director: Wingate Smith; Second Unit Director: Cliff Lyons; Properties: Jack Colconda; Sound: Clem Portman, Frank Webster; Special Effects: Jack Caffee; Miniatures: Ray Kellogg; Second Unit Director of Photography: Archie Stout; Costume Researcher: D. R. O. Hatswell; Wardrobe: Wesley Jeffries, Adele Parmenter; Stunts: Chuck Hayward, Bryan "Slim" Hightower, Billy Jones, Eddie Juaragui, Fred Kennedy, Cliff Lyons, Frank McGrath, Post Park, Gil Perkins, Ray Thomas; Locations: Moab, Monument Valley and Spanish Valley, Utah; Production Dates: November 14 to mid–December 1949; Argosy Pictures Corporation–RKO Radio Pictures; 86 minutes.

CAST: Ben Johnson (Travis Blue), Joanne Dru (Denver), Harry Carey, Jr. (Sandy), **Ward Bond** (Elder Jonathan Wiggs), Charles Kemper (Uncle Shiloh Clegg), Alan Mowbray (Dr. A. Locksley Hall), Jane Darwell (Sister Ledeyard), Ruth Clifforf (Fleuretty Phyffe), Russell Simpson (Adam Perkins), Kathleen O'Malley (Prudence Perkins), James Arness (Floyd Clegg), Francis Ford (Mr. Peachtree), Fred Libby (Reese Clegg), Jim Thorpe (Navaho), Mickey Simpson (Jesse Clegg), Cliff Lyons (Marshal of Crystal City), Hank Worden (Luke Clegg), Don Summers (Sam Jenkins), Movita (Young Navaho Indian).

Rio Grande (November 15, 1950)

CREDITS: Director: John Ford; Producers: John Ford, Merian C. Cooper; Screenplay: James Kevin McGuinness; Based on the story by James Warner Bellah; Director of Photography: Bert Glennon; Editor: Jack Murray; Assistant Editor: Barbara Ford; Musical Score: Victor Young; Art Director: Frank Hotaling; Set Decorator: John McCarthy, Jr., Charles S. Thompson; Costume Design: Adele Palmer; Makeup: Bob Mark; Hair Stylist: Peggy Gray; Assistant Director: Wingate Smith; Second Unit Director: Cliff Lyons; Second Unit Director of Photography: Archie Stout; Properties: Dudley Holmes; Sound: Earl Crain, Sr.,

Howard Lawson; Special Effects: Howard Lydecker, Theodore Lydecker; Orchestrators: Sidney Cutner, Leo Shuken; Driver: Norm Taylor; Uniforms: D. R. O. Hatswell; Technical Advisor: Philip Kieffer; Stunts: Jerry Brown, Everett Creach, Chuck Hayward, John Hudkins, Fred Kennedy, Cliff Lyons, Frank McGrath, Chuck Roberson; Bob Rose, Barlow Simpson, Norm Taylor, Terry Wilson, Jack N. Young; Stand-in for John Wayne: Sid Davis; Production Dates: mid–June to late July 1950; Locations: Moab and Mexican Hat, Utah; Argosy Pictures Corporation–Republic Pictures; 105 minutes.

CAST: **John Wayne** (Lieutenant Colonel Kirby Yorke), Maureen O'Hara (Mrs. Kathleen Yorke), Ben Johnson (Trooper Travis Tyree), Claude Jarman, Jr. (Trooper Jefferson "Jeff" Yorke), Harry Carey, Jr. (Trooper Daniel "Sandy" Boone), Chill Wills (Dr. Wilkins), J. Carrol Naish (Lieutenant General Philip Sheridan), Victor McLaglen (Sergeant Major Timothy Quincannon), Grant Withers (U.S. Deputy Marshal), Peter Ortiz (Captain St. Jacques), Steve Pendleton (Captain Prescott), Karolyn Grimes (Margaret Mary), Alberto Morin (Lieutenant), Stan Jones (Sergeant), Fred Kennedy (Trooper Heinze), Sons of the Pioneers: Ken Curtis, Tommy Doss, Hugh Farr, Karl Farr, Shug Fisher, Lloyd Perryman (Regimental Musicians), Cliff Lyons (Soldier), Jack Pennick (Sergeant), Chuck Roberson (Officer/Indian), Barlow Simpson (Indian Chief), Patrick Wayne (Boy), Lee Morgan (Bit).

The Quiet Man (September 14, 1952)

CREDITS: Director: John Ford; Producers: John Ford, Merian C. Cooper; Screenplay: Frank S. Nugent, John Ford; Based on a story by Maurice Walsh; Director of Photography: Winton C. Hoch; Editor: Jack Murray; Musical Score: Victor Young; Art Director: Frank Hotaling; Set Decorators: John McCarthy, Jr., Charles S. Thompson; Costumes: Adele Palmer; Wardrobe: Neva Bourne, Adele Palmer, Robert Ramsey, Ted Towey; Makeup: James R. Barker, Bob Mark, Web Overlander (for John Wayne); Hair Stylists: Peggy Gray, Fay Smith; Unit Manager: Lee Lukather; Assistant Directors: Wingate Smith, Edward O'Fearna, Albert Podlansky; Second Unit Directors: Patrick Ford, **John Wayne**; Sound: T. A. Carmen, Howard Wilson, Daniel J. Bloomberg, David H. Moriarty, W. O. Watson; Special Effects: Howard Lydecker, Theodore Lydecker; Assistant Editor: Barbara Ford; Editorial Department: Al Horowitz; Camera Operators: Arthur Graham; Second Unit Director of Photography: Archie Stout; Process Photographer: Bud Thackery; Camera Department: Bill Wade; Musical Director: Ray Roberts; Orchestrators: Leo Arnaud, R. Dale Butts, Sidney Cutner, Leo Shuken, Stanley Wilson; Best Boy: Ray Bensfield; Grips: Ben Bishop, Bob Harrison, Ben Moran; Electrician: Paul Guerin; Gaffer: Bob Staffer; Props: Dudley Holmes, John McCarthy; Construction: F. B. Gibbs, Gordon Lantz; Painter: Lou Shields; Drapery: Francis Frank; Art Department: Ralph Oberg; Poster Artist: Clement Hurel; Stunts: Patrick Ford, Bryan "Slim" Hightower, Billy Jones, Fred Kennedy, Bert LeBaron, Bob Morgan, Post Park, Bob Rose, Terry Wilson; Riding Double

for John Wayne: Joe Fair; Transportation: Fred Manning, Slim Metcalfe, Frenchie Valin; Technicolor Consultant: Francis Cugat; Location Manager: J. T. Bourke; Technical Advisors: D. R. O. Hatswell, Father Stack (religion); Chief Engineer: D. J. Bloomberg; Morning Operations: Michael Eason; Publicist: Mort Goodman; Accountant: Harry Williams; Studio Physician: N. E. Gourson; Studio First Aid: Fred Vinson; Stock Room: Martin Horwitz; Head Wrangler: Bill Jones; Labor Department: Pete Matsk; Film Library: E. Schroeder; Script Supervisor: Meta Stern; Projectionist: Hal Swanson; Production Dates: early June to late August 1951; Locations: County Mayo and County Galway, Ireland; Argosy Pictures Corporation–Republic Pictures; 129 minutes.

CAST: **John Wayne** (Sean Thornton), Maureen O'Hara (Mary Kate Danaher), Barry Fitzgerald (Michaleen Og Flynn), **Ward Bond** (Father Peter Lonergan), Victor McLaglen (Squire "Red" Will Danaher), Mildred Natwick (The Widow Sarah Tillane), Francis Ford (Dan Tobin), Eileen Crowe (Mrs. Elizabeth Playfair), May Craig (Fishwoman with Basket at Station), Arthur Shields (The Rev. Cyril Playfair), Charles B. Fitzsimons (Hugh Forbes), James O'Hara, aka James Lilburn (Father Paul), Sean McClory (Owen Glynn), Jack McGowran (Ignatius Feeney), Eric Gorman (Costello, Engine Driver), Kevin Lawless (Train Fireman), Paddy O'Donnell (Railway Porter), Frank Baker, Pat O'Malley (Men in Bar), Tony Canzoneri (Boxing Second), Ruth Clifford (Mother), Maureen Coyne (Dan Tobin's Daughter, Ireland), Mimi Doyle (Dan Tobin's Daughter, United States), Ken Curtis (Dermot Fahy), Douglas Evans (Ring Physician), Robert Foy (Man Driving Cart Across River), Jim McVeigh (Man Following Carr Across River), Sam Harris (General), D. R. O. Hatswell (Guppy), John Horan (Man at Railway Station), David Hughes (Police Constable), Billy Jones (Bugler), Tiny Jones (Nell, Maid), Mae Marsh (Father Paul's Mother), Jim Morrin (Roof Thatcher), Al Murphy (Boxing Referee), Michael O'Brian (Musha Musha Man), Frank O'Connor (Ringside Photographer), Web Overlander (Hugh Bailey, Stationmaster), Bob Perry (Trooper Thorn's Ringside Trainer), Darla Ridgeway (Girl), Freddy Ridgeway (Girl), Jack Roper (Tony Gardello, Boxer), Philip Stainton (Anglican Bishop), Harry Tenbrook (Police Sergeant Hannan), Harry Tyler (Pat Cohan, Publican), Melinda Wayne (Girl on Wagon at Horse Race), Michael Wayne (Teenage Boy at Races), Patrick Wayne (Boy on Wagon at Horse Race), Toni Wayne (Teenage Girl at Races), Hank Worden (Trainer in Flashback), Colin Kenny (Pub Extra).

The Long Gray Line (February 9, 1955)

CREDITS: Director: John Ford; Producer: Robert Arthur; Screenplay: Edward Hope; Based on the book by Marty Maher and Nardi Reeder Campion; Directors of Photography: Charles Lawton, Jr., Charles Lang; Editor: William A. Lyon; Musical Score: George Duning, W. Franke Harling; Art Director: Robert Peterson; Set Decorator: Frank Tuttle; Costume Design: Jean Louis; Makeup: Clay Campbell, Robert J. Schiffer; Hair Stylist: Helen Hunt; Assistant Directors:

Wingate Smith, Jack Corrick; Sound: George Cooper, John P. Livadary; Sound Re-recordist: Richard Olson; Camera Operator: Emil Oster; Music Supervisor and Conductor: Morris Stoloff; Technicolor Consultant: Francis Cugat; Technical Advisors: Lieutenant Colonel George McIntyre, Major George Pappas; Production Dates: March 15 to May 17, 1954; Columbia Pictures Corporation; 138 minutes.

CAST: Tyrone Power (Martin "Marty" Maher), Maureen O'Hara (Mary O'Donnell), Robert Francis (James N. Sundstrom, Jr.), Donald Crisp (Old Martin), **Ward Bond** (Captain Herman J. Koehler), Betsy Palmer (Kitty Carter), Philip Carey (Charles "Chuck" Dotson), William Leslie (James Nilsson "Red" Sundstrom), Harry Carey, Jr. (Dwight Eisenhower), Patrick Wayne (Abner "Cherub" Overton), Sean McClory (Dinny Maher), Peter Graves (Corporal Rudolph Heinz), Milburn Stone (Captain John Pershing), Erin O'Brien-Moore (Mrs. Koehler), Walter D. Ehlers (Mike Shannon), Willis Bouchey (Major Thomas), Don Barclay (McDonald), Dona Cole (Peggy), Chuck Courtney (Whitey Larson), Lisa Davis (Nell), Diane DeLaire (Nurse), Harry Denny (Priest), Mimi Doyle (Nun), Robert Ellis (Cadet Short), Bess Flowers (Football Fan at Army-Navy Game), Tom Hennesy (Cadet Dotson), John Herrin (Cadet Ramsey), Robert F. Hoy (Cadet Kennedy), Philip Kieffer (Superintendent), Robert Knapp (Lieutenant), Jean Moorhead (Girl), Martin Milner (Jim O'Carberry), Donald Murphy (Army Captain), James O'Hara (Cadet Thorne), Pat O'Malley (Priest), Jack Pennick (Recruiting Officer), Russell P. Reader (Commandant of Cadets), Robert Roark (Cadet Pirelli), Mickey Roth (Cadet Stern), Kevin Schultz, Keith Schultz (Kitty's Infant Son), Jim Sears (Knute Rockne), Mickey Simpson (New York Policeman), Elbert Steele (The President), Harry Tenbrook (Waiter), Norm Van Brocklin (Gus Dorias), Ken Curtis (Specialty), Mary Benoit, Richard Bishop, Jack Ellis, Fritz Ford, Raoul Freeman, Leon McLaughlin, Jack Mower (Bits).

Mister Roberts (December 4, 1955)

CREDITS: Directors: John Ford, Mervyn LeRoy, Joshua Logan, **Ward Bond**; Producer: Leland Hayward; Screenplay: Frank S. Nugent, Joshua Logan; Based on the play by Thomas Heggen and Joshua Logan and the novel by Thomas Heggen; Director of Photography: Winton C. Hoch; Editor: Jack Murray; Musical Score: Franz Waxman; Art Director: Art Loel; Set Decorator: William L. Kuehl; Costume Design: Moss Mabry; Makeup: Gordon Bau, Robert J. Schiffer; Production Manager: Norman A. Cook; Assistant Director: Wingate Smith; Sound: Earl Crain, Sr.; Sound Recordist: William A. Mueller; Assistant Camera: Cliff Shirpser; Orchestrator: Leonid Raab; Conductor: Franz Waxman; Stunts: Philip Crawford, Jack Lewis; Technical Advisors: Commander Merle MacBain, John Dale Price; Naval Liaison: Frank Coghlan, Jr.; Locations: Hawaii, Midway Island, Pacific Ocean; Production Dates: late August to mid–November 1954; Warner Bros. Pictures; 123 minutes.

CAST: Henry Fonda (Lieutenant [j.g.] Douglas A. "Doug" Roberts), James Cagney (Captain Morton),

William Powell (Lieutenant "Doc"), Jack Lemmon (Ensign Frank Thurlowe Pulver), Betsy Palmer (Lieutenant Ann Girard), **Ward Bond** (Chief Petty Officer Dowdy), Philip Carey (Mannion), Nick Adams (Reber), Perry Lopez (Rodrigues), Ken Curtis (Yeoman 3rd Class Dolan), Robert Roark (Insig-nia), Harry Carey, Jr. (Stefanowski), Patrick Wayne (Bookser), Frank Aletter (Gerhart), Tige Andrews (Wiley), Fritz Ford (Lindstrom), Jim Moloney (Kennedy), Buck Kartalian (Mason), Denny Niles (Gilbert), William Henry (Lieutenant Billings), Francis Connor (Cochran), William Hudson (Olson), Shug Fisher (Johnson), Stubby Kruger (Schlemmer), Danny Borzage (Jonesy), Harry Tenbrook (Cookie), Jim Murphy (Taylor), Kathleen O'Malley, Maura Murphy, Mimi Doyle, Jeanne Murray, Lonnie Pierce (Nurses), Martin Milner (Shore Patrol Officer), Gregory Walcott (Shore Patrolman), James Flavin (Military Policeman), Jack Pennick (Marine Sergeant), Duke Kahanamoku (Native Chief), George Brangier (French Colonial Officer), Clarence E. Frank (Naval Officer), Carolyn Tong (Bookser's Native Romance).

Screen Directors Playhouse: "Rookie of the Year" (December 7, 1955)

CREDITS: Director: John Ford; Executive Producer: Sidney Van Keuren; Teleplay: Frank S. Nugent; Based on a story by W. R. Burnett; Director of Photography: Hal Mohr; Editor: Marsh Hendry; Art Director: William Ferrari; Production Supervisor: Sidney Van Keuren; Production Coordinator: William Sterling; Hal Roach Studios–NBC-TV; 29 minutes.

CAST: **John Wayne** (Mike Cronin), Vera Miles (Ruth Dahlberg), **Ward Bond** (Larry "Buck" Goodhue, alias Buck Garrison), James Gleason (Ed Shafer), Patrick Wayne (Lyn Goodhue), Willis Bouchey (Mr. Cully), Harry Tyler (Mr. White), William Forrest (Mr. Walker), Robert Lyden (Willie), Tiger Fafara (Bobby), Charles Ferguson (Phil).

"The Red, White and Blue Line" (1955)

CREDITS: Director: John Ford; Screenplay: Edward Hope; Director of Photography: Charles Lawton, Jr.; Includes scenes from *The Long Gray Line*; United States Treasury Department–Columbia Pictures; 10 minutes.

CAST: Tyrone Power, Maureen O'Hara, Donald Crisp, Betsy Palmer, William Leslie (Themselves), **Ward Bond** (Narrator).

The Searchers (March 13, 1956)

CREDITS: Director: John Ford; Executive Producer: Merian C. Cooper; Associate Producer: Patrick Ford; Screenplay: Frank S. Nugent; Based on the novel by Alan LeMay; Director of Photography: Winton C. Hoch; Editor: Jack Murray; Musical Score: Max Steiner; Art Directors: James Basevi, Frank Hotaling; Set Decorator: Victor A. Gangelin; Costume Design: Charles Arrico; Wardrobe: Frank Beetson, Jr., Ann Peck; Makeup: Web Overlander; Hair Stylist: Fae M.

Smith; Production Manager: Lowell J. Farrell; Assistant Directors: Wingate Smith, Gary Nelson; Sound: Hugh McDowell, Jr., Howard Wilson; Properties: Dudley Holmes; Special Effects: George Brown; Second Unit Camera: Alfred Gilks; Orchestrator: Murray Cutter; Stunts: Bill Cartledge, Philip Crawford, Dick Dial, Chuck Hayward, Bryan "Slim" Hightower, John Hudkins, Fred Kennedy, Cliff Lyons, Frank McGrath, Chuck Roberson, Dale Van Sickel, Henry Wills, Terry Wilson, Billy Yellow, Jack N. Young; Script Supervisor: Robert Gary; Technicolor Consultant: James Gooch; Locations: California, Utah, Colorado, Alberta; Production Dates: mid–June to mid–August 1955; C. V. Whitney Pictures–Warner Bros. Pictures; 119 minutes.

CAST: **John Wayne** (Ethan Edwards), Jeffrey Hunter (Martin Pawley), Vera Miles (Laurie Jorgensen), **Ward Bond** (The Rev. Captain Samuel Johnson Clayton), Natalie Wood (Debbie Edwards), John Qualen (Lars Jorgensen), Olive Carey (Mrs. Jorgensen), Henry Brandon (Chief Cicatriz, aka "Scar"), Ken Curtis (Charlie McCorry), Harry Carey, Jr. (Brad Jorgensen), Antonio Moreno (Emilio Gabriel Fernandex y Figueroa), Hank Worden (Mose Harper), Beulah Archuletta (Wild Goose Flying in the Night Sky, aka "Look"), Walter Coy (Aaron Edwards), Dorothy Jordan (Martha Edwards), Pippa Scott (Lucy Edwards), Patrick Wayne (Lieutenant Greenhill), Lana Wood (Debbie Edwards, younger), Danny Borzage (Accordionist at Funeral), Ruth Clifford (Deranged Woman at Fort), Tommy Doss, Lloyd Perryman (Wedding Musicians), Nacho Galindo (Mexican Bartender), Chuck Hayward (Man at Wedding), Robert Lyden (Ben Edwards), Cliff Lyons (Colonel Greenhill), Peter Mamakos (Jerem Futterman), Mae Marsh (Dark Cloaked Woman at Fort), Jack Pennick (Sergeant at Fort), Chuck Roberson (Ranger at Wedding), Chief Thundercloud (Comanche Chief), William Steele (Rider in Posse), Pipe Line Begishe, Exactly Sonnie Betsuie, Pete Grey Eyes, Feather Hat, Jr., Jack Tin Horn, Harry Black Horse, Away Luna, Bob Many Mules, Smile White Sheep, Many Mules Son, Percy Shooting Star, Billy Yellow (Comanches), Frank McGrath, Terry Wilson (Bits).

The Wings of Eagles (February 22, 1957)

CREDITS: Director: John Ford; Producer: Charles Schnee; Associate Producer: James E. Newcom; Screenplay: Frank Fenton, William Wister Haines; Based on the life and writings of Frank W. "Spig" Wead; Director of Photography: Paul C. Vogel; Editor: Gene Ruggiero; Musical Score: Jeff Alexander; Art Directors: Malcolm Brown, William A. Horning; Set Decorators: F. Keogh Gleason, Edwin B. Willis; Wardrobe: Walter Plunkett; Makeup: William Tuttle; Assistant Director: Wingate Smith; Sound: Wesley C. Miller; Special Effects: A. Arnold Gillespie, Warren Newcombe; Orchestrator: Arthur Morton; Stunts: Fred Graham, Chuck Hayward, John Hudkins, Cliff Lyons, Paul Mantz, Frank McGrath, Bob Morgan, Chuck Roberson, Ronnie Rondell, Jr., Paul Stader, Dale Van

Sickel, Jack Williams, Terry Wilson; Technical Advisors: John Dale Price, John Keye; Color Consultant: Charles K. Hagedon; Locations: U.S. Naval Air Station, Pensacola, Florida; U.S.S. *Philippine Sea*; Production Dates: September 10 to October 4, 1956; Metro-Goldwyn-Mayer; 110 minutes.

CAST: **John Wayne** (Frank W. "Spig" Wead), Dan Dailey ("Jughead" Carson), Maureen O'Hara (Min Wead), **Ward Bond** (John Dodge), Ken Curtis (John Dale Price), Edmund Lowe (Admiral Moffett), Kenneth Tobey (Captain Herbert Allen Hazard), James Todd (Jack Travis), Barry Kelley (Captain Jock Clark), Sig Ruman (Manager), Henry O'Neil (Captain Spear), Willis Bouchey (Barton), Dorothy Jordan (Rose Brentmann), Tige Andrews (Arizona Pincus), Danny Borzage (Pete), Olive Carey (Bridy O' Faolain), Franklyn Farnum (Man Outside Movie Theater), James Flavin (MP at Garden Party), Mimi Gibson (Lila Wead), Fred Graham (Officer in Brawl), Sam Harris (Patient), William Henry (Naval Aide), Louis Jean Heydt (Dr. John Keye), Stuart Holmes (Producer), Janet Lake, May McAvoy (Nurses), William Paul Lowery (Commodore, Wead's Baby), Mae Marsh (Nurse Crumley), Alberto Morin (Manager), Forbes Murray (Congressman), Peter Ortiz (Lieutenant Charles Dexter), Jack Pennick (Joe McGuffey), Chuck Roberson (Officer), Evelyn Rudie (Doris Wead), Arthur Salzfass (Navy Pilot), Harry Strang (Bartender), William Tracy (Air Officer), Charles Trowbridge (Admiral Crown), Dale Van Sickel, Terry Wilson (Naval Officers), Harlan Warde (Executive Officer), Blue Washington (Bartender at Officers' Club), Veda Ann Borg, Christopher James, Cliff Lyons (Bits).

"The Growler Story" (1957)

CREDITS: Director: John Ford; Producer: Mark Armistead; Cinematography: Pacific Fleet Combat Camera Group; Editor: Jack Murray; Assistant Editor: Barbara Ford; Locations: Hawaii; South Pacific; Production Dates: November–December 1956; United States Navy; 29 minutes.

CAST: **Ward Bond** (Quincannon), Ken Curtis (Captain Howard W. Gilmore), Dan Dailey (Narrator), U.S. Navy personnel (supporting and extra roles).

The Horse Soldiers (July 1959)

CREDITS: Director: John Ford; Producers and Screenplay: John Lee Mahin, Martin Rackin; Based on the novel by Harold Sinclair; Director of Photography: William Clothier; Editor: Jack Murray; Musical Score: David Buttolph; Art Director: Frank Hotaling; Set Decorator: Victor Gangelin; Properties: Sam Gordon; Makeup: Web Overlander; Hair Stylist: Fae M. Smith; Production Manager: Allen K. Wood; Assistant Directors: Wingate Smith, Ray Gosnell, Jr.; Sound Mixer: Jack Solomon; Special Effects: Augie Lohman; Wardrobe: Frank Beetson, Jr., Ann Peck; Stunts: Jim Burke, Everett Creach; Dick Dial, Chuck Hayward, Tom Hennesy, John Hudkins, Fred Kennedy, Jack Lewis, Cliff Lyons, Ted White, Jack N. Young; Script Supervisors: Meta Stern, Stanley Sheuer; Location Manager: John Veitch; Locations: Texas, Louisiana, Mississippi; Premiere: Shreveport, Louisiana, June 18, 1959; Production Dates: late October 1958 to January 8, 1959; The Mirisch Corporation–United Artists; 119 minutes.

CAST: **John Wayne** (Colonel John Marlowe), William Holden (Major Henry "Hank" Kendall), Constance Towers (Miss Hannah Hunter of Greenbriar), Judson Pratt (Sergeant Major Kirby), Hoot Gibson (Sergeant Brown), Ken Curtis (Corporal Wilkie), Willis Bouchey (Colonel Phil Secord), Bing Russell (Dunker, Yankee Soldier Amputee), O. Z. Whitehead (Otis "Hoppy" Hopkins), Hank Worden (Deacon Clump), Chuck Hayward (Union Captain), Denver Pyle (Jackie Jo), Strother Martin (Virgil), Basil Ruysdael (The Reverend), Carleton Young (Colonel Jonathan Miles, CSA), William Leslie (Major Richard Gray), William Henry (Confederate Lieutenant), Walter Reed (Union Officer), Anna Lee (Mrs. Buford), William Forrest (General Steve Hurlburt), Ron Hagerthy, William Wellman, Jr. (Buglers), Russell Simpson (Acting Sheriff Henry Goodbody), Althea Gibson (Lukey, Hannah Hunter's Maid), Sarge Allen (Union Officer), Danny Borzage (Ned), Otis Courville, Fred Kennedy (Soldiers), Richard Cutting (General William Tecumsah Sherman), Fred Graham (Union Soldier), Sam Harris, Stuart Holmes (Passengers to Newton Station), Stan Jones (General Ulysses S. Grant), Roy Kennedy (Wrangler), Jack Pennick (Sergeant Major "Mitch" Mitchell), Charles Seel (Newton Station Bartender), Jan Stine (Union General).

Wagon Train: "The Colter Craven Story" (November 23, 1960)

CREDITS: Director: John Ford; Producer: Howard Christie; Teleplay: Tony Paulson; Original Story: John Ford; Director of Photography: Benjamin H. Kline; Editor: Marston Fay; Musical Theme: Jerome Moross; Musical Score and Supervisor: Stanley Wilson; Art Director: Martin Obzina; Set Decorator: Ralph Sylos; Makeup: Jack Barron, Florence Bush; Assistant Director: James H. Brown; Sound: David H. Moriarty; Costume Supervisor: Vincent Dee; Editorial Supervisor: David J. O'Connell; Revue Productions–NBC; 53 minutes.

CAST: **Ward Bond** (Major Seth Adams); Robert Horton (Flint McCullough), Frank McGrath (Charlie Wooster), Terry Wilson (Bill Hawks), Carleton Young (Dr. Colter Craven), Anna Lee (Mrs. Allyris Craven), Paul Birch (General Ulysses Simpson "Sam" Grant), Ken Curtis (Kyle Cleatus), Cliff Lyons (Creel Weatherby), Chuck Hayward (Quentin Cleatus), Dennis Rush (Jamie), Willis Bouchey (Mr. Grant), John Carradine (Park Cleatus), **John Wayne** [as "Michael Morris"] (General William Tecumseh Sherman), Richard H. Cutting (Colonel Lollier), Annelle Hayes (Mrs. Grant), Mae Marsh (Mrs. Jesse Grant), Jack Pennick (Drill Sergeant Tim Molloy), Chuck Roberson (Junior), Charles Seel (Mort), Hank Worden (Hank).

The Man Who Shot Liberty Valance (April 22, 1962)

CREDITS: Director: John Ford; Producers: John Ford, Willis Goldbeck; Screenplay: James Warner Bellah, Willis Goldbeck; Based on the story by Dorothy M. Johnson; Director of Photography: William H. Clothier; Editor: Otho Lovering; Musical Score: Cyril J. Mockridge; Art Directors: Eddie Imazu, Hal Pereira; Set Decorators: Sam Comer, Darryl Silvera; Costume Design: Edith Head, Ron Talsky; Makeup: Wally Westmore; Hair Stylist: Nellie Manley; Unit Production Manager: Don Robb; Assistant Director: Wingate Smith; Construction Coordinator: Gene Lauritzen; Sound: Charles Grenzbach, Philip Mitchell; Process Photography: Farciot Edouart; Assistant Editor: Stu Linder; Musical Conductor: Irvin Talbot; Orchestrators: Jack Hayes, Leo Shuken; Still Photographer: Denis Cameron; Stunts: John Epper, Chuck Hayward, Tom Hennesy, Bryan "Slim" Hightower, John Hudkins, Eddie Juaregui, Ted Mapes, Louise Montana, Montie Montana, Bob Morgan, Hal Needham, Chuck Roberson, Jack Williams; Locations: Janss Conejo Ranch, Thousand Oaks, California; Paramount Pictures; 123 minutes.

CAST: James Stewart (Ransom Stoddard), **John Wayne** (Tom Doniphon), Vera Miles (Hallie Stoddard), Lee Marvin (Liberty Valance), Edmond O'Brien (Dutton Peabody), Andy Devine (Marshal Link Appleyard), Ken Murray (Doc Willoughby), John Carradine (Major Cassius Starbuckle), Jeanette Nolan (Nora Ericson), John Qualen (Peter Ericson), Willis Bouchey (Jason Tully, Conductor), Carleton Young (Maxwell Scott), Woody Strode (Pompey), Denver Pyle (Amos Carruthers), Strother Martin (Floyd), Lee Van Cleef (Reese), Robert F. Simon (Handy Strong), O. Z. Whitehead (Herbert Carruthers), Paul Birch (Major Winder), Joseph Hoover (Charlie Hasbrouck, Reporter for *The Star*), Mario Arteaga, Chuck Hayward, Chuck Roberson, Jack Williams (Henchmen), Leonard Baker (Man), Danny Borzage, Duke Fishman, Ralph Volkie (Townsmen), Buddy Roosevelt (Townsman in Diner), Larry Finley (Bar X Man), Shug Fisher (Kaintuck), Bryan "Slim" Hightower (Shotgun), Earle Hodgins (Clute Humphries), Eddie Juaregui, Charles Morton (Drummers), Anna Lee (Mrs. Prescott), Jacqueline Malouf (Lietta Appleyard), Ted Mapes (Highpockets), Monte Montana (Politician on Horseback), Bob Morgan (Roughrider), Jack Pennick (Jack, Barman), Charles Seel (Election Council President), Tom Smith (Barfly), Max Wagner (Poker Game Dealer), Charles Akins, Gertrude Astor, Robert Donner, Helen Gibson, Sam Harris, William Henry, Stuart Holmes, Jack Kenny, Eva Novak, Dorothy Phillips, Stephanie Pond-Smith, Slim Talbot, Blackie Whiteford (Bits).

How the West Was Won (February 20, 1963)

CREDITS: Directors: John Ford, Henry Hathaway, George Marshall, Richard Thorpe; Producer: Bernard Smith; Screenplay: James R. Webb, John Gay; Based on the series "How the West Was Won" in *Life* magazine; Director of Photography: William H. Daniels, Milton R. Krasner, Charles Lang, Joseph LaShelle; Editor: Harold F. Kress; Musical Score: Alfred Newman; Art Directors: George W. Davis, William Ferrari, Addison Hehr; Set Decorators: Henry Grace, Don

Greenwood, Jr., Jack Mills; Costume Design: Ron Talsky; Makeup: William Tuttle; Hair Stylist: Sydney Guilaroff; Hair Designer: Jay Sebring; Cinerama Production Supervisor: Thomas Conroy; Assistant Directors: George Marshall, Jr., William McGarry, Robert Saunders, William Shanks, Wingate Smith; Second Unit Director: Richard Talmadge; Recording Supervisor: Franklin Milton; Sound Editor: Van Allen James; Special Effects: Bob Overbeck; Special Visual Effects: A. Arnold Gillespie, Robert R. Hoag; Camera Operator: Bill Johnson; Assistant Camera Operator: Owen Marsh; Second Unit Director of Photography: Harold E. Wellman; Second Unit Camera Operator: James V. King; Grip: Pete G. Papanickolas; Assistant Set Costumer: Robert Fuca; Color Consultant: Charles K. Hagedon; Negative Cutter: Mike Henry; Musical Conductor: Alfred Newman; Associate Conductor: Robert Armbruster: Music Coordinator: Robert Emmett Dolan; Music Associate and Choir Director: Ken Darby; Musicians: Bob Bain (guitar), Carl Fortina (concertina), Tommy Morgan (harmonica); Folk Singer: Dave Guard; Choral Singer: Paul Salamunovich; Stunts: Rick Arnold, May Boss, Polly Burson, Frank Cordell, Everett Creach, John Epper, Richard Farnsworth, Sol Gorss, Fred Graham, Johnny Hagner, Donna Hall, Chuck Hayward, Charles Horvath, Loren Janes, Roy Jensen, Leroy Johnson, Eddie Juaregui, Cliff Lyons, Ted Mapes, Troy Melton, Louise Montana, Bob Morgan, Boyd "Red" Morgan, Hal Needham, Harvey Parry, Gil Perkins, Carl Pitti, Rusty Richards, Chuck Roberson, Victor Romito, Ronnie Rondell, Jr., Danny Sands, Dean Smith, Richard Talmadge, Bob Terhune, Ken Terrell, Autry Ward, Troy Ward, Jack Williams, Henry Wills, Jack N. Young, Joe Yrigoyen; Locations: Arizona, California, Colorado, Illinois, Kentucky, South Dakota, Utah; Cinerama Productions Corporation–Metro-Goldwyn-Mayer; 162 minutes.

CAST: Carroll Baker (Eve Prescott), Lee J. Cobb (Marshal Lou Ramsey), Henry Fonda (Jethro Stuart), Carolyn Jones (Julie Rawlings), Karl Malden (Zebulon Prescott), Gregory Peck (Cleve Van Valen), George Peppard (Zeb Rawlings), Robert Preston (Roger Morgan), Debbie Reynolds (Lilith Prescott), James Stewart (Linus Rawlings), Eli Wallach (Charlie Gant), **John Wayne** (General William Tecumseh Sherman), Richard Widmark (Mike King), Brigid Bazlen (Dora Hawkins), Walter Brennan (Colonel Jeb Hawkins), David Brian (Lilith's Attorney), Andy Devine (Corporal Peterson), Raymond Massey (Abraham Lincoln), Agnes Moorehead (Rebecca Prescott), Harry Morgan (General Ulysses S. Grant), Thelma Ritter (Agatha Clegg), Mickey Shaughnessy (Deputy Stover), Russ Tamblyn (Confederate Deserter), Spencer Tracy (Narrator), Rodolfo Acosta (Gant Gang Member), Mark Allen (Colin Harvey), Beulah Archuletta (Indian Woman), Robert Banas (Dance Hall Dancer), Willis Bouchey (Surgeon), Charlie Briggs (Flying Arrow Barker), Paul Bryar (Auctioneer's Assistant), Walter Burke (Wagon Poker Player), Polly Burson (Stock Player), Kim Charney (Sam Prescott), Ken Curtis (Corporal Ben), John Damler, Robert Nash (Lawyers), Christopher Dark, James Griffith, Carleton Young (Poker Players with

Cleve), Kem Dibbs (Blacksmith), Craig Duncan (James Marshall), Ben Black Elk, Sr. (Arapaho Chief), Jay C. Flippen (Huggins), Sol Gorss, Ken Terrell, Lee Van Cleef (River Pirates), Barry Harvey (Angus Harvey), William Henry (Staff Officer), Jerry Holmes (Railroad Clerk), Roy Jenson, Harvey Parry, Gil Perkins, Victor Romito (Henchmen), Claude Johnson (Jeremiah Rawlings), Jack Lambert, Harry Dean Stanton (Gant Henchmen), John Larch (Grimes), Stanley Livingston (Prescott Rawlings), J. Edward McKinley (Auctioneer), Bob Morgan (Member of Train Robbery Gang), Cliff Osmond (Bartender), Tudor Owen (Parson Alec Harvey), Jack Pennick (Corporal Murphy), Red Perkins (Union Soldier), Buddy Red Bow (Native Man), Chuck Roberson, William Wellman, Jr. (Officers), Jamie Ross (Bruce Harvey), Gene Roth (Riverboat Poker Player), Bryan Russell (Zeke Prescott), Danny Sands (Trapeze Man), Joe Sawyer (Riverboat Officer), Jeffrey Sayre (Auction Spectator), Clinton Sundberg (Hylan Seabury), Karl Swenson (Train Conductor), Harry Wilson (Cattleman at Barricade), Tom Greenway, Harry Monty, Boyd "Red" Morgan, Walter Reed (Bits).

Donovan's Reef (June 12, 1963)

CREDITS: Director and Producer: John Ford; Screenplay: James Edward Grant, Frank S. Nugent; Based on a story by Edmund Beloin and James Michener; Director of Photography: William H. Clothier; Editor: Otho Lovering; Musical Score: Cyril J. Mockridge; Art Directors: Eddie Imazu, Hal Pereria; Set Decorators: Sam Comer, Darryl Silvera; Costume Design: Edith Head; Makeup: Wally Westmore; Hair Stylist: Nellie Manley; Unit Production Manager: Don Robb; Assistant Director: Wingate Smith; Sound: Charles Grenzbach, Hugo Grenzbach; Process Photography: Farciot Edouart; Special Photographic Effects: Paul K. Lerpae; Musical Conductor: Irvin Talbot; Orchestrators: Jack Hayes, Leo Shuken; Stunts: Jerry Gatlin, Duke Green, Tom Hennesy, Cliff Lyons, Boyd "Red" Morgan, Hal Needham, Leo C. Richmond, Chuck Roberson, Wally Rose; Technicolor Consultant: Richard Mueller; Still Photographer: Bernie Abramson; Locations: Kauai, Hawaii; John Ford Productions–Paramount Pictures; 109 minutes.

CAST: **John Wayne** (Michael Patrick "Guns" Donovan), Lee Marvin (Thomas Aloysius "Boats" Gilhooley), Elizabeth Allen (Ameilia Dedham), Jack Warden (Dr. William Dedham), Cesar Romero (Marquis Andre de Lage), Dick Foran (Australian Navy Officer Sean O'Brien), Dorothy Lamour (Miss Lafleur), Marcel Dalio (Father Cluzeot), Mike Mazurki (Sergeant Monk Menkowicz), Jacqueline Malouf (Lelani Dedham), Cherylene Lee (Sarah "Sally" Deadham), Jeffrey Byron, aka Tim Stafford (Luki Deadham), Edgar Buchanan (Boston Attorney Francis X. O'Brien), Jon Fong (Mister Eu), John Alderson (Officer), Frank Baker (Captain Martin), Clyde Cook (Australian Officer), Carmen Estrabeau (Sister Gabrielle), Harold Fong (Swimsuit Seller), Dan Ford, John Stafford (Children), H. W. Gim (Chinese Man), Duke Green (Mate), Frank Hagney, Leslie Sketchley (Chief Petty Officers), Sam Harris, Fred Jones, Carl M. Leviness,

Mae Marsh, Scott Seaton, Sara Taft (Family Council Members), Tom Harris, Ron Nyman (Naval Officers), June Y. Kim, Midori (Servants), Richard Kipling, King Lockwood (Lawyers), Cliff Lyons (Australian Navy Officer), Yvonne Peattie (Sister Matthew), John Qualen (Deckhand), Chuck Roberson (Festus), Charles Seel (Grand Uncle Sedley Atterbury Pennyfeather), Ralph Volkie (James), Aissa Wayne (Native Girl), Patrick Wayne (Australian Navy Lieutenant), Lee Wood (Islander), Michelle Mazurki (Bit).

Appendix B
The Films of Ward Bond

The films are listed in order of their general release dates. An asterisk [*] indicates that Ward Bond is not billed in the on-screen credits. A plus sign [+] indicates that Bond's scenes were deleted from the final cut.

Words and Music (August 18, 1929) **Ward Bond** (Ward*); **John Wayne**, Lois Moran, David Percy, Helen Twelvetrees; directed by James Tinling; Fox Film Corporation; 81 minutes

Salute (September 1, 1929) **Ward Bond** (Midshipman Harold); **John Wayne**, George O'Brien, Helen Chandler, Stepin Fetchit; directed by **John Ford**; Fox Film Corporation; 84 minutes

So This Is College (November 8, 1929) **Ward Bond** (USC Player Number 30*); Elliott Nugent, Robert Montgomery, Cliff Edwards, Sally Starr; directed by Sam Wood; Metro-Goldwyn-Mayer; 98 minutes

The Lone Star Ranger (January 5, 1930) **Ward Bond** (Townsman*); George O'Brien, Sue Carol, Walter McGrail, Warren Hymer; directed by A. F. Erickson; Fox Film Corporation; 64 minutes

Born Reckless (June 6, 1930) **Ward Bond** (Sergeant); Edmund Lowe, Catherine Dale Owen, Frank Albertson, Marguerite Churchill; directed by Andrew Bennison and **John Ford**; production began in early 1930; Fox Film Corporation; 82 minutes

Good News (August 23, 1930) **Ward Bond** (Football Player*); Mary Lawlor, Stanley Smith, Bessie Love, Cliff Edwards; directed by Nick Grinde; production began in early 1930; Metro-Goldwyn-Mayer; 78 minutes

Up the River (October 12, 1930) **Ward Bond** (Inmate*); Spencer Tracy, Claire Luce, Warren Hymer, Humphrey Bogart; directed by **John Ford**; Fox Film Corporation; 85 minutes

Doorway to Hell (October 18, 1930) **Ward Bond** (Policeman*); Lew Ayres, Charles Judels, Dorothy Mathews; James Cagney; directed by Archie Mayo; production dates: August 1930; Warner Bros. Pictures; 78 minutes

The Big Trail (November 1, 1930) **Ward Bond** (Sid Bascom*); **John Wayne**, Marguerite Churchill, El Brendel, Tully Marshall; directed by Raoul Walsh; production began: spring 1930; Fox Film Corporation; 125 minutes [original 70mm version: 158 minutes]

A Connecticut Yankee (April 6, 1931) **Ward Bond** (Queen's Knight*); Will Rogers, William Farnum, Maureen O'Sullivan, Myrna Loy; directed by David Butler; production dates: November 24, 1930 to mid–January 1931; Fox Film Corporation; 95 minutes

Three Girls Lost (April 19, 1931) **Ward Bond** (Airline Steward*); **John Wayne**, Loretta Young, Lew Cody, Joan Marsh; directed by Sidney Lanfield; production dates: December 18, 1930 to mid–January 1931; Fox Film Corporation; 80 minutes

Quick Millions (May 3, 1931) **Ward Bond** (Cop*); Spencer Tracy, Marguerite Churchill, Sally Eilers, George Raft; directed by Rowland Brown; production dates: January 26 to late February 1931; Fox Film Corporation; 72 minutes

The Brat (September 20, 1931) **Ward Bond** (bit*); Sally O'Neil, Alan Dinehart, Frank Albertson, J. Farrell MacDonald; directed by **John Ford**; Fox Film Corporation; 67 minutes.

The Spider (September 27, 1931) **Ward Bond** (Cop*); Edmund Lowe, Lois Moran, El Brendel, George E. Stone; directed by Kenneth McKenna and William Cameron Menzies; production dates: mid–June to early July 1931; Fox Film Corporation; 59 minutes

Sob Sister (October 25, 1931) **Ward Bond** (Ward, a Cop*); James Dunn, Linda Watkins, Minna Gombell, George E. Stone; directed by Alfred Santell; production dates: August 3 to mid–September 1931; Fox Film Corporation; 67 minutes

Over the Hill (November 29, 1931) **Ward Bond** (Detective Escort*); Mae Marsh, James Dunn, Sally Eilers, Edward Crandell; directed by Henry King; production dates: early April to early May and August 31 to mid–October 1931; Fox Film Corporation; 89 minutes

Blonde Crazy (December 3, 1931) **Ward Bond** (Highway Patrolman*); James Cagney, Joan Blondell, Louis Calhern, Noel Francis; directed by Roy Del Ruth; production dates: early June to July 8, 1931; Warner Bros. Pictures; 79 minutes

Maker of Men (December 18, 1931) **Ward Bond** (Pat*); **John Wayne**, Jack Holt, Richard Cromwell, Joan Marsh; directed by Edward Sedgwick; production dates: October 6–26, 1931; Columbia Pictures Corporation; 71 minutes

Arrowsmith (December 26, 1931) **Ward Bond** (Cop*); Ronald Colman, Helen Hayes, Richard Bennett, Myrna Loy; directed by **John Ford**; production began early September 1931; Samuel Goldwyn Company–United Artists; 99 minutes

The Greeks Had a Word for Them (February 13, 1932) **Ward Bond** (Taxi Driver*); Joan Blondell, Madge Evans, Ina Claire, David Manners; directed by Lowell Sherman; production completed early October 1931; Samuel Goldwyn Company–United Artists; 79 minutes

High Speed (April 2, 1932) **Ward Bond** (Ham); Buck Jones, Loretta Sayers, Wallace MacDonald, Mickey Rooney; directed by D. Ross Lederman; production dates: November 24 to December 7, 1931; Columbia Pictures Corporation; 62 minutes

Careless Lady (April 3, 1932) **Ward Bond** (Cop*); Joan Bennett, John Boles, Minna Gombell, Weldon Heyburn; directed by Kenneth MacKenna; production dates: January 14 to mid–February 1932; Fox Film Corporation; 68 minutes

The Trial of Vivienne Ware (May 1, 1932) **Ward Bond** (Officer Johnson*); Joan Bennett, Donald Cook, Richard "Skeets" Gallagher, Zasu Pitts; directed by William K. Howard; production dates: February 10 to early March 1932; Fox Film Corporation; 56 minutes

Bachelor's Affairs (June 26, 1932) **Ward Bond** (Cop*); Adolphe Menjou, Minna Gombell, Arthur Pierson, Joan Marsh; directed by Alfred L. Werker; production dates: April 15 to mid–May 1932; Fox Film Corporation; 64 minutes

Hello Trouble (July 15, 1932) **Ward Bond** ("Heavy" Kennedy); Buck Jones, Lina Basquette, Russell Simpson, Otto Hoffman; directed by Lambert Hillyer; production dates: April 15–30, 1932; Columbia Pictures Corporation; 67 minutes

Hold 'Em Jail (September 16, 1932) Ward Bond (Football Player*); Bert Wheeler, Robert Woolsey, Edna Mae Oliver, Robert Armstrong; directed by Norman Taurog; RKO Radio Pictures; 66 minutes

White Eagle (October 7, 1932) **Ward Bond** (Henchman Bart); Buck Jones, Barbara Weeks, Robert Ellis, Jason Robards, Sr.; directed by Lambert Hillyer; production dates: June 13–25, 1932; Columbia Pictures Corporation; 64 minutes

Rackety Rax (October 23, 1932) **Ward Bond** ("Brick" Gilligan); Victor McLaglen, Greta Nissen, Nell O'Day, Alan Dinehart; directed by Lambert Hillyer; production dates: August 18 to late September 1932; Fox Film Corporation; 70 minutes

Virtue (October 25, 1932) **Ward Bond** (Frank); Carole Lombard, Pat O'Brien, Shirley Grey, Mayo Methot; directed by Edward Buzzell; production

dates: August 23 to September 12, 1932; Columbia Pictures Corporation; 68 minutes

Air Mail (November 3, 1932) **Ward Bond** (Joe Barnes*); Ralph Bellamy, Gloria Stuart, Pat O'Brien, Slim Summerville; directed by **John Ford**; Universal Pictures; 84 minutes

Flesh (December 8, 1932) **Ward Bond** (Muscles Manning*); Wallace Beery, Ricardo Cortez, Karen Morley, Jean Hersholt; directed by **John Ford**; production dates: September 26 to late October 1932; Metro-Goldwyn-Mayer; 96 minutes

Sundown Rider (December 30, 1932) **Ward Bond** (Gabe Powers); Buck Jones, Barbara Weeks, Pat O'-Malley, Niles Welch; directed by Lambert Hillyer; production dates: September 9–20, 1932; Columbia Pictures Corporation; 65 minutes

Lucky Devils (February 3, 1933) **Ward Bond** (unidentified role*); William Boyd, Dorothy Wilson, William Gargan, Creighton Chaney [Lon Chaney, Jr.]; directed by Ralph Ince; RKO Radio Pictures; 64 minutes

State Trooper (February 10, 1933) **Ward Bond** (unidentified role*); Regis Toomey, Evalyn Knapp, Barbara Weeks, Raymond Hatton; directed by D. Ross Lederman; production dates: December 1–15, 1932; Columbia Pictures Corporation; 68 minutes

Obey the Law (March 11, 1933) **Ward Bond** (Kid Paris); Leo Carrillo, Dickie Moore, Lois Wilson, Henry Clive; directed by Benjamin Stoloff; production dates: November 8–22, 1932; Bryan Foy Productions–Columbia Pictures Corporation; 64 minutes

Unknown Valley (May 5, 1933) **Ward Bond** (Elder Snead); Buck Jones, Cecelia Parker, Wade Boteler, Frank McGlynn, Sr.; directed by Lambert Hillyer; production dates: December 20, 1932, to January 3, 1933; Columbia Pictures Corporation; 69 minutes

When Strangers Marry (May 25, 1933) **Ward Bond** (Billy McGuire); Jack Holt, Lilian Bond, Arthur Vinton, Gustav von Seyffertitz; directed by Clarence G. Badger; production dates: January 3 to February 4, 1933; Columbia Pictures Corporation; 65 minutes

Heroes for Sale (June 17, 1933) **Ward Bond** (Red); Richard Barthelmess, Aline MacMahon, Loretta Young, Robert Barrat; directed by William A. Wellman; Warner Bros.–First National Pictures; 76 minutes

The Wrecker (July 10, 1933) **Ward Bond** (Cramer); Jack Holt, Genevieve Tobin, George E. Stone, Sidney Blackmer; directed by Albert S. Rogell; production dates: May 8–28, 1933; Columbia Pictures Corporation; 72 minutes

Lady for a Day (September 13, 1933) **Ward Bond** (Mounted Policeman*); Warren William, May Robson, Guy Kibbee, Glenda Farrell; directed by Frank Capra; production dates: May 9 to June 6, 1933; Columbia Pictures Corporation; 96 minutes

Police Car 17 (September 30, 1933) **Ward Bond** (Bumps O'Neil); Tim McCoy, Evalyn Knapp, Edwin Maxwell, DeWitt Jennings; directed by Lambert Hillyer; production dates: June 15–24, 1933; Columbia Pictures Corporation; 57 minutes

Wild Boys of the Road (October 7, 1933) **Ward Bond** (Red*); Frankie Darro, Edwin Phillips, Rochelle Hudson, Dorothy Coonan Wellman; directed by William A. Wellman; Warner Bros.–First National Pictures; 68 minutes

College Coach (November 4, 1933) **Ward Bond** (Assistant Coach*); Dick Powell, Ann Dvorak, Pat O'Brien, Arthur Byron, **John Wayne**; directed by William A. Wellman; Warner Bros. Pictures; 76 minutes

Straitaway (December 22, 1933) **Ward Bond** (Hobo); Tim McCoy, Sue Carol, William Bakewell, Lafe McKee; directed by Lambert Hillyer; production dates: October 23 to November 2, 1933; Columbia Pictures Corporation; 58 minutes

Son of a Sailor (December 23, 1933) **Ward Bond** (Joe*); Joe E. Brown, Jean Muir, Frank McHugh, Thelma Todd; directed by Lloyd Bacon; Warner Bros.–First National Pictures; 73 minutes

The Fighting Code (December 30, 1933) **Ward Bond** (Krull); Buck Jones, Diane Sinclair, Richard Alexander, Alfred P. James; directed by Lambert Hillyer; production dates: February 22 to March 6, 1933; Columbia Pictures Corporation; 65 minutes

Frontier Marshal (January 19, 1934) **Ward Bond** (Ben Murchison); George O'Brien, Irene Bentley, George E. Stone, Alan Edwards; directed by Lewis Seiler; production dates: late September to mid–October 1933; Fox Film Corporation; 66 minutes

School for Romance (January 31, 1934) **Ward Bond** (Husband); Lou Holtz, Billie Seward, Betty Grable, Lois January; directed by Archie Gottler; Columbia Pictures Corporation; 20 minutes

Speed Wings (February 5, 1934) **Ward Bond** (Henchman*); Tim McCoy, Evalyn Knapp, William Bakewell, Vincent Sherman; directed by Otto Brower; production dates: November 17 to December 5, 1933; Columbia Pictures Corporation; 61 minutes

It Happened One Night (February 23, 1934) **Ward Bond** (Bus Driver*); Clark Gable, Claudette Colbert, Walter Connolly, Roscoe Karns; directed by Frank Capra; production dates: November 13 to December 22, 1933; retakes: January 8–12, 1934; Columbia Pictures Corporation; 105 minutes

The Poor Rich (February 26, 1934) **Ward Bond** (Motor Cop); Edward Everett Horton, Edna Mae Oliver, Andy Devine, Thelma Todd; directed by Edward Sedgwick; production dates: November 6–29, 1933; Universal Pictures; 77 minutes

The Fighting Ranger (March 17, 1934) **Ward Bond** (Dave); Buck Jones, Dorothy Revier, Frank Rice, Bradley Page; directed by George B. Seitz; production dates: March 9–18, 1934; Columbia Pictures Corporation; 60 minutes

Voice in the Night (April 6, 1934) **Ward Bond** (Bob Hall); Tim McCoy, Billie Seward, Joseph Crehan, Kane Richmond; directed by Charles C. Coleman; production dates: January 16–27, 1934; Columbia Pictures Corporation; 59 minutes

Whirlpool (April 10, 1934) **Ward Bond** (Farley); Jack Holt, Jean Arthur, Donald Cook, Allen Jenkins; directed by Roy William Neill; production dates: January 31 to February 20, 1934; Columbia Pictures Corporation; 80 minutes

Crime of Helen Stanley (April 20, 1934) **Ward Bond** (Jack Baker); Ralph Bellamy, Shirley Grey, Gail Patrick, Kane Richmond; directed by D. Ross Lederman; production dates: March 2–13, 1934; Columbia Pictures Corporation; 58 minutes

I'll Tell the World (April 21, 1934) **Ward Bond** (Dirigible Officer*); Lee Tracy, Gloria Stuart, Roger Pryor, Onslow Stevens; directed by Edward Sedgwick; production dates: February 12 to March 2, 1934; Universal Pictures Corporation; 77 minutes

The Most Precious Thing in Life (June 5, 1934) **Ward Bond** (Head Coach Smith); Richard Cromwell, Jean Arthur, Donald Cook, Anita Louise; directed by Lambert Hillyer; production dates: March 6–26, 1934; Columbia Pictures Corporation; 67 minutes

The Circus Clown (June 13, 1934) **Ward Bond** (Audience Member*); Joe E. Brown, Patricia Ellis, Dorothy Burgess, Don Dillaway; directed by Ray Enright; production began February 12, 1934; Warner Bros.–First National Pictures; 63 minutes

Here Comes the Groom (June 22, 1934) **Ward Bond** (Second Cop); Jack Haley, Mary Boland, Neil Hamilton, Patricia Ellis; directed by Edward Sedgwick; production began April 16, 1934; Paramount Pictures; 66 minutes

A Man's Game (June 16, 1934) **Ward Bond** (Dave); Tim McCoy, Evalyn Knapp, DeWitt Jennings, John Dilson; directed by D. Ross Lederman; production dates: April 4–14, 1934; Columbia Pictures Corporation; 56 minutes

The Defense Rests (July 15, 1934) **Ward Bond** (Gooch); Jack Holt, Jean Arthur, Nat Pendleton, Raymond Walburn; directed by Lambert Hillyer; production dates: May 9–28, 1934; Columbia Pictures Corporation; 70 minutes

The Affairs of Cellini (August 24, 1934) **Ward Bond** (Palace Guard); Constance Bennett, Fredric March, Frank Morgan, Fay Wray; directed by Gregory La Cava; production dates: February 5 to March 5, 1934; 20th Century Pictures–United Artists; 80 minutes

Chained (August 31, 1934) **Ward Bond** (Ship Steward*); Joan Crawford, Clark Gable, Otto Kruger, Stewart Irwin; directed by Clarence Brown; production dates: late May to July 7, 1934; Metro-Goldwyn-Mayer; 74 minutes

The Human Side (September 1, 1934) **Ward Bond** (Cop); Adolphe Menjou, Doris Kenyon, Charlotte Henry, Reginald Owen; directed by Edward Buzzell; production dates: June 18 to July 16, 1934; Universal Pictures; 70 minutes

Girl in Danger (September 11, 1934) **Ward Bond** (Wynkoski); Ralph Bellamy, Shirley Grey, J. Carrol Naish, Arthur Hohl; directed by D. Ross Lederman; production dates: June 4–13, 1934; Columbia Pictures Corporation; 57 minutes

Death on the Diamond (September 14, 1934) **Ward Bond** (Police Guard*); Robert Young, Madge Evans, Nat Pendleton, Ted Healy; directed by Edward Sedgwick; production dates: mid–July to August 1, 1934; Metro-Goldwyn-Mayer; 71 minutes

6 Day Bike Rider (October 20, 1934) **Ward Bond** (First Officer*); Joe E. Brown, Maxine Doyle, Frank McHugh, Gordon Westcott; directed by Lloyd Bacon; production began July 9, 1934; Warner Bros.–First National Pictures; 69 minutes

Against the Law (October 25, 1934) **Ward Bond** (Tony Rizzo); Johnny Mack Brown, Sally Blaine, Arthur Hohl, George Meeker; directed by Lambert Hillyer; production dates: August 24 to September 7, 1934; Columbia Pictures Corporation; 61 minutes

Men of the Night (November 18, 1934) **Ward Bond** (Detective John Connors); Bruce Cabot, Judith Allen, Charles Sabin, John Kelly; directed by Lambert Hillyer; production dates: September 21 to October 4, 1934; Columbia Pictures Corporation

Broadway Bill (November 30, 1934) **Ward Bond** (Morgan's Henchman*); Warner Baxter, Myrna Loy, Walter Connolly, Helen Vinson; directed by Frank Capra; production dates: June 18 to August 16, 1934; Columbia Pictures Corporation; 104 minutes

Grand Old Girl (January 18, 1935) **Ward Bond** (Coach Clark*); May Robson, Mary Carlisle, Fred MacMurray, Alan Hale; directed by John S. Robertson; production dates: September 19 to mid–October 1934; RKO Radio Pictures; 72 minutes

Under Pressure (February 2, 1935) **Ward Bond** (Prize Fighter*); Edmund Lowe, Victor McLaglen, Florence Rice, Charles Bickford; directed by Raoul Walsh; production dates: September 7 to October 13 and December 3–31, 1934; Fox Film Corporation; 72 minutes

Devil Dogs of the Air (February 9, 1935) **Ward Bond** (Jimmy, Senior Instructor); James Cagney, Pat O'Brien, Margaret Lindsay, Frank McHugh; directed by Lloyd Bacon; production began October 1, 1934; Cosmopolitan Productions–Warner Bros. Pictures; 85 minutes

One New York Night (March 3, 1935) **Ward Bond** (Actor*); Franchot Tone, Una Merkel, Conrad Nagel, Harvey Stephens; directed by Jack Conway; production dates: February 15 to March 2, 1935; Metro-Goldwyn-Mayer; 71 minutes

Times Square Lady (March 8, 1935) **Ward Bond** (Dugan*); Robert Taylor, Virginia Bruce, Helen Twelvetrees, Isabel Jewel; directed by George B. Seitz; production dates: January 22 to February 9, 1935; Metro-Goldwyn-Mayer; 68 minutes

The Crimson Trail (March 11, 1935) **Ward Bond** (Luke Long); Buck Jones, Polly Ann Young, Paul Fix, Carl Stockdale; directed by Alfred Raboch; Buck Jones Productions–Universal Pictures; 60 minutes

Strangers All (April 1, 1935) **Ward Bond** (Ward, Assistant Director*); May Robson, Preston Foster, William Bakewell, Samuel S. Hinds; directed by Charles Vidor; production dates: January 30 to February 27, 1935; RKO Radio Pictures; 70 minutes

Black Fury (May 18, 1935) **Ward Bond** (Mac, Company Policeman); Paul Muni, Karen Morley, William Gargan, Barton MacLane; directed by Michael Curtiz; production began October 20, 1934; Warner Bros.–First National Pictures; 94 minutes

Fighting Shadows (April 18, 1935) **Ward Bond** (Brad Harrison); Tim McCoy, Robert Allen, Geneva Mitchell, Si Jenks; directed by David Selman; production dates: January 28 to February 13, 1935; Columbia Pictures Corporations; 58 minutes

G-Men (May 4, 1935) **Ward Bond** (Gunman at Train Station*); James Cagney, Margaret Lindsay, Ann Dvorak, Robert Armstrong; directed by William Keighley; production dates: February 20 to April 1, 1935; Warner Bros. Pictures; 85 minutes

Go Into Your Dance (April 20, 1935) **Ward Bond** (Herman Lahey*); Al Jolson, Ruby Keeler, Glenda Farrell, Barton MacLane; directed by Archie Mayo; Warner Bros. Pictures; 89 minutes

Mary Jane's Pa (April 27, 1935) **Ward Bond** (Roughneck Leader*); Aline MacMahon, Guy Kibbee, Tom Brown, Robert McWade; directed by William Keighley; Warner Bros.–First National Pictures; 70 minutes

The Headline Woman (May 15, 1935) **Ward Bond** (Johnson); Heather Angel, Roger Pryor, Ford Sterling, Conway Tearle; directed by William Nigh; production began April 12, 1935; Mascot Pictures; 71 minutes

Justice of the Range (May 25, 1935) **Ward Bond** (Bob Brennan); Tim McCoy, Billie Seward, Guy Usher, George "Gabby" Hayes; directed by Ford Beebe; production dates: March 12–23, 1935; Columbia Pictures Corporation; 58 minutes

Murder in the Fleet (May 27, 1935) **Ward Bond** ("Heavy" Johnson*); Robert Taylor, Jean Parker, Ted Healy, Una Merkel; directed by Edward Sedgwick; production dates: March 28 to April 17, 1935; Metro-Goldwyn-Mayer; 69 minutes

Calm Yourself (June 28, 1935) **Ward Bond** (Detective*); Robert Young, Madge Evans, Betty Furness, Ralph Morgan; directed by George B. Seitz; production dates: May 8–28, 1935; Metro-Goldwyn-Mayer; 70 minutes

She Gets Her Man (August 5, 1935) **Ward Bond** (Chick); Zasu Pitts, Hugh O'Connell, Helen Twelvetrees, Lucien Littlefield; directed by William Nigh; production dates: June 20 to July 8, 1935; Universal Pictures; 65 minutes

Little Big Shot (September 7, 1935) **Ward Bond** (Kell's Henchman); Sybil Jason, Glenda Farrell, Robert Armstrong, Edward Everett Horton; directed by Michael Curtiz; Warner Bros. Pictures; 72 minutes

His Night Out (October 1, 1935) **Ward Bond** (Lanky); Edward Everett Horton, Irene Hervey, Jack LaRue, Robert McWade; directed by William Nigh; production dates: August 2 to September 11, 1935; Universal Pictures; 67 minutes

Waterfront Lady (October 5, 1935) **Ward Bond** (Jess); Ann Rutherford, Frank Albertson, J. Farrell MacDonald, Barbara Pepper; directed by Joseph Santley; Mascot Pictures; 70 minutes

The Last Days of Pompeii (October 18, 1935) **Ward Bond** (Murmex of Carthage, Gladiator*); Preston Foster, Alan Hale, Basil Rathbone, Louis Calhern; directed by Ernest B. Schoedsack and Merian C. Cooper; production dates: May 14 to mid–July 1935; RKO Radio Pictures; 96 minutes

Three Kids and a Queen (October 21, 1935) **Ward Bond** (Detective*); May Robson, Henry Armetta, Herman Bing, Frankie Darro; directed by Edward Ludwig; production dates: July 29 to August 27, 1935; Universal Pictures; 90 minutes

Western Courage (October 29, 1935) **Ward Bond** (Lacrosse); Ken Maynard, Geneva Mitchell, Charles K. French, Betty Blythe; directed by Spencer Gordon

Bennet; production dates: September 10–23, 1935; Larry Darmour Productions–Columbia Pictures Corporation; 61 minutes

Guard That Girl (November 2, 1935) **Ward Bond** (Budge Edwards); Robert Allen, Florence Rice, Barbara Kent, Arthur Hohl; directed by Lambert Hillyer; production dates: July 16 to August 3, 1935; Columbia Pictures Corporation; 67 minutes

I Found Stella Parish (November 16, 1935) **Ward Bond** (Roman Soldier in Play*); Kay Francis, Ian Hunter, Paul Lukas, Sybil Jason; directed by Mervyn LeRoy; production began August 19, 1935; Warner Bros.–First National Pictures; 85 minutes

Broadway Hostess (December 7, 1935) **Ward Bond** (Lucky's Henchman*); Wini Shaw, Genevieve Tobin, Lyle Talbot, Allen Jenkins; directed by Frank McDonald; production began August 9, 1935; Warner Bros. Pictures; 68 minutes

Too Tough to Kill (December 20, 1935) **Ward Bond** (Danny); Victor Jory, Sally O'Neil, Johnny Arthur, Robert Gleckler; directed by D. Ross Lederman; production dates: September 23 to October 5, 1935; Columbia Pictures Corporation; 58 minutes

We're Only Human (December 27, 1935) **Ward Bond** (Bank Robber*); Preston Foster, Jane Wyatt, James Gleason, Arthur Hohl; directed by James Flood; production dates: mid–September to late October 1935; RKO Radio Pictures; 69 minutes

Hitch Hike Lady (December 28, 1935) **Ward Bond** (Motorcycle Officer); Alison Skipworth, Mae Clarke, Arthur Treacher, James Ellison; directed by Aubrey Scotto; production dates: November 5–19, 1935; Republic Pictures; 77 minutes

Two in the Dark (January 10, 1936) **Ward Bond** (Policeman*); Walter Abel, Margot Grahame, Wallace Ford, Alan Hale; directed by Benjamin Stoloff; production dates: October 22 to mid–November 1935; RKO Radio Pictures; 74 minutes

Muss 'Em Up (February 14, 1936) **Ward Bond** ("John Doe," Gangster); Preston Foster, Margaret Callahan, Alan Mowbray, Ralph Morgan; directed by Charles Vidor; production dates: November 5 to December 7, 1935; RKO Radio Pictures; 70 minutes

The Leathernecks Have Landed (February 17, 1936) **Ward Bond** (Tex); Lew Ayres, Isabel Jewel, James Ellison, James Burke; production dates: late November 1935 to February 1936; Republic Pictures; 67 minutes

Boulder Dam (March 7, 1936) **Ward Bond** (Pa's Guest*); Ross Alexander, Patricia Ellis, Lyle Talbot, Eddie Acuff; directed by Frank McDonald; production dates: October 21 to November 20, 1935; Warner Bros. Pictures; 70 minutes

Colleen (March 21, 1936) **Ward Bond** (Sweeney, Second Officer *); Dick Powell, Ruby Keeler, Jack Oakie, Joan Blondell; directed by Alfred E. Green; production began November 5, 1935; Warner Bros. Pictures; 89 minutes

Pride of the Marines (April 2, 1936) **Ward Bond** (Gunner Brady); Charles Bickford, Florence Rice, Robert Allen, Thurston Hall; directed by D. Ross Lederman; production dates: January 10 to February 3, 1936; Columbia Pictures Corporation; 64 minutes

The First Baby (April 2, 1936) **Ward Bond** (bit*); Johnny Downs, Shirley Deane, Jane Darwell, Hattie McDaniel; directed by Lewis Seiler; production dates: March 2 to late March 1936; 20th Century–Fox Film Corporation; 75 minutes

The Case Against Mrs. Ames (May 8, 1936) **Ward Bond** (Newspaper Buyer*); Madeleine Carroll, George Brent, Arthur Treacher, Alan Baxter; directed by William A. Seiter; production began March 1936; Walter Wanger Productions–Paramount Pictures; 85 minutes

Avenging Waters (May 8, 1936) **Ward Bond** (Marve Slater); Ken Maynard, Beth Marion, John Elliott, Zella Russell; directed by Spencer Gordon Bennet; production dates: February 29 to March 14, 1936; Larry Darmour Productions–Columbia Pictures Corporation; 56 minutes

Fatal Lady (May 15, 1936) **Ward Bond** (American Stage Manager*); Mary Ellis, Walter Pidgeon, John Halliday, Ruth Donnelly; directed by Edward Ludwig; production completed March 11, 1936; Walter Wanger Productions–Paramount Pictures; 73 minutes

The Cattle Thief (May 26, 1936) **Ward Bond** (Ranse Willard); Ken Maynard, Geneva Mitchell, Roger Williams, James A. Marcus; directed by Spencer Gordon Bennet; production dates: December 9–24, 1935; Larry Darmour Productions–Columbia Pictures Corporation; 58 minutes

The Bride Walks Out (July 10, 1936) **Ward Bond** (Taxi Driver*); Barbara Stanwyck, Gene Raymond, Robert Young, Hattie McDaniel; directed by Leigh Jason; production dates: late April to late May 1936; Edward Small Productions–RKO Radio Pictures; 81 minutes

High Tension (July 17, 1936) **Ward Bond** (Husky Man*); Brian Donlevy, Glenda Farrell, Norman Foster, Hattie McDaniel; directed by Allan Dwan; production dates: April 27 to late May 1936; 20th Century–Fox Film Corporation; 63 minutes

White Fang (July 17, 1936) **Ward Bond** (Thief*); Michael Whalen, Jean Muir, Charles Winninger, John Carradine; directed by David Butler; production dates: late March to early May 1936; 20th Century–Fox Film Corporation; 70 minutes

Crash Donovan (August 1, 1936) **Ward Bond** (The Drill Master); Jack Holt, John "Dusty" King, Nan Grey, Eddie Acuff; directed by William Nigh; production dates: March 30 to May 7, 1936; retakes began June 8, 1936; Universal Pictures; 70 minutes

Second Wife (August 21, 1936) **Ward Bond** (Politician*); Gertrude Michael, Walter Abel, Erik Rhodes, Emma Dunn; directed by Edward Killy; production dates: June 24 to mid–July 1936; RKO Radio Pictures; 59 minutes

They Met in a Taxi (September 9, 1936) **Ward Bond** (Policeman*); Chester Morris, Fay Wray, Raymond Walburn, Lionel Stander; directed by Alfred E. Green; production dates: June 10 to July 8, 1936; Columbia Pictures Corporation; 70 minutes

The Man Who Lived Twice (September 25, 1936) **Ward Bond** (John "Gloves" Baker); Ralph Bellamy, Marian Marsh, Thurston Hall, Isabel Jewell; directed by Harry Lachman; production dates: July 11–29, 1936; Columbia Pictures Corporation; 73 minutes

The Big Game (October 9, 1936) **Ward Bond** (Gambler*); Phillip Huston, James Gleason, June Travis, Bruce Cabot; directed by George Nichols, Jr., and Edward Killy; production dates: July 25 to mid–August 1936; RKO Radio Pictures; 74 minutes

Without Orders (October 23, 1936) **Ward Bond** (Tim Casey); Sally Eilers, Robert Armstrong, Frances Sage, Charley Grapewin; directed by Lew Landers; production dates: August 3 to late August 1936; RKO Radio Pictures; 64 minutes

Legion of Terror (November 1, 1936) **Ward Bond** (Don Foster); Bruce Cabot, Marguerite Churchill, Crawford Weaver, Charles C. Wilson; directed by Charles C. Coleman; production dates: August 24–September 10, 1936; Columbia Pictures Corporation; 63 minutes

The Accusing Finger (November 17, 1936) **Ward Bond** (Prison Guard*); Paul Kelly, Marsha Hunt, Robert Cummings, Harry Carey; directed by James P. Hogan; Paramount Pictures; 62 minutes

Conflict (November 29, 1936) **Ward Bond** (Gus "Knockout" Carrigan); **John Wayne**, Jean Rogers, Tommy Bupp, Bryant Washburn; directed by David Howard; production began mid–September 1936; Universal Pictures; 60 minutes

Woman-Wise (January 22, 1937) **Ward Bond** (Kramer*); Rochelle Hudson, Michael Whalen, Thomas Beck, Alan Dinehart; directed by Allan Dwan; production dates: October 26 to mid November 1936; 20th Century–Fox Film Corporation; 62 minutes

The Devil's Playground (January 24, 1937) **Ward Bond** (Sidecar Wilson); Richard Dix, Dolores del Rio, Chester Morris, George McKay; directed by Erle C. Kenton; production dates: September 8 to October 19, 1936; Columbia Pictures Corporation; 74 minutes

You Only Live Once (January 29, 1937) **Ward Bond** (Casey*); Sylvia Sidney, Henry Fonda, Barton MacLane, Jerome Cowan; directed by Fritz Lang; production dates: September 30 to mid–November 1936 and early January 1937; Walter Wanger Productions–United Artists; 86 minutes

When's Your Birthday? (February 19, 1937) **Ward Bond** (Detective*); Joe E. Brown, Marian Marsh, Fred Keating, Edgar Kennedy; directed by Harry Beaumont; David L. Loew Productions–RKO Radio Pictures; 75 minutes

Park Avenue Logger (March 16, 1937) **Ward Bond** (Paul Sangar); George O'Brien; Beatrice Roberts, Willard Robertson, Bert Hanlon; directed by David Howard; production dates: early December to December 22, 1936; George A. Hirliman Productions–RKO Radio Pictures; 67 minutes

23½ Hours Leave (March 21, 1937) **Ward Bond** (Top Sergeant Burke); James Ellison, Terry Walker, Morgan Hill, Arthur Lake; directed by John G. Blystone; production dates: January 4 to February 3, 1937; Douglas MacLean Productions–Grand National Pictures; 72 minutes

The Soldier and the Lady (April 7, 1937) **Ward Bond** (Tartar Chief*); Anton Walbrook, Elizabeth Allan, Akim Tamiroff, Margot Grahame; directed by George Nichols, Jr.; production dates: November 19

to December 28, 1936; RKO Radio Pictures; 85 minutes

Night Key (May 2, 1937) **Ward Bond** (Fingers); Boris Karloff, Jean Rogers, Warren Hull, Alan Baxter; directed by Lloyd Corrigan; production dates: January 18 to February 16, 1937; Universal Pictures; 68 minutes

They Gave Him a Gun (May 7, 1937) **Ward Bond** (M.P.*); Spencer Tracy, Gladys George, Franchot Tone, Edgar Dearing; directed by W. S. Van Dyke; production dates: mid–February to April 5, 1937; Metro-Goldwyn-Mayer; 94 minutes

The Go Getter (May 22, 1937) **Ward Bond** (Logger*); George Brent, Anita Louise, Charles Winninger, John Eldredge; directed by Busby Berkeley; production began mid–December 1936; Cosmopolitan Productions–Warner Bros. Pictures; 92 minutes

The Wildcatter (June 6, 1937) **Ward Bond** (Johnson); Scott Kolk, Jean Rogers, Russell Hicks, Milburn Stone; directed by Lewis D. Collins; production began February 22, 1937; Universal Pictures; 58 minutes

Mountain Music (June 18, 1937) **Ward Bond** (G-Man); Bob Burns, Martha Raye, John Howard, George "Gabby" Hayes; directed by Robert Florey; production dates: early March to early May 1937; Paramount Pictures; 76 minutes

A Fight to the Finish (June 30, 1937) **Ward Bond** (Eddie Hawkins); Don Terry, Rosalind Keith, George McKay, Wade Boteler; directed by Charles C. Coleman; production dates: April 19 to May 2, 1937; Columbia Pictures Corporation; 58 minutes

The Singing Marine (July 3, 1937) **Ward Bond** (First Sergeant*); Dick Powell, Doris Weston, Lee Dixon, Allen Jenkins; directed by Ray Enright; production began late January 1937; Warner Bros. Pictures; 105 minutes

Marry the Girl (July 13, 1937) **Ward Bond** (Motorcycle Policeman*); Mary Boland, Frank McHugh, Hugh Herbert, Allen Jenkins; directed by William C. McGann; Warner Bros. Pictures; 68 minutes

Topper (July 16, 1937) **Ward Bond** (Eddie, Cab Driver*); Constance Bennett, Cary Grant, Roland Young, Billie Burke; directed by Norman Z. McLeod; production dates: late March to late May 1937; Hal Roach Studios–Metro-Goldwyn-Mayer; 97 minutes

Dead End (August 27, 1937) **Ward Bond** (Doorman); Sylvia Sidney, Joel McCrea, Humphrey Bogart, Claire Trevor; directed by William Wyler; production dates: May 4 to mid–July 1937; Samuel Goldwyn Company–United Artists; 93 minutes

Escape By Night (September 1, 1937) **Ward Bond** (Peter "Spudsy" Baker); William Hall, Ann Nagel, Dean Jagger, Murray Alper; directed by Hamilton McFadden; production began July 7, 1937; Republic Pictures; 64 minutes

The Game That Kills (September 21, 1937) **Ward Bond** (Tom Ferguson); Charles Quigley, Rita Hayworth, John Gallaudet, J. Farrell McDonald; directed by D. Ross Lederman; production dates: May 4–26, 1937; Columbia Pictures Corporation; 55 minutes

Music for Madame (October 8, 1937) **Ward Bond** (Violets*); Nino Martini, Joan Fontaine, Alan Hale, Billy Gilbert; directed by John G. Blystone; production dates: June 10 to July 29, 1937; Jesse L. Lasky Feature Play Company–RKO Radio Pictures; 81 minutes

The Westland Case (October 31, 1937) **Ward Bond** (Connors*); Preston Foster, Frank Jenks, Carol Hughes, Barbara Pepper; directed by Christy Cabanne; Crime Club Productions–Universal Pictures; 62 minutes

Fight for Your Lady (November 5, 1937) **Ward Bond** (Mr. Walton*); John Boles, Jack Oakie, Ida Lupino, Margot Grahame; directed by Benjamin Stoloff; production dates: mid–July to mid–August 1937; RKO Radio Pictures; 66 minutes

Of Human Hearts (February 11, 1938) **Ward Bond** (Laughing Man in Church*); Walter Huston, James Stewart, Beulah Bondi, John Carradine; directed by Clarence Brown; production dates: October 18 to December 20, 1937; Metro-Goldwyn-Mayer; 103 minutes

Penitentiary (February 8, 1938) **Ward Bond** (Red, Prison Barber*); Walter Connolly, John Howard, Jean Parker, Robert Barrat; directed by John Brahm; production dates: October 26 to November 22, 1937; Columbia Pictures Corporation; 74 minutes

The Kid Comes Back (February 12, 1938) **Ward Bond** (Spike*); Wayne Morris, Barton MacLane, June Travis, "Slapsie" Maxie Rosenbloom; directed by B. Reeves Eason; production began November 2, 1937; Warner Bros. Pictures; 60 minutes

Born to Be Wild (February 16, 1938) **Ward Bond** (Bill Purvis); Ralph Byrd, Doris Weston, Robert Emmett Keane, Ben Hewlett; directed by Joseph Kane; production dates: December 17, 1937 to January 5, 1938; Republic Pictures; 66 minutes

Bringing Up Baby (February 18, 1938) **Ward Bond** (Motorcycle Cop*); Katherine Hepburn, Cary Grant, Charles Ruggles, Walter Catlett; directed by Howard Hawks; production dates: September 23, 1937 to January 6, 1938; RKO Radio Pictures; 102 minutes

Hawaii Calls (March 11, 1938) **Ward Bond** (Muller); Bobby Breen, Ned Sparks, Gloria Holden, Warren Hull; directed by Edward F. Cline; production dates: November 5 to mid–December 1937; Bobby Breen Productions–RKO Radio Pictures; 91 minutes

Over the Wall (April 2, 1938) **Ward Bond** (Eddie Edwards); Dick Foran, June Travis, John Litel, George E. Stone; directed by Frank McDonald; production began July 29, 1937; Cosmopolitan Productions–Warner Bros. Pictures; 67 minutes

Mr. Moto's Gamble (April 7, 1938) **Ward Bond** (Biff Moran); Peter Lorre, Keye Luke, Dick Baldwin, Lynn Bari; directed by James Tinling; production dates: January 10 to mid–February 1938; 20th Century–Fox Film Corporation; 72 minutes

The Adventures of Marco Polo (April 15, 1938) **Ward Bond** (Mongol Guard*); Gary Cooper, Sigrid Gurie, Basil Rathbone, Alan Hale; directed by Archie Mayo; production dates: June 16 to early September 1937; Samuel Goldwyn Company–United Artists; 104 minutes

Flight into Nowhere (April 19, 1938) **Ward Bond** (Taylor, Dispatcher); Jack Holt, Dick Purcell, Julie Bishop, James Burke; directed by Lewis D. Collins; production dates: January 20 to February 8, 1938;

Larry Darmour Productions–Columbia Pictures Corporation; 63 minutes

Gun Law (May 13, 1938) **Ward Bond** (Pecos); George O'Brien, Rita Oehman, Ray Whitley, Paul Everton; directed by David Howard; production began mid–March 1938; RKO Radio Pictures; 60 minutes

Numbered Woman (May 22, 1938) **Ward Bond** (Detective); Sally Blane, Lloyd Hughes, Mayo Methot, J. Farrell McDonald; directed by Karl Brown; production began early April 1938; Monogram Pictures; 63 minutes

Reformatory (June 20, 1938) **Ward Bond** (Mac Grady); Jack Holt, Bobby Jordan, Grant Mitchell, Frankie Darro; directed by Lewis D. Collins; production dates: April 25 to May 8, 1938; Larry Darmour Productions–Columbia Pictures Corporation; 61 minutes

Prison Break (July 12, 1938) **Ward Bond** (Big Red Kincaid); Barton MacLane, Glenda Farrell, Paul Hurst, Edward Pawley; directed by Arthur Lubin; production dates: May 23 to mid–June 1938; Universal Pictures; 72 minutes

Professor Beware (July 29, 1938) **Ward Bond** (Motorcycle Cop*); Harold Lloyd, Phyllis Welch, Raymond Walburn, Lionel Stander; directed by Elliott Nugent; production dates: late November 1937 to mid–January 1938; Harold Lloyd Productions–Paramount Pictures; 95 minutes

The Amazing Doctor Clitterhouse (July 30, 1938) **Ward Bond** (Tug); Edward G. Robinson, Claire Trevor, Humphrey Bogart, Allen Jenkins; directed by Anatole Litvak; production dates: late February to early April 1938; Warner Bros.–First National Pictures; 87 minutes

You Can't Take It with You (November 3, 1938) **Ward Bond** (Mike, Detective*); Jean Arthur, Lionel Barrymore, James Stewart, Edward Arnold; directed by Frank Capra; production dates: April 25 to June 29, 1938; Columbia Pictures Corporation; 126 minutes

Fugitives for a Night (September 23, 1938) **Ward Bond** (Gambler*); Frank Albertson, Eleanor Lynn, Allan Lane, Bradley Page; directed by Leslie Goodwins; RKO Radio Pictures; 63 minutes

The Law West of Tombstone (November 18, 1938) **Ward Bond** (Mulligan P. Martinez); Harry Carey, Tim Holt, Evelyn Brent, Allan Lane; directed by Glenn Tryon; production dates: early September to early October 1938; RKO Radio Pictures; 73 minutes

Submarine Patrol (November 25, 1938) **Ward Bond** (Seaman Olaf Swanson); Richard Greene, Nancy Kelly, Preston Foster, George Bancroft; directed by **John Ford**; production dates: late June to late August 1938; 20th Century–Fox Film Corporation; 95 minutes

Going Places (December 1, 1938) **Ward Bond** (Clarence, Policeman*); Dick Powell, Anita Louise, Allen Jenkins, Ronald Reagan; directed by Ray Enright; production dates: early August to late September 1938; Warner Bros. Pictures; 84 minutes

Son of Frankenstein (January 13, 1939) **Ward Bond** (Gendarme at Gate*); Basil Rathbone, Boris

Karloff, Bela Lugosi, Lionel Atwill; directed by Rowland V. Lee; production dates: November 7, 1938 to January 4, 1939; Universal Pictures; 99 minutes

They Made Me a Criminal (January 28, 1939) **Ward Bond** (Lenihan); John Garfield, *Dead End* Kids, Claude Rains, Ann Sheridan; directed by Busby Berkeley; production dates: mid–August to mid–October and early November 1938; Warner Bros. Pictures; 92 minutes

Made for Each Other (February 10, 1939) **Ward Bond** (Jim Hatton*); Carole Lombard, James Stewart, Charles Coburn, Lucile Watson; directed by John Cromwell; production dates: late August to late October 1938; Selznick International Pictures; 92 minutes

Pardon Our Nerve (February 24, 1939) **Ward Bond** (Kid Ramsey); Lynn Bari, June Gale, Guinn "Big Boy" Williams, Edward Brophy; directed by H. Bruce Humberstone; production dates: September 17 to mid–October 1938; 20th Century–Fox Film Corporations; 65 minutes

The Oklahoma Kid (March 11, 1939) **Ward Bond** (Wes Handley); James Cagney, Humphrey Bogart, Rosemary Lane, Donald Crisp; directed by Lloyd Bacon; production dates: late September to mid–December 1938; Warner Bros. Pictures; 85 minutes

Trouble in Sundown (March 24, 1939) **Ward Bond** (Dusty); George O'Brien, Rosalind Keith, Ray Whitley, Chill Wills; directed by David Howard; production began mid–February 1939; RKO Radio Pictures; 60 minutes

Dodge City (April 8, 1939) **Ward Bond** (Bud Taylor); Errol Flynn, Olivia de Havilland, Ann Sheridan, Bruce Cabot; directed by Michael Curtiz; production began early November 1938; Warner Bros. Pictures; 104 minutes

Mr. Moto in Danger Island (April 7, 1939) **Ward Bond** (Sailor Sam, Wrestler*); Peter Lorre, Jean Hersholt, Amanda Duff, Warren Hymer; directed by Herbert I. Leeds; production dates: late November to late December 1938; 20th Century–Fox Film Corporation; 64 minutes

Union Pacific (May 5, 1939) **Ward Bond** (Track-layer*); Barbara Stanwyck, Joel McCrea, Akim Tamiroff, Robert Preston; directed by Cecil B. DeMille; production dates: late October 1938 to late January 1939; Paramount Pictures; 135 minutes

Confessions of a Nazi Spy (May 6, 1939) **Ward Bond** (American Legionnaire*); Edward G. Robinson, Francis Lederer, George Sanders, Paul Lukas; directed by Anatole Litvak; production dates: February 1 to March 18, 1939; Warner Bros.–First National Pictures; 104 minutes

The Return of the Cisco Kid (April 28, 1939) **Ward Bond** (Accused Rustler); Warner Baxter, Lynn Bari, Cesar Romero, Henry Hull; directed by Herbert I. Leeds; production dates: February 22 to March 27, 1939; 20th Century–Fox Film Corporation; 70 minutes

The Kid from Kokomo (May 23, 1939) **Ward Bond** (Ladislaus "Tiger" Klewicki); Pat O'Brien, Wayne Morris, Joan Blondell, Sidney Toler; directed by Lewis Seiler; production dates: early December 1938 to mid–

January 1939; Warner Bros.–First National Pictures; 93 minutes

The Girl from Mexico (June 2, 1939) **Ward Bond** (Mexican Pete, Wrestler); Lupe Velez, Donald Woods, Leon Errol, Donald MacBride; directed by Leslie Goodwins; production dates: early March to March 28, 1939; RKO Radio Pictures; 71 minutes

Young Mr. Lincoln (June 9, 1939) **Ward Bond** (John Palmer Cass); Henry Fonda, Alice Brady, Marjorie Weaver, Arleen Whelan; directed by **John Ford**; production dates: early March to mid–April 1939; Cosmopolitan Productions–20th Century–Fox Film Corporation; 100 minutes

Waterfront (July 15, 1939) **Ward Bond** (Matt Hendler); Gloria Dickson, Dennis Morgan, Marie Wilson, Sheila Bromley; directed by Terry O. Morse; production dates: February 11 to mid–March 1939; Warner Bros. Pictures; 59 minutes

Frontier Marshal (July 28, 1939) **Ward Bond** (Town Marshal); Randolph Scott, Nancy Kelly, John Carradine, Lon Chaney, Jr.; directed by Allan Dwan; production dates: June 10 to July 11, 1939; 20th Century–Fox Film Corporation; 71 minutes

Dust Be My Destiny (September 16, 1939) **Ward Bond** (Thug*); John Garfield, Priscilla Lane, Alan Hale, Frank McHugh; directed by Lewis Seiler; production began late April 1939; Warner Bros. Pictures; 88 minutes

Heaven with a Barbed Wire Fence (November 3, 1939) **Ward Bond** (Hunk); Jean Rogers, Raymond Walburn, Glenn Ford, Richard Conte; directed by Ricardo Cortez; production dates: June 8–31 and July 20–26, 1939; 20th Century–Fox Film Corporation; 62 minutes

Drums Along the Mohawk (November 10, 1939) **Ward Bond** (Adam Hartman); Claudette Colbert, Henry Fonda, Edna May Oliver, John Carradine; directed by **John Ford**; production dates: June 28 to late August 1939; 20th Century–Fox Film Corporation; 104 minutes

Gone with the Wind (December 1939) **Ward Bond** (Tom, Yankee Captain); Clark Gable, Vivien Leigh, Leslie Howard, Thomas Mitchell; directed by Victor Fleming; production dates: December 10, 1938; January 26 to February 15, 1939; March 2 to July 1, 1939; and mid–July to November 11, 1939; Selznick International Pictures–Metro-Goldwyn-Mayer; 238 minutes

The Cisco Kid and the Lady (December 29, 1939) **Ward Bond** (Walton); Cesar Romero, Marjorie Weaver, Chris Pin-Martin, George Montgomery; directed by Herbert I. Leeds; production began September 11, 1939; 20th Century–Fox Film Corporation; 74 minutes

Mexican Spitfire (January 12, 1940) **Ward Bond** (Policeman*); Lupe Velez, Leon Errol, Donald Woods, Linda Hayes; directed by Leslie Goodwins; production began late September 1939; RKO Radio Pictures; 67 minutes

The Grapes of Wrath (March 15, 1940) **Ward Bond** (Policeman); Henry Fonda, Jane Darwell, John Carradine, Charley Grapewin; directed by **John Ford**; production dates: October 4 to November 16, 1939; 20th Century–Fox Film Corporation; 128 minutes

Little Old New York (February 9, 1940) **Ward Bond** (Regan, Shipyard Owner); Alice Faye, Fred MacMurray, Richard Greene, Brenda Joyce; directed by Henry King; 20th Century–Fox Film Corporation; 100 minutes

Virginia City (March 23, 1940) **Ward Bond** (Confederate Sergeant*); Errol Flynn, Miriam Hopkins, Randolph Scott, Humphrey Bogart; directed by Michael Curtiz; production began late October 1939; Warner Bros. Pictures; 121 minutes

Buck Benny Rides Again (May 31, 1940) **Ward Bond** (Outlaw); Jack Benny, Ellen Drew, Eddie "Rochester" Anderson, Andy Devine; directed by Mark Sandrich; production began late October 1939; Paramount Pictures; 82 minutes

The Mortal Storm (June 14, 1940) **Ward Bond** (Franz); Margaret Sullivan, James Stewart, Robert Young, Frank Morgan; directed by Frank Borzage; production dates: February 8 to mid–April 1940; Metro-Goldwyn-Mayer; 100 minutes

Sailor's Lady (July 5, 1940) **Ward Bond** (Shore Patrolman); Nancy Kelly, Jon Hall, Joan Davis, Dana Andrews; directed by Allan Dwan; production dates: January 15 to mid–February 1940; 20th Century–Fox Film Corporation; 67 minutes

Kit Carson (August 30, 1940) **Ward Bond** (Ape); Jon Hall, Lynn Bari, Dana Andrews, Harold Huber; directed by George B. Seitz; production began May 1940; Edward Small Productions–United Artists; 97 minutes

City for Conquest (September 21, 1940) **Ward Bond** (Policeman*); James Cagney, Ann Sheridan, Donald Crisp, Frank McHugh; directed by Anatole Litvak; production began May 31, 1940; Warner Bros. Pictures; 104 minutes

The Long Voyage Home (November 11, 1940) **Ward Bond** (Yank); **John Wayne**, Thomas Mitchell, Ian Hunter, Barry Fitzgerald; directed by **John Ford**; production began April 17, 1940; Argosy Pictures–Walter Wanger Productions–United Artists; 105 minutes

Santa Fe Trail (December 28, 1940) **Ward Bond** (Townley); Errol Flynn, Olivia de Havilland, Raymond Massey, Ronald Reagan; directed by Michael Curtiz; production dates: mid–July to mid–September 1940; Warner Bros. Pictures; 110 minutes

Tobacco Road (March 7, 1941) **Ward Bond** (Lov Bensey); Charley Grapewin, Marjorie Rambeau, Gene Tierney, Dana Andrews; directed by **John Ford**; production dates: late November to late December 1940; 20th Century–Fox Film Corporation; 84 minutes

A Man Betrayed (March 7, 1941) **Ward Bond** (Floyd); **John Wayne**, Frances Dee, Edward Ellis, Wallace Ford; directed by John H. Auer; production began January 3, 1941; Republic Pictures; 82 minutes

The Shepherd of the Hills (July 18, 1941) **Ward Bond** (Wash Gibbs); **John Wayne**, Betty Field, Harry Carey, Beulah Bondi; directed by Henry Hathaway; production dates: early September to mid–November 1940; Paramount Pictures; 98 minutes

Manpower (August 9, 1941) **Ward Bond** (Eddie Adams); Edward G. Robinson, Marlene Dietrich, George Raft, Alan Hale; directed by Raoul Walsh; production dates: late March to mid–May 1941; Warner Bros. Pictures; 103 minutes

Sergeant York (September 7, 1941) **Ward Bond** (Ike Botkin); Gary Cooper, Walter Brennan, Joan Leslie, Stanley Ridges; directed by Howard Hawks; production dates: February 3 to May 1, 1941; Warner Bros. Pictures; 134 minutes

Doctors Don't Tell (September 22, 1941) **Ward Bond** (Barney Millen); John Beal, Florence Rice, Edward Norris, Douglas Fowley; directed by Jacques Tourneur; production dates: July to early August 1941; Republic Pictures; 65 minutes

The Maltese Falcon (October 18, 1941) **Ward Bond** (Detective Tom Polhaus); Humphrey Bogart, Mary Astor, Gladys George, Peter Lorre; directed by John Huston; production dates: June 9 to July 18, 1941; retakes: August 8 and September 10, 1941; Warner Bros. Pictures; 101 minutes

Swamp Water (November 16, 1941) **Ward Bond** (Tim Dorson); Walter Brennan, Walter Huston, Anne Baxter, Dana Andrews; directed by Jean Renoir; production dates: July 14 to late August and September 3, 1941; 20th Century–Fox Film Corporation; 88 minutes

Know for Sure (1941) **Ward Bond** (Patient*); Samuel S. Hinds, Tim Holt, Edwin Maxwell, J. Carrol Naish; directed by Lewis Milestone; Research Council of Academy of Motion Picture Arts and Sciences–United States Public Health Service; 23 minutes

Will Bill Hickok Rides (January 21, 1942) **Ward Bond** (Sheriff Edmunds); Constance Bennett, Bruce Cabot, Warren William, Walter Catlett; directed by Ray Enright; production dates: early September to late October 1941; Warner Bros. Pictures; 82 minutes

The Falcon Takes Over (May 29, 1942) **Ward Bond** (Moose Malloy*); George Sanders, Lynn Bari, James Gleason, Allen Jenkins; directed by Irving Reis; production dates: early November to December 1, 1941; RKO Radio Pictures; 65 minutes

Ten Gentlemen from West Point (June 26, 1942) **Ward Bond** (Sergeant Scully); George Montgomery, Maureen O'Hara, John Sutton, Laird Cregar; directed by Henry Hathaway; production dates: December 26, 1941 to March 18, 1942; 20th Century–Fox Film Corporation; 102 minutes

Sin Town (September 25, 1942) **Ward Bond** (Rock Delaney); Constance Bennett, Broderick Crawford, Patric Knowles, Anne Gwynne; directed by Ray Enright; production dates: August 12 to late September 1942; Universal Pictures; 73 minutes

Gentleman Jim (November 25, 1942) **Ward Bond** (John L. Sullivan); Errol Flynn, Alexis Smith, Jack Carson, Alan Hale; directed by Raoul Walsh; production dates: May 20 to July 23, 1942; Warner Bros. Pictures; 104 minutes

Hello Frisco, Hello (March 26, 1943) **Ward Bond** (Sharkey); Alice Faye, John Payne, Jack Oakie, Laird Cregar; directed by H. Bruce Humberstone; production dates: November 2, 1942 to early January 1943; retakes began January 21, 1943; 20th Century–Fox Film Corporation; 99 minutes

Hitler: Dead or Alive (April 3, 1943) **Ward Bond** (Steve Maschick); Dorothy Tree, Warren Hymer, Paul

Fix, Bobby Watson; directed by Nick Grinde; production began August 6, 1942; previewed (Chicago) November 12, 1942; Ben Judel–Charles House Productions; 70 minutes

Slightly Dangerous (April 1943) **Ward Bond** (Jimmy); Lana Turner, Robert Young, Walter Brennan, Eugene Pallette; directed by Wesley Ruggles; production dates: early September to late November 1942; Metro-Goldwyn-Mayer; 94 minutes

They Came to Blow Up America (May 7, 1943) **Ward Bond** (FBI Chief Craig); George Sanders, Anna Sten, Dennis Hoey, Ludwig Stossel; directed by Edward Ludwig; production dates: December 5 to late December 1942; 20th Century–Fox Film Corporation; 73 minutes

The Sullivans (February 3, 1944) **Ward Bond** (Lieutenant Commander Robinson); Anne Baxter, Thomas Mitchell, Selena Royle, Trudy Marshall; directed by Lloyd Bacon; production dates: early September to mid–November 1943; 20th Century–Fox Film Corporation; 112 minutes

A Guy Named Joe (March 1944) **Ward Bond** (Al Yackey); Spencer Tracy, Irene Dunne, Van Johnson, Lionel Barrymore; directed by Victor Fleming; production dates: February 15 to late September 1943; retakes: November 10 to late November 1943; Metro-Goldwyn-Mayer; 122 minutes

Home in Indiana (July 1944) **Ward Bond** (Jed Bruce); Walter Brennan, Charlotte Greenwood, Charles Dingle, Lon McCallister; directed by Henry Hathaway; production dates: early September 1943 to mid–January 1944; 20th Century–Fox Film Corporation; 106 minutes

Tall in the Saddle (September 29, 1944) **Ward Bond** (Robert Garvey); **John Wayne**, Ella Raines, George "Gabby" Hayes, Paul Fix; directed by Edwin L. Marin; production dates: mid–April to mid–June 1944; RKO Radio Pictures; 87 minutes

They Were Expendable (December 20, 1945) **Ward Bond** ("Boats" Mulcahy, C.B.M.); **John Wayne**, Robert Montgomery, Donna Reed, Jack Holt; directed by **John Ford**; production dates: February 23 to mid–June 1945; Metro-Goldwyn-Mayer; 135 minutes

Dakota (December 25, 1945) **Ward Bond** (Jim Bender); **John Wayne**, Vera Ralston, Walter Brennan, Paul Fix; directed by Joseph Kane; production dates: July 17 to late August 1945; Republic Pictures; 82 minutes

Canyon Passage (July 17, 1946) **Ward Bond** (Honey Bragg); Dana Andrews, Brian Donlevy, Susan Hayward, Hoagy Carmichael; directed by Jacques Tourneur; production dates: mid–August to mid–December 1945; Universal Pictures; 92 minutes

My Darling Clementine (December 3, 1946) **Ward Bond** (Morgan Earp); Henry Fonda, Linda Darnell, Victor Mature, Walter Brennan; directed by **John Ford**; production dates: April 1 to mid–June 1946; 20th Century–Fox Film Corporation; 97 minutes

It's a Wonderful Life (January 7, 1947) **Ward Bond** (Bert the Cop); James Stewart, Donna Reed, Lionel Barrymore, Thomas Mitchell; directed by Frank Capra; production dates: April 15 to July 27 1946; Liberty Films–RKO Radio Pictures; 130 minutes

Unconquered (October 10, 1947) **Ward Bond** (John Fraser); Gary Cooper, Paulette Goddard, Howard Da Silva, Boris Karloff; directed by Cecil B. DeMille; production dates: early June 1946, July 29 to November 8, 1946, December 10 and 30, 1946, and May 5, 1947; Paramount Pictures; 146 minutes

The Fugitive (November 3, 1947) **Ward Bond** (James Calvert, "El Gringo"); Henry Fonda, Dolores del Rio, Pedro Armendariz, J. Carrol Naish; directed by **John Ford**; production dates: early December 1946 to late January 1947; Argosy Pictures Corporation–RKO Radio Pictures; 104 minutes

Fort Apache (March 9, 1948) **Ward Bond** (Sergeant Major Michael O'Rourke); **John Wayne**, Henry Fonda, Shirley Temple, Pedro Armendariz; directed by **John Ford**; production dates: July 24 to late September 1947; Argosy Pictures Corporation–RKO Radio Pictures; 125 minutes

Tap Roots (August 25, 1948) **Ward Bond** (Hoab Dabney); Van Heflin, Susan Hayward, Boris Karloff, Julie London; directed by George Marshall; production dates: June 3 to mid–August 1947; Walter Wanger Productions–Universal Pictures; 109 minutes

The Time of Your Life (September 3, 1948) **Ward Bond** (McCarthy, a "blatherskite"); James Cagney, William Bendix, Wayne Morris, Broderick Crawford; directed by H. C. Potter; production dates: early May to early August 1947 and mid–April 1948; William Cagney Productions–United Artists; 109 minutes

3 Godfathers (December 1, 1948) **Ward Bond** (Perley "Buck" Sweet); **John Wayne**, Pedro Armendariz, Harry Carey, Jr., Ben Johnson; directed by **John Ford**; production dates: early May to early June 1948; Argosy Pictures Corporation–Metro-Goldwyn-Mayer; 106 minutes

Joan of Arc (December 22, 1948) **Ward Bond** (La Hire); Ingrid Bergman, Francis L. Sullivan, J. Carrol Naish, Gene Lockhart; directed by Victor Fleming; production dates: September 16 to mid–December 1947 and February 16–25, 1948; Sierra Pictures–RKO Radio Pictures; 145 minutes

Singing Guns (March 15, 1950) **Ward Bond** (Sheriff Jim Caradac); Vaughn Monroe, Ella Raines, Walter Brennan, Jeff Corey; directed by R. G. Springsteen; Palomar Pictures–Republic Pictures; 91 minutes

Riding High (April 12, 1950) **Ward Bond** (Lee); Bing Crosby, Coleen Gray, Charles Bickford, William Demarest; directed by Frank Capra; production dates: March 14 to mid–May 1949; Paramount Pictures; 112 minutes

Wagon Master (April 19, 1950) **Ward Bond** (Elder Jonathan Wiggs); Ben Johnson, Joanne Dru, Harry Carey, Jr., Alan Mowbray; directed by **John Ford**; production dates: November 14 to mid–December 1949; Argosy Pictures Corporation–RKO Radio Pictures; 86 minutes

Kiss Tomorrow Goodbye (August 4, 1950) **Ward Bond** (Inspector Charles Weber); James Cagney, Barbara Payton, Luther Adler, Barton MacLane; directed by Gordon Douglas; production dates: April 15 to mid–May 1950; William Cagney Productions–Warner Bros. Pictures; 102 minutes

Operation Pacific (January 27, 1951) **Ward Bond**

(Commander John T. "Pop" Perry); **John Wayne**, Patricia Neal, Philip Carey, Paul Picerni; directed by George Waggner; production dates: August 29 to late October 1950; Warner Bros. Pictures; 111 minutes

The Great Missouri Raid (February 1951) **Ward Bond** (Major Marshal Trowbridge); Wendell Corey, Macdonald Carey, Ellen Drew, Bruce Bennett; directed by Gordon Douglas; production dates: late May to early July 1950; Paramount Pictures; 84 minutes

Only the Valiant (April 13, 1951) **Ward Bond** (Corporal Timothy Gilchrist); Gregory Peck, Barbara Payton, Gig Young, Lon Chaney, Jr.; directed by Gordon Douglas; production dates: late July to early September 1950; William Cagney Productions–Warner Bros. Pictures; 105 minutes

Bullfighter and the Lady (April 26, 1951) **Ward Bond** (Narrator*); Robert Stack, Gilbert Roland, Virginia Grey, Katy Jurado; directed by Budd Boetticher; production dates: May 29 to July 15, 1950; Republic Pictures; 124 minutes

On Dangerous Ground (February 12, 1952) **Ward Bond** (Walter Brent); Ida Lupino, Robert Ryan, Ed Begley, Ian Wolfe; directed by Nicholas Ray; production dates: March 20 to May 10, 1950 and August 7–9, 1951; RKO Radio Pictures; 82 minutes

Hellgate (September 5, 1952) **Ward Bond** (Lieutenant Tod Voorhees); Sterling Hayden, Joan Leslie, James Arness, Peter Coe; directed by Charles Marquis Warren; production dates: March 25 to mid–April 1952; Commander Films Corporation–Lippert Pictures; 87 minutes

The Quiet Man (September 14, 1952) **Ward Bond** (Father Peter Lonergan); **John Wayne**, Maureen O'Hara, Barry Fitzgerald, Victor McLaglen; directed by **John Ford**; production dates: early June to late August 1951; Argosy Pictures Corporation–Republic Pictures; 129 minutes

Thunderbirds (November 27, 1952) **Ward Bond** (Lieutenant John McCreery); John Derek, John Drew Barrymore, Mona Freeman, Gene Evans; directed by John H. Auer; production dates: late April to late May 1952; Republic Pictures; 98 minutes

The Moonlighter (September 19, 1953) **Ward Bond** (Cole Gardner); Barbara Stanwyck, Fred MacMurray, William Ching, Jack Elam; directed by Roy Rowland; production dates: mid–April to mid–May 1953; Joseph Bernhard Productions–Warner Bros. Pictures; 77 minutes

Hondo (November 25, 1953) **Ward Bond** (Buffalo Baker); **John Wayne**, Geraldine Page, Michael Pate, James Arness; directed by John Farrow; production dates: June 11 to early August 1953; Wayne–Fellows Productions–Warner Bros. Pictures; 83 minutes

Blowing Wild (December 16, 1953) **Ward Bond** (Dutch Peterson); Gary Cooper, Barbara Stanwyck, Ruth Roman, Anthony Quinn; directed by Hugo Fregonese; production dates: early February to early April 1953; United States Pictures–Warner Bros. Pictures; 90 minutes

Gypsy Colt (April 2, 1954) **Ward Bond** (Frank MacWade); Donna Corcoran, Frances Dee, Larry Keating, Lee Van Cleef; directed by Andrew Marton; production dates: July 7 to late July 1953; Metro-Goldwyn-Mayer; 72 minutes

Johnny Guitar (May 27, 1954) **Ward Bond** (John McIvers); Joan Crawford, Sterling Hayden, Mer-cedes McCambridge, Ernest Borgnine; directed by Nicholas Ray; production dates: mid–October to mid–December 1953; Republic Pictures; 110 minutes

The Bob Mathias Story (October 24, 1954) **Ward Bond** (Coach Jackson); Bob Mathias, Melba Mathias, Howard Petrie, Ann Doran; directed by Francis D. Lyon; production began early June 1954; Allied Artists Pictures; 80 minutes

The Long Gray Line (February 9, 1955) **Ward Bond** (Captain Herman J. Koehler); Tyrone Power, Maureen O'Hara, Robert Francis, Donald Crisp; directed by **John Ford**; production dates: March 15 to May 17, 1954; Columbia Pictures Corporation; 138 minutes

A Man Alone (October 17, 1955) **Ward Bond** (Sheriff Gil Corrigan); Ray Milland, Mary Murphy, Raymond Burr, Arthur Space, Lee Van Cleef; directed by Ray Milland; production began early April 1955; Republic Pictures; 96 minutes

Mister Roberts (December 4, 1955) **Ward Bond** (Chief Petty Officer Dowdy); Henry Fonda, James Cagney, William Powell, Jack Lemmon; directed by **John Ford** and Mervyn LeRoy; production dates: late August to mid–November 1954; Warner Bros. Pictures; 123 minutes

The Searchers (March 13, 1956) **Ward Bond** (The Rev. Captain Samuel Johnston Clayton); **John Wayne**, Jeffrey Hunter, Natalie Wood, Henry Brandon; directed by **John Ford**; production dates: mid–June to mid–August 1955; C. V. Whitney Pictures–Warner Bros. Pictures; 119 minutes

Dakota Incident (July 23, 1956) **Ward Bond** (Senator Blakely); Linda Darnell, Dale Robertson, John Lund, Regis Toomey; directed by Lewis R. Foster; production dates: mid–December 1955 to early January 1956; Republic Pictures; 88 minutes

Pillars of the Sky (October 12, 1956) **Ward Bond** (Dr. Joseph Holden); Jeff Chandler, Dorothy Malone, Lee Marvin, Sydney Chaplin; directed by George Marshall; production dates: August 18 to late September 1955; Universal International Pictures; 95 minutes

The Halliday Brand (January 1957) **Ward Bond** (Big Dan Halliday); Joseph Cotton, Viveca Lindfors, Betsy Blair, Bill Williams; directed by Joseph H. Lewis; Collier Young Associates–United Artists; 79 minutes

The Wings of Eagles (February 22, 1957) **Ward Bond** (John Dodge); **John Wayne**, Dan Dailey, Maureen O'Hara, Ken Curtis; directed by **John Ford**; production dates: late July to late September 1956; Metro-Goldwyn-Mayer; 110 minutes

China Doll (December 3, 1958) **Ward Bond** (Father Cairns); Victor Mature, Li Hua Li, Bob Mathias, Stuart Whitman; directed by Frank Borzage; production began August 15, 1957; Batjac Productions–United Artists; 99 minutes

Alias Jesse James (March 20, 1959) **Ward Bond** (Major Seth Adams*); Bob Hope, Rhonda Fleming,

Wendell Corey, Gloria Talbot; directed by Norman Z. McLeod; production dates: late September to late October and November 18–19, 1958; Hope Enterprises–United Artists; 92 minutes
    Rio Bravo (April 4, 1959) **Ward Bond** (Pat Wheeler);

John Wayne, Dean Martin, Ricky Nelson, Walter Brennan; directed by Howard Hawks; production dates: early May to mid–July 1958; Armada Productions–Warner Bros. Pictures; 141 minutes

Appendix C
The Television Performances
of Ward Bond

The Silver Theater: "My Brother's Keeper" (February 20, 1950) **Ward Bond**; Conrad Nagel (host), Glenn Corbett, Beverly Tyler, Patrick Sexton; directed by Frank Telford; Jerry Fairbanks Productions–CBS; 30 minutes
    Schlitz Playhouse of Stars: "Apple of His Eye" (February 29, 1952) **Ward Bond**; Henry Jones, June Lockhart; Meridian Productions–CBS; 60 minutes
    The Gulf Playhouse: "You Can Look It Up" (October 10, 1952) **Ward Bond**; produced by Frank Telford; NBC; 30 minutes
    General Electric Theater: "Winners Never Lose" (March 15, 1953) **Ward Bond**; Murray Alper, Frankie Darro, Wallace Ford, Pat O'Brien; directed by James V. Kern; Revue Studios–CBS; 30 minutes
    The Ford Television Theatre: "Gun Job" (December 17, 1953) **Ward Bond** (Hank Fetterman); Philip Carey, Ellen Drew, Peter Whitney, John Maxwell; directed by Ted Post; Ford Motor Company–NBC; 30 minutes
    Suspense: "The Hunted" (June 29, 1954) **Ward Bond** (Bill Meeker); John Kerr, Jane Du Frayne, Steve Parker; directed by Robert Mulligan; CBS; 30 minutes
    The Ford Television Theatre: "Segment" (October 21, 1954) **Ward Bond** (Police Lieutenant Ben Annetti); William Bendix. Rosemary DeCamp, Joanne Woodward, Alan Baxter; directed by Marc Daniels and Franklin J. Schaffner; Screen Gems–NBC; 30 minutes
    Cavalcade of America: "The Marine Who Was Two Hundred Years Old" (January 4, 1955) **Ward Bond** (Lou Diamond); John Clift, James Flavin, Gregg Palmer, Norma Varden; ABC; 30 minutes
    Climax!: "The Mohave Kid" (January 27, 1955) **Ward Bond** (Sheriff); John Lupton, Ricardo Montalban, Barbara Ruick; directed by Anthony Barr; CBS; 60 minutes
    The Christophers: "Washington as a Young Man" (November 20, 1955) **Ward Bond**; Father James G. Keller (host), Joe E. Brown, Ruth Hussey; ABC; 30 minutes

Screen Directors Playhouse: "Rookie of the Year" (December 7, 1955) **Ward Bond** (Buck Goodhue, alias Buck Garrison); **John Wayne**, Vera Miles, James Gleason, Patrick Wayne; directed by **John Ford**; Hal Roach Studios–NBC; 30 minutes
    Schlitz Playhouse of Stars: "Plague Ship" (May 11, 1956) **Ward Bond**; Jon Shepodd; Meridian Productions–CBS; 30 minutes
    Schlitz Playhouse of Stars: "Moment of Vengeance" (September 28, 1956) **Ward Bond**; Gene Nelson; Meridian Productions–CBS; 30 minutes
    Cavalcade of America: "Once a Hero" (December 11, 1956) **Ward Bond** (Harvey Kendall); Ben Johnson, Richard Eyer, Sarah Selby, Michael Winkelman; directed by Lee Sholem; ABC; 60 minutes
    Wagon Train: "The Willy Moran Story" (September 18, 1957) **Ward Bond** (Major Seth Adams); Robert Horton, Ernest Borgnine, Marjorie Lord, Beverly Washburn; directed by Herschel Daugherty; Revue Productions–NBC; 60 minutes
    The Steve Allen Show: "NBC Fall Preview" (September 22, 1957) **Ward Bond**; Steve Allen (host), Rosemary Clooney, Robert Cummings, Eddie Fisher; NBC; 60 minutes
    Wagon Train: "The Jean LeBec Story" (September 25, 1957) **Ward Bond** (Major Seth Adams); Robert Horton, Frank McGrath, Ricardo Montalban, Joanna Moore; directed by Sidney Lanfield; Revue Productions–NBC; 60 minutes
    Wagon Train: "The John Cameron Story" (October 2, 1957) **Ward Bond** (Major Seth Adams); Robert Horton, Frank McGrath, Carolyn Jones, Michael Rennie; directed by George Waggner; Revue Productions–NBC; 60 minutes
    Wagon Train: "The Ruth Owens Story" (October 9, 1957) **Ward Bond** (Major Seth Adams); Robert Horton, Frank McGrath, Terry Wilson, Shelley Winters; directed by Robert Florey; Revue Productions–NBC; 60 minutes
    Wagon Train: "The Les Rand Story" (October 16, 1957) **Ward Bond** (Major Seth Adams); Robert Hor-

ton, Frank McGrath, Terry Wilson, Sterling Hayden; directed by Robert Florey; Revue Productions–NBC; 60 minutes

Wagon Train: "The Nels Stack Story" (October 23, 1957) **Ward Bond** (Major Seth Adams); Robert Horton, Frank McGrath, Terry Wilson, Joanne Dru; directed by Don Weis; Revue Productions–NBC; 60 minutes

Wagon Train: "The Emily Rossiter Story" (October 30, 1957) **Ward Bond** (Major Seth Adams); Robert Horton, Frank McGrath, Terry Wilson, Mercedes McCambridge; directed by Sidney Lanfield; Revue Productions–NBC; 60 minutes

Wagon Train: "The John Darro Story" (November 6, 1957) **Ward Bond** (Major Seth Adams); Robert Horton, Frank McGrath, Terry Wilson, Eddie Albert; directed by Mark Stevens; Revue Productions–NBC; 60 minutes

Wagon Train: "The Charles Avery Story" (November 13, 1957) **Ward Bond** (Major Seth Adams); Robert Horton, Frank McGrath, Farley Granger, Henry Brandon; directed by Bernard Girard; Revue Productions–NBC; 60 minutes

Wagon Train: "The Mary Halstead Story" (November 20, 1957) **Ward Bond** (Major Seth Adams); Robert Horton, Frank McGrath, Terry Wilson, Agnes Moorehead; directed by Jus Addiss; Revue Productions–NBC; 60 minutes

Wagon Train: "The Zeke Thomas Story" (November 27, 1957) **Ward Bond** (Major Seth Adams); Robert Horton, Frank McGrath, Terry Wilson, Gary Merrill; directed by John Brahm; Revue Productions–NBC; 60 minutes

Wagon Train: "The Riley Gratton Story" (December 4, 1957) **Ward Bond** (Major Seth Adams); Robert Horton, Guy Madison, Malcolm Adderbury, Karen Steele; directed by John Brahm; Revue Productions–NBC; 60 minutes

Wagon Train: "The Clara Beauchamp Story" (December 11, 1957) **Ward Bond** (Major Seth Adams); Robert Horton, Frank McGrath, Terry Wilson, Nina Foch; directed by Earl Bellamy; Revue Productions–NBC; 60 minutes

Wagon Train: "The Julie Gage Story" (December 18, 1957) **Ward Bond** (Major Seth Adams); Robert Horton, Frank McGrath, Terry Wilson, Anne Jeffreys; directed by Sidney Lanfield; Revue Productions–NBC; 60 minutes

Wagon Train: "The Cliff Grundy Story" (December 25, 1957) **Ward Bond** (Major Seth Adams); Robert Horton, Frank McGrath, Terry Wilson, Dan Duryea; directed by George Waggner; Revue Productions–NBC; 60 minutes

Wagon Train: "The Luke O'Malley Story" (January 1, 1958) **Ward Bond** (Major Seth Adams); Robert Horton, Frank McGrath, Terry Wilson, Keenan Wynn; directed by Mark Stevens; Revue Productions–NBC; 60 minutes

The Steve Allen Show (January 5, 1958) **Ward Bond**; Steve Allen (host), Robert Horton, Sam Cooke, Abbe Lane; NBC; 60 minutes

Wagon Train: "The Jesse Cowan Story" (January 8, 1958) **Ward Bond** (Major Seth Adams); Robert Horton, Frank McGrath, Terry Wilson, George Montgomery; directed by Sidney Lanfield; Revue Productions–NBC; 60 minutes

Wagon Train: "The Gabe Carswell Story" (January 15, 1958) **Ward Bond** (Major Seth Adams); Robert Horton, Frank McGrath, Terry Wilson, James Whitmore; directed by Earl Bellamy; Revue Productions–NBC; 60 minutes

Wagon Train: "The Honorable Don Charlie Story" (January 22, 1958) **Ward Bond** (Major Seth Adams); Robert Horton, Frank McGrath, Terry Wilson, Cesar Romero; directed by David Butler; Revue Productions–NBC; 60 minutes

Wagon Train: "The Dora Gray Story" (January 29, 1958) **Ward Bond** (Major Seth Adams); Robert Horton, Frank McGrath, Terry Wilson, Linda Darnell; directed by Arnold Laven; Revue Productions–NBC; 60 minutes

Wagon Train: "The Annie MacGregor Story" (February 5, 1958) **Ward Bond** (Major Seth Adams); Robert Horton, Frank McGrath, Terry Wilson, Jeannie Carson; directed by Mark Stevens; Revue Productions–NBC; 60 minutes

Wagon Train: "The Bill Tawnee Story" (February 12, 1958) **Ward Bond** (Major Seth Adams); Robert Horton, Frank McGrath, Terry Wilson, Macdonald Carey; directed by David Butler; Revue Productions–NBC; 60 minutes

Wagon Train: "The Mark Hanford Story" (February 26, 1958) **Ward Bond** (Major Seth Adams); Robert Horton, Frank McGrath, Terry Wilson, Tom Tryon; directed by Jerry Hopper; Revue Productions–NBC; 60 minutes

Wagon Train: "The Bernal Sierra Story" (March 12, 1958) **Ward Bond** (Major Seth Adams); Robert Horton, Frank McGrath, Terry Wilson, Gilbert Roland; directed by David Butler; Revue Productions–NBC; 60 minutes

Wagon Train: "The Marie Dupree Story" (March 19, 1958) **Ward Bond** (Major Seth Adams); Robert Horton, Frank McGrath, Terry Wilson, Debra Paget; directed by Richard Bartlett; Revue Productions–NBC; 60 minutes

Wagon Train: "A Man Called Horse" (March 26, 1958) **Ward Bond** (Major Seth Adams); Robert Horton, Frank McGrath, Terry Wilson, Ralph Meeker; directed by Sidney Lanfield; Revue Productions–NBC; 60 minutes

Wagon Train: "The Sarah Drummond Story" (April 2, 1958) **Ward Bond** (Major Seth Adams); Robert Horton, Frank McGrath, Terry Wilson, June Lockhart; directed by Richard Bartlett; Revue Productions–NBC; 60 minutes

Wagon Train: "The Sally Potter Story" (April 9, 1958) **Ward Bond** (Major Seth Adams); Robert Horton, Vanessa Brown, Jocelyn Brando, Martin Milner; directed by David Butler; Revue Productions–NBC; 60 minutes

Wagon Train: "The Daniel Barrister Story" (April 16, 1958) **Ward Bond** (Major Seth Adams); Robert Horton, Frank McGrath, Terry Wilson, Charles Bickford; directed by Richard Bartlett; Revue Productions–NBC; 60 minutes

Wagon Train: "The Major Adams Story: Part 1" (April 23, 1958) **Ward Bond** (Major Seth Adams); Robert Horton, Frank McGrath, Terry Wilson, Virginia Grey; directed by Mark Stevens; Revue Productions–NBC; 60 minutes

Wagon Train: "The Major Adams Story: Part 2" (April 30, 1958) **Ward Bond** (Major Seth Adams); Robert Horton, Frank McGrath, Terry Wilson, Virginia Grey; directed by Mark Stevens; Revue Productions–NBC; 60 minutes

Wagon Train: "The Charles Maury Story" (May 7, 1958) **Ward Bond** (Major Seth Adams); Robert Horton, Frank McGrath, Terry Wilson, Charles Drake; directed by Allen H. Miner; Revue Productions–NBC; 60 minutes

Wagon Train: "The Dan Hogan Story" (May 14, 1958) **Ward Bond** (Major Seth Adams); Robert Horton, Frank McGrath, Terry Wilson, Jock Mahoney; directed by Richard Bartlett; Revue Productions–NBC; 60 minutes

Wagon Train: "The Ruttledge Monroe Story" (May 21, 1958) **Ward Bond** (Major Seth Adams); Robert Horton, Frank McGrath, Terry Wilson, John Drew Barrymore; directed by Richard Bartlett; Revue Productions–NBC; 60 minutes

Wagon Train: "The Rex Montana Story" (May 28, 1958) **Ward Bond** (Major Seth Adams); Robert Horton, Frank McGrath, Terry Wilson, Forrest Tucker; directed by Jesse Hibbs; Revue Productions–NBC; 60 minutes

Wagon Train: "The Cassie Tanner Story" (June 4, 1958) **Ward Bond** (Major Seth Adams); Robert Horton, Frank McGrath, Terry Wilson, Marjorie Main; directed by Mark Stevens; Revue Productions–NBC; 60 minutes

Wagon Train: "The John Wilbot Story" (June 11, 1958) **Ward Bond** (Major Seth Adams); Robert Horton, Frank McGrath, Terry Wilson, Dane Clark; directed by Mark Stevens; Revue Productions–NBC; 60 minutes

Wagon Train: "The Monte Britton Story" (June 18, 1958) **Ward Bond** (Major Seth Adams); Robert Horton, Frank McGrath, Terry Wilson, Ray Danton; directed by Mark Stevens; Revue Productions–NBC; 60 minutes

Wagon Train: "The Sacramento Story" (June 25, 1958) **Ward Bond** (Major Seth Adams); Robert Horton, Marjorie Main, Dan Duryea, Margaret O'Brien; directed by Richard Bartlett; Revue Productions–NBC; 60 minutes

Wagon Train: "Around the Horn" (October 1, 1958) **Ward Bond** (Major Seth Adams); Robert Horton, Frank McGrath, William Bendix, Ernest Borgnine; directed by Herschel Daughtery; Revue Productions–NBC; 60 minutes

Wagon Train: "The Juan Ortega Story" (October 8, 1958) **Ward Bond** (Major Seth Adams); Robert Horton, Frank McGrath, Terry Wilson, Dean Stockwell; directed by David Swift; Revue Productions–NBC; 60 minutes

Wagon Train: "The Jennifer Churchill Story" (October 15, 1958) **Ward Bond** (credit only); Robert Horton, Rhonda Fleming, Andy Clyde, Paul Maxey; directed by Jerry Hopper; Revue Productions–NBC; 60 minutes

Wagon Train: "The Tobias Jones Story" (October 22, 1958) **Ward Bond** (Major Seth Adams); Robert Horton, Frank McGrath, Lou Costello, Beverly Washburn; directed by Herschel Daugherty; Revue Productions–NBC; 60 minutes

Wagon Train: "The Liam Fitzmorgan Story" (October 28, 1958) **Ward Bond** (credit only); Robert Horton, Cliff Robertson, Audrey Dalton, Rhys Williams; directed by Herschel Daugherty; Revue Productions–NBC; 60 minutes

The Christophers: "Bring Out Their Greatness" (October 28, 1958) **Ward Bond**; Father James G. Keller (host), Gigi Perreau; ABC; 30 minutes

Wagon Train: "The Doctor Willoughby Story" (November 5, 1958) **Ward Bond** (Major Seth Adams); Frank McGrath, Terry Wilson, Jane Wyman, Alan Marshall; directed by Allen H. Miner; Revue Productions–NBC; 60 minutes

Wagon Train: "The Bije Wilcox Story" (November 19, 1958) **Ward Bond** (Major Seth Adams); Robert Horton, Frank McGrath, Terry Wilson, Chill Wills; directed by Abner Biberman; Revue Productions–NBC; 60 minutes

General Electric Theater: "A Turkey for the President" (November 23, 1958) **Ward Bond**; Ronald Reagan, Nancy Davis; Revue Studios–CBS; 30 minutes

Wagon Train: "The Millie Davis Story" (November 26, 1958) **Ward Bond** (Major Seth Adams); Robert Horton, Frank McGrath, James Coburn, Nancy Gates; directed by Jerry Hopper; Revue Productions–NBC; 60 minutes

Wagon Train: "The Sakae Ito Story" (December 3, 1958) **Ward Bond** (Major Seth Adams); Robert Horton, Frank McGrath, Terry Wilson, Sessue Hayakawa; directed by Herschel Daugherty; Revue Productions–NBC; 60 minutes

Wagon Train: "The Tent City Story" (December 10, 1958) **Ward Bond** (Major Seth Adams); Robert Horton, Frank McGrath, Terry Wilson, Peter Coe; directed by Richard Bartlett; Revue Productions–NBC; 60 minutes

Wagon Train: "The Beauty Jamison Story" (December 17, 1958) **Ward Bond** (Major Seth Adams); Robert Horton, Virginia Mayo, Russell Johnson, Charles Tannen; directed by Richard Bartlett; Revue Productions–NBC; 60 minutes

Wagon Train: "The Mary Ellen Thomas Story" (December 24, 1958) **Ward Bond** (Major Seth Adams); Robert Horton, Frank McGrath, Terry Wilson, Patty McCormack; directed by Virgil W. Vogel; Revue Productions–NBC; 60 minutes

Wagon Train: "The Dick Richardson Story" (December 31, 1958) **Ward Bond** (Major Seth Adams); Frank McGrath, Terry Wilson, John Ericson, Lyle Talbot; directed by David Butler; Revue Productions–NBC; 60 minutes

Wagon Train: "The Kitty Angel Story" (January 7, 1959) **Ward Bond** (Major Seth Adams); Robert Horton, Frank McGrath, Terry Wilson, Anne Baxter; directed by James Neilson; Revue Productions–NBC; 60 minutes

Wagon Train: "The Flint McCullough Story" (January 14, 1959) **Ward Bond** (credit only); Robert Horton, Everett Sloane, Charles Cooper, Milton Frome; directed by Allen H. Miner; Revue Productions–NBC; 60 minutes

Wagon Train: "The Hunter Malloy Story" (January 21, 1959) **Ward Bond** (Major Seth Adams); Frank McGrath, Terry Wilson, Lloyd Nolan, Troy Donahue; directed by Allen H. Miner; Revue Productions–NBC; 60 minutes

Wagon Train: "The Ben Courtney Story" (January 28, 1959) **Ward Bond** (credit only); Robert Horton, Stephen McNally, Rachel Ames, Richard Hale; directed by Abner Biberman; Revue Productions–NBC; 60 minutes

Wagon Train: "The Ella Lindstrom Story" (February 4, 1959) **Ward Bond** (Major Seth Adams); Robert Horton, Bette Davis, Robert Fuller, Susan Henning; directed by Allen H. Miner; Revue Productions–NBC; 60 minutes

Wagon Train: "The Last Man" (February 11, 1959) **Ward Bond** (Major Seth Adams); Robert Horton, Frank McGrath, Terry Wilson, Dan Duryea; directed by James Neilson; Revue Productions–NBC; 60 minutes

Wagon Train: "The Old Man Charvanaugh Story" (February 18, 1959) **Ward Bond** (Major Seth Adams); Robert Horton, Frank McGrath, J. Carrol Naish, L. Q. Jones; directed by Virgil W. Vogel; Revue Productions–NBC; 60 minutes

Wagon Train: "The Annie Griffith Story" (February 25, 1959) **Ward Bond** (Major Seth Adams); Robert Horton, Frank McGrath, Terry Wilson, Jan Sterling; directed by Jerry Hopper; Revue Productions–NBC; 60 minutes

Wagon Train: "The Jasper Cato Story" (March 4, 1959) **Ward Bond** (Major Seth Adams); Robert Horton, Frank McGrath, Terry Wilson, Brian Donlevy; directed by Arthur Hiller; Revue Productions–NBC; 60 minutes

Wagon Train: "The Vivian Carter Story" (March 11, 1959) **Ward Bond** (Major Seth Adams); Robert Horton, Frank McGrath, Phyllis Thaxter, Lorne Greene; directed by Joseph Pevney; Revue Productions–NBC; 60 minutes

Wagon Train: "The Conchita Vasquez Story" (March 18, 1959) **Ward Bond** (Major Seth Adams); Robert Horton, Anna Maria Alberghetti, John Goddard, Joyce Meadows; directed by Aaron Spelling; Revue Productions–NBC; 60 minutes

Wagon Train: "The Sister Rita Story" (March 25, 1959) **Ward Bond** (Major Seth Adams); Robert Horton, Frank McGrath, Terry Wilson, Vera Miles; directed by Joseph Pevney; Revue Productions–NBC; 60 minutes

Wagon Train: "The Matthew Lowry Story" (April 1, 1959) **Ward Bond** (Major Seth Adams); Robert Horton, Frank McGrath, Terry Wilson, Richard Anderson; directed by Jack Arnold; Revue Productions–NBC; 60 minutes

Wagon Train: "The Swift Cloud Story" (April 8, 1959) **Ward Bond** (Major Seth Adams); Robert Horton, Rafael Campos, Alan Baxter, Henry Brandon; directed by Virgil W. Vogel; Revue Productions–NBC; 60 minutes

Wagon Train: "The Vincent Eaglewood Story" (April 15, 1959) **Ward Bond** (Major Seth Adams); Robert Horton, Frank McGrath, Terry Wilson, Wally Cox; directed by Jerry Hopper; Revue Productions–NBC; 60 minutes

Wagon Train: "The Clara Duncan Story" (April 22, 1959) **Ward Bond** (Major Seth Adams); Robert Horton, Angie Dickinson, Eduardo Ciannelli, Robert Clarke; directed by Jerry Hopper; Revue Productions–NBC; 60 minutes

Wagon Train: "The Duke LeMay Story" (April 29, 1959) **Ward Bond** (Major Seth Adams); Robert Horton, Frank McGrath, Terry Wilson, Cameron Mitchell; directed by Virgil W. Vogel; Revue Productions–NBC; 60 minutes

Wagon Train: "The Kate Parker Story" (May 6, 1959) **Ward Bond** (Major Seth Adams); Robert Horton, Virginia Grey, Royal Dano, Ruta Lee; directed by Tay Garnett; Revue Productions–NBC; 60 minutes

Wagon Train: "The Steve Campden Story" (May 13, 1959) **Ward Bond** (Major Seth Adams); Robert Horton, Frank McGrath, Terry Wilson, Ben Cooper; directed by Christian Nyby; Revue Productions–NBC; 60 minutes

Wagon Train: "Chuck Wooster, Wagonmaster" (May 20, 1959) **Ward Bond** (Major Seth Adams); Robert Horton, Frank McGrath, Terry Wilson, Harry Carey, Jr.; directed by Virgil W. Vogel; Revue Productions–NBC; 60 minutes

Wagon Train: "The Jose Maria Moran Story" (May 27, 1959) **Ward Bond** (Major Seth Adams); Robert Horton, Frank McGrath, Terry Wilson, Robert Loggia; directed by Tay Garnett; Revue Productions–NBC; 60 minutes

Wagon Train: "The Andrew Hale Story" (June 3, 1959) **Ward Bond** (Major Seth Adams); Robert Horton, Frank McGrath, John McIntire, Clu Gulager; directed by Virgil W. Vogel; Revue Productions–NBC; 60 minutes

Wagon Train: "The Rodney Lawrence Story" (June 10, 1959) **Ward Bond** (Major Seth Adams); Robert Horton, Frank McGrath, Terry Wilson, Dean Stockwell; directed by Virgil W. Vogel; Revue Productions–NBC; 60 minutes

Wagon Train: "The Steele Family" (June 17, 1959) **Ward Bond** (Major Seth Adams); Robert Horton, Frank McGrath, Terry Wilson, Penny Edwards; directed by Christian Nyby; Revue Productions–NBC; 60 minutes

Wagon Train: "The Jenny Tannen Story" (June 24, 1959) **Ward Bond** (Major Seth Adams); Robert Horton, Frank McGrath, Terry Wilson, Ann Blyth; directed by Christian Nyby; Revue Productions–NBC; 60 minutes

Wagon Train: "The Stagecoach Story" (September 30, 1959) **Ward Bond** (Major Seth Adams); Robert Horton, Frank McGrath, Clu Gulager, Debra Paget; directed by William Whitney; Revue Productions–NBC; 60 minutes

Wagon Train: "The Greenhorn Story" (October 7, 1959) **Ward Bond** (Major Seth Adams); Robert Horton, Frank McGrath, Terry Wilson, Mickey Rooney; directed by Bretaigne Windust; Revue Productions–NBC; 60 minutes

Wagon Train: "The C. L. Harding Story" (October 14, 1959) **Ward Bond** (Major Seth Adams); Robert Horton, Frank McGrath, Johnny Cash, Claire Trevor; directed by Herschel Daugherty; Revue Productions–NBC; 60 minutes

Wagon Train: "The Estaban Zamora Story" (October 21, 1959) **Ward Bond** (Major Seth Adams); Robert Horton, Ernest Borgnine, Robert Armstrong, Leonard Nimoy; directed by Bretaigne Windust; Revue Productions–NBC; 60 minutes

Wagon Train: "The Elizabeth McQueeney Story" (October 28, 1959) **Ward Bond** (Major Seth Adams); Robert Horton, Frank McGrath, Terry Wilson, Bette Davis; directed by Allen H. Miner; Revue Productions–NBC; 60 minutes

Wagon Train: "The Martha Barham Story" (November 4, 1959) **Ward Bond** (Major Seth Adams); Robert Horton, Ann Blyth, Henry Brandon, Warren Oates; directed by James Neilson; Revue Productions–NBC; 60 minutes

Wagon Train: "The Cappy Darrin Story" (November 11, 1959) **Ward Bond** (Major Seth Adams); Frank McGrath, Terry Wilson, Ed Wynn, Tyler McVey; directed by Virgil W. Vogel; Revue Productions–NBC; 60 minutes

Wagon Train: "The Felizia Kingdom Story" (November 18, 1959) **Ward Bond** (Major Seth Adams); Robert Horton, Frank McGrath, Terry Wilson, Judith Anderson; directed by Joseph Pevney; Revue Productions–NBC; 60 minutes

Wagon Train: "The Jess MacAbbee Story" (November 25, 1959) **Ward Bond** (Major Seth Adams); Robert Horton, Frank McGrath, Terry Wilson, Andy Devine; directed by David Butler; Revue Productions–NBC; 60 minutes

Wagon Train: "The Danny Benedict Story" (December 2, 1959) **Ward Bond** (Major Seth Adams); Robert Horton, Frank McGrath, Terry Wilson, Brandon De Wilde; directed by Herschel Daugherty; Revue Productions–NBC; 60 minutes

Wagon Train: "The Vittorio Bottecelli Story" (December 16, 1959) **Ward Bond** (Major Seth Adams); Robert Horton, Frank McGrath, Terry Wilson, Elizabeth Montgomery; directed by Jerry Hopper; Revue Productions–NBC; 60 minutes

Wagon Train: "The St. Nicholas Story" (December 23, 1959) **Ward Bond** (Major Seth Adams); Robert Horton, Frank McGrath, Terry Wilson, Robert Emhardt; directed by Bretaigne Windust; Revue Productions–NBC; 60 minutes

Wagon Train: "The Ruth Marshall Story" (December 30, 1959) **Ward Bond** (Major Seth Adams); Robert Horton, Luana Patten, Henry Amargo, Mike Keene; directed by Richard Bartlett; Revue Productions–NBC; 60 minutes

Wagon Train: "The Lita Foladaire Story" (January 6, 1960) **Ward Bond** (Major Seth Adams); Robert Horton, Diane Brewster, Evelyn Brent, Kent Smith; directed by Jerry Hopper; Revue Productions–NBC; 60 minutes

Wagon Train: "The Colonel Harris Story" (January 13, 1960) **Ward Bond** (Major Seth Adams); Robert Horton, Frank McGrath, Terry Wilson, John Howard; directed by Virgil W. Vogel; Revue Productions–NBC; 60 minutes

Wagon Train: "The Marie Brant Story" (January 20, 1960) **Ward Bond** (Major Seth Adams); Robert Horton, Frank McGrath, Terry Wilson, Jean Hagen; directed by Virgil W. Vogel; Revue Productions–NBC; 60 minutes

Wagon Train: "The Larry Hanify Story" (January 27, 1960) **Ward Bond** (credit only); Robert Horton, Frank McGrath, Terry Wilson, Tommy Sands; directed by Ted Post; Revue Productions–NBC; 60 minutes

Wagon Train: "The Clayton Tucker Story" (February 10, 1960) **Ward Bond** (Major Seth Adams); Robert Horton, Frank McGrath, Terry Wilson, Jeff Morrow; directed by Virgil W. Vogel; Revue Productions–NBC; 60 minutes

Wagon Train: "The Benjamin Burns Story" (February 17, 1960) **Ward Bond** (Major Seth Adams); Robert Horton, Frank McGrath, Terry Wilson, J. Carrol Naish; directed by Virgil W. Vogel; Revue Productions–NBC; 60 minutes

Wagon Train: "The Ricky and Laura Bell Story" (February 24, 1960) **Ward Bond** (Major Seth Adams); Robert Horton, Frank McGrath, James Gregory, June Lockhart; directed by Allen H. Miner; Revue Productions–NBC; 60 minutes

Wagon Train: "The Tom Tuckett Story" (March 2, 1960) **Ward Bond** (Major Seth Adams); Robert Horton, Frank McGrath, Terry Wilson, Ben Cooper; directed by Herschel Daugherty; Revue Productions–NBC; 60 minutes

Wagon Train: "The Tracy Sadler Story" (March 9, 1960) **Ward Bond** (Major Seth Adams); Robert Horton, Frank McGrath, Terry Wilson, Elaine Stritch; directed by Ted Post; Revue Productions–NBC; 60 minutes

Wagon Train: "The Alexander Portlass Story" (March 16, 1960) **Ward Bond** (Major Seth Adams); Robert Horton, Frank McGrath, Terry Wilson, Peter Lorre; directed by Jerry Hopper; Revue Productions–NBC; 60 minutes

Wagon Train: "The Christine Elliot Story" (March 23, 1960) **Ward Bond** (Major Seth Adams); Robert Horton, Frank McGrath, Terry Wilson, Phyllis Thaxter; directed by Herschel Daugherty; Revue Productions–NBC; 60 minutes

Wagon Train: "The Joshua Gilliam Story" (March 30, 1960) **Ward Bond** (Major Seth Adams); Robert Horton, Frank McGrath, Terry Wilson, Dan Duryea; directed by Virgil W. Vogel; Revue Productions–NBC; 60 minutes

Wagon Train: "The Maggie Hamilton Story" (April 6, 1960) **Ward Bond** (Major Seth Adams); Robert Horton, Frank McGrath, Leonard Nimoy, Susan Oliver; directed by Allen H. Miner; Revue Productions–NBC; 60 minutes

Wagon Train: "The Jonas Murdock Story" (April 13, 1960) **Ward Bond** (Major Seth Adams); Robert

Horton, Frank McGrath, Terry Wilson, Noah Beery, Jr.; directed by Virgil W. Vogel; Revue Productions–NBC; 60 minutes

Wagon Train: "The Amos Gibbon Story" (April 20, 1960) **Ward Bond** (Major Seth Adams); Robert Horton, Frank McGrath, Terry Wilson, Charles Aidman; directed by Joseph Pevney; Revue Productions–NBC; 60 minutes

Wagon Train: "Trial for Murder: Part 1" (April 27, 1960) **Ward Bond** (Major Seth Adams); Robert Horton, Henry Daniell, Henry Hull, William Schallert; directed by Virgil W. Vogel; Revue Productions–NBC; 60 minutes

Wagon Train: "Trial for Murder: Part 2" (April 27, 1960) **Ward Bond** (Major Seth Adams); Robert Horton, Henry Daniell, Henry Hull, William Schallert; directed by Virgil W. Vogel; Revue Productions–NBC; 60 minutes

Wagon Train: "The Countess Baranof Story" (May 11, 1960) **Ward Bond** (Major Seth Adams); Robert Horton, Frank McGrath, Terry Wilson, Taina Elg; directed by Ted Post; Revue Productions–NBC; 60 minutes

Wagon Train: "The Dick Jarvis Story" (May 18, 1960) **Ward Bond** (Major Seth Adams); Robert Horton, Frank McGrath, Terry Wilson, Tom Nolan; directed by Jerry Hopper; Revue Productions–NBC; 60 minutes

Wagon Train: "The Dr. Swift Cloud Story" (May 25, 1960) **Ward Bond** (Major Seth Adams); Robert Horton, Frank McGrath, Rafael Campos, Henry Brandon; directed by Virgil W. Vogel; Revue Productions–NBC; 60 minutes

Wagon Train: "The Luke Grant Story" (June 1, 1960) **Ward Bond** (Major Seth Adams); Robert Horton, Frank McGrath, Terry Wilson, Donald Woods; directed by Christian Nyby; Revue Productions–NBC; 60 minutes

Wagon Train: "The Charlene Brenton Story" (June 8, 1960) **Ward Bond** (Major Seth Adams); Robert Horton, Frank McGrath, Terry Wilson, Raymond Bailey; directed by Virgil W. Vogel; Revue Productions–NBC; 60 minutes

Wagon Train: "The Sam Livingston Story" (June 15, 1960) **Ward Bond** (Major Seth Adams); Robert Horton, Frank McGrath, Terry Wilson, Charles Drake; directed by Joseph Pevney; Revue Productions–NBC; 60 minutes

Wagon Train: "The Shad Bennington Story" (June 22, 1960) **Ward Bond** (Major Seth Adams); Robert Horton, Frank McGrath, Terry Wilson, David Wayne; directed by Joseph Pevney; Revue Productions–NBC; 60 minutes

Wagon Train: "Wagons Ho!" (September 28, 1960) **Ward Bond** (Major Seth Adams); Robert Horton, Frank McGrath, Terry Wilson, Mickey Rooney; directed by Herschel Daugherty; Revue Productions–NBC; 60 minutes

Wagon Train: "The Horace Best Story" (October 5, 1960) **Ward Bond** (Major Seth Adams); Robert Horton, Frank McGrath, Terry Wilson, George Gobel; directed by Jerry Hopper; Revue Productions–NBC; 60 minutes

Wagon Train: "The Albert Farnsworth Story" (October 12, 1960) **Ward Bond** (Major Seth Adams); Robert Horton, Frank McGrath, Terry Wilson, Charles Laughton; directed by Herschel Daugherty; Revue Productions–NBC; 60 minutes

Wagon Train: "The Allison Justis Story" (October 19, 1960) **Ward Bond** (Major Seth Adams); Robert Horton, Frank McGrath, Terry Wilson, Gloria DeHaven; directed by Ted Post; Revue Productions–NBC; 60 minutes

Wagon Train: "The Jose Morales Story" (October 26, 1960) **Ward Bond** (Major Seth Adams); Robert Horton, Frank McGrath, Lee Marvin, Lon Chaney, Jr.; directed by Virgil W. Vogel; Revue Productions–NBC; 60 minutes

Wagon Train: "Princess of a Lost Tribe" (November 2, 1960) **Ward Bond** (Major Seth Adams); Robert Horton, Frank McGrath, Terry Wilson, Raymond Massey; directed by Richard Whorf; Revue Productions–NBC; 60 minutes

Wagon Train: "The Cathy Eckhardt Story" (November 9, 1960) **Ward Bond** (Major Seth Adams); Robert Horton, Frank McGrath, Terry Wilson, Martin Landau; directed by Sutton Roley; Revue Productions–NBC; 60 minutes

Wagon Train: "The Bleymier Story" (November 16, 1960) **Ward Bond** (Major Seth Adams); Robert Horton, Frank McGrath, Terry Wilson, Dan Duryea; directed by Virgil W. Vogel; Revue Productions–NBC; 60 minutes

Wagon Train: "The Colter Craven Story" (November 23, 1960) **Ward Bond** (Major Seth Adams); **John Wayne**, Anna Lee, Ken Curtis, John Carradine; directed by **John Ford**; Revue Productions–NBC; 60 minutes

Wagon Train: "The Jane Hawkins Story" (November 30, 1960) **Ward Bond** (Major Seth Adams); Robert Horton, Frank McGrath, Terry Wilson, Myrna Fahey; directed by R. G. Springsteen; Revue Productions–NBC; 60 minutes

Wagon Train: "The Candy O'Hara Story" (December 7, 1960) **Ward Bond** (Major Seth Adams); Robert Horton, Frank McGrath, Terry Wilson, Joan O'Brien; directed by Tay Garnett; Revue Productions–NBC; 60 minutes

Wagon Train: "The River Crossing" (December 14, 1960) **Ward Bond** (Major Seth Adams); Robert Horton, Frank McGrath, Terry Wilson, Charles Aidman; directed by Jesse Hibbs; Revue Productions–NBC; 60 minutes

Wagon Train: "The Roger Bigelow Story" (December 21, 1960) **Ward Bond** (Major Seth Adams); Robert Horton, Frank McGrath, Terry Wilson, Robert Vaughn; directed by Jerry Hopper; Revue Productions–NBC; 60 minutes

Wagon Train: "The Patience Miller Story" (January 11, 1961) **Ward Bond** (credit only); Robert Horton, Frank McGrath, Rhonda Fleming, Michael Ansara; directed by Mitchell Leisen; Revue Productions–NBC; 60 minutes

Wagon Train: "Weight of Command" (January 25, 1961) **Ward Bond** (Major Seth Adams); John McIntire (credit only), Robert Horton, Frank McGrath,

Terry Wilson; directed by Herschel Daugherty; Revue Productions–NBC; 60 minutes

Wagon Train: "**Path of the Serpent**" (February 8, 1961) **Ward Bond** (credit only); Robert Horton, Frank McGrath, Terry Wilson, Noah Beery, Jr.; directed by Virgil W. Vogel; Revue Productions–NBC; 60 minutes

Wagon Train: "**The Beth Pearson Story**" (February 22, 1961) **Ward Bond** (Major Seth Adams); Robert Horton, Frank McGrath, Terry Wilson, Virginia Grey; directed by Virgil W. Vogel; Revue Productions–NBC; 60 minutes

Wagon Train: "**The Nancy Palmer Story**" (March 7, 1961) **Ward Bond** (credit only); Robert Horton, Frank McGrath, Audrey Meadows, Jack Cassidy; directed by John English; Revue Productions–NBC; 60 minutes

Chapter Notes

Preface

1. Joseph McBride, *Searching for John Ford: A Life* (New York: St. Martin's Press, 2001), p. 6.
2. Maureen O'Hara with John Nicoletti, *'Tis Herself: A Memoir* (New York: Simon & Schuster, 2004), p. 142.

Introduction

1. Joseph McBride, *Searching for John Ford*, p. 3.
2. Bill Libby, "The Old Wrangler Rides Again," *Cosmopolitan*, March 1964.
3. Ronald L. Davis, *John Ford: Hollywood's Old Master* (Norman, Oklahoma: University of Oklahoma Press, 1995), p. xi.
4. Ronald L. Davis, p. xii.

Chapter 1

1. "The Late Ward Bond Had a Pioneer Heritage," Benkelman, Nebraska, weekly newspaper, 1960.
2 C. L. Ketler, "Ward Bond and the Bond Family," Benkelman, Nebraska, weekly newspaper, 26 February 1953.

Chapter 2

1. Randy Roberts and James S. Olson, *John Wayne: American* (Lincoln, Nebraska: University of Nebraska Press, 1997), p. 8.
2. Maurice Zolotow, *Shooting Star: A Biography of John Wayne* (New York: Simon & Schuster, 1974).
3. Ronald L. Davis, p. 33.
4. Dan Ford, *Pappy: The Life of John Ford* (Englewood Cliffs, New Jersey: Prentice-Hall, Inc., 1979), p. 14.
5. Joseph McBride, *Searching for John Ford*, p. 85.
6. Dan Ford, p. 14.

7. Peter Bogdanovich, *John Ford* (Berkeley: University of California Press, 1978), pp. 39–40.
8. Peter Bogdanovich, *John Ford*, p. 40.
9. Peter Bogdanovich, *John Ford*, p. 40.
10. Ronald L. Davis, p. 35.
11. Dan Ford, p. 19.
12. Peter Bogdanovich, *John Ford*, p. 43.
13. Dan Ford, p. 22.
14. Dan Ford, p. 24.
15. Dan Ford, p. 29.
16. Dan Ford, p. 34.
17. Peter Bogdanovich, *John Ford*, p. 44.
18. Dan Ford, p. 39.
19. Peter Bogdanovich, *John Ford*, p. 47.
20. Joseph McBride, *Searching for John Ford*, p. 156.
21. Dan Ford, p. 41.
22. Peter Bogdanovich, *John Ford*, p. 50.
23. Joseph McBride, *Searching for John Ford*, p. 161.
24. Peter Bogdanovich, *John Ford*, p. 50.
25. Dan Ford, pp. 48–49.
26. Dan Ford, p. 49.
27. Dan Ford, pp. 49–50.
28. Peter Bogdanovich, *John Ford*, p. 51.
29. Joseph McBride, *Searching for John Ford*, p. 171.
30. Joseph McBride, *Searching for John Ford*, p. 32.
31. Joseph McBride, *Searching for John Ford*, p. 171.
32. Woody Strode and Sam Young, *Goal Dust: The Warm and Candid Memoirs of a Pioneer Black Athlete and Actor* (Lanham, Maryland: Madison Books, 1990), pp. 189–190.
33. Dan Ford, p. 51.
34. Randy Roberts and James S. Olson, pp. 76–77.
35. Joseph McBride, *Searching for John Ford*, p. 45.

36. Peter Bogdanovich, *John Ford*, p. 52.
37. Joseph McBride, *Searching for John Ford*, p. 185.
38. Harry Carey, Jr., *Company of Heroes: My Life as an Actor in the John Ford Stock Company* (Metuchen New Jersey: Scarecrow Press, 1994), p. 72.
39. Bill Clinton, *My Life* (New York: Alfred A. Knopf, 2004), p. 539.
40. Ward Bond, Letter to Mr. and Mrs. J. W. Bond, Los Angeles, California, 5 March 1930.
41. Greil Marcus, *The Dustbin of History* (Cambridge: Harvard University Press, 1995), p. 212.
42. Ward Bond, Letter to Mr. and Mrs. J. W. Bond, Hotel del Ming, Yuma, Arizona, 19 April 1930.
43. Gary Wills, *John Wayne's America: The Politics of Celebrity* (New York: Simon & Schuster, 1997), p. 48.
44. Peter Bogdanovich, *John Ford*, p. 52.
45. Larry Swindell, *Spencer Tracy* (New York: New American Library, 1969), pp. 74–75.
46. Peter Bogdanovich, *John Ford*, p. 52.
47. Larry Swindell, p. 83.
48. Joseph McBride, *Searching for John Ford*, p. 175.
49. Gary Wills, p. 65.
50. "'I Come Ready': An Interview with John Wayne," *Film Heritage*, Summer 1975.
51. Joseph McBride, *Searching for John Ford*, p. 184.
52. Scott Eyman, *Print the Legend: The Life and Times of John Ford* (New York: Simon & Schuster, 1999), p. 128.
53. Peter Bogdanovich, *John Ford*, p. 55.
54. Ward Bond, Letter to Mr. and Mrs. J. W. Bond, Los Angeles, California, 27 July 1931.
55. Joseph McBride, *Searching for John Ford*, p. 187.
56. Donald Shepherd and Robert Slatzer, *Duke: The Life and Times of*

John Wayne (New York: Citadel Press, 2002), p. 143.
57. Gary Wills, p. 59.

Chapter 3

1. Joseph McBride, *Searching for John Ford*, p. 280.
2. Ronald L. Davis, p. 72.
3. Joseph McBride, *Searching for John Ford*, p. 195.
4. Ward Bond, Letter to Mr. and Mrs. J. W. Bond, Columbia Studios, Hollywood, California, 4 January 1933.
5. Peter Bogdanovich, *John Ford*, pp. 55–57.
6. Peter Bogdanovich, *John Ford*, p. 57.
7. Boris Karloff, Interview, Chateau Marmont, Hollywood, California, 1957.
8. Randy Roberts and James S. Olson, p. 136.
9. Dan Ford, p. 76.
10. Peter Bogdanovich, *John Ford*, p. 59.
11. Joseph McBride, *Searching for John Ford*, p. 211.
12. Scott Eyman, pp. 146–147.
13. Bryan B. Sterling and Frances Sterling, *Will Rogers in Hollywood* (New York: Crown, 1984), p. 133.
14. Dan Ford, p. 76.
15. Joseph McBride, *Searching for John Ford*, p. 179.
16. Dan Ford, p. 84.
17. Scott Eyman, p. 155.
18. Joseph McBride, *Searching for John Ford*, p. 223.
19. Joseph McBride, *Searching for John Ford*, pp. 193–194.
20. Dan Ford, p. 96.
21. Dan Ford, p. 97.
22. Ronald L. Davis, p. 79.
23. Joseph McBride, *Searching for John Ford*, p. 258.
24. Dan Ford, p. 99.
25. *Pride of the Marines* pressbook, Columbia Pictures Corporation, 1936, p. 9.
26. Katharine Hepburn, *Me: Stories of My Life* (New York: Alfred A. Knopf, 1991).
27. Peter Bogdanovich, *John Ford*, pp. 67–68.
28. Scott Eyman, p. 182.
29. Dan Ford, p. 100.
30. Peter Bogdanovich, *John Ford*, p. 68.
31. Dan Ford, p. 78.
32. Dan Ford, p. 78.
33. Dan Ford, p. 79.
34. Dan Ford, p. 103.
35. Peter Bogdanovich, *John Ford*, p. 69.
36. Dan Ford, p. 110.
37. Dan Ford, p. 113.

38. Dan Ford, p. 113.
39. Peter Bogdanovich, *John Ford*, p. 69.
40. Ronald L. Davis, p. 89.

Chapter 4

1. Ronald L. Davis, pp. 98–99.
2. "I Come Ready," pp. 18–19.
3. Bob Thomas, ed., *Directors in Action: Selections from* Action, *the Official Magazine of the Directors Guild of America* (Indianapolis: Bobbs-Merrill Company, 1973), p. 166.
4. Dan Ford, p. 124.
5. Randy Roberts and James S. Olson, p. 147.
6. Randy Roberts and James S. Olson, p. 149.
7. Dan Ford, p. 125.
8. Joseph McBride, *Searching for John Ford*, p. 163.
9. "Employment Agreement Between Hal Roach Studios, Inc., and Victor McLaglen," Hal E. Roach Studios, Culver City, California, 12 November 1938, p. 3.
10. Dan Ford, p. 128.
11. Gary Wills, p. 71.
12. *The Size of Legends, The Soul of Myth, The Man Who Shot Liberty Valance* Centennial Collection DVD, Paramount Home Entertainment, 2009.
13. Harry Carey, Jr., p. 73.
14. Dan Ford, p. 128.
15. Gary Wills, p. 91.
16. Randy Roberts and James S. Olson, pp. 161–162.
17. Tag Gallagher, *John Ford: The Man and His Films* (Berkeley: University of California Press, 1986) p. 162.
18. James Cagney, *Cagney by Cagney* (New York: Doubleday and Company, Inc., 1976), pp. 84–85.
19. Dan Ford, pp. 117–118.
20. Dan Ford, p. 119.
21. Dan Ford, pp. 130–131.
22. Dan Ford, p. 134.
23. Dan Ford, p. 138.
24. Dan Ford, pp. 138–139.
25. Ronald L. Davis, pp. 103–104.
26. Dan Ford, p. 115.
27. Peter Bogdanovich, *John Ford*, p. 74.
28. Joseph McBride, *Searching for John Ford*, p. 270.
29. Thomas Schatz, *The Genius of the System: Hollywood Filmmaking in the Studio Era* (New York: Pantheon Books, 1988), p. 180.
30. *The Daily Worker*, 9 January 1940.
31. Dan Ford, p. 142.
32. Peter Bogdanovich, *John Ford*, pp. 76–77.
33. Scott Eyman, p. 218.

34. Peter Bogdanovich, *John Ford*, p. 78.
35. John Ford, Letter to Darryl F. Zanuck, Hollywood, California, December 1939.
36. Ronald L. Davis, p. 6.
37. Dan Ford, p. 146.
38. Dan Ford, p. 149.
39. Joseph McBride, *Searching for John Ford*, pp. 274–275.
40. Randy Roberts and James S. Olson, p. 179.
41. Henry Fonda, *Fonda: My Life* (New York: Signet, 1982), p. 190.
42. *New York Times*, 19 August 1940.
43. Joseph McBride, *Searching for John Ford*, p. 317.
44. Peter Bogdanovich, *John Ford*, p. 78.
45. Ronald L. Davis, p. 119.
46. Dan Ford, p. 155.
47. Randy Roberts and James S. Olson, p. 186.
48. James Cagney, p. 96.
49. James Cagney, p. 194.
50. Steven Bach, *Marlene Dietrich: Life and Legend* (New York: William Morrow and Company, 1992), pp. 257–258.
51. Henry Brandon, Discussion with Scott Allen Nollen, St. Paul, Minnesota, July 1988.
52. Randy Roberts and James S. Olson, p. 196.
53. Peter Bogdanovich, *John Ford*, p. 80.
54. Joseph McBride, *Searching for John Ford*, p. 316.
55. Joseph McBride, *Searching for John Ford*, p. 317.
56. Ronald L. Davis, p. 121.
57. *Hollywood Reporter*, 6 March 1941, p. 10.
58. Joseph McBride, *Searching for John Ford*, p. 315.
59. Maureen O'Hara, p. 64.
60. Maureen O'Hara, p. 65.
61. Maureen O'Hara, p. 68.
62. Joseph McBride, *Searching for John Ford*, p. 326.
63. Joseph McBride, *Searching for John Ford*, p. 333.
64. Anna Lee, Discussion with Scott Allen Nollen, Hollywood, California, 12 August 1989.
65. Maureen O'Hara, p. 69.
66. Randy Roberts and James S. Olson, p. 202.
67. Ward Bond, Telegram to John Ford, Los Angeles, California, 25 November 1941.

Chapter 5

1. Joseph McBride, *Searching for John Ford*, p. 343.

2. Gary Wills, p. 107.
3. Dan Ford, p. 162.
4. Dan Ford, p. 164.
5. Maureen O'Hara, pp. 71–72.
6. Maureen O'Hara, p. 90.
7. Joseph McBride, *Searching for John Ford*, p. 343.
8. Joseph McBride, *Searching for John Ford*, p. 343.
9. Randy Roberts and James S. Olson, p. 211.
10. John Ford, Letter to Darryl F. Zanuck, Moana Hotel, Honolulu, Hawaii, April 1942.
11. Randy Roberts and James S. Olson, p. 219.
12. Dan Ford, p. 172.
13. Dan Ford, p. 172.
14. Henry Fonda, pp. 144–147.
15. Peter Bogdanovich, *John Ford*, p. 82.
16. Randy Roberts and James S. Olson, p. 215.
17. Randy Roberts and James S. Olson, p. 223.
18. Mary Ford, Letter to John Ford, Hollywood, California, 1 June 1943.
19. Joseph McBride, *Searching for John Ford*, p. 367.
20. Mary Ford, Letter to John Ford, Hollywood, California, 18 November 1943.
21. Mary Ford, Letter to John Ford, Hollywood, California, 25 December 1943.
22. John T. McManus, "Speaking of Movies: Reaction's Rump," *PM*, 14 February 1944.
23. Randy Roberts and James S. Olson, p. 250.
24. Joseph McBride, *Searching for John Ford*, p. 390.
25. Joseph McBride, *Searching for John Ford*, pp. 393–394.
26. Joseph McBride, *Searching for John Ford*, p. 396.
27. Joseph McBride, *Searching for John Ford*, p. 397.
28. Joseph McBride, *Searching for John Ford*, p. 401.
29. Harry Carey, Jr., p. 133.
30. Joseph McBride, *Searching for John Ford*, p. 392.
31. Harry Carey, Jr., p. 76.
32. Harry Carey, Jr., p. 78.
33. Patrick Ford, Letter to John Ford, Hollywood, California, 4 February 1944.
34. Ben Barzman, "The Duke and Me," *Los Angeles Magazine*, January 1989.
35. Randy Roberts and James S. Olson, pp. 262–263.
36. Maureen O'Hara, p. 100.
37. Maureen O'Hara, p. 102.
38. Maureen O'Hara, p. 102.
39. Dan Ford, p. 200.

40. Joseph McBride, *Searching for John Ford*, p. 409.
41. Randy Roberts and James S. Olson, p. 272.
42. Dan Ford, p. 201.
43. Joseph McBride, *Searching for John Ford*, p. 409.
44. Randy Roberts and James S. Olson, pp. 270–271.
45. Joseph McBride, *Searching for John Ford*, p. 408.
46. Dan Ford, p. 199.
47. Randy Roberts and James S. Olson, p. 268.
48. Joseph McBride, *Searching for John Ford*, p. 410.

Chapter 6

1. Joseph McBride, *Hawks on Hawks* (Berkeley: University of California Press, 1982), p. 116.
2. Ronald L. Davis, p. 202.
3. Dan Ford, pp. 206–207.
4. Dan Ford, p. 207.
5. Randy Roberts and James S. Olson, pp. 278–279.
6. Dan Ford, p. 208.
7. Dan Ford, p. 210.
8. Peter Bogdanovich, *John Ford*, pp. 84–85.
9. John Ford, Letter to Frank Capra, Hollywood, California, 29 March 1946.
10. Andrew Sarris, *The John Ford Movie Mystery* (Bloomington: Indiana University Press, 1975).
11. Joseph McBride, *Searching for John Ford*, p. 432.
12. Tom and Sara Pendergast, eds., *The St. James Encyclopedia of Popular Culture* (Detroit: St. James Press, 2000), p. 429.
13. Harry Carey, Jr., p. 80.
14. Joseph McBride, *Hawks on Hawks*, p. 116.
15. James D'Arc, "Howard Hawks and the Great Paper Chase," *Projections* 6, 1996.
16. Joseph McBride, *Hawks on Hawks*, p. 123.
17. Gerald Mast, *Howard Hawks, Storyteller* (New York: Oxford University Press, 1984), pp. 51–54 and 329.
18. Dan Ford, p. 212.
19. Joseph McBride, *Searching for John Ford*, p. 437.
20. Joseph McBride, *Searching for John Ford*, p. 438.
21. Joseph McBride, *Searching for John Ford*, p. 438.
22. Joseph McBride, *Searching for John Ford*, p. 440.
23. Peter Bogdanovich, *John Ford*, p. 85.
24. Joseph McBride, *Searching for John Ford*, p. 440.

25. Maureen O'Hara, pp. 103–104.
26. Maureen O'Hara p. 124.

Chapter 7

1. Joseph McBride, *Searching for John Ford*, p. 291.
2. Dan Ford, pp. 214–215.
3. Joseph McBride, *Searching for John Ford*, p. 450.
4. Peter Bogdanovich, *John Ford*, p. 86.
5. Scott Eyman, p. 336.
6. Dan Ford, p. 217.
7. Dan Ford, p. 217.
8. Joseph McBride, *Searching for John Ford*, pp. 454–455.
9. Scott Eyman, p. 299.
10. Joseph McBride, *Searching for John Ford*, pp. 451–452.
11. Joseph McBride, *Searching for John Ford*, p. 446.
12. Joseph McBride, *Searching for John Ford*, p. 456.
13. Peter Bogdanovich, *John Ford*, p. 86.
14. Randy Roberts and James S. Olson, p. 294.
15. Gaylyn Studlar and Matthew Bernstein, eds., *John Ford Made Westerns: Filming the Legend in the Sound Era* (Bloomington: Indiana University Press, 2001), pp. 155–156.
16. Scott Eyman, p. 341.
17. Joseph McBride, *Searching for John Ford*, p. 439.
18. Harry Carey, Jr., p. 8.
19. Harry Carey, Jr., p. 11.
20. Harry Carey, Jr., p. 15.
21. Ronald L. Davis, p. 221.
22. Joseph McBride, *Searching for John Ford*, p. 443.
23. Harry Carey, Jr., pp. 28–29.
24. Harry Carey, Jr., p. 29.
25. Harry Carey, Jr., p. 133.
26. Harry Carey, Jr., p. 34.
27. Harry Carey, Jr., pp. 39–40.
28. Harry Carey, Jr., p. 43.
29. Dan Ford, p. 223.
30. Randy Roberts and James S. Olson, p. 312.
31. Randy Roberts and James S. Olson, pp. 304–305.
32. Ronald L. Davis, p. 221.
33. John Ford, Letter to James Warner Bellah, Hollywood, California, 15 July 1948.
34. Joseph McBride, *Searching for John Ford*, p. 458.
35. Harry Carey, Jr., p. 55.
36. Harry Carey, Jr., p. 57, 63.
37. Peter Bogdanovich, *John Ford*, p. 87.
38. Gaylyn Studlar and Matthew Bernstein, eds., pp. 158–160.
39. Harry Carey, Jr., p. 67.
40. Harry Carey, Jr., p. 71.

41. Peter Bogdanovich, "The Duke's Gone West," *New York*, 25 June 1979.

42. Dan Ford, p. 230.

Chapter 8

1. Richard Warren Lewis, "*Playboy* Interview with John Wayne," *Playboy*, May 1971.

2. Henry Brandon, Discussion with Scott Allen Nollen, St. Paul, Minnesota, July 1988.

3. Gary Wills, p. 195.

4. Randy Roberts and James S. Olson, p. 332.

5. Gary Wills, pp. 197–198.

6. "I Come Ready," p. 32.

7. Randy Roberts and James S. Olson, p. 343.

8. Gary Wills, p. 199.

9. Scott Eyman, p. 344.

10. Harry Carey, Jr., p. 8.

11. Joseph McBride, *Searching for John Ford*, p. 474.

12. Gary Wills, p. 29.

13. Joseph McBride, *Searching for John Ford*, p. 476.

14. Joseph McBride, *Searching for John Ford*, p. 476.

15. Joseph McBride, *Searching for John Ford*, p. 477.

16. Anna Lee, Discussion with Scott Allen Nollen, Hollywood, California, 12 August 1989.

17. Scott Eyman, pp. 358–359.

18. Michael F. Blake, "He Was Their Stage Coach," *Los Angeles Times*, 28 May 1999.

19. *Los Angeles Times*, March 1949.

20. Michael F. Blake.

21. Michael F. Blake.

22. Bryan Burrough, *The Big Rich: The Rise and Fall of the Greatest Texas Oil Fortunes* (New York: Penguin Press, 2009), p. 176.

23. Gary Wills, p. 154.

24. Randy Roberts and James S. Olson, p. 320.

25. Gary Wills, p. 149.

26. Gary Wills, p. 156.

27. Joseph McBride, *Searching for John Ford*, p. 489.

28. Scott Eyman, p. 361.

29. Ethel Waters with Charles Samuels, *His Eye Is on the Sparrow: An Autobiography* (New York: Doubleday and Company, Inc., 1951), pp. 271–272.

30. Scott Eyman, p. 305.

Chapter 9

1. Harry Carey, Jr., pp. 86–87.

2. Harry Carey, Jr., p. 99.

3. Harry Carey, Jr., p. 86.

4. Harry Carey, Jr., p. 89, 94.

5. Harry Carey, Jr., p. 94.

6. Harry Carey, Jr., pp. 99–100.

7. Ronald L. Davis, p. 234.

8. Dan Ford, p. 231.

9. Joseph McBride, *Searching for John Ford*, p. 497.

10. Peter Bogdanovich, John Ford, p. 88.

11. Dan Ford, p. 232.

12. Dan Ford, p. 232.

13. Maureen O'Hara, p. 137.

14. Joseph McBride, *Searching for John Ford*, p. 503.

15. Gary Wills, p. 186.

16. Maureen O'Hara, p. 139.

17. Harry Carey, Jr., p. 117.

18. Maureen O'Hara, p. 140.

19. Gary Wills, p. 189.

20. Randy Roberts and James S. Olson, p. 325.

21. Ronald L. Davis, p. 246.

22. *Hollywood Reporter*, 18 July 1951, p. 3; 25 July 1951, p. 6.

23. John Ford, Letter to John Wayne, Song-Dong, near Mo Prong, Korea, 19 January 1951.

24. John Wayne, Western Union telegram to John Ford, North Hollywood, California, 30 January 1951.

25. Joseph McBride, *Searching for John Ford*, p. 504.

26. Dan Ford, p. 237.

27. Joseph McBride, *Searching for John Ford*, p. 480.

28. Joseph McBride, *Searching for John Ford*, p. 485.

29. Maureen O'Hara, p. 159.

30. Maureen O'Hara, p. 141.

31. Gary Wills, p. 248.

32. Dan Ford, pp. 243–244.

33. *The Making of* The Quiet Man, Republic Entertainment, Inc., DVD, 1999.

34. *Directed by John Ford*, Turner Entertainment-American Film Institute, 2006.

35. Dan Ford, p. 244.

36. Gary Wills, p. 245.

37. Maureen O'Hara, p. 166.

38. *The Making of* The Quiet Man.

39. Joseph McBride, *Searching for John Ford*, p. 515.

40. Joseph McBride, *Searching for John Ford*, p. 513.

41. Randy Roberts and James S. Olson, pp. 366–367.

42. Gary Wills, p. 246.

43. Gary Wills, p. 247.

44. Joseph McBride, *Searching for John Ford*, p. 509.

Chapter 10

1. Dan Ford, p. 268.

2. Joseph McBride, *Searching for John Ford*, p. 551.

3. Joseph McBride, *Searching for John Ford*, p. 493.

4. Joseph McBride, *Searching for John Ford*, p. 493.

5. Joseph McBride, *Searching for John Ford*, p. 522.

6. Randy Roberts and James S. Olson, p. 369.

7. Joseph McBride, *Searching for John Ford*, p. 533.

8. *Frank Sinatra in Concert at the Royal Festival Hall*, Reprise DVD, 1971.

9. John Howlett, *Frank Sinatra* (Philadelphia: Courage Books, 1980), p. 71.

10. John Ford, Letter to John Wayne, Nairobi, Kenya, Africa, December 1952.

11. Randy Roberts and James S. Olson, p. 407.

12. Dan Ford, p. 259.

13. Randy Roberts and James S. Olson, p. 348.

14. Randy Roberts and James S. Olson, p. 401.

15. John Wayne, Letter to John Ford, Carmago, Mexico, 17 June 1953.

16. Randy Roberts and James S. Olson, p. 403.

17. Randy Roberts and James S. Olson, p. 403.

18. *The Making of* Hondo, Paramount Home Entertainment DVD, 2005.

19. *Johnny Guitar* pressbook, Republic Pictures Corporation, 1954, p. 8.

20. Harry Carey, Jr., p. 133.

21. John Wayne, Telegram to John Ford, Hollywood, California, 1 February 1954.

22. Harry Carey, Jr., p. 130.

23. Maureen O'Hara, p. 188.

24. Maureen O'Hara, p. 190

25. Ronald L. Davis, p. 9.

26. Maureen O'Hara, p. 193.

27. Maureen O'Hara, p. 187.

28. Randy Roberts and James S. Olson, p. 299.

29. Ronald L. Davis, p. 265.

30. Harry Carey, Jr., p. 132.

31. Harry Carey, Jr., p. 136.

32. Harry Carey, Jr., p. 137.

33. Harry Carey, Jr., p. 137.

34. Tag Gallagher, p. 339.

35. Joseph McBride, *Searching for John Ford*, p. 539.

36. *Time*, February 1956.

37. Ronald L. Davis, pp. 266–267.

38. Joseph McBride, *Searching for John Ford*, p. 545.

39. Harry Carey, Jr., p. 145.

40. Harry Carey, Jr., pp. 145–146.

41. Dan Ford, p. 265.

42. Harry Carey, Jr., p. 147.

43. Harry Carey, Jr., p. 148.

44. Harry Carey, Jr., p. 148.

45. Harry Carey, Jr., p. 152.

46. Harry Carey, Jr., p. 152.
47. Harry Carey, Jr., p. 153.
48. Harry Carey, Jr., p. 156.
49. Harry Carey, Jr., p. 156.
50. Jack Lemmon, Commentary, *Mister Roberts* DVD, Warner Home Video, 1998.
51. Jack Lemmon.
52. Ronald L. Davis, p. 270.
53. Peter Bogdanovich, *John Ford*, p. 142.
54. *Mister Roberts* DVD, Warner Home Video, 1998.
55. Dan Ford, p. 269.

Chapter 11

1. Harry Carey, Jr., p. 8.
2. *A Turning of the Earth: John Ford, John Wayne and* The Searchers, Warner Bros. Entertainment DVD, 2006.
3. Ronald L. Davis, pp. 273–274.
4. The Searchers: *An Appreciation*, Warner Bros. Entertainment DVD, 2006.
5. Harry Carey, Jr., p. 165.
6. Bill Libby.
7. Harry Carey, Jr., pp. 167–168.
8. Chuck Roberson, Chuck, *Fall Guy* (Vancouver: Hancock House, 1980), p. 160.
9. Harry Carey, Jr., p. 168.
10. Harry Carey, Jr., p. 172.
11. Joseph McBride, *Searching for John Ford*, p. 555.
12. Harry Carey, Jr., p. 170, 173.
13. Harry Carey, Jr., p. 174.
14. Joseph McBride, *Searching for John Ford*, p. 556.
15. Henry Brandon, Letter to Scott Allen Nollen, North Hollywood, California, 30 December 1988.
16. Henry Brandon, Letter, 30 December 1988.
17. *A Turning of the Earth: John Ford, John Wayne and* The Searchers.
18. Harry Carey, Jr., p. 158,170.
19. Joseph McBride, *Searching for John Ford*, p. 557.
20. Joseph McBride, *Searching for John Ford*, p. 557.
21. Joseph McBride, *Searching for John Ford*, p. 557.
22. *A Turning of the Earth: John Ford, John Wayne and* The Searchers.
23. Peter Bogdanovich, *John Ford*, pp. 92–93.
24. Henry Brandon, Discussion, July 1988.
25. The Searchers: *An Appreciation*.
26. The Searchers: *An Appreciation*.
27. John Wayne, Letter to John Ford, Hollywood, California, 28 November 1955.
28. John Wayne, Letter, 28 November 1955.

29. Ronald L. Davis, p. 283.
30. Gary Wills, p. 249.
31. Dan Ford, p. 276.
32. John Ford, Letter to John Wayne, Hollywood, California, 26 December 1956.
33. John Ford, Letter to John Wayne, Hollywood, California, 25 January 1957.

Chapter 12

1. Randy Roberts and James S. Olson, p. 121.
2. Bill Libby.
3. Harry Carey, Jr., p. 190.
4. James Rosin, Wagon Train: *The Television Series* (Philadelphia: Autumn Road, 2008), pp. 18–19.
5. James Rosin, p. 19.
6. James Rosin, p. 21.
7. Huston, John, *An Open Book* (New York: Knopf, 1980).
8. Pilar Wayne with Alex Thorleifson, *My Life with the Duke: John Wayne* (New York: New English Library, Ltd., 1989).
9. Pilar Wayne.
10. Pilar Wayne.
11. Lawrence Grobel, *The Hustons* (New York: Scribners, 1989), p. 451.
12. James Rosin, pp. 29–30.
13. *Daily Variety*, 12 January 1959.
14. Joseph McBride, *Searching for John Ford*, p. 587.
15. John Ford, Letter to John Wayne, Hollywood, California, February 1958.
16. Orson Welles and Peter Bogdanovich, *This Is Orson Welles* (Cambridge, Massachusetts: Da Capo Press, 1998).
17. Joseph McBride, *Searching for John Ford*, p. 593.
18. James Rosin, p. 27.
19. Joseph McBride, *Hawks on Hawks*, p. 130.
20. Dan Ford, p. 281.
21. Dan Ford, p. 281.
22. Anna Lee, Discussion with Scott Allen Nollen, Hollywood, California, 12 August 1989.
23. Dan Ford, p. 283.
24. Nicholas Meyer, Discussion with Scott Allen Nollen, Hollywood, California, 17 October 2011.
25. James Rosin, p. 29.
26. James Rosin, p. 34.
27. Joseph McBride, *Searching for John Ford*, p. 611.
28. James Rosin, p. 34.
29. Dan Ford, p. 288.

Chapter 13

1. Gary Wills, p. 202.
2. Harry Carey, Jr., p. 129.

3. Joseph McBride, *Searching for John Ford*, p. 604.
4. Joseph McBride, *Searching for John Ford*, p. 604.
5. Joseph McBride, *Searching for John Ford*, p. 605.
6. Woody Strode, p. 199.
7. Woody Strode, p. 201.
8. Woody Strode, p. 201.
9. Woody Strode, p. 202.
10. Woody Strode, p. 203.
11. Woody Strode, pp. 203–204.
12. Woody Strode, p. 204.
13. J. P. Coursodon, "Notes of a Press Attache: John Ford in Paris, 1966," *Film Comment*, July–August 1994.
14. Gaylyn Studlar and Matthew Bernstein, eds., p. 75.
15. Scott Eyman, pp. 478–479.
16. Gary Wills, p. 225.
17. Frankie Avalon, Telephone discussion with Scott Allen Nollen, February 2008.
18. Dan Ford, p. 287.
19. John McCabe, Letter to Scott Allen Nollen, Mackinac Island, Michigan, Autumn 1989.
20. Gary Wills, p. 217.
21. Woody Strode, pp. 207–208.
22. Woody Strode, p. 209.
23. Woody Strode, p. 209.
24. Harry Carey, Jr., p. 178.
25. Harry Carey, Jr., p. 185.
26. Harry Carey, Jr., p. 186.
27. Woody Strode, p. 202.
28. Henry Brandon, Discussion, July 1988.
29. Harry Carey, Jr., p. 190.
30. Harry Carey, Jr., p. 190.
31. James Rosin, p. 36.
32. Harry Carey, Jr., p. 190.
33. Harry Carey, Jr., p. 191.
34. Harry Carey, Jr., p. 191.
35. Joseph McBride, *Searching for John Ford*, p. 617.
36. Scott Eyman, p. 483.
37. John Wayne, Telegram to Peter Lawford, Hollywood, California, 9 November 1960.
38. Joseph McBride, *Searching for John Ford*, p. 619.
39. James Rosin, p. 35.
40. Joseph McBride, *Searching for John Ford*, p. 615.
41. Pilar Wayne, pp. 153 154.
42. Ronald L. Davis, pp. 301–302.
43. James Rosin, p. 37.
44. James Rosin, p. 37.
45. James Rosin, pp. 41–42.
46. John Wayne, Telegram to President John F. Kennedy, Tanganyika, Africa, 4 February 1961.
47. Gaylyn Studlar and Matthew Bernstein, eds., pp. 24–25.
48. Scott Eyman, p. 490.
49. *The Size of Legends, The Soul of Myth, The Man Who Shot Liberty*

Valance Centennial Collection DVD, Paramount Home Entertainment, 2009.

50. Joseph McBride, *Searching for John Ford*, p. 627.

51. Joseph McBride, *Searching for John Ford*, p. 630.

52. Woody Strode, pp. 210–211.

53. Woody Strode, pp. 211–212.

54. *The Size of Legends, The Soul of Myth.*

55. *Directed by John Ford.*

56. *The Size of Legends, The Soul of Myth.*

57. Joseph McBride, *Searching for John Ford*, p. 623.

58. Scott Eyman, pp. 491–492.

59. *The Size of Legends, The Soul of Myth.*

60. Joseph McBride, *Searching for John Ford*, p. 633.

61. *Directed by John Ford.*

62. Edmond O'Brien, Letter to John Ford, 22 February 1962.

63. Andrew Sarris.

64. Sammy Davis, Jr., Letter to John Wayne, Prince of Wales Theatre, London, England, 29 August 1961.

65. Paul Newman, Letter to John Wayne, New York, New York, 20 December 1961.

66. Joseph McBride, *Searching for John Ford*, p. 638.

67. Harry Carey, Jr., p. 192.

Chapter 14

1. Bill Libby.

2. Ronald L. Davis, p. 311.

3. Frank Capra, *The Name Above the Title: An Autobiography* (New York: MacMillan, 1971).

4. Maureen O'Hara, p. 236.

5. Woody Strode, p. 216.

6. Woody Strode, p. 218.

7. Joseph McBride, *Searching for John Ford*, p. 652.

8. Peter Bogdanovich, *John Ford*, p. 104.

9. Howard Fast, *Being Red: A Memoir* (New York: M. E. Sharp, Inc., 1994).

10. Woody Strode, p. 220.

11. Bill Libby.

12. Dan Ford, p. 301.

13. Bernard Tavernier, translated by Tag Gallagher, "John Ford a' Paris: Notes d' un Attache de Press," *Positif,* March 1967.

14. Scott Eyman, p. 503.

15. Harry Carey, Jr., p. 203.

16. Peter Bogdanovich, *John Ford*, p. 106.

17. Harry Carey, Jr., p. 194.

18. Joseph McBride, *Searching for John Ford*, p. 643.

19. Bill Libby.

20. Harry Carey, Jr., p. 204.

21. Scott Eyman, p. 514.

22. Dan Ford, p. 307

23. John Wayne, Western Union telegram to Nat "King" Cole, Hollywood, California, 22 December 1964.

24. Pilar Wayne, p. 196.

25. *Time,* 1 March 1965.

26. Randy Roberts and James S. Olson, p. 526.

27. Joseph McBride, *Searching for John Ford*, p. 663.

28. Ronald L. Davis, p. 333.

29. Joseph McBride, *Searching for John Ford*, p. 663.

30. Dan Ford, p. 310.

31. John Ford, Letter to Alnah Johnson, Vietnam, 1968.

32. Scott Eyman, p. 538.

33. Gary Wills, p. 231.

34. Gary Wills, p. 233.

35. Joseph McBride, *Hawks on Hawks*, p. 116.

36. Joseph McBride, *Hawks on Hawks*, p. 133.

37. Joseph McBride, *Hawks on Hawks*, p. 140.

38. Gary Wills, p. 270.

39. Sammy Davis, Jr., Letter to John Wayne, 11 February 1969.

40. Joan Crawford, Letter to John Wayne, New York, New York, 3 February 1970.

41. Lyndon B. Johnson, Telegram to John Wayne, The White House, Washington, D.C., 8 April 1970.

42. John Ford, Letter to Katherine Hepburn, Hollywood, California, 2 October 1970.

43. James Cagney, Letter to John Wayne, Verney Farm, Stanfordville, New York, 30 November 1970.

44. Joseph McBride, *Searching for John Ford*, p. 688.

45. Joseph McBride, *Searching for John Ford*, p. 687.

46. Harry Carey, Jr., p. 205.

47. Anna Lee, Discussion.

48. Bill Libby.

49. Woody Strode, p. 249.

50. Joseph McBride, *Searching for John Ford*, p. 718.

Bibliography

Primary Sources

Interviews, Discussions and Reminiscences

Avalon, Frankie. Telephone discussion with Scott Allen Nollen, February 2008.

Bogdanovich, Peter. Commentary, *The Man Who Shot Liberty Valance*. Centennial Collection DVD. Paramount Home Entertainment, 2009.

Brandon, Henry. Discussions with Scott Allen Nollen, St. Paul, MN, and North Hollywood, CA, July 1988– March 1989.

Erickson, Glenn. Commentary, *On Dangerous Ground* DVD. Warner Bros., 2006.

Ford, John. Interview in Bogdanovich, Peter. *John Ford.* Berkeley: University of California Press, 1978.

Hawks, Howard. Interview in McBride, Joseph. *Hawks on Hawks.* Berkeley: University of California Press, 1982.

Hoey, Michael A. Discussion with Scott Allen Nollen, San Clemente, CA, 12–15 October 2011.

Karloff, Boris. Interview, Chateau Marmont, Hollywood, CA, 1957.

Lee, Anna. Discussion with Scott Allen Nollen, Hollywood, CA, 12 August 1989.

Lemmon, Jack. Commentary, *Mister Roberts* DVD. Warner Home Video, 1998.

Meyer, Nicholas. Discussion with Scott Allen Nollen, Hollywood, CA, 17 October 2011.

Letters and Telegrams

Bond, Ward. Letter to Mr. and Mrs. J. W. Bond, Los Angeles, CA, 5 March 1930, from the Estate of Ward Bond.

_____. Letter to Mr. and Mrs. J. W. Bond, Hotel del Ming, Yuma, AZ, 19 April 1930, from the Estate of Ward Bond.

_____. Letter to Mr. and Mrs. J. W. Bond, Los Angeles, CA, 27 July 1931, from the Estate of Ward Bond.

_____. Letter to Mr. and Mrs. J. W. Bond, Columbia Studios, Hollywood, CA, 4 January 1933, from the Estate of Ward Bond.

_____. Telegram to John Ford, Los Angeles, CA, 25 November 1941.

Brandon, Henry. Letter to Scott Allen Nollen, North Hollywood, CA, 30 December 1988.

_____. Letter to Scott Allen Nollen, North Hollywood, CA, April 1989.

Cagney, James. Letter to John Wayne, Verney Farm, Stanfordville, NY, 30 November 1970.

Crawford, Joan. Letter to John Wayne, New York, 3 February 1970.

Davis, Sammy Jr. Letter to John Wayne, Prince of Wales Theatre, London, England, 29 August 1961.

_____. Letter to John Wayne, 11 February 1969.

Ford, John. Letter to Alnah Johnson, Vietnam, 1968.

_____. Letter to Darryl F. Zanuck, Hollywood, CA, December 1939.

_____. Letter to Darryl F. Zanuck, Moana Hotel, Honolulu, HI, April 1942.

_____. Letter to Frank Capra, Hollywood, CA, 29 March 1946.

_____. Letter to James Warner Bellah, Hollywood, CA, 15 July 1948.

_____. Letter to John Wayne, Song-Dong, near Mo Prong, Korea, 19 January 1951.

_____. Letter to John Wayne, Nairobi, Kenya, Africa, December 1952.

_____. Letter to John Wayne, Hollywood, CA, 26 December 1956.

_____. Letter to John Wayne, Hollywood, CA, 25 January 1957.

_____. Letter to John Wayne, Hollywood, CA, February 1958.

_____. Letter to Katherine Hepburn, Hollywood, CA, 2 October 1970.

Ford, Mary. Letter to John Ford, Hollywood, CA, 1 June 1943.

_____. Letter to John Ford, Hollywood, CA, 20 October 1943.

_____. Letter to John Ford, Hollywood, CA, 18 November 1943.

Ford, Mary. Letter to John Ford, Hollywood, CA, 25 December 1943.

Ford, Patrick. Letter to John Ford, Hollywood, CA, 4 February 1944.

Gerard, Philip R. Letter to Evelyn Karloff, 20 February 1969.

Hoey, Michael A. Letter to Scott Allen Nollen, San Clemente, CA, 21 February 2011.

Huston, John. Letter to Scott Allen Nollen, Puerto Vallarta, Jalisco, Mexico, 15 February 1982.

Johnson, President Lyndon B. Telegram to John Wayne, The White House, Washington, DC, 8 April 1970.

Lee, Anna. Letter to Scott Allen Nollen, Hollywood, CA, 3 August 1989.

McCabe, John. Letter to Scott Allen Nollen, Mackinac Island, MI, Autumn 1989.

Newman, Paul. Letter to John Wayne, New York, 20 December 1961.

O'Brien, Edmond. Letter to John Ford, 22 February 1962.

Wayne, John. Letter to John Ford, Parreah, UT, 1 August 1943.

_____. Letter to John Ford, Carmago, Mexico, 17 June 1953.

_____. Letter to John Ford, Hollywood, CA, 28 November 1955.

_____. Telegram to John Ford, Hollywood, CA, 1 February 1954.

_____. Telegram to Peter Lawford, Hollywood, CA, 9 November 1960.

_____. Telegram to President John F. Kennedy, Tanganyika, Africa, 4 February 1961.

_____. Western Union telegram to John Ford, North Hollywood, CA, 30 January 1951.

_____. Western Union telegram to Nat "King" Cole, Hollywood, CA, 22 December 1964.

Original Studio Documents

"Employment Agreement Between Hal Roach Studios, and Victor McLaglen." Hal E. Roach Studios, Culver City, CA, 12 November 1938.

"Minimum Contract for Artists, One Week Minimum Employment," Hal Roach Studios, and Ward Bond, for *Mister Cinderella*. Hal E. Roach Studios, Culver City, CA, May 1936.

Original Studio and News Service Publicity Materials

Johnny Guitar pressbook. Republic Pictures, 1954.

"Life's Worth Living" (*Doctor Bull*) still photograph. Fox Film, 1933, photo number 114–115.

Mister Roberts, *Playbill* for the Alvin Theatre. New York, 23 February 1948.

Myrna Loy and Gene Markey wedding still photograph and accompanying snipe, 3 January 1946, photo number F256-S-36.

Pride of the Marines pressbook. Columbia Pictures, 1936.

The Searchers pressbook. Warner Bros., 1956.

Seven Sinners press release. Universal Pictures, 1940.

The Trial of Vivienne Ware still photograph. Fox Film, 1932, photo number How-12-56.

Ward Bond, Mrs. Pat O'Brien, Hugh Herbert and Van Heflin on *The Shamrock Special* still photograph and accompanying publicity snipe, 17 March 1949.

William Fox Presents The Iron Horse, *a John Ford Production*. New York: The Gordon Press, 1924.

Original Personal Documents and Photographs

Affidavit of Birth, Hollywood, County of Los Angeles, State of California, signed by John Wayne and notarized by Paul M. La Cava, 15 May 1972.

Authenticated Birth Record, State of Iowa, Madison County, issued to Marion Robert Morrison, 11 March 1950.

Certificate of Marriage, County of Los Angeles, State of California, issued to Marion Mitchell Morrison and Josephine Alicia Saenz, 24 June 1933.

McLaglen family portrait and accompanying notes, England, 1919.

Motion Picture Studio Mechanics' Membership Card, No. 34854, issued to brother Duke Morrison by Local No. 37, Hollywood and Culver City, CA, Season 1929-1930.

Standard Certificate of Birth, County of Madison, City of Winterset, Marion Robert Morrison, date of birth 26 May 1907, filed 31 December 1907.

Wagon Train, "Wagons Ho!" candid photograph and accompanying inscription, from the Estate of Ward Bond, 1960.

Memoirs

Cagney, James. *Cagney by Cagney*. New York: Doubleday, 1976.

Capra, Frank. *The Name Above the Title: An Autobiography*. New York: Macmillan, 1971.

Carey, Harry, Jr. *Company of Heroes: My Life as an Actor in the John Ford Stock Company*. Metuchen, NJ: Scarecrow, 1994.

Clinton, Bill. *My Life*. New York: Alfred A. Knopf, 2004.

Fast, Howard. *Being Red: A Memoir*. New York: M. E. Sharp, 1994.

Fonda, Henry. *Fonda: My Life*. New York: Signet, 1982.

Hepburn, Katharine. *Me: Stories of My Life*. New York: Alfred A. Knopf, 1991.

Huston, John. *An Open Book*. New York: Knopf, 1980.

O'Hara, Maureen, with John Nicoletti. *'Tis Herself: A Memoir*. New York: Simon and Schuster, 2004.

Roberson, Chuck. *Fall Guy*. Vancouver: Hancock House, 1980.

Strode, Woody, and Sam Young. *Goal Dust: The Warm and Candid Memoirs of a Pioneer Black Athlete and Actor*. Lanham, MD: Madison Books, 1990.

Temple-Black, Shirley. *Child Star: An Autobiography*. New York: McGraw-Hill, 1988.

Thomas, Bob, ed. *Directors in Action: Selections from Action, the Official Magazine of the Directors Guild of America*. Indianapolis: Bobbs-Merrill, 1973.

Walsh, Raoul. *Each Man in His Time: The Life Story of a Director*. New York: Farrar, Straus and Giroux, 1974.

Waters, Ethel, with Charles Samuels. *His Eye Is on the Sparrow: An Autobiography*. New York: Doubleday, 1951.

Wayne, Pilar, with Alex Thorleifson. *My Life with the Duke: John Wayne*. New York: New English Library, 1989.

Welles, Orson, and Peter Bogdanovich. *This Is Orson Welles*. Cambridge, MA: Da Capo Press, 1998.

Films and Television Programs

The American West of John Ford. Mill Creek Entertainment DVD, 2005.

Behind the Cameras: Monument Valley. The Searchers 50th Anniversary 2-Disc Special Edition DVD. Warner Bros., 2006.

Behind the Cameras: Setting Up Production. The Searchers 50th Anniversary 2-Disc Special Edition DVD. Warner Bros., 2006.

Darryl F. Zanuck: 20th Century Filmmaker. Van Ness Films–Twentieth Television–A&E Network, 1995.

Directed by John Ford. Turner Entertainment–American Film Institute, 2006.

Ford, John. *Ford at Fox*. DVD box set. Beverly Hills, CA: 20th Century–Fox, 2007.

Frank Sinatra in Concert at the Royal Festival Hall, Reprise DVD, 1971.

John Ford Goes to War. Image Entertainment, 2005.
John Wayne's The Alamo. MGM Restored Edition Laserdisc, 1992.
The John Wayne Stock Company: Ward Bond. Hondo DVD. Paramount Home Entertainment, 2005.
The Making of Hondo. *Hondo* DVD. Paramount Home Entertainment, 2005.
The Making of The Quiet Man. Republic Entertainment, DVD, 1999.
The Making of Rio Grande. Republic Entertainment, DVD, 1999.
Mr. Moto Meets Mr. Chan: The Making of Mr. Moto's Gamble. *The Mr. Moto Collection, Volume Two* DVD. 20th Century–Fox, 2007.
The Searchers: *An Appreciation.* The Searchers 50th Anniversary 2-Disc Special Edition DVD. Warner Bros., 2006.
The Size of Legends, The Soul of Myth. The Man Who Shot Liberty Valance Centennial Collection DVD. Paramount Home Entertainment, 2009.
A Turning of the Earth: John Ford, John Wayne and The Searchers. The Searchers 50th Anniversary 2-Disc Special Edition DVD. Warner Bros., 2006.
Wagon Train: The Complete First Season DVD set. NBC Universal, 2009.
Wagon Train: The Complete Season Two DVD set. NBC Universal, 2010.
Wagon Train: The Complete Third Season DVD set. NBC Universal, 2011.
Wagon Train: The Complete Season Four DVD set. NBC Universal, 2011.

Secondary Sources

Anderson, Lindsay. *About John Ford.* New York, McGraw-Hill, 1981.
Bach, Steven. *Marlene Dietrich: Life and Legend.* New York: William Morrow, 1992.
Basinger, Jeanine. *Shirley Temple.* New York: Pyramid Communications, 1975.
Bogdanovich, Peter. *John Ford.* Berkeley: University of California Press, 1978.
Burrough, Bryan. *The Big Rich: The Rise and Fall of the Greatest Texas Oil Fortunes.* New York: Penguin Press, 2009.
Davis, Ronald L. *John Ford: Hollywood's Old Master.* Norman: University of Oklahoma Press, 1995.
Everson, William K. *A Pictorial History of the Western Film.* Secaucus, NJ: The Citadel Press, 1969.
Eyman, Scott. *Print the Legend: The Life and Times of John Ford.* New York: Simon and Schuster, 1999.
Ford, Dan. *Pappy: The Life of John Ford.* Englewood Cliffs, NJ: Prentice-Hall, 1979.
Gallagher, Tag. *John Ford: The Man and His Films.* Berkeley: University of California Press, 1986.
Grobel, Lawrence. *The Hustons.* New York: Scribners, 1989.
Howlett, John. *Frank Sinatra.* Philadelphia: Courage Books, 1980.
Marcus, Greil. *The Dustbin of History.* Cambridge: Harvard University Press, 1995.
Mast, Gerald. *Howard Hawks, Storyteller.* New York: Oxford University Press, 1984.
McBride, Joseph. *Searching for John Ford: A Life.* New York: St. Martin's, 2001.
McCabe, John. *Cagney.* New York: Carroll and Graf, 1997.
Nollen, Scott Allen. *Boris Karloff: A Gentleman's Life.* Baltimore: Midnight Marquee Press, 1999.
_____. *Boris Karloff: A Critical Account of His Screen, Stage, Radio, Television, and Recording Work.* Jefferson, NC: McFarland, 1988.
_____. *The Cinema of Sinatra: The Actor, on Screen and in Song.* Baltimore: Luminary Press, 2003.
_____. *Sir Arthur Conan Doyle at the Cinema.* Jefferson, NC: McFarland, 1996.
_____. *Warners Wiseguys: All 112 Films That Robinson, Cagney and Bogart Made for the Studio.* Jefferson, NC: McFarland, 2008.
Pendergast, Tom, and Sara Pendergast, eds. *The St. James Encyclopedia of Popular Culture.* Detroit: St. James Press, 2000.
Place, J. A. *The Western Films of John Ford.* Secaucus, NJ: Citadel Press, 1974.
_____. *The Non-Western Films of John Ford.* Secaucus, NJ: Citadel Press, 1979.
Roberts, Randy, and James S. Olson. *John Wayne: American.* Lincoln: University of Nebraska Press, 1997.
Rosin, James. *Wagon Train: The Television Series.* Philadelphia: Autumn Road, 2008.
Sarris, Andrew. *The John Ford Movie Mystery.* Bloomington: Indiana University Press,1975.
Schatz, Thomas. *The Genius of the System: Hollywood Filmmaking in the Studio Era.* New York: Pantheon Books, 1988.
Shepherd, Donald, and Robert Slatzer. *Duke: The Life and Times of John Wayne.* New York: Citadel Press, 2002.
Sinclair, Andrew. *John Ford: A Biography.* New York: Lorrimer, 1984.
Sterling, Bryan B., and Frances Sterling. *Will Rogers in Hollywood.* New York: Crown,1984.
Studlar, Gaylyn, and Matthew Bernstein, eds. *John Ford Made Westerns: Filming the Legend in the Sound Era.* Bloomington: Indiana University Press, 2001.
Swindell, Larry. *Spencer Tracy.* New York: New American Library, 1969.
Watts, Jill. *Hattie McDaniel: Black Ambition, White Hollywood.* New York: Harper Collins, 2005.
Wills, Gary. *John Wayne's America: The Politics of Celebrity.* New York: Simon and Schuster, 1997.
Zolotow, Maurice. *Shooting Star: A Biography of John Wayne.* New York: Simon and Schuster, 1974.

Periodicals

Barzman, Ben. "The Duke and Me," *Los Angeles Magazine,* January 1989.
Blake, Michael F. "He Was Their Stage Coach," *Los Angeles Times,* 28 May 1999.
Bogdanovich, Peter. "The Duke's Gone West," *New York,* 25 June 1979.
Coursodon, J. P. "Notes of a Press Attache: John Ford in Paris, 1966," *Film Comment,* July-August 1994.
D'Arc, James. "Howard Hawks and the Great Paper Chase," *Projections* 6, 1996.
Film Daily, 1928–1959.
"Filmland Stars Do G.I. Benefit," *Los Angeles Times,* 27 February 1949.
Hollywood Reporter, 1931–1972.
"'I Come Ready': An Interview with John Wayne," *Film Heritage,* Summer 1975.
Ketler, C. L. "Ward Bond and the Bond Family," Benkelman, NE, weekly newspaper, 26 February 1953.
"The Late Ward Bond Had a Pioneer Heritage," Benkelman, NE, weekly newspaper, 1960.
Lewis, Richard Warren. "*Playboy* Interview with John Wayne," *Playboy,* May 1971.

Libby, Bill. "The Old Wrangler Rides Again," *Cosmopol-*
   itan, March 1964.
"The Man with the Trigger-Happy Tongue," *TV Guide*,
   14 June 1958.
McManus, John T. "Speaking of Movies: Reaction's
   Rump," *PM*, 14 February 1944.
Motion Picture Herald, 1931–1959.
New York Times, 1928–1973.
Nollen, Scott Allen. "John Ford, Howard Hawks and the
   John Wayne Image," *Movie Collector's World*, No. 273,
   18 September 1987.

"Some on Acad. Bd. Would K.O. Rule Barring Oscar to
   Reds," *Daily Variety*, 12 January 1959.
"Story of Ward Bond's Success and of His Ultimate Pass-
   ing," Benkelman, NE, weekly newspaper, 1960.
Tavernier, Bernard, translated by Tag Gallagher. "John
   Ford a' Paris: Notes d' un Attache de Press," *Positif*,
   March 1967.
Time, February 1956, 1 March 1965.
Variety, 1928–1973.

Index

Numbers in **_bold italics_** indicate pages with photographs